San Francisco

"All you've got to do is decide to go
and the hardest part is over.

So go!"

TONY WHEELER, COFOUNDER – LONELY PLANET

THIS EDITION WRITTEN AND RESEARCHED BY

Alison Bing,
Sara Benson, John A Vlahides

Contents

(left) **F-Market Street-car p174** Travel to the Castro in retro style.

(above) **Alamo Square p186** Check out the Haight's 'Painted Ladies.'

(right) **22nd St Parklet p164** Stop and take in the passing Mission scene.

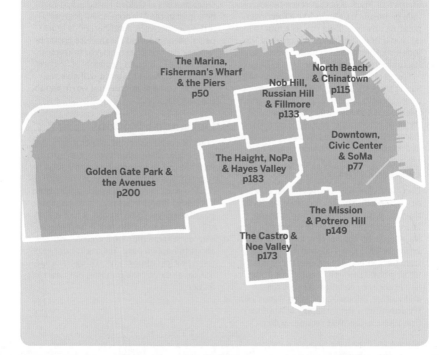

The Marina, Fisherman's Wharf & the Piers p50

North Beach & Chinatown p115

Nob Hill, Russian Hill & Fillmore p133

Downtown, Civic Center & SoMa p77

The Haight, NoPa & Hayes Valley p183

Golden Gate Park & the Avenues p200

The Mission & Potrero Hill p149

The Castro & Noe Valley p173

Welcome to San Francisco

Grab your coat and a handful of glitter, and enter the land of fog and fabulousness. So long, inhibitions; hello, San Francisco.

Natural Highs

California is one grand, sweeping gesture, a long arm cradling the Pacific. But then there's San Francisco, that seven-by-seven-mile peninsula that looks like a forefinger pointing upwards. Take this as a hint to look up: you'll find San Francisco's crooked Victorian rooflines, wind-sculpted treetops and fog tumbling over the Golden Gate Bridge.

Heads are perpetually in the clouds atop San Francisco's 43 hills. Cable cars provide easy access to Russian and Nob Hills and splendid panoramas atop Coit Tower. But the most exhilarating highs are earned on Telegraph Hill's garden-lined stairway walks and windswept hikes around Land's End.

Food & Drink

Every available Bay Area–invented technology is needed to make dinner decisions in this city, with the most restaurants and farmers markets per capita in North America, supplied by pioneering local organic farms. In 1906 City Hall banned women from bars, effectively driving the action underground through Prohibition. Today San Francisco celebrates its speakeasies and vintage saloons – and with Wine Country providing a steady supply of America's finest hooch, the West remains wild.

Neighborhood Microclimates

Microclimates add a touch of magic realism to San Francisco: when it's drizzling in the outer reaches of Golden Gate Park, it may be sunny in the Mission. A few degrees' difference between neighborhoods grants permission for salted caramel ice cream in Dolores Park or a hasty retreat to tropical heat inside California Academy of Sciences' rainforest dome. This town will give you goose bumps one minute and warm you to the core the next.

Outlandish Notions

Consider permission permanently granted to be outlandish: other towns may surprise you, but in San Francisco you will surprise yourself. Good times and social revolutions tend to start here, from manic gold rushes to blissful hippie be-ins. If there's a skateboard move yet to be busted, a technology still unimagined, a poem left unspoken or a green scheme untested, chances are it's about to happen here. Yes, right now: this town has lost almost everything in earthquakes and dot-com gambles, but never its nerve.

Why I Love San Francisco

By Alison Bing, Author

On my way from Hong Kong to New York, I stopped in San Francisco for a day. I walked from the Geary St art galleries up Grant Ave to Waverly Place, just as temple services were starting. The breeze smelled like incense and roast duck. In the basement of City Lights bookstore, near the Muckraking section, I noticed a sign painted by a 1920s cult: 'I am the door.' It's true. San Francisco is the threshold between East and West, body and soul, fact and fiction. That was 18 years ago. I'm still here. You have been warned.

For more about our authors, see p344.

For more about our authors, see p344.

Top: Victorian houses in the Haight

San Francisco's
Top 10

Golden Gate Bridge *(p59)*

1 Other suspension bridges impress with engineering, but none can touch the Golden Gate Bridge for showmanship. On sunny days it transfixes crowds with its radiant glow – thanks to 25 daredevil painters, who reapply 1000 gallons of International Orange paint weekly. When fog rolls in, the bridge performs its disappearing act: now you see it, now you don't and, abracadabra, it's sawn in half. Return tomorrow for its dramatic unveiling, just in time for the morning commute.

◉ *The Marina, Fisherman's Wharf & the Piers*

Golden Gate Park *(p202)*

2 You may have heard that San Francisco has a wild streak a mile wide but it also happens to be 4.5 miles long. Golden Gate Park lets San Franciscans do what comes naturally: roller-discoing, drum-circling, petting starfish, sniffing orchids and racing bison toward the Pacific. It's hard to believe these 1017 acres of lush terrain were once just scrubby sand dunes and that San Franciscans have successfully preserved this stretch of green since 1866, ousting casinos and resorts. BELOW: CONSERVATORY OF FLOWERS, GOLDEN GATE PARK

◉ *Golden Gate Park & the Avenues*

WENDY CONNETT / GETTY IMAGES ©

DAVID CLAPP / GETTY IMAGES ©

DNY59 / GETTY IMAGES ©

5

Alcatraz (p52)

3 From its 19th-century founding to hold Civil War deserters and Native American dissidents, to its closure by Bobby Kennedy in 1963, Alcatraz was America's most notorious prison. No prisoner is known to have escaped alive – but after entering D-Block solitary and hearing carefree city life humming across the bay, the 1.25-mile swim through riptides seems worth a shot. For maximum chill factor, book the spooky twilight jailhouse tour. On the return ferry to San Francisco, freedom never felt so good.

⊙ *The Marina, Fisherman's Wharf & the Piers*

Cable Cars (p43)

4 White-knuckle grips on worn wooden benches give away San Francisco novices. Lurching uphill, you may exhale when the bell signals the summit. But what goes up all 338ft of San Francisco's Nob Hill must come down. Maybe now is not the best time to mention that the brakes are still hand-operated or that this Victorian steampunk invention has hardly changed since 1873. Once you reach the terminus, you're ready to take the next giddy ride standing, nothing between you and eternity but a creaky hand strap.

⊙ *Cable Cars*

Coit Tower (p117)

5 Wild parrots may mock your progress up Telegraph Hill but, really, they can't expect to keep scenery like this to themselves. Filbert St Steps pass improbable cliffside gardens and boardwalk cottages to reach SF's singular monument to independent thinking: Coit Tower. Firefighting, cigar-smoking tomboy heiress Lillie Hitchcock Coit commissioned this art deco tower honoring fire-fighters, and San Francisco muralists captured 1930s city life in the lobby frescoes. The murals and panoramic viewing platform show San Francisco as it was and still remains: a city of many outlandish viewpoints, all worth considering.

⊙ *North Beach & Chinatown*

Marine Life at Fisherman's Wharf (p56)

6 Sea lions have lived the Californian dream since 1989, when they brought harems to Pier 39 yacht docks for sunning and canoodling. After disappearing in 2009, their return in 2010 was greeted with cheers and a brass band. Sharks circle nearby at Aquarium of the Bay, where the only barrier between visitors and bay waters is a glass tube. A less ominous underwater world can be glimpsed at the newly restored Aquatic Park Bathhouse, where jellyfish flutter across 1930s mosaics.

⊙ *The Marina, Fisherman's Wharf & the Piers*

Neighborhood Boutiques (p38)

7 Typewriters, necklaces made of shattered windshields: shopping looks like installation art in San Francisco's indie boutiques. Although SF has spawned mega-retailers – Levi Strauss, Pottery Barn and the Gap are all headquartered downtown – zoning restrictions limit chain retailers in the city's neighborhoods. Where other cities might plunk another mall, here you'll find Victorian storefronts selling Icelandic gamelan music and Mayan-inspired dresses. Local designers win pride of place on shelves and killer sale racks put mall mark-ups to shame. RIGHT: PIEDMONT BOUTIQUE, THE HAIGHT

🛍 *Shopping*

LAURENT SAUVEL / GETTY IMAGES ©

NIKREATIVE / ALAMY ©

SILICONVALLEYSTOCK / ALAMY ©

Exploratorium *(p62)*

8 Time-warping, perception-altering, consciousness-expanding... the Exploratorium is a total trip. Hear salt sing, stimulate your appetite with color and find out what cows see when they look at you, through hands-on exhibits created by MacArthur Genius Grant winners. Manhattan Project nuclear physicist Frank Oppenheimer founded the Exploratorium in 1969 to explore science, art and human perception and you can actually simulate '60s flashbacks as you grope barefoot through the Tactile Dome. After Dark events are truly illuminating, with glowing cocktails in the Ultraviolet Room.

👁 *The Marina, Fisherman's Wharf & the Piers*

Ferry Building (p79)

9 San Francisco's monument to food stands proud on Saturdays, when star chefs troll farmers market stalls for rare heirloom varietals and foodie babies blissfully teethe on organic apricots. Local farmers and food trucks have dedicated followings any rock star would envy, so anticipate waits for organic Dirty Girl tomatoes and Namu's sustainable Korean steak tacos. Pass the time exchanging recipe tips, then haul your picnic to Pier 2. With feet dangling over the sparkling bay and culinary bounty in hand, lunch and life exceed expectations.

👁 *Downtown, Civic Center & SoMa*

Mission Bars (p161)

10 Circa 1849, a San Francisco bar crawl that began with smiles and a 10¢ whiskey from barman Shanghai Kelly could end two days later, waking from a drugged sleep on a vessel bound for Patagonia. Today Mission revelers can relax and pick their own poison: microbrews and organic cocktails in restored Gold Rush saloons, cult California wines and Pantone-color-coded bar menus in midcentury lounges, and enough tequila and late-night tacos to keep you asleep to Patagonia and back. ABOVE: ELIXIR, THE MISSION

🍷 *The Mission & Potrero Hill*

What's New

SFJAZZ Center

Tonight could be the night the roof blows clean off the West Coast's sleek new landmark jazz center, with thunderous stomps and rapturous whoops for the latest jazz legends in residence. America's second jazz center is number one for sheer bravado, with the country's top talents riffing on Hunter S Thompson lyrics and skateboarders performing feats with backbeats. (p194)

Exploratorium

San Francisco's weird science showcase has a new waterfront home on Pier 15, with mind-altering new exhibits and sensational special-effects photo-ops on Fog Bridge. (p62)

Dogpatch Creative Corridor

Hop the T streetcar to 22nd St to discover local designers, wineries, the new Museum of Craft & Design and a chocolate laboratory. (p155)

Parklets Everywhere

Ever since San Francisco art-collective Rebar started repurposing parking spaces as public mini-parks, driftwood benches and potted palms have sprouted up where cars once idled citywide.

SFMOMA Expansion

A half-billion-dollar expansion is in the works through 2016 at San Francisco Museum of Modern Art (SFMOMA) to accommodate a donation of 1100 modern masterworks. (p85)

Radical Food Mission

The Mission is out to prove local, seasonal and sustainable doesn't mean predictable, with organic microbrewed-beer ice cream or muffins with softboiled farm egg surprises inside. (p155)

Potrero Gulch Galleries

Potrero's Design District is branching out from sofas into art, with some of SF's best contemporary art galleries taking up residence around arts hub SOMArts. (p153)

NoPa Crawl

Upstart cafes and indie retailers along Divisidero Street offer new ways to kill time (aka 'work remotely') between Alamo Square picnics and happy-hour bar bites. (p183)

Green Rules

America's greenest city already has mandatory composting and recycling citywide, and now plastic bags are banned at stores and restaurants – a fine excuse to score a souvenir tote-bag.

Bay Bridge

After 14 years, repairs to the eastern span of the Bay Bridge are complete – but the western span is getting all the attention. Artist Leo Villareal's installation of 25,000 twinkling LED lights along the western span will make you swear the Bay Bridge is winking at you. The light show starts nightly after dusk and runs until March 2015.

For more recommendations and reviews, see **lonelyplanet. com/usa/san-francisco**

Need to Know

For more information, see Survival Guide (p285)

Currency
US dollar ($)

Language
English

Visas
The US Visa Waiver program allows nationals of 37 countries to enter the US without a visa.

Money
ATMs widely available; credit cards accepted at most hotels, stores and restaurants. Farmers markets, food trucks and some bars are cash-only.

Cell Phones
Most US cell phones (apart from the iPhone) operate on CDMA, not the European standard GSM; check compatibility with your phone service provider.

Time
Pacific Standard Time (GMT/UTC minus eight hours)

Tourist Information
SF Visitor Information Center (Map p320; ☎415-391-2000, www.onlyinsanfrancisco. com; Market & Powell Sts, lower level, Hallidie Plaza; ⊙9am-5pm Mon-Fri, to 3pm Sat & Sun; ⛟Powell-Mason, Powell-Hyde, Ⓜ & Ⓑ Powell St) Muni Passports, last-minute vacancy listings and accommodations deals.

Daily Costs
Budget: less than $100
➡ Dorm bed $25–$30
➡ Burrito $6–$8
➡ Food-truck dishes $5–$10
➡ Mission murals free
➡ Live music at Hotel Utah/ Bottom of the Hill $5–$12
➡ Castro Theatre show $11

Midrange: $100– $250
➡ Motel/downtown hotel $80–$180
➡ Ferry Building meal $15–$35
➡ Bar bites meal $20–$45
➡ Thursday Exploratorium After Dark/Academy of Sciences NightLife $15/12
➡ Symphony rush tickets $20
➡ Muni Passport $14

Top End: $250+
➡ Boutique hotel $150–$380
➡ Chef's tasting menu $65–$140
➡ City Pass (Muni, cable cars plus four attractions) $84
➡ Alcatraz night tour $37
➡ Opera orchestra seats $30–$94

Advance Planning
Two months before Book your reservations at Chez Panisse or French Laundry; start walking to build stamina for Coit Tower climbs and Mission bar crawls.

Three weeks before Book Alcatraz tour, Chinatown History Tour or Precita Eyes Mission Mural Tour.

One week before Search for tickets to American Conservatory Theater, SF Symphony or SF Opera and find out what else is on next weekend.

Useful Websites
SF Bay Guardian (www.sfbg. com) Hot tips on local entertainment, arts, politics.

SFGate (www.sfgate.com) *San Francisco Chronicle* news and event listings.

7x7 (www.7x7.com) Trend-spotting SF restaurants, bars and style.

Craigslist (http://sfbay. craigslist.org) SF-based source for jobs, dates, free junk.

Lonely Planet (www.lonely-planet.com/san-francisco) Destination information, hotel bookings, traveler forum.

WHEN TO GO

June and July bring fog and chilly 55°F weather to SF; August, September and October are best for warm weather, street fairs and harvest cuisine.

Arriving in San Francisco

San Francisco Airport (SFO) Fast rides to downtown SF on BART cost $8.25; door-to-door shuttle vans cost $15 to $17; express bus fare to Temporary Transbay Terminal is $5; taxis cost $35 to $50.

Oakland International Airport (OAK) Take the AirBART shuttle ($3) to Coliseum station to catch BART to downtown SF ($3.85); take a shared van to downtown SF for $27 to $35; or pay $55 to $70 for a taxi to SF destinations.

Temporary Transbay Terminal (Howard & Main Sts) Greyhound buses arrive/depart downtown SF's temporary depot (until 2017) at Howard & Main Sts.

Emeryville Amtrak station (EMY) Located outside Oakland, this depot serves west coast and nationwide train routes; Amtrak runs free shuttles to/from San Francisco's Ferry Building and Caltrain.

For much more on **arrival** see p286

Getting Around

For Bay Area transit options, departures and arrivals, call 511 or check www.511.org. A detailed Muni Street & Transit Map is available free online.

➡ **Cable cars** Frequent, slow and scenic, from 6am to 1am daily. Single rides cost $6; for frequent use, get a Muni Passport ($14/day).

➡ **Muni streetcar & bus** Reasonably fast but schedules vary wildly by line; infrequent after 9pm. Fares cost $2.

➡ **BART** High-speed transit to East Bay, Mission St, SFO and Millbrae, where it connects with Caltrain.

➡ **Taxi** Fares cost about $2.75 per mile; meters start at $3.50.

For much more on **getting around** see p287

Sleeping

San Francisco offers stylish rooms at a price: $120 to $200 midrange, plus 15.5% hotel tax (hostels exempt) and $35 to $50 for overnight parking. Some downtown hotels cost less but proceed with caution: west of Mason is the sketchy, depressing Tenderloin. Motels are better options for parking, and hostels offer value for solo travelers but no privacy.

Useful Websites

➡ **B&B San Francisco** (www.bbsf.com) Personable, privately owned B&Bs and neighborhood inns.

➡ **SF Visitor Information Center Reservations** (www.onlyinsanfrancisco. com) Vacancies and deals; indispensible in high season and during major conventions.

➡ **Lonely Planet** (www. lonelyplanet.com/usa/ san-francisco/hotels) Expert author reviews, user feedback, booking engine.

For much more on **sleeping** see p239

TOP THREE SF TOURS

➡ Precita Eyes Mission Mural Tours (p294)
➡ Sea Foraging Adventures (p294)
➡ Chinatown Alleyway Tours (p295)

Top Itineraries

Day One

Telegraph Hill & Waterfront (p115 & p50)

Grab a leather strap on the **Powell-Mason cable car** and hold on: you're in for hills and thrills. Hop off at **Washington Square Park**, and parrots squawk encouragement as you hike up to **Coit Tower** for WPA murals and giddy, 360-degree panoramas. Take scenic **Filbert Street Steps** to the **Embarcadero** and wander across Fog Bridge to explore the freaky Tactile Dome at the **Exploratorium**.

Lunch Try the local oysters and Dungeness crab at the Ferry Building (p79).

Alcatraz & North Beach (p50 & p115)

Catch your pre-booked ferry to **Alcatraz**, where D-block solitary raises goosebumps and library books were censored for kissing and curses. Make your island prison break (checking out the **Golden Gate Bridge** views on the trip back) and take the Powell-Mason cable car to North Beach, where you can read freely at free-speech landmark **City Lights** and mingle with San Francisco's freest spirits at the **Beat Museum**.

Dinner Reserve ahead for North Beach's best pasta at Cotogna (p89).

North Beach (p115)

Since you just escaped prison, you're tough enough to handle too-close-for-comfort comics at **Cobb's Comedy Club**, or razor-sharp drag satire at **Beach Blanket Babylon**. Toast the wildest night in the west with potent Pisco sours at **Comstock Saloon**.

Day Two

Chinatown (p115)

Take the **California cable car** to pagoda-topped Grant Street for eye-opening **Red Blossom** tea tasting, then a jaw-dropping history of Chinatown at **Chinese Historical Society of America**. Wander temple-lined **Waverly Place** and notorious **Ross Alley** to find your fortune at **Golden Gate Fortune Cookie Company**.

Lunch Hail dim sum carts for dumplings at City View (p126).

Fisherman's Wharf (p50)

To cover the waterfront, take the **Powell-Hyde cable car** past zigzagging **Lombard St** to **Aquatic Park Bathhouse**, where an underwater world unfolds in 1930s murals and mosaics. Save the world from Space Invaders at **Musée Mécanique**, or enter underwater stealth mode inside a real WWII submarine: **USS Pampanito**. Watch sea lions cavort as the sun fades over **Pier 39**, then hop the vintage **F-line streetcar**.

Dinner Inspired NorCal fare at Rich Table (p189) satisfies and surprises.

Hayes Valley (p183)

Troll boutiques before your concert at **San Francisco Symphony** or **SFJAZZ Center**, and toast your good fortune with California bubbly in the bar at **Jardinière**.

The Embarcadero and the Bay Bridge

Day Three

Golden Gate Park (p200)

 Hop the N Judah to Golden Gate Park to see carnivorous plants enjoying insect breakfasts at **Conservatory of Flowers** and dahlias wet with dew in the **Dahlia Garden**. Follow Andy Goldworthy's artful sidewalk fault lines to find Oceanic masks and faultless tower-top views at the **MH de Young Museum**, then take a walk on the wild side inside the rainforest dome of the **California Academy of Sciences**. Enjoy a moment of Zen with green tea at the **Japanese Tea Garden** and bliss out in the secret redwood grove at the **San Francisco Botanical Garden**.

> **Lunch** Surfers hit Outerlands (p211) for grilled cheese and organic soup.

The Richmond (p200)

 Beachcomb **Ocean Beach** up to the **Beach Chalet** to glimpse 1930s WPA murals celebrating Golden Gate Park. Follow the **Coastal Trail** past **Sutro Baths** and **Land's End** for **Golden Gate Bridge** vistas and priceless paper artworks at **Legion of Honor**.

> **Dinner** Organic Cal-Moroccan feasts satisfy cravings at Aziza (p210).

Japantown (p133)

Psychedelic posters and top acts make for rock-legendary nights at the **Fillmore**, or get in the swing with jazz greats performing nightly at **Yoshi's**.

Day Four

The Mission (p149)

 Stroll 24th St past mural-covered bodegas to **Balmy Alley**, where the Mission muralist movement began in the 1970s. Stop for a 'secret breakfast' (bourbon and cornflake) ice cream sundae at **Humphry Slocombe**, then head up Valencia to Ritual Coffee Roasters. Pause for pirate supplies and Fish Theater at **826 Valencia** and duck into **Clarion Alley**, the Mission's outdoor graffiti-art gallery. See San Francisco's first building, Spanish adobe **Mission Dolores**, and visit the memorial to native Ohlone who built it.

> **Lunch** Get La Taqueria (p155) burritos to go and enjoy in Dolores Park.

The Haight (p183)

Spot Victorian 'Painted Ladies' around **Alamo Square** and browse **NoPa boutiques**. Stroll the green Panhandle park to Stanyan, then window-shop your way down hippie-historic **Haight Street** past record stores, vintage emporiums, drag designers and **Bound Together Anarchist Book Collective**.

> **Dinner** Early walk-ins may score amazing small plates at Frances (p177).

The Castro (p173)

 Sing along to show tunes pounded out on the Mighty Wurlitzer organ before shows at deco-fabulous **Castro Theatre**. Party boys cruise over to 440 Castro, while straight-friendly crowds clink glasses at **Blackbird**.

If You Like...

Museums

Exploratorium Hands-on exhibitions test scientific theories in a vast new home at Pier 15. (p62)

MH de Young Museum Global art and craft masterworks with provocative ideas and enviable hand–eye coordination. (p203)

Asian Art Museum Sightsee halfway across the globe in an hour, from romantic Persian miniatures to daring contemporary Chinese installation art. (p81)

Legion of Honor Iconic impressionist paintings, a sensational modern collection of 90,000 graphic artworks and weekend organ recitals amid Rodin sculptures. (p205)

Cartoon Art Museum Original drawings by comics legends, from R Crumb and Edward Gorey to Spiderman. (p85)

Freebies

Stern Grove Festival Free concerts at Golden Gate Park's natural amphitheater, from Afrobeat jazz to SF Opera. (p34)

Hardly Strictly Bluegrass Festival Elvis Costello, Gillian Welch, banjo legend Earl Scruggs and other headliners play for free on three stages at Golden Gate Park. (p34)

Cable Car Museum Observe the inner workings of San Francisco's transport icon, which remains largely unchanged since its 1873 invention. (p136)

Amoeba Music concerts Rockers, DJs and hip-hop heroes give free shows in-store. (p194)

THOMAS WINZ / GETTY IMAGES ©

Vesuvio (p130) in Jack Kerouac Alley, North Beach

Giants Baseball Catch a glimpse of the action and join the party at the Embarcadero waterfront promenade behind left field. (p41)

Vista Points

Coit Tower Up Greenwich St stairs, atop Telegraph Hill, inside the 1930s tower and atop the viewing platform: 360-degree panoramas. (p117)

Land's End Shipwrecks, Golden Gate Bridge views and wind-blown Monterey pines line the scenic hike from Sutro Baths to Legion of Honor. (p205)

Sterling Park Poetic views of the Golden Gate Bridge from atop Russian Hill are worth jumping off the Powell-Hyde cable car to find. (p136)

Corona Heights Park Rocky outcropping with views over the Haight, Castro and Mission to the great bay beyond. (p175)

Local Hangouts

Trouble Coffee Soggy wet-suited surfers sit on driftwood parklet benches, while beachcombers warm up inside at the scavenged-wood coffee bar. (p212)

Coffee to the People The quadruple-shot Freak Out with hemp milk could wake the Grateful Dead at this radical Haight coffeehouse. (p188)

Cafe Flore Glassed-in Castro corner venue that serves coffee with a side of local eye candy. (p177)

Dolores Park Athletes, radical politicos, quasi-professional tanners, performance artists and toddlers: on sunny days, they all converge on this grassy hillside. (p151)

Japantown The unofficial living room of film festival freaks, Lolita Goths, anime aficionados and grandmas who fought for civil rights. (p138)

Movie Locations

Nob Hill What a ride: Steve McQueen's muscle car goes flying over the summit in *Bullitt* and somehow lands in SoMa. (p136)

Ocean Beach The moody, windswept beach sets the scene for turbulent romance in Woody Allen's 2013 *Blue Jasmine*. (p206)

Sutro Baths San Francisco's splendid, dandified ruin made a suitable setting for the May–December romance in *Harold and Maude*. (p205)

Human Rights Campaign Action Center & Store Harvey Milk's camera shop in the movie *Milk* was the actual Castro location, now home to the GLBT civil rights organization. (p181)

Bay Bridge Oops: when Dustin Hoffman sets out for Berkeley in *The Graduate,* he is heading the wrong way across the bridge.

Alcatraz Even America's highest-security prison can't contain Clint Eastwood, who plots to escape with a spoon and razor-sharp wits in *Escape from Alcatraz.* (p52)

Fort Point Hitchcock was right: swirling noir-movie fog and giddy Golden Gate views make for a thrilling case of *Vertigo*. (p61)

Avant-Garde Architecture

California Academy of Sciences Renzo Piano's LEED-certified green landmark, capped with a 'living roof' of California wildflowers. (p203)

MH de Young Museum Pritzker Prize–winning Swiss architects Herzog & de Meuron clad the museum in copper, which is slowly oxidizing green to match park scenery. (p203)

Contemporary Jewish Museum Daniel Libeskind's creatively repurposed SF power station makes a powerful statement with a blue steel addition to form the Hebrew letter for life. (p86)

Federal Building Natural lighting and air circulation lighten the mood inside this government building – and save taxpayer dollars. (p87)

Animals in Urban Habitats

Bison in Golden Gate Park Great shaggy beasts safely stampede toward the Pacific in their park paddock. (p202)

Sea lions at Pier 39 These beach bums have been sticking it to the man since 1989, claiming squatters' rights to millionaires' yacht slips. (p56)

Wild parrots at Telegraph Hill By city decree, SF's official birds are the renegade parrots that turn Telegraph treetops red, yellow, green and blue. (p117)

Knock-kneed shorebirds at Crissy Field Once this airstrip was home to WWII warbirds, but it's been converted back into a coastal marshland sanctuary for shorebirds. (p60)

For more top San Francisco spots, see the following:

➡ Eating (p26)
➡ Drinking & Nightlife (p30)
➡ Entertainment (p33)
➡ Shopping (p38)
➡ Sports & Activities (p41)

PLAN YOUR TRIP IF YOU LIKE...

Mission bookstore cats Great vacation reads await discovery on piled tables in **Borderlands** but you'll have to convince the hairless cats to move. (p163)

Hidden Alleyways

Balmy Alley Hot topics and artistic talents have surfaced since the 1970s in this alley covered in art by SF muralistas. (p151)

Spofford Alley Revolutions were plotted and bootlegger gun battles waged here – but peace has brought Chinese orchestras and mah jong games. (p120)

Jack Kerouac Alley This byway named after the Beat author is inscribed with his poetry, right on the road. (p118)

Bob Kaufman Alley A quiet alley, named for the spoken-word artist who kept an anti-war vow of silence for 12 years. (p119)

Ross Alley Ladies who entered this notorious alley once risked their reputations, but now the most colorful characters are on the alleyway murals. (p120)

Macondray Lane A shady, cottage-lined lane was the perfect setting for a mysterious landlady in Armistead Maupin's *Tales of the City.* (p136)

Getting Naked

Baker Beach When the fog rolls into the clothing-optional north end of the beach, you'll get goose bumps in the most unusual places. (p61)

Pride Parade A handful of rainbow glitter is all you need to get out there and show some pride. (p22)

Bay to Breakers Racers streak across town wearing nothing but shoes and fanny packs to stash sunscreen. (p21)

Folsom St Fair As you'll notice, it's possible to get tattooed and pierced absolutely everywhere here – but don't stare unless you're prepared to compare. (p22)

Jane Warner Plaza You've arrived in the Castro when you spot nudists casually chatting at bistro tables at the F-line streetcar turnaround. (p175)

Historic Sites

Mission Dolores The first building in San Francisco was this Spanish adobe mission, built by conscripted Ohlone and Miwok labor. (p151)

Alcatraz 'The Rock' was a Civil War jail, an A-list gangster penitentiary, and contested territory between Native Americans and the FBI. (p52)

City Lights Publishing poetry got City Lights founder Lawrence Ferlinghetti arrested – and won a landmark case for free speech. (p131)

Chinese Historical Society of America Julia Morgan built the elegant, tile-roofed brick Chinese YWCA, which now highlights turning points in Asian-American history. (p119)

City Hall History keeps getting made under this rotunda – the first 1960s sit-in, the first publicly gay elected official, the first citywide composting law. (p87)

Sutro Baths Once Victorians in wooly bathing suits filled the pools, but now Sutro Sam the otter has the run of this glorious ruin. (p205)

Portsmouth Square The Gold Rush, dirty politics, kangaroo trials and burlesque shows all kicked off around Portsmouth Square. (p123)

Beaches

Baker Beach This cove was once an army base, but now it's packed with families, fishers and, at the north end, nudists. (p61)

Ocean Beach Beachcombing and bonfires are the preferred activities at SF's 4-mile Pacific Ocean beach, where riptides limit swimming. (p206)

Crissy Field Windsurfing, fishing and casual paddling are much easier in this Bay cove than at blustery Ocean Beach. (p60)

Month by Month

February

Lion-dancing, freakishly warm days and alt-rock shows provide sudden relief from February drizzle.

☆ Noise Pop

Winter blues, be gone: discover your new favorite indie band and catch rockumentary premieres and rockin' gallery openings during the Noise Pop Festival (www.noisepop.com); last week of February.

Lunar New Year Parade

Chase the 200ft dragon, lion dancers and frozen-smile runners-up for the Miss Chinatown title during Lunar New Year celebrations (www.chineseparade.com).

April

Reasonable room rates and weekends crammed with cultural events make for an excellent start to San Francisco spring.

Perpetual Indulgence in Dolores Park

Easter Sunday is an all-day event with Sisters of Perpetual Indulgence in Dolores Park, from a morning Easter egg hunt to the Hunky Jesus Contest, for those who prefer their messiahs muscle-bound.

Cherry Blossom Festival

Japantown blooms and booms in April when the Cherry Blossom Festival (www.nccbf.org) turns out *taiko* drums, homegrown hip-hop, food stalls and street shrines.

☆ San Francisco International Film Festival

The nation's oldest film festival is still looking stellar, with 325 films, 200 directors and star-studded premieres; held end of April to early May at Sundance Kabuki Cinema.

May

As inland California warms up, fog settles over the Bay Area – but goose bumps haven't stopped the naked joggers and conga lines yet.

Bay to Breakers

Run costumed or naked from Embarcadero to Ocean Beach for Bay to Breakers, while joggers dressed as salmon run upstream. Race registration costs $58–89.50; held third Sunday in May.

Carnaval San Francisco

Brazilian or just faking it with a wax and a tan? Shake your tail feathers in the Mission and conga through the inevitable fog during Carnaval (www.carnavalsf.com); last weekend of May.

June

Since 1970, Pride has grown into a month-long extravaganza, with movie premieres and street parties culminating in the million-strong Pride Parade.

✨ Haight Ashbury St Fair

Free music on two stages, plus macramé, tie-dye and herbal brownies surreptitiously for sale: all that's missing is free love. Held every mid-June since 1978, when Harvey Milk helped make the first Haight St Fair happen.

☆ SF Jazz Festival

Minds are blown by jazz greats and upstarts play career-defining sets during the SF Jazz Festival (www. sfjazz.org), which features Grammy winners and crossover global talents; it is held late June at SFJAZZ Center and other venues around the city.

☆ San Francisco International LGBT Film Festival

Here, queer and ready for a premiere for three decades, the oldest, biggest lesbian/gay/bisexual/transgender (GLBT) film fest anywhere screens 250 films from 25 countries over two weeks in the second half of June (www. frameline.org).

✨ Pride Parade

Come out wherever you are: SF goes wild for GLBT pride (http://sfpride.org) on the last Sunday of June, with 1.2 million people, seven stages, tons of glitter and ounces of thongs at the Pride Parade. Crowds cheer same-sex newlyweds, gays in uniform and inspired drag.

July

Wintry summer days make bundling up advisable, but don't miss July

barbecues and outdoor events, including charity hikes, free concerts and fireworks.

✨ Independence Day

July 4 explodes with Fisherman's Wharf fireworks even in summer fog, celebrating San Francisco's enthusiastic dedication to life, liberty and the pursuit of happiness no matter the climate – economic, political or meteorological.

🏃 AIDS Walk

Until AIDS takes a hike, you can: this 10km fundraiser hike (www.aidswalk. net/sanfran) benefits 26 AIDS organizations. In nearly three decades, $81 million has been raised to fight the pandemic and support those living with HIV. Held the third Sunday in July.

☆ Stern Grove Festival

Music for free among the redwood and eucalyptus trees every summer since 1938. Stern Grove concerts include world music and jazz, but the biggest events are July performances by SF Ballet and SF Symphony and August arias from SF Opera.

August

Finally San Francisco fog rolls back and permits sunsets on Ocean Beach, just in time for one last glorious summer fling in Golden Gate Park.

☆ Outside Lands

Golden Gate Park is a magnet for three days of major acts and debauchery

at Wine Lands, Beer Lands and star-chef food trucks; tickets $105/250 1/3 days (www.sfoutsidelands.com).

September

Warm weather arrives at last and SF celebrates with more outrageous antics than usual, including public spankings and Shakespearean declarations of love.

✨ Folsom St Fair

Bondage enthusiasts emerge from dungeons worldwide for San Francisco's wild street party, with public spankings for charity, leather, nudity and beer; held last Sunday of September, at Folsom St between 7th and 11th Sts.

☆ SF Shakespeare Festival

The play's the thing in the Presidio, outdoors and free of charge on sunny September weekends during the Shakespeare Festival. Kids' summer workshops are also held for budding Bards, culminating in great performances throughout the Bay Area.

October

Expect golden sunshine and events for all kinds of aficionados.

☆ Alternative Press Expo

SF's indie comics convention (www.comic-con. org/ape) has a punk-rock DIY spirit and fantastic undiscovered talents shyly signing hand-stapled comics and original art mid-October.

(Top) Children's band, Lunar New Year Parade (p21)

(Bottom) Elvis impersonators taking part in Bay to Breakers (p21)

ROBERTO SONCIN GEROMETTA / GETTY IMAGES ©

GETTY IMAGES ©

☆ Litquake

Stranger-than-fiction literary events take place the second week of October during SF's literary festival (www.litquake.org), with authors leading lunchtime story sessions and spilling trade secrets over drinks at the legendary Lit Crawl.

☆ Hardly Strictly Bluegrass Festival

The West goes wild for free bluegrass (p34) at Golden Gate Park, with three days of concerts and three stages of headliners; held early October.

November

Party to wake the dead and save the planet as San Francisco celebrates its Mexican history and green future.

✯ Día de los Muertos

Zombie brides and Aztec dancers in feather regalia party like there's no tomorrow on Día de los Muertos (www.dayofthedeadsf.org), paying respects to the dead along the 24th St parade route on November 2.

✯ Green Festival

Energy-saving spotlights are turned on green cuisine, technology, fashion and booze during the three-day, mid-November Green Festival (www.green festivals.org).

With Kids

San Francisco has the fewest kids per capita of any US city and, according to SPCA data, about 32,000 more dogs than children live here. Yet many locals make a living entertaining kids – from Pixar animators to video game designers – and this town is full of attractions for young people.

Loof Carousel (p86) at Yerba Buena Gardens

Alcatraz & the Piers

Prison tours of Alcatraz (p52) fascinate kids and keep them on their best behavior for hours. The Exploratorium's (p62) award-winning, hands-on exhibits explore the science of skateboarding and glow-in-the-dark animals, and the toilet-shaped water fountain is a lesson in visual perception kids won't forget. Free the world from Space Invaders at Musée Mechanique (p57), then troll the waterfront for fish-wiches and obligatory 'I Escaped Alcatraz' souvenir tees.

Freebies

See SF history at the free Cable Car Museum (p136), and take free mechanical pony rides and peeks inside vintage stagecoaches at the Wells Fargo History Museum (p82). At the piers, the Exploratorium (p62) offers free photo-ops at the Fog Bridge and outdoor exhibits and there are free chocolate-factory tours at TCHO Chocolate (p73). For treats, Buyer's Best Friend Mercato (p131) offers free locally made candy in North Beach and kids score free toys in exchange for a bartered song, drawing or poem at 826 Valencia (p151).

The Wild Side

Penguins, buffalo and white alligators call Golden Gate Park (p202) home. Chase butterfies through the rainforest dome, pet starfish in the petting zoo and squeal in the Eel Forest at the California Academy of Sciences (p203). Meet San Francisco's resident sea lions at Pier 39 (p56) or brave the shark tunnel at Aquarium of the Bay (p58). San Francisco Zoo (p206) is out of the way but worth the trip for monkeys, lemurs and giraffes. Tree Frog Treks (p295) organizes scientific play-dates and nature discovery day-camps.

Cable Cars & Boats

When junior gearheads demand to know how cable cars work, the Cable Car Museum (p136) lets them glimpse the inner workings for themselves. Take cable car joyrides from downtown to Aquatic Park to enter submarine stealth mode aboard the USS *Pampanito* (p58) and climb aboard vintage steamships at Maritime National Historical Park (p57). Future sea captains will enjoy model-ship regattas on weekends at Spreckels Lake in Golden Gate Park (p202).

Warm Days

On sunny Sundays when Golden Gate Park is mostly closed to traffic, rent paddleboats at Stow Lake (p204) or strap on some rentals at Golden Gate Park Bike & Skate (p214). Crissy Field (p60) is a better bet for kid-friendly beaches than Ocean Beach, where fog and strong currents swiftly end sand-castle-building sessions. Hit Chinatown for teen-led Chinatown Alleyways Tours (p295), cookies at Golden Gate Fortune Cookie Company (p132) and a long-tailed dragon model at Chinatown Kite Shop (p132), then let it rip at Crissy Field.

Playgrounds

Golden Gate Park (p202) Swings, monkey bars, play castles with slides, hillside slides and a vintage carousel.

Dolores Park (p151) Jungle gym, Mayan pyramid, picnic tables.

Mission Playground Soccer, public pool, water features in summer.

Yerba Buena Gardens (p87) Grassy Downtown playground with carousel, surrounded by museums, cinemas and kid-friendly dining.

Portsmouth Square (p123) Chinatown's outdoor play-room.

Duboce Park Sandy playground between Castro community center and dog park.

Old St Mary's Square (p123) Skateboarders and play equipment.

Weird & Creepy

Carnivorous flowers have insect breath at Conservatory of Flowers (p204) and kids will be holding their own breath as they slip below decks on the submarine USS

NEED TO KNOW

➡ **Change facilities** Best public facilities are at Westfield San Francisco Centre (p110) and San Francisco Main Library (p293).

➡ **Emergency care** San Francisco General Hospital (p293).

➡ **Babysitting** Available at high-end hotels or American Child Care (www.americanchildcare.com/san_francisco.html).

➡ **Strollers & car seats** Bring your own or hire from a rental agency like **Travel BaBees** (☑877-922-2337; www.travelbabees.com).

➡ **Diapers & formula** Available citywide at Walgreens.

➡ **Kiddie menus** Mostly in cafes and downtown diners; call ahead about dietary restrictions.

Pampanito (p58). For pirate supplies, don't miss 826 Valencia (p151), and for assorted hummingbird bones, organic play-dough and shadow puppets, hit the Paxton Gate children's store (p170). Spooky sunset tours of Alcatraz (p52) will keep kids on their best behavior for weeks to come.

Museums & Interactive

San Francisco Children's Creativity Museum (p86) allows future tech moguls to design their own video games and animations, while the Exploratorium's (p62) interactive displays help kids figure out the physics of skateboarding for themselves. Kids are highly encouraged to explore art in San Francisco, with free admission to kids aged 12 and under at Asian Art Museum (p81), Legion of Honor (p205), MH de Young Museum (p203), Museum of the African Diaspora (p86) and Contemporary Jewish Museum (p86).

Boulette's Larder (p94)

Eating

*Other US cities boast bigger monuments, but San Francisco packs more
flavor. Chef Alice Waters set the Bay Area standard for organic, sustainable,
seasonal food back in 1971 at Chez Panisse, and today you'll find
California's pasture-raised meats and organic produce proudly featured
on Korean, Mexican, Chinese, Moroccan, Japanese and Vietnamese menus.
Congratulations: you couldn't have chosen a better time or place for dinner.*

Fine Dining

Reservations Most SF restaurants have online
reservations through their websites or OpenTable
(www.opentable.com), but if the system shows no
availability, call the restaurant directly – some seats
may be held for phone reservations and walk-ins,
and there may be last-minute cancellations or
room at the bar. Landmark restaurants like French
Laundry (p232) and Chez Panisse (p219) and small,
celebrated SF bistros like Rich Table (p189) and
Frances (p177) offer limited seating, so call a month
ahead and take what's available.

Walk-ins Best bets are restaurant-dense areas
like the Mission, Japantown, the Avenues or North
Beach.

Local & sustainable To taste the difference that local, organic, sustainably sourced ingredients make,
try restaurants with the 🌿 icon.

Dietary restrictions Mention any dietary limita-
tions when reserving and you'll be cheerfully
accommodated.

California casual Nice jeans are acceptable and personable interactions appreciated. Service is well-informed and friendly, never snooty.

Bargain Gourmet

Street food The best street eats are at farmers market stalls, and food trucks and pop-ups in the Mission. For in-house street food, hit mom-and-pop eateries in the Avenues and the gritty, gourmet Tenderloin.

Gourmet for less Even at upscale SF restaurants, you'll find affordable bar menus and midweek deals.

Corkage Restaurants without liquor licenses typically offer free corkage, but otherwise it's usually $15 to $20 – a bargain when you consider wine mark-up is three to four times wholesale costs.

Deals Look out for deals at top SF restaurants at Blackboard Eats (www.blackboardeats.com) and during Dine About Town (www.sanfrancisco.travel/dine/dine-about-town) in June and January.

Nontraditional Dining

POP-UP RESTAURANTS

By night, guest chefs commandeer SF galleries, bars and cafes with creative pop-up menus. The downside: pop-ups often charge restaurant prices but without advance menus, quality control, health-inspected facilities or professional service. Bring cash and arrive early: most pop-ups don't accept credit cards and popular dishes run out fast.

Look for announcements on **EaterSF** (http://sf.eater.com), **Grub Street San Francisco** (http://sanfrancisco.grubstreet.com) and **Inside Scoop** (http://insidescoopsf.sfgate.com) for upcoming pop-ups. For a curated pop-up experience, check the Off the Grid (p67) prix fixe dining schedule at Fort Mason.

DESTINATION DINING POP-UPS

Outstanding in the Field (https://outstandinginthefield.com) Dinners with guest star chefs like Alice Waters and this Bay Area–based crew pop up in the unlikeliest places – strawberry fields, sea caves, sand bars – to bring diners to the source of their food.

ForageSF (www.foragesf.com) Wild Kitchen events are foraging trips ending with a communal foraged-food meal.

FOOD TRUCKS & CARTS

Look for prominently displayed permits as guarantee of proper food preparation, refrigeration and regulated working conditions.

NEED TO KNOW

Price Ranges

The following price ranges apply, exclusive of drink, tax and tip:

➡ **$$$** over $20 a meal
➡ **$$** $10–$20 a meal
➡ **$** under $10 a meal

Tipping

Together, tax and tip add 25% to 30% to the bill. SF follows the US tipping standard: 20% to 25% is generous, 15% minimum, unless something went horribly wrong with service. Many restaurants add 18% service charge for parties of six or more.

Surcharges

Some restaurants tack on 3% to 4% surcharge (or $1 to $2 per guest) to cover the cost of providing healthcare to restaurant employees as required by SF law. If you don't appreciate the surcharge, say so in a restaurant review online.

Just don't blame your server, who may not actually be benefiting. In a 2013 scandal, the city found 50 restaurants were pocketing surcharge fees earmarked for employee healthcare – 12 pocketed more than $100K each. The city published the list at www.sfgate.com and fined the restaurants heavily.

Opening Hours

Many restaurants are open seven days a week, though some close Sunday and/or Monday night. Lunch is usually noon to 3pm; dinner starts around 5:30pm with last service 9pm to 9:30pm weekdays or 10pm weekends. Exceptions are noted in reviews.

Feedback

Get local opinions and share your own experience at **Chowhound** (www.chowhound.chow.com/boards/1) and SF-based **Twitter** (www.twitter.com) and **Yelp** (www.yelp.com).

SF's largest gathering of gourmet trucks is Off the Grid (p67), where 30-plus food trucks circle their wagons. Trucks and carts are cash-only businesses and lines for popular trucks can take 10 to 20 minutes.

For the best gourmet to go, try empanadas from **El Sur** (http://www.elsursf.com/), clamshell buns stuffed with duck and mango from **Chairman** (www.thechairmantruck.com), free-range herbed roast chicken from **Roli Roti** (www.roliroti.com) and dessert from Kara's Cupcakes (p70) and the **Créme Bruleé Cart** (www.twitter.com/cremebruleecart).

You can track food trucks at **Roaming Hunger** (www.roaminghunger.com/sf/vendors) or on **Twitter** (@MobileCravings/sf-foodtrucks,@streetfoodsf). Plan ahead for the annual **Street Food Festival** (www.sfstreetfoodfest.com).

DIY DINING

For California-fresh ingredients, you can't beat SF farmers markets, Rainbow Grocery (p161) and Bi-Rite (p161). Downtown are several handy Whole Foods (www.wholefoodsmarket.com) and Trader Joes (www.traderjoes.com) stores.

FARMERS MARKETS

NorCal idealists who headed back to the land in the 1970s started the nation's organic farming movement. Today the local bounty can be sampled in the US city with the most farmers markets per capita.

Ferry Plaza Farmers Market Map p319 (☑415-291-3276; www.cuesa.org; ⊙10am-2pm Tue & Thu, from 8am Sat) The Ferry Building market showcases California-grown, organic produce, artisan meats and gourmet prepared foods at moderate-to-premium prices.

Alemany Farmers Market (http://sfgsa.org; ⊙Sat dawn to dusk) City-run Alemany has offered bargain prices for local and organic produce every Saturday year-round since 1945, plus stalls with ready-to-eat foods.

Heart of the City Farmers Market Map p322 (www.hocfarmersmarket.org; United Nations Plaza; ⊙7am-5pm Wed & Sun, to 2:30pm Fri) This market has local produce (some organics), including lesser-known varietals, plus prepared-food stalls. Bargain prices.

Castro Farmers Market Map p336 (www.pcfma.com; Market St at Noe St; ⊙4-8pm Wed, Mar-Sep) Local and organic produce and artisan foods at moderate prices with live folk music March through December.

HANDS-ON COOKING EVENTS

Spots fill up quickly at DIY cooking events, so subscribe to the organizations' email lists and act fast.

18 Reasons Map p328 (☑415-568-2710; www.18reasons.org; 3674 18th St; classes & events $5-35; ⊙varies by event; 🚼; 🚌22, 33, Ⓜ J) Go gourmet at this Bi-Rite–affiliated community food nonprofit, which offers deliciously educational events: *shochu* tastings, knife-skills and cheesemaking workshops and California cuisine classes. Mingle with fellow foodies at regular family-friendly Wednesday soup suppers and Thursday happy hours, and check the website for low-cost classes with cookbook authors, sommeliers and guest chefs.

La Cocina Map p328 (☑415-824-2729; www.lacocinasf.org; 2948 Folsom St; classes $80; ⊙varies by event; 🚼; 🚌14, 49, Ⓑ24th St Mission) San Francisco keeps food inspiration coming at this culinary nonprofit, which offers 2.5-hour, expert-led cooking workshops on making simple Nepalese *momos* (dumplings), complex Mexican *mole* (cocoa-based sauce) and your own signature cupcake. Proceeds provide training and kitchens for low-income culinary entrepreneurs. Don't miss August's Street Food Festival (p28), featuring hundreds of vendors – including La Cocina's gourmet graduates.

Eating by Neighborhood

➡ **The Marina, Fisherman's Wharf & the Piers** Seafood, fusion and food trucks at the Embarcadero.

➡ **Downtown, Civic Center & SoMa** Vietnamese and tandoori in the Tenderloin; bar bites, tasting menus and sandwiches at SoMa.

➡ **North Beach & Chinatown** Pizza, pasta, experimental Californian in North Beach.

➡ **The Mission & Potrero Hill** Tacos, Italian-Californian fusion, vegetarian, pop-up restaurants in the Mission.

➡ **The Castro & Noe Valley** Bistros and burgers in the Castro.

➡ **The Haight, NoPa & Hayes Valley** Market menus, Japanese *izakaya*, dessert in Hayes Valley.

➡ **Golden Gate Park & the Avenues** Dim sum, Dungeness crab, modern Moroccan and surfer cuisine in the Avenues.

Lonely Planet's Top Choices

Coi (p125) Wild tasting menus featuring foraged morels, wildflowers and Pacific seafood are like licking the California coastline.

Benu (p97) Fine dining meets DJ styling in ingenious remixes of Eastern classics and the best ingredients in the West.

La Taqueria (p155) Some of SF's most memorable meals, wrapped in foil and under $8.

Rich Table (p189) Tasty, inventive California fare with French fine-dining finesse makes you feel clever by association.

Outerlands (p211) Organic surfer fare with all the right moves, hearty enough to take on big waves.

Best for NorCal Cuisine

Coi (p125) See above.

Rich Table (p189) See above.

Outerlands (p211) See above.

Chez Panisse (p219) Alice Waters' Berkeley bistro has championed local, sustainable, fabulous food since 1971.

Outstanding in the Field (p27) California roots cuisine served by star chefs at pioneering organic farms.

Jardinière (p189) Mood-altering, luxuriant meals cater to California's decadent appetites.

Best Meals under $10

La Taqueria (p155) See above.

Off the Grid (p67) First course: empanadas; next course: pork-belly bun; cupcakes for dessert.

Rosamunde Sausage Grill (p186) Sausages with gourmet fixings and Toronado microbrews.

Blue Barn Gourmet (p70) Guilty-pleasure truffle brie sandwiches and healthy master-cleanse salads.

Liguria Bakery (p124) Foccacia hot from the 100-year-old oven.

La Palma Mexicatessen (p161) Beyond tacos: Salvadoran *pupusas* and stuffed *huaraches* handmade with organic masa.

Best Cal-Fusion

Benu (p97) See above.

Namu Gaji (p159) Organic Korean surfer soul food at communal tables.

Slanted Door (p94) Cal-Vietnamese Marin shaking beef with Bay views.

Mr. Pollo (p160) Bargain prix-fixe ranges from Venezuelan *arepas* to California wild salmon belly.

Radish (p158) Cal-Creole brunches bring mardi gras to the Mission.

Mission Chinese (p160) Tiki pork belly and other hipster Cal-Chinese inventions.

Best Al Fresco Frisco

Boulette's Larder (p94) Sunny market-inspired lunches at the Ferry Building waterfront.

Greens (p70) Sitting on the dock of the bay, with chili that'll distract you from the Golden Gate Bridge.

Beach Chalet (p212) Toast the bison with bubbly over brunches in Golden Gate Park's heated backyard.

Mission Cheese (p155) Gloat over your California goat cheese selections and trend-spot Mission street fashion.

Warming Hut (p71) Let's Be Frank hot dogs and sustainable tuna sandwiches under the Golden Gate Bridge.

Cafe Flore (p177) Brunch on the glassed-in patio at the center of the gay universe.

Best Gourmet Gifts

Heath Ceramics (p111) Top SF chefs' tableware of choice, handmade in Sausalito.

Bi-Rite (p161) SF's best-curated selection of local artisan chocolates, cured meats and small-production wines.

Rainbow Grocery (p161) Vast selection of NorCal's finest coffees, cheeses and organic airplane snacks.

Le Sanctuaire (p110) Gellants, spherifiers, foaming agents and other mad-scientist dinner ingredients.

Global Exchange (p182) Fair-trade, handcrafted place settings showcase SF's thoughtful cosmopolitan tastes.

Drinking & Nightlife

No matter what you're having, SF bars, cafes and clubs are here to oblige. But why stick to your usual, when there are California wines, Bay spirits, microbrews and local roasts to try? Adventurous drinking is abetted by local bartenders, who've been making good on Gold Rush saloon history. SF baristas take their cappuccino-foam-drawings seriously and DJs invent their own software around here.

Cocktails

Tonight you're gonna party like it's 1899. Gone are the mad scientist's mixology beakers of two years ago: today SF's drink historians are judged by their absinthe fountains and displays of swizzle sticks from defunct ocean liners. All that authenticity-tripping over cocktails may sound self-conscious, but after enjoying strong pours at vintage saloons and speakeasies, consciousness is hardly an issue.

Cost Happy-hour specials or well drinks run $6 to $7 and gourmet choices with premium hooch run $8 to $15.

Local spirits Top-shelf SF Bay liquor includes St George gin, 1512 bourbon, Old Potrero whiskey and Hangar vodka.

Tip With $1 to $2 per drink, bartenders return the favor with heavy pours next round – that's why it's called getting tip-sy.

Wine

To get a glass of the good stuff, you don't need to commit to a bottle or escape to Wine Country. San Francisco restaurants and wine bars are increasingly offering top-notch, small-production California wines *alla spina* (on tap). Organically grown, sustainable and biodynamic wines feature on most SF lists.

Wine Country deals Plan your trip to Napa or Sonoma for late fall, when you can taste new releases and score harvest specials.

Food-truck pairings Consult the bar's Twitter feed or Facebook page – or see what trucks are around at www.roaminghunger.com/sf/vendors or @Mobile Cravings/sf-food-trucks on Twitter.

Cult wine retailers Bi-Rite (p161), PlumpJack Wines (p73) and California Wine Merchant (p71) sell hard-to-find wines at reasonable prices.

Beer

SF's first brewery (1849) was built before the city and beer has been the default beverage ever since.

Cost $4 to $7 a pint for draft microbrews, $2 PBRs (Pabst Blue Ribbon) – plus $1 tip.

Beer gardens Drink in the great outdoors at Biergarten (p192), Zeitgeist (p161) and Beach Chalet (p212).

House brews Doesn't get more local than beer brewed onsite at Anchor Brewing (p171), 21st Amendment (p97), Magnolia Brewpub (p188), Southern Pacific (www.southernpacificbrewing.com) and Social (p212).

Meet brewers SF Brewers' Guild (www.sfbrewersguild.org) hosts meet-ups with local brewers.

Cafe Scene

When San Francisco couples break up, the thorniest issue is: who gets the cafe? San Franciscans are fiercely loyal to specific roasts and baristas – especially in the Mission and North Beach – and the majority of first internet dates meet on neutral coffee grounds. When using free cafe wi-fi, remember: order something every hour, deal with interruptions graciously and don't leave laptops unattended.

Cost $2 for American coffee and $3 to $5 for espresso drinks.

Tip Leave a buck in the tip jar for espresso drinks, especially when staying a while.

Cell phones Texting is fine, but phone calls are many baristas' pet peeve.

Clubbing

DJs set the tone at clubs in SF, where the right groove gets everyone on the dance floor – gay, straight and a glorious swath of whatever. You'll usually only wait 10 minutes to get in anywhere, unless you're stumbling drunk.

Cost Most clubs charge $10 to $20 at the door. For discounted admission, show up before 10pm or sign up on the club's online guest list (look for a VIP or RSVP link). Seating may be reserved for bottle service at high-end clubs.

Dress code SF is pretty casual, though club bouncers do turn away people wearing flip-flops, shorts or T-shirts (unless they're spiffy), especially at swing and salsa clubs.

Late night Many clubs close around last call, though EndUp (p104) rages til dawn.

Drinking by Neighborhood

➡ **The Marina, Fisherman's Wharf & the Piers** Straight bars in the Marina.

➡ **Downtown, Civic Center & SoMa** Dives, chichi lounges, old-school gay bars in Civic Center & the Tenderloin; art lounges, wine bars, men's cruising bars and clubs in SoMa.

➡ **North Beach & Chinatown** Barbary Coast saloons, eccentric bars, Italian cafes and retro lounges in North Beach.

➡ **The Mission & Potrero Hill** Hipster saloons, friendly wine bars, salsa clubs, women's and trans bars in the Mission.

➡ **The Castro & Noe Valley** Gay bars in the Castro.

➡ **The Haight & Hayes Valley** Mean whiskey, serious beer and boho lounges in the Haight; wine bars in Hayes Valley.

➡ **Golden Gate Park & the Avenues** Irish and tiki bars in the Richmond.

NEED TO KNOW

Smoking

Not legal indoors. Some bars have smoking patios, including Rye (p100), Bar Agricole (p101) and Irish Bank (p99), or backyards, such as El Rio (p167), Wild Side West (p171) and Zeitgeist (p161) – otherwise, you'll be puffing on the sidewalk.

Opening Hours

Downtown and SoMa bars draw happy hour crowds 4 to 7pm; otherwise, bars are hopping by 9pm, with last call 10:30 to 11:30pm weekdays and 1:30am weekends. Clubs kick in around 10pm and many close at 2am.

Websites

To find out what's up where this weekend, check free weeklies **SF Weekly** (www.sfweekly.com) and **San Francisco Bay Guardian** (www.sfbg.com), and troll upcoming events on **Squid List** (www.squidlist.com/events), **UrbanDaddy** (www.urbandaddy.com/home/sfo) and **Thrillist** (www.thrillist.com).

PLAN YOUR TRIP DRINKING & NIGHTLIFE

Lonely Planet's Top Choices

Bar Agricole (p101) Drink your way to a history degree with well-researched cocktails – anything with hellfire bitters earns honors.

Smuggler's Cove (p193) Roll with the rum punches at this Barbary Coast shipwreck bar.

Comstock Saloon (p127) Vintage wild west saloon with potent, period-perfect concoctions and dainty bar bites.

Toronado (p189) Beer for every season and any reason – summer ales, holiday barley-wines, Oktoberfest wheats.

Hôtel Biron (p193) Walk-in closet wine-bar with small, standout selection.

Best Cocktails

Bar Agricole (p101) See Top Choices above.

Smuggler's Cove (p193) See Top Choices above.

Comstock Saloon (p127) See Top Choices above.

Rickhouse (p98) Impeccable bourbon drinks in chic shotgun-shack atmosphere.

Trick Dog (p161) Midcentury-modern designer cocktails in a Pantone palette.

Bourbon & Branch (p99) Not since Prohibition have secret passwords and gin knowledge been this handy.

Best Wine Bars

Hôtel Biron (p193) See Top Choices above.

RN74 (p101) Rajat Parr's wine menu is a collector's wish-list, with small plate pairings from Michael Mina.

20 Spot (p162) Instant mellow, with Eames rockers, deviled duck eggs and 100 wines.

Terroir Natural Wine Merchant (p101) Red, white and green: sustainably produced wines from cult winemakers.

Barrique (p98) Roll out the barrel: no labels, no pretensions, just good times with terrific local wines on tap.

St. Vincent (p163) Smart pairings and adventurous tastings around sociable communal tables.

Best for Beer

Toronado (p189) See Top Choices above.

Zeitgeist (p161) Surly lady bartenders tap 40 microbrews and street-food vendors cure late-night munchies.

City Beer Store & Tasting Room (p103) Beer sommeliers earn the title here with expert-led tastings, brewing and pairing tips.

Specs Museum Cafe (p127) Blow off steam with Anchor Steam by the pitcher in the nautical back-alley bar.

Biergarten (p192) A shipping-container bar keeps this beer garden well-watered.

Irish Bank (p99) Downtown's secret Emerald Isle getaway offers properly poured Guinness and fish 'n' chips in cozy snugs.

Best Dance Clubs

Endup (p104) Offers epic 24-hour dance sessions in an urban-legendary SoMa gay club since 1973.

DNA Lounge (p103) Known for booty-shaking mashups, Tranny-shacking drag and roof-raising live acts like Prince.

Cat Club (p102) Something for everyone: '80s one-hit wonders, '90s mega-pop and go-go bondage.

El Rio (p167) Get down and funky in the Mission and flirt internationally in the backyard.

Starlight Room (p106) Classy dates and morning-after drag-show brunches 21 floors above Union Square.

Rickshaw Stop (p100) Beats won't quit at this all-ages, all-orientations, all-fabulous shoebox club.

Best Cafes

Caffe Trieste (p127) Legendary North Beach cafe, fueling epic Beat poetry and weekend accordion jams since the '50s.

Ritual Coffee Roasters (p161) Heady roasts, local art and seats among burlap coffee bags in a cult roastery-cafe.

Réveille (p130) Sunny flatiron cafe with stellar espresso drinks, decadent pastries and sidewalk people-watching.

Sightglass Coffee (p103) This SoMa roastery looks industrial but serves small-batch roasts from family farms.

Blue Bottle Coffee Company (p193) The back-alley garage that kicked off the Third Wave coffee roastery craze.

The Magic Flute, presented by the San Francisco Opera (p105)

☆ Entertainment

SF is one of the top five US cities for the number of creative types per square mile – and when all those characters take the stage, look out. Though the city has a world-famous orchestra, opera, film festival, theater and ballet, the SF scene isn't all about marquee names: you can see cutting-edge dance, comedy and music for the price of an IMAX movie.

Comedy & Spoken Word

For laughs, try campy Beach Blanket Babylon (p130), Marsh monologues (p167) or historic Cobb's Comedy Club (p131) – or get onstage with BATS Improv (p72) comedy workshops.

Literary types should check out SF's annual Litquake (p23), San Francisco Main Library (p88) and Booksmith (p194) readings, plus **Literary Death Match** (www.literarydeathmatch. com). Hemlock Tavern (p106) and Edinburgh Castle (p99) are liquid-literary legends.

Dance

SF supports the longest-running US ballet company, San Francisco Ballet (p105), and multiple independent troupes at Yerba Buena Center for the Arts (p107). Experimental styles are championed at Oberlin Dance Collective (p163), **Kunst Stoff** (Map p324; www. kunst-stoff.org; 26 7th St, San Francisco Dance Center) and Root Division (p155). **Dancers' Group** (www.dancersgroup.org) keeps a comprehensive calendar.

NEED TO KNOW

Arts Calendar

Check **KQED Community** (http://events.kqed.org) for free and family event listings.

Discounts

Sign up at **Gold Star Events** (www.goldstarevents.com) for discounts on comedy, theater, concerts and opera.

Half-Price Tickets

Visit **TIX Bay Area** (Map p320; www.tixbayarea.org) or the Union Square ticket booth for cheap tickets for same-day or next-day shows.

Film

Cinemaniacs adore SF's vintage movie palaces, including the Roxie (p163), Castro (p181) and Balboa (p213) cinemas. Summers bring monthly **Dolores Park Movie Night** (www.doloresparkmovie.org).

Festivals Beyond SF International Film Festival (http://festival.sffs.org), SF hosts LGBT (p22), Jewish and Arab Film Festivals.

Tickets Most tickets run $10 to $13, with weekday matinees around $8.

Live Music

Eclectic SF clubs host funk, reggae, bluegrass and punk; check online calendars.

Bluegrass Hear the original music of San Francisco's Gold Rush at Hardly Strictly Bluegrass Festival (www.hardlystrictlybluegrass.com) and on public radio's Bluegrass Signal (http://kalw.org/programs/bluegrass-signal).

Funk & Hip-Hop Oakland has tougher rap and faster beats, but SF plays it loose and funky at Mezzanine (p107) and Independent (p194).

Jazz Major jazz talents are in residence year-round at SFJAZZ Center (p194), and perform at Yoshi's (p144) and The Chapel (p166).

Punk Punk's not dead at SUB-Mission (p167) and Slim's (p107).

Rock Psychedelic rock legends played at the Fillmore (p144), but alt-rock takes the stage at Outside Lands fest (www.sfoutsidelands.com), Warfield (p107) and the Great American Music Hall (p106).

Opera & Classical Music

Between San Francisco Opera (p105) seasons, hear opera by the Grammy-winning, 12-man chorus **Chanticleer** (www.chanticleer.org; dates vary) and San Francisco's **Pocket Opera Company** (www.pocketopera.org; February through June).

Michael Tilson Thomas conducts the nine-time Grammy-winning San Francisco Symphony (p105), and **San Francisco Performances** (www.performances.org) hosts world-class classical performances at Herbst Theater.

Symphony & opera season Typically runs September through June; check SF Classical Voice (www.sfcv.org) for dates.

Free music SF Opera and SF Symphony perform gratis at Stern Grove Festival (www.sterngrove.org); check http://noontimeconcerts.org for donation-requested concerts.

Bargain tickets SF Opera offers America's least expensive opera tickets ($10–50); SF Symphony offers rush tickets and open rehearsal tickets ($20–25).

Theater

Before winning Tonys and a Pulitzer Prize, *Angels in America* got its wings at the American Conservatory Theater (p105). In summer, the **San Francisco Mime Troupe** (www.sfmt.org) performs free political-comedy satire in Dolores Park, while the SF Shakespeare Festival (www.sfshakes.org) is held gratis in the Presidio.

Theatre Bay Area (www.theatrebayarea.org) is a comprehensive calendar of 100 Bay Area theater companies.

Broadway shows See SF listings at www.shnsf.com.

Tickets Marquee shows run $35 to $150, but same-day, half-price tickets are often available. Indie theater runs $10 to $30.

Entertainment by Neighborhood

➡ **Downtown & Civic Center** Symphony, opera, theater, live music, spoken word and comedy.

➡ **North Beach & Chinatown** Comedy, live music and spoken word.

➡ **The Mission, SoMa & Potrero Hill** Dance, live music, experimental theater and spoken word.

➡ **Golden Gate Park & the Avenues** Free opera, theater and concerts.

Lonely Planet's Top Choices

San Francisco Symphony (p105) Sets the tempo for modern classical, with guests like Jessye Norman, Metallica and Rufus Wainwright.

SFJAZZ Center (p194) Top talents reinvent standards and create new works inspired by mariachis, Hunter S Thompson texts and even skateboards.

Castro Theatre (p181) Organ overtures and revivals with enthusiastic audience participation raise this art deco cinema's roof.

American Conservatory Theater (p105) Daring theater, from operas by Tom Waits and William S Burroughs to controversial David Mamet plays.

San Francisco Opera (p105) Divas like Renée Fleming bring down the house with classics and contemporary works including *Nixon in China*.

Best Live Music Venues

San Francisco Symphony (p105) See Top Choices above.

SFJAZZ Center (p194) See Top Choices above.

San Francisco Opera (p105) See Top Choices above.

Fillmore Auditorium (p144) Rock-legendary since the '60s, with the psychedelic posters to prove it.

Great American Music Hall (p106) Marquee acts in a historic, intimate venue that was once a bordello.

Yoshi's (p144) Jazz greats improvise nightly and you're along for the ride in this legendary club.

Best for Theater & Dance

American Conservatory Theater (p105) See Top Choices above.

San Francisco Ballet (p105) Elegant lines and gorgeous original staging from America's oldest ballet company.

Oberlin Dance Collective (p163) Style and substance in balance, with muscular, meaningful, original choreography.

Yerba Buena Center for the Arts (p107) Modern dance troupes throw down and represent SF's cutting edge.

Intersection for the Arts (p107) Playwrights debut original work, and jazz composers, writers and artists collaborate.

Best for Movies

Castro Theatre (p181) See Top Choices.

San Francisco International Film Festival Breakthrough indies and stealth Oscar favorites premiere here, with directors from Afghanistan to Uganda and movie-star Q&As.

Sundance Kabuki Cinema (p145) Balcony bars, reserved seating and zero ads make great films better.

Roxie Cinema (p163) Offers cult classics, documentary premieres and indie films not yet distributed in a vintage cinema.

Balboa Theatre (p213) Art deco cinema features first-run and art-house films, plus family matinees.

Best Free Entertainment

Hardly Strictly Bluegrass Festival (see opposite) See bluegrass legends like Alison Krauss jam alongside Elvis Costello, Patti Smith and Dwight Yoakam – for free.

Stern Grove Festival (see opposite) SF Opera divas and symphony soloists perform in the great outdoors.

San Francisco Mime Troupe (p34) Social satire, Kabuki and musical comedy make scenes in Dolores Park.

San Francisco Shakespeare Festival (see opposite) Audiences warm to *The Winter's Tale* at foggy Presidio performances.

Amoeba (p194) Free in-store concerts by legends, plus new and cult acts.

Best for Laughs

Cobb's Comedy Club (p131) Comics from the streets to Comedy Central test risky new material.

Beach Blanket Babylon (p130) Laugh your wig off with San Francisco's over-the-top Disney-drag cabaret.

Punch Line (p106) Breakthrough comedians like Ellen Degeneres, Chris Rock and Margaret Cho started here.

Marsh (p167) Monologues range from uproarious to heartbreaking, sometimes in the same act.

⭐ GLBT

Doesn't matter where you're from, who you love or who's your daddy: if you're here and queer, welcome home. San Francisco is America's pinkest city, and though New York Marys may call it the retirement home of the young – the sidewalks roll up early here – there's nowhere better to be out and proud.

Gay/Lesbian/Bi/Trans Scene

In San Francisco, you don't need to trawl the urban underworld for a gay scene. The intersection of 18th and Castro is the historic center of the gay world, but dancing queens head to SoMa for thump-thump clubs.

So where are all the ladies? They're busy scamming on their exes' exes at the Lexington Club (p162), screening documentaries at **Artists' Television Access** (www.atasite.org) or raising kids in Noe Valley and Bernal Heights. The Mission is the preferred 'hood of alt-chicks, dykes, trans FTMs (female-to-males) and flirty femmes.

Gender need not apply in SF, where even the DMV acknowledges trans identities. Drag shows are beloved San Francisco institutions, though you'll never need a professional reason to cross gender lines here – next to baseball, gender-bending is SF's favorite sport.

Party Planning

On Sundays in the 1950s, SF bars held gay old times euphemistically known as 'tea dances' – and Sundays remain the most happening nights in town.

Trannyshack (www.trannyshack.com) SF's finest monthly drag throw-downs at DNA, hosted by legendary dragmother Heklina.

Cockblock (www.cockblocksf.com) Les/gay 'homolicious' dance party mayhem breaks out at Rickshaw Stop.

Faetopia (http://faetopia.com) Bringing fabulous faerie magick to SF with glam street theater, cuddle cinema, feyboy art grants and sliding-scale donation parties.

Juanita More (www.juanitamore.com) This drag superstar throws fierce parties attended by hot boys, especially for Pride.

Comfort & Joy (http://playajoy.org) The Queer Burning Man collective lists happening dance parties and creative community events.

Honey Soundsystem Map p324 (www.honeysoundsystem.com) Kick-ass dance party – from obscure disco B-sides to German techno.

Go Bang! (www.facebook.com/GoBANGSF) Atomic-scale disco inferno tears through SF, including Cafe Flore.

GLBT by Neighborhood

➡ **Downtown, SoMa & Civic Center** Raging dance clubs, leather bars, drag shows and men's sex clubs in SoMa; bars, trans venues and queer theater in the Tenderloin.

➡ **The Mission & Potrero Hill** Women's and trans bars, arts venues and community spaces in the Mission.

➡ **The Castro & Noe Valley** Gay history, activism and men's cruising bars in the Castro; GLBT family scene in Noe Valley.

Lonely Planet's Top Choices

Pride The most extravagant celebration on the planet culminates in Pink Saturday parties and an exhilarating 1.2-million-strong Pride Parade.

Human Rights Campaign Action Center & Store (p181) Been there, signed the petition, bought the T-shirt supporting civil rights at Harvey Milk's camera storefront.

Castro Theatre (p181) San Francisco International LGBT Film Festival premieres here as well as audience-participatory cult classics.

GLBT History Museum (p175) Proud moments and historic challenges, captured for posterity.

Aunt Charlie's (p100) Knock-down, drag-out winner for gender-bending shows and dance-floor freakiness.

Best for Gay Old Times with Straight Friends

Pride See Top Choices above.

GLBT History Museum (p175) See Top Choices above.

Trannyshack Mind-blowing genderfreakery, glitter gutter-mouths, art-project costumes: now you know why SF drag is better.

SF International LGBT Film Festival (p22) Worldwide queer premieres, from Argentina to Vietnam.

Faetopia Because the world needs a little extra fairie magick.

Under One Roof (p110) Buy souvenirs from volunteers to support AIDS charities.

Best for Women

Lexington Club (p162) Accidentally hit on your ex-girlfriend's ex-girlfriend? Blame it on the Lex Hex.

Wild Side West (p171) Cheers to queers and beers in the backyard garden.

El Rio (p167) Mix it up with world music mixes, free oysters and SF's flirtiest patio.

Women's Building (p152) Glorious murals crown this community institution.

Brava Theater (p167) Original shows by, for and about lesbians and transwomen.

Cafe (p180) Grrrrl power takes over the Castro weekly.

Best for Men

Aunt Charlie's (p100) See Top Choices above.

Eagle (p104) Landmark SoMa leather rocker bar, as friendly/sleazy as you wanna be.

Stud (p104) Low visibility and the tantalizing aroma of bourbon and testosterone: guaranteed good times.

Rickshaw Stop (p100) Freak beats keep sweaty 18-plus crowds up past their bedtimes.

Endup (p104) Hit your groove Saturday night and work it until Monday.

Lookout (p180) Gay and ready to play in the Castro, with people-watching perch.

Best Daytime Scene

Dolores Park (p151) Sun and cityscapes at grassy Gay Beach, plus protests and Hunky Jesus Contests.

PLAN YOUR TRIP GLBT

NEED TO KNOW

News & Events

San Francisco Bay Times has good resources for trans events; **Bay Area Reporter** for news and listings; free **Gloss Magazine** for nightlife.

Women's Community Venues

Women's Building (p152) for organizations; **Lyon-Martin Women's Health Services** (p294) for health and support; **Brava Theater** (p167) for arts.

Support & Activism

LYRIC (www.lyric.org) for queer youth; **Human Rights Campaign Action Center & Store** (p181) for political organizing; **GLBT History Museum** (p175) for context; **Transgender Law Center** for civil rights activism and support; **Homobile** for a safe, non-profit GLBT taxi service; **Under One Roof** (p110) purchases support local AIDS organizations.

Baker Beach (p61) Only Baker Beach regulars knew you could get goosebumps there.

Cafe Flore (p177) The best people-watching on the gay planet: blind dates, parents showing support for GLBT kids, dogs in drag.

Harvey Milk & Jane Warner Plazas (p175) Come out and hang out under the giant rainbow flag.

Samovar Tea Lounge (p180) Clean & sober hangout with wi-fi and flirting over rare teas.

Zinc Details (p148), Pacific Heights

🛍 Shopping

All those rustic dens, well-stocked spice racks and fabulous outfits don't just pull themselves together – San Franciscans scour their city for them. Eclectic originality is San Francisco's signature style and that's not one-stop shopping. But consider the thrill of the hunt: while shopping in SF, you can watch fish theater, make necklaces from zippers and trade fashion tips with drag queens.

Downtown Malls & Shopping Hubs

Union Square Ringed by department stores and luxury boutiques: Neiman Marcus, Macy's, Saks, Louis Vuitton, Levi's.

Westfield Centre Under a vast dome are Bloomingdale's and Nordstrom, but also cult stores like Vans, Kate Spade, Art of Shaving and Mango.

Crocker Galleria Specialty gifts, non-profit Under One Roof, Tomboy Tailors and Thursday farmers markets (www.thecrockergalleria.com).

Powell St Lined with flagship stores and bargains: Gap, Uniqlo, H&M, Urban Outfitters, DSW.

Unconventional Retail

Indie designers and vintage shops supply original style on SF's most boutique-studded streets: Haight, Valencia, Hayes, upper Grant, Fillmore, Union and Polk. For further adventures in retail, don't miss the following shopping events:

Monster Drawing Rally (www.soex.org)
Artists scribble furiously and audience members snap up their work while still wet; February.

Noise Pop (www.noisepop.com) Concerts and rock-star pop-up shops; February.

Litquake (www.litquake.com) Score signed books and grab drinks with authors afterwards; September.

Alternative Press Expo (www.comic-con. org/ape) Comics, drawings, zines and crafts, plus workshops with comics artists; October.

Artpad (www.artpadsf.com) Independent art fair with live bands, rooftop video screenings and artistic mayhem.

Celebration of Craftswomen (www.womens building.org) Local craftswomen show off their skills and support the Women's Building; held at Fort Mason in December.

Shopping by Neighborhood

➜ **The Marina, Fisherman's Wharf & the Piers** Date outfits, girly accessories, wine and design in the Marina.

➜ **Downtown & Civic Center** Department stores, global megabrands, discount retail and an Apple store.

➜ **The Hills & Japantown** Home design, stationery, toys, accessories and anime in Japantown; designer clothes, jewelry and decor in Pacific Heights and Russian Hill.

➜ **The Mission & Potrero Hill** Bookstores, local design collectives, artisan foods, art galleries, hipster tees, vintage whatever.

➜ **The Haight, NoPa & Hayes Valley** Local designers, decor, sweets and shoes in Hayes Valley; quirky gifts and accessories in NoPa; head shops, music, vintage, and skate and snow gear in the Haight.

NEED TO KNOW

Business Hours

Most stores are open daily from 10am to 6 or 7pm, though hours often run 11am to 8pm Saturdays and 11am to 6pm Sundays. Stores in the Mission and the Haight tend to open later and keep erratic hours; many Downtown stores stay open until 8pm or 9pm.

Sales Tax

Combined SF city and CA state sales taxes tack 9.5% onto the price of your purchase. This tax is not refundable.

Returns

Try before you buy and ask about return policies. Many stores offer returns for store credit only, so when in doubt, consider a gift certificate. In California, they never expire and you can often use them online.

Websites

Check **Urban Daddy** (www.urbandaddy. com) for store openings and pop-ups; Thrillist (p31) for guy gifts and gadgets; **Refinery 29** (www.refinery29.com) for sales and trends; and **Daily Candy** (www.daily candy.com) for SF finds and deals.

Lonely Planet's Top Choices

City Lights (p131) If you can't find nirvana in the Poetry Chair upstairs, try Lost Continents in the basement.

826 Valencia (p151) Your friendly neighborhood pirate-supply store and publishing house; proceeds support on-site youth literacy programs.

Under One Roof (p110) Volunteers ring up goods donated by local designers with sincere thanks – all proceeds support local AIDS organizations.

Heath Ceramics (p111) The local, handmade tableware of choice for SF's star chefs, in essential modern shapes and appetizing earthy colors.

Park Life (p213) Making museum stores jealous with rising-star artists out back and limited-edition art books and design oddities in front.

Reliquary (p198) Well-traveled indie-movie-star style and retro boho-chic; no clove cigarettes required.

Best SF Fashion Designers

Gravel & Gold (p169) Hand-silkscreened patterns on nubby cotton frocks and smocks go from beach to gallery.

Betabrand (p169) Limited-edition clothing inspired by SF obsessions: disco balls, sharks, beards.

Goorin Brothers Hats (p195) Dapper fedoras, coy cloches and tattooed caps to fit your every alter ego.

Nooworks (p169) '80s new wave designs reinvented with edgy art-schooled graphics.

Dema (p170) Flattering vintage silhouettes in African-print cottons and psychedelic paisley silks.

Aggregate Supply (p170) Pop-art windbreakers and tees from Turk+Taylor.

Best for Éclectic SF Decor

Heath Ceramics (p111) See Top Choices above.

Park Life (p213) See Top Choices above.

Accident & Artifact (p170) Spools, homespun indigo, altered topographical maps: decor beyond design magazines.

General Store (p213) All the NorCal beach-house essentials: Pendleton blankets, geodesic dome planters, surfboard-shaped cutting boards.

Global Exchange (p182) Fair trade fabulous – handwoven cotton hammocks, kantha quilts, recycled glass bowls.

Viracocha (p166) Typewriters, driftwood lamps, bottled messages and other decor for incorrigible romantics.

Best for the Person Who Has Everything

826 Valencia (p151) See Top Choices above.

Electric Works (p86) Artist multiples, including original works by Paul Madonna and Trina Robbins for $40.

Good Vibrations (p170) Adult toys, with informed staff and zero judgment.

New People (p146) Ninja shoes, Lolita Goth petticoats, and the latest in wooden speakers at this Japantown showcase.

Piedmont Boutique (p195) Drag like you mean it, honey: boas, fake-fur bootie shorts, airplane earrings.

Loved to Death (p195) Goth jewelry, macabre Victoriana and taxidermied everything.

Sports & Activities

San Franciscans love the outdoors, and their historic conservation efforts have protected acres of parks, beaches and woodlands for all to enjoy. This city lives for sunny days spent biking, skating, surfing and facing fierce competition. Foggy days are spent at arts workshops and on trapezes, but nights are for dancing and Giants games.

Spectator Sports

See the Giants play baseball on their home turf at AT&T Park (p113). You might be able catch some Giants action for free at the Embarcadero waterfront boardwalk. As of fall 2014 you'll need to head an hour south to see the 49ers play football in their new stadium in Santa Clara.

Tickets Book through team websites or try Ticketmaster (www.ticketmaster.com). If games are sold out, search the 'Tickets' category on www.craigslist.org.

Sports coverage *San Francisco Chronicle* (www.sfgate.com) offers complete coverage, but *The Examiner* (www.sfexaminer.com) also has sports stats and predictions.

Outdoor Activities

On sunny weekends, SF is out kite-flying, surfing or biking. Even on foggy days, don't neglect sunscreen: UV rays penetrate SF's thin cloud cover.

BICYCLING

Every weekend thousands of cyclists cross Golden Gate Bridge (p59) to explore the Marin Headlands and Mt Tamalpais. Since the '70s, Mt Tam has remained the Bay Area's ultimate mountain-biking challenge.

Many SF streets have bicycle lanes and major parks have bike paths. The safest places to cycle in SF are Golden Gate Park (car-free on Sundays), the Embarcadero and wooded Presidio. SF's most beloved street-biking route is the green-painted, flat bike lane connecting Market St and Golden Gate Park called the Wiggle (www.sfbike.org/?wiggle).

City biking maps San Francisco Bicycle Coalition (www.sfbike.org) produces *San Francisco Biking/ Walking Guide,* which outlines the Wiggle route and shows how to avoid traffic and hills.

Route planning Put your smart phone to work finding the perfect route using the San Francisco Bike Route Planner (http://amarpai.com/bikemap).

Critical Mass To claim bicylists' right of way on city streets, join the Critical Mass protest-parade on the last Friday of the month. Some motorists are unsympathetic with this interruption in rush-hour traffic, so use caution and stand down if someone flips you off from a passing car.

Riding naked World Naked Bike Ride (www.sfbikeride.org) takes place in early June to protest the US dependence on fossil fuels.

GOLF

Tee up and enjoy mild weather, clipped greens and gorgeous views on SF's top public courses (see box text, p215).

RUNNING

Crissy Field (p60) has a 2.5-mile jogging track, and trails run 3 miles through Golden Gate Park (p202) from the Panhandle to Ocean Beach. The Presidio (p64) offers ocean breezes through eucalyptus trees. Some of SF's major races, like Bay to Breakers, are more festive than serious.

NEED TO KNOW

Free Outdoor Activities

Lawn bowling, lindy-hopping, disc golf: try something new gratis at Golden Gate Park (p202).

Gear

From mountaineering to diving, gear up at Sports Basement (p74).

Group Activities

Join groups kayaking, surfing and camping through www.meetup.com or **University of California San Francisco's Outdoors Programs** (📞415-476-2078; www.outdoors.ucsf.edu).

Rainy Day Adventures

Head to the Marina to Planet Granite rock-climbing gym (p76) and House of Air trampoline park (p76), learn trapeze at **Circus Center Trapeze** (Map p342; 📞415-759-8123; www.circuscenter.org; 755 Frederick St; 2hr workshop $40; ⊙class times vary; 🚇; 🚌6, 33, 71, Ⓜ️N) or hit Yerba Buena Center Ice Skating & Bowling (p114).

SKATING & SKATEBOARDING

SF is the home of roller disco and the skateboard magazine *Thrasher*. Inline skaters skate the Embarcadero Friday nights and disco-skate in Golden Gate Park (p202) on Sundays. Golden Gate Park Bike & Skate (p214) rents inline and four-wheeled roller skates in good weather.

Potrero del Sol/La Raza Skatepark (p172) has ramps for kids and bowls for pros. Haight St is urban skating at its obstacle-course best, especially the downhill slide from Baker to Pierce.

For signature SF skateboards and skate gear, hit Mission Skateboards (p170) and SFO Snowboarding & FTC Skateboarding (p195); for decks and trucks, Upper Playground (p198).

Water Sports & Activities

SAILING

Sailing is best April through August, and classes and rentals are available from Spinnaker Sailing (p114) or City Kayak (p114). Newbies may feel more comfortable on a catamaran with Adventure Cat (p74) or a booze cruise with Red & White Fleet (p74).

Whale-watching season peaks mid-October through December, when the mighty mammals are easy to spot from Point Reyes (p234). Book whale-watching tours through Oceanic Society Expeditions (p74).

SURFING & WINDSURFING

About a 90-minute drive south of SF, Santa Cruz is NorCal's top surf destination for kooks (newbies) and pros alike. For challenging (and shark-prone) swells, try Stinson Beach in Marin County. SF's Ocean Beach (p206) is surfed by locals at daybreak in winter but these Pacific swells aren't for beginners. Mavericks big-wave surfing competition held each February in Half Moon Bay (30 minutes south of SF) is strictly for pros.

A safer bet is bay windsurfing and bodysurfing off the beach at Crissy Field (p60). Hit up Mollusk (p213) for specialty boards and gear. Check the **surf report** (415-273-1618) before you suit up.

SWIMMING

Ocean Beach (p206) is best for walking – the Pacific undertow is dangerous. Hardy swimmers brave chilly Bay waters at Aquatic Park (p57) or Baker Beach (p61; nude around the northern end). Head to Santa Cruz for calmer waters and warmer beaches.

Local pools Koret Pool (Map p338) and Embarcadero YMCA (p114) have well-kept pools; city pool schedules are listed at www.parks.sfgov.org.

Alcatraz Sharkfest Swim Swim 1.5 miles from Alcatraz to Aquatic Park. Entry is $175; check Envirosports (www.envirosports.com) for info.

Dance

Learn to lindy-hop (p214) at Golden Gate Park, tango at Mission Cultural Center (p171) and vogue at Oberlin Dance Collective (p163). Many music venues offer dance classes before the evening's entertainment, including Bimbo's 356 Club (p130).

Sports & Activities by Neighborhood

➡ **The Marina, Fisherman's Wharf & the Piers** Running, biking, windsurfing, kayaking, skating and yoga in the Marina.

➡ **The Mission, SoMa & Potrero Hill** Arts, dance, skateboarding and yoga in the Mission; swimming, kayaking and sailing in SoMa.

➡ **Golden Gate Park & the Avenues** Surfing, biking, swimming, golf and archery in the Avenues.

Cable car going down Hyde St

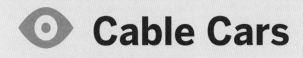 # Cable Cars

A creaking hand brake seems to be the only thing between you and cruel fate as your 15,000-pound cable car picks up speed downhill, careening toward oncoming traffic. But Andrew Hallidie's 1873 contraptions have held up miraculously well on San Francisco's breakneck slopes, and groaning brakes and clanging brass bells only add to the carnival-ride thrills.

History

Legend has it that the idea of cable cars occurred to Andrew Hallidie in 1869, as he watched a horse carriage struggle up Jackson St – until one horse slipped on wet cobblestones and the carriage went crashing downhill. Such accidents were considered inevitable on steep San Francisco hills, but Hallidie knew better. His father was the Scottish inventor of wire cable, which Hallidie had used for hauling ore from mines during the Gold Rush. If hemp-and-metal cable

could haul rocks through High Sierra snowstorms, it could transport San Franciscans through fog.

'Wire rope railway' wasn't a name that inspired confidence and skeptical city planners granted the inventor just three months to make his contraption operational by August 1, 1873. Hallidie missed his city deadline by four hours when his cable car was poised on Jones St, ready for the descent. The cable car operator was terrified, and Hallidie himself is said to have grabbed the brake and steered the car downhill.

NEED TO KNOW

Operating Hours

Cable car lines operate from about 6am to 1am daily, with scheduled departures every three to 12 minutes; for detailed schedules, see http://transit.511.org.

Cost

If you're planning to stop en route, get a Muni Passport; one-way tickets cost $6, with no on-and-off privileges.

Boarding

The Powell St and California St cable car turnarounds usually have queues (which thankfully move fast). To skip the queue, head further up the line and jump on when the cable car stops. Cable cars may make rolling stops, especially on downhill runs. To board on hills, act fast: leap onto the baseboard and grab the closest leather hand strap.

Stops

Cable cars stop at almost every block on the California St and Powell-Mason lines, and every block on the north–south stretches of the Powell-Hyde line; see www.sfmuni.com for maps.

Child Safety

This Victorian mode of transport is certainly not childproof. You won't find car seats or seat belts on these wooden benches; kids love the open-air seating in front, but holding small children securely inside the car is safer.

Accessibility

Cable cars are not accessible for people with disabilities.

By the 1890s, 53 miles of track crisscrossed the city. Hallidie became a rich man and even ran for mayor. But despite his civic contributions and US citizenship, he was defamed as an opportunistic Englishman and lost the race. He remained a lifelong inventor, earning 300 patents and becoming a prominent member of the California Academy of Sciences.

THE CABLE CAR LADY TO THE RESCUE

The Powell-Hyde turnaround at Fisherman's Wharf is named for botany enthusiast Friedel Klussmann. She became better known as 'The Cable Car Lady' in 1947, when she began rallying her local ladies' gardening club against the mayor's plans to replace the two Powell St cable car lines with buses. Her campaign was derided by the mayor, who mocked his opponent as a dotty, sentimental Luddite.

Klussmann and her fellow gardeners responded to harsh words with hard numbers: cable cars brought in more tourism dollars than the city spent on upkeep, and buses were less effective and more costly. The dispute was brought to a public vote: the mayor lost to the ladies by a landslide. When the insolvent California St line was imperiled in 1952, the Cable Car Lady fought to rescue it. Upon Klussmann's death at age 90 in 1986, cable cars citywide were draped in black.

Technology & Operation

Today the cable car seems more like a steampunk carnival ride than modern transport, but it remains key to conquering San Francisco's highest hills. Cable cars can't move in reverse, and require burly gripmen and one buff gripwoman to lean hard on hand-operated brakes to keep them from careening downhill. The city receives many applicants for this job but 80% fail the strenuous tests of upper-body strength and hand-eye coordination, and rarely reapply.

Although cables groan piteously with uphill effort, they seldom fray and have rarely broken in more than a century of near-continuous operation. The key to the cable car's amazing safety record is the cable grip wheel: clips click into place and gradually release to prevent cables from slipping. To watch this clever Victorian technology in action, visit the Cable Car Museum (p136).

Powell-Hyde Cable Car

The ascent up Nob Hill feels like the world's longest roller-coaster climb – but on the Powell-Hyde cable car (red signs), the biggest thrills are still ahead. This cable car bobs up and down hills, with the Golden Gate Bridge popping in and out of view on Russian Hill. Hop off the cable car at Lombard St to walk the zig-zagging route to North Beach. Otherwise, stop and smell the roses along stairway walks to shady Macondray Lane and blooming Ina Coolbrith Park.

San Francisco's Cable Cars

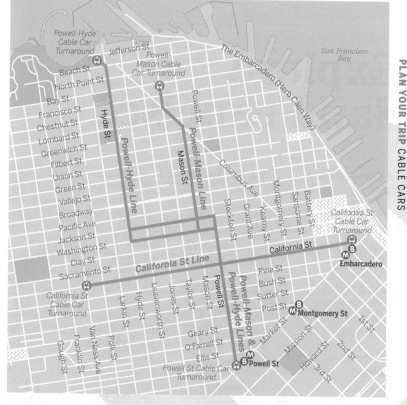

Powell-Mason Cable Car

The Powell-Hyde line may have multimillion-dollar vistas but the Powell-Mason line (yellow signs) has more culture. Detour atop Nob Hill for San Francisco–invented martinis with 360-degree panoramas at Top of the Mark, then resume the ride to Chinatown. The route cuts through North Beach at Washington Square, where you're surrounded by pizza possibilities and Diego Rivera murals. The terminus at Bay and Taylor Sts is handy to visit two truly riveting attractions: the USS *Pampanito* and Musée Mécanique.

California St Cable Car

History buffs and crowd-shy visitors prefer San Francisco's oldest cable car line: the California St cable car, in operation since 1878. This divine ride west heads through Chinatown past Old St Mary's Cathedral and climbs Nob Hill to Grace Cathedral. Hop off at Polk St for Swan Oyster Depot, tempting boutiques and cocktail bars. The Van Ness Ave terminus is a few blocks west of Alta Plaza Park and Lafayette Parks, which are both ringed by stately Victorians. From here, brave the gauntlet of Fillmore St boutiques to Japantown.

Explore San Francisco

SAN FRANCISCO'S
TOP SIGHTS

Neighborhoods at a Glance

1 The Marina, Fisherman's Wharf & the Piers p50

Since the Gold Rush, this waterfront has been the point of entry for new arrivals. It remains a major attraction for sea lion antics and getaways to and from Alcatraz. To the west, the Marina has chic boutiques in a former cow pasture and organic dining along the waterfront. At the adjoining Presidio, you'll encounter Shakespeare on the loose and public nudity on a former army base.

2 Downtown, Civic Center & SoMa p77

Downtown has all the urban amenities: art galleries, swanky hotels, first-run theaters, a mall and XXX cinemas. Civic Center is a zoning conundrum, with great performances

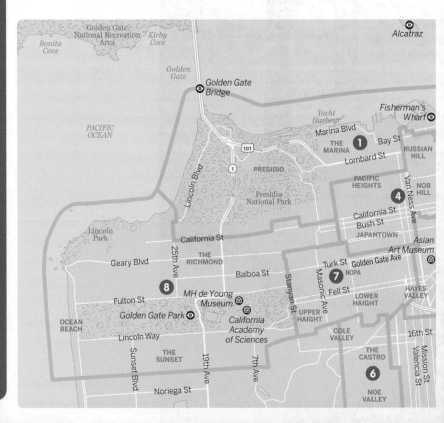

and Asian art treasures on one side of City Hall and dive bars and soup kitchens on the other. Some are drawn to South of Market (SoMa) for high technology, others for high art, but everyone gets down and dirty on the dance floor.

❸ North Beach & Chinatown p115

In North Beach, wild parrots circle over Italian cafes and bohemian bars. On the main streets of Chinatown, dumplings and rare teas are served under pagoda roofs, but its historic back alleys are filled with temple incense, mah jong tile clatter and distant echoes of revolution.

❹ Nob Hill, Russian Hill & Fillmore p133

Russian and Nob Hills are the stomping grounds of millionaires and urban hikers,

with cable cars delivering customers to hilltop bars and high-fashion boutiques. When you see sushi picnics, anime-inspired fashion and the legendary Fillmore, you'll know you've arrived in Japantown.

❺ The Mission & Potrero Hill p149

The best way to enjoy the Mission is with a book in one hand and a burrito in the other, amid murals, sunshine and the usual crowd of documentary filmmakers and novelists. Largely Latin American 24th St also attracts Southeast Asians, lesbians and dandies. Silicon Valley refugees take to Potrero Hill, while barflies and artists lurk in the valleys below.

❻ The Castro & Noe Valley p173

Rainbow flags wave their welcome to party boys, career activists and leather daddies in the Castro, while over the hill in Noe Valley megastrollers brake for bakeries and boutiques, as moms load up on sleek shoes and strong coffee.

❼ The Haight, NoPa & Hayes Valley p183

Hippies reminisce in the Haight, land of flower-power souvenirs, anarchist comic books and skateboards. Eat at trendy NoPa bistros and try on local designs in Hayes Valley, where Zen monks and jazz legends drift down the sidewalks.

❽ Golden Gate Park & the Avenues p200

Around Golden Gate Park, hardcore surfers and gourmet adventurers find a home where the buffalo roam, with the MH de Young's tower rising above it all. The foggy Avenues offer authentic Irish bars, organic Cali-Moroccan cuisine and Japanese convenience stores.

The Marina, Fisherman's Wharf & the Piers

THE MARINA & COW HOLLOW | FISHERMAN'S WHARF & THE PIERS | THE PRESIDIO

Neighborhood Top Five

1 Strolling across the **Golden Gate Bridge** (p59) just as the fog clears, revealing magnificent views of downtown San Francisco with sailboats plying the waves below.

2 Feeling cold winds blow through **Alcatraz** (p52) and imagining the misery of prison life.

3 Giggling at the shenanigans of braying and barking sea lions at **Pier 39** (p56).

4 Poking into hidden courtyards and finding indie boutiques along **Union St** (p73).

5 Marveling at 19th-century arcade games at the **Musée Mécanique** (p57).

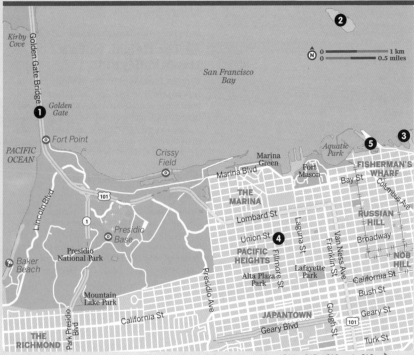

For more detail of this area, see Map p314, p315, p316 and p318 ➡

Explore the Marina, Fisherman's Wharf & the Piers

Fisherman's Wharf is the epicenter of tourism in San Francisco; the few remaining fishermen moor their boats around Pier 45. Locals don't usually visit the Wharf because it's entirely geared to tourists. Budget two hours to a half-day maximum. Weekends it gets packed by early afternoon: come in the morning to avoid crowds. Summertime fog usually clears by midday (if it clears at all), so save the Golden Gate Bridge for the early afternoon – but be forewarned that afternoon fog blows in around 4pm. Carry a jacket and don't wear shorts, unless you're here during the rare heat wave (locals spot the tourists by their short pants). Most people walk further than they anticipate: wear comfortable shoes and sunscreen. Cow Hollow and the Marina have good boutique-shopping strips, bars and restaurants. Explore them later in the day, after working hours but while shops are still open, when the busy sidewalks provide a glimpse of the Marina crowd.

Local Life

→ **Nature walks** San Franciscans love the outdoors – joggers and dog walkers flock to the waterfront trails at Crissy Field and the wooded hills of the Presidio for ocean breezes and knockout views.

→ **Barhopping** The Marina District bars on Fillmore St, from Union St to Chestnut St, are ground zero for party-girl sorority sisters and the varsity jocks who love them. Not all locals approve.

→ **City views** For dramatic views of Fisherman's Wharf and the San Francisco skyline – and a break from the crowds – hop on a ferry at Pier 39.

Getting There & Away

→ **Streetcar** Historic F Market streetcars run along Market St, then up the Embarcadero waterfront to Fisherman's Wharf.

→ **Cable car** The Powell-Hyde and Powell-Mason lines run up Powell St to the Wharf; the Mason line is quicker but the hills are better on the Hyde line.

→ **Bus** Major routes to the Wharf and/or the Marina from downtown include the 19, 30, 47 and 49.

→ **Parking** At the Wharf, there are garages at Pier 39 and Ghiradelli Square (enter on Beach St, between Larkin and Polk Sts). At the Marina, there's parking at Crissy Field and Fort Mason. The Presidio is the only place where it's easy to park – and free.

Lonely Planet's Top Tip

To escape the crowds, head west of Ghirardelli Square. Make your way to Aquatic Park, then cut west along the waterfront path, through Fort Mason to the Marina Green. Aim for the bobbing masts of the yacht club, along Marina Blvd, stopping to explore the piers but keeping your eye on the prize: the Golden Gate Bridge.

Best Places to Eat

→ Gary Danko (p67)
→ A16 (p70)
→ Betelnut (p70)
→ Greens (p70)
→ Friday night food trucks (p67)

For reviews, see p64 →

Best Places to Drink

→ Buena Vista Cafe (p71)
→ Gold Dust Lounge (p71)
→ Pier 23 (p72)
→ Brazen Head (p71)
→ California Wine Merchant (p71)

For reviews, see p71 →

Best for Waterfront Vistas

→ Golden Gate Bridge (p59)
→ Warming Hut (p71)
→ Crissy Field (p60)
→ Municipal pier at Aquatic Park (p57)
→ Sea lions at Pier 39 (p56)

For reviews, see p63 →

TOP SIGHT
ALCATRAZ

Alcatraz: for almost 150 years, the name has given the innocent chills and the guilty cold sweats. Over the years it's been the nation's first military prison, a forbidding maximum-security penitentiary and disputed territory between Native American activists and the FBI. So it's no surprise that the first step you take off the ferry and onto 'the Rock' seems to cue ominous music: dunh-dunh-dunnnnh!

Early History

It all started innocently enough back in 1775, when Spanish lieutenant Juan Manuel de Ayala sailed the *San Carlos* past the 12-acre island that he called Isla de Alcatraces (Isle of the Pelicans). In 1857 a new post on Alcatraz became the first US West Coast fort and it soon proved handy as a holding pen for Civil War deserters, insubordinates and the court-martialed. Among the prisoners were Native American scouts and 'unfriendlies,' including 19 Hopis who refused to send their children to government boarding schools, where speaking Hopi and practicing their religion were punishable by beatings. By 1902 the four cell blocks of wooden cages were rotting, unsanitary and ill-equipped for the influx of US soldiers convicted of war crimes in the Philippines. The army began building a new concrete military prison in 1909, but upkeep was expensive and the US soon had other things to worry about: WWI, financial ruin and flappers.

Prison Life

In 1922, when the 18th Amendment to the Constitution declared selling liquor a crime, rebellious Jazz Agers weren't prepared to give up their tipple – and gangsters kept the booze coming. Authorities were determined to make a public example of criminal ringleaders and in 1934 the Federal Bureau of Prisons took over Alcatraz as a prominent showcase for its crime-fighting efforts. The Rock averaged only 264 inmates, but its roster read like a list of America's Most Wanted. A-list criminals doing time on Alcatraz included Chicago crime boss Al 'Scarface' Capone, dapper kidnapper George 'Machine Gun' Kelly, hot-headed Harlem mafioso and some-time-poet 'Bumpy' Johnson and Morton Sobell, the military contractor found guilty of Soviet espionage along with Julius and Ethel Rosenberg.

Today, first-person accounts of daily life in the Alcatraz lockup are included on the excellent self-guided audio tour. But take your headphones off for just a moment and you'll notice the sound of care-free city life traveling from across the water: this is the torment that made perilous escapes into riptides worth the risk. Although Alcatraz was considered escape-proof, in 1962 the Anglin brothers and Frank Morris stuffed their beds with dummies, floated away on a makeshift raft and were never seen again. Security and upkeep proved prohibitively expensive and finally the island prison was abandoned to the birds in 1963.

Indian Occupation

Native Americans claimed sovereignty over the island in the '60s, noting that Alcatraz had long been used by the Ohlone people as a spiritual retreat. But federal authorities refused their proposal to turn Alcatraz into a Native American study center. Then on the eve of Thanksgiving, 1969, 79 Native American activists broke a Coast Guard blockade to enforce their claim. Over the next 19 months, some 5600 Native Americans would visit the occupied island. Public support eventually pressured President Richard Nixon to restore Native territory and strengthen self-rule for Native nations in 1970. Each Thanksgiving Day since 1975, an 'Un-Thanksgiving' ceremony has been held at dawn on Alcatraz, with Native leaders and supporters showing their determination to reverse the course of colonial history. After the government regained control of the island, it became a national park and by 1973 it had already become a major tourist draw. Today the cell blocks' 'Home of the free Indian land' water-tower graffiti and rare wildlife are all part of the attraction.

NEED TO KNOW

When visiting by day, to avoid crowds book the day's first or last boat. You need only reserve the outbound boat, not the return, so take your time.

Weather changes fast and it's often windy and much colder on Alcatraz, so wear extra layers, long pants and a cap.

Visiting Alcatraz means walking – a lot. The ferry drops you off at the bottom of a 130ft-high hill, which you'll have to ascend to reach the cell block. The ¼-mile path is paved, but if you're out of shape you'll be panting by the top. Alternatively, ride the twice-hourly tram from dock to cell house. Wear sturdy shoes, as you may want to explore some of the unpaved bird-watching trails.

Most people spend two to three hours; bring lunch with you to linger longer.

ALCATRAZ

Book a ferry from Pier 33 and ride 1.5 miles across the bay to explore America's most notorious former prison. The trip itself is worth the money, providing stunning views of the city skyline. Once you've landed at the **Ferry Dock & Pier** 1, you begin the 580-yard walk to the top of the island and prison; if you're out of shape, there's a twice-hourly tram.

As you head toward the **Guardhouse** 2, notice the island's steep slope; before it was a prison, Alcatraz was a fort. In the 1850s, the military quarried the rocky shores into near-vertical cliffs. Ships could then only dock at a single port, separated from the main buildings by a sally port (a drawbridge and moat in what became the guardhouse). Inside, peer through floor grates to see Alcatraz' original prison.

Volunteers tend the brilliant **Officer's Row Gardens** 3 – an orderly counterpoint to the overgrown rose bushes surrounding the burned-out shell of the **Warden's House** 4. At the top of the hill, by the front door of the **Main Cellhouse** 5, beauty shots unfurl all around, including a **view of the Golden Gate Bridge** 6. Above the main door of the administration building, notice the **historic signs & graffiti** 7, before you step inside the dank, cold prison to find the **Frank Morris cell** 8, former home to Alcatraz' most notorious jail-breaker.

TOP TIPS

➡ Book at least two weeks prior for self-guided daytime visits, longer for ranger-led night tours. For info on garden tours, see www.alcatraz gardens.org.

➡ Be prepared to hike; a steep path ascends from the ferry landing to the cell block. Most people spend two to three hours on the island. You need only reserve for the outbound ferry; take any ferry back.

➡ There's no food (just water) but you can bring your own; picnicking is allowed at the ferry dock only. Dress in layers as weather changes fast and it's usually windy.

JOHN VLAHIDES ©

Historic Signs & Graffiti
During their 1969–71 occupation, Native Americans graffitied the water tower: 'Home of the Free Indian Land.' Above the cellhouse door, examine the eagle-and-flag crest to see how the red-and-white stripes were changed to spell 'Free.'

Warden's House
Fires destroyed the warden's house and other structures during the Indian Occupation. The government blamed the Native Americans; the Native Americans blamed agents provocateurs acting on behalf of the Nixon Administration to undermine public sympathy.

Parade Grounds

DAVID CLAPP / GETTY IMAGES ©

Ferry Dock & Pier
A giant wall map helps you get your bearings. Inside nearby Bldg 64, short films and exhibits provide historical perspective on the prison and details about the Indian Occupation.

View of Golden Gate Bridge
The Golden Gate Bridge stretches wide on the horizon. Best views are from atop the island at Eagle Plaza, near the cellhouse entrance, and at water level along the Agave Trail (September to January only).

Main Cellhouse
During the mid-20th century, the maximum-security prison housed the day's most notorious troublemakers, including Al Capone and Robert Stroud, the 'Birdman of Alcatraz' (who actually conducted his ornithology studies at Leavenworth).

6

Power House

Recreation Yard

Water Tower

5

Officers' Club

8

Frank Morris Cell
Peer into cell 138 on B-Block to see a re-creation of the dummy's head that Frank Morris left in his bed as a decoy to aid his notorious – and successful – 1962 escape from Alcatraz.

7

Lighthouse

3

4

Guard Tower

2

1

Guardhouse
Alcatraz' oldest building dates to 1857 and retains remnants of the original drawbridge and moat. During the Civil War the basement was transformed into a military dungeon – the genesis of Alcatraz as prison.

Officer's Row Gardens
In the 19th century soldiers imported topsoil to beautify the island with gardens. Well-trusted prisoners later gardened – Elliott Michener said it kept him sane. Historians, ornithologists and archaeologists choose today's plants.

TOP SIGHT
FISHERMAN'S WHARF

Truth be told, you won't find many fishermen at Fisherman's Wharf. Though some still moor here, they're difficult to spot beyond the blinking neon and side-by-side souvenir shops. The Wharf may not be the 'real San Francisco,' but it's always lively and holds a few surprises. Stick near the waterfront, where sea lions bray, street performers scare unsuspecting passersby, and an aquarium and carousel entice wide-eyed kids. Once you've explored tall ships, consulted mechanical fortune tellers and eaten the obligatory clam chowder in a sourdough-bread bowl, high-tail it away to more authentic neighborhoods.

Pier 39

The focal point of Fisherman's Wharf isn't the waning fishing fleet but the carousel, carnival-like attractions, shops and restaurants of **Pier 39** (Map p314; www.pier39.com; Beach St & the Embarcadero; 🚹; 🚌47, 🚋Powell-Mason, Ⓜ F). Developed in the 1970s to revitalize tourism, the pier draws thousands of tourists daily but it's really just a big outdoor shopping mall. On the plus side, its visitors center rents strollers, stores luggage and has free phone-charging stations.

By far the best reason to walk the pier is to spot the famous sea lions, who took over this coveted waterfront real estate in 1989. These unkempt squatters have been making a public display ever since and now they're San Francisco's favorite mascots. The valuable boat slips accommodate as many as 1300 sea lions that 'haul out' onto the docks between January and July. Follow signs along the pier's western edge – you can't miss 'em.

DON'T MISS...

➡ Sea lions at Pier 39

➡ Musée Mécanique

➡ San Francisco Maritime National Historic Park

➡ Aquatic Park

PRACTICALITIES

➡ Map p314

➡ www.fishermans wharf.org

➡ Embarcadero & Jefferson St waterfront, from Pier 29 to Van Ness Ave

➡ 🚌19, 30, 47, 49, 🚋Powell-Mason, Powell-Hyde, Ⓜ F

San Francisco Maritime National Historical Park

Four historic Bay Area ships are floating museums at the **Maritime National Historical Park** (Map p314; www.nps.gov/safr; 499 Jefferson St, Hyde St Pier; adult/child $5/free; ☺9:30am-5pm Oct-May, to 5:30pm Jun-Sep; ♿; ☐19, 30, 47, ☐Powell-Hyde, ☐F), the Wharf's most authentic attraction. Moored along the Hyde St Pier, standouts include the 1891 schooner *Alma* and the 1890 steamboat *Eureka*. Also check out the paddlewheel tugboat *Eppleton Hall* and the iron-hulled *Balclutha*, which brought coal to San Francisco. It's free to walk out along the pier; pay only to board ships.

National Parks Visitors Center

San Francisco grew from its docks. This 10,000 sq ft **visitors center** (Map p314; ☎415-447-5000; www.nps.gov/safr; 499 Jefferson St; ☺9:30am-5:30pm; ♿; ☐19, 30, 47, ☐Powell-Hyde) FREE for the nearby historical park details how it happened, in a permanent exhibit that recreates a 19th-century waterfront. Also on display is a rich collection of maritime artifacts, from a giant 1850s lighthouse lens to scale models of 19th-century schooners. Kids love running around the vast space. Rangers provide maps and information about the surrounding area's trails and walks.

Musée Mécanique

A flashback to penny arcades, the **Musée Mécanique** (Map p314; www.museemechanique.org; Pier 45, Shed A; ☺10am-7pm; ♿; ☐47, ☐Powell-Mason, Powell-Hyde, ☐F) houses a mind-blowing collection of vintage mechanical amusements. Sinister, freckle-faced Laughing Sal has creeped out kids for over a century, but don't let this manic mannequin deter you from the best arcade west of Coney Island. A quarter lets you start brawls in Wild West saloons, peep at belly dancers through a vintage Mutoscope and even learn a cautionary tale about smoking opium.

Aquatic Park

Fisherman's Wharf eccentricity is mostly staged, but at **Aquatic Park** (Map p314; northern end of Van Ness Ave; ♿; ☐19, 30, 47, ☐Powell-Hyde) FREE it's the real deal: extreme swimmers dive into the bone-chilling waters of the bay in winter, while oblivious old men cast fishing lines and listen to AM-radio sport. Aside from being the city's principal swimming beach (bathrooms but no lifeguard), the park is ideal for people-watching and sandcastle-building. For perspective on the Wharf, wander out along the enormous pier at the foot of Van Ness Ave.

WHAT THE...?

Look out for the notorious 'Bushman' of Pier 39, who lurks behind branches of eucalyptus, then leaps out and shouts 'Ugga bugga!' to scare the bejeezus out of unsuspecting tourists and hit them up for change. If you spot him first, stick around and watch how others react.

It's hard to resist waterfront restaurants and their breathtaking views but you really should, unless only for drinks and appetizers. Aside from places we recommend, Wharf restaurants are way overpriced and the food can't compare to what's available in nearby neighborhoods. Go simple – maybe a cup of chowder or some crab Louis from the fish stands at the foot of Taylor St.

FISHERMEN AT PIER 47

A few third- and fourth-generation fishermen remain in the bay, but to survive the drop in salmon and other local stocks some now use their boats for tours, surviving off the city's new lifeblood: tourism. Find the remaining fleet around Pier 47.

Maritime Museum (Aquatic Park Bathhouse)

The **Maritime Museum** (Aquatic Park Bathhouse; Map p316; www.maritime.org; 900 Beach St; ⊙10am-4pm; ♿; ☐19, 30, 47, ☐Powell-Hyde) FREE was built as a casino and public bathhouse in 1939 by the Depression-era Works Projects Administration (WPA). Beautifully restored murals depict the mythical lands of Atlantis and Mu and the handful of exhibits include maritime ephemera and dioramas – the full cadre of exhibits won't be in place until 2016. Note the entryway slate carvings by celebrated African American artist Sargent Johnson and the back veranda's sculptures by Beniamino Bufano.

USS Pampanito

The **USS Pampanito** (Map p314; ☑415-775-1943; www.maritime.org/pamphome.htm; Pier 45; adult/child $12/6; ⊙9am-8pm Thu-Tue, to 6pm Wed; ♿; ☐19, 30, 47, ☐Powell-Hyde, Ⓜ️F), a WWII-era US navy submarine, completed six wartime patrols, sank six Japanese ships, battled three others and lived to tell the tale. Submariners' stories of tense moments in underwater stealth mode will have you holding your breath, and all those cool brass knobs and mysterious hydraulic valves make 21st-century technology seem overrated.

SS Jeremiah O'Brien

Hard to believe the historic 10,000-ton **SS Jeremiah O'Brien** (Map p314; www.ss jeremiahobrien.org; Pier 45; adult/child $12/6; ⊙9am-4pm; ♿; ☐19, 30, 47, ☐Powell-Hyde, Ⓜ️F) was turned out by San Francisco's ship builders in under eight weeks. Harder still to imagine how she dodged U-boats on a mission delivering supplies to Allied forces on D-Day. Of the 2710 Liberty ships launched during WWII, only this one is still fully operational. Check the website for upcoming four-hour cruises.

Aquarium of the Bay

Sharks circle overhead, manta rays sweep by and seaweed sways all around at **Aquarium of the Bay** (Map p314; www.aquariumofthebay.com; Pier 39; adult/child/family $18/10/50; ⊙9am-8pm summer, 10am-6pm winter; ♿; ☐49, ☐Powell-Mason, Ⓜ️F), where you wander through glass tubes surrounded by sea life from San Francisco Bay. Not for the claustrophobic, perhaps, but the thrilling fish-eye view leaves kids and parents wide-eyed. Kids love the critters and touch-pools upstairs.

San Francisco Carousel

A chariot awaits to whisk you and the kiddies past the Golden Gate Bridge, Alcatraz and other SF landmarks hand-painted onto this Italian **carousel** (Map p314; www.pier39.com; Pier 39; admission $3; ⊙11am-7pm; ♿; ☐47, ☐Powell-Mason, Ⓜ️F), twinkling with 1800 lights, at the bayside end of Pier 39.

Ghirardelli Square

Willy Wonka would tip his hat to Domingo Ghirardelli, whose business became the West's largest chocolate factory in 1893. After the company moved to the East Bay, developers reinvented the factory as a mall and ice-cream parlor in 1964. Today, **Ghirardelli Square** (Map p314; www.ghirardellisq.com; 900 North Point St; ⊙10am-9pm; ☐19, 30, 47, ☐Powell-Hyde) has entered its third incarnation as a boutique timeshare/spa complex with wine-tasting rooms. The square looks quite spiffy with local boutiques, Kara's Cupcakes and, of course, Ghirardelli Ice Cream (p67).

GOLDEN GATE BRIDGE, THE MARINA & PRESIDIO

The city's most spectacular icon towers 80 stories above the roiling waters of the Golden Gate, the narrow entrance to San Francisco Bay. Hard to believe SF's northern gateway lands not into a tangle of city streets but into the Presidio, an army base turned national park, where forested paths and grassy promenades look largely as they have since the 19th century.

Golden Gate Bridge

San Francisco's famous suspension bridge, painted a signature shade called International Orange, was almost nixed by the navy in favor of concrete pylons and yellow stripes. Joseph B Strauss rightly receives praise as the engineering mastermind behind this iconic marvel, but without the aesthetic intervention of architects Gertrude and Irving Murrow and incredibly quick work by daredevil workers, this 1937 landmark might have been just another traffic bottleneck.

How It Came to Be

Nobody thought it could happen. Not until the early 1920s did the City of San Francisco seriously investigate building a bridge over the treacherous, windblown strait. The War Department owned the land on both sides and didn't want to take chances with ships: safety and solidity were its goals. But the green light was given to the counterproposal by Strauss and the Murrows for a subtler suspension span, economic in form, that harmonized with the natural environment. Before the War Department could insist on an eyesore, laborers dove into the treacherous riptides of

DON'T MISS...

→ Fort Point
→ Cross-section of suspension cable, behind Bridge Pavilion visitors center
→ Midday summer fog clearing; bridge towers emerging through clouds
→ Municipal pier behind the Warming Hut

PRACTICALITIES

→ Map p318
→ www.goldengate bridge.org/visitors
→ off Lincoln Blvd
→ northbound free, southbound toll $6, billed electronically to vehicle's license plate; for details, see www.goldengate.org/tolls
→ ▣28, all Golden Gate Transit buses

BEST PLACES TO SEE IT

Cinema buffs believe Hitchcock had it right: seen from below at Fort Point, the bridge induces a thrilling case of *Vertigo*. Fog aficionados prefer the lookout at Vista Point in Marin, on the bridge's sunnier northern side, to watch gusting clouds rush through the bridge cables. Better still, find your way into the Marin Headlands. Crissy Field is a key spot to appreciate the span in its entirety, with windsurfers and kite-fliers adding action to your snapshots. Unlike the Bay Bridge, the Golden Gate allows pedestrians and cyclists.

On the foggiest days, up to one million gallons of water, in the form of fog, blow through the Golden Gate hourly.

Docents lead 45-minute walking tours (adult/child $13/10, April to October, six times daily from 10:30am to 3:30pm) revealing fascinating details about the bridge. Reserve online at www.goldengatebridge75.org. Tours depart the Roundhouse, beside the toll plaza. Afterward pose for souvenir pictures.

the bay and got the bridge underway in 1933. Just four years later workers balanced atop swaying cables to complete what was then the world's longest suspension bridge – nearly 2 miles long, with 746ft suspension towers, higher than any construction west of New York.

Crossing the Bridge

For onsite information, stop into the **Bridge Pavilion Visitors Center** (Map p318; 415-426-5220; www.ggnpc.org; Golden Gate Bridge toll plaza; 9am-7pm Jun-Aug, 9am-6pm Sep-May).

Pedestrians take the eastern sidewalk. Dress warmly! From the parking area and bus stop (off Lincoln Blvd), a pathway leads past the toll plaza, then it's 1.7 miles across. If 3.4 miles round-trip seems too much, bus to the north side via Golden Gate Transit, then walk back (for exact instructions, see www.goldengatebridge.org/visitors). Note: pedestrian access is open summer 5am to 9pm, winter 5am to 6:30pm.

By bicycle, from the toll plaza parking area: ride toward the Roundhouse then follow signs to the western sidewalk, reserved for bikes only. (Caution: locals pedal fast; avoid collisions.) Bicycles cross 24 hours but travel the eastern sidewalk certain hours; see www.goldengatebridge.org.

From the toll plaza, it's 4.5 miles to Sausalito; ferry back to SF via **Golden Gate Ferry** (415-455-2000, 511; http://goldengateferry.org) (to downtown) or Blue & Gold Fleet (p75) (to Fisherman's Wharf). Bikes are allowed on ferries.

Muni bus 28 runs west from Fort Mason (Laguna & Bay Sts) to the toll plaza, then cuts south down 19th Ave, intersecting with the N-Judah metro line at Judah St. Marin County–bound Golden Gate Transit buses (routes 10, 70, 80 and 101; $4 one-way) are the fastest, most comfortable way from downtown; disembark at the toll plaza. On Sundays only, Muni bus 76 travels from downtown, crosses the bridge and loops through the spectacular Marin Headlands.

Parking at the toll plaza is extremely limited. Find additional parking west along Lincoln Blvd.

Crissy Field

War is for the birds at **Crissy Field** (Map p318; www.crissyfield.org; 1199 East Beach; 30, PresidioGo Shuttle – Crissy Field Rte), a military airstrip turned waterfront nature preserve with knockout Golden Gate views. Where military aircraft once zoomed in for landings, bird-watchers now huddle in the silent rushes of a reclaimed tidal marsh. Joggers pound beachside trails and the only security alerts are raised by puppies suspiciously sniffing surfers. On foggy days, stop by the certified-green Warming Hut (p71) to browse regional-nature books and warm up with fair-trade coffee.

Baker Beach
Picnic amid wind-sculpted pines, fish from craggy rocks or frolic nude at mile-long **Baker Beach** (Map p318; ☺sunrise-sunset; [P]; ☐29, PresidiGo Shuttle – Presidio Hills Rte), with spectacular views of the bridge. Crowds come weekends, especially on fog-free days; arrive early. For nude sunbathing (mostly straight girls and gay boys), head to the north end. Families in clothing stick to the south end, nearer the parking lot. Mind the currents and the c-c-cold water.

Presidio Base
Explore that splotch of green on the map between Baker Beach and Crissy Field and discover unusual delights. What began as a Spanish fort built by conscripted Ohlone people in 1776 is now a treasure trove of oddities, set in an urban national park, **Presidio of San Francisco.** (Map p318; ☑415-561-4323; www.nps.gov/prsf; ☺dawn-dusk; [P]; ☐28, 43)

Begin your adventures at the parade grounds to gather hiking maps and shuttle bus schedules at the **visitors center** (www.presidio.gov; Montgomery St & Lincoln Blvd, Bldg 105; ☺10am-4pm Thu-Sun; ☐PresidiGo Shuttle (Crissy Field Rte)) (call ahead; it's slated to move), then explore the barracks. This is where Jerry Garcia began and ended his ignominious military career by going AWOL nine times in eight months, before being twice court-martialed and co-founding the Grateful Dead. Mickey Mouse fans head to the Walt Disney Family Museum, while fans of the macabre hike to the **Pet Cemetery** off Crissy Field Ave, where handmade tombstones mark final resting places of hamsters and kitties. East of the parade grounds, towards the Palace of Fine Arts, lies the **Letterman Campus**, home to nonprofits and *Star Wars* creator George Lucas's Lucas Arts (now owned by Disney) – offices are closed to visitors but you can pay respects to the Yoda statue outside.

To find site-specific temporary art, such as environmental-artist Andy Goldsworthy's *Wood Line* (between Lovers Lane and Presidio Blvd), consult **Presidio Trust** (Map p318; ☑415-561-5300; www.presidio.gov; Bldg 103, Montgomery St at Lincoln Blvd; ☺information 8am-5pm Mon-Fri, gallery 11am-5pm Wed-Sun; ☐PresidiGo Shuttle), which publishes good hiking maps to scenic overlooks and is open days that the adjacent visitors center is closed.

Free **PresidiGo** (☑415-561-2739; www.presidio.gov/shuttle) FREE buses loop the park, via two routes, from the **Presidio Transit Center** (Map p318; 215 Lincoln Blvd). Service runs every 30 minutes, 6:30am to 7:30pm weekdays, 11am to 6:30pm weekends. There's weekday-only service to downtown, free to the public 9:30am to 4pm and 7:30pm to 8pm. Download maps and schedules from the PresidiGo website.

Fort Point
Fort Point (Map p318; ☑415-556-1693; www.nps.gov/fopo; Marine Dr; ☺10am-5pm Fri-Sun; [P]; ☐28) FREE came about after an eight-year makeover from a small Spanish fort to a triple-decker, brick-walled US military fortress. Completed in 1861 with 126 cannons, just in time to protect the bay against certain invasion by Confederate soldiers during the Civil War...or not, as it turned out. Without a single shot having been fired, Fort Point was abandoned in 1900 and became neglected once the Golden Gate Bridge was built overhead – engineers added an extra span to preserve it. The site now has some great Civil War displays and knockout panoramic viewing decks.

TOP SIGHT
EXPLORATORIUM

Is there a science to skateboarding? Do toilets really flush counterclockwise in Australia? Find answers to questions you wish you'd learned in school at San Francisco's dazzling hands-on science museum. Combining science with art, the Exploratorium nudges you to question how you know what you know. As thrilling as the exhibits is the setting: a 9-acre, glass-walled pier jutting over San Francisco Bay, with vast outdoor portions you can explore for free, 24 hours a day.

Covering a whopping 330,000 sq feet of indoor-outdoor space, the 600-plus exhibits have buttons to push, cranks to ratchet and dials to adjust, all tinkered together by artists and scientists at the in-house building shop. Try on a punk hairdo, courtesy of the static-electricity station. Turn your body into the gnomon of a sundial. Slide, climb and feel your way – in total darkness – through the labyrinth of the thrilling **Tactile Dome** (☏415-528-4444; www.exploratorium.edu; $15, reservations & separate ticket required; ⏰10am-5pm Tue-Sun, 6pm-10pm Thu adults only).

In 2013 the Exploratorium moved from the Marina to Pier 15, a brand-new solar-powered space, built in concert with scientific agencies, including the National Oceanic & Atmospheric Administration (NOAA), which hard-wired the entire pier with sensors delivering real-time data on weather, wind, tides and the bay. See the data flow in at your final stop, the glass-enclosed Observatory Gallery.

DON'T MISS

➡ Tactile Dome (reservations required)

➡ 'Visualizing the Bay' exhibit

➡ Tinkering Studio

➡ Plankton exhibit

➡ Two-faced Mirror

PRACTICALITIES

➡ Map p315

➡ ☏415-528-4444

➡ www.exploratorium.edu

➡ Pier 15

➡ adult/child $25/19, Thu evening $15

➡ ⏰10am-5pm Tue-Sun, to 10pm Wed, adults 18+ only Thu 6pm-10pm

➡ ♿

➡ Ⓜ F

⊙ SIGHTS

⊙ The Marina & Cow Hollow

The Marina generally refers to everything north of busy Lombard St, west of Van Ness Ave, and east of the Presidio; Cow Hollow refers to the area around Union St, just south of Lombard, on the slope below Pacific Heights.

FORT MASON CENTER   CULTURAL PRECINCT
Map p316 (📞415-345-7500; www.fortmason.org; cnr Marina Blvd & Laguna St; 🅿; 🚌22, 28, 30) San Francisco takes subversive glee in turning military installations into venues for nature, fine dining and out-there experimental art. Evidence: Fort Mason, once a former shipyard and embarkation point for WWII troops, now a vast cultural center and gathering place for community events.

Mess halls are replaced by vegan-friendly Greens (p70), a Zen-community-run restaurant. Warehouses now contain cutting-edge theater at the Magic (p72), home base of prize-winning playwright Sam Shepard, and improvised comedy workshops at BATS Improv (p72). The Herbst Pavilion hosts major arts events and fashion shows – see the website for upcoming events.

WAVE ORGAN   MONUMENT
Map p316 (www.exploratorium.edu/visit/wave-organ; Marina Small Craft Harbor jetty; ⊙daylight hours; ♿; 🚌22, 30) FREE A project of the Exploratorium (p62), the Wave Organ is a sound sculpture of PVC tubes and concrete pipes capped with found marble from San Francisco's old cemetery, built into the tip of the yacht-harbor jetty. Depending on the waves, tide and time, the tones emitted sound like nervous humming from a dinnertime line-chef or spooky heavy breathing over the phone in a slasher film.

CHURCH OF ST MARY THE VIRGIN   CHURCH
Map p316 (📞415-921-3665; www.smvsf.org; 2325 Union St; ⊙9am-5pm Sun-Fri; 🚌22, 41, 45) You'd expect to see this rustic Arts and Crafts–style building on the slopes of Tahoe, not Pacific Heights, but this episcopal church is full of surprises. The structure dates from 1891 but the church has kept pace with its progressive-minded parish, with homeless-community outreach and 'Unplugged' all-acoustic Sunday services.

VEDANTA SOCIETY   TEMPLE
Map p316 (📞415-922-2323; www.sfvedanta.org; 2963 Webster St; ⊙closed to public; 🚌22, 41, 45) Meandering the Marina, you'll pass Mexican-inspired art deco, Victorian mansions, generic bay-windowed boxes – and, hello, what's this? A riotous 1905 mish-mash of architectural styles, with red turrets representing major world religions and the Hindu-inspired Vedanta Society's organizing principle: 'the oneness of existence.' The society founded a new temple in 1959 but its original architectural conundrum remains.

OCTAGON HOUSE   HISTORICAL BUILDING
Map p316 (📞415-441-7512; 2645 Gough St; admission by donation $3; ⊙noon-3pm 2nd & 4th Thu & 2nd Sun of month, closed Jan; 🚌41, 45) Crafty architects are always trying to cut corners on clients and here architect William C McElroy succeeded. This is among the last examples of a brief San Franciscan vogue for octagonal houses in the 1860s, when some believed that catching direct sunlight from eight angles was healthful. Three afternoons monthly, you can peruse collections of colonial antiques and peek inside a time capsule that McElroy hid under the stairs.

⊙ Fisherman's Wharf & the Piers

FISHERMAN'S WHARF   LANDMARK
See p56.

EXPLORATORIUM   MUSEUM
See p62.

ⓘ FISHERMAN'S WHARF PROMENADES

What's beautiful at Fisherman's Wharf are the bay views. When walking west of Pier 39, avoid the inland streets and instead hug the shoreline and stride broad promenades and docks jutting over the bay. Plunk down at benches to picnic (beware seagulls!). Near Pier 41, with sea lions in view, locate the huge topographical model of the entire Bay Area to wrap your head around this gorgeous vast geography.

⊙ The Presidio

PRESIDIO   LANDMARK
The Presidio includes the following sights: Baker Beach (p61), Crissy Field (p60), Presidio Base (p61) and Fort Point (p61).

GOLDEN GATE BRIDGE   BRIDGE
See p59.

PALACE OF FINE ARTS   MONUMENT
Map p318 (www.lovethepalace.org; Palace Dr; ☐28, 30, 43) FREE Like a fossilized party favor, this romantic, ersatz Greco-Roman ruin is the memento San Francisco kept from the 1915 Panama–Pacific International Exposition. The original was built of wood, burlap and plaster as a picturesque backdrop, designed by celebrated Berkeley architect Bernard Maybeck, then later reinforced.

By the 1960s it was crumbling. The structure was recast in concrete, so future generations could gaze up at the rotunda relief to glimpse 'Art under attack by materialists, with idealists leaping to her rescue.' Further renovations have restored the palace to its initial glory. Pose for pictures by the swan lagoon.

SWEDENBORGIAN CHURCH   CHURCH
Map p318 (☐415-346-6466; www.sfsweden borgian.org; 2107 Lyon St; ☺hours vary; ☐3, 43)

HOW TO KNOW IF IT'S FOGGY AT THE COAST

San Francisco is famous for summertime microclimates. Downtown may be sunny and hot, while the Golden Gate is fogged-in and 20°F (10°C) colder. Thanks to satellite imagery, you can view the fog line over the California coast (during daylight hours) and immediately know if clouds are hugging the shoreline and – most importantly – how warmly to dress before trekking to the Golden Gate Bridge. Go to the **National Oceanic & Atmospheric Administration** (NOAA; www.wrh.noaa.gov/mtr) website for San Francisco, navigate to 'Satellite imagery' and click on '1km visible satellite' for Monterey, California. SF is the thumb-shaped peninsula, surrounded by bays to its right. Voilà!

Radical ideals in the form of distinctive buildings make beloved SF landmarks; this standout 1894 example is the collaborative effort of 19th-century Bay Area progressive thinkers, such as naturalist John Muir, California Arts and Crafts leader Bernard Maybeck and architect Arthur Page Brown.

Inside, nature is everywhere – in hewn-maple chairs, mighty madrone trees supporting the roof and in scenes of Northern California that took muralist William Keith 40 years to complete. Church founder Emanuel Swedenborg was an 18th-century Swedish theologian, scientist and occasional conversationalist with angels; he believed humans are spirits in a material world unified by nature, love and luminous intelligence – a lovely concept, embodied in an equally lovely building. Enter the church through a modest brick archway and pass into a garden sheltered by trees from around the world.

WALT DISNEY FAMILY MUSEUM   MUSEUM
Map p318 (☐415-345-6800; www.waltdisney. org; 104 Montgomery St, Presidio; adult/student/ child $20/15/12; ☺Wed-Mon 10am-6pm, last entry 5pm; ℙ♿; ☐43, PresidiGo Shuttle) An 1890s military barracks houses 10 galleries that chronologically tell the exhaustively long story of Walt Disney's life. Opened 2009, the museum gets high marks for design, integrating 20,000 sq ft of contemporary glass-and-steel exhibition space with the original 19th-century brick building, but it's definitely geared toward grown-ups and will bore kids after an hour (too much reading).

In typical Disney style, exhibits are impeccably presented, with lavish detail in a variety of media, including a jaw-dropping scale model of Disneyland that will delight die-hard Mouseketeers, but budgeteers may prefer to save their $20 toward a trip to Anaheim. Discount coupons often available; check online.

✕ EATING

The fishing fleet unloads its catch at Fisherman's Wharf; mid-November to June, the specialty is Dungeness crab. Wharf restaurants are generally mediocre and expensive. If you're a serious foodie, explore the Wharf before

lunch, from west to east (if you're arriving by cable car, ride the Powell-Hyde line), then go to the Ferry Building, either on foot (1-mile/20-minute walk) or F-Market streetcar, which goes directly there.

In the Marina: good restaurants line Chestnut St, from Fillmore to Divisadero Sts, and Union St, between Fillmore St and Van Ness Ave. There's also good-priced ethnic fare on Lombard St, if you're willing to hunt. Greens (p70) gives reason to trek to Fort Mason.

✕ Fisherman's Wharf

FISHERMAN'S WHARF
CRAB STANDS SEAFOOD $

Map p314 (Foot of Taylor St; mains $5-15; ⓂF) Brawny-armed men stir steaming cauldrons of Dungeness crab at several side-by-side take-away crab stands at the foot of Taylor St, the epicenter of Fisherman's Wharf. Crab season typically runs winter through spring, but you'll find shrimp and other seafood year-round.

Instead of dining on the giant, noisy, crowded plaza, either head east along the waterfront to the Pier 43 Promenade to find benches where you can sit; or if you don't mind standing to eat, look behind the crab stalls, between 8 & 9 Fisherman's Wharf, for swinging glass doors marked 'Passageway to the Boats' and amble out the docks to eat in view of the boats that hauled in your lunch.

FISHERMAN'S WHARF
FOOD TRUCKS FOOD TRUCKS $

Map p314 (2850 Jones St; ☎47, ☐Powell-Mason, ⓂF) Three side-by-side food trucks provide perfect alternatives to the Wharf's overpriced restaurants. **Carmel Pizza** (Map p314; ☑415-676-1185; www.carmelpizza.com; 2826 Jones St; pizzas $10-18; ⊘noon-2pm & 5-8pm Mon, Tue, Thu, noon-9pm Fri & Sat, noon-6pm Sun; ☎47, ☐Powell-Mason, ⓂF) bakes gooey-delicious single-serving pizza in a wood-fired oven. **Codmother** (Map p314; ☑415-606-9349; 2824 Jones St; mains $5-10; ⊘11:30am-7pm Mon-Sat; ☎47, ☐Powell-Mason, Ⓜ F) serves note-perfect fish and chips, plus Baja-style fish tacos. **Tanguito** (Map p314; ☑415-577-4223; 2850 Jones St; dishes $3-12; ⊘11am-7pm Tue-Sun; ☎47, ☐Powell-Mason, Ⓜ F) makes its own Argentinian-style empanadas with chicken or steak, stellar

ⓘ FINDING WATERFRONT ADDRESSES

When searching for waterfront addresses, note: even-numbered piers lie *south* of the Ferry Building, odd-numbered piers *north* of the Ferry Building. All even-numbered piers are south of Market St.

saffron rice and even paella (if you can wait 45 minutes). Note early close times and outdoor-only seating.

BOUDIN BAKERY BAKERY $

Map p314 (www.boudinbakery.com; 160 Jefferson St; dishes $7-15; ⊘11am-9:30pm; ☎47, ⓂF) Dating to 1849, Boudin was one of the first five businesses in San Francisco and still uses the same yeast starter in its sourdough bread. Though you can definitely find better bread elsewhere, Boudin's food court remains a Wharf staple for clam chowder in a hollowed-out bread bowl.

The best reason to come is the remarkably well-curated **bread-baking museum**, which chronicles SF's role in the Gold Rush and the city's long love affair with sourdough. Though there's usually a $3 museum admission charge, employees tell us you're welcome to peek inside for free if nobody's manning the door.

PAT'S CAFE AMERICAN $

Map p334 (☑415-776-8735; 2330 Taylor St; mains $8-12; ⊘7:30am-2:30pm daily; ⓐ; ☐30, ☐Powell-Mason) Just beyond the tourist hubbub, this cute little storefront diner serves classic-American food – scrambles, pancakes and waffles for breakfast; hot pastrami and club sandwiches for lunch – to locals and out-of-towners who appreciate no-fuss cooking, cheerful service and the easy location between the Wharf and North Beach.

IN-N-OUT BURGER BURGERS $

Map p314 (☎800-786-1000; www.in-n-out.com; 333 Jefferson St; meals under $10; ⊘10:30am-1am Sun-Thu, to 1:30am Fri & Sat; ⓐ; ☐30, 47, ☐Powell-Hyde) Gourmet burgers have taken SF by storm, but In-N-Out has had a good thing going for 60 years: prime chuck beef processed on-site, plus fries and shakes made with ingredients you can pronounce, all served by employees paid a living wage. Consider ordering yours off the menu 'animal style,' cooked in mustard with grilled onions.

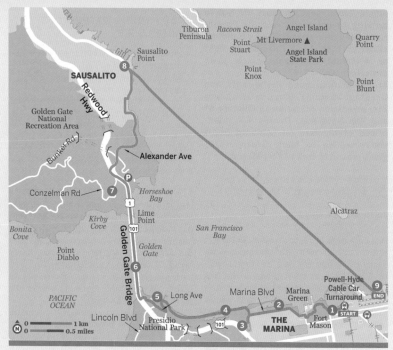

Neighborhood Walk
Freewheeling Over the Bridge

START MARITIME MUSEUM
FINISH PIER 41
LENGTH 8 MILES; TWO TO FOUR HOURS

Built in Streamline Moderne style, the 1939 ❶ **Maritime Museum** (p58) resembles an art deco ocean liner. Head behind the building to the sandy shore along Aquatic Park and dip your toes into the icy bay.

Joggers, Frisbee-throwers and kite-fliers congregate at ❷ **Marina Green**. A right turn bisects two boat marinas; at the end is the curious Wave Organ. Flash back to the 1915 Panama–Pacific International Expo at the ❸ **Palace of Fine Arts** (p64). Hear how your voice echoes inside. Watch kids chase swans, while you pose for photos beside gorgeous Greco-Roman arches.

Head to ❹ **Crissy Field** (p60) to watch windsurfers and kiteboarders attempt one of SF's windiest beaches. Take the Golden Gate Promenade, a foot-and-bike path skirting the field, toward Fort Point. Fuel up on organic sandwiches and coffee at

❺ **Warming Hut** (p71). Afterwards, backtrack to Long Ave and hang a sharp right up super-steep Lincoln Blvd toward the bridge.

With everyone craning their necks, it's no surprise bicycles sometimes collide on the ❻ **Golden Gate Bridge** (p59); keep your eyes peeled. Before crossing, stop at the visitors center and see the exhibits. You'll be grateful you brought a windbreaker if the fog suddenly blows.

Just across the bridge, turn left onto Conzelman Rd and ascend the ❼ **Marin Headlands** (p225) to look down on the bridge from a former WWII bunker, Battery Spencer – pedal up the giant hill or walk your bike. Or just enjoy the views and pedal past. Swanky ❽ **Sausalito** (p221), with bayside vistas and galleries aplenty, is ideal for a stroll to stretch the legs, but first get the ferry schedule at the dock to coordinate your timing.

Ferry from Sausalito back to ❾ **Pier 41** at Fisherman's Wharf, or if you're headed downtown, board a boat to the Ferry Building.

GHIRARDELLI ICE CREAM — ICE CREAM $

Map p314 (☎415-771-4903; www.ghirardelli.com; 900 North Point St, Ghirardelli Square; ice creams $4-9; ⊗10am-11pm Sun-Thu, 10am-midnight Fri & Sat; 🚻; 🚌19, 30, 47, 🚋Powell-Hyde) Mr Ghirardelli sure makes a swell sundae. The legendary Cable Car comes with Rocky Road ice cream, marshmallow topping and enough hot fudge to satisfy a jonesing chocoholic.

EAGLE CAFE — AMERICAN $$

Map p314 (☎415-433-3689; www.eaglecafe.com; Pier 39, 2nd fl, Ste 103; mains $10-20; ⊗7:30am-9pm; 🚻; 🚌47, 🚋Powell-Mason) Good for breakfast or a no-fuss lunch at Pier 39, the Eagle's straightforward fare includes pancakes and omelets, crab-salad sandwiches, burgers etc. Views are good, the prices right for families and it takes reservations, which you should make on weekends to spare yourself (long) waits.

★GARY DANKO — CALIFORNIAN $$$

Map p314 (☎415-749-2060; www.garydanko.com; 800 North Point St; 3-/5-course menus $73/107; ⊗5:30-10pm; 🚌19, 30, 47, 🚋Powell-Hyde) Gary Danko wins James Beard Awards for his impeccable haute California cuisine. Smoked-glass windows prevent passersby from tripping over their tongues at the exquisite presentations – roasted lobster with trumpet mushrooms, blushing duck breast and rhubarb compote, lavish cheeses and trios of crèmes brûlées. Reservations a must.

Best to order the chef's three- to five-course menu – and why not start with champagne? From the first bite of oysters and caviar, to the gift-wrapped tiny chocolates handed you on leaving, this is one meal to remember.

SCOMA'S — SEAFOOD $$$

Map p314 (☎415-771-4383; www.scomas.com; Pier 47; mains $28-42; ⊗11:30am-10pm; 🅿; 🚋Powell-Hyde; Ⓜ F) A flashback to the 1960s, with waiters in white dinner jackets, pine-paneled walls decorated with signed photographs of forgotten celebrities, and windows overlooking the docks – Scoma's is the Wharf's long-standing top choice for seafood. Little changes except prices. Expect classics like cioppino and lobster Thermidor – never groundbreaking, always good – that taste better when someone else buys.

The restaurant accepts limited reservations but always accommodates walk-ins and has a retro-cool cocktail lounge where you can wait for your table.

FOOD TRUCK FRIDAYS

The most happening Friday-night food scene is at **Off the Grid** (Map p316; www.offthegridsf.com; most dishes $5-10; ⊗5-10pm Fri; 🚌22, 28), SF's largest mobile-gourmet hootenanny, with 40 Bay Area food trucks assembled in the parking lot of Fort Mason Center. Arrive before 6:30pm or expect 20-minute waits for the Chairman's clamshell buns stuffed with duck and mango, Roli Roti's free-range herbed roast chicken, and dessert from the Crème Brûlée Man. Cash only. Take dinner to nearby docks for Golden Gate Bridge sunsets.

FORBES ISLAND — GRILL $$$

Map p314 (☎415-951-4900; www.forbesisland.com; Pier 41; mains $27-39; ⊗5pm-late; 🚻; 🚌47, Ⓜ F) No man is an island, except for an eccentric millionaire named Forbes Thor Kiddoo. A miniature lighthouse, thatched hut, waterfall, sandy beach and swaying palms transformed his moored houseboat into the Hearst Castle of the bay. Today this bizarre domicile is a gently rocking romantic restaurant, strong on grilled meats and atmosphere. Reservations essential.

Take the putt-putt boat taxi from the west side of Pier 39; landlubbers dining below deck should bring motion-sickness meds.

✖ The Marina

PLUTO'S FRESH FOOD — AMERICAN $

Map p316 (☎415-775-8867; www.plutosfreshfood.com; 3258 Scott St; mains $6-12; ⊗11am-10pm; 🅿 🚻; 🚌28, 30, 43) When you're hungry for a wholesome meal but don't want to fuss, Pluto's serves good food fast, with build-your-own salads, stick-to-your-ribs mac 'n' cheese, and carved-to-order roast beef and turkey with all the fixings. Order at the counter, then snag a seat. Wholesome kids' meals cost just $3.75.

ROAM ARTISAN BURGER — BURGERS $

Map p316 (☎415-440-7626; www.roamburgers.com; 1785 Union St; burgers $6-8; ⊗11:30am-10pm; 🚻; 🚌41, 45) 🍽 Obsessive about ingredients, Roam serves burgers of beef, bison and turkey, all locally grown and sustainably farmed.

SABRINA DALBESIO / GETTY IMAGES ©

DAVID PARKER / ALAMY ©

1. Palace of Fine Arts (p64)
Intended as a temporary feature, this ersatz Greco-Roman ruin became a permanent fixture in the 1960s.

2. Mingle (p73)
Pick up some local couture at this boutique in Cow Hollow.

3. Buena Vista Cafe (p71)
Once a haunt of cannery workers and sailors, this Fisherman's Wharf bar remains a city favorite.

4. Golden Gate Bridge (p59)
At nearly 2 miles in length, the bright-orange bridge remains the city's most iconic sight.

STICKNEY DESIGN / GETTY IMAGES ©

For the classic, stick to juicy grass-fed beef served on a fresh-baked bun with housemade pickles. Don't ask for Coke: Roam makes its own organic sodas, plus stellar milkshakes with ice cream from Sonoma. There's also a branch on **Fillmore** (Map p331; www.roamburgers.com; 1923 Fillmore St; ◷11:30am-10pm; ☐1, 3, 22).

BLUE BARN GOURMET　　SANDWICHES, SALADS $

Map p316 (📞415-441-3232; www.bluebarngourmet.com; 2105 Chestnut St; $9-12; ◷11am-8:30pm Sun-Thu, to 8pm Fri & Sat; 🖊🖐; ☐22, 28, 30, 43) 🍃 Toss aside ordinary salads. For $9.25, build a mighty mound of organic produce, topped with six fixings: artisan cheeses, caramelized onions, heirloom tomatoes, candied pecans, pomegranate seeds, even Meyer grilled sirloin. For something hot, try toasted panini oozing with Manchego cheese, fig jam and salami.

REAL FOOD　　DELI $

Map p316 (📞415-567-6900; www.realfoodco.com; 3060 Fillmore St; ◷8am-9pm; 🖊; ☐22, 41, 45) 🍃 This organic grocery's deli is packed with housemade foods, including respectable sushi, roasted-eggplant-and-tomato salad, free-range herb-turkey sandwiches and organic gingerbread. On sunny days, grab a patio seat.

LUCCA DELICATESSEN　　DELI $

Map p316 (📞415-921-7873; http://luccadeli.com; 2120 Chestnut St; ◷9am-6:30pm Mon-Fri, 9am-6pm Fri & Sat; ☐28, 30, 43) Open since 1929, this classic Italian deli is the perfect spot to assemble picnics for Marina Green. Besides perfect prosciutto and salami, nutty cheeses and fruity Chiantis, expect made-to-order sandwiches on fresh-baked Acme bread, including yummy meatball subs. There's hot homemade soup from 11am to 3pm.

JUDY'S CAFE　　BREAKFAST $

Map p316 (📞415-922-4588; www.judyscafesf.com; 2268 Chestnut St; mains $9-13; ◷7am-4pm; 🖐; ☐30) Locals queue up for giant breakfasts at Judy's, a storefront diner with standout sourdough French toast, enormous omelets and great pumpkin bread. Expect to wait; cash only.

KARA'S CUPCAKES　　BAKERY, DESSERT $

Map p316 (📞415-563-2223; www.karascupcakes.com; 900 North Point; cupcakes $3; ◷10am-8pm Sun-Thu, 10am-10pm Fri & Sat; ☐28, 30, 49, 🚋Powell-Hyde, Powell-Mason) 🍃 Proustian

nostalgia washes over fully grown adults as they bite into cupcakes that recall childhood magician-led birthday parties. Varieties range from yummy chocolate marshmallow to classic carrot cake with cream-cheese frosting, all meticulously calculated for maximum glee.

A16　　ITALIAN $$

Map p316 (📞415-771-2216; www.a16sf.com; 2355 Chestnut St; pizza $12-18, mains $18-26; ◷lunch Wed-Fri, dinner daily; ☐28, 30, 43) Like a high-maintenance date, this Neapolitan pizzeria demands reservations, then haughtily makes you wait in the foyer. The housemade mozzarella *burrata* and chewy-but-not-too-thick-crust pizza make it worth your while. Skip the spotty desserts and concentrate on adventurous appetizers, including house-cured *salumi* platters and delectable marinated tuna.

BETELNUT　　ASIAN $$

Map p316 (📞415-929-8855; www.betelnutrestaurant.com; 2030 Union St; dishes $7-13; ◷11:30am-10pm Sun-Thu, to 11pm Fri & Sat; ☐22, 41, 45) Palm-frond ceiling fans whirl overhead at high-energy Betelnut, a Marina District spin on the Chinese beer house, whose fiery pan-Asian street foods are designed to pair with house-label brews and fresh-fruit cocktails. Standouts: Szechuan string beans, Celia's lettuce cups and succulent glazed pork ribs. Plan to share. Up-tempo beats set a party mood, perfect before a night out. Make reservations.

⭐**GREENS**　　VEGETARIAN, CALIFORNIAN $$

Map p316 (📞415-771-6222; www.greensrestaurant.com; Bldg A, Fort Mason Center, cnr Marina Blvd & Laguna St; lunch $15-17, dinner $17-24; ◷lunch Tue-Sat, dinner Mon-Sat, brunch Sun; 🖊; ☐28) 🍃 Career carnivores won't realize there's zero meat in the hearty black-bean chili with crème fraîche and pickled jalapeños, or in that roasted eggplant *panino* (sandwich) packed with hearty flavor from ingredients mostly grown on a Zen farm in Marin. On sunny days, get yours to go and enjoy it on a wharf-side bench, but if you're planning on proper weekend dinner or Sunday brunch, make reservations.

MAMACITA　　MEXICAN $$

Map p316 (📞415-346-8494; www.mamacitasf.com; 2317 Chestnut St; dishes $10-18; ◷5:30-late Mon-Thu, 5pm-late Fri-Sun; ☐30) One of the city's best for sit-down Mexican makes everything from scratch – tortillas, tamales and two dozen fresh-daily sauces for wide-ranging dishes, from spit-roasted goat to duck *carnitas*. The knock-out cocktail menu lists 60 tequilas, which explains the room's deafening roar. Make reservations.

ROSE'S CAFÉ
ITALIAN, CALIFORNIAN **$$**

Map p316 (☏415-775-2200; www.rosescafesf. com; 2298 Union St; mains lunch $10-17, dinner $17-28; ☺8am-10pm; ☏; ☒22, 41, 45) Follow your salads and housemade soups with rich organic polenta with gorgonzola and thyme, or a simple grass-fed beef burger, then linger over espresso or tea. Shop if you must, but return to this sunny corner cafe from 4pm to 6pm for half-price wine by the glass. Great breakfasts, too.

✖ The Presidio

WARMING HUT
CAFE, SANDWICHES **$**

Map p318 (☏415-561-3040; 983 Marine Dr, The Presidio; dishes $4-6; ☺9am-5pm; ☑ ☒; ☒PresidiGo Shuttle (Crissy Field Rte)) Wetsuited windsurfers and Crissy Field kite-fliers recharge with fair-trade coffee, organic pastries and organic hot dogs at the Warming Hut while browsing field guides and sampling honey from Presidio honeybees. Ingeniously insulated with recycled denim, this eco-shack below the Golden Gate Bridge evolved from a heartwarming concept: all purchases fund Crissy Field's ongoing conversion from US army airstrip to wildlife preserve.

🍷 DRINKING & NIGHTLIFE

Fisherman's Wharf bars cater almost entirely to tourists but can be good fun, if pricy. If you're at a Wharf hotel but prefer a local scene, head a mile up Polk St (p143). Clustered around Fillmore and Greenwich Sts, Marina District watering holes – which author Armistead Maupin called 'breeder bars' – cater to frat boys and bottle blonds.

★BUENA VISTA CAFE
BAR

Map p314 (☏415-474-5044; www.thebuenavista. com; 2765 Hyde St; ☺9am-2am Mon-Fri, 8am-2am Sat & Sun; ☒19, 47, ☒Powell-Hyde) Warm your cockles with a prim little goblet of bitter-creamy Irish coffee, introduced to America at this destination bar that once served sailors and cannery workers. The creaky Victorian floor manages to hold up carousers and families alike, served community-style at round tables overlooking the cable-car turnaround at Victoria Park.

GOLD DUST LOUNGE
BAR

Map p314 (☏415-397-1695; www.golddustsf. com; 165 Jefferson St; ☺8am-2am; ☒47, ☒Powell-Mason, MF) The Gold Dust is so beloved by San Franciscans that when it lost its lease on the Union Square building it had occupied since the 1930s, then reopened in 2013 at the Wharf – with the same precarious Victorian brass chandeliers and the same twangy rockabilly band – the mayor officially declared it 'Gold Dust Lounge Day.'

This is likely the only Wharf bar where you may spot an actual local; come for strong drink and a dose of red-velvet nostalgia.

CALIFORNIA WINE MERCHANT
WINE BAR

Map p316 (www.californiawinemerchant.com; 2113 Chestnut St; ☺10am-midnight Mon-Wed, 10am-1:30am Thu-Sat, 11am-11pm Sun; ☒22, 30, 43) Part wine store, part wine bar, this small shop on busy Chestnut St caters to neighborhood wine aficionados, with a daily-changing list of 30 wines by the glass, available in half pours. Arrive early to score a seat, or stand and gab with the locals.

BRAZEN HEAD
PUB

Map p316 (☏415-921-7600; www.brazenheadsf. com; 3166 Buchanan St; ☺5pm-1am; ☒28, 30) You have to know where you're going to find the Brazen Head, a tiny pub with low lighting and cozy nooks, where hand-holding couples dine on good onion soup and pepper steak.

LIGHTNING TAVERN
BAR

Map p316 (☏415-704-1875; 1875 Union St; ☺4pm-2am Mon-Fri, noon-2am Sat-Sun; ☒41, 45) Edison-bulb chandeliers and laboratory equipment lend a mad-scientist backdrop for bartenders, who serve $10 combos of high-end spirits with a pint back (think Jameson and Guinness), plus cocktails by the pitcher (think messy night out). Dig the giant mural of the Bay Bridge being struck by lightning, which is how you may feel after a few hours here. Keep your buzz in check with tasty tater tots.

MATRIXFILLMORE LOUNGE
Map p316 (www.matrixfillmore.com; 3138 Fillmore St; ⊗8pm-2am Wed-Mon; ⬚22, 28, 30, 43) The neighborhood's most notorious upmarket pick-up joint provides a fascinating glimpse into the lives of single Marina swankers. Treat it as a comic sociological study, while enjoying stellar cocktails, blazing fireplace and sexy lounge beats – if, that is, you can get past the door. Bring your credit card.

BUS STOP BAR
Map p316 (☑415-567-6905; 1901 Union St; ⊗10am-2am; ⬚41, 45) Bus Stop has 18 flickering TV screens, two pool tables and a manly crowd that roars when their team scores. If your girlfriend wants to shop but you must watch the game, wait here as she trawls surrounding Union St boutiques.

☆ ENTERTAINMENT

PIER 23 LIVE MUSIC
Map p315 (☑415-362-5125; www.pier23cafe.com; Pier 23; admission from free-$10; ⊗shows 5-7pm Tue, 6-8pm Wed, 7-10pm Thu, 8pm-midnight Fri & Sat, 4-8pm Sun; Ⓜ F) It resembles a surf shack, but this old waterfront restaurant on Pier 23 regularly features R&B, reggae, Latin bands, mellow rock and the occasional jazz pianist. Wander out to the bayside patio to soak in views. The dinner menu features pier-worthy options like batter-fried oysters and whole roasted crab.

LOU'S FISH SHACK LIVE MUSIC
Map p314 (☑415-771-5687; www.lousfishshack.com; 300 Jefferson St; admission free; ⊗shows 8:30pm-midnight Fri & Sat, 4-8pm Sun; ⬚; ⬚30, 47, ⬚Powell-Mason, Ⓜ F) Lou's presents live blues on Friday and Saturday nights and Sunday afternoons. Primarily a restaurant, it also has a few bar tables near the bandstand and tiny dance floor, making it a good backup when you're staying nearby and want to hear live music but don't want to travel. And unlike bona fide blues bars, Lou's welcomes kids.

MAGIC THEATER THEATER
Map p316 (☑415-441-8822; www.magictheatre.org; 3rd fl, Bldg D, Fort Mason Center, cnr Marina Blvd & Laguna St; tickets $25-55; ⬚28) The Magic is known for taking risks and staging provocative plays by playwrights such as Bill Pullman, Terrence McNally, Edna O'Brien, David Mamet and longtime playwright-in-residence Sam Shepard. If you're interested in seeing new theatrical works and getting under the skin of the Bay Area theater scene, the Magic is an excellent starting point. Check the calendar.

BATS IMPROV THEATER
Map p316 (☑415-474-8935; www.improv.org; 3rd fl, bldg B, Fort Mason Center, cnr Marina Blvd & Laguna St; admission $17-20; ⊗shows 8pm Fri & Sat; ⬚28) Bay Area Theater Sports explores all things improv, from audience-inspired themes to whacked-out musicals at completely improvised weekend shows. Or take center stage yourself at an improv-comedy workshop (held on weekday nights and weekend afternoons). Think fast: classes fill quickly. Admission prices vary depending on the show/workshop.

🛍 SHOPPING

Wharf shopping yields 'I Escaped Alcatraz' T-shirts, Golden Gate Bridge fridge magnets and miniature cable cars – the latter, perfect only-in-SF souvenirs; the best are of wood or metal. However, unless you're hunting for Christmas ornaments in July, there's (far) better shopping nearby on Polk St (Russian Hill) and in the Marina. First choice for Marina shopping is Cow Hollow – Union St between Gough and Fillmore Sts – where you'll find indie boutiques and upmarket chains; watch for shops hidden in courtyards. Second choice is Chestnut St, between Fillmore and Divisadero Sts, where chains like Apple, Gap and Pottery Barn sit beside boutiques catering almost exclusively to wealthy stay-at-home moms.

🛍 Fisherman's Wharf & Piers

ELIZABETHW PERFUME
Map p314 (www.elizabethw.com; 900 North Point St; ⊗10am-9pm Mon-Sat, 10am-7pm Sun; ⬚19, 30, 47, ⬚Powell-Hyde) Local scent-maker elizabethW supplies the tantalizing aromas of changing seasons without the sweaty brows or frozen toes. 'Sweet Tea' smells like a Georgia porch in summertime; 'Vetiver'

like autumn in Maine. For a true SF fragrance, 'Leaves' is as audaciously green as Golden Gate Park in January.

TCHO CHOCOLATE FOOD

Map p315 (☑415-981-0189; www.tcho.com; Pier 17; ◎9:30am-5:30pm Mon-Fri, 10am-5:30pm Sat-Sun; Ⓜ) ✎ The dirty little secret of the chocolate trade is that much of the world's cocoa-bean supply is harvested using questionable labor practices. Not so at TCHO, which stamps every bar 'no slavery' and partners directly with co-ops and farmers in Ghana to source fair-trade beans for its luxurious, high-cacao chocolates that cost more, but that you can feel good about consuming – never mind your diet.

The Pier 17 store is also its factory; free one-hour chocolate-factory tours (daily 10:30am and 2:30pm, reservation required, book online) let you sample the entire line.

SEASONS GIFTS, SOUVENIRS

Map p314 (☑415-398-2944; www.seasonssf.com; Pier 39, Level 2; ◎10am-7pm Sun-Thu, 10am-9pm Fri & Sat; Ⓜ) The Wharf is full of tchotchke shops but this is the mother of them all: it offers a wild array of quality Christmas and Halloween ornaments; statuary of saints; Disney-character salt-and-pepper shakers; hurdy-gurdies for make-your-own music boxes; commemorative spoons and shot glasses; and enough ceramic houses to build an entire city beneath your next holiday tree.

🏠 The Marina & Presidio

★MINGLE CLOTHING, ACCESSORIES

Map p316 (www.mingleshop.com; 1815 Union St; ◎11am-6pm; 🚍41, 45) To break free of Gap-khaki monotony and H&M trends, mingle with SF designers. Local couturiers stock this boutique with hot Cleopatra-collar dresses, mod ring-buckled bags and plaid necklaces, for less than you'd pay for Marc Jacobs on mega-sale. Men emerge date-ready in dark tailored denim and black Western shirts with white piping – the SF version of a tux.

MY ROOMMATE'S CLOSET WOMEN'S CLOTHING

Map p316 (www.myroommatescloset.com; 3044 Fillmore St; ◎11am-6pm, noon-5pm Sun; 🚍22, 41, 45) All the half-off bargains and none of the clawing dangers of a sample sale. Stocks

constantly change but have included cloud-like Catherine Malandrino chiffon party dresses, executive Diane Von Fürstenberg wrap dresses, and designer denim at prices approaching reality.

PAST PERFECT ANTIQUES, HOUSEWARES

Map p316 (☑415-929-7651; 2246 Lombard St; ◎11am-7pm; 🚍22, 41, 45) So this is how Pacific Heights eccentrics fill up those mansions: Fornasetti face plates, Danish teak credenzas and Lucite champagne buckets. Past Perfect is a collective so prices vary wildly – some sellers apparently believe their belongings owe them back rent, while others are happy just to unload their ex's mother's prized spoon collection.

UKO CLOTHING, ACCESSORIES

Map p316 (☑415-252-7719; www.ukosf.com; 2070 Union St; ◎11am-6:30pm Mon-Sat, noon-5:30pm Sun; 🚍22, 41, 45) Laser-cut, draped and micro-pleated are the fashion-forward signatures of Uko's inventive garments for men and women. Get bonus fashion IQ points for clever jackets with hidden pockets-within-pockets and silver drop earrings that add an exclamation point to your look.

CHLOE ROSE WOMEN'S CLOTHING, ACCESSORIES

Map p316 (www.chloeroseboutique.com; 1824 Union St; 🚍41, 45) If your airline lost your luggage and you're pouting about not having that perfect party dress to wear to dinner, take heart: Chloe Rose will restore your sexy silhouette and doll you up with such pretty jewelry that you can tell the airline to write you a check instead.

PLUMPJACK WINES WINE

Map p316 (www.plumpjackwines.com; 3201 Fillmore St; ◎11am-8pm Mon-Sat, to 6pm Sun; 🚍22, 28, 30, 43) Discover a new favorite California vintage for under $25 at the distinctive wine boutique that won partial-owner and former mayor Gavin Newsom respect from even Green Party gourmets. A more knowledgeable staff is hard to find anywhere in SF and they'll set you up with the right bottles to cross party lines. PlumpJack Wines also has a store in **Noe Valley**.

★ATYS HOUSEWARES

Map p316 (www.atysdesign.com; 2149b Union St; ◎11am-6:30pm Mon-Sat, noon-6pm Sun; 🚍22, 41, 45) Tucked away in a courtyard, this design showcase offers version 2.0 of essential household items: a mirrored coat rack, a rechargeable flashlight that turns a wineglass into a lamp, and a zero-emissions, solar-powered toy airplane.

DRESS
WOMEN'S CLOTHING

Map p316 (📞415-440-3737; www.shopdress online.com; 2271 Chestnut St; ⏰10:30am-6:30pm Mon-Sat, noon-5pm Sun; 🚍28, 30, 43) A tiny shop for girly-girls with big clothing allowances, Dress draws from leading contemporary designers, such as Diane von Fürstenberg and Rag & Bone, to piece together eclectic inventory that ranges from casual weekend wear to fancy cocktail dresses, rendered prettier with the good selection of locally designed jewelry, including many one-of-a-kind pieces.

TOSS DESIGNS
ACCESSORIES, GIFTS

Map p316 (📞415-440-8677; www.tossdesigns. com; 2185 Chestnut St; ⏰10am-7pm Mon-Sat, 10:30am-6:30pm Sun) If you've bought too much and need an extra bag, but can't bear schlepping an ugly disposable carry-on, Toss has you covered with a good selection of reasonably priced day-bags, all colorfully patterned in bold stripes or prints, some with matching hip flasks so you can tipple while you tote. Cashmere, candles and Waspy hostess gifts complete the collection.

★SPORTS BASEMENT
OUTDOOR GEAR

Map p318 (📞415-437-0100; www.sportsbase ment.com; 610 Old Mason St; ⏰9am-9pm Mon-Fri, 8am-8pm Sat & Sun; 🚍43, PresidiGo Shuttle (Crissy Field Route)) When you're wondering where to rent gear for that last-minute trip to Yosemite or Tahoe, or if you just like digging through odd lots of sporting goods at closeout prices, this 80,000-sq-ft sports-and-camping equipment emporium is a must-visit. Once a US army post exchange, it's inside the Presidio and there's talk of turning it into a new museum space: call ahead.

JACK'S
MEN'S CLOTHING

Map p316 (📞415-409-6114; www.jackssf.com; 2260 Chestnut St; ⏰10:30am-6:30pm; 🚍28, 30, 43) Jack's dresses Marina dudes in sexy denim by Hudson, Agave and J Brand. But we most like the screen-print T-shirts, emblazoned with logos of Bay Area sports teams, present and past, from the A's to the Seals – not cheap at $40 but perfect souvenirs for fans.

🏃 SPORTS & ACTIVITIES

🏃 Fisherman's Wharf

BLAZING SADDLES
BICYCLING

Map p314 (📞415-202-8888; www.blazing saddles.com; 2715 Hyde St; bike hire per hour $8-15, per day $32-88; electric bikes per day $48-88; ⏰8am-7:30pm; 🚲; 🚋Powell-Hyde) Blazing Saddles is tailored to visitors, with a main shop on Hyde St and seven rental stands around Fisherman's Wharf, convenient for biking the Embarcadero or to the Golden Gate Bridge. They also rent electric bikes and offer 24-hour return service – a big plus. Reserve online for a 10% discount; rental includes all extras (bungee cords, packs etc).

The **Downtown location** (Map p322; 📞415-202-8888; www.blazingsaddles.com; 433 Mason St; bike hire per hour $8-15, per day $32-88; electric bikes per day $48-88; ⏰8am-7:30pm) is convenient to many hotels.

OCEANIC SOCIETY EXPEDITIONS
WHALE WATCHING

Map p316 (📞415-474-3385; www.oceanic society.org; 3950 Scott St; whale-watching trips per person $120-125; ⏰office 8:30am-5pm Mon-Fri, trips Sat & Sun; 🚍30) The Oceanic Society runs top-notch, naturalist-led, ocean-going weekend boat trips – sometimes to the Farallon Islands – during both whale-migration seasons. Cruises depart from the yacht harbor and last all day. Kids must be 10 years or older. Reservations required.

ADVENTURE CAT
SAILING

Map p314 (📞415-777-1630; www.adventurecat. com; Pier 39; adult/child $35/15, sunset cruise $50; 🚲; 🚍47, MF) There's no better view of San Francisco than from the water, especially at twilight on a fogless evening aboard a sunset cruise. Adventure Cat uses catamarans, with a windless indoor cabin for grandmums and a trampoline between hulls for bouncy kids. Three daily cruises depart March through October; weekends-only in November.

RED & WHITE FLEET
BAY CRUISE

Map p314 (📞415-673-2900; www.redandwhite. com; Pier 43½; adult/child $28/18; 🚲; 🚍47, MF) A one-hour bay cruise with Red & White lets you see the Golden Gate Bridge from water level. Brave the wind and sit on the

THE BAY BY BOAT

Some of the best views of San Francisco are from the water – if the weather is fair, we highly recommend you take a boat ride. Here's a list of tour boats and ferry rides that will get you out on the bay and provide some stellar photo opps too. Be forewarned: it's always at least 10 degrees cooler on the bay's chilly waters. Bring a jacket.

➔ **Bay cruises** The quickest way to familiarize yourself with the view from the bay is aboard a narrated one-hour cruise that loops beneath the Golden Gate Bridge. Red & White Fleet operates multiple trips from Pier 43½; Blue & Gold Fleet operates from Pier 41 and also offers 30-minute trips aboard its high-speed Rocketboat. (Note: Blue & Gold's Alcatraz-themed cruise only sails *around* the island, not to it.)

➔ **Sailboat tours** If you prefer sailboats to ferries, hit the bay aboard the Adventure Cat – a catamaran with trampoline between hulls – for a 90-minute bay cruise or sunset sail. Or charter a private sailboat, with our without skipper, from Spinnaker Sailing (p114).

➔ **Paddle tours** Explore the bay's calm eastern shoreline in canoe or kayak from City Kayak (p114), which guides tours, including full-moon paddles, and rents boats to experienced paddlers.

➔ **Whale-watching tours** To go beyond the Golden Gate and onto the open ocean, we most recommend the excellent trips operated by the Oceanic Society.

➔ **Guided tours** Various companies offer tours for niche audiences. SF Winery Cruise shuttles between wine-tasting rooms on both sides of the bay. Ride the Ducks uses amphibious vehicles – thrilling for little kids.

➔ **Alcatraz trips** Only one ferry operator (p291) is licensed to sail to Alcatraz and you'll need advance reservations, but other ferries sail nearby, providing a fleeting glimpse of the notorious island.

➔ **Sausalito & Tiburon trips** It's a quick ferry ride to these neighboring waterside villages across the bay from SF. For more, see p221.

➔ **Angel Island trips** Spend the day hiking and picnicking at this state park in the middle of the bay. For more, see p228.

➔ **Oakland trips** Ferries land at Jack London Square, where you can eat bayside and have a beer at historic Heinold's First & Last Chance Saloon, whose sloping bar has been operating since 1883.

➔ **Alameda trips** Ferry to Oakland's small-town neighbor and go wine-and-spirits tasting. Rosenblum Cellars is adjacent to the ferry landing. Or bring a bike and pedal to wineries and distilleries that lie a little further afield.

outdoor upper deck. Audio tours in multiple languages provide narrative. On-board alcohol subdues naysayers.

BLUE & GOLD FLEET BOAT TOUR
Map p314 (☎415-705-8200; www.blueandgold fleet.com; Pier 41; adult/child 60-min ferry tour $26/18; 30-min Rocketboat ride $24/16 ; ☎) See the bay up close aboard a one-hour round-trip cruise to the Golden Gate Bridge or on a 30-minute high-speed thrill ride aboard the fleet's Rocketboat (May to October only). Blue & Gold also operates regularly scheduled ferry service to Sausalito, Tiburon and Angel Island, all departing from Pier 41 at Fisherman's Wharf.

SF WINERY CRUISE BOAT TOUR
(☎415-935-9600; www.sfwinerycruise.com; $165; ☉tours depart 11:30am Sat & Sun) Wine is the focus of this four-hour tour, which crosses the bay aboard a vintage 1958 motor yacht that doubles as a tasting bar. Begin with onshore wine-tasting, followed by champagne toasts and hors d'oeuvres as you ferry to nearby Treasure Island and two small onshore tasting rooms. At day's end, you return glass in hand to Pier 39. Reservations essential.

RIDE THE DUCKS BOAT TOUR
Map p314 (☎877-887-8225; http://sanfrancisco. ridetheducks.com; 2766 Taylor St, cnr Jefferson St; adult/child $29-34/22-25) The Ducks

90-minute tour is limited to the Wharf, North Beach, Chinatown and eastern waterfront. What's special is the conveyance: an amphibious vehicle – bus to boat – that launches for a short loop south of the Bay Bridge. Bring ear plugs: passengers get kazoo-like, noisy 'quackers' and blow them often – delightful for kids, potentially tedious for parents.

🏂 The Presidio

HOUSE OF AIR   TRAMPOLINING
Map p318 (☑415-345-9675; www.houseofairsf. com; 926 Old Mason St, Crissy Field; adult/child $14/10; ☺10am-9pm Mon, 11am-7pm Tue, 11am-9pm Wed & Thu, 10am-10pm Fri & Sat, 10am-8pm Sun; 🚼; 🚌28) If you ever resented your gym teacher for not letting you jump like you wanted on the trampoline, finally you can get your way at this incredible trampoline park, the multiple jumping areas of which include the Matrix, where you can literally bounce off the walls on 42 attached trampolines the size of a basketball court. Kids get dedicated play areas. Reservations strongly recommended, especially on weekends.

PLANET GRANITE   ROCK-CLIMBING
Map p318 (☑415-692-3434; www.planetgranite. com; 924 Old Mason St, Crissy Field; day use adult/ child $15-19/12; ☺6am-11pm Mon-Fri, 8am-8pm Sat, 8am-6pm Sun; 🚌28) Take in spectacular bay views through glass walls as you ascend false-rock structures inside this kick-ass 25,000-sq-ft climbing center – ideal for training before climbs at Yosemite. Master top ropes of 45ft or test your strength ascending giant boulders and vertical-crack climbing walls; finish in the full gym or stretch in a yoga session. Check website for schedules.

PRESIDIO GOLF COURSE   GOLF
Map p318 (☑415-561-4661; www.presidiogolf. com; Arguello Blvd & Finley Rd; 18 holes SF resident $65-85, non-resident $125-145; ☺sunrise-sunset; 🚌33) Whack balls with military-style precision on the course once reserved exclusively for US forces. The Presidio course, now operated by Arnold Palmer Enterprises, overlooks the bay and is considered one of the country's best. Book up to 30 days in advance on the website, which sometimes lists specials too. Rates include cart.

Downtown, Civic Center & SoMa

FINANCIAL DISTRICT & JACKSON SQUARE | UNION SQUARE | SOMA | CIVIC CENTER & THE TENDERLOIN

Neighborhood Top Five

1 Taking a bite out of the Northern California food scene at the **Ferry Building** (p79) – showcase for the Bay Area's small-batch food purveyors and organic farmers – while soaking up incredible bay views.

2 Squealing with glee aboard the **cable cars**, and congratulating yourself for not wearing shorts and freezing your butt off.

3 Ooh-ing and ahh-ing as you travel 6000 years back in time at the **Asian Art Museum**. (p81)

4 Hearing impresario Michael Tilson Thomas conduct Mahler or Beethoven at the Grammy-winning **San Francisco Symphony** (p105).

5 Wandering out along Pier 14 after nightfall to gaze upon the dazzling **Bay Bridge Lights**.

For more detail of this area, see Map p319, p320, p322 and p324 ➡

Lonely Planet's Top Tip

Most tourists begin their trips at Powell St but often get stuck waiting in the long lines at the Powell St cable car turnaround at Market St, held hostage by panhandlers and bad street performers. Either queue up for the Powell St cable car well before noon or get your fix on the lesser-traveled California St line.

Best Places to Eat

➡ Ferry Building (p79)

➡ Benu (p97)

➡ Slanted Door (p94)

➡ Cotogna (p89)

➡ Kokkari (p92)

For reviews, see p89 ➡

Best Places to Drink

➡ Rickhouse (p98)

➡ Barrique (p98)

➡ Edinburgh Castle (p99)

➡ Cantina (p98)

➡ Bloodhound (p101)

For reviews, see p98 ➡

Best Live Performances

➡ San Francisco Symphony (p105)

➡ San Francisco Opera (p105)

➡ Café Royale (p106)

➡ Biscuits & Blues (p106)

For reviews, see p105 ➡

Explore Downtown

Grab food at the Ferry Building, amble the waterfront, then board the California St cable car. From Nob Hill, transfer to Wharf-bound cables or walk northeast into Chinatown; alternatively stay aboard until Polk St, then walk west to Pacific Heights or south toward the Asian Art Museum. Montgomery St is the axis of the Financial District. Civic Center refers to the buildings behind City Hall which abut the less-than-savory Tenderloin. Shoppers and gallery-hoppers will love Union Square. Come nightfall, SoMa nightclubs encourage outrageous behavior.

A word of warning: most first-time visitors are thrown by the grittiness of some downtown areas, including lower Powell St. Downtown is generally safe, but streets west of Powell and south of Geary are rife with panhandlers and junkies. For in-person directions, pop by the Visitor Information Center down the escalator from the Powell St cable-car turnaround.

Local Life

➡ **Markets** The farmers markets at the Ferry Building draw food-savvy locals.

➡ **Waterfront walks** Locals walk south toward the Bay Bridge for expansive vistas and public art.

➡ **Cheap eats** The Tenderloin is full of cheap ethnic restaurants but walking here is not for the faint of heart: when in doubt, taxi.

Getting There & Away

➡ **Streetcar** Historic F-Market streetcars run above Market St, between the Castro and Fisherman's Wharf.

➡ **Cable car** Powell-Hyde and Powell-Mason lines link Downtown with the Wharf (Mason is shorter, Hyde more scenic); the California St line runs perpendicular, over Nob Hill.

➡ **Bus** Market St–bound Muni lines serve Downtown: 2, 5, 6, 14, 21, 30, 31, 38, 41, 45 and 71. In SoMa, the 30 and 45 run down 4th St from the Marina and Union Square; the 14 runs through SoMa to the Mission. The 27 runs from the Mission to Nob Hill via SoMa; the 47 runs along Harrison St through SoMa, up Van Ness to Fisherman's Wharf; the 19 runs up 8th and Polk Sts to the Wharf.

➡ **Metro** J, K/T, L, M and N metro lines run under Market St. The N continues to the Caltrain station, connecting SoMa to the Haight and Golden Gate Park. The T runs from Downtown, via SoMa, stopping along 3rd St.

➡ **BART** Downtown stations are Embarcadero, Montgomery and Powell.

FEARGUS COONEY / GETTY IMAGES ©

TOP SIGHT
FERRY BUILDING & SURROUNDS

Other towns have gourmet ghettos, but San Francisco puts its love of food front and center at the Ferry Building. The once-grand port was overshadowed by a 1950s elevated freeway until 1989, when the road turned out to be less than earthquake-proof. The freeway above the waterfront was demolished and the Ferry Building again emerged as the symbol of San Francisco. Only now, it's become its own destination, marking your arrival onto America's most-happening food scene.

Ferry Building

Like a grand salute, the Ferry Building's trademark 240ft tower greeted dozens of ferries daily after its 1898 inauguration. But with the opening of the Bay Bridge and Golden Gate, ferry traffic subsided in the 1930s. Then the new overhead freeway obscured the building's stately facade and car fumes turned it black. Only after the 1989 earthquake did city planners snap to and realize what they'd been missing: with its grand halls and bay views, this was the perfect place to develop a new public commons.

Even before building renovations were completed in 2003, the Ferry Plaza Farmers Market (p28) began operating out front on the sidewalk. While some complained the prices were higher than at other markets, there was no denying this one offered seasonal, gourmet treats and local specialty foods not found elsewhere. Artisanal goat cheese, fresh-pressed California olive oil, wild boar and organic vegetables soon captured the imagination of SF's professional chefs and semiprofessional eaters.

DON'T MISS...

➜ Food stalls in the Ferry Building's grand arrivals hall

➜ The Embarcadero waterfront promenades

➜ Wild parrots at Justin Herman Plaza

➜ Views of SF from a departing ferry

➜ Vaillancourt Fountain

PRACTICALITIES

➜ Map p319

➜ 📞415-983-8000

➜ www.ferrybuilding marketplace.com

➜ Market St & the Embarcadero

➜ ⏱10am-6pm Mon-Fri, 9am-6pm Sat, 11am-5pm Sun

➜ 🚌2, 6, 9, 14, 21, 31, Ⓜ F, J, K, L, M, N, T

The area's most thrilling sight is the view across to the famous wild parrots of Telegraph Hill. From Justin Herman Plaza, follow the poplar trees leading north to lush Sue Bierman Park (Map p319; cnr Clay & Drumm Sts), a patch of green where you can picnic and watch squawking green birds zip through the branches.

FARMERS MARKET

Saturday morning's farmers market (p28) presents the best people-watching – it's not uncommon to spot an occasional celebrity – but arrive early if you're shopping, as the best items sell fast.

Today the organic gourmet action also continues indoors, where select local shops sell wild-harvested mushrooms, gold-leaved chocolates, sustainably farmed oysters and caviar, as well as myriad other temptations. Standout shops and restaurants provide further reasons to miss your ferry.

Justin Herman Plaza

The plaza (p82) at the foot of Market St, across the Embarcadero from the Ferry Building, may lack visual aesthetics – the Vaillancourt Fountain was intentionally designed to be ugly, mirroring the freeway that once roared above – but Justin Herman Plaza draws big crowds. Lunchtime concert-goers, Critical Mass protesters, lawn bowlers, wintertime ice-skaters, Friday-night roller skaters and internet-daters screening potential mates from behind the fountain's wall of water all flock here.

Bay Bridge Lights

Leave it to San Francisco to turn one of its bridges into a psychedelic spectacle. In 2013, lighting artist Leo Villareal strung 25,000 LED lights onto the bridge's vertical suspension cables, transforming the span into a 1.8-mile-long show – the world's largest display of LED lights. From sunset until 2am they swirl, shimmer and pulse in never-repeating patterns that create wild optical illusions. One minute the span is transformed into an aquarium, with schools of fish swimming above traffic; the next minute the cables are like jets of water, spraying vertically in fifty-story-high fountains. You could stare at it for hours – we certainly have. Here's hoping the installation is made permanent. For more, see baylights.org.

Rincon Park

A sliver of green south of the Ferry Building, Rincon Park borders the bay, with a wide promenade luring hand-holding sweethearts, families with strollers and kids with skateboards. The centerpiece is a five-story-high bow-and-arrow sculpture called 'Cupid's Span,' its giant yellow bow rising from native bunch grasses. From a distance, the vertical arrow and pulled string mirror the Bay Bridge cables. Up close, the giant yellow bow resembles a marooned galleon. We're not sure if it's technically legal to climb, but there's always someone shimmying up for souvenir photos. Come nightfall, amateur photographers line their tripods along the park's bayside promenade to shoot images of the bridge's dazzling lights, especially nights of the full moon, which rises directly behind the bridge, its reflection shimmering on the water.

TOP SIGHT
ASIAN ART MUSEUM

One of the largest, most comprehensive collections of Asian art outside Asia covers 6000 years and thousands of miles of terrain. A trip through the galleries is a treasure-hunting expedition, from racy Rajasthan palace paintings to the largest collection of Japanese sculptural baskets outside Japan to the jewel-box gallery of lustrous Chinese jade – just don't bump into those priceless Ming vases.

The Asian Art Museum has amassed 18,000 prime examples of the region's ingenuity and artistry. Consider the diplomatic backbends curators made to put such diverse collections into proper perspective. Where the UN falters, this museum succeeds in bringing Taiwan, China and Tibet together, uniting Pakistan and India and striking harmonious balance between Japan, Korea and China. Granted, the Chinese collection takes up two wings and South Asia only one, but that healthy cultural competition has served to encourage donations of South Asian artifacts. Given the city's 150-year history as North America's gateway to Asia, the collection is also quintessentially San Franciscan, drawing on longstanding local ties and distinguished local collections.

The building is another feat of diplomacy. Italian architect Gae Aulenti's clever repurposing of the old San Francisco Main Library left intact the much-beloved building's Beaux Arts exterior, and the entryway's travertine arches and polished stone interior staircase. Two new plazas for exhibitions and events were added inside, and in 2013 two 19th-century Japanese bronze lions took the podiums outside.

For a proper tour of the collection, ascend the single-file escalator to the top floor. The curatorial concept is to follow the evolution of Asian art and culture from the top floor down, beginning on the 3rd floor with South Asia and then – wait, isn't that Iran, followed by the Sikh kingdoms, then Indonesia? By the time you've cruised past the Zoroastrian artifacts, Javanese puppets and countless Buddhas, all theological quibbles will yield to astonishment – and possibly exhaustion. If museums wear you out – or you're short on time – find art from your favorite Asian country, or head directly for the highlighted masterworks and special exhibitions.

The Asian also emphasizes educational programs, which keep pan-generational crowds thronging the place. Hands-on workshops for kids and evening lectures with noted art historians are boons for parents and couples on date night.

Make a day of it with lunch at **Cafe Asia** (Map p322; www.asianart.org/visit/cafe-asia; 200 Larkin St; mains $5-14; ☺10am-4:30pm Tue, Wed, Fri-Sun, to 8:30pm Thu), where sunny days mean sipping rooibos tea or guava lemonade on the balcony terrace. February to September, on Thursday evenings 5pm to 9pm, hipsters run the show, with urban-contemporary event series; lineups vary, but imagine DJs spinning Japanese hip-hop, tattoo artists giving live demos, sake-makers pouring brews and crafty types making Chinese paper lanterns to ward off hungry ghosts.

DON'T MISS...

➡ 3000-year-old Chinese ritual bronzes

➡ Rare Japanese scrolls and screens

➡ Gilt-bronze Buddha from the year 338

➡ Architectural detail on the building's facade

➡ Cafe Asia

PRACTICALITIES

➡ Map p322

➡ ☎415-581-3500

➡ www.asianart.org

➡ 200 Larkin St

➡ adult/student/child $12/8/free, 1st Sun of month free

➡ ☺10am-5pm Tue-Sun, to 9pm Thu Feb-Sep

➡ ⓂCivic Center, ⒷCivic Center

82

◉ SIGHTS

The Financial District centers around Montgomery St – the 'Wall St of the West' – and bleeds into Jackson Square, the city's oldest neighborhood, with low-slung brick buildings and high-end antiquarians. Union Square refers to the square proper *and* the surrounding neighborhood; it's the principal retail-shopping and hotel district. South of Market (SoMa) was formerly the warehouse district, but massive construction projects are transforming it into the new downtown; the area around 3rd and Mission is chockablock with museums and galleries, but most of SoMa's long blocks lack sights and are tedious to walk without a specific destination. Civic Center refers to the governmental buildings by City Hall; the surrounding neighborhood, the Tenderloin, is a study in urban grit.

◉ Financial District & Jackson Square

FERRY BUILDING   LANDMARK
See p79.

JUSTIN HERMAN PLAZA   PLAZA
See p80.

TRANSAMERICA PYRAMID & REDWOOD PARK   NOTABLE BUILDING
Map p319 (www.thepyramidcenter.com; 600 Montgomery St; ⊙9am-6pm Mon-Fri; ⓂEmbarcadero, ⒷEmbarcadero) The defining feature of San Francisco's skyline was built during the jet age, atop the wreck of a whaling ship abandoned in the 1849 Gold Rush, at the site of a saloon frequented by Mark Twain and the newspaper office where Sun Yatsen drafted his Proclamation of the Republic of China.

Architect William Pereira maximized light in the narrow streets below with his pyramid design, but even before its 1972 inauguration his pointy office tower was derided as Pereira's Prick. Critics claimed Pereira's Hollywood special-effects background was too apparent in the 853ft streamlined tower, which looked ready for blastoff. But others found the quirky landmark perfectly suited to SF. Even the haters love Redwood Park, the half-acre redwood stand beneath the Pyramid.

Another redeeming feature was the view – note, past tense. Since September 11, the view deck at the top has been closed for 'security reasons.' If you're determined to get virtually queasy witnessing the Pyramid's slight half-foot sway in a strong wind, visit the virtual observation deck online.

JACKSON SQUARE   NEIGHBORHOOD
(www.jacksonsquaresf.com; around Jackson & Montgomery Sts; ⓂEmbarcadero, ⒷEmbarcadero) Jackson Square – bounded by Washington, Columbus, Pacific and Sansome – was once the waterfront docks. Italianate brick buildings with tall windows and cast-iron shutters housed whiskey dealers, lawyers, loan offices and other Barbary Coast denizens. Now the province of upscale interior-design showrooms, ad agencies and antiques dealers, the low-slung architecture is a refreshing counterpoint to surrounding skyscrapers.

Current tenants are more subtle about wheedling money from unsuspecting consumers than were previous occupants during the 19th century. Notorious saloon owner Shanghai Kelly and madam Miss Piggot once conked new arrivals on the head and delivered them to ships in need of crew. (Despite their efforts, many ships were abandoned as sailors left to seek their fortune in San Francisco.)

AP HOTALING WAREHOUSE   HISTORICAL BUILDING
Map p319 (451-55 Jackson St; ⓂEmbarcadero, ⒷEmbarcadero) 'If, as they say, God spanked the town/For being over-frisky/Why did He burn His churches down/And spare Hotaling's whiskey?' The snappiest comeback in SF history was this saloon-goers' retort after Hotaling's 1866 whiskey warehouse survived the 1906 earthquake and fire. Many considered this divine retribution for Barbary Coast debauchery. A bronze plaque with this ditty graces the resilient Italianate building.

WELLS FARGO HISTORY MUSEUM   MUSEUM
Map p319 (☎415-396-2619; www.wellsfargohistory.com; 420 Montgomery St; ⊙9am-5pm Mon-Fri; ⚓; ⓂMontgomery, ⒷMontgomery) **FREE** The evolution of San Francisco is inextricably linked to the Gold Rush, and this spiffy little museum pays homage to the much-romanticized era, with emphases on stagecoaches, the Pony Express and bank-

DOWNTOWN ROOFTOP GARDENS

Above the busy sidewalks, there's a serene world of unmarked public rooftop gardens that grant perspective on Downtown's skyscraper-canyons. They're called 'privately owned public-open spaces,' or POPOs. Local public-advocacy group **SPUR** (www.spur.org) publishes a complete list; its smartphone app lists them all. Here's a short list of favorites:

One Montgomery Terrace (Map p320; 50 Post St/1 Montgomery St; ☺10am-6pm Mon-Sat; MMontgomery, BMontgomery) Great Market St views of old and new SF. Enter through Crocker Galleria, take the elevator to the top, then ascend stairs; or enter Wells Fargo at One Montgomery and take the elevator to 'R.'

Sun Terrace (Map p319; 343 Sansome St; ☺10am-6pm Mon-Fri; MEmbarcadero, BEmbarcadero) Knockout vistas of the Financial District and Transamerica Pyramid from atop a slender art-deco skyscraper. Take the elevator to 15.

Fairmont San Francisco (Map p332; 950 Mason St; ☺24hr; ⬜1, ⬜California St, Powell-Hyde, Powell-Mason) Traverse the lobby toward the Pavilion Room, then out glass doors to a deliciously kitsch rooftop courtyard – our favorite.

ing. Notwithstanding blatant PR for Wells Fargo, the exhibits are remarkably well curated, including detailed histories of 19th-century travel in the American West.

Wells Fargo was in 1866 the world's largest operator of stagecoaches, and here you can peer inside two that are marvelously preserved. Upstairs, climb aboard a recreated coach and hear recorded stories, while the kids ride a free mechanical pony. If you're nearby, it merits a look – especially with little ones.

◉ Union Square

UNION SQUARE   SQUARE
Map p320 (intersection of Geary, Powell, Post & Stockton Sts; ⬜Powell-Mason, Powell-Hyde, MPowell, BPowell) Louis Vuitton is more top-of-mind than the Emancipation Proclamation, but Union Square – now bordered by high-end department stores and boutiques – was named for pro-Union Civil War rallies held here 150 years ago. Plop down on a bench, with espresso from Emporio Rulli (p97), for perfect people-watching. Find half-price theater tickets at the TIX Bay Area booth.

Just beyond the square's northeast corner, on Stockton St, locate the **Ruth Asawa Fountain** (Map p320; 335 Stockton St, Grand Hyatt steps) – Asawa being one of SF's most esteemed artists – and note the relief's tiny detail of civic icons and SF landmarks. Each was fashioned from bread dough by 250 different people – from famous artists to little

children – then cast by the artist in bronze. When in 2013, Apple Inc. submitted plans for its new store at Post and Stockton Sts, it assumed the fountain would be removed, but local outcry was so great, Apple was, at this writing, redrawing its plans.

49 GEARY   ART GALLERY
Map p320 (☎415-788-9818; www.sfada.com; 49 Geary St; ☺10:30am-5:30pm Tue-Fri, 11am-5pm Sat; MPowell, BPowell) **FREE** Pity the collectors silently nibbling endive in austere Chelsea galleries – at 49 Geary, openings mean unexpected art, goldfish-shaped crackers and outspoken crowds. Four floors of galleries feature standout international and local works including eclectic, eye-popping photography ranging from the 19th to 21st century at Fraenkel Gallery to sculptor Seth Koen's minimalist pieces at Gregory Lind. For quieter contemplation, visit weekdays.

77 GEARY   ART GALLERY
Map p320 (77 Geary St; ☺10:30am-5:30pm Tue-Fri, 11am-5pm Sat; MPowell, BPowell) **FREE** The most intriguing art often appears in what seems the wrong place: 77 Geary's unmarked entryway confirms this. Get seduced on the mezzanine by contemporary painting and sculpture at **Patricia Sweetow Gallery** (www.patriciasweetowgallery.com). Upstairs at **Rena Bransten Gallery** (www.renabranstengallery.com), sensitive meets sensation in shows like Hung Liu's mirage-like portraits of found ancestors, and collaged stills from 'unwatchable' movies by Polyester cult-sensation John Waters.

SAN FRANCISCO'S HOMELESS: WHAT'S THE DEAL?

It's inevitable: Panhandlers *will* ask you for spare change during your visit to San Francisco, especially around Union Square and most downtown tourist attractions.

The city's mild climate, history of tolerance and extensive social services have rendered it a magnet for the homeless, whose numbers are estimated up to 10,000 – the highest in the USA. Many say the issue dates to the 1960s, when then-governor Ronald Reagan slashed funding to mental hospitals, drug-rehab programs and low-income housing programs, policies he continued as president.

The city's recent mayors have confronted the homeless issue in creative ways, with varying success. Willie Brown proposed seizing homeless people's shopping carts – a notorious failure. Gavin Newsom's controversial 'Care, not Cash' policy replaced cash payments with social services; his 'Sit/Lie Ordinance,' approved by voters in 2010, made it illegal to sit or lie on the sidewalk between 7am and 11pm. The latter has gone largely unenforced. Current mayor Ed Lee seems to be skirting the problem; he discontinued the City Hall position of 'Homeless Czar,' focusing instead on downtown business development.

The bottom line is that nobody knows how to address the homeless issue, and until they do, panhandlers aren't going away. Whether you offer money or food is your choice, but generally a polite 'No, thank you' suffices.

POWELL ST CABLE CAR TURNAROUND
LANDMARK

Map p320 (cnr Powell & Market Sts; MPowell, BPowell) Stand awhile at Powell and Market Sts and spot arriving cable-car operators leaping out, gripping the trolleys' chassis and slooowly rotating the car atop a revolving wooden platform. Cable cars can't go backwards and this is the terminus of Powell St lines. Riders queue up mid-morning to early evening for the famous moving historic landmarks, providing a captive audience for panhandlers, street performers and preachers on megaphones.

Some find the scene colorful, others unnerving. If you're worried about time, count heads and do math: cable cars hold 60 people (29 seated, 31 standing), but depart carrying fewer to leave room to board passengers to board en route. They depart every five to ten minutes at peak times. Powell-Mason cars are quickest to the Wharf, but Powell-Hyde cars traverse more terrain and hills.

PALACE HOTEL
HISTORICAL BUILDING

Map p320 (☑415-512-1111; www.sfpalace.com; 2 New Montgomery St; MMontgomery, BMontgomery) The city's most storied hotel dates back a century. Visit by day to see the opulent Garden Court's luminous stained-glass ceiling and Austrian-crystal chandeliers, then peek into the **Pied Piper Bar** to see Maxfield Parrish's mural of the Pied Piper. Afterward have drinks across the street at House of Shields (p103) and see the gorgeous mahogany back bar, which was originally intended to frame Parrish's mural but proved too small.

In 2013, the Palace's present owner, Kyo-Ya Hotels, removed the Parrish mural to sell at auction but locals pitched a fit and management returned the painting to its proper place.

The Palace opened in 1875 and was gutted during the 1906 earthquake and fire. Opera star Enrico Caruso was staying here that day and reportedly ran into the street, swearing he'd never return to San Francisco. The current building opened in 1909. Ten years later, Woodrow Wilson gave his League of Nations speech here and in 1923 US President Warren G Harding died upstairs.

CROCKER BANK BUILDING
HISTORIC BUILDING

Map p320 (1 Montgomery St; ⊙9am-6pm Mon-Fri, to 4pm Sat; MMontgomery, BMontgomery) FREE Designed by Willis Polk and built in 1908, the former Crocker Bank Headquarters (now Wells Fargo) has one of the city's most lavish interiors, with rows of white-marble columns beneath a coffered ceiling ornamented with rosettes. Hunched gargoyles support marble check-writing tables with inkwells cradled by winged statuettes. No photos, lest the guards pounce. The roof is a public garden.

BOHEMIAN CLUB
HISTORICAL BUILDING

Map p320 (624 Taylor St; ☐2, 3, 38, ☐Powell-Mason, Powell-Hyde) The most infamous, secretive club in all San Francisco was founded in the 19th century by bona fide bohemians, but they couldn't afford the upkeep so allowed the ultra-rich to join. On the Post St side of the ivy-covered club, look for the plaque honoring Gold Rush–era author Bret Harte, which depicts characters from his works.

On the plaque's extreme right is 'The Heathen Chinee.' It's not a racist attack – au contraire – but a reference to the eponymous 1870 satirical poem Harte wrote mocking anti-Chinese sentiment in Northern California. Ironically, upon publication the poem had the opposite effect and became a rallying cry against Chinese immigration. Things are seldom what they seem at the Bohemian Club. Today's member roster lists an odd mix of power elite and famous artists: apparently both George W Bush and Bob Weir are current members.

WESTIN ST FRANCIS HOTEL
GLASS ELEVATORS VIEWPOINT
Map p320 (☎415-397-7000; www.westin.com; 335 Powell St; Ⓜ Powell, Ⓑ Powell) For a bird's-eye view of Union Square, aim for the front desk (in the new building), find the glass-walled tower elevators in the corner and soar 32 stories for drop-dead vistas. Shhh! Don't tell 'em we told you.

XANADU GALLERY: FOLK ART
INTERNATIONAL NOTABLE BUILDING
Map p320 (☎415-392-9999; www.folkartintl.com; 140 Maiden Lane; ⊙10am-6pm Tue-Sat; Ⓜ Powell, Ⓑ Powell) Shrink the Guggenheim, plop it inside a brick box with sunken Romanesque archway and voilà: Frank Lloyd Wright's 1949 Circle Gallery Building, now Xanadu Gallery. The nautilus shell ramp in the atrium leads you on a world tour of high-end folk art, from Fijian war clubs to mounted nose ornaments from the Andes.

JAMES FLOOD BUILDING HISTORICAL BUILDING
Map p320 (cnr Market & Powell Sts; Ⓜ Powell, Ⓑ Powell) This 1904 stone building survived the 1906 earthquake and retains its original character, notwithstanding the Gap downstairs. Upstairs, long labyrinthine marble hallways are lined with frosted-glass doors, just like a noir movie set. No coincidence: in 1921 the SF office of infamous Pinkerton Detective Agency hired a young investigator named Dashiell Hammett, author of the 1930 noir classic *The Maltese Falcon*.

LOTTA'S FOUNTAIN MONUMENT
Map p320 (intersection of Market & Kearny Sts; Ⓜ Montgomery, Ⓑ Montgomery) Lotta Crabtree made a killing as San Francisco's diminutive opera diva and never forgot the city that paid for her trademark cigars. In 1875, at 28, the already-rich performer commissioned this cast-metal pillar (thrice her size) with a spigot fountain (now dry) as a present to San Francisco – useful gift indeed during the 1906 fire, when it became downtown's sole water source.

⊙ SoMa

SAN FRANCISCO MUSEUM OF
MODERN ART MUSEUM
Map p324 (SFMOMA; ☎415-357-4000; www.sfmoma.org; 151 3rd St; Ⓜ Montgomery, Ⓑ Montgomery) San Francisco Museum of Modern Art (SFMOMA) was destined from its start in 1935 to become an eclectic, unconventional museum. But when it moved into architect Mario Botta's light-filled brick box in 1995, it became clear just how far this museum was prepared to push the art world. The new museum showed its backside to New York and leaned full-tilt towards the western horizon.

Undergoing a massive 235,000-sq-ft expansion, the museum is closed until early 2016.

CARTOON ART MUSEUM MUSEUM
Map p324 (☎415-227-8666; www.cartoonart.org; 655 Mission St; adult/student $7/5, 1st Tue of month 'pay what you wish' ; ⊙11am-5pm Tue-Sun; Ⓜ Montgomery, Ⓑ Montgomery) Founded on a grant from Bay Area cartoon legend Charles M Schultz of *Peanuts* fame, this bold museum isn't afraid of the dark, racy or political, including R Crumb drawings from the '70s and a retrospective of political cartoons from the *Economist* by Kevin 'Kal' Kallaugher. Lectures and openings are rare opportunities to mingle with comic legends, Pixar studio heads, and obsessive collectors.

Introducing this place to comics fans would be an insult: of course you recognize John Romita's amazing Spiderman cover drawings and you were probably raised on the alphabet from Edward Gorey's *Gashlycrumb Tinies*, starting with 'A is for Amy who fell down the stairs/B is for Basil assaulted by bears...' But even fans will learn something from lectures about 1930s efforts to unionize overworked women animators, and shows on underground comics legends like Spain Rodriguez and Trina Robbins.

CONTEMPORARY
JEWISH MUSEUM   MUSEUM

Map p324 (☏415-344-8800; www.thecjm.org; 736 Mission St; adult/child $10/free, after 5pm Thu $5; ☺11am-5pm Fri-Tue, 1-8pm Thu; MMontgomery, BMontgomery) That upended brushed-steel box balancing improbably on one corner isn't a sculpture, but a gallery for the Contemporary Jewish Museum, a major new SF landmark derived from a former power substation. Exhibits are thoughtfully curated, heavy-hitting and compelling, investigating ideas and ideals through the lens of artists and social figures as diverse as Andy Warhol, Gertrude Stein and Harry Houdini.

The museum opened 2008 but had been around since 1984. Before Daniel Libeskind signed on to design New York's much-debated September 11 memorial, his design for this museum was already causing murmurs in SF, with its blue-steel cladding and shape drawn from the Hebrew word *l'chaim* – 'to life' – a fine idea in theory but one best appreciated from a helicopter. The steel structure is merged with the 1907 brick facade of the Jesse St power substation, an early industrial structure charmingly decorated with cherubs and garlands.

MUSEUM OF THE AFRICAN
DIASPORA   MUSEUM

Map p324 (MOAD; ☏415-358-7200; www.moadsf. org; 685 Mission St; adult/student/child $10/5/ free; ☺11am-6pm Wed-Sat, noon-5pm Sun; MMontgomery, BMontgomery) Exploring four main themes – origins, movement, adaptation and transformation – MOAD assembles a standout international cast of characters to tell the epic story of diaspora, including a moving video of slave narratives, told by Maya Angelou. Standouts among quarterly changing exhibits have included Romare Bearden's graphic riffs on trains, jazz and family; and quilts by India's Siddi community, descended from 16th-century African slaves.

The gift shop carries colorful handicrafts, jewelry and unusual kids' toys from Africa.

ELECTRIC WORKS   ART GALLERY

Map p324 (☏415-626-5496; www.sfelectric works.com; 1360 Mission St; ☺11am-6pm Tue-Fri, to 5pm Sat; ⊟14, MVan Ness) FREE In the gallery/printmaking studio that calls itself 'The Land of Yes,' anything is possible – including David Byrne's diagrams revealing the overlap between hairstyles and long division, Talia Greene's portraits of Victorians with beards of swarming bees and Sandow Birk's modern take on Dante's *Inferno,* starring traffic-jammed LA as hell and San Francisco as a foggy purgatory.

The small, select gallery store is what museum stores ought to be, with arty must-haves – beeswax crayons, Klein bottles, vintage Chinese toys from the Cultural Revolution and sculpted marble soda cans; the sale of some books and prints benefits nonprofits.

CALIFORNIA HISTORICAL
SOCIETY MUSEUM   MUSEUM

Map p324 (☏415-357-1848; www.californiahisto ricalsociety.org; 678 Mission St; suggested donation $5; ☺museum noon-5pm Tue-Sun; library noon-5pm Wed-Fri ; MMontgomery, BMontgomery) Get the lowdown on California at this exhibition space devoted entirely to the state's history. Galleries show themed highlights from the museum's vast collection of a million-plus photographs, paintings and ephemera. Recent exhibits have examined the Golden State's reputation for movies, fresh food and the good life via silent-movie posters, vintage fruit labels and tourism brochures – and how that mythology washes with reality.

History buffs: make time for the fascinating **research library** and gain access to rare books, photos and manuscripts. The library has the definitive collection on the Northern California American Civil Liberties Union and People's Temple, among other California-centric subjects. Call ahead if you want to research specific topics so staff can pull appropriate materials from vaults.

CHILDREN'S CREATIVITY MUSEUM   MUSEUM

Map p324 (☏415-820-3320; www.zeum.org; 221 4th St; admission $11; ☺10am-4pm Wed-Sun Sept-May, Tues-Sun Jun-Aug; ⚑; MPowell, BPowell) No velvet ropes or hands-off: kids have free reign, with high-tech art displays double-daring them to make their own music videos, claymation movies and soundtracks. Jump into live-action video games and sign up for workshops with Bay Area superstar animators, techno-whizzes and robot-builders. The only non-tech, non-screen activity is the vintage-1906 **Loof Carousel** outside, operating until 5:30pm daily; one $4 ticket covers two rides.

YERBA BUENA GARDENS   PARK

Map p324 (☑415-820-3550; www.yerbabuena
gardens.com; 3rd & Mission Sts; ⊙sunrise-10pm;
🚻; MMontgomery, BMontgomery) Flanked
by Yerba Buena Center for the Arts and
the Metreon shopping mall, the gardens
bring much-needed spot green to concrete
SoMa, perfect for playtime with the kiddies, downtime while gallery-hopping or
for clandestine trysts behind the fountain.
Free noontime concerts in summer feature
world music, hip-hop and jazz.

The show-stopping centerpiece is Hou-
ston Cornwell and Joseph De Pace's sleek
Martin Luther King Jr Memorial Fountain,
a wall of water that runs over the Reverend's immortal words: '...until justice rolls
down like waters and righteousness like a
mighty stream.'

A pedestrian bridge over Howard St
links the popular esplanade to an often
overlooked playground and family entertainment complex. Kids won't want to miss
this complex, which includes the hands-on
Children's Creativity Museum and carousel,
a small bowling alley and an ice rink.

ELI RIDGWAY   ART GALLERY

Map p324 (☑415-777-1366; www.eliridgway.com;
172 Minna St; ⊙11am-6pm Tue-Sat; 🚌14, 30, 45,
BMontgomery, MMontgomery) **FREE** Meticulously made-in-San Francisco works make
you stop, think and marvel at Eli Ridgway:
Jacqueline Kiyomi Gordon's sculptural installations are actually speakers projecting
eerie outdoor sounds into the gallery, Cas-
tenada/Reiman's architectural landscapes
are constructed from piled landscape
paintings and Sean McFarland's 'impossible landscape' photographs are actually
snapshots of buildings cut and rearranged
into distorted but convincing cityscapes.

CROWN POINT PRESS   ART GALLERY

Map p324 (☑415-974-6273; www.crownpoint.
com; 20 Hawthorne St; ⊙10am-5pm Mon, to 6pm
Tue-Sat; BMontgomery, MMontgomery) **FREE**
Crown Point Press printmakers work with
artists to turn singular visions into large-
scale paper multiples. When master printmakers are at work, you're often invited to
watch – and if you want to make your own,
you can pick up how-to books and tools.

Bet you didn't think anyone could capture Chuck Close's giant portraits, Wayne
Thiebaud's Pop Art pastries or Australian
Aboriginal artist Dorothy Napangardi's
dreamings on paper. Yet here they are:

🛈 BIKE OR WALK?

Downtown's hilly terrain and many
transit routes make walking ideal;
but South of Market's long flat blocks
and minimal transit make bicycle the
preferred transport – consult the SF
Bicycle Coalition (www.sfbike.org) for
best routes.

color, woodcut portraits produced by carv-
ing and printing 51 separate blocks of
wood; color gravures within glass pastry
cases; and salt tracings of Mina Mina in
mesmerizing sugar-lift etchings. Such are
the mysterious powers of Crown Point.

FEDERAL BUILDING   NOTABLE BUILDING

Map p324 (90 7th St; MCivic Center, BCivic
Center) The revolutionary green design of
this government-office building by 2005
Pritzker Architecture Prize–winner Thom
Mayne means huge savings in energy –
and taxpayer dollars. Ingenious layouts
eliminate internal political battles over
corner offices, providing direct sunlight,
natural ventilation and views for 90% of
work stations. Detractors decry it a fortress but it adds green distinction to the
otherwise bland industrial skyline of SoMa
warehouses.

⊙ Civic Center & the Tenderloin

ASIAN ART MUSEUM   MUSEUM

See p81.

CITY HALL   HISTORICAL BUILDING

Map p322 (☑art exhibit line 415-554-6080; tour
info 415-554-6023; www.ci.sf.ca.us/cityhall; 400
Van Ness Ave; ⊙8am-8pm Mon-Fri, tours 10am,
noon & 2pm; 🚻; MCivic Center, BCivic Center)
FREE That mighty beaux arts dome pretty
much covers San Francisco's grandest am-
bitions and fundamental flaws. Designed in
1915 to outdo Paris for flair and outsize the
capitol in Washington, DC, the dome – the
world's fifth largest – was unsteady until its
retrofit after the 1989 earthquake, when ingenious technology enabled it to swing on
its base without raising alarm.

The gold leafing on the dome's exterior
is a reminder of dot-com-era excess. But
from the inside, the splendid rotunda has

DOWNTOWN, CIVIC CENTER & SOMA SIGHTS

ringing acoustics, and if that dome could talk, it would tell of triumph and tragedy. Anti-McCarthy sit-in protesters were hosed off the grand staircase in 1960 but finally ran McCarthy out of town. Supervisor Harvey Milk and Mayor George Moscone were assassinated here in 1978. And in 2004, cheers rang around the world for families and friends of the 4037 same-sex couples who celebrated their marriages here, thanks to Mayor Newsom's short-lived challenge to California marriage law (the latter overturned by the Supreme Court in 2013). Take the elevator one flight down to discover intriguing public art exhibitions, which range from photographs of senior subcultures to work by blind artists.

Free docent-led tours meet at the tour kiosk near the Van Ness Ave entrance, but City Hall is best seen in action. For insight into how San Francisco's government works – or doesn't – the Board of Supervisors meets Tuesdays at 2pm in City Hall; check the agenda and minutes online. Theoretically, visitors may be removed for 'boisterous' behavior, but this being San Francisco, democracy in action can get pretty rowdy without fazing seen-it-all security guards.

For the best perspective on the massive dome's elegant detail, lie down on the grand marble staircase beneath the rotunda and look straight up. Seriously.

GLIDE MEMORIAL UNITED METHODIST CHURCH   CHURCH
Map p322 (☎415-674-6090; www.glide.org; 330 Ellis St; ◉celebrations 9am & 11am Sun; ⓂPowell, ⒷPowell) The 100-member Glide gospel choir kicks off Sunday celebrations with a warm welcome for whomever comes through the door – the diverse, 1500-plus congregation includes many who'd once lost all faith in faith. After the celebration ends, the congregation keeps inspiring, providing a million free meals a year and housing for formerly homeless families – now that's hitting a high note.

SAN FRANCISCO MAIN LIBRARY   NOTABLE BUILDING
Map p322 (☎415-557-4400; www.sfpl.org; 100 Larkin St; ◉10am-6pm Mon & Sat, 9am-8pm Tue-Thu, noon-5pm Fri & Sun; ♿; ⓂCivic Center, ⒷCivic Center) The vast skylight dome sheds plenty of light through San Francisco's Main Library. Besides its ragtag masses of San Franciscans and some of their favorite books, the library quietly hosts an excellent high-profile author-reading and lecture series, plus intriguing ephemera exhibits in the 6th-floor Skylight Gallery.

And this being San Francisco, the library actively appeals to broad audiences – to wit the African American Center, Chinese Center, James C Hormel Gay & Lesbian Center and the Center for San Francisco History. Artistic touches include Alice Ay-

SOUTH PARK OR BUST

'Dot-com' was the magic word in San Francisco in the mid-'90s, when venture capitalists and 20-something techies plotted website launches in cafes ringing **South Park** (Map p324; S Park St; Ⓜ4th St). But when online pet food and ice cream delivery services failed to deliver profits, South Park became a dot-com ghost town, adding yet another bust to its checkered history.

Speculation is nothing new to South Park, which was planned by a real-estate developer in the 1850s as a bucolic gated community. A party to honor Crimean War victory was thrown here in 1855 in the hopes of attracting some of San Francisco's Gold Rush millionaires – but it degenerated into a cake-throwing food fight and the development never took off. But this turf proved fertile ground for wild ideas: as a plaque around the corner indicates, 601 3rd St was the **birthplace of Jack London**, best-selling author of The Call of the Wild, White Fang and other Wild West adventure stories.

After WWII, Filipino American war veterans formed a quiet community here – at least until dot-com HQs suddenly moved in and out of the neighborhood. South Park offices weren't vacant for long before Web 2.0 moved in, including a scrappy start-up with an outlandish notion that soon everyone would be communicating in online haiku. Twitter has since moved its operations and 500 million users to Market St.

cock's spiral staircase between the 5th and 6th floors, and artist Ann Chamberlain's 2nd-floor wallpaper made of cards from the old card catalog, with running commentary provided by 200 San Franciscans.

LUGGAGE STORE GALLERY   ART GALLERY

Map p322 (📞415-255-5971; www.luggagestore gallery.org; 1007 Market St; ☺noon-5pm Wed-Sat; MCivic Center, BCivic Center) A dandelion pushing through sidewalk cracks, this plucky nonprofit gallery has for two decades brought signs of life to one of the toughest blocks in the Tenderloin. Art sprawls across the spacious 2nd-floor gallery, rising above the street without losing sight of it: this was the launching pad for renowned graffiti satirists – which is why the door is camouflaged by spray paint.

Two Luggage Store regulars you might recognize around town are Rigo and Brazilian duo Ogemeos. Rigo did the 'One Tree' mural that looks like a one-way sign by the 101 Fwy on-ramp in SoMa. And the Ogemeos did the mural of a defiant kid holding a lit firecracker atop the gallery building. With such oddly touching works, poetry nights and monthly performing-arts events, this place puts the tender in the Tenderloin.

UNITED NATIONS PLAZA   SQUARE

Map p322 (Market St, btwn Hyde & Leavenworth Sts; ☺6am-midnight; MCivic Center, BCivic Center) This vast brick-paved triangle commemorates the signing of the UN charter in San Francisco. It offers a clear view of City Hall, sundry Scientologists drumming up converts and the odd drug deal in progress. Thankfully, the wonderful Heart of the City Farmers Market (p28) provides a fresher perspective on the Tenderloin.

EATING

Make reservations whenever possible for Downtown restaurants. The Ferry Building houses multiple food vendors under one roof, with chef-operated lunch counters, high-end take-out, and a farmers market Tuesdays and Thursdays from 10am to 2pm and Saturdays from 8am to 2pm. At dinnertime, Downtown and South of Market are best known for high-end restaurants, but lunchtime eateries cater to office workers, with

meals around $10. The Financial District is dead at nighttime, when only midrange and top-end houses stay open. The Tenderloin (west of Powell St, south of Geary St, north of Market St) feels sketchy and rough, but as always in San Francisco, superior dining rewards the adventurous. Some cheap eats in the 'Loin close earlier than their posted hours.

✖ Financial District & Jackson Square

MIXT GREENS   SALADS $

Map p319 (www.mixtgreens.com; 120 Sansome St; salads $8-11; ☺10:30am-3pm Mon-Fri; 🖉; MMontgomery, BMontgomery) 🍃 Stockbrokers line up out the door for the generous organic salads with zingy dressings. Add humanely raised meat and you've a meal for an omnivore. Grab a stool, or order to-go and eat outdoors beside office workers at St Mary's Square, up California St.

★COTOGNA   ITALIAN $$

Map p319 (📞415-775-8508; www.cotognasf.com; 470 Pacific Ave; mains $14-26; ☺11:30am-11:30pm Mon-Sat, 11:30am-2:30pm & 5-9pm Sun; 🖉; 🚋10, 12) Chef-owner Michael Tusk won the 2011 James Beard Award for best chef. Ever since, it's been hard to book a table at Cotogna (and its fancier big sister Quince next door), but it's worth planning ahead to be rewarded with authentic, wood-fired rustica Italian cooking that magically balances a few pristine flavors in pastas, tender-to-the-tooth pizzas and rotisserie meats.

1. Yerba Buena Gardens (p87)
A welcome patch of green amongst the SoMa concrete, this park links an arts center, recreation areas and the Children's Creativity Museum.

2. Bar Agricole (p101)
A James Beard Award–winner, this bar is at the forefront of San Francisco's cocktail scene: stop by for a well-researched drink and some bar bites.

3. City Hall (p87)
Designed in 1915, the City Hall's mighty beaux arts dome has been retrofitted with technology that allows it to swing on its base during earthquakes.

Every bottle of wine costs $40. The $24 prix-fixe menu is a steal. To avoid reservations and waits Monday to Saturday, come between 3pm and 5pm for late lunch.

BOCADILLOS
BASQUE $$

Map p319 (☎415-982-2622; www.bocasf.com; 710 Montgomery St; dishes $8-17; ◎7am-10pm Mon-Fri, 5-10:30pm Sat; ◻1, 10, 12, 41) Forget multipage menus and giant portions; choose between two small sandwiches on toasted rolls, with green salad, for just $12 (lunchtime only) at this downtown favorite for Mediterranean tapas, offshoot of Michelin-starred Pipérade. For dinner, juicy lamb burgers, snapper ceviche and Catalan sausages are just-right Basque bites, enhanced with good wine by the glass. There's breakfast, too. Anticipate deafening noise at peak times.

GEORGE'S
SEAFOOD, MEDITERRANEAN $$

Map p319 (☎415-956-6900; www.georgessf.com; 415 Sansome St; mains $16-26; ◎11am-10pm Mon-Fri, 5pm-10pm Sat; ◻1, 10, 12, 41, ◻California St) An anomaly downtown, George's has the casual, inviting vibe of a small, moderately priced neighborhood restaurant. The menu focuses on sustainably harvested seafood, with nods to the Mediterranean – standouts include polenta-crusted calamari, deliciously simple sautéed trout, Dungeness crab rolls (in season) at lunch and housemade pastas at dinner, including feather-light gnocchi. Reservations advised. Afternoons, there's a limited menu.

BARBACCO
ITALIAN $$

Map p319 (☎415-955-1919; www.barbaccosf. com; 220 California St; mains lunch $10-13, dinner $11-17; ◎11:30am-3pm & 5-10pm Mon-Fri, 5-10pm Sat; ◻California St, ◻Embarcadero, ◻Embarcadero) A lunch counter for the new millennium, Barbacco's best seats are stools along the open kitchen. Otherwise, seating is at communal tables lining the exposed-brick wall. Plan to share earthy-delicious small plates – fried brussels sprouts, bruschetta of house-cured sardines and lemon-aioli egg salad, and chicken thighs braised with olives. For a splashier meal, book its next-door upmarket sister Perbacco.

Barbacco's iPad wine list is annoying (don't downtowners go out to lunch to get away from their screens?) but includes 3oz pours at fair prices, allowing you to taste multiple varietals without going broke.

KOKKARI
GREEK $$$

Map p319 (☎415-981-0983; www.kokkari.com; 200 Jackson St; mains $21-35; ◎lunch Mon-Fri, dinner daily; ◻; ◻1, 10, 12, 41) This is one Greek restaurant where you'll want to lick your plate instead of break it, with starters like grilled octopus with a zing of lemon and oregano, and a signature lamb, eggplant and yogurt moussaka as rich as the Pacific Stock Exchange. Reserve ahead to avoid waits, or make a meal of hearty Mediterranean appetizers at the happening bar.

WAYFARE TAVERN
AMERICAN $$$

Map p319 (☎415-772-9060; www.wayfaretavern. com; 558 Sacramento St; lunch mains $18-28; dinner mains $24-38; ◎11am-11pm Mon-Sat, 5pm-11pm Sun; ◻1, 10, 12, ◻California St, ◻Montgomery) The decor nods to Colonial Americana and old San Francisco, with exposed brick and polished wood, barkeeps in white jackets, trophy heads on the wall,and enough decorative bric-a-brac to cause frissons over potential earthquakes. The cooking – deviled eggs, buttermilk fried chicken, steak tartare, pot roast – gives excellent insight into the traditional-American culinary repertoire. Book two to three weeks ahead.

During cocktail hour, the backslapping-businessman clientele can get loud; sit upstairs.

✖ Union Square

GALETTE 88
CREPES $

Map p320 (www.galettesf.com; 88 Hardie Pl; crepes $9-11; ◎11:30am-2:30pm Mon-Fri, 4pm-9pm Wed & Thu; ◻; ◻Montgomery, ◻Montgomery) Down a tiny alley, this Spartan storefront creperie draws big lunchtime crowds for authentic, Brittany-style savory buckwheat gallettes, with fillings from simple ham and cheese to vegan-friendly ratatouille, and sweet desert crepes, including the classic Nutella and bananas.

BOXED FOODS
SANDWICHES, SALADS $

Map p320 (www.boxedfoodscompany.com; 245 Kearny St; dishes $8-10; ◎8am-3pm Mon-Fri; ◻; ◻Montgomery, ◻Montgomery) ◗ Organic, local, seasonal ingredients make outrageously flavorful lunches, whether the zesty strawberry salad with mixed greens, walnuts and tart goat cheese, or the Boxed BLT, with crunchy applewood smoked bacon. Get yours to go to the Transamerica Pyramid Redwood Park or grab a table out back.

ALFRESCO DINING ON WARM NIGHTS

During the odd heat wave in SF, when it's too hot to stay indoors without air-con (which nobody in SF has) and warm enough to eat outside, two Downtown streets become the go-to destinations for dining alfresco: **Belden Place** (www.belden-place. com) and Claude Lane. Both are pedestrian alleyways lined with restaurants, which set up side-by-side tables in the street, creating scenes remarkably like Paris in summertime. The food is marginally better on Claude Lane, notably at sexy Gitane (p95) and Cafe Claude (p93). But the scene on Belden is more colorful, especially at restaurants Plouf, B44, Tiramisu and Café Bastille – which are otherwise not outstanding, but so much fun.

MURACCI'S CURRY
JAPANESE $

Map p320 (www.muraccis.com; 307 Kearny St; dishes $8-11; ⊙11am-7pm Mon-Thu, to 6pm Fri; Ⓜ; ⓂMontgomery, ⒷMontgomery) Warm up foggy days with steaming curry-topped *katsu* (pork cutlet), grilled chicken rice-plate or classic Japanese comfort-food curry – neither spicy nor sharp but gently tingling, faintly sweet and powerfully savory. Order at the counter and wait for your name to be called.

BREAD & COCOA
CAFE, SANDWICHES $

Map p320 (www.breadandcocoa.com; 199 Sutter St; dishes $6-9; ⊙7am-5pm Mon-Fri, 8:30am-5pm Sat & Sun; Ⓜ; ⓂMontgomery, ⒷMontgomery) 🍴 Local, artisanal ingredients add zing to sandwiches, such as roast-chicken panini with pesto, and tangy Humboldt Fog cheese with prosciutto, organic tomato and arugula. For $8 to $10 they're not huge, but their flavor sure is.

CAFE CLAUDE
FRENCH $$

Map p320 (☎415-392-3505; www.cafeclaude. com; 7 Claude Lane; mains $10-20; ⊙11:30am-10:30pm Mon-Sat, 5:30pm-10:30pm Sun; ⓂMontgomery, ⒷMontgomery) Hidden down a little alleyway, Cafe Claude is the perfect French cafe, with zinc bar, umbrella tables outside and staff chattering *en français*. Lunch is served till a civilized 5pm and jazz combos play Thursday to Saturday dinner. Expect classics like coq au vin and steak tartare, always good, if not great – it's the romantic scene that's so special.

SWEET WOODRUFF
CAFE, CALIFORNIAN $$

Map p320 (☎415-292-9090; www.sweetwood ruffsf.com; 798 Sutter St; dishes $8-13; ⊙11am-9:45pm; 🚌2, 3, 27) 🍴 Little sister to ground-breaking, Michelin-starred Sons & Daughters, this storefront quick-bites bar uses top-end seasonal-regional ingredients

for its short, small-plates menu, with dishes like roasted padron peppers with fromage blanc, and sea-urchin baked potatoes with bacon – ideal for a nosh while shopping or before bar-hopping.

There's no waiter service (you fetch your own cutlery) and no stove, just an oven and hot plate (which explains the limited offerings); in exchange, the cafe provides a window into the SF culinary scene without demanding serious cash.

FARMERBROWN
NEW AMERICAN $$

Map p320 (☎415-409-3276; www.farmerbrown sf.com; 25 Mason St; mains $14-24; ⊙5:30-10pm Tue-Thu, to 11pm Fri & Sat, to 9pm Sun; brunch bar 10am-2pm Sat-Sun; ⓂPowell, ⒷPowell) 🍴 This rebel from the wrong side of the block dishes up mean seasonal watermelon margaritas with a cayenne-salt rim (genius), ribs that stick to yours and coleslaw with a kick that'll leave your lips buzzing. Chef-owner Jay Foster works with local organic and African American farmers to provide food with actual soul, in a setting that's rusted and cleverly repurposed as a shotgun shack.

Expect harried service – it's always busy – and Afro-funk beats to match the uptempo crowd.

FLEUR DE LYS
FRENCH $$$

Map p320 (☎415-673-7779; www.hubertkeller.com; 777 Sutter St; menus $72-98; ⊙dinner Mon-Sat; Ⓜ; ⓂPowell, ⒷPowell) Long before celebrity chef Hubert Keller expanded to Vegas and *Top Chef Masters*, this was the ultimate over-the-top SF destination, the swanky dining room a sultan's tent draped with magnificent fabric, a fitting backdrop for princely repasts artfully prepared, with a king's ransom of luxury ingredients from caviar to truffles. Vegetarians also get royal treatment, with five-course feasts for a remarkable $72.

EATING AT THE FERRY BUILDING

Slanted Door (Map p319; ☎415-861-8032; www.slanteddoor.com; 1 Ferry Bldg; lunch $15-28, dinner $19-42; ☺lunch & dinner; ⓂEmbarcadero, ⒷEmbarcadero) San Francisco's most effortlessly elegant restaurant harmonizes California ingredients, continental influences and Vietnamese flair. Owner-chef Charles Phan enhances top-notch ingredients with bright flavors, heaping local Dungeness crab atop cellophane noodles, and garlicky Meyer Ranch 'shaking beef' on watercress. And oh, the views. Book two weeks ahead for lunch, a month for dinner – or call at 5:30pm for last-minute cancellations.

La Mar Cebicheria (Map p319; ☎415-397-8880; www.lamarcebicheria.com; Pier 1½, The Embarcadero; lunch mains $13-20, dinner $21-32; ☺lunch & dinner; ⓂEmbarcadero, ⒷEmbarcadero) Big and bustling, La Mar has spectacular bay views and a snappy electric-blue and polished-wood decor. The key ingredient in its collaged plates of Peruvian ceviche is leche de tigre, the 'milk of the tiger,' a marinade of lime, chili and brine that 'cooks' the fish without a fire and is said to have aphrodisiac properties.

Hog Island Oyster Company (Map p319; ☎415-391-7117; www.hogislandoysters.com; 1 Ferry Bldg; 6 oysters $16-20; ☺11:30am-8pm Mon-Fri, 11am-6pm Sat & Sun; ⓂEmbarcadero, ⒷEmbarcadero) 🌱 Slurp the bounty of the North Bay, with a view of the East Bay, at this Ferry Building favorite for sustainably farmed oysters. Take yours au naturel, with caper beurre blanc, spiked with bacon and paprika or perhaps classic-style, with lemon and shallots. Mondays and Thursdays between 5pm and 7pm are happy hours indeed for shellfish fans, with half-price oysters and $4 pints.

Boulette's Larder (Map p319; ☎415-399-1155; www.bouletteslarder.com; 1 Ferry Bldg; mains $18-23; ☺Larder: 8am-2:30pm Mon, Tue, Thu & Fri, 10am-2:30pm Sun, Bouli Bar: 11am-3pm Tue-Sat, 5-9pm Tue-Fri; ⓂEmbarcadero, ⒷEmbarcadero) Dinner theater doesn't get more literal than brunch at Boulette's communal table, strategically placed inside a working kitchen in view of the Bay Bridge, amid a swirl of chefs preparing fancy French take-out dinners for commuter gourmands. At the adjoining Bouli Bar, a wood-fired oven produces smoky-delicious pizzas and flatbreads, served in a casual dining room facing the main hall. Find spices and mixes to-go at the pantry shop.

Il Cane Rosso (Map p319; ☎415-391-7599; www.canerossosf.com; 1 Ferry Bldg; mains breakfast $5-9, lunch & dinner $9-14; ☺9am-9pm; ⓂEmbarcadero, ⒷEmbarcadero) Il Cane Rosso serves seasonal-regional, earthy-delicious breakfasts, and simple soul-satisfying lunches and dinners in a tiny space that seats you in the kitchen. If it's warm, snag an outdoor bayside table. Menus change daily (look online) and you can't book, but this is great food for not much money.

Mijita (Map p319; ☎415-399-0814; www.mijitasf.com; 1 Ferry Bldg; dishes $4-8; ☺10am-7pm Mon-Thu, to 8pm Fri-Sat, 8:30am-3pm Sun; ☝🚼; ⓂEmbarcadero, ⒷEmbarcadero) At this order-at-the-counter taco shop, James Beard Award–winning Traci Des Jardins adapts her Mexican grandmother's standbys, using fresh local produce for tangy-savory jicama-and-grapefruit salad with pumpkin seeds, and sustainably harvested fish cooked with minimal oil for seriously addictive Baja fish tacos. Wash it down with melon agua frescas (fruit-flavored drinks), as envious seagulls circle above your outdoor bayside table.

Gott's Roadside (Map p319; www.gotts.com; 1 Ferry Bldg; burgers $8-11; ☺10:30am-10pm; 🚼; ⓂEmbarcadero, ⒷEmbarcadero) 🌱 Gott's keeps it simple with juicy hamburgers made from sustainably farmed Niman Ranch beef, plus rare-seared ahi-tuna burgers, Cobb salads and multiple varieties of crispy-delicious fries, including sweet potato and garlic. Order at the counter and they'll give you a pager that beeps when your order is ready. Tops for no-fuss meals and families on a budget.

GITANE
BASQUE, MEDITERRANEAN $$$

Map p320 (☑415-788-6686; www.gitanerestaurant.com; 6 Claude Lane; mains $22-34; ☺5:30-10:30pm, bar till midnight Mon-Wed, 5:30-11:30pm, bar till 1am Thu-Sat; ☑; MMontgomery, BMontgomery) Slip out of the Financial District and into something more comfortable at this sexy jewel-box – a low-lit mash-up of French boudoir and '70s chic, with lipstick-red lacquered ceilings reflecting tasseled silks, tufted leather and velvet snugs. Inspired by Southern Spain's Andalucia region, the menu includes standouts like Petrale sole with chorizo sausage and pickled garlic, and pancetta-wrapped rabbit loin with braised escargots.

Make reservations and dress sharp. Or drop by for craft cocktails at the swank little bar.

✗ Civic Center & the Tenderloin

BRENDA'S FRENCH
SOUL FOOD
CREOLE, SOUTHERN $

Map p322 (☑415-345-8100; www.frenchsoulfood.com; 652 Polk St; mains lunch $9-13, dinner $11-17; ☺8am-3pm Mon-Tue, to 10pm Wed-Sat, to 8pm Sun; ☐19, 31, 38, 47, 49) Chef-owner Brenda Buenviaje blends New Orleans–style Creole cooking with French technique to create 'French soul food.' Expect updated classics like red beans and rice, serious biscuits and grits, amazing Hangtown fry (eggs scrambled with bacon and fried oysters), good shrimp-stuffed po' boys, and fried chicken served with collard greens and hot-pepper jelly. Take the fire off the spicy cooking with sweet-watermelon tea.

Two doors down, Brenda operates a takeout sandwich shop with her watermelon pickles – great gifts for the foodies on your list.

FARM:TABLE
AMERICAN $

Map p322 (☑415-292-7089; www.farmtablesf.com; 754 Post St; dishes $6-9; ☺7:30am-2pm Mon-Fri, 8am-3pm Sat, 9am-3pm Sun; ☐2, 3, 27, 38) ✐ A tiny storefront with one wooden communal table inside, two tables and a stand-up counter outside, farm:table uses seasonal, regional organics in its foodie-smart breakfasts and lunches, posting the daily-changing menu on Twitter (@farm table). Good place to chill with locals. Great coffee. Cash only.

PAGOLAC
VIETNAMESE $

Map p322 (☑415-776-3234; 655 Larkin St; mains $7-9; ☺5-9:30pm Tue-Sun; ☐19, 38, 47, 49) Smack in the hard heart of the Tenderloin, this inviting nook is warm with low light and friendly faces. The special tasting menu of seven courses of beef is a must for serious carnivores, but sugarcane shrimp and barbecued chicken make tasty alternatives. Pagolac also does good *pho* (Vietnamese soup) with meatballs and *bo tai chanh* (lemon-marinated rare steak slices).

CAFE ZITOUNA
MOROCCAN $

Map p322 (☑415-673-2622; www.sfcafezitouna.com; 1201 Sutter St; mains $8-15; ☺11:30am-8:30pm Tue-Thu & Sat-Sun, 2pm-9pm Fri; ☐2, 3, 19, 47, 49) Hearty couscous platters, lamb stew, kebabs and shawarma are specialties at modest Zitouna, a spotlessly clean window-lined cafe serving big plates of Moroccan cooking, redolent with smoky spices. The humble chef-owner hails from Tunisia, his wife from Morocco – and everything, *merguez* (lamb sausage) to mint tea, is homemade. Tops for cheap eats. They sometimes close at 8pm: call ahead.

KATANA-YA
JAPANESE $

Map p322 (☑415-771-1280; 430 Geary St; dishes $7-12; ☺11:30am-1:15am; MPowell, BPowell) A glorified closet of a restaurant, Katana-Ya is the place for a late-night bite after the theater or bar-hopping. The broth in its steaming bowls of udon and ramen is so savory that it's almost dense. Avoid the bland sushi. After a night's drinking, the curries seem to have curative properties. Expect waits at peak times.

SAI JAI THAI
THAI $

Map p322 (☑415-673-5774; www.saijaithairestaurant.com; 771 O'Farrell St; mains $7-14; ☺11am-10:45pm; ☑; ☐19, 38, 47, 49) Mom and the cooks shout at each other in Thai, hardly anyone speaks English and the room is grungy, but the classic cooking's spot on. Try the pork-shoulder fried rice. Just make sure when they ask how hot, you reply, 'Spicy like for Thai people!' Alas, no beer and cash only. Free delivery to downtown hotels.

SHALIMAR
INDIAN $

Map p322 (☑415-928-0333; www.shalimarsf.com; 532 Jones St; dishes $5-10; ☺noon-midnight; ☑; ☐27, 38) Follow your nose to tandoori chicken straight off the skewer and naan bread still bubbling from the oven at this fluorescent-lit, linoleum-floored downtown Indian dive. Watch and learn as foodies, who demand five-star service elsewhere, meekly fetch their own water pitchers and tamarind sauce from the fridge.

SAIGON SANDWICH SHOP
VIETNAMESE $

Map p322 (415-474-5698; saigon-sandwich.com; 560 Larkin St; sandwich $3.50; 7am-5pm; 19, 31) Order your $3.50 *banh mi* (Vietnamese sandwich) when the ladies of the Saigon call you, or you'll get skipped. Act fast and be rewarded with a baguette piled high with your choice of roast pork, chicken, pâté, meatballs and/or tofu, plus pickled carrots, cilantro, jalapeño and thinly sliced onion.

MILLENNIUM
VEGETARIAN $$$

Map p322 (415-345-3900; www.millennium restaurant.com; 580 Geary St; set menu $42-72; 5:30-9:30pm Sun-Thu, to 10:30pm Sat & Sun; ; 2, 3, 27, 38) If all vegetarian cuisine could be this satisfying and opulent, cattle could roam San Francisco streets without garnering a second glance. Though Millennium appears initially a classic French brasserie, it is très San Francisco, with smartly elegant dishes made from the season's best produce for multicourse feasts. Reservations advised.

SoMa

DOTTIE'S
TRUE BLUE CAFÉ
AMERICAN, BREAKFAST $

Map p324 (http://dotties.biz; 28 6th St; mains $7-12; 7:30am-3pm Thu-Mon; Powell, Powell) Consider yourself lucky if you queue up less than half an hour and get hit up for change only once – but fresh baked goods come to those who wait at Dottie's. Cinnamon pancakes, grilled cornbread, scrambles with whiskey fennel sausage and anything else off the griddle are tried and true blue.

BUTLER & THE CHEF
FRENCH $

Map p324 (415-896-2075; www.thebutler andthechefbistro.com; 155a S Park St; brunch mains $9-12; 8am-3pm Tue-Sat, 10am-3pm Sun; 10, 30, 45, 2nd & King Sts) Find authentic French-cafe classics among the SoMa warehouses at this lunch-only South Park favorite. Tables are tiny: mind your elbows or they'll wind up in your French onion soup, made properly with rich beef stock and a real *crouton* topped with melting Gruyère.

TIN VIETNAMESE
VIETNAMESE $

Map p324 (415-882-7188; www.tinsf.com; 937 Howard St; mains $7.50-11; 11:30am-3pm & 5:30-10pm Mon-Sat; 14, 27) Two blocks from the convention center's overpriced tourist restaurants, hole-in-the-wall Tin caters to SoMa locals, with consistently good pho, rice plates and rice-noodle bowls topped with lemongrass chicken, shrimp-and-pork fried spring rolls, and other fragrant Vietnamese classics. There's beer and wine, too, however limited.

ZERO ZERO
PIZZA $$

Map p324 (415-348-8800; www.zerozerosf. com; 826 Folsom St; pizzas $10-19; 11:30am-2:30pm & 5:30-10pm Mon-Thu, to 11pm Fri, 11:30am-11pm Sat, 11:30am-10pm Sun; Powell, Powell) The name is a throw-down of Neapolitan pizza credentials – '00' flour is used exclusively for Naples' famous puffy-edged crust – and these pies deliver on that promise, with inspired SF-themes toppings. The Geary is an exciting offering involving Manila clams, bacon and chilies, but the real crowd-pleaser is the Castro, which, as you might guess, is turbo-loaded with house-made sausage.

CITIZEN'S BAND
CALIFORNIAN $$

Map p324 (415-556-4901; www.citizensbandsf. com; 1198 Folsom St; mains lunch $9-13, dinner $13-24; 11:30am-2pm & 5:30-10pm Tue-Thu, till 11pm Fri, 10am-2pm & 5:30-11pm Sat, til 9:30pm Sun; Civic Center, Civic Center) The menu is retro-American diner with a California difference: mac 'n' cheese with Sonoma jack cheese and optional truffle, wedge-lettuce salads with local Point Reyes blue cheese, and local Snake River kobe beef burgers (the best in town). Don't miss small-production local wines and after-lunch treats from the on-premises cupcake shop Pinky's.

TROPISUEÑO
MEXICAN $$

Map p324 (415-243-0299; www.tropisueno. com; 75 Yerba Buena Lane; mains lunch $6-12, dinner $11-16; 11am-10:30pm; Powell, Powell) Last time you enjoyed casual Mexican dining this much, there were probably balmy ocean breezes and hammocks involved. Instead, you're steps away from SoMa's museums, savoring *al pastor* (marinated pork) burritos with mesquite salsa and grilled pineapple, sipping margaritas with chili-salted rims.

QUICK BITES WHILE SHOPPING

A few of our favorite places to recharge between boutiques:

Cafe Claude (p93) The ideal spot to collapse with your shopping bags when you realize it's 4pm and you've forgotten to eat lunch – and, oh, wouldn't a glass of wine be nice, too?

Rotunda (Map p320; ☑415-249-2720; www.neimanmarcus.com; 150 Stockton St; mains $18-26; ⊙10am-7pm Mon-Sat, noon-6pm Sun; ☂; MPowell, BPowell) Favored by ladies in Chanel suits, who come for lobster club sandwiches, French champagne and proper afternoon tea beneath the gorgeous stained-glass dome at Neiman Marcus.

Mocca on Maiden Lane (Map p320; ☑415-956-1188; 175 Maiden Lane; mains $10-15; ⊙10am-5:30pm; MPowell, BPowell) Order steak sandwiches, seafood salads and cheesecake inside, then carry outside to umbrella tables lining a chic pedestrian alley; cash only.

Bio (Map p320; ☑415-362-0255; www.biologiquesf.com; 75 O'Farrell St; dishes $5-10; ⊙8am-6pm; ☂; MPowell, BPowell) Healthful sandwiches, vegan salads, gluten-free quiches and multiple varieties of kombucha, but no seating (picnic at Union Square).

Emporio Rulli (Map p320; ☑415-433-1122; www.rulli.com; Union Square; ⊙7am-7pm; MPowell, BPowell) Artisanal Italian pastries, powerful espresso and prosciutto sandwiches at outdoor tables in Union Square.

The rustic-organic decor and location are upscale, but prices are near what you'd pay in the Mission – give or take a buck and a BART ride.

BASIL THAI CANTEEN   THAI $$
Map p324 (☑415-552-3963; www.basilcanteen.com; 1175 Folsom St; mains $10-14; ⊙11:30am-2:30pm & 5-10pm Mon-Fri, 5-10pm Sat-Sun; ☂; ☐9, 12, 47) Inside a brick-walled former brewery, Basil Canteen is perfect before a night at SoMa's bars and clubs, with excellent cocktails and reasonably priced, brilliantly spiced Thai cooking, including a variety of snack plates, ideal for sharing. Reservations advised.

21ST AMENDMENT BREWERY   AMERICAN $$
Map p324 (☑415-369-0900; http://21st-amendment.com; 563 2nd St; mains $10-20; ⊙kitchen 11:30am-10pm Mon-Sat, 10am-10pm Sun; bar till midnight; ☂; ☐10, M2nd & King) Perfectly placed before Giants games, 21st Amendment brews stellar IPA and (wow!) watermelon wheat beer. The respectable bar-and-grill menu – burgers, pizza, chops, sandwiches, salads – checks your buzz, but the cavernous space is so loud, nobody'll notice you're shouting. Bring the kids: for desert there's root-beer ice-cream floats, with homemade root beer. Ground zero for techies who lunch.

★BENU   CALIFORNIAN FUSION $$$
Map p324 (☑415-685-4860; www.benusf.com; 22 Hawthorne St; mains $26-42; ⊙5:30-10pm Tue-Sat; ☐10, 12, 14, 30, 45) SF has refined fusion cuisine over 150 years, but no one rocks it quite like chef/owner Corey Lee (formerly of Napa's French Laundry), who remixes local, sustainable fine-dining staples and Pacific Rim flavors with a SoMa DJ's finesse. This is contemporary California dining at its highest echelon. Its only flaw is the pretentiously casual room, which doesn't match the stupendously regal cooking.

Dungeness crab and black truffle custard bring such outsize flavor to faux-shark's fin soup, you'll swear there's Jaws in there. The tasting menu is steep ($180) and beverage pairings add $150, but you won't want to miss star sommelier Yoon Ha's flights of fancy – including a rare 1968 Madeira with your soup.

BOULEVARD   CALIFORNIAN $$$
Map p324 (☑415-543-6084; www.boulevardrestaurant.com; 1 Mission St; mains $30-40; ⊙11:30am-2pm & 5:30-10pm Mon-Thu, to 10:30 Fri & Sat; MEmbarcadero, BEmbarcadero) The quake-surviving, 1889 belle epoque Audiffred Building is a fitting locale for James Beard Award–winning Boulevard, which remains one of San Francisco's most reliable

and effortlessly graceful restaurants. Chef Nancy Oakes has an easy touch with classics like simple juicy pork chops; finesses Dungeness crab salad with fresh basil, watermelon and yogurt; and ends East–West coastal rivalries with Maine lobster stuffed inside California squid.

Her latest venture, **Prospect** (Map p324; ☑415-247-7770; www.prospectsf.com; 300 Spear St), provides a swank alternative if Boulevard is booked.

🍷 DRINKING & ⚓ NIGHTLIFE

Most nightclubs are in SoMa, but they're dispersed across a large area. Don't get stuck walking in heels. The highest concentration of bars and clubs is around 11th and Folsom Sts; the SoMa scene pops weekends, dies weekdays. Financial District bars pack Wednesdays through Fridays, 5pm to 8pm, then die and close by midnight. A downside to Downtown drinking is the scene: too-loud dudes in suits and after-hours office drama between co-workers; it gets sloppy on Fridays. For grit and cheaper libation, hit the the Tenderloin – aka the Trendy-loin – and swill with 20-something hipsters. Drink prices rise as you move towards the Financial District, exceeding $10 east of Powell St.

🍷 Financial District & Jackson Square

BARRIQUE
WINE BAR

Map p319 (☑415-421-9200; www.barriquesf.com; 461 Pacific Ave; ☺3pm-10pm Sun & Mon, noon-midnight Tue-Sat ; ☐10, 12, 41) 🍴 Farm-to-table is to restaurants what Barrique is to wine bars. Here your glass of high-end, small-batch vino comes straight from the cask, directly from Sonoma, sans label. There's a bottle list, but stick to barrel tastings for the full experience. There's good people-watching up front, but we prefer the white-leather sofas, near the casks, to watch blending in action.

The fruit-forward, high-alcohol wine-making style is very Californian – zinfandel and pinot noir are specialties. Cheese and charcuterie plates – artisinal and organic, natch – keep your buzz in check.

TAVERNA AVENTINE
BAR

Map p319 (☑415-981-1500; www.aventinesf.com; 582 Washington St; ☺11:30am-10pm Mon-Tue, to midnight Thu-Fri, 8:30pm-2am Sat; ☐1, 10, 12, 41) In the days of the Barbary Coast, the Aventine's 150-year-old building fronted on the bay – you can still see salt-water marks on the brick walls downstairs. But the action happens upstairs, where high ceilings, brick walls and repurposed wood lend a vintage vibe and bartenders mix bourbon and Scotch cocktails in the old-new fashion.

The place packs for happy hour, from 3pm to 7pm Monday to Friday.

BIX
BAR

Map p319 (☑415-433-6300; www.bixrestaurant.com; 56 Gold St; ☺bar 4:30pm-midnight ; ☐1, 10, 12, 41) Down an alleyway at Jackson Square, Bix evokes 1930s supper clubs, with mahogany paneling and white-jacketed barmen shaking martinis. The restaurant's good – order the tuna tartare – but the bar is great, with nightly live piano and sometimes jazz. Look sharp and swagger.

🍷 Union Square

★RICKHOUSE
BAR

Map p320 (www.rickhousebar.com; 246 Kearny St; ☺5pm-2am Mon, 3pm-2am Tue-Fri, 6pm-2am Sat; Ⓜ Montgomery, Ⓑ Montgomery) Like a shotgun shack plunked downtown, Rickhouse is lined floor-to-ceiling with repurposed whisky casks imported from Kentucky and backbar shelving from an Ozark Mountains nunnery that once secretly brewed hooch. The emphasis is (naturally) on whiskey, specifically hard-to-find bourbons. Come with a posse and order Pisco Punch, served vintage-style in a garage-sale punch bowl, with cups dangling off the side.

CANTINA
BAR

Map p320 (www.cantinasf.com; 580 Sutter St; ☺5pm-2am Mon-Sat, 2pm-2am Sun; ☐2, 3, 38, ☐Powell-Mason, Powell-Hyde) All the Latin-inspired cocktails (think tequila, cachaça and pisco) are made with fresh juice – there's not even a soda gun behind the bar – at this mixologist's dream bar that's mellow enough weeknights for quiet conversation. The local crowd includes many off-duty bartenders – always a good sign. DJs spin on weekends.

HUSH-HUSH HOOCH

Psst – keep a secret? Speakeasies, those Prohibition-era underground gin joints, still exist in SF, and **Bourbon & Branch** (415-346-1735; www.bourbonandbranch.com; Wed-Sat by reservation) is one of the best. You can make a reservation via phone or the website to get directions to the secret location (an unmarked door in the Tenderloin) and the password for entry. Inside, studded leather banquettes, mirrored oak tables and red velvet walls evoke the roaring 1920s. The original speakeasy basement – complete with bullet holes and secret escape routes – and the room hidden behind the fake bookcase are perfect for those super-private parties. Keep it under your hat.

BURRITT ROOM   LOUNGE

Map p320 (www.mystichotel.com; 417 Stockton St; ⊙5pm-1am Sun-Thu, till 2am Fri-Sat; MMontgomery, BMontgomery) Upstairs at the Mystic Hotel, the Burritt Room works shabbychic, with distressed-wood paneling and century-old tile floors, red-velvet sofas, brick walls and gaudy chandeliers that create the effect of an abandoned building co-opted by swank squatters, who prefer champagne cocktails over swill and punchbowls over pints.

Celeb-chef Charlie Palmer bought the place in 2012, adding a pretty-good (if pricy) tavern with meat-heavy menu, but the bar's the real draw.

TUNNEL TOP   BAR

Map p320 (601 Bush St; ⊙5pm-2am Mon-Sat; MMontgomery, BMontgomery) You can't tell who's local and who's not in this happening, chill two-story bar with exposed beams, beer-bottle chandelier and a little mezzanine where you can spy on the crowd. The owners are French, and their Gallic friends throng the place, tapping their toes to conscious hip-hop and boom-boom house music, the SF soundtrack. Cash only.

CLOCK BAR   LOUNGE

Map p320 (415-397-9222; www.michaelmina. net; 335 Powell St, Westin St Francis Hotel; ⊙4pm-2am; Powell-Mason, Powell-Hyde, MPowell, BPowell) If it's in season, it goes into the glass at this top-end mixology bar, the brainchild of celeb-chef Michael Mina. Ooh and aah over truffled popcorn while sampling knockout cocktails at cozy leather-and-wood snugs. Arrive early or reserve ahead, or expect to stand. Dress sharp.

IRISH BANK   PUB

Map p320 (www.theirishbank.com; 10 Mark Lane; ⊙11:30am-2am; MMontgomery, BMontgomery) Perfectly pulled pints and thick-cut fries with malt vinegar, plus juicy burgers, brats and anything else you could possibly want with lashings of mustard are staples at this cozy Irish pub. There are tables beneath a big awning in the alley out front, ideal for smokers – even on a rainy night.

OTIS LOUNGE   BAR

Map p320 (www.otissf.com; 25 Maiden Ln; ⊙4pm-2am; MMontgomery, BMontgomery) Surprising such a down-to-earth bar exists on chichi Maiden Lane. Bartenders play R&B and hip-hop from their iPods for a diverse crowd who come for fresh-juice cocktails and $5 sangria. The place is tiny – make a beeline for the little upstairs mezzanine. Best weeknights; otherwise it's shoulder-to-shoulder and not worth a cover.

JOHN'S GRILL   BAR

Map p320 (www.johnsgrill.com; 63 Ellis St; ⊙11am-10pm; Powell-Mason, Powell-Hyde, MPowell, BPowell) It could be the martinis, low lighting or *Maltese Falcon* statuette upstairs, but something about Dashiell Hammett's favorite bar lends itself to hardboiled tales of lost love and true crimes, confessed while chewing toothpicks. That is, until the tourists filling the joint snap you back into the present.

Civic Center & the Tenderloin

EDINBURGH CASTLE   BAR

Map p322 (415-885-4074; www.castlenews. com; 950 Geary St; ⊙5pm-2am; 19, 38, 47, 49) SF's finest old-school monument to drink nods to Scotland with darts, billiards, rock bands, trivia nights, occasional literary readings and, of course, wasted locals acting out. The jukebox blares the

Trainspotting soundtrack, when DJs aren't spinning glam, pop, punk or soul, and some bloke brings 'round fish-and-chips wrapped in newspaper. Oi!

LUSH LOUNGE
GAY BAR

Map p322 (☑415-771-2022; www.thelushlounge sf.com; 1221 Polk St; ☐2, 3, 19, 38, 47, 49) Snag a wooden table by the steel-front fireplace and order anything in stemware – martinis are the specialty (15 different kinds), but we highly recommend the lemon drops, cosmos and other such girly drinks that kick men's asses. Lush Lounge marks the line on Polk where grit ends and hip begins. Ideal for couples and small groups of all sexual persuasions.

RYE
BAR

Map p322 (☑415-474-4448; www.ryesf.com; 688 Geary St; ⊙6pm-2am; ☐2, 3, 27, 38) Rye's stark-style design mixes concrete, steel and polished wood, and its leather sofas are a sexy spot for a basil gimlet or anything made with herb-infused spirits or fresh-squeezed juice. The smokers patio is a cage on the sidewalk and offers a glimpse of who's inside. Rye packs after 10pm; arrive early.

SUGAR CAFE
CAFE, LOUNGE

Map p322 (☑415-441-5678; www.sugarcafesf. com; 679 Sutter St; ⊙10am-midnight Mon, 10am-2am Tue-Thu, 8am-2am Fri & Sat; ☎; ☐2, 3, 27, 38) Cafe by day, lounge bar by night, Sugar's uptempo vibe plays to students from the art college down the street. It's one of few internet cafes near Union Square and in the afternoons everyone hunches over laptops, sipping coffee and cocktails made with fresh-squeezed juice, nibbling sweets and snacks. Internet terminals cost $6/hr.

LE COLONIAL
NIGHTCLUB

Map p322 (☑415-931-3600; www.lecolonialsf. com; 20 Cosmo Pl; ⊙dinner nightly from 5:30pm; club 7-10pm Mon-Thu, 9:30pm-2am Fri-Sat; ☐2, 3, 38, ⓦPowell-Mason, Powell-Hyde) Time-travel to colonial French Vietnam at this swanky downtowner with attentive service and tasty, if overpriced, Southeast Asian cooking. The draw is the scene: after 10pm Friday and Saturday, the 2nd-floor lounge becomes a nightclub. Make a night of it with dinner or head directly to the pink-lit bar, with its rattan decor and low-slung stools, and order a Singapore sling.

The sometimes-touristy, dressed-up crowd varies, but after 10pm skews toward 20- and 30-somethings.

RUBY SKYE
NIGHTCLUB

Map p322 (www.rubyskye.com; 420 Mason St; admission $10-30; ⊙9pm-late Fri & Sat; ⓜPowell, ⒷPowell) The city's premier-name nightclub occupies a vintage theater reminiscent of classic NY clubs, with reserveable balcony boxes. The who's-who of the world's DJs play here – Danny Tenaglia, Dimitri from Paris, Christopher Lawrence and Paul Van Dyk. The (very) mainstream crowd gets messy (hence gruff security) but when your fave DJ's playing, who cares? The sound system kicks ass.

CELLAR
NIGHTCLUB

Map p322 (www.cellarsf.com; 685 Sutter St; cover varies; ☐2, 3, 27, 38) The slightly grungy, subterranean Cellar has two dance floors with dueling sound systems. It's best weeknights when you want to party but don't want to fuss with fancier clubs. Recommended when there's no cover (check the website); otherwise, it's not worth $10.

RICKSHAW STOP
NIGHTCLUB

Map p322 (☑415-861-2011; www.rickshawstop. com; 155 Fell St; admission $5-35; ⊙variable; ⓜVan Ness) Finally a club where 18- to 21-year-olds can (sometimes) get in for the high-school prom they wish they'd attended. DIY-looking, red-velvet curtains line this former black-box TV studio and the changing lineup appeals to alterna-20-somethings who style life on a shoestring. Thursday's Popscene (18-plus) is always happening. Other nights range from Bollywood to lesbian. Check online.

WHISKEY THIEVES
BAR

Map p322 (☑415-506-8331; 839 Geary St; ⊙1pm-2am; ☐38) Brave junkies on the sidewalk for the incredible selection of unusual whiskeys at this Tenderloin dive, where the backbar is subdivided by category – Irish, Scotch, Bourbon and Rye. Seven dollars buys a shot plus a PBR. Party-kid hipsters get shitfaced fast, feeding the jukebox between rounds of pool.

AUNT CHARLIE'S
GAY BAR

Map p322 (☑415-441-2922; www.auntcharlies lounge.com; 133 Turk St; admission $5; ⓜPowell, ⒷPowell) On Downtown's worst block, divey-chic Aunt Charlie's brings vintage

OLD-SCHOOL TRAVELER FAVORITES

Downtown is chockablock with tourist joints that fit the bill under certain circumstances – like when you're traveling with screaming hungry kids and you just want to have a couple of cocktails and be left alone, but realize you're on vacation and should go somewhere atmospheric. Fear not: we've got you covered.

Tommy's Joynt (Map p322; ☑415-775-4216; www.tommysjoynt.com; 1101 Geary St; mains $6-11; ☺11am-2am; 🚻; 🚌38, 47, 49) Open and unchanged since 1947 – with enough ephemera and animal heads on the walls to prove it – Tommy's is the classic for *hofbrau* (cafeteria-style) meals of turkey, corned beef and buffalo stew.

Johnny Foley's (Map p320; ☑415-954-0777; www.johnnyfoleys.com; 243 O'Farrell St; mains $14-24; ☺11:30am-1:30am; 🚻; ⓂPowell, ⒷPowell) Great-looking vintage bar and grill, with subway-tile floors and carved woodwork, live music nightly and passable Irish-pub grub.

Lefty O'Doul's (Map p320; ☑415-982-8900; www.leftyodouls.biz; 333 Geary St; mains $7-11; ☺7am-2am; 🚻; ⓂPowell, ⒷPowell) Floor-to-ceiling kitsch, baseball memorabilia, sports on TV, live music and *hofbrau* – Lefty's is tourist central, a blast on game nights.

pulp-fiction covers to life with the Hot Boxxx Girls, the city's best classic drag show, on Friday and Saturday nights at 10pm (call for reservations). Thursday is Tubesteak Connection ($5), when bathhouse anthems, vintage porn and early '80s disco draw throngs of art-school gay boys. Other nights, it's a classic dump.

🍷 SoMa

⭐BAR AGRICOLE   BAR
Map p324 (☑415-355-9400; www.baragricole. com; 355 11th St; ☺6-10pm Sun-Wed, 6pm-late Thu-Sat; 🚌9, 12, 27, 47) Drink your way to a history degree with well-researched cocktails: Bellamy Scotch Sour with egg whites passes the test, but Tequila Fix with lime, pineapple gum and hellfire bitters earns honors. And what an overachiever – for its modern wabi-sabi design, with natural materials and sleek deck, Agricole won a James Beard Award.

Bar bites here are a proper pig-out, including pork pâté with aspic, fried farm egg and crispy pork belly.

⭐BLOODHOUND   BAR
Map p324 (www.bloodhoundsf.com; 1145 Folsom St; ☺4pm-2am; 🚌12, 14, 19, 27, 47) The murder of crows painted on the ceiling is definitely an omen: nights at Bloodhound often assume mythic proportions. Vikings would feel at home amid these white walls and antler chandeliers, while bootleggers

would appreciate the reclaimed barnwood walls and top-shelf booze served in Mason jars. Shoot pool or chill on leather couches until your jam comes on the jukebox – it won't be long.

RN74   RESTAURANT BAR
Map p324 (☑415-543-7474; www.michaelmina. net; 301 Mission St; ☺11:30am-1am Mon-Fri, 5pm-1am Sat, 5-11pm Sun; ⓂEmbarcadero, ⒷEmbarcadero) Wine collectors and encyclopedia authors must envy the Rajat Parr–designed wine menu at RN74, a succinct, sweeping volume that manages to include obscure Italian and Austrian entries, long-lost French vintages and California's most definitive account of cult wines. Settle into a couch for the duration of your self-guided wine adventure and don't skip bar-menu food pairings by star chef Michael Mina.

TERROIR NATURAL
WINE MERCHANT   WINE BAR
Map p324 (terroirsf.com; 1116 Folsom St; ☺2pm-2am Mon-Thu, noon-2am Fri-Sat, 2pm-9pm Sun; 🚌12, 19, 27, 47; ⒷCivic Center) 🍷 Whether red or white, the wine is green – Terroir specializes in natural-process, organic and biodynamic vinos, with impressive lists from key French and Italian producers. Quality doesn't come cheap – expect $10 to $16 a glass– but you'll discover lesser-known cult wines in an unpretious environment, styled with reclaimed wood and mismatched vintage furniture. Sit upstairs.

LOCAL KNOWLEDGE

THOUGHTS FROM A TOP-FLIGHT SOMMELIER

Drinking in the Bay Area Scenery
Even though I worked in Napa, I still find the tasting rooms along Silverado Trail full of surprises, including some exceptional white wines. Everyone knows about the well-researched wine list at RN74, but have you had its cocktails? Rye is also on top of its mixology and Bar Agricole doesn't serve beginner cocktails – they're strong enough that you have to respect them with little sips and know they're going to take three times as long to finish.

Pop-up Pairings
All the food trucks and pop-up restaurants in San Francisco let you play around with the pairing possibilities, without a big investment. Look for Sonoma's versatile coastal pinot noirs and cool-climate chardonnays that aren't over-oaked, so they're better at the table. Mr Pollo doesn't have a license yet and complex flavors like [chef] Manny's empanadas present a great creative corkage challenge.

How Wine Pairing is Like Air Traffic Control
Finding room on the palate for wine is like landing a plane: it works better if you have a wide airstrip. [Benu] chef Corey Lee has me taste menu items early on and asks what four flavors come to the forefront. Once all those flavors are perfectly aligned, that creates a solid platform for wine – it just takes aim.

Becoming a Wine Aficionado
Look, I was raised in a nonwine culture, in Seoul, Korea. Growing up, we never had wine at the table. I had to learn everything, but I worked hard and enjoyed it. Nothing is innate. Just keep drinking.

Yoon Ha is Head Sommelier at Benu (p97).

CAT CLUB   CLUB
Map p324 (www.catclubsf.com; 1190 Folsom St; admission $5 after 10pm; ⊘9pm-3am Tue-Sun; MCivic Center, BCivic Center) You never really know your friends till you've seen them belt out A-ha's 'Take on Me' at 1984, Cat Club's Thursday-night retro dance party, where the euphoric bi/straight/gay/undefinable scene is like some sweaty, surreal John Hughes movie. Tuesdays it's karaoke, Wednesdays Bondage-a-Go-Go, Fridays Goth and Saturdays '90s power pop – but confirm online, lest you dress the wrong part.

111 MINNA   BAR, CLUB
Map p324 (www.111minnagallery.com; 111 Minna St; admission free-$15; MMontgomery, BMontgomery) A superhero to rescue the staid Downtown scene, 111 Minna is a streetwise art gallery and cafe by day (7:30am to 5pm, Monday through Friday) that transforms into a happening lounge space and club by night (evening hours vary). After-work events are networky but usually interesting, lasting until 9pm, when dance parties take the back room by storm.

At monthly Sketch Tuesdays (free), artists make work for sale to the audience.

WATERBAR   BAR
Map p324 (www.waterbarsf.com; 399 The Embarcadero; ⊘11:30am-9:30pm Sun-Mon, to 10pm Tue-Sat; MFolsom, BEmbarcadero) Waterbar's giant glass-column aquariums and picture-window vistas of the Bay Bridge lights are SF's surest way to impress a date over drinks. Leave the dining room to Silicon Valley strivers trying hard to impress investors and make a beeline for the oval bar, where seating is closer, plates and prices smaller, and oysters surround carved ice sculptures.

HARLOT   CLUB
Map p324 (www.harlotsf.com; 46 Minna St; admission free-$20; ⊘5pm-2am Wed-Fri, from 9pm Sat, sometimes Sun from 4pm; MMontgomery, BMontgomery) Back when SoMa was the stomping ground of sailors, alleys were named for working girls and Harlot pays them homage. Vampire bordello is the vibe here, with intense red lighting, velvet curtains revealing exposed-brick walls and

table-sized photos of pinups wearing nothing but boa constrictors. Watch where you put down that cocktail.

Before 9pm it's a lounge, but after that the sound system pumps – it's usually house but occasionally electronica and indie rock. Weekends get suburban, but everyone cuts loose, so who cares? RSVP online and dress funky to get past doormen.

CLUB OMG   BAR, DJ, DANCE
Map p324 (www.clubomgsf.com; 43 6th St; admission free to $10; ⏱5pm-2am Mon-Fri, 7pm-2am Sat, variable Sun; MPowell) Tiny OMG draws a mixed gay-straight 20-to-30-something crowd to a grungy SoMa block for its mod turquoise-Lucite bar and fab dancefloor with overhead planetarium dome onto which DJs project wild LED light shows. Expect house, techno, occasional dubstep and '80s–'90s pop. Never mind the junkies outside.

HOUSE OF SHIELDS   BAR
Map p324 (www.thehouseofshields.com; 39 New Montgomery St; ⏱2pm-2am Mon-Fri, from 3pm Sat-Sun; MMontgomery, BMontgomery) Flash back 100 years at this brilliantly restored mahogany bar with original c 1908 chandeliers hanging from high ceilings and old-fashioned cocktails without the frippery. This is the one bar in SF that slumming Nob Hill socialites and Downtown bike messengers can agree on – especially after a few $5 cocktails in dimly lit corners.

DNA LOUNGE   NIGHTCLUB
Map p324 (www.dnalounge.com; 375 11th St; admission $3-25; ⏱9pm-3am Fri & Sat, other nights vary; 12, 27, 47) One of SF's last mega clubs hosts live bands and big-name DJs, with two floors of late-night dance action just seedy enough to be interesting. Saturdays bring Bootie, the kick-ass original mash-up party (now franchised worldwide) and sometimes epic drag at Trannyshack; Monday's 18-and-over Goth dance party is (naturally) called Death Guild. Check the online calendar. Early arrivals may hear crickets.

MONARCH   BAR, CLUB
Map p324 (www.monarchsf.com; 101 Sixth St; cover varies; ⏱5:30pm-2am Mon-Fri, from 8pm Sat-Sun; 14) A boom-town club on a nasty SoMa block, slick Monarch sports a tiny main-floor bar, downstairs black-box dance hall, killer sound system and party-ready DJs. The room sizzles when sexy circus-

burlesque performers contort on the trapeze over the bar. New-money techies earn cred here; Monarch plays to them, with craft cocktails aptly named 'Ruling Class' and 'Kingmaker.' Check online calendar.

CITY BEER STORE & TASTING ROOM   BAR
Map p324 (www.citybeerstore.com; 1168 Folsom St; ⏱noon-10pm Tue-Sat, to 6pm Sun; 12, 14, 19) Sample from 300 exceptional local and Belgian microbrewed beers in 6-to-20oz pours at SF's top beer store. Create your own tastings of stouts or ales, or pick at random and discover lesser-known artisanal brews. Pair with cheese and salami plates or assemble a mixed six-pack to go.

SIGHTGLASS COFFEE   CAFE
Map p324 (www.sightglasscoffee.com; 270 7th St; ⏱7am-7pm Mon-Sat, from 8am Sun; BCivic Center) San Francisco's newest cult coffee is roasted in a SoMa warehouse – and if you're in the neighborhood, you won't need to be told where to find it. Follow the wafting aromas through the big wooden doors to discover signature Owl's Howl Espresso and sample the family-grown, high-end 100% bourbon-shrub coffee.

BUTTER   BAR
Map p324 (www.smoothasbutter.com; 354 11th St; ⏱6pm-2am Wed-Sat, from 8pm Sun; 9, 12, 47) Lowbrow and loving it: everyone's chasing Tang cocktails with PBR and wailing to rock anthems here, while across the street at VIP clubs they're still politely waiting for the good times to start. You'll never pay $10 for a drink at this tiny, happening bar, leaving plenty of cash for nasty-delicious junk food – Tater Tots, corn dogs and deep-fried Twinkies.

Check the website for events with even cheaper drinks, including infamous Trailer Trash Thursdays and genuinely sloppy Sunday karaoke.

83 PROOF   BAR
Map p324 (www.83proof.com; 83 1st St; ⏱2pm-midnight Mon & Tue, 2pm-2am Wed-Fri, 8pm-2am Sat; MMontgomery, BMontgomery) On average weeknights when the rest of Downtown is dead, you may have to shout to be heard over 83's flirtatious, buzzing crowd. High ceilings make room for five shelves of top-shelf spirits behind the bar, so trust your bartender to make a mean cucumber martini or basil gimlet that won't hurt at work tomorrow.

SOMA GAY BARS

A generation ago, no self-respecting straight person would have been caught dead South of Market after dark. But as go the gays, so goes the party, and now straight bars and clubs have overrun what was once exclusively 'mo turf. Lately internet cruising has decimated crowds and some nights are dead, but the following stalwarts anchor the gay drinking scene, which jams on weekends.

Eagle Tavern (Map p324; ☎415-626-0880; www.sfeagle.com; 398 12th St; admission $5-10; ☺noon-2am; ☐9, 12, 27, 47) Sunday afternoons, all roads in the gay underground lead to the Eagle and the crowd gets hammered on all-you-can-drink beer ($10) from 3pm to 6pm. Wear leather – or act like a whore – and blend right in; arrive before 3pm to beat long lines. Thursdays bring mixed crowds for rockin' bands; Fridays and Saturdays range from bondage to drag. Check online.

Powerhouse (Map p324; www.powerhouse-sf.com; 1347 Folsom St; ☺4pm-2am; ☐12, 47) Thursdays through Sundays are best at Powerhouse, an almost-rough-trade SoMa bar for leathermen, shirtless gym queens and the occasional porn star. Draft beer is cheap and specials keep the crowd loose. Smokers grope on the (too-smoky) back patio, while oddballs lurk in the corners.

Stud (Map p324; ☎415-252-7883; www.studsf.com; 399 9th St; admission $5-8; ☺5pm-3am; ☐12, 19, 27, 47) The Stud has rocked the gay scene since 1966. Anything goes at Meow Mix Tuesday drag variety shows; Wednesdays bring raunchy comedy and karaoke. But Friday's the thing, when the party 'Some-thing' brings bizarre midnight drag, pool-table crafts and dance-ready beats. Saturdays, various DJs spin – kick-ass GoBang is among the best. Check the online calendar.

Lone Star Saloon (Map p324; ☎415-863-9999; www.lonestarsaloon.com; 1354 Harrison St; ☺noon-2am; ☐9, 12, 27, 47) Like bears to a honeycomb, big guys with fur fill the Lone Star, but if you're skinny and smooth, you'll likely call it the Go-home-alone Star. There's a huge back patio and competitive pool table but no women-specific bathroom – this is a guys' scene. Busiest Thursday through Sunday.

Hole in the Wall (Map p324; www.holeinthewallsaloon.com; 1369 Folsom St; ☺noon-2am; ☐9, 12, 47) When the Hole moved here, it lost its legendary filthiness because it would otherwise have lost its license. But it still has the wildest erotic poster collection in SF – and remains ground zero for sexy weirdos shooting pool and pinball and swinging from chains dangling over the bar.

DADA
BAR

Map p324 (www.dadasf.com; 86 2nd St; ☺4pm-2am Mon-Wed, from 3pm Thu & Fri, from 7pm Sat; MMontgomery, BMontgomery) Happy-hour flavored martinis for $5 to $7 until 9pm and rotating local art shows take the commercial edge off Downtown and restore the art-freak factor to SoMa. The high ceilings can make the scene loud when the DJ gets going, but that doesn't stop impassioned debates about the future of photography.

1015 FOLSOM
NIGHTCLUB

Map p324 (www.1015.com; 1015 Folsom St; admission $10-20; ☺10pm-2am Thu-Sat; ☐12) Among the city's biggest clubs, 'Ten-Fifteen' draws huge 20-something crowds for weekend DJ headliners and serious dancers for Saturday Pura Latin nights.

The main hall is enormous, and four other dance floors mean you'll lose your posse if you're momentarily entranced by videos projected onto the 400ft water wall. Sound purists: 1015's basement has one of SF's best systems.

Be prepared for a pat-down before you enter; there's a serious no-drugs (or weapons) policy. Usually free before 10:15pm, though drinks run $10 to $15; see online calendar. Public transit is hard to come by and adjacent 6th St is sketchy: plan to taxi.

ENDUP
GAY CLUB

Map p324 (www.theendup.com; 401 6th St; admission $5-20; ☺10pm-4am Mon-Thu, 11pm-11am Fri, 10pm Sat-4am Mon; ☐12, 27, 47) Anyone left sketching on the streets after 2am weekends is subject to the magnetic pull of the EndUp's marathon dance sessions. It's the only club with a 24-hour license and though straight people do come, it remains best known for its gay Sunday tea dances, in full force since 1973. You could feasibly arrive Saturday night and leave Monday morning.

Forget the Golden Gate Bridge: once you EndUp watching the sunrise over the freeway ramp here, you've officially arrived in SF.

☆ ENTERTAINMENT

☆ Financial District, Union Square & Civic Center

★ SAN FRANCISCO SYMPHONY
CLASSICAL MUSIC

Map p322 (☑box office 415-864-6000; www.sf symphony.org; Grove St, btwn Franklin St and Van Ness Ave; M Van Ness, B Civic Center) The SF Symphony often wins Grammys, thanks to celebrity-conductor and musical-director Michael Tilson Thomas, the world's foremost Mahler impresario. When he's not conducting, other famous names take the baton. The orchestra is joined by the Grammy-winning Symphony Chorus for serious choral works, such as Beethoven's *Missa solemnis*. During summer and at Christmas, look for stars like Bernadette Peters, Pink Martini and Peabo Bryson.

The best sound is in the cheap seats in the center terrace, but the loge is most comfy and glam and has the best sight lines. If you're on a budget, sit in the front section of AA, BB, HH or JJ or behind the stage in the center terrace – the sound doesn't blend evenly, but you get the musicians' perspective and look into the conductor's eyes (likewise in pricier side terrace seats). Call the rush-ticket hotline (☑415-503-5577) after 6:30pm to find out whether the box office has released $20 next-day tickets, which you must pick up in person on the day of performance: choose the side terrace over the front orchestra – unless you want to be 10ft from the strings, but the sound is uneven so close to the stage. Preorder your intermission drinks to beat the line. For bird's-eye views of City Hall, head to the second-tier lobby and stand outside on the flying-saucer-like balconies.

★ SAN FRANCISCO OPERA
OPERA

Map p322 (☑415-864-3330; www.sfopera.com; War Memorial Opera House, 301 Van Ness Ave; tickets $10-350; B Civic Center, M Van Ness) SF has been obsessed with opera since the Gold Rush and it remains a staple on the social calendar. Blue bloods like Ann Getty *always* book the Tuesday A-series – the best nights to spot fabulous gowns and tuxedos. If you're walking by during a performance, wander into the box-office lobby and watch the stage monitors for a teaser.

The gorgeous 1932 hall is cavernous and echoey, but there's no more glamorous seat in SF than the velvet-curtained boxes, complete with champagne service. The best midrange seats for sight lines and sound are in the front section of the dress circle. The balcony has the best sound but you'll need binoculars to see the stage, unless you come on 'Opera Vision' nights, when a huge screen shows the action on stage. (Don't sit directly beneath the flickering high-def monitors; if you come to the opera to get away from TV, you'll hate the balcony during these performances.) On a budget? Hang in the back of the hall with die-hard opera buffs: starting at 10am, the box office sells 150 standing-room spots ($10, cash only); two hours before curtain, they release 50 more. Snag an empty seat after intermission, when somnambulant seniors go home. Preorder intermission cocktails at reserved tables in the lower-lobby cafe. Smokers and thrill-seekers: head to the Grand Tier outdoor terrace to overlook City Hall and Downtown's twinkling lights – one of SF's best nighttime views.

SAN FRANCISCO BALLET
DANCE

Map p322 (☑415-861-5600, tickets 415-865-2000; www.sfballet.org; War Memorial Opera House, 301 Van Ness Ave; tickets $10-120; M Van Ness) The San Francisco Ballet is America's oldest ballet company and the first to premier the *Nutcracker,* which it performs annually. In San Francisco, its home is the War Memorial Opera House (and has the same seating chart as the opera), but it also appears at other venues now and then; check the website.

★ AMERICAN CONSERVATORY THEATER
THEATER

Map p322 (ACT; ☑415-749-2228; www.act-sf.org; 415 Geary St; ☑38, ☑Powell-Mason, Powell-Hyde) Breakthrough shows destined for London or New York sometimes pass muster at the turn-of-the-century Geary Theater, which has hosted ACT's landmark productions of Tony Kushner's *Angels in America* and Robert Wilson's *Black Rider*, with a libretto by William S Burroughs and music by the Bay Area's own Tom Waits.

In 2012, ACT purchased the Strand Theater at 1127 Market St, scheduled to open in late 2014.

CAFÉ ROYALE   LOUNGE
Map p322 (☑415-441-4099; www.caferoyale-sf. com; 800 Post St; ⊙4pm-2am; 🚍2, 3, 27, 38) **FREE** A Parisian tiled floor and semicircular fainting couches lend atmosphere and acoustics to this artsy-cool lounge, which hosts live jazz, film screenings, theatrical presentations, readings by local writers and sometimes even belly dancing. Otherwise it's a cute cafe and wine bar with good drink prices, a pool table and an entirely local crowd. The kitchen serves food till 10pm.

BISCUITS & BLUES   LIVE MUSIC
Map p322 (☑415-292-2583; www.biscuitsand blues.com; 401 Mason St; admission $5-25; ⊙music 8-11:30pm Wed-Sat, from 7pm Sun; 🚍Powell, 🅱Powell) With a steady lineup of top-notch blues and jazz talent, Biscuits & Blues has rightly earned a reputation as one of America's best blues clubs. And the name isn't a gimmick – the joint serves hot biscuits, catfish and chicken for the full Southern experience ($15 minimum food purchase at weekend 8pm shows). Make reservations. Acts sometimes perform on Tuesdays and Sundays.

STARLIGHT ROOM   LIVE MUSIC, DANCING
Map p320 (☑415-395-8595; www.starlight roomsf.com; 450 Powell St, 21st fl; cover varies; ⊙8:30pm-2am Tue-Sat, brunch Sun; 🚍Powell-Mason, Powell-Hyde, 🅼Powell, 🅱Powell) Views are mesmerizing from the 21st floor of the Sir Francis Drake Hotel, where khaki-clad tourists and couples on date night let down their hair and dance to live bands (weekends) or DJs (weekdays). Sundays, there's a kooky drag-show brunch (make reservations).

HEMLOCK TAVERN   LIVE MUSIC
Map p322 (☑415-923-0923; www.hemlock tavern.com; 1131 Polk St; cover free-$10; 🚍2, 3, 19, 47, 49) When you wake up tomorrow with peanut shells in your hair (weren't they on the floor?) and a stiff neck from rocking too hard to the Family Curse (weren't they great?), you'll know it was another wild night at the Hemlock. Weekday nights, occasional literary readings are anything but staid among this motley crowd of raucous San Franciscans.

GREAT AMERICAN MUSIC HALL   LIVE MUSIC
Map p322 (☑415-885-0750; www.gamh.com; 859 O'Farrell St; admission $12-35; ⊙box office 10:30am-6pm Mon-Fri & on show nights; 🚍19, 38, 47, 49) Once a bordello, the rococo Great American Music Hall is one of SF's coolest places for shows. A balcony with table seating rims the main standing-room floor area, the sound system is top-notch and there are food and drinks. Music ranges from rock, alt-rock and country to jazz and blues.

PUNCH LINE   COMEDY
Map p319 (☑415-397-4337; www.punchline comedyclub.com; 444 Battery St; admission $12-25, plus two-drink minimum; ⊙shows 8pm Tue-Thu & Sun, 8pm & 10pm Fri & Sat; 🅼Embarcadero, 🅱Embarcadero) Known for launching promising talent (including Robin Williams, Chris Rock, Ellen DeGeneres and David Cross), this historic standup venue is small enough for you to see into performers' eyes. Strong drinks keep you laughing, even when jokes sometimes bomb.

EMBARCADERO CENTER CINEMA   CINEMA
Map p319 (☑415-267-4893; www.landmark theatres.com; 1 Embarcadero Center, Promenade Level; adult/child $10.50/8.25; 🅼Embarcadero, 🅱Embarcadero) Forget blockbusters – here locals queue up for the latest Almodóvar film and whatever won best foreign film at the Oscars. The snack bar caters to discerning tastes with good local coffee, fair-trade chocolate and popcorn with real butter.

PANDORA KARAOKE   KARAOKE
Map p322 (☑415-359-1888; www.pandora karaoke.com; 177 Eddy St; ⊙6pm-2am Tue-Sun; 🅱Powell, 🅼Powell) Liquor up and sing too loudly at this downtown karaoke lounge, on a gritty block of the Tenderloin, with a public bar and themed private rooms (reserve ahead) that aptly showcase booze brands and too-cute kitsch like Hello Kitty. At the later-than-average happy hour (8pm to 9pm), room-rental prices drop 50% and drink specials keep you belting.

WARFIELD LIVE MUSIC

Map p322 (☑888-929-7849; www.thewar fieldtheatre.com; 982 Market St; ⊘box office 10am-4pm Sun & 90min before shows; ⓂPowell, ⒷPowell) Famous names play this former vaudeville theater, including the Beastie Boys and PJ Harvey; when Furthur (formerly the Grateful Dead) plays, the balcony fills with pot smoke.

☆ SoMa

SLIM'S LIVE MUSIC

Map p324 (☑415-255-0333; www.slims-sf.com; 333 11th St; tickets $12-30; ⊘5pm-2am; 🚌9, 12, 27, 47) Guaranteed good times by Gogol Bordello, Tenacious D, the Expendables and AC/DShe (a hard-rocking female tribute band) fit the bill at this midsized club, owned by R&B star Boz Skaggs. Shows are all-ages, though shorties may have a hard time seeing once the floor starts bouncing. Reserve dinner for an additional $25 and score seats on the small balcony.

MEZZANINE LIVE MUSIC

Map p324 (☑415-625-8880; www.mezzaninesf. com; 444 Jessie St; admission $10-40; ⓂPowell, ⒷPowell) Big nights come with bragging rights at the Mezzanine, with one of the city's best sound systems and crowds hyped for breakthrough hip-hop and R&B shows by Wyclef Jean, Quest Love, Method Man, Nas and Snoop Lion (né Dogg). Mezzanine also hosts throwback new-wave nights and classic alt bands like the Dandy Warhols and Psychedelic Furs. Check the calendar.

YERBA BUENA CENTER FOR THE ARTS LIVE MUSIC

Map p324 (YBCA; ☑415-978-2787; www.ybca.org; 700 Howard St; tickets free-$35; ⓂPowell, ⒷPowell) Rock stars would be jealous of art stars at YBCA openings, which draw overflow crowds of impeccably hip art groupies to see anything from live hip-hop by Mos Def, to 1960s smut film festivals, to Vik Muniz' documentary on making art from trash. Most touring dance and jazz companies perform at YBCA's main theater (across the sidewalk from the gallery).

ASIASF NIGHTCLUB

Map p324 (☑415-255-2742; www.asiasf.com; 201 9th St; per person from $39; ⊘7-11pm Wed & Thu, 7pm-2am Fri, 5pm-2am Sat, 7-10pm Sun,

reservation line 1-8pm; ⓂCivic Center, ⒷCivic Center) First ladies of the world, look out: these dazzling Asian ladies can out-hostess you in half the time and half the clothes. Cocktails and Asian-inspired dishes are served with a tall order of sass and one little secret: your servers are drag stars. Every hour, they dance atop the bar, working it like a runway on fire.

The house choreographer worked with Michael and Janet Jackson, so when pop starts to pound, it's look out, Lady Gaga. Teasing is all in good fun, so don't take it seriously if (OK, when) your server flirts with your date or threatens to steal your shoes. Gaggles of girlfriends squeal and blushing straight businessmen play along, but once the inspiration and drinks kick in, everyone mixes it up on the downstairs dance floor. The three-course menu runs $39–54 (depending on seating time); cocktails cost around $10. And honey, those tips are well earned.

INTERSECTION FOR THE ARTS THEATER

Map p324 (☑415-626-2787; www.theinter section.org; 925 Mission St; admission $5-20; 🚡Powell-Mason, Mason-Hyde, ⓂPowell, ⒷPowell) Watch this nonprofit arts space – since its founding in 1965, riveting and entirely unforeseen events have unfolded at Intersection. Hot jazz drawn from Latin, Asian and African American traditions punctuates the calendar of theater premieres by noted playrights, including adapted works by Pulitzer Prize–winner Junot Díaz, National Book Award–winner Denis Johnson and American Book Award–winning poet Jessica Hagedorn.

SAN FRANCISCO'S NEW SKYLINE

At this writing, dozens of cranes tower above San Francisco in a full-scale boom that includes construction of a new Central Subway line from South of Market to Chinatown. The crowning project is the new Transbay Transit Tower – at 1070ft the tallest building on the entire West Coast and eventual landing point of California's high-speed rail project. SF is looking more and more like NY. For the latest on the fast-changing skyline, see http://socketsite.com

DANCE AT YERBA BUENA CENTER FOR THE ARTS

Big names in the art world play Yerba Buena Center for the Arts, but the biggest, boldest moves in town are made across the sidewalk. The theater main stage at Yerba Buena hosts the annual **Ethnic Dance Festival** (www.sfethnicdancefestival.org) and the regular season of **Liss Fain Dance** (www.lissfaindance.org), San Francisco's champions of muscular modern movement. Better yet, you never have to wait long for an encore, because three other major SF dance companies perform their home seasons on this stage.

Alonzo King's Lines Ballet (415-863-3040; www.linesballet.org) Long, lean dancers perform complicated, angular movements that showcase their impeccable technical skills. Recent shows have included a knockout kung-fu-meets-ballet joint work with Shaolin monks, which explored a synthesis of Eastern and Western forms, pairing dance with martial arts. King also offers classes and workshops.

Smuin Ballet (415-912-1899; www.smuinballet.org; box office phone line 1-5pm Tue-Fri) Smuin riled the dance world in 2009 when it dubbed its work 'Ballet, but Entertaining' – as if the form wasn't – but the tag line captures the troupe's populist spirit. Balletic in form, works are by turns wacky and humorous, poignant and touching, always with mass appeal – ideal for those who find interpretive dance too precious.

Joe Goode Performance Group (415-561-6565; www.joegoode.org) An early adaptor of narrative performance art into dance, maverick Joe Goode has an international reputation and a rigorous national touring schedule, yet regularly graces the Yerba Buena stage. His dancers are phenomenal exponents of their craft – and they're not kept silent: in Joe Goode works, the dancers use their voices as well as their bodies.

Intersection won a major grant to transform the former SF Chronicle building into a space for innovation and cultural transformation, and the ground-floor gallery installations regularly make good on that promise. Check the website for openings, workshops, lectures, and jazz in the streets Friday at noon with Off the Grid food trucks (see website for details).

HOTEL UTAH SALOON
LIVE MUSIC

Map p324 (415-546-6300; www.hotelutah.com; 500 4th St; shows free-$10; 11:30am-2am; 47, M4th & King Sts) The ground-floor bar of this Victorian hotel became ground zero of the underground scene in the '70s, when upstarts Whoopi Goldberg and Robin Williams took the stage – now it's a sure bet for Monday Night Open Mics, indie-label debuts and local favorites like Riot Earp, Saucy Monkey and the Dazzling Strangers.

Back in the '50s the bartender graciously served Beats, grifters and Marilyn Monroe but snipped the ties of businessmen when they leaned across the bar; now you can wear whatever, as long as you're buying, but there's a $20 credit-card minimum.

BRAINWASH
LIVE MUSIC, LAUNDROMAT

Map p324 (415-861-3663; www.brainwash.com; 1122 Folsom St; 7am-10pm Mon-Thu, 7am-11pm Fri & Sat, 8am-10pm Sun; ; MCivic Center) The barfly's eternal dilemma between going out or doing laundry is finally solved at this bar-cafe with live music most nights and comedy Thursdays. Last wash is at 8:30pm and the kitchen closes at 9pm, so plan your presoaking and order of Wash Load Nachos accordingly.

AMC LOEWS METREON 16
CINEMA

Map p324 (415-369-6201; www.amctheatres.com; 101 4th St; adult/child $12.50/9.75; MPowell, BPowell) Housed in a mega-entertainment complex, the 16-screen Metreon has comfortable reclining seats with clear views of digital projection screens, plus 3D screenings ($4 extra per ticket) and an IMAX theater ($6 extra per ticket or $7 for 3D screenings). The cinema occupies the top floor of a mall complex with a pretty-good food court.

🛍 SHOPPING

Union Square is the city's principal shopping district, with scores of boutiques and department stores, most chains. Expect a mash-up of major names from Abercrombie to Zara. The shopping area's borders are (roughly) Powell St

(west), Sutter St (north), Kearny St (east) and Market St (south); the epicenter of the Union Square shopping area is along Post St, near Grant Ave. Stockton St crosses Market St and becomes 4th St, passing by Apple and Old Navy before arriving at City Target at Mission St.

⌂ Union Square

ORIGINAL LEVI'S STORE CLOTHING, ACCESSORIES
Map p320 (☎415-501-0100; www.us.levi.com; 815 Market St; ◉10am-9pm Mon-Sat, 11am-8pm Sun; ☐Powell-Mason, Powell-Hyde, MPowell, BPowell) The flagship store in Levi Strauss' hometown sells classic jeans that fit without fail, plus limited-edition pairs made of tough Japanese selvage and eco-organic cotton denim. Scour the impressive discount racks (30% to 60% off) but don't hold out for sales – denim fanatics tweet their finds, so rare lines like 1950s prison-model denim sell fast. Hemming costs $10.

UNIQLO CLOTHING
Map p320 (www.uniqlo.com; 111 Powell St; ◉10am-9pm Mon-Sat, 11am-8pm Sun; MPowell, BPowell) Japanese retailer Uniqlo made a mighty splash in 2013 with its first West Coast store, and suddenly everyone in SF was wearing denim jeans in colors not seen since the 1980s and shiny horizontally channeled down jackets that scrunch to the size of a coffee mug. Easy to understand why: Uniqlo's zingy wardrobe basics don't break the bank.

MACY'S DEPARTMENT STORE
Map p320 (www.macys.com; 170 O'Farrell St; ◉10am-9pm Mon-Sat, 11am-7pm Sun; ☐Powell-Mason, Powell-Hyde, MPowell, BPowell) Five floors of name brands, plus a basement food court and daily-operating post office together occupy a full city block. The men's store is across Stockton Street and easy to navigate, but women will have to brave the perfume police and slightly insulting free-makeover offers to reach shoe sales (totally worth it).

GUMP'S JEWELRY, HOUSEWARES
Map p320 (www.gumps.com; 135 Post St; ◉10am-6pm Mon-Sat, noon-5pm Sun; MMontgomery, BMontgomery) San Francisco's original department store opened in 1861, importing luxury items from the Far East. Today it's famous for jade, silk, rugs, porcelain and housewares – if you're a guest in someone's home and want to express your gratitude with the perfect high-end hostess gift, something from Gump's will always impress.

BRITEX FABRICS FABRICS
Map p320 (www.britexfabrics.com; 146 Geary St; ◉10am-6pm Mon-Sat; ☐Powell-Mason, Powell-Hyde, MPowell, BPowell) Only *Project Runway* can compete with Britex's fashion drama. First floor: designers bicker over dibs on caution-orange chiffon. Second floor: glam rockers dig through velvet goldmines. Third floor: Hollywood stylists squeal 'To die for!' over '60s Lucite buttons. Top floor: fake fur flies and remnants roll as costumers prepare for Burning Man, Halloween and your average SF weekend.

BARNEYS DEPARTMENT STORE
Map p320 (www.barneys.com; 77 O'Farrell St; ◉10am-7pm Mon-Sat, 11am-6pm Sun; ☐Powell-Mason, Powell-Hyde, MPowell, BPowell) The high-end New York fashion staple known for inspired window displays and up-to-70%-off sales has hit the West Coast. Barneys showcases emerging designers, plus well-priced, well-fitted sportswear on its co-op label and exclusive ecoconscious lines by Philip Lim, Theory and its own affordable Green Label, focusing on clean lines with a clean conscience.

MARGARET O'LEARY CLOTHING, ACCESSORIES
Map p320 (www.margaretoleary.com; 1 Claude Lane; ◉10am-5pm Tue-Sat; MMontgomery, BMontgomery) Ignorance of the fog is no excuse in San Francisco, but should you confuse SF for LA (the horror!) and neglect to pack the obligatory sweater, Margaret O'Leary will sheathe you in knitwear, no questions asked. The San Francisco designer's specialties are warm, whisper-light cardigans in cashmere, organic cotton or ecominded bamboo yarn.

The Pacific Heights flagship store (p147) is open daily.

DSW SHOES
Map p320 (www.dsw.com; 111 Powell St; ◉10am-9pm Mon-Sat, to 8pm Sun; ☐Powell-Mason, Powell-Hyde, MPowell, BPowell) The basement clearance section is where recovering shoe hounds come after they've sworn that they've bought their last pair for the season. Diligent research has uncovered 40% to 60% off Marc Jacobs flats, Betsy Johnson wedges and an inexplicable bonanza of limited-edition Pumas.

LOEHMANN'S CLOTHING, ACCESSORIES

Map p320 (www.loehmanns.com; 222 Sutter St; ⊙9am-8pm Mon-Sat, 11-7 Sun; MMontgomery, BMontgomery) The most revealing Downtown fashion choice isn't what shoes you wear, but which floor you choose in this discount designer superstore. North Beach artists drift to the middle floor for almost-free Free People smocks; Pacific Heights charity fundraisers hit the top floor for discounted Prada shirtdresses; and gift shoppers converge around 40%-off red-tagged Kate Spade clutches in main-floor accessories.

Pace yourself: women's shoes and an impressive men's section are across the street.

H&M CLOTHING, ACCESSORIES

Map p320 (www.hm.com; 150 Powell St; ⊙10am-9pm Mon-Sat, to 8pm Sun; ☐Powell-Mason, Powell-Hyde, MPowell, BPowell) What IKEA is to home furnishing, H&M is to fashion: suspiciously affordable, perpetually crowded, not really made for the long haul and perfect for parties. Its limited-edition runs and special collections mean you won't have to worry that your closet looks exactly like everyone else's – unless you bought it at IKEA.

There are several H&Ms in town but Powell St is biggest, with a vast men's section.

ICEBREAKER CLOTHING

Map p320 (www.icebreaker.com; 170 Post St; ⊙10am-8pm Mon-Sat, 11am-6pm Sun; BMontgomery, MMontgomery) Think fast: what's the only material that keeps you warm when wet? That's right: wool. And New Zealand-based Icebreaker makes some of the best, using fine-weave merino in its simple, wardrobe basics – long underwear, snug-fit sweaters and toasty-warm hoodies – ideal for damp and chilly San Francisco. We speak from experience: these garments travel well.

LE SANCTUAIRE FOOD, DRINK

Map p320 (☑415-986-4216; www.le-sanctuaire.com; 315 Sutter St, 5th fl; ⊙by appointment 10:30am-4:30pm Mon-Fri; ☐Powell-Mason, Powell-Hyde, MMontgomery) Mad scientists, thrill seekers and professional chefs get buzzed, speakeasy-style (read: appointment only) at this culinary curiosity shop. Here you'll find anchovy juice, spherifiers to turn fruit into caviar, salt for curing meats and, of course, that hallmark of molecular gastronomy: foaming agents.

Check the website for classes on making smoked watermelon with vacuum sealers and using liquid nitrogen to make powdered lard – alas, suspending disbelief with gellants isn't on the schedule.

UNDER ONE ROOF GIFTS, HOUSEWARES

Map p320 (☑415-502-2300; www.underoneroof.org; Shop 13, Crocker Galleria, 50 Post St; ⊙10am-6pm Mon-Fri, to 5pm Sat; MMontgomery, BMontgomery) All the fabulous gifts under this roof are donated by local designers and businesses, so AIDS service organizations get 100% of the proceeds from your etched San Francisco–skyline martini glasses and adorable Jonathan Adler vase. Those sweet sales clerks are volunteers, so show them love for raising $11 million to date.

WESTFIELD SAN FRANCISCO CENTRE DEPARTMENT STORE

Map p320 (www.westfield.com/sanfrancisco; 865 Market St; ⊙10am-8:30pm Mon-Sat, to 7pm Sun; ⛟; ☐Powell-Mason, Powell-Hyde, MPowell, BPowell) Wait, is this suburbia? Sure looks it inside this nine-level chain-store city, with Bloomingdale's and Nordstrom, plus 400 retailers and multiplex theater. Supposedly the mall has a 'distinctive boutique' concept, which translates to same stuff, smaller stores. Best reasons to brave this behemoth: post-holiday sales, H&M's Spanish cousin Mango, bathrooms (including lounges with baby-changing tables) and respectable food court.

🔒 Financial District

FERRY PLAZA WINE MERCHANT FOOD, DRINK

Map p319 (www.fpwm.com; 1 Ferry Bldg; ⊙11am-8pm Mon, 10am-8pm Tue, 10am-9pm Wed-Fri, 8am-8pm Sat, 10am-7pm Sun; MEmbarcadero, BEmbarcadero) Stock up on California wines after you've sipped a few, swishing and spitting to maintain your capacity to taste. Savvy staff describe wine in fun, informative ways, ensuring a good time. The bar is jammed Saturdays, but otherwise staff take time to suggest pairings and exciting new releases.

RECCHIUTI CHOCOLATES FOOD, DRINK

Map p319 (www.recchiuticonfections.com; 1 Ferry Bldg; ⊙10am-7pm Mon-Fri, 8am-6pm Sat, 10am-5pm Sun; MEmbarcadero, BEmbarcadero) No San Franciscan can resist Recchiuti: Pacific

Heights parts with old money for its *fleur de sel* caramels; Noe Valley's child foodie prodigies prefer S'more Bites to the campground variety; and the Mission splurges on chocolates designed by developmentally disabled artists from Creativity Explored – part of the proceeds benefit the nonprofit gallery.

★ **HEATH CERAMICS**　　HOUSEWARES

Map p319 (www.heathceramics.com; 1 Ferry Bldg; ⊙10am-7pm Mon-Fri, 8am-6pm Sat, 11am-5pm Sun; Ⓜ Embarcadero, Ⓑ Embarcadero) No local, artisanal SF restaurant tablescape is complete without handmade modern Heath stoneware, thrown by local potters in Heath's Sausalito studio since 1948. Chef Alice Waters has served her definitive California fare on Heath dishware for decades – hence the popular Chez Panisse ceramics in earthy, food-friendly shades. Pieces are priced for fine dining except studio seconds, sold here on weekends.

SUR LA TABLE　　HOUSEWARES

Map p319 (www.surlatable.com; 1 Ferry Bldg; ⊙9am-7pm Mon-Fri, from 8am Sat, from 10am Sun; Ⓜ Embarcadero, Ⓑ Embarcadero) Can't fathom life without an espresso maker and citrus reamer? You'll never need to, thanks to these understanding salespeople. For the hippie gourmet, there's a windowsill grow-light for sprouting, ahem, herbs, and for the young aspiring chef, a cupcake-frosting set. Look for free demos that show how to master technique with your new gear.

JAPONESQUE　　HOUSEWARES

Map p319 (☑415-391-8860; 824 Montgomery St; ⊙10:30am-5:30pm Tue-Fri, 11am-5pm Sat; ▣10, 12, 41) Wabi-sabi is not something you smear on sushi, but the fine appreciation for imperfect, organic forms and materials. Experience this first-hand at Japonesque. Owner Koichi Hara stocks antique Japanese bamboo baskets and ceramics, alongside Ruth Rhoten's molten silver vases and Hiromichi Iwashita's graphite-coated, chiseled-wood panels that look like bonfire embers.

FOG CITY NEWS　　BOOKS, CHOCOLATE

Map p319 (www.fogcitynews.com; 455 Market St; ⊙9am-6pm Mon-Fri, noon-5pm Sat; Ⓜ Embarcadero, Ⓑ Embarcadero) The perfect stopover before a long flight, Fog City stocks a huge

EDEN & EDEN

Detour from reality at **Eden & Eden** (Map p334; www.edenandeden.com; 560 Jackson St; ⊙10am-7pm Mon-Fri, 10am-6pm Sat; Ⓜ Kearny St), a Dadaist design boutique, where anchors float on silk dresses, clouds rain on pillows, architectural blueprints serve as placemats and Ozzy Osbourne has been transformed into a stuffed mouse wearing batwings. Prices are surprisingly down to earth for far-out, limited-edition finds from local and international designers.

variety of domestic and international magazines and newspapers, plus one of the city's most diverse selections of chocolates – a whopping 200 bars. Historic photos of SF line the walls between the old wooden racks.

EMBARCADERO CENTER　　MALL

Map p319 (embarcaderocenter.com; btwn Sacramento and Clay Sts, from Drumm to Battery Sts; ⊙10am-7pm Mon-Fri, 10am-6pm Sat, noon-5pm Sun; Ⓜ Embarcadero, Ⓑ Embarcadero) The skyscrapers of the Embarcadero Center, joined by overhead walkways, form a four-block-long, '70s-futurist urban-sprawl mall, with chain-store branches like Gap and Ann Taylor catering to downtown business people. If you're nearby, it's worth a look (mostly for the architecture – head to the Promenade Level) but not a special trip, except to the arthouse Embarcadero Center Cinema (p106).

🔒 Civic Center & the Tenderloin

KAYO BOOKS　　BOOKSTORE

Map p322 (www.kayobooks.com; 814 Post St; ⊙11am-6pm Thu-Sat; ▣2, 3, 27, 38) Juvenile delinquents will find an entire section dedicated to their life stories here, where vintage pulp, true crime and erotica titles ending in exclamation points (including succinct *Wench!*) induced John Waters' endorsement on NPR. You might find a first-edition Dashiell Hammett gumshoe caper, wayward nun's tale filed under Catholic Guilt or *Women's Medical Problems* in the Bizarre Nonfiction section.

LOCAL KNOWLEDGE

MADE IN SAN FRANCISCO

San Francisco is a crafty town, with many designers and artisans, but finding them can be tricky, especially when you're shopping downtown against a backdrop of megabrands. That's why we love **SF Made** (www.sfmade.org), an umbrella organization of SF-based manufacturers, which publishes a handy map to help you pinpoint locally based retailers that carry items you won't find anywhere else. Alternatively, download the smartphone app ShopNear.me and find local, indie shops nearest your location.

GYPSY ROSALIE'S   FASHION

Map p322 (☑415-771-8814; 1215 Polk St; ⊙10am-5:30pm Mon-Sat, 11am-5pm Sun; ☒2, 3, 19, 38, 47, 49) In SF you never know when you'll be invited to a fancy-dress party. Rosalie's works you a look, with the city's most fabulous selection of wigs, from serious cuts for real ladies, to over-the-top bouffants fit for a queen, plus beaded, spangled vintage gowns so garish, so tacky, that you'll either run away horrified or rush to try everything on.

MAGAZINE   MAGAZINES

Map p322 (www.themagazinesf.com; 920 Larkin St; ⊙noon-7pm Mon-Sat; ☒19, 38, 47, 49) No place carries a better selection of vintage magazines. The Magazine's old wooden shelves contain everything from 1940s pinup mags, 1970s *Vanity Fair* and decades-old issues of *Playboy*, to the *Saturday Evening Post*, *Tiger Beat* and pulp novels with titles like *Aliens Ate My Baby*. Most cost a mere 35¢.

🛍 SoMa

SFMOMA MUSEUM STORE   BOOKS, GIFTS

Map p324 (☑415-357-4035; www.sfmoma.org/museumstore; 51 Yerba Buena Lane; ⊙11am-7pm Mon-Sat, noon-5pm Sun; ♿; Ⓜ Powell, Ⓑ Powell) Design fetishists may have to be pried away from MOMA's display cases, which brim with cereal bowls looking like spilt milk, Pantone color-swatch espresso cups and watches with a face to match Mario Botta's black-and-white SFMOMA facade. Contem-

porary art books keep aspiring collectors absorbed and William Wegman's videos of dogs spelling out the alphabet entrance kids.

This location is temporary until 2016, when the store will relocate back to the museum.

★ JEREMY'S   CLOTHING, ACCESSORIES

Map p324 (www.jeremys.com; 2 South Park St; ⊙11am-6pm Mon-Wed & Fri-Sat, to 8pm Thu, noon-6pm Sun; ☒10, Ⓜ2nd & King) No South Park excursion would be complete without bargain-hunting at Jeremy's. Runway-modeling, window displays and high-end customer returns translate to jaw-dropping bargains on major designers. The racks get picked over fast, but you may score an Armani suit for over half off if you're quick. Brave the fitting-room lines – returns are possible for store credit but only within seven days.

SAN FRANCISCO RAILWAY MUSEUM GIFT SHOP   GIFTS

Map p324 (☑415-974-1948; www.streetcar.org/museum; 77 Steuart St; ⊙10am-6pm Tue-Sun; ☒Embarcadero, Ⓑ Embarcadero) If all those vintage streetcars have inspired imagination, find souvenir trains at this tiny free Municipal Railway museum that showcases all things MUNI, including model streetcars, vintage posters, baseball caps and T-shirts emblazoned with transit tags, including our favorite: 'Information gladly given, but safety requires avoiding unnecessary conversation.'

BRANCH   HOUSEWARES

Map p324 (www.branchhome.com; 345 9th St; ⊙9:30am-5:30pm Mon-Fri; ☒12, 14) ✐ When you're looking for original home decor with a sustainable edge, it's time to Branch out. Whether you're in the market for a cork chaise lounge, beechwood-fiber bath towel or a tiny bonsai in a reclaimed breath-mint tin, Branch has you covered – and yes, they ship.

MADAME S & MR S LEATHER   CLOTHING, ACCESSORIES

Map p324 (www.madame-s.com; 385 8th St; ⊙11am-7pm; ☒12, 19, 27, 47) Only in San Francisco would you find an S&M superstore, with such musts as suspension stirrups, latex hoods and, for that special someone, a chrome-plated codpiece. If you've been a very bad puppy, there's an entire department catering to you here, and gluttons for punishment will find home-decor inspiration in Dungeon Furniture.

GENERAL BEAD
JEWELRY, GIFTS

Map p324 (www.generalbead.net; 637 Minna St; ☺noon-6pm; MCivic Center, BCivic Center) Blind beading ambition may seize you among the racks of bagged bulk beads, where visions of DIY holiday gifts for the entire family appear like mirages: multitiered necklaces, sequined seascapes, mosaic frames, even lampshades. To practice restraint, order smaller quantities downstairs from the bead-bedecked staff behind the counter, who will ring up your sale on bejeweled calculators.

ISDA & CO OUTLET
CLOTHING, ACCESSORIES

Map p324 (www.isda-and-co.com; 21 South Park St; ☺10am-6pm Mon-Sat; ⬚10, M2nd & King) Sharp SF urban professionals aren't born into casual Friday elegance – they probably clawed their way up through racks of artfully draped shirts and sculpted cardigans at this local designer outlet. Colors are mostly variations on a graphite-gray theme, but the lean silhouette is shamelessly flattering.

METREON
MALL

Map p324 (www.westfield.com/metreon; 135 4th St; ☺7am-10pm Mon-Fri, 8am-10pm Sat, 8am-9pm Sun; MPowell, BPowell) Architecturally like an airport terminal, Metreon houses a City Target, multiplex cinema, and pretty-good food court. What's best here is outside: Yerba Buena Gardens.

🏃 SPORTS & ACTIVITIES

★ AT&T PARK
BASEBALL

(☎415-972-2000, tour 415-972-2400; http://sanfrancisco.giants.mlb.com; AT&T Park; tickets $8-200, tour tickets adult/senior/child/ $20/15/10; ☺tour 10:30am & 2:30pm; 👶; MN, T) The San Francisco Giants won the World Series in 2010 and 2012 and play 81 home games, April to October. Games pack huge crowds, despite this being one of America's most

WORTH A DETOUR

DETOUR: SOUTH BEACH TO MISSION BAY

South Beach, the eastern waterfront around the Bay Bridge, was until not so long ago an industrial wasteland of dilapidated docks. Then came the 1985 Downtown Plan, a new metro (the T-line), condominium towers, baseball stadium (AT&T Park, home of the World Series–winning Giants) and a wide waterfront promenade linking the stadium with Fisherman's Wharf. In 2013, the America's Cup sailboat race brought further redevelopment, including the **Brannan St Wharf** (Map p324), a new bayside park between Piers 30 and 38.

The easiest way to explore is on bicycle – the Embarcadero is entirely flat – or to walk 30 minutes south of the Ferry Building. En route, pass the SFFD's c 1915 Fire Boat House and South Beach's three last-remaining waterfront dives (however gentrified). Stop for beer. At the ballpark, hug the shoreline alongside sailboats at McCovey Cove and suddenly you're beside the field, looking through the fence – on game days, at eye level with the players. Stay for an inning. Return downtown via metro from 2nd and King Streets.

On bicycle, keep going: Cut inland along either side of Mission Creek, past houseboats and kayakers, through a new shoreline park, lush with diverse riparian flora planted to restore the natural ecosystem. At the railroad tracks beneath the freeway, by UCSF's Mission Creek Campus (epicenter of biotech research), cut west on 16th St for the backdoor route to the Mission and Castro or return downtown by heading north via 7th St, through SoMa.

To see an un-gentrified slice of the waterfront, detour south to the **Ramp** (Map p330; ☎415-621-2378; www.theramprestaurant.com; 855 Terry Francois St; mains $10-15; ☺lunch 11am-3:30pm Mon-Fri, 9:30am-4pm Sat-Sun; bar 11am-9pm; MMariposa) for drinks and food. Sit at rickety umbrella tables on a pier abutting an industrial dry dock and sip Bloodies while you scope the dynamic cross-section of locals. The food's OK – sandwiches, salads and barbecue – but it's the place that's captivating, revealing a side of SF tourists never see (though as of this writing, Woody Allen had just shot scenes for a film here, so the secret may be out). Bands play at 5:30pm on weekends – salsa on Saturdays is a blast. It's over by 8pm. Just don't fall off your bike on the way home.

expensive ballparks – the average cost for a family of four, including food and beer, is $237. Season-ticket holders sell unwanted tickets through the team's Double Play Ticket Window on the website.

On nongame days behind-the-scenes **tours** cover the clubhouse, dugout and field. Discover a mini-replica of the field, the world's largest baseball glove, and a kids' play structure within that giant Coke bottle masquerading as sculpture. Bonus: on the park's east side, you can stand at the archways on the waterfront side and watch innings for free.

SPINNAKER SAILING   BOATING

Map p324 (415-543-7333; www.spinnaker-sailing.com; Pier 40, South Beach Harbor; skippered charters from $382, lessons from $300; 10am-5pm; Brannan) Do 'luff,' 'cringle' and 'helms-a-lee' mean anything to you? If yes, captain a boat from Spinnaker and sail into the sunset. If not, charter a skippered vessel or take classes and learn to talk like a sailor – in a good way.

CITY KAYAK   KAYAKING

Map p324 (415-294-1050; www.citykayak.com; Pier 40, South Beach Harbor; kayak rentals per hr $35-65, 3hr lesson & rental $59, tours $65-75; Brannan) You haven't seen San Francisco until you've seen it from the water. Newbies to kayaking can take lessons and venture calm waters near the Bay Bridge, alone or escorted; experienced paddlers can brave

choppy currents beneath the Golden Gate (conditions permitting; get advice first). We especially love the romantic, calm-water moonlight tours. Check website for details.

EMBARCADERO
YMCA   HEALTH & FITNESS, SWIMMING

Map p324 (415-957-9622; www.ymcasf.org/embarcadero; 169 Steuart St; day pass $15; 5:30am-9:45pm Mon-Fri, 8am-7:45pm Sat, 9am-5:45pm Sun; Embarcadero, Embarcadero) The Embarcadero YMCA has knockout bay views from its gym floor and its policy of no TVs, amplified music or cell phones means zero distractions. The full-service facility includes 25m pool, co-ed hot tub, basketball courts, extensive gym equipment and separate men's and women's sauna and steam. Towels included. Bring a lock or use free small lockers outside the locker rooms.

YERBA BUENA CENTER
ICE SKATING & BOWLING   ICE SKATING, BOWLING

Map p324 (415-820-3532; www.skatebowl.com; 750 Folsom St; skating adult/child $10/8, skate rental $3, bowling per game $5, shoe rental $4; 10am-10pm Sun-Thu, to midnight Fri & Sat; Powell, Powell) Built on the rooftop of the Moscone Convention Center, the ice and bowling centers are big draws for families. Unlike most rinks, this one is bright, naturally lit with walls of windows; the bowling alley has just 12 hard-to-book lanes but serves beer. Check website or call for skating times.

North Beach & Chinatown

Neighborhood Top Five

1 Wandering **Chinatown alleyways** (p120) to hear mah jong tiles, temple gongs and Chinese orchestras – the sounds of a community that's survived fire, earthquakes and even politicians.

2 Climbing Filbert St steps past heckling par-

rots and fragrant gardens to panoramic **Coit Tower** (p117).

3 Reflecting in the Poet's Chair and celebrating free speech at **City Lights** (p131).

4 Time-traveling through the old Chinatown at the **Chinese Historical Society of America** (p119) in the

historic Julia Morgan-designed Chinatown YWCA.

5 Picking up where Jack Kerouac left off at historic Beat hangouts: **Li Po** (p130), **Vesuvio** (p130) and **Caffe Trieste** (p127).

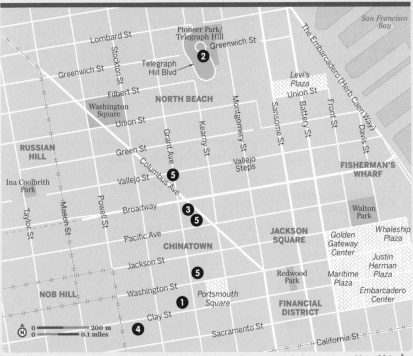

For more detail of this area, see Map p334 ➡

Lonely Planet's Top Tip

Wild hawks and parrots circle above North Beach as though looking for a parking spot. The weekend parking situation is so dire that locals avoid North Beach and Chinatown – forgetting there's public parking underneath Portsmouth Square. You may also luck into a spot at Good Luck Parking Garage, where spots are stenciled with fortune-cookie wisdom: 'You are not a has-been.'

✕ Best Places to Eat

➡ Coi (p125)

➡ Z & Y (p126)

➡ Liguria Bakery (p124)

➡ Ristorante Ideale (p125)

➡ Jai Yun (p127)

For reviews, see p124 ➡

🍷 Best Places to Drink

➡ Specs Museum Cafe (p127)

➡ Caffe Trieste (p127)

➡ Comstock Saloon (p127)

➡ Réveille (p130)

➡ 15 Romolo (p127)

For reviews, see p127 ➡

◉ Best for Artistic Inspiration

➡ City Lights (p131)

➡ Chinese Culture Center (p119)

➡ Coit Tower (p117)

➡ Bob Kaufman Alley (p119)

➡ Li Po (p130)

➡ Jack Kerouac Alley (p118)

For reviews, see p118 ➡

Explore North Beach & Chinatown

From downtown, enter Dragon's Gate onto Chinatown's main tourist drag, Grant Ave. Hard to believe this pagoda-topped, souvenir-shopping strip was once notorious brothel-lined Dupont St – at least until you see the fascinating displays at Chinese Historical Society of America. Duck into Chinatown's historic alleyways to glimpse a neighborhood that's survived against daunting odds and detour for dim sum at City View. Cross into North Beach via Jack Kerouac Alley and City Lights bookstore, San Francisco's free-speech landmark and home of the Beat literary movement. Fuel up with espresso at Caffe Trieste for your North Beach Beat walking tour, and hike garden-lined Filbert St steps to giddy panoramas and daring murals at Coit Tower. Descend for a bar crawl or dinner at Coi.

Local Life

➡**Hangouts** Join regular crowds of writers at Caffe Trieste (p127), martial arts masters at Washington Square (p118) and skaters at Old St Mary's Square (p123).

➡**Foodie discoveries** Even been-there, eaten-that San Franciscans find new taste sensations at Z & Y (p126), Red Blossom Tea Company (p132) and Jai Yun (p127).

➡**Local celebrity sightings** Keep an eye out for Robin Williams at Cobb's Comedy Club (p131), Sean Penn at Tosca Cafe (p127), Francis Ford Coppola at Columbus Tower (p118) and Tom Waits and Carlos Santana at 101 Music (p131).

➡**Five-dollar bargains** Fly a butterfly kite from Chinatown Kite Shop (p132), rummage sale toy bins at Double Punch (p132) and carbo-load at Liguria Bakery. (p124)

Getting There & Away

➡**Bus** Key routes passing through Chinatown and North Beach are 1, 10, 12, 30, 39, 41 and 45.

➡**Cable car** From Downtown or the Wharf, take the Powell-Mason and Powell-Hyde lines through Chinatown and North Beach. The California St cable car passes through the southern end of Chinatown.

ALLAN BAXTER / GETTY IMAGES ©

The exclamation point on San Francisco's skyline is Coit Tower, the stark white deco tower that eccentric heiress Lillie Hancock Coit left a fortune to build as a monument to San Francisco firefighters. The tower has been a lightning rod for controversy for its colorful, provocative 1930s Works Project Administration (WPA) murals – but there's no debating the 360-degree panoramas from Coit Tower's viewing platform.

WPA Murals & Viewing Platform

Coit Tower's lobby murals are positioned high above the city but grounded in the realities of California's Great Depression. They show San Franciscans at work and play, lining up at soup kitchens and organizing dock-workers' unions, partying despite Prohibition and reading books – including manifestos by Karl Marx – in Chinese, Italian and English.

Today, San Franciscans embrace the tower and its murals as symbols of the city's openness to all perspectives. For a 360-degree outlook 210ft above San Francisco, take the elevator up to the tower's open-air platform. To glimpse murals hidden inside the stairwell, join a free tour at 11am Saturdays.

Telegraph Hill

In the 19th century, a ruthless entrepreneur began quarrying and blasting away roads here, and this garden-lined cliffside boardwalk became the main uphill route. City Hall eventually stopped the quarrying of Telegraph Hill, but the view of the bay from **Filbert St steps** is still (wait for it) dynamite. The steep climb leads past hidden cottages along **Napier Lane**, sweeping Bay Bridge vistas and colorful **wild parrot flocks**.

DON'T MISS...

➡ WPA murals

➡ 360-degree viewing platform panorama

➡ Filbert St steps

PRACTICALITIES

➡ Map p334

➡ ☏415-362-0808

➡ http://sfrecpark.org/destination/telegraph-hill-pioneer-park/coit-tower

➡ Telegraph Hill Blvd

➡ elevator entry (non-resident) adult/child $7/5

➡ ☺10am-5:30pm Mar-Sep, 9am-4:30pm Oct-Feb

➡ ☐39

⊙ SIGHTS

Standing atop the Filbert St steps, you can understand what Italian fishermen, Beat poets and wild parrots saw in North Beach: tough climbs and giddy vistas, a place that was more sky than ground, an area that was civilized but never entirely tamed. Coit Tower punctuates the scenery, lifting North Beach out of the fog of everyday life. Across Columbus Ave is Chinatown, survivor of gold booms and busts, anti-Chinese riots and bootlegging wars, trials by fire and earthquake. Yet Chinatown repeatedly made history, providing labor for America's first cross-country railroad, creating original Chinatown deco architecture and leading the charge for China's revolution and US civil rights.

⊙ North Beach

COIT TOWER   HISTORICAL BUILDING
See p117.

JACK KEROUAC ALLEY   STREET
Map p334 (btwn Grant & Columbus Aves; ☒1, 10, 12, 30, 45, ☒Powell-Hyde, Powell-Mason) 'The air was soft, the stars so fine, the promise of every cobbled alley so great...' This ode by the *On the Road* and *Dharma Bums* author is embedded in his namesake alley, a fittingly poetic and slightly seedy shortcut between Chinatown and North Beach via Kerouac haunts City Lights and Vesuvio – Kerouac took literature, Buddhism and beer seriously.

BEAT MUSEUM   MUSEUM
Map p334 (☒1-800-537-6822; www.kerouac. com; 540 Broadway; admission adult/student $8/5; ☺10am-7pm Tue-Sun; ☒; ☒10, 12, 30, 41, 45, ☒Powell-Hyde, Powell-Mason) The Beat goes on and on at this obsessive collection of SF literary-scene ephemera c 1950–69. The banned edition of Allen Ginsberg's *Howl* is the ultimate free-speech trophy and the 1961 check for $10.08 that Jack Kerouac wrote to a liquor store has a certain dark humor, but those cheesy Kerouac bobble-head dolls take the cake as the real head-shakers.

Enter the museum through a turnstile in the adjoining museum store and pass a 1949 Hudson roadster covered with dust accumulated over 4000 miles of driving coast-to-coast for the filming of 2012's *On the Road* movie. Grab a ramshackle reclaimed theater seat redolent with the accumulated odors of literary giants, pets and pot to watch fascinating films about the Beat era's leading artists and free thinkers. Upstairs are shrines to individual Beats with first-hand remembrances and artifacts, including first editions of books that expanded the American outlook to include the margins.

Downstairs in the store, you can buy poetry chapbooks and obscure Beat titles you won't find elsewhere; entry to this part is free and so are readings held here (check website). Guided Beat tours are offered Friday, Saturday and Sunday, covering the museum, Beat history and literary alleys in two hours (adult/student $30/25).

COLUMBUS TOWER   HISTORICAL BUILDING
Map p334 (916 Kearny St; ☒1, 10, 12, 20, 35, 41, ☒California St) Built by shady political boss Abe Ruef in 1905, Columbus Tower was finished just in time to be reduced to its steel skeleton in the 1906 earthquake. The new copper cladding was still shiny in 1907 when not-so-honest Abe was convicted of bribing city supervisors. By the time he emerged bankrupt from San Quentin State Prison, the cupola was oxidizing green.

Grammy-winning folk group The Kingston Trio bought the tower in the 1960s and the Grateful Dead recorded in the basement. Since the 1970s, Columbus Tower has been owned by Francis Ford Coppola, and film history has been made here by Coppola's American Zoetrope filmmaking studio, *The Joy Luck Club* director Wayne Wang and Academy Award–winning actor/director Sean Penn. Ground-floor Zoetrope Cafe features Coppola wines and decent desserts – as a character famously advised in Coppola's film *The Godfather*, take the cannoli.

WASHINGTON SQUARE   PARK
Map p334 (Columbus Ave & Union St; ☒30, 39, 41, 45, ☒Powell-Mason) Wild parrots, tai chi masters and nonagenarian churchgoing *nonnas* (grandmothers) are the company you'll keep on this lively patch of lawn. The parrots keep their distance in the treetops, but like anyone else in North Beach, they can probably be bribed into friendship with a focaccia from Liguria Bakery (p124) on the square's northeast corner.

WORTH A DETOUR

BOB KAUFMAN ALLEY

What, you mean your hometown doesn't have a street named after an African American Catholic-Jewish-voodoo anarchist Beat poet who refused to speak for 12 years? The man revered in France as the 'American Rimbaud' was a major poet who helped found the legendary *Beatitudes* magazine in 1959 and a spoken-word bebop jazz artist who was never at a loss for words. Yet he felt compelled to take a Buddhist vow of silence after John F Kennedy's assassination that he kept until the end of the Vietnam War.

Kaufman's life was hardly pure poetry: he was a teenage runaway, periodically found himself homeless, was occasionally jailed for picking fights in rhyme with police, battled methamphetamine addiction with varying success and once claimed his goal was to be forgotten. Yet like the man himself, the hidden **Bob Kaufman Alley** (Map p334; off Grant Ave near Filbert St; ☐30, 39, 41, 45, ☐Powell-Mason) named in his honor is offbeat, streetwise and often profoundly silent.

The park's 1897 statue of Ben Franklin is a non sequitur and the taps below his feet falsely advertise mineral water from Vichy, France. This puzzling public artwork was donated by certifiable SF eccentric Henry D Cogswell, who made his fortune fitting miners with gold fillings. Originally the monument was topped by Cogswell himself, but after it was mocked as ugly and toppled by self-appointed art critics in 1894, Ben Franklin was raised in the dentist's stead. Cogswell buried a time capsule under this monument in 1879, and in accordance with his instructions, a century later it was opened to reveal an early women's liberation manifesto, a San Francisco Chinese-language newspaper and sundry dental tools.

SAINTS PETER & PAUL CHURCH   CHURCH
Map p334 (☑415-421-0809; www.stspeterpaul. san-francisco.ca.us; 666 Filbert St; ☉7:30am-4pm; ☐30, 39, 41, 45, ☐Powell-Mason) Wedding cake was the apparent inspiration for this 1924 triple-decker cathedral with lacy white towers. The church holds Catholic masses in Italian, Chinese and Spanish and pulls triple wedding shifts on Saturdays. Joe DiMaggio and Marilyn Monroe had wedding photos taken here, but they weren't permitted to marry in the church because both had been divorced (they got hitched at City Hall).

The church is also a North Beach literary landmark, with poetry by Dante in a glittering mosaic inscription over the grand triple entryway that brings to mind Beat poets and Beatles: 'The glory of Him who moves all things/Penetrates and glows throughout the universe.'

⊙ Chinatown

CHINESE CULTURE CENTER   ART GALLERY
Map p334 (☑415-986-1822; www.c-c-c.org; 3rd fl, Hilton Hotel, 750 Kearny St; suggested donation $5, tours adult/student $30/25; ☉10am-4pm Tue-Sat; ☐; ☐1, 8X, 10, 12, 30, 35, 41, ☐California St, Powell-Mason, Powell-Hyde) You can see all the way to China from the Hilton's 3rd floor inside this cultural center, which hosts exhibits ranging from showcases of China's leading brush-painters to Xian Rui ('fresh-arp') cutting-edge installations, recently featuring video art exploring gender identity in Chinese culture. In odd-numbered years, don't miss Present Tense Biennial, where 30-plus Bay Area artists present personal takes on Chinese culture.

Check the center's online schedule for upcoming concerts, hands-on arts workshops for adults and children, Mandarin classes and genealogy services.

CHINESE HISTORICAL SOCIETY OF AMERICA   MUSEUM
Map p334 (CHSA; ☑415-391-1188; www.chsa.org; 965 Clay St; adult/child $5/2, 1st Thu of month free; ☉noon-5pm Tue-Fri, 11am-4pm Sat; ☐1, 30, 45, ☐California St) Picture what it was like to be Chinese in America during the Gold Rush, the transcontinental railroad construction or the Beat heyday in this 1932 landmark, built as Chinatown's YWCA by Julia Morgan (also chief architect of Hearst Castle). The nation's largest Chinese American historical institute is a treasury of artifacts tracing personal journeys from China that made American history.

Chinatown Alleyways

Forty-one historic alleyways packed into Chinatown's 22 blocks have seen it all since 1849: gold rushes and revolution, incense and opium, fire and icy receptions. These narrow backstreets are lined with towering buildings because there was nowhere to go but up in Chinatown after 1870, when laws limited Chinese immigration, employment and housing.

Waverly Place

Off Sacramento St are the flag-festooned balconies of Chinatown's historic temples, where services have been held ever since 1852 – even in 1906, while the altar was still smoldering at Tien Hau Temple (p123). Downstairs are noodle shops, laundries and traditional Chinese apothecaries.

Ross Alley

Ross Alley was known as Mexico, Spanish and Manila St after the women who staffed its notorious back-parlor brothels. Colorful characters now fill alleyway murals and anyone can make a fortune the easy way at Golden Gate Fortune Cookie Company (p132).

Spofford Alley

As sunset falls on sociable Spofford Alley, you'll hear clicking mah jong tiles and a Chinese orchestra warming up. But generations ago, you might have overheard Sun Yat-sen and his conspirators at number 36 plotting the 1911 overthrow of China's last dynasty.

Commercial St

Across Portsmouth Square from San Francisco's City Hall, this euphemistically named hot spot caught fire in 1906. The city banned the 25¢ Chinese brothels of Commercial St in favor of 'parlor houses,' where basic services were raised to $3.

1. Waverly Place 2. Ross Alley 3. Tien Hau Temple (p123)

Neighborhood Walk
North Beach Beat

START CITY LIGHTS BOOKSTORE
END LI PO
LENGTH 1.5 MILES; TWO HOURS

At ❶ **City Lights bookstore** (p131), home of Beat poetry and free speech, pick up something to inspire your journey into literary North Beach – Ferlinghetti's *San Francisco Poems* and Ginsberg's *Howl* are popular choices.

Head to ❷ **Caffe Trieste** (p127) for potent espresso and opera on the jukebox in the back booth, where Francis Ford Coppola allegedly drafted *The Godfather*.

At ❸ **Washington Square** (p118), you'll spot parrots in the treetops and octogenarians in tai-chi tiger stances on the lawn: pure poetry in motion. At the corner, focaccia hot from a 100-year-old oven makes ❹ **Liguria Bakery** (p124) a worthy pit stop.

Quiet ❺ **Bob Kaufman Alley** (p119) was named for the legendary street-corner poet, who broke a 12-year vow of silence when he walked into a North Beach cafe and recited his poem *All Those Ships That Never Sailed:* 'Today I bring them back/Huge and transitory/And let them sail/Forever.'

At the ❻ **Beat Museum** (p118) don't be surprised to hear a Dylan jam session by the front door or see a nude Allen Ginsberg onscreen inside: the Beat goes on here in rare form.

Begin your literary bar crawl at ❼ **Specs** (p127) amid merchant-marine memorabilia, tall tales and pitchers of Anchor Steam.

On the Road author Jack Kerouac once blew off Henry Miller to go on a bender, until ❽ **Vesuvio** (p130) bartenders ejected him into the street now named for him: ❾ **Jack Kerouac Alley** (p118). Note the words of Chinese poet Li Po embedded in the alley: 'In the company of friends, there is never enough wine.'

Follow the lead of Kerouac and Ginsberg and end your night under the laughing Buddha at ❿ **Li Po** (p130) – there many not be enough wine, but there's plenty of beer.

NORTH BEACH & CHINATOWN

Sleuthing by CHSA historians continues to uncover lost-and-found artifacts, including Jake Lee's fascinating 1960s watercolors of Chinese American history. Rotating art exhibits are held in CHSA's graceful red-brick, green-tile-roofed landmark building; check CHSA's website for openings and events.

PORTSMOUTH SQUARE — PARK

Map p334 (http://sfrecpark.org/destination/portsmouth-square; 733 Kearny St; ; 1, 8X, 10, 12, 30, 35, 41, California St, Powell-Hyde, Powell-Mason) Chinatown's unofficial living room is named after John B Montgomery's sloop, which staked the US claim on San Francisco here in 1846. This is where the Gold Rush began and where San Francisco's first city hall took over burlesque Jenny Lind Theater in 1852. The resident deity is the Goddess of Democracy, a bronze replica of the statue Tiananmen Square protesters made in 1989.

The action begins early and runs late in Portsmouth Square, where tai chi practitioners greet the dawn with outstretched arms and a lively night market is held during Chinese New Year and in summer (July to October). Each afternoon, toddlers rush the playground slides and tea-drinking crowds gather at the kiosk under the pedestrian bridge to joke and discuss the day's news. Checkers and chess played on concrete tables in gazebos late into the evening aren't just games but year-round obsessions, come rain or shine.

OLD ST MARY'S CATHEDRAL & SQUARE — CHURCH

Map p334 (415-288-3800; www.oldsaintmarys.org; 660 California St; 11am-6pm Mon-Tue, to 7pm Wed-Fri, 9am-6:30pm Sat, 9am-4:30pm Sun; 1, 30, 45, California St) California's first cathedral was built in 1854 by an Irish entrepreneur determined to give wayward San Francisco some religion – despite its location on brothel-lined Dupont St. Hence the stern admonition on the clock tower: 'Son, observe the time and fly from evil.' The 1906 earthquake miraculously spared the church's brick walls but destroyed a bordello across the street, making room for St Mary's Square.

Eventually the archdiocese abandoned attempts to convert Dupont St and handed the church over to America's first Chinese community mission, run by the activism-oriented Paulists. During WWII, Old St Mary's served 450,000 members of the US armed services as a recreation center and cafeteria.

Today, skateboarders do tricks of a different sort in the park, under the watchful eye of Beniamino Bufano's 1929 pink-granite-and-steel statue of Chinese revolutionary Sun Yat-sen.

CHINESE TELEPHONE EXCHANGE — HISTORICAL BUILDING

Map p334 (743 Washington St; 1, 30, 45, California St, Powell-Hyde, Powell-Mason) California's earliest adopters of advanced technology weren't in Silicon Valley but right here in Chinatown. This triple-decker tiled pagoda revolutionized communication in 1894. To connect callers, switchboard operators spoke fluent English and five Chinese dialects and memorized at least 1500 Chinatown residents by name, residence and occupation. Managers lived onsite and kept the switchboard operating 365 days a year.

Since anyone born in China was prohibited by law from visiting San Francisco throughout the 1882–1943 Chinese Exclusion era, this switchboard was the main means of contact with family and business partners in China for 60 years. The exchange operated until 1949 and the landmark was bought and restored by Bank of Canton in 1960.

TIEN HAU TEMPLE — TEMPLE

Map p334 (Tin How Temple; 125 Waverly Place; donation customary; hours vary; 1, 30, 45, California St, Powell-Mason, Powell-Hyde) There was no place to go but up in Chinatown in the 19th century, when laws restricted where Chinese San Franciscans could live and work. Atop barber shops, laundries and neighborhood associations lining Waverly Place, temples were built, their brightly painted balconies festooned with flags and lanterns. Tien Hou Temple was built in 1852 and its altar miraculously survived the 1906 earthquake.

To drop by and pay your respects, look for the narrow doorway with the sign that says 'Tin How' under the yellow balcony and follow the scent of sandalwood incense up three flights of stairs. Entry is free, but it's customary to leave an offering for temple upkeep. No photography is allowed inside the temple.

DRAGON'S GATE
MONUMENT

Map p334 (intersection of Grant Ave & Bush St; 🚌1, 8X, 30, 45, 🚋California St) Enter the Dragon archway and you'll find yourself on the street formerly known as Dupont in its notorious red-light heyday. Sixty years before the family-friendly overhaul of the Las Vegas Strip, Look Tin Eli and a group of forward-thinking Chinatown businessmen pioneered the approach here in Chinatown, replacing seedy attractions with more tourist-friendly ones.

After consultation with architects and community groups, Dupont St was transformed into Grant Ave, freshly adorned with deco-chinoiserie dragon lamps and tiled pagoda rooftops, and police were reluctantly persuaded to enforce the 1914 Red Light Abatement Act in Chinatown. By the time this gate was donated by Taiwan in 1970, grandly proclaiming that 'everything in the world is in just proportions,' Chinatown finally had a main street that did the community greater justice.

GOOD LUCK PARKING GARAGE
LANDMARK

Map p334 (735 Vallejo St; 🚌10, 12, 30, 41, 45, 🚋Powell-Mason) Each parking spot at this garage comes with fortune-cookie wisdom stenciled onto the asphalt: 'The time is right to make new friends' or 'Stop searching forever: happiness is just next to you.' These omens are supplied by artists Harrell Fletcher and Jon Rubin, who also gathered local residents' photographs of Chinese and Italian ancestors to grace the entry like heraldic emblems.

EATING

North Beach

★ LIGURIA BAKERY
BAKERY $

Map p334 (🞎415-421-3786; 1700 Stockton St; focaccia $4-5; ⊗8am-1pm Mon-Fri, from 7am Sat; 🚼👶; 🚌8X, 30, 39, 41, 45, 🚋Powell-Mason) Bleary-eyed art students and Italian grandmothers are in line by 8am for cinnamon-raisin focaccia hot out of the 100-year-old oven, leaving 9am dawdlers a choice of tomato or classic rosemary/garlic and 11am stragglers out of luck. Take yours in wax paper or boxed for picnics – but don't kid yourself that you're going to save some for later. Cash only.

CINECITTÀ
PIZZA $

Map p334 (🞎415-291-8830; www.cinecittares taurant.com; 663 Union St; pizzas $12-15; ⊗noon-10pm Sun-Thu, to 11pm Fri & Sat; 🚼👶; 🚌8X, 30, 39, 41, 45, 🚋Powell-Mason) Follow tantalizing aromas into this eatery for thin-crust Roman pizza, made from scratch by Roman owner Romina. Local loyalties are divided between the Roman Travestere (fresh mozzarella, arugula and prosciutto) and Neapolitan O Sole Mio (capers, olives, mozzarella and anchovies). Local brews are on tap, house wine is $5 from 3pm to 7pm and Romina's tiramisu is San Francisco's best.

MOLINARI
DELI $

Map p334 (🞎415-421-2337; www.molinarisalame. com; 373 Columbus Ave; sandwiches $5-8; ⊗9am-5:30pm Mon-Fri, 7:30am-5pm Sat; 🚌8X, 30, 39, 41, 45, 🚋Powell-Mason) Grab a number and a crusty roll, and when your number rolls around, wise-cracking deli staff in paper hats will stuff it with translucent sheets of *prosciutto di Parma,* milky buffalo mozzarella, tender marinated artichokes or slabs of the legendary house-cured salami (the city's best). Eat yours hot from the panini press at sidewalk tables or Washington Square.

MAMA'S
BRUNCH $

Map p334 (🞎415-362-6421; www.mamas-sf. com; 1701 Stockton St; brunch mains $7.95-13.50; ⊗8am-3pm Tue-Sun; 👶; 🚌8X, 🚋Powell-Mason) Generations of North Beachers have entrusted the most important meal of the day to Mama and Papa Sanchez, whose sunny Victorian storefront diner has offered definitive cures for barbaric Barbary Coast hangovers for 50 years. Local farm-egg omelettes and *kugelhopf* (house-baked brioche) French toast are cure-alls, but weekend specials like Dungeness-crab eggs benedict make waits down the block worthwhile.

BRIOCHE BAKERY
BAKERY, SANDWICHES $

Map p334 (🞎415-765-0412; http://briochecafe. com; 210 Columbus Ave; pastries $2-6, sandwiches $8.50-10; ⊗7am-8pm; 🛜👶👶; 🚌8X, 10, 12, 30, 45, 🚋Powell-Mason, Powell-Hyde) When Gold Rush miners found gold they treated themselves to 'Frenchy food' along San Francisco's Barbary Coast. Now you too can strike it rich here with flaky cinnamon twists and not-too-sweet *pain au chocolat* (chocolate croissants). Return for decadent North Beach–inspired tartines with *prosciutto di Parma,* avocado, pear and herbed ricotta, drizzled with honey.

ℹ️ CHINATOWN HERITAGE WALKING TOURS

Local-led, kid-friendly **Chinatown Heritage Walking Tours** (📞415-986-1822; www. c-c-c.org; adult/child $30/25; ⊙tours 10am, noon & 2pm Tue-Sat) guide visitors through the living history and mythology of Chinatown in two hours, winding through back-streets to key historic sights: Golden Gate Fortune Cookie Factory, Tien Hau Temple and Portsmouth Square. Tour themes include The Tale of Two Chinatowns, covering Chinatown's daily life and cultural influence, and From Dynasty to Democracy, which explores Chinatown's role in the US civil rights movement and international human rights struggles. All proceeds support Chinatown community programming at the Chinese Culture Center; bookings can be made online or by phone. Groups of four or more should book two days in advance.

MARA'S ITALIAN PASTRY
PASTRY $

Map p334 (📞415-397-9435; 503 Columbus Ave; pastries $2-6; ⊙7am-10:30pm Sun-Thu, to midnight Fri-Sat; 🚌8X, 30, 39, 41, 45, 🚋Powell-Mason) Join early risers for shots of Illy espresso and *crostata* (jam tart), or wander in at night between bars and Beach Blanket Babylon for *torta di mandorla* (almond-meal tart with layer of jam) and choco-late-chip-ricotta cannoli. Twice-baked, extra-crunchy biscotti are an acquired taste for non-Italians – try dunking them in *vin santo* – but pine-nut-studded chewy pignoli are cross-cultural crowd-pleasers.

MARIO'S BOHEMIAN CIGAR STORE CAFE
CAFE $

Map p334 (📞415-362-0536; 566 Columbus Ave; sandwiches $7.50-11; ⊙10am-10pm; 🚌8X, 30, 39, 41, 45, 🚋Powell-Mason) A Boho North Beach holdout on Washington Square Park, Mario's gave up smoking in the 1970s and turned to piping-hot panini. The oven-baked onion foccacia sandwiches are satisfying but mostly a pretense to people-watch while glugging wine by the carafe and pints of Anchor Steam served by art-schooled wait staff.

TONY'S COAL-FIRED PIZZA & SLICE HOUSE
PIZZA $

Map p334 (📞415-835-9888; www.tonyspizza napoletana.com; 1556 Stockton St; slices $3.75-5; ⊙noon-11pm Wed-Sun; 🚌8X, 30, 39, 41, 45, 🚋Powell-Mason) Fuggedaboudit, New York pizza loyalists: in San Francisco, you can grab a cheesy, thin-crust slice from nine-times world champion pizza-slinger Tony Gemignani. What, you were expecting meat-ball subs and Kosher salt shakers? Done. Difference is, here you can take that slice to sunny Washington Square, and watch tai chi practice and wild parrots year-round. Sorry, Manhattan – whaddayagonnado?

RISTORANTE IDEALE
ROMAN, ITALIAN $$

Map p334 (📞415-391-4129; www.idealerestau rant.com; 1315 Grant Ave; pasta $15-18; ⊙5:30-10:30pm Mon-Thu, to 11pm Fri-Sat, 5-10pm Sun; 🚌8X, 10, 12, 30, 41, 45, 🚋Powell-Mason) Other North Beach restaurants fake Italian accents, but this trattoria has Italians in the kitchen, on the floor and at the table. Roman chef Maurizio Bruschi serves authentic, al dente *bucatini ammatriciana* (tube pasta with tomato-pecorino sauce and house-cured pancetta) and ravioli and gnocchi handmade in-house ('of course!'). Ask Tuscan staff to recommend well-priced wine and everyone goes home happy.

⭐COI
CALIFORNIAN $$$

Map p334 (📞415-393-9000; www.coirestaurant. com; 373 Broadway; set menu $175; ⊙5:30-10pm Wed-Sat; 🅿; 🚌8X, 30, 41, 45, 🚋Powell-Mason) 🍴 Chef Daniel Patterson's restlessly imaginative eight-course tasting menu is like licking the California coastline: purple ice-plant petals are strewn atop warm duck's tongue, and wild-caught Monterey Bay abalone appears in a tidepool of pea shoots. The 70s-retreat-inspired decor belies the freshness of the constantly changing seasonal menu and adventurous wine pairings ($105; generous enough for two to share).

Reserve ahead, especially for winemaker dinners ($150 including wine pairing). No need to worry about tip or parking: 18% service is added and valet parking available.

CAFE JACQUELINE
FRENCH $$$

Map p334 (📞415-981-5565; 1454 Grant Ave; souf-flés $15-25 per person; ⊙5:30-11pm Wed-Sun; 🚌8X, 30, 39, 41, 45, 🚋Powell-Mason) The secret terror of top chefs is the classic French soufflé, but Chef Jacqueline's perfectly puffy creations float across the tongue like fog over the Golden Gate Bridge. With the right person across the tiny wooden table to share that seafood soufflé, dinner could hardly get more romantic – until you order the chocolate or seasonal berry version for dessert.

PARK TAVERN
CALIFORNIAN **$$$**

Map p334 (☎415-989-7300; www.parktavernsf.com; 1652 Stockton St; mains dinner $21-33, brunch $12-16; ☺5:30-11pm Mon-Thu, 11:30am-12:30am Fri, 10:30am-midnight Sat-Sun; ☒8X, 30, 39, 41, 45, ☐Powell-Mason) An instant Washington Square institution, this women-run, Kiwi-founded bistro cheekily updates Italian-accented standards with California ingredients: gnocchi with golden chanterelles, venison carpaccio with bone marrow and capers, polenta cakes with truffled salsa verde. Brunch brings oatmeal-raisin pancakes slathered with cherry-bourbon preserves and grapefruit mimosas. Never mind the noise; have a Negroni and some Brussels-sprout chips and join the happy din.

✖ Chinatown

CITY VIEW
DIM SUM **$**

Map p334 (☎415-398-2838; 662 Commercial St; dishes $3-8; ☺11am-2:30pm Mon-Fri, from 10am Sat & Sun; ☒8X, 10, 12, 30, 45, ☐California St) Take your seat in the sunny dining room and your pick from carts loaded with delicate shrimp and leek dumplings, garlicky Chinese broccoli, tangy spare ribs, coconut-dusted custard tarts and other tantalizing dim sum. Arrive before or after the midday lunch rush, so you don't have to flag down speeding carts to peek inside those fragrant bamboo steamers.

ℹ HOW TO TELL ITALIAN IMPOSTERS

When choosing an Italian restaurant in North Beach, use this rule of thumb: if a host has to lure you inside with, 'Ciao, bella!', keep walking. Ditto for any restaurant with a gimmicky or too-obvious name – Stinking Rose and Mona Lisa are every bit as touristy as you'd expect. Try smaller neighborhood restaurants on side streets off Grant Ave and Washington St, where staff gossip in Italian.

Z & Y
SICHUAN, CHINESE **$$**

Map p334 (☎415-981-8988; www.zandyrestaurant.com; 655 Jackson St; mains $9-18; ☺11am-10pm Mon-Thu, to 11pm Fri-Sun; ☒8X, ☐Powell-Mason, Powell-Hyde) Graduate from ho-hum sweet-and-sour and middling mu shu to sensational Szechuan dishes that go down in a blaze of glory. Warm up with spicy pork dumplings and heat-blistered string beans, take on the house-made tantan noodles with peanut-chili sauce, and leave lips buzzing with fish poached in flaming chili oil and buried under red Szechuan chili-peppers. Go early; expect a wait.

GREAT EASTERN RESTAURANT
CHINESE, DIM SUM **$$**

Map p334 (☎415-986-2500; http://greateastern restaurant.net; 649 Jackson St; mains $8-20; ☺10am-11pm Mon-Thu, 9am-midnight Sat-Sun; ♿; ☒8X, ☐Powell-Mason, Powell-Hyde) Eat your way across China in this classic tiled Chinatown restaurant, from northern Peking duck to southern pan-fried shrimp and chive dumplings. President Obama stopped by Great Eastern for takeout, and weekend dim-sum throngs around noon may make you wish for your own secret-service escort – call ahead for reservations or come around 1pm as brunch crowds stagger out happy.

HOUSE OF NANKING
CHINESE **$$**

Map p334 (☎415-421-1429; 919 Kearny St; mains $9-15; ☺11am-10pm Mon-Fri, noon-10pm Sat, noon-9pm Sun; ☒8X, 10, 12, 30, 45, ☐Powell-Mason) Meekly suggest an interest in seafood, nothing deep-fried, perhaps some greens and your server nods, grabs the menu and returns laden with Shanghai specialties: fragrant sautéed pea shoots with scallops, garlicky noodles and black-bean-glazed eggplant. Expect bossy service, a wait for a shared table and a strict cash-only policy – but also bright, fresh flavors at reasonable prices.

YUET LEE
CHINESE, SEAFOOD **$$**

Map p334 (☎415-982-6020; 1300 Stockton St; mains $8-17.50; ☺11am-3am Wed-Sat & Mon, to midnight Sun; ♿; ☒8X, 10, 12, 30, 41, 45, ☐Powell-Mason) With a radioactive-green paint job and merciless fluorescent lighting, this Chinese seafood diner isn't for first dates, but for drinking buddies and committed couples who have nothing to hide and are willing to share batter-fried, salt-and-pepper calamari and tender roast duck.

BANQUETS AT JAI YUN

Wedding banquets in Shanghai got a lot less lavish when Chef Nei moved to San Francisco and opened **Jai Yun** (Map p334; ☑415-981-7438; 680 Clay St; from $65 per person; ⏱by reservation only 6:30-9:30pm; ☒8X, ☒California St), where he serves 12- to 22-course market-fresh feasts. There's no menu, since the chef creates his Shanghai-style fare based on what's freshest that day – but fingers crossed, your banquet will include ethereal abalone that floats over the tongue like a kite over Crissy Field, housemade rice noodles with cured pancetta, and lacy, paper-thin pickled lotus root. Never mind that the restaurant has more mirrors than a Bruce Lee movie and creepy dining-room surveillance cameras – all attention is on sophisticated, fascinating flavors. Prices are based on party size: with 5–10 people, meal price starts at $65 per person; for 3–4 prices start at $80 per person; and for two the price begins at $98 per person. Pay more and you can pile on even more courses. Mention any food allergies or aversions when you book. Wine selection is limited, so bring your own and pay corkage. Dessert is a token sweet but you won't miss it after such feasts.

🍷 DRINKING & NIGHTLIFE

🍸 North Beach

★COMSTOCK SALOON
BAR

Map p334 (☑415-617-0071; www.comstocksaloon.com; 155 Columbus Ave; ⏱4pm-2am Sat-Thu, from noon Fri; ☒8X, 10, 12, 30, 45, ☒Powell-Mason) Welcome to the Barbary Coast, where cocktails at this Victorian saloon remain period-perfect: Pisco Punch is made with pineapple gum and martini-precursor Martinez features gin, vermouth, bitters and maraschino liqueur. Call ahead to claim booths or tufted-velvet parlor seating, so you can hear dates when mezzanine ragtime-jazz bands play. Daytime drinking is rewarded Fridays, when lunch is free with two-drink purchase.

The adjacent street-corner dining room is the kind of place you might take a madam for late-night dinners of decadent roast duck pot pie or the naughty rabbit three-way (terrine, rillette, chicken-fried).

★SPECS MUSEUM CAFE
BAR

Map p334 (☑415-421-4112; 12 William Saroyan Pl; ⏱5pm-2am; ☒8X, 10, 12, 30, 41, 45, ☒Powell-Mason) What do you do with a drunken sailor? Here's your answer. The walls are plastered with merchant-marine mementos and you'll be plastered too if you try to keep up with the salty old-timers holding court in back. Surrounded by nautical memorabilia, your order is obvious: pitcher of Anchor Steam, coming right up.

★CAFFE TRIESTE
CAFE

Map p334 (☑415-392-6739; www.caffetrieste.com; 601 Vallejo St; ⏱6:30am-10pm Sun-Thu, to 11pm Fri & Sat; ☎; ☒8X, 10, 12, 30, 41, 45) Poetry on bathroom walls, opera on the jukebox, live accordion jams weekly and sightings of Beat poet laureate Lawrence Ferlinghetti: this is North Beach at its best, since the 1950s. Linger over a legendary espresso and scribble your screenplay under the Sicilian mural just as young Francis Ford Coppola did. Perhaps you've heard of the movie: it was called *The Godfather*.

TOSCA CAFE
BAR

Map p334 (☑415-986-9651; www.toscacafesf.com; 242 Columbus Ave; ⏱5pm-2am Tue-Sun; ☒8X, 10, 12, 30, 41, 45, ☒Powell-Mason) Regulars Sean Penn, Bobby DeNiro and Sofia Coppola could base their next character studies on regulars sipping *caffe corretto* (espresso 'corrected' with liquor) in these retro red-leather booths. Under new ownership, SF's sultry film-noir bar now has restored 1930s murals, a revived menu and, as always, jukebox opera to set the mood.

15 ROMOLO
BAR

Map p334 (☑415-398-1359; www.15romolo.com; 15 Romolo Pl; ⏱5pm-2am Mon-Fri, 11:30am-3:30pm & 5pm-2am Sat-Sun; ☒8X, 10, 12, 30, 41, 45, ☒Powell-Mason) What a wild-west saloon should be: down an alley flanked by burlesque joints, with dangerously delicious cocktails straight out of a long-lost Tim Burton Gothic western. The Inflorescence is a knockout potion of tequila,

DAVID CLAPP / GETTY IMAGES ©

DIANA MAYFIELD / GETTY IMAGES ©

1. Filbert St Steps (p117)
Parrots squawk as pedestrians ascend Telegraph Hill, passing hidden cottages and gardens to reach Coit Tower.

2. Dragon's Gate (p124)
Marking the entrance to Chinatown, this gate at the intersection of Grant Ave and Bush St greets visitors to this bustling area.

3. City Lights (p131)
One of the world's most famous bookstores, this North Beach institution was at the center of the Beat movement.

chartreuse, lemon, Earl Grey bitters and foamy egg whites, but you'll lose your head over the Anne Boleyn, with gin, Aperol and Lillet Rose.

Happy hour runs 5:00pm to 7:30pm daily, and spiffy, hearty dishes like lamb pot pie and bone marrow fritters are served until 1:30am – but bear in mind bathrooms are limited.

VESUVIO   BAR

Map p334 (☎415-362-3370; www.vesuvio.com; 255 Columbus Ave; ⏱6am-2am; ☐8X, 10, 12, 30, 41, 45, ☐Powell-Mason) Guy walks into a bar, roars and leaves. Without missing a beat, the bartender says to the next customer, 'Welcome to Vesuvio, honey – what can I get you?' Jack Kerouac blew off Henry Miller to go on a bender here, and after joining neighborhood characters on the stained-glass mezzanine for microbrews or Kerouacs (rum, tequila and OJ), you'll get why.

SALOON   BAR

Map p334 (☎415-989-7666; www.sfblues.net/Saloon.html; 1232 Grant Ave; weekend cover $2-5; ⏱noon-2am; ☐8X, 10, 12, 30, 41, 45, ☐Powell-Mason) Blues in a red saloon that's been jumping since 1861: what more do you need on a North Beach night? When the rest of San Francisco burned in 1906, loyal patrons saved the Saloon by dousing it with buckets of hooch. Today it's the oldest bar in SF, and blues and rock bands perform nightly and from 4pm weekend afternoons. Cash only.

Chinatown

LI PO   BAR

Map p334 (☎415-982-0072; www.lipolounge.com; 916 Grant Ave; ⏱2pm-2am; ☐8X, 30, 45, ☐Powell-Mason, Powell-Hyde) Beat a hasty retreat to red vinyl booths where Allen Ginsberg and Jack Kerouac debated the meaning of life alongside a bemused golden Buddha. Enter the vintage 1937 faux-grotto doorway and dodge red lanterns to place your order: Tsing Tao beer or sweet, sneaky-strong Chinese mai tai made with *baiju* (rice liquor). Bathrooms and random DJ appearances are in the basement.

RÉVEILLE   CAFE

Map p334 (☎415-789-6258; http://reveille coffee.com; 200 Columbus St; ⏱7am-6pm Mon-Fri, 8am-6pm Sat, 8am-5pm Sun; ♿☻; ☐8X, 10, 12, 30, 41, 45, ☐Powell-Mason) If this sunny flatiron storefront doesn't instantly lighten your mood, cappuccino with a foam-art heart will. Réveille's coffee is like San Francisco on a good day: nutty and uplifting, without a trace of bitterness. Check the circular marble counter for just-baked chocolate-chip cookies and sticky buns. No wi-fi makes for easy conversation and sidewalk-facing counters offer some of SF's best people-watching.

BUDDHA LOUNGE   BAR

Map p334 (☎415-362-1792; 901 Grant Ave; ⏱1pm-2am Mon-Sat; ☐8X, 30, 45, ☐Powell-Mason, Powell-Hyde) Vintage red neon promises evenings worthy of WWII sailors on shore leave. Drink in the atmosphere, but stick to basic well drinks and beer straight from a laughing Buddha bottle. Cue selections on the eclectic jukebox (Outkast, The Clash), ask the bartender for dice and you're in for the duration. Bathrooms are in the former opium-den basement. Cash only.

☆ ENTERTAINMENT

BEACH BLANKET BABYLON   LIVE MUSIC

Map p334 (BBB; ☎415-421-4222; www.beach blanketbabylon.com; 678 Green St; admission $25-100; ⏱shows 8pm Wed, Thu & Fri, 6:30pm & 9:30pm Sat, 2pm & 5pm Sun; ☐8X, ☐Powell-Mason) Snow White searches for Prince Charming in San Francisco: what could possibly go wrong? The Disney-spoof musical-comedy cabaret has been running since 1974, but topical jokes keep it outrageous and production numbers involving wigs big as parade floats are gasp-worthy. Pop icons and heads of state are spoofed by actors in campy costumes – even when President Obama, Queen Elizabeth and SF Giants attended.

Spectators must be over 21 to handle racy humor, except at cleverly sanitized Sunday matinees. Reservations essential; arrive one hour early for best seats.

BIMBO'S 365 CLUB   LIVE MUSIC

Map p334 (☎415-474-0365; www.bimbos365 club.com; 1025 Columbus Ave; tickets from $22; ⏱shows vary; ☐8X, 30, 39, 41, 45, ☐Powell-Mason) This vintage-1931 speakeasy plays fast and loose with strong drink, a polished parquet dance floor where Rita Hayworth once high-kicked in the chorus line, bawdy bar murals and intimate live shows by the likes of Adele, Beck, The Flaming Lips and Sandra Bernhard. Cash only and bring change to tip the ladies' powder room attendant – this is a classy joint.

COBB'S COMEDY CLUB COMEDY

Map p334 (☑415-928-4320; www.cobbscomedyclub.com; 915 Columbus Ave; admission $12.50-45, plus two-drink minimum; ◷shows 7:30/8pm & 10pm; ᰦ8X, 30, 39, 41, 45, ᰦPowell-Mason) There's no room to be shy at Cobb's, where bumper-to-bumper shared tables make an intimate (and vulnerable) audience. The venue is known for launching local talent and giving big-name acts from Dave Chappelle to Louis CK a place to try risky new material. Check the website for shows and comically twisted events – Father's Day Burlesque Brunch, anyone?

🔒 SHOPPING

🔒 North Beach

★ CITY LIGHTS BOOKSTORE

Map p334 (☑415-362-8193; www.citylights.com; 261 Columbus Ave; ◷10am-midnight; ᰦ8X, 10, 12, 30, 41, 45, ᰦPowell-Mason, Powell-Hyde) 🖋 'Abandon all despair, all ye who enter,' orders the sign by the door to City Lights bookstore by founder and San Francisco poet laureate Lawrence Ferlinghetti. This commandment is easy to follow upstairs in the sunny **Poetry Room**, with its piles of freshly published verse, a designated **Poet's Chair** and literary views of laundry strung across Jack Kerouac Alley.

Poetic justice has been served here since 1957, when City Lights won a landmark free speech ruling over publishing Allen Ginsberg's incendiary epic poem 'Howl', and went on to publish Charles Bukowski, Angela Davis and Zapatista Subcomandante Marcos, among others. City Lights publications are showcased on the mezzanine, while the nonfiction cellar is organized by provocative themes like Stolen Continents, Muckraking and Commodity Aesthetics. When you abandon despair, you make more room for books.

ARIA ANTIQUES, COLLECTIBLES

Map p334 (☑415-433-0219; 1522 Grant Ave; ◷11am-6pm Mon-Sat, noon-5pm Sun; ᰦ8X, 30, 39, 41, 45, ᰦPowell-Mason) Find inspiration for your own North Beach epic poem on Aria's weathered wood counters, piled with anatomical drawings of starfish, castle keys lost in gutters a century ago, rusty numbers pried from French village walls and 19th-century letters still in their wax-sealed envelopes. Hours are erratic whenever owner/chief scavenger Bill Haskell is out treasure-hunting, so call ahead.

101 MUSIC MUSIC

Map p334 (☑415-392-6369; 1414 Grant Ave; ◷10am-8pm Tue-Sat, from noon Sun; ᰦ8X, 30, 39, 41, 45, ᰦPowell-Mason) You'll have to bend over those bins to let DJs and hardcore collectors pass (and, hey, wasn't that Tom Waits?!), but among the $5–20 discs are obscure releases (Songs for Greek Lovers) and original recordings by Nina Simone, Janis Joplin and San Francisco's own anthem-rockers, Journey.

AL'S ATTIRE CLOTHING, ACCESSORIES

Map p334 (☑415-693-9900; www.alsattire.com; 1300 Grant Ave; ◷11am-7pm Mon-Sat, noon-6pm Sun; ᰦ8X, 10, 12, 30, 41, 45, ᰦPowell-Mason) Hepcats and slick chicks get their threads at Al's, where vintage styles are reinvented in noir-novel twill, dandy high-sheen cotton and midcentury flecked tweeds. Prices aren't exactly bohemian, but turquoise wing-tips are custom-made to fit your feet and svelte hand-stitched jackets have silver-screen star quality. Ask about custom orders for weddings and other shindigs.

BUYER'S BEST FRIEND MERCATO FOOD, DRINK

Map p334 (☑415-223-3912; www.bbfdirect.com; 450 Columbus Ave; ◷11am-10pm; ᰦ8X, 30, 39, 41, 45, ᰦPowell-Mason) Free samples of local artisan food and drink make tasty snacks and effective sales ploys – before you know it, you've had a light meal of Dang coconut chips, agave-sweetened Amella caramels and Teatulia lemongrass tea and bought Sixth Course fennel-pollen chocolates and GLOB kids' veggie finger-paints. Spend enough and chipper staff will throw in free organic energy bars.

ROCK POSTERS & COLLECTIBLES ANTIQUES

Map p334 (☑415-956-6749; www.rockposters.com; 1851 Powell St; ◷10am-6pm Mon-Sat; ᰦ8X, 30, 39, 41, 45, ᰦPowell-Mason) Anyone who loves vintage music must visit this trippy temple to classic rock gods. Nostalgia isn't cheap here: expect to pay hundreds for

TEA TASTING

Several Grant Ave tea importers let you sample tea free, but the hard sell may begin before you finish sipping. For a more relaxed, enlightening teatime experience, Red Blossom Tea Company (p132) offers half-hour tea immersion classes with tastings and tips on preparing tea for maximum flavor ($30 for up to four participants). Drop-in classes may be available weekdays but call ahead on weekends; seating is limited.

first-run psychedelic Fillmore concert posters featuring Jimi Hendrix or the Grateful Dead. But you can still find deals on handbills for 1970s San Francisco acts like Santana, Dead Kennedys and Sly and the Family Stone.

DOUBLE PUNCH   TOYS, ART

Map p334 (www.doublepunch.com; 1821 Powell St; ⊘11am-7pm Mon-Sat, to 6pm Sun; 🚍8X, 30, 39, 41, 45, 🚋Powell-Mason) Art and collectible toys line these walls, making Double Punch doubly dangerous for collectors with kids. Upstairs gallery artworks are by emerging local artists (San Francisco Art Institute is nearby), while limited-edition toys include official-issue Kubricks from local studios Pixar and LucasFilm. Prices run high for David Choe's hand-painted wooden warriors but check the $5 bargain bin for kid-friendly finds.

🏯 Chinatown

GOLDEN GATE FORTUNE
COOKIE COMPANY   FOOD, DRINK

Map p334 (☎415-781-3956; 56 Ross Alley; ⊘8am-6pm; 🚍30, 45, 🚋Powell-Mason, Powell-Hyde) Make a fortune in San Francisco at this bakery, where cookies are stamped from vintage presses and folded while hot – much as they were in 1909, when fortune cookies were invented for San Francisco's Japanese Tea Garden (p204). Write your own fortunes for custom cookies (50¢ each) or get bags of regular or risqué cookies. Cash only; 50¢ tip per photo.

RED BLOSSOM TEA COMPANY   TEA

Map p334 (☎415-395-0868; www.redblossomtea.com; 831 Grant Ave; ⊘10am-6:30pm Mon-Sat, to 6pm Sun; 🚍1, 10, 12, 30, 35, 41, 🚋Powell-Mason, Powell-Hyde, California St) Crook your pinky: it's always teatime at Red Blossom, featuring 100 specialty teas imported by brother-sister team Alice and Peter Luong. Sniff shiny canisters lining wooden shelves, ask about seasonal blends and try premium blends before you buy. For gourmet gifts, go with namesake blossoms – tightly wound balls of tea that unfurl into flowers in hot water.

CLARION MUSIC CENTER   MUSIC

Map p334 (☎415-391-1317; www.clarionmusic.com; 816 Sacramento St; ⊘11am-6pm Mon-Fri, 9am-5pm Sat; 🚍1, 30, 45, 🚋California St) Minor chords played on *erhu* (Chinese two-stringed instrument) pluck at your heartstrings as you walk through Chinatown's alleyways; here you can try your hand at the bow on a rosewood student model. With impressive ranges of congas, gongs and hand-carved drums, you could become your own multiculti, one-man band. Check the website for concerts, workshops and demonstrations by masters.

CHINATOWN KITE SHOP   GIFTS

Map p334 (☎415-989-5182; www.chinatownkite.com; 717 Grant Ave; ⊘10am-8pm; 👶; 🚍1, 10, 12, 30, 35, 41, 🚋Powell-Hyde, Powell-Mason, California St) Be the star of Crissy Field and wow any kids in your life with a fierce 9ft-long flying dragon, a pirate-worthy wild parrot (SF's city bird), surreal floating legs or a flying panda bear that looks understandably stunned. Pick up a two-person, papier-mâché lion dance costume and invite a date to bust ferocious moves with you next lunar new year.

FAR EAST FLEA MARKET   GIFTS

Map p334 (☎415-989-8588; 729 Grant Ave; ⊘10am-9:30pm; 🚍1, 10, 12, 30, 35, 41, 🚋Powell-Mason, Powell-Hyde, California St) The shopping equivalent of crack, this bottomless store is dangerously cheap and certain to make you giddy and delusional. Of course you can get that $8.99 samurai sword through airport security! There's no such thing as too many bath toys, bobble-heads and Chia Pets! Step away from the $1 Golden Gate Bridge snow globes while there's still time...

Nob Hill, Russian Hill & Fillmore

NOB & RUSSIAN HILLS | JAPANTOWN & PACIFIC HEIGHTS

Neighborhood Top Five

1 Stepping off the Powell-Hyde cable car atop twisty **Lombard St** (p135) and thrilling to spectacular hilltop vistas.

2 Marveling at afternoon fog blowing through the Golden Gate, from atop **George Sterling Park** (p136).

3 Soaking naked in silence in communal Japanese baths at **Kabuki Springs & Spa** (p148).

4 Eating sushi and catching big-name jazz acts at **Yoshi's** (p144).

5 Shopping for Japanime and kooky ephemera at the vintage-'60s **Japan Center** (p146).

For more detail of this area, see Map p331 and p332 ➡

Lonely Planet's Top Tip

Cable cars serve Russian and Nob Hills, but the Powell St lines have notoriously long waits at their terminuses. Alternatively take the California St line, which rarely has queues. Ride west from the foot of Market St to Van Ness Ave, then walk to Pacific Heights and Japantown. Instead of taking busy California St west of Van Ness, walk along pretty Sacramento St (one block north of California), detouring through Lafayette Park.

✖ Best Places to Eat

→ Acquerello (p142)

→ Swan Oyster Depot (p139)

→ Tataki (p142)

→ Out the Door (p143)

→ Leopold's (p139)

For reviews, see p139 ➡

🍷 Best Places to Drink

→ Tonga Room (p143)

→ Amélie (p143)

→ Hi-Lo Club (p143)

→ 1300 on Fillmore (p144)

→ Social Study (p144)

For reviews, see p143 ➡

👁 Best Places for Live Music

→ Yoshi's (p144)

→ Boom Boom Room (p144)

→ Fillmore Auditorium (p144)

→ Red Devil Lounge (p144)

→ Sheba Piano Lounge (p145)

For reviews, see p144 ➡

Explore the Hills & Japantown

Tackle Japantown and Pacific Heights together – they're adjacent and connect via Fillmore St. Start at the intersection of Geary Blvd and Fillmore St, wander Japantown, then go north on Fillmore to window-shop spiffy boutiques. Continue uphill till the street becomes residential, around Jackson St, then walk west to Alta Plaza Park for knockout hilltop city-view picnics – there's a fantastic playground, too.

Russian and Nob Hills are likewise adjacent, but their ultra-steep gradients render them harder to explore on foot if you're out of shape. Fortunately they're accessible via cable car. Nob Hill stands between downtown and Chinatown; Russian Hill abuts Fisherman's Wharf and North Beach. Consider exploring the hills with these other neighborhoods. Polk St is the happening shopping and nightlife strip near Russian Hill; Fillmore St, in Pacific Heights, is swankier by day, quieter by night.

Local Life

→**Jazz** The city's jazz clubs lie south of Geary St, along Fillmore St; wander between piano bars and jazz clubs before deciding which you like best.

→**Cinema** Locals come to Japantown for dinner and a movie at Sundance Kabuki Cinema, which serves food and wine in its main theater.

→**Shopping** Most visitors only see the inside of the mall at Japan Center but there's also shopping *outside* the mall, along Post St, from Webster St to Laguna St.

→**Canines** Dog lovers flock to Alta Plaza Park for a pug parade – awww! – on the first Sunday of the month, 1pm to 4pm.

Getting There & Away

→**Bus** The 1, 2, 3 and 38 connect Downtown with Japantown; the 22 connects Japantown with the Marina and the Mission. Buses 10 and 12 link Downtown with the Hills; the 10 continues to Pacific Heights. The 27 connects Mission, SoMa and Downtown to Nob Hill. Buses 41 and 45 connect Downtown to Russian Hill and Cow Hollow.

→**Cable car** The Powell-Hyde cable car serves Russian and Nob Hills; the Powell-Mason line serves Nob Hill; and the California line runs between downtown, Nob Hill and the easternmost edge of Pacific Heights.

→**Parking** Street parking is difficult but possible. Find garages at Japan Center on Fillmore St (between Geary and Post Sts) and Post St (between Webster and Buchanan Sts).

JIM CORWIN / GETTY IMAGES ©

TOP SIGHT
LOMBARD ST

You've seen its eight switchbacks in 1000 photographs and maybe a few movies and TV shows, too. Hitchcock used it in *Vertigo*, MTV shot episodes of *The Real World* here and Barbra Streisand and Ryan O'Neal came flying down the twisty street in the classic-cinema car chase in *What's Up, Doc?* Everyone knows Lombard St as the 'world's crookedest street,' but is it really true?

Russian Hill, as it descends Lombard St, has a natural 27% grade – too steep in the 1920s for automobiles to ascend. Lombard St property owners decided to install a series of curves. The result is what you see today: a red-brick street with eight sweeping turns, divided by lovingly tended flower beds and 250 steps rising on either side.

Once the street appeared on postcards in the 1950s, the tourist board dubbed it the 'world's crookedest street,' which is factually incorrect. Vermont St, on Potrero Hill, between 20th and 22nd Sts, deserves this cred but don't bother trekking across town: Lombard St is (way) prettier. To avoid throngs of tourists, come early morning, but chances are it'll be foggy; for sun-lit pictures, time your visit for late morning (the hill faces east).

Don't try anything funny. The recent clampdown on renegade skaters means that the Lombard St thrills featured in the *Tony Hawk's Pro Skater* video game will remain strictly virtual, at least until the cops get slack. Until 2008, every Easter Sunday for seven years adults had arrived at the crest of Lombard St toting plastic toy tricycles for the annual Bring Your Own Big Wheel Race. But after vehement complaints from kill-joy residents, the art-prankster organizers moved their toy-joyride to – where else? – Vermont St. Check http://bringyourownbigwheel.com for the latest.

DON'T MISS...

➡ Snapping pictures from the bottom of the hill, looking up

➡ Arriving via the Powell-Hyde cable car

➡ Seeing Lombard St from Coit Tower, the next hill over

PRACTICALITIES

➡ Map p332

➡ 900 block of Lombard St

➡ 🚋Powell-Hyde

◉ SIGHTS

◉ Nob & Russian Hills

LOMBARD ST STREET
See p135.

GRACE CATHEDRAL CHURCH
Map p332 (☑415-749-6300; www.gracecathe dral.org; 1100 California St; suggested donation adult/child $3/2, Sun services free; ⊙8am-6pm, services 8:30am & 11am Sun; ☐1, ☐California St) This Episcopal church has been rebuilt three times since the Gold Rush; the current French-inspired, reinforced concrete cathedral took 40 years to complete. The spectacular stained-glass windows include a series dedicated to human endeavor, including Albert Einstein uplifted in swirling nuclear particles. Check website for events on the indoor labyrinth, including meditation services and yoga.

Grace's commitment to pressing social issues is embodied in its AIDS Memorial Chapel, with a bronze altarpiece by artist-activist Keith Haring, his signature figures angels taking flight – especially powerful since this was his last work before his 1990 death from AIDS. Day and night, spot yogis walking the outdoor, inlaid stone labyrinth, meant to guide restless souls through three spiritual stages: releasing, receiving and returning.

CABLE CAR MUSEUM HISTORIC SITE
Mapp332(☑415-474-1887;www.cablecarmuseum .org;1201 Mason St; ⊙10am-6pm Apr-Sep, to 5pm Oct-Mar; ☐; ☐Powell-Mason, Powell-Hyde) FREE Grips, engines, braking mechanisms... if these warm your gearhead heart, you'll be besotted by the Cable Car Museum, inside the city's still-functioning cable-car barn. See three original 1870s cable cars and watch cables whir over massive bull wheels – as awesome a feat of physics now as when invented by Andrew Hallidie in 1873.

MACONDRAY LANE STREET
Map p332 (btwn Jones & Leavenworth Sts; ☐41, 45, ☐Powell-Mason, Powell-Hyde) The scenic route down from Ina Coolbrith Park – via steep stairs, past gravity-defying wooden cottages – is so charming, it looks like something from a novel. And so it is: Armistead Maupin used this as the model for Barbary Lane in his *Tales of the City* series.

GEORGE STERLING PARK PARK
Map p332 (www.rhn.org/pointofinterestparks. html; Greenwich & Hyde Sts; ☐; ☐Powell-Hyde) 'Homeward into the sunset/Still unwearied we go/Till the northern hills are misty/With the amber of afterglow.' Poet George Sterling's *City by the Sea* is almost maudlin – that is, until you watch the sunset over the Golden Gate Bridge from his namesake hilltop park.

Sterling was a great romancer of all San Francisco offered – nature, idealism, free love and opium – and was frequently broke. But as toast of the secretive, elite Bohemian Club, San Francisco's high society indulged the poet in his eccentricities, which included carrying a lethal dose of cyanide as a reminder of life's transience. Broken by his ex-wife's suicide and loss of his best friend, novelist Jack London, the 'King of Bohemia' apparently took this bitter dose in 1926 inside his apartment at the club. Afterward, his influential friends named this park – with zigzagging paths and stirring, Sterling views – for him.

If you're not breathless from these hilltop vistas, play tennis on the adjacent public court named after San Francisco's Alice Marble, the 1930s tennis champ who recovered from tuberculosis to win Wimbledon and serve during WWII as a US secret agent among Nazis. Sure puts a little post-tennis panting into perspective, doesn't it?

DIEGO RIVERA GALLERY GALLERY
Map p332 (☑415-771-7020; www.sfai.edu; 800 Chestnut St; ⊙9am-5pm; ☐30, ☐Powell-Mason) FREE Diego Rivera's 1931 *The Making of a Fresco Showing a Building of a City* is a *trompe l'oeil* fresco within a fresco, showing the artist himself, pausing to admire his work, as well as the work in progress that is San Francisco. The fresco covers an entire wall in the Diego Rivera Gallery at the San Francisco Art Institute.

For a memorable San Francisco aspect, head to the terrace cafe for espresso and panoramic bay views.

INA COOLBRITH PARK PARK
Map p332 (Vallejo & Taylor Sts; ☐Powell-Mason) On San Francisco's literary scene, all roads eventually lead to Ina Coolbrith, California's first poet laureate; colleague of Mark Twain and Ansel Adams; mentor to Jack London, Isadora Duncan, George Sterling and Charlotte Perkins Gilman; and lapsed Mormon (she kept secret that her uncle was

Mormon-prophet Joseph Smith). The tiny park is a fitting honor – long on romance and exclamation-inspiring vistas.

Climb past gardens, decks and flower-framed apartments, and when fog blows, listen for the whooshing in the treetops.

JACK KEROUAC'S LOVE SHACK HISTORIC SITE
Map p332 (29 Russell St; ☐41, 45, ☐Powell-Hyde) This modest house on a quiet alley was the source of major literature *and* drama from 1951 to 1952, when Jack Kerouac shacked up with Neal and Carolyn Cassady and their baby daughter to pound out his 120ft-long scroll draft of *On the Road*.

Jack and Carolyn became lovers at her husband Neal's suggestion, but Carolyn frequently kicked them both out – though Neal was allowed to move back for the birth of their son John Allen Cassady (named for Jack, and Allen Ginsberg).

MASONIC AUDITORIUM CULTURAL BUILDING
Map p332 (☐415-776-7457; www.masonicaudito rium.com; 1111 California St; ☐10am-3pm Mon-Fri; ☐1, ☐California St) Conspiracy theorists, jazz aficionados and anyone exploring immigrant roots must know the Masonic Auditorium. Built as a temple to freemasonry in 1958, the building hosts headline acts and, every other Tuesday, mass US-citizenship swearing-in ceremonies.

If you're looking for confirmation that California is run by a secret club, here you have it: many of the nation's founding fathers were Freemasons, including George Washington, and the same can be said about California's. It's all captured in the modernist stained-glass windows, which depict founders of freemasonry in California and their accomplishments – if you can decipher the enigmatic symbols and

---

STAIRWAY WALKS

To appreciate San Francisco's brilliant vistas means ascending her hills. Sure, you could ride a cable car, but you'd miss all those marvelous staircases hidden behind hedgerows and backyard gardens cascading with fragrant flowers. Better to walk.

Here's a short list of our favorite staircases. Add some to your itinerary and be rewarded with knockout views – and strong thighs. Take care on damp days, when wet leaves render some routes slippery. And keep your eyes peeled for the famous wild parrots zipping between hilltops – you'll hear them before you see them.

Filbert St Steps, Telegraph Hill (Map p334; ☐39) Famous wooden staircase through backyard gardens, with brilliant East Bay vistas. Start at Coit Tower and find the route through the bushes. Careful not to confuse with adjacent Greenwich St steps – also beautiful but concrete. Tired afterward? Board the F-Market Streetcar at Greenwich and the Embarcadero.

Francisco St Steps, Telegraph Hill (Map p334) The high route from the Wharf to North Beach. Between 150 and 155 Francisco St, traverse the courtyard, ascend to Grant Ave, then turn left to Jack Early Park and climb higher for Golden Gate-to-Bay Bridge panoramas. Descend via Grant Av to North Beach.

Lyon St Steps, Pacific Heights Two blocks, between Broadway and Green St, flanked by forests and glamorous mansions – including Senator Dianne Feinstein's. Jaw-dropping bay and Marina views. Popular with stair-runners and coffee klatches. Connects Cow Hollow with Pacific Heights.

Baker St Steps, Pacific Heights Quiet alternative to adjacent Lyon Street's social and fitness scene. Two hundred steep, narrow steps between Broadway and Vallejo St, dense with greenery flanking the Getty mansions. Note: no handrail.

Vallejo St Steps, Russian Hill (Map p332) Connects North Beach with Russian Hill. Ideal for working off a pasta dinner. Ascend Vallejo toward Mason St; stairs rise toward Jones St, passing Ina Coolbrith Park (p136). Sit at the top for brilliant views of the Bay Bridge lights, then continue west to Polk St for nightlife.

16th Ave Steps, Golden Gate Heights Well off the beaten path on the western side of Twin Peaks but famous for its brilliant tile mosaics. See tiledsteps.org. To appreciate the artwork, ascend. Start at 1700 16th Avenue, at Moraga St. Most easily reached by car.

snippets of fabric embedded in the glass. The frieze below the windows has soil and gravel samples from all 58 California counties, plus Hawaii for some reason known only to those in on the secret handshake. Downstairs a visitors center reveals some of the society's intriguing secrets.

PACIFIC-UNION CLUB   HISTORICAL BUILDING

Map p332 (1000 California St; ⬜California St) The only Nob Hill mansion to survive the 1906 earthquake and fire is this neoclassical brownstone, which despite its grandeur lacks architectural imagination. Today it's a private men's club. The exclusive roster lists newspaper magnates, both Hewlett and Packard of Hewlett-Packard, several US secretaries of defense and government contractors (insert conspiracy theory here).

Democrats, people of color and anyone under 45 are scarce on the published list, but little else is known about the 800-odd membership: members can be expelled for leaking information. Cheeky cross-dressing protesters have pointed out there's no specific ban on transgender or transvestite visitors supping in its main dining room or walking through the front door – privileges denied to women.

⊙ Japantown & Pacific Heights

PEACE PAGODA   MONUMENT

Map p331 (Peace Plaza, Japan Center; ⬜22, 38) When in 1968 San Francisco's sister city of Osaka, Japan, made a gift of Yoshiro Taniguchi's five-tiered concrete stupa, the city seemed stupefied about what to do with the minimalist monument, clustering boxed shrubs around its stark nakedness. But with well-placed cherry trees and low, hewn-rock benches in the plaza, the pagoda is finally in its element, *au naturel*.

RUTH ASAWA FOUNTAINS   MONUMENT

Map p331 (Buchanan St Pedestrian Mall, at Post St; ⬜2, 3, 38) Splash in the fountain and stay awhile: celebrated sculptor and former WWII internee Ruth Asawa designed these fountains to be lived in, not observed from polite distance. Bronze origami dandelions sprout from polished-pebble pools, with built-in benches for bento-box picnics. On warm days along this wind-tunnel pedestrian block, kids frolic while weary shoppers recharge with footbaths.

IKENOBO IKEBANA SOCIETY   GALLERY

Map p331 (🖉415-567-1011; Suite 150 Kinokuniya Bldg, Japan Center, 1581 Webster St; ⊙9:30am-5:30pm Tue-Sat; ⬜2, 3, 22, 38) FREE The largest, oldest society outside Japan for *ikebana* (the Japanese art of flower-arranging) has the displays to prove it: a curly willow tickling a narcissus in an abstract *jiyubana* (freestyle) arrangement, or traditional seven-part *rikka* landscape featuring pine and iris. Even shoppers hell-bent on iron teapots and *maneki neko* (waving kitty) figurines can't resist looking.

COTTAGE ROW   STREET

Map p331 (off Bush St btwn Webster & Fillmore Sts; ⬜2, 3, 22, 38) Detour to days of yore, when San Francisco was a sleepy seaside fishing village, before houses got all uptight, upright and Victorian. Easygoing 19th-century California clapboard cottages hang back along a brick-paved pedestrian promenade, where plum trees and bonsai take center stage. Homes are private but the mini-park is public, good for sushi picnics.

KONKO CHURCH   CHURCH

Map p331 (🖉415-931-0453; www.konkofaith.org; 1909 Bush St; ⊙8am-6pm Mon-Sat, to 1pm Sun; ⬜2, 3) Inside this low-roofed, high-modernist church, you'll find a handsome blond-wood sanctuary with lofty beamed ceiling, vintage photographs of Konko events dating back 80 years, and friendly Reverend Joanne Tolosa, who'll answer questions about Shinto-inspired beliefs, then leave you to contemplation.

On New Year's Day, visitors jot down a remembrance, regret and wish on a slip of paper, affix it to a tree and receive blessings with sacred rice wine.

HAAS-LILIENTHAL HOUSE   HISTORICAL BUILDING

(Map p331; 🖉415-441-3004; www.sfheritage.org/haas-lilienthal-house; 2007 Franklin St; adult/child $8/5; ⊙noon-3pm Wed & Sat, 11am-4pm Sun; ⬜10, 12, 27, 47, 49) A grand Queen Anne–style Victorian with its original 1886 splendor still intact, this family mansion looks like a Clue game come to life – Colonel Mustard could certainly have committed murder with a rope in the dark-wood ballroom, or Miss Scarlet with a candlestick in the red-velvet parlor. One-hour tours are led by docents devoted to Victoriana.

AUDIUM
SOUND SCULPTURE

Map p331 (415-771-1616; www.audium.org; 1616 Bush St; admission $20; performances 8:30pm Fri & Sat, arrive by 8:15pm; 2, 3, 19, 38, 47, 49, California St) Sit in total darkness as Stan Shaff plays his hour-plus compositions of sounds emitted by his sound chamber, which sometimes degenerate into 1970s sci-fi sound effects before resolving into oddly endearing Moog synthesizer wheezes. The Audium was specifically sculpted in 1962 to produce bizarre acoustic effects and eerie soundscapes that only a true stoner could enjoy for two solid hours.

EATING

Japan Center is packed with pretty-good Japanese restaurants; also find intriguing eats along Post St and in the Buchanan Mall, across Post St. Upper Fillmore St is lined with diverse restaurants. Along Hyde St, on Russian Hill, you'll be glad you climbed to prime picnic spots and neighborhood bistros, but if walking afterward seems anticlimactic, hop a cable car.

Nob & Russian Hills

CHEESE PLUS
DELI $

Map p332 (www.cheeseplus.com; 2001 Polk St; sandwiches $9; 10am-7pm; 10, 12, 19, 27, 47, 49) Foodies, rejoice: here's one deli where they won't blink if you request aged, drunken chèvre instead of provolone on your sandwich. The specialty is classic grilled cheese, made with artisan *fromage du jour*, but for $9 get a salad loaded with oven-roasted turkey and sustainable Niman Ranch bacon.

ZA
PIZZA $

Map p332 (415-771-3100; www.zapizzasf.com; 1919 Hyde St; noon-9:30pm Sun-Wed, to 10:30pm Thu-Sat; 41, 45, Powell-Hyde) You don't get gourmet, cornmeal-dusted, thin-crust slices like this every day. Pizza lovers brave uphill climbs for pizza piled with fresh toppings, a pint of Anchor Steam and a cozy bar setting – all for under $10.

SWENSEN'S
ICE CREAM $

Map p332 (www.swensensicecream.com; 1999 Hyde St; noon-10pm Tue-Thu, to 11pm Fri-Sun; 41, 45, Powell-Hyde) Bite into your ice-cream cone, and get an instant brain-freeze and hit of nostalgia besides. Oooh-ouch, that peppermint stick really takes you back, doesn't it? The 16oz root-beer floats are the 1950s version of Prozac, but the classic hot fudge sundae is pure serotonin with sprinkles on top.

ZARZUELA
TAPAS $$

Map p332 (2000 Hyde St; dishes $8-10; 5:30pm-10pm Tue-Thu, to 10:30pm Fri-Sat; 41, 45, Powell-Hyde) Smack on the Powell-Hyde cable, Zarzuela is the long-shining star among several fine restaurants along Hyde St, on Russian Hill proper. Real Spanish tapas include terrific paella and classic garlic-prawns, plus unusual dishes like braised quail and Madrid-style tripe. Ochre-washed walls and terra-cotta tile set a simple backdrop for dynamic cooking No reservations: expect 30- to 45-minute waits after 6pm.

SWAN OYSTER DEPOT
SEAFOOD $$

Map p332 (415-673-1101; 1517 Polk St; dishes $10-20; 8am-5:30pm Mon-Sat; 1, 19, 47, 49, California St) Superior flavor without the superior attitude of typical seafood restaurants – Swan's downside is an inevitable wait for the few stools at the vintage lunch counter, but the upside of high turnover is incredibly fresh seafood.

Sunny days, place your order to go, browse Polk St boutiques, then breeze past the line to pick up crab salad with Louie dressing and the obligatory top-grade oysters with mignonette sauce. Hike or bus up to George Sterling Park (p136) for superlative seafood with ocean views.

LEOPOLD'S
GERMAN $$

Map p332 (www.leopoldssf.com; 2400 Polk St; mains $13-17; dinner 5:30pm-10pm Sun-Thu, to 11pm Fri-Sat; brunch 11:30am-2:30pm Sat-Sun; 19, 41, 45, 47, 49) Polk Street was traditionally called Polkstrasse for its German immigrants. Leopold's pays homage with lip-schmacking Austrian–German Alpine cooking, served beer-hall style at pinewood booths. The 20-something crowd gets deafeningly loud, but after a boot full of beer you'll hardly notice. Hearty specialties include hearty chicken soup with dumplings, goulash, schnitzel, flatbread and housemade salumi – *lecker!* No reservations; expect waits.

1. Fillmore St
This thoroughfare in Pacific Heights plays host to the neighborhood's best boutiques and cafes.

2. Cherry Blossom Festival (p21)
Japantown blooms and booms during this April festival, which culminates in a colorful parade.

3. Peace Pagoda (p138)
The centerpiece of Japantown's plaza, this concrete stupa marks the friendship between Osaka and SF.

4. Lombard St (p135)
The eight sweeping turns of this steep Russian Hill street make it one of SF's most photographed sights.

★ACQUERELLO   CALIFORNIAN, ITALIAN $$$
Map p332 (☑415-567-5432; www.acquerello.com; 1722 Sacramento St; 3-/5-course menu $82/110; ⊙5:30-9:30pm Tue-Sat; 🚌1, 19, 47, 49, 🚃California St) A converted chapel is a fitting location for a meal that'll turn Italian culinary purists into true believers in Cal-Italian cuisine. Chef Suzette Gresham's generous pastas and ingenious seasonal meat dishes include heavenly quail salad, devilish lobster *panzerotti* and venison loin chops. Suave maitre d'hotel Giancarlo Paternini indulges every whim, even providing black-linen napkins if you're worried about lint.

An anteroom where brides once steadied nerves is now lined with limited-production Italian vintages.

✖ Japantown & Pacific Heights

CROWN & CRUMPET   CAFE $
Map p331 (☑415-771-4252; www.crownandcrumpet.com; 1746 Post St; dishes $9-11, afternoon tea $22; ⊙11am-6pm daily; 👶; 🚌2, 3, 22, 38) In this cafe inside New People (p146), designer style and rosy cheer usher tea-time into the 21st century: girlfriends rehash hot dates over scones with strawberries and tea, and dads and daughters clink porcelain cups after choosing from 24 kinds of tea. Weekend reservations recommended.

NIJIYA SUPERMARKET   JAPANESE, SUSHI $
Map p331 (☑415-563-1901; www.nijiya.com; 1737 Post St; 🚌2, 3, 22, 38) Picnic under the Peace Pagoda with sushi or teriyaki bento boxes fresh from the deli counter, swig Berkeley-brewed Takara Sierra Cold sake from the drinks aisle and have change from a $20 for mango-ice-cream-filled *mochi* (chewy Japanese cakes with savory or sweet fillings). Tip: By the door, there's a microwave for customers' use.

GROVE   AMERICAN $
Map p331 (☑415-474-1419; 2016 Fillmore St; dishes $8-12; ⊙7am-11pm; 🛜👶; 🚌1, 3, 22) Rough-hewn recycled wood, bric-a-brac in the rafters and a stone fireplace lend a ski-lodge aesthetic to this Fillmore St cafe, where Pacific Heights locals recover from hangovers with made-to-order breakfasts, hunch over laptops with salads and sandwiches, and gab fireside with warm-from-the-oven cookies and hot cocoa. There's another branch in the **Marina** (☑415-474-4843; www.thegrovesf.com; 2250 Chestnut St; ⊙7am-11pm Mon-Fri, 8am-11pm Sat & Sun).

BENKYODO   JAPANESE $
Map p331 (☑415-922-1244; www.benkyodocompany.com; 1747 Buchanan St; dishes $1-10; ⊙8am-5pm Mon-Sat; 🚌2, 3, 22, 38) The perfect retro lunch counter cheerfully serves an old-school egg-salad sandwich or pastrami for $5, but the real draw is the $1.25 *mochi* made in-house daily – come early for popular varieties of green tea and chocolate-filled strawberry. Cash only.

SOPHIE'S CREPES   DESSERT $
Map p331 (Ste 275, Japan Center, 1581 Webster St; dishes $4-8; ⊙11am-9pm Sun-Thu, to 10pm Fri & Sat; 🚌2, 3, 22, 38) Crowds line up for Sophie's made-to-order crepes and sundaes. As interesting as the ice-cream selection (try the red bean) are the occasional posses of Lolita Goth girls, who take their fashion cues from filmmaker Tim Burton.

STATE BIRD PROVISIONS   CALIFORNIAN, SMALL PLATES $$
Map p331 (☑415-795-1272; statebirdsf.com; 1529 Fillmore St; ⊙5:30pm-10pm Mon-Thu, to 11pm Fri-Sat; 🚌22, 38) We're flummoxed why in 2013 James Beard dubbed State Bird America's best new restaurant. Yes, the food is thrilling, a play on dim sum, wildly inventive with seasonal-regional ingredients and esoteric flavors like, say, fennel pollen or garum, but the open-kitchen-dominated room is downright drab and so crowded that parvenu foodie-hipsters without reservations stand to eat, blocking the door.

If you're curious to see the Emperor's new clothes, book exactly 60 days ahead, or arrive by 5pm for a coveted walk-in, stand-up spot. Prices are deceptive; all those small plates add up.

TATAKI   JAPANESE, SUSHI $$
(Map p331; ☑415-931-1182; www.tatakisushibar.com; 2815 California St; dishes $12-20; ⊙lunch Mon-Fri, dinner daily; 🚌1, 24) 🐟 Pioneering sushi chefs Kin Lui and Raymond Ho rescue dinner and the oceans with sustainable delicacies: silky Arctic char drizzled with yuzu-citrus replaces at-risk wild salmon; and the Golden State Roll is a local hero, featuring spicy, line-caught scallop, Pacific tuna, organic-apple slivers

and edible 24-karat gold. It's tiny, off the beaten path and accepts no reservations, but merits the trip.

PIZZERIA DELFINA   PIZZA $$

Map p331 (☑415-440-1189; www.pizzeriadelfina.com; 2406 California St; pizzas $11-17; ⊙5-10pm Mon, 11am Tue-Thu, 11:30am-11pm Fri, noon-11pm Sat, noon-10pm Sun; ☑1, 3, 22) Pizzeria Delfina derives success from simplicity: fresh-from-the-farm ingredients in copious salads and house-cured meats on tender-to-the-tooth, thin-crusted pizzas – this is one place you actually *want* anchovies on your pizza. Inside gets loud; sit on the sidewalk. Expect a wait at peak meal times; come early or late.

WOODHOUSE FISH CO   SEAFOOD $$

Map p331 (www.woodhousefish.com; 1914 Fillmore St; mains $13-26; ⊙11:30am-10pm; ☑2, 3, 22) If being near the ocean makes you crave seafood but you (rightly) don't want to eat at the Wharf, Woodhouse's classic New England–style seafood provides a better alternative, with no-fuss meals of crab and lobster rolls, fried clams, fish and chips and traditional SF-style *cioppino* (seafood stew), complete with bib. No reservations. There's another branch in the **Castro** (Map p328; www.woodhousefish.com; 2073 Market St; ⊙11:30am-9:30pm).

SAPPORO-YA   JAPANESE $$

Map p331 (☑415-563-7400; Ste 202, 1581 Webster St; noodles $8-11; ⊙11am-11pm Mon-Sat, to 10pm Sun; ☑2, 3, 22, 38) Locals favor this 2nd-floor noodle house for no-fuss meals of homemade ramen, served in big earthenware bowls on Formica tables in a room that's barely changed since the 1970s. Giant-sized combination dinners complete the menu but noodles are the thing here.

OUT THE DOOR   VIETNAMESE $$$

Map p331 (☑415-923 9575; www.outthedoors.com; 2232 Bush St; mains lunch $12-18, dinner $18-28; ⊙8am-4:30pm Mon-Fri, 8am-3pm Sat & Sun, 5:30pm-10pm daily; ☑2, 3, 22) Offshoot of the famous Slanted Door (p94), this casual outpost jump-starts early shopping with stellar French beignets and Vietnamese coffee, or salty-sweet Dungeness crab frittatas. Lunchtime's rice plates and noodles are replaced at dinner with savory clay-pot meats and fish. Make reservations.

🍷 DRINKING & NIGHTLIFE

🍷 Nob & Russian Hills

⭐ TONGA ROOM   LOUNGE

Map p332 (www.tongaroom.com; Fairmont San Francisco, 950 Mason St; cover $5-7; ⊙5-11:30pm Sun, Wed & Thu, 5:30pm-12:30am Fri & Sat; ☑1, ☒California St, Powell-Mason, Powell-Hyde) Tonight's San Francisco weather: 100% chance of tropical rainstorms every 20 minutes, but only around the top-40 band playing on the island in the middle of the indoor pool – you're safe in your grass hut. For a more powerful hurricane, order one in a plastic coconut. Come before 8pm to beat the cover charge.

HI-LO CLUB   BAR

Map p332 (http://hilosf.com; 1423 Polk St; ⊙4pm-2am Mon-Sat; ☑1, 19, 47, 49, ☒California St) A must-visit on any Polk St pub crawl, the Hi-Lo plays trashy-fancy, with peeling paint, tarnished-tin ceilings and distressed-wood floors that make it resemble a candlelit squat. The classic cocktails showcase lesser-known craft spirits, never brand names – don't ask for Absolut! – and the soundtrack is vintage soul, rock and punk. Come early; otherwise it's packed – and loud.

AMÉLIE   BAR

Map p332 (www.ameliesf.com; 1754 Polk St; ⊙5:30pm-2am; ☑1, 10, 12, 19, 27, 47, 49, ☒Powell-Hyde, California St) This *très* cool neighborhood wine bar, with sexy lipstick-red counters, serves well-priced vintages – happy-hour (5:30pm to 7pm) flights of three cost just $10 – and delish cheese and charcuterie plates. Weekends get too crowded (make reservations); weekdays it's an ideal spot to cozy up with your sweetheart.

BIGFOOT LODGE   THEME BAR

Map p332 (www.bigfootlodge.com; 1750 Polk St; ⊙3pm-2am; ☑10, 12, 27, 47, 49, ☒Powell-Hyde, California St) Log-cabin walls, antler chandeliers, taxidermy animals everywhere you look – you'd swear you were at a state-park visitors center, if not for all the gigglydrunk 20-somethings. If you're looking for your gay boyfriend, he's wandered across the street to the Cinch.

TOP OF THE MARK
BAR, DANCING

Map p332 (www.topofthemark.com; 999 California St; cover $10-15; ◷5pm-midnight Sun-Thu, 4pm-1am Fri & Sat; ◲1, ◲California St) So what if it's touristy? Nothing beats twirling in the clouds in your best cocktail dress to a full jazz orchestra on the city's highest dance floor. Call ahead to ensure a band is playing the night you're coming. Expect $15 drinks.

CINCH
GAY BAR

Map p332 (http://cinchsf.com; 1723 Polk St; ◷9am-2am Mon-Fri, from 6am Sat & Sun; ◲1, 19, 27, 47, 49, ◲California St) The last of the old-guard Polk St gay bars still has an old-timey saloon vibe, with pool, pinball, free popcorn and a big smokers patio where you get yelled at if you spark a joint (but people do it anyway).

🍷 Japantown & Pacific Heights

SOCIAL STUDY
CAFE, BAR

Map p331 (http://socialstudysf.com; 1795 Geary Blvd; ◷5pm-11pm Mon, from 10am Tue-Sun; 📶; ◲22, 38) Part cafe, part bar, Social Study draws an upbeat collegiate crowd for strong coffee and good beer, wi-fi and board games. An alternative to booze bars, it's ideal for a post-movie tête-à-tête or catch-up time with friends.

1300 ON FILLMORE
LOUNGE

Map p331 (www.1300fillmore.com; 1300 Fillmore St; ◷4:30pm-10pm Sun-Thu, to midnight Fri & Sat; ◲22, 31, 38) Reviving swank south of Geary, 1300 on Fillmore's enormous heavy doors open into a double-high living-room space, with oriental rugs, tufted-leather sofas and floor-to-ceiling, black-and-white portraits of jazz luminaries. On Fridays, jazz plays at 8:30pm. There's good Southern-inspired food, and on Sundays gospel brunch (reservations required) – big with the after-church crowd.

DOSA
BAR

Map p331 (📞415-441-3672; www.dosasf.com; 1700 Fillmore St; ◷5pm-11pm; ◲2, 3, 22, 38) Baubled glittering chandeliers hang from high ceilings at Dosa, an otherwise expensive (but good) Indian restaurant with a happening bar scene of sexy, non-snooty locals. It's good for snazzy cocktails, but if you're wearing dumpy clothes you'll feel out of place.

HARRY'S BAR
BAR

Map p331 (www.harrysbarsf.com; 2020 Fillmore St; ◷4pm-2am Mon-Thu, from 11:30am Fri-Sun; ◲1, 3, 22) Cap off a shopping trip at Harry's mahogany bar with freshly muddled *mojitos* or Bloody Marys made properly with horseradish. A Pacific Heights mainstay, Harry's appeals to aging debutantes who love getting politely hammered.

☆ ENTERTAINMENT

YOSHI'S
JAZZ, LIVE MUSIC

Map p331 (📞415-655-5600; www.yoshis.com; 1300 Fillmore St; ◷shows 8pm and/or 10pm Tue-Sun, dinner Tue-Sun; ◲22, 31) San Francisco's definitive jazz club draws the world's top talent and hosts appearances by the likes of Leon Redbone and Nancy Wilson, along with occasional classical and gospel acts. Make a night of it with top-notch sushi in the swingin' restaurant up front. Students: ask about half-off tickets.

Best to book in advance – if you're a group, consider the round high-back booths (table numbers 30 to 40) but there's not a bad seat.

FILLMORE AUDITORIUM
LIVE MUSIC

Map p331 (📞415-346-6000; http://thefillmore.com; 1805 Geary Blvd; admission $15-50; ◷box office 10am-4pm Sun, 7:30-10pm show nights; ◲22, 38) Jimi Hendrix, Janis Joplin, the Doors – they all played the Fillmore. Now you might catch the Indigo Girls, Duran Duran or Tracy Chapman in the historic 1250-capacity, standing-room theater (if you're polite and lead with the hip, you might squeeze up to the stage). Don't miss the priceless collection of psychedelic posters in the upstairs gallery.

BOOM BOOM ROOM
LIVE MUSIC, DANCING

Map p331 (📞415-673-8000; www.boomboomblues.com; 1601 Fillmore St; admission $5-15; ◷4pm-2am Tue-Sun; ◲22, 38) Jumping since the '30s, Boom Boom is a relic from the Fillmore's heyday – dig the old photos lining the walls. The black-box room ain't fancy – just a bar, stage, tables and dance floor – but rocks six nights a week with blues, soul and New Orleans funk by top touring talent. Shows start 'round 9pm.

RED DEVIL LOUNGE
LIVE MUSIC

Map p332 (📞415-921-1695; www.reddevillounge.com; 1695 Polk St; cover $5-25; ◷nights vary; 📶; ◲1, 19, 27, 47, 49, ◲California St) The up-and-

FILLMORE ST JAZZ BAR CRAWL

The Fillmore St Jazz District was dubbed the 'Harlem of the West' in the '40s and '50s, when Ella Fitzgerald and Duke Ellington played clubs near Fillmore and Geary. The 'hood fell victim to urban blight in the '70s and '80s, but lately has bounced back, particularly since the opening of Yoshi's (p144) and the **Jazz Heritage Center** (Map p331; www.jazzheritagecenter.org; 1320 Fillmore St).

Start the evening at Geary and Fillmore and head south, listening at doors of clubs to find what turns you on. John Lee Hooker's Boom Boom Room (p144) marks the gateway to the neighborhood. For something quieter and more intimate, **Sheba Piano Lounge** (Map p331; www.shebapianolounge.com; 1419 Fillmore St; ☺5pm–midnight, later on weekends) has a fireplace, plus piano jazz and sometimes jazz ensembles. Even if you don't catch an act at Yoshi's, pop into the lobby-level Lush Life Gallery to see ephemera of jazz greats. End with drinks on tufted-leather sofas at 1300 on Fillmore, where photos of jazz luminaries line the walls.

coming and formerly famous (think Vanilla Ice and Sugar Hill Gang) play this intimate shotgun club. Your once-fave stars may have lost their luster, but the strong drinks haven't. Mondays are movie nights, Tuesdays open mic. Bands play Wednesday to Saturday.

ENCORE KARAOKE LOUNGE   KARAOKE LOUNGE

Map p332 (☎415-775-0442; www.encorekara okesf.com; 2nd fl, 1550 California St; ☺3pm–2am, karaoke from 8pm Mon-Thu, from 5pm Fri-Sun; ☐1, 19, 27, 47, 49, ☒California St) What a dump. Still, it's hard to resist this throwback-to-1970s rumpus room, crammed with low-slung, swiveling stitched-Naugahyde chairs and a happy-tipsy crowd of raucous Karaoke-philes who cheer when you nail it but talk when you suck.

SUNDANCE KABUKI CINEMA   CINEMA

Map p331 (☎415-929-4650; www.sundance cinemas.com; 1881 Post St; adult/child $9.50-15/9; ☐2, 3, 22, 38) 🌿 Cinema-going at its best. Reserve a stadium seat, belly up to the bar, and order wine and surprisingly good food to enjoy during the film. A multiplex initiative by Robert Redford's Sundance Institute, Kabuki features big-name flicks and festivals – and it's green, with recycled-fiber seating, reclaimed-wood decor and local chocolates and booze. Validated parking available.

Note: expect a $1 to $3 surcharge to see a movie not preceded by commercials.

CLAY THEATER   CINEMA

Map p331 (☎415-267-4893; www.landmarkthea tres.com; 2261 Fillmore St; adult/child & matinee $10.50/8; ☐1, 3, 10, 22, 24) In business since 1913, the single-screen Clay regularly screens a mix of both independent and for-eign films. On Saturdays (and occasionally Fridays) at midnight, look for classics like *Rocky Horror Picture Show*.

NEW PEOPLE CINEMA   CINEMA

Map p331 (☎415-525-8600; www.newpeople world.com; New People, 1746 Post St; tickets $12; ☐2, 3, 22, 38) See current-release Japanese films, anime and documentaries at this underground 143-seat theater with HD projection and kick-ass sound. Also hosts the SF and Asian American Film Festivals.

🛍 SHOPPING

Near Russian Hill, Polk St (from California St to Broadway) is great for browsing indie boutiques. Japantown is packed with kitschy-fun gift shops and authentic Japanese wares. Fillmore St, in Pacific Heights, caters to an upmarket demographic (hence its nickname, Specific Whites); there's fab shopping between Bush and Jackson Sts – continue to Broadway for brilliant bay views. For more high-end indie boutiques, head to Presidio Heights – Sacramento St, west of Presidio Ave.

🛍 Nob & Russian Hills

STUDIO   GIFTS, ARTS & CRAFTS

Map p332 (www.studiogallerysf.com; 1815 Polk St; ☺11am-7pm Wed-Fri, to 6pm Sat & Sun, by appointment Mon & Tue; ☐1, 19, 47, 49, ☒California St) Spiff up your pad with locally made art at great prices. For a visual remembrance of your visit to SF, Studio is the place, with a mishmash of small prints of local haunts by Elizabeth Ashcroft and architectural etchings by Alice Gibbons, plus paintings of local land- and city-scapes. Monthly receptions are open to the public.

VELVET DA VINCI
JEWELRY

Map p332 (www.velvetdavinci.com; 2015 Polk St; ⊙11am-6pm Tue-Sat, to 4pm Sun; ⊒10, 12, 19, 27, 47, 49, ⊟Powell-Hyde) At this jewelry gallery, you can actually see the ideas behind the handcrafted gems: Lynn Christiansen puts her food obsessions into a purse that looks like whipped cream and Enric Majoral's Mediterranean meditations yield rings that appear to be made of sand. Six to eight shows annually mean an ever-changing collection of contemporary-art jewelry from around the world.

FAVOR
JEWELRY, GIFTS

Map p332 (www.shopatfavor.com; 500 Sutter St, ste 101; ⊙10am-6pm Mon-Sat, to 5pm Sun; Ⓜ Powell) Local designer Caramia Viscick nods to the past with snappy retro-cool jewelry, including lapel pins of hand-carved resin with inset vintage images, chunky beaded bracelets of art deco–era Bakelite, and necklaces made from repurposed chandelier crystals and cast-off hotel keys. The look is playful and girly and some pieces are gender-neutral – in SF, at least.

CITY DISCOUNT
HOUSEWARES

Map p332 (☑415-771-4649; 1542 Polk St; ⊙10am-7pm Mon-Fri, 11am-6pm Sat-Sun; ⊒1, 19, 47, 49, ⊟California St) Bargains never tasted so sweet: heart-shaped Le Creuset casseroles, frighteningly effective Microplane graters, Brika espresso makers and other specialty gourmet gear, all at 30% to 50% off the prices you'd pay downtown. Hard-to-find appliance replacement parts, parchment paper and cooking tips are all readily available from dedicated-foodie counter staff.

MOLTE COSE
CLOTHING, ACCESSORIES

Map p332 (www.moltecose.com; 2036 Polk St; ⊙11am-6pm Mon-Sat, noon-5pm Sun; ⊒10, 12, 19, 47, 49) Thrilling for browsers, Molte Cose's imaginative, unpredictable collection of vintage bric-a-brac ranges from French stemware to Royal typewriters that double as set decoration for displays of frilly dresses, elegant lingerie, cufflinks, shaving kits, hip flasks and super-cute kids' gear, including hoodies emblazoned with unicorns flying over the Golden Gate.

PICNIC
CLOTHING, HOMEWARES

Map p332 (www.picnicsf.com; 1806-8 Polk St; ⊒19, 27, 47, 49, ⊟Powell-Hyde) The kind of boutique young moms hope to find when they're out for a girly-girl afternoon, Picnic caters to women of childbearing age, who say c-u-u-u-t-e! to the pretty tops, smart skirts, baby clothes, children's toys, handcrafted jewelry and cozy home decor.

CRIS
CLOTHING, ACCESSORIES

Map p332 (☑415-474-1191; 2056 Polk St; ⊙11am-6pm Mon-Sat, from noon Sun; ⊒10, 12, 19, 47, 49, ⊟Powell-Hyde) The sharpest windows on Polk St are consistently at Cris, a consignment shop specializing in contemporary high-end fashion by big-name designers like Balenciaga, Lanvin, Marni, Alexander Wang and Chloé, all in beautiful condition and at amazing prices, carefully curated by an elegant Frenchwoman with an eagle's eye and duchess's taste. Also great for handbags by Prada, Dolce & Gabbana, yada-yada-yada...

JOHNSON LEATHERS
LEATHER

Map p332 (www.johnsonleather.com; 1833 Polk St; ⊙11am-6pm Tue-Sat; ⊒10, 12, 19, 27, 47, 49) If you've been looking for a new leather jacket – the ideal garment in chilly SF – Johnson custom-tailors classic cuts, built to last. Their materials and craftsmanship are so reliable, so durable, they outfit both the SFPD's motorcycle patrolmen *and* the Hell's Angels.

⌂ Japantown & Pacific Heights

JAPAN CENTER
MALL

Map p331 (www.sfjapantown.org; 1625 Post St; ⊙10am-midnight; ⊒2, 3, 22, 38) Entering this oddly charming mall is like walking onto a 1960s Japanese movie set – the fake-rock waterfall, indoor wooden pedestrian bridges, rock gardens and curtained wooden restaurant entryways have hardly aged since 1968. The mall covers three square blocks but you'll also find Japantown shops outside, along Buchanan and Post Sts.

★ NEW PEOPLE
CLOTHING, GIFTS

Map p331 (www.newpeopleworld.com; 1746 Post St; ⊙noon-7pm Mon-Sat, to 6pm Sun; ⊒2, 3, 22, 38) An eye-popping three-story emporium devoted to Japanese art and pop culture, New People is reason alone to visit Japantown. At **New People Shop**, find funky *kawaii* (Japanese for all things cute), like origami kits and cute-as-Pikachu Japanimation cards and t-shirts. Try on Lolita fashions (imagine *Alice in Wonderland*) at 2nd-floor **Baby the Stars Shine Bright** and traditional Japanese clothing emblazoned with contemporary graphics at **Sou-Sou**.

Get inspired by contemporary artists at **Superfrog Gallery**, then recharge over tea at Crown & Crumpet (p142).

NEST   HOUSEWARES, GIFTS

Map p331 (www.nestsf.com; 2300 Fillmore St; ☺10:30am-6pm Mon-Sat, from 11am Sun; ☐1, 3, 10, 22, 24) Make your nest cozier with one-of-a-kind accessories from this well-curated collection, including Provençal quilts, beaded jewelry, craft kits and papier-mâché trophy heads for the kids' room, and mesmerizing century-old bric-a-brac and toys.

BENEFIT   BEAUTY PRODUCTS

Map p331 (www.benefitcosmetics.com; 2117 Fillmore St; ☺10am-7pm Mon-Fri, 9am-6:30pm Sat, 10am-6pm Sun; ☐1, 3, 22) Get cheeky with BeneTint, the dab-on liquid blush made from roses, or raise eyebrows with Brow Zings tinted brow wax – they're two of Benefit's signature products invented in San Francisco by the twin-sister team. Surgery is so LA: in SF, overnight Angelinas swear by LipPlump and Lindsay Lohan dark-eye-circles are cured with Ooh La Lift. There's another store in the **Marina** (Map p316; ☑415-567-1173; 2219 Chestnut St; ☺10am-7pm Sun-Tue, 10am-8pm Wed-Fri, 9am-7pm Sat ; ☐28, 30, 43).

CLARY SAGE ORGANICS   BEAUTY PRODUCTS, WOMEN'S CLOTHING

Map p331 (www.clarysageorganics.com; 2241 Fillmore St; ☺10am-7pm Mon-Sat, 11am-6pm Sun; ☐1, 3, 10, 22, 24) Clary Sage designs its own line of yoga-wear and will kit you out with effortlessly flattering organic-California-cotton tunics, organic plant-based cleansers and lotions with light, delectable scents, and homeopathic flower-essence stress remedies.

BROOKLYN CIRCUS   MEN'S CLOTHING, SHOES

Map p331 (thebkcircus.com; 1521 Fillmore St; ☺noon-7pm Tue-Sun; ☐22, 38) Stylish men who skew casual appreciate Brooklyn Circus's classic American aesthetic. Find wool-and-leather varsity-letter jackets, snappy

shirts and hats and quality US-made shoes, including high-top leather PF Flyers and Red Wing boots.

ALICE & OLIVIA   WOMEN'S CLOTHING

Map p331 (www.aliceandolivia.com; 2259 Fillmore St; ☺11am-7pm Mon-Fri, 10am-6pm Sat, 11am-6pm Sun; ☐1, 3, 10, 22, 24) NYC-based designer Stacey Bendet makes perfect party dresses and gorgeous hand-beaded gowns for pretty girls prepping for the ball. Racks display only size 2; larger sizes are kept hidden in back like Cinderella.

MARGARET O'LEARY   CLOTHING, ACCESSORIES

Map p331 (☑415-771-9982; 2400 Fillmore St; ☺10am-6pm Mon-Sat, 11am-5pm Sun; ☐1, 3, 10, 22, 24) At her flagship store, San Francisco local Margaret O'Leary showcases whisper-light cardigans of cashmere, organic cotton or eco-minded bamboo yarn.

KINOKUNIYA BOOKS & STATIONERY   BOOKSTORE

Map p331 (☑415-567-7625; www.kinokuniya.com/us; Japan Center, 1581 Webster St; ☺10:30am-8pm; ☐22, 38) Like warriors in a showdown, the bookstore, stationery and manga divisions of Kinokuniya compete for your attention. Only you can decide where your loyalties lie: with stunning photography books and Harajuku fashion mags upstairs, vampire comics downstairs or the stationery department's *washi* paper, supersmooth Sakura gel pens and pig notebooks with the motto 'what lovely friends, they will bring happy.'

SANKO COOKING SUPPLY   CERAMICS, HOUSEWARES

Map p331 (www.shop.sankosf.com; 1758 Buchanan St; ☺9:30am-5:30pm Mon-Sat, 11:30am-5pm Sun; ☐2, 3, 22, 38) The elegant owner serves you tea while you browse aisle upon aisle of Japanese ceramics, tea pots, sake sets, tableware and cookware at this extraordinary Japantown shop. Where else, we ask, can you find restaurant-grade plastic sushi suitable for display?

MARC BY MARC JACOBS   CLOTHING, ACCESSORIES

Map p331 (www.marcjacobs.com; 2142 Fillmore St; ☺11am-7pm; ☐1, 3, 22) The USA's hippest designer usually charges prices to match, but here alongside the $800 jackets and $300 sandals are accessories under $25 – chunky resin bangles, snappy belts and limited-edition clutches.

SOKO HARDWARE
HOUSEWARES

Map p331 (📞415-931-5510; 1698 Post St; ⏰9am-5:30pm Mon-Sat; 🚌2, 3, 22, 38) *Ikebana,* bonsai, tea ceremony and Zen rock-garden supplies are all here at fair prices.

KATSURA GARDEN
GARDEN

Map p331 (📞415-931-6209; Japan Center, 1581 Webster St; ⏰10am-5:30pm Mon, Thu-Fri; 11am-5:30pm Sat, 11am-5pm Sun; 🚌2, 3, 22, 38) For a special gift, consider a bonsai. Katsura Garden will set you up with a miniature juniper that looks like it grew on a windswept molehill, or a stunted maple that next autumn will shed five tiny, perfect red leaves.

ICHIBAN KAN
GIFTS

Map p331 (📞415-409-0472; www.ichibankanusa.com; Ste 540, 22 Peace Plaza, Japan Center; ⏰10am-8pm; 🚌2, 3, 22, 38) How can you survive without penguin soy-sauce dispensers, 'Men's Pocky' chocolate-covered pretzels, extra-spiky Japanese hair wax, soap dishes with feet and the ultimate in gay gag gifts, the handy 'Closet Case' – all for under $5.

KOHSHI
GIFTS

Map p331 (www.kohshisf.com; Ste 335, Japan Center, 1737 Post St; ⏰11am-7pm; 🚌2, 3, 22, 38) Fragrant Japanese incense for every purpose, from long-burning sandalwood for meditation to cinnamon-tinged Gentle Smile to atone for laundry left too long, plus lovely gift ideas: gentle charcoal soap, cups that look like crumpled paper, and purple Daruma figurines for making wishes.

JONATHAN ADLER
HOUSEWARES

Map p331 (www.jonathanadler.com; 2133 Fillmore St; ⏰10am-6pm Mon-Sat, noon-5pm Sun; 🚌1, 3, 22) Vases with handlebar mustaches and cookie jars labeled 'Quaaludes' may seem like holdovers from a Big Sur bachelor pad c 1974, but they're snappy interior inspirations from California pop potter (and *Top Design* judge) Jonathan Adler. Don't worry whether that leather pig footstool matches your midcentury couch – as Adler says, 'Minimalism is a bummer.'

ZINC DETAILS
HOUSEWARES

Map p331 (www.zincdetails.com; 1905 Fillmore St; ⏰11am-7pm Mon-Sat, noon-6pm Sun; 🚌2, 3, 22) Pacific Heights chic meets Japantown mod at Zinc Details, with items like orange lacquerware salad-tossers, a sake dispenser that looks like a Zen garden boulder and bird-shaped soy dispensers, all noteworthy for their smart designs and artful presentations.

CROSSROADS
CLOTHING, ACCESSORIES

Map p331 (www.crossroadstrading.com; 1901 Fillmore St; ⏰11am-7pm Sun-Thu, to 8pm Fri-Sat; 🚌2, 3, 22, 38) Pssst, fashionistas: you know those designers you see lining Fillmore St? Many of their creations wind up at Crossroads for a fraction of retail, thanks to Pacific Heights clotheshorses who ditch last season's wardrobe here. That's why this Crossroads is better than others in the city. For better deals, trade in your old clothes for credit.

🏃 SPORTS & ACTIVITIES

⭐ KABUKI SPRINGS & SPA
SPA

Map p331 (📞415-922-6000; www.kabukisprings.com; 1750 Geary Blvd; admission $25; ⏰10am-9:45pm, co-ed Tue, women only Wed, Fri & Sun, men only Mon, Thu & Sat; 🚌22, 38) Our favorite urban retreat is a spin on communal, clothing-optional Japanese baths. Scrub yourself down with salt in the steam room, soak in the hot pool, then the cold plunge and reheat in the sauna. Silence is mandatory, fostering a meditative mood – if you hear the gong, it means Shhhh!

The look befits the location – slightly dated Japanese modern, with vaulted lacquered-wood ceilings, tile mosaics and low lighting. Men and women alternate days, except co-ed Tuesdays, when bathing suits are required (arrive before 5pm to beat the line). Plan two hours' minimum, plus a 30-to-60-minute wait at peak times (add your name to the waitlist, then go next door to slurp noodles or catch a movie; when you return, breeze right in). Communal bathing discounted with massage appointments; book ahead and come on the gender-appropriate day.

The Mission & Potrero Hill

Neighborhood Top Five

1 Seeing garage doors, billboards and storefronts transformed into canvases with over 400 **Mission murals** (p151 & p152).

2 Watching puffer fish completely immersed in their roles inside the Fish Theater at **826 Valencia** (p151).

3 Playing, tanning, picnicking and protesting entire days away in **Dolores Park** (p151).

4 Immersing yourself in history at San Francisco's oldest building, **Mission Dolores** (p151).

5 Joining local design, wine and chocolate already in progress in **Dogpatch's Creative Corridor** (p166).

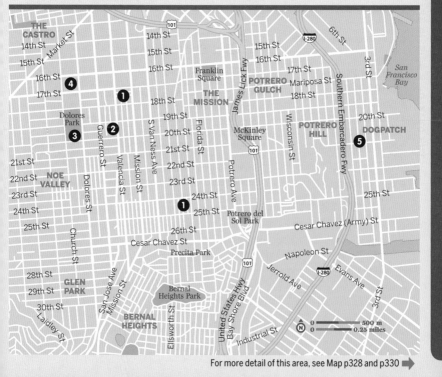

For more detail of this area, see Map p328 and p330 ➡

Lonely Planet's Top Tip

The Mission is packed with bars and clubs and although you should be fine in the daytime, it's not always the safest area to walk alone in at night. Recruit a friend and be alert in the Mission east of Valencia, in Potrero Hill below 18th St and around deserted Dogpatch warehouses. Don't bring the bling – this isn't LA – and don't leave belongings unattended.

✕ Best Places to Eat

➡ La Taqueria (p155)
➡ Craftsman & Wolves (p155)
➡ Ichi Sushi (p159)
➡ Commonwealth (p160)
➡ Namu Gaji (p159)
➡ Humphry Slocombe (p158)

For reviews, see p155 ➡

🍷 Best Places to Drink

➡ Elixir (p161)
➡ Trick Dog (p161)
➡ Zeitgeist (p161)
➡ Ritual Coffee Roasters (p161)
➡ 20 Spot (p162)
➡ Rock Bar (p162)

For reviews, see p161 ➡

Explore the Mission & Potrero Hill

Get to know San Francisco from the inside out, from pirate stores to mural-covered Mission alleys. Score a whole new look at Mission boutiques and book ahead at local venues for the ultimate SF souvenir: a new talent, discovered at a hands-on cooking class, arts workshop, dancing or rock-climbing lesson. Combine epic bar crawls with taco tastings and end up salsa dancing with suave strangers at Mission clubs.

Local Life

➡**Learn something new** Upcycle office supplies into art at SCRAP (p170), concoct edible perfumes at 18 Reasons (p28), skate the bowl at Potrero del Sol/La Raza Skatepark (p172) and tell likely stories at 826 Valencia (p151).

➡**Do dessert** After another lap of Mission murals, you're ready for Mission Pie (p159), boozy ice cream at Humphry Slocombe (p158), tea cakes from Tartine (p159) and salted caramel eclairs from Craftsman & Wolves (p155).

➡**Look the part** Define your own streetwise Mission style with local designers at Gravel & Gold (p169), Betabrand (p169), Nooworks (p169), Dema (p170) and Aggregate Supply (p170).

Getting There & Away

➡**Bus** The 14 runs from Downtown to the Mission District along Mission St. The 22 runs from Mission to the Marina, bus 49 follows Mission St and Van Ness Ave to the wharf, while the 33 links Potrero and the Mission to the Castro, the Haight and Golden Gate Park.

➡**Streetcar** The J streetcar heads from Downtown through the Mission. The T Muni line from Downtown via SoMa stops along 3rd St between 16th and 22nd, in Potrero's Dogpatch district.

➡**BART** Stations at 16th and 24th Sts serve the Mission.

◉ SIGHTS

The Mission is a crossroads of contradictions and at its heart is Mission St, San Francisco's faded 'miracle mile' of deco cinemas now occupied by 99¢ stores and shady characters, surrounded by colorful murals and trendsetting restaurants. West of Mission St, Valencia St has quirky boutiques and cultural centers. Further east, Potrero Hill has become a bedroom community for Silicon Valley tech execs, with art and culinary schools taking over warehouses downhill in Potrero Gulch and in waterfront Dogpatch.

★ BALMY ALLEY
MURALS

Map p328 (☎415-285-2287; www.precitaeyes. org; btwn 24th & 25th Sts; ☐10, 12, 27, 33, 48, Ⓑ24th St Mission) Inspired by Diego Rivera's 1930s San Francisco murals and outraged by US foreign policy in Central America, Mission artists set out in the 1970s to transform the political landscape, one mural-covered garage door at a time. Balmy Alley brought personal perspectives to international events, with Mujeres Muralistas (Women Muralists) and Placa ('mark-making') transforming back-alley fences into a united artistic front.

Today, a one-block walk down Balmy Alley leads past three decades of murals, from an early memorial for El Salvador activist Archbishop Óscar Romero to an homage to Frida Kahlo, Georgia O'Keefe and other pioneering women artists. Precita Eyes restores these murals, commissions new ones by San Francisco artists and runs muralist-led tours that cover 50 to 70 Mission murals within an eight-block radius of Balmy Alley. On November 1, the annual Mission parade Día de los Muertos (Day of the Dead) begins here.

★ 826 VALENCIA
CULTURAL SITE

Map p328 (☎415-642-5905; www.826valencia. org; 826 Valencia St; ⊗noon-6pm; ⊛; ☐14, 33, 49, ⓂJ, Ⓑ16th St Mission) Avast, ye scurvy scalawags! If ye be shipwrecked without yer eye patch or McSweeney's literary anthology, lay down ye dubloons and claim yer booty at this here nonprofit Pirate Store. Below decks, kids be writing tall tales for dark nights asea, and ye can study making video games and magazines and suchlike, if that be yer dastardly inclination. Arrrr!

This eccentric pirate supply store selling eye patches, spyglasses and McSweeney's literary magazines fronts a nonprofit offering free writing workshops and tutoring for youth. 'No buccaneers! No geriatrics!' warns the sign above the vat of sand where kids rummage for buried pirates' booty. Found treasure is theirs to keep, in exchange for barter at the front counter – a song, maybe, or a knock-knock joke.

Step behind the velvet curtain into the Fish Theater, where a bug-eyed puffer fish is immersed in Method acting. The ichthyoid antics may not be quite up to Sean Penn standards, but as the sign says, 'Please don't judge the fish.' Check the calendar for evening writing workshops ranging from perfume-inspired fiction to video game scripts.

DOLORES PARK
PARK

Map p328 (www.doloresparkworks.org; Dolores St, btwn 18th & 20th Sts; ⊛⛹; ☐14, 33, 49, Ⓑ16th St Mission, ⓂJ) Semiprofessional tanning, taco picnics and a Hunky Jesus Contest every Easter: welcome to San Francisco's sunny side. Dolores Park has something for everyone, from street ball and tennis to the Mayan pyramid playground (sorry kids: no human sacrifice allowed). Political protests and other favorite local sports happen year-round and there are free movie nights and Mime Troupe performances in summer.

Climb to the upper southwest corner for the best views of downtown, framed by palm trees. Flat patches are generally reserved for soccer games, cultural festivals, candlelight vigils and ultimate Frisbee. Second-hand highs copped near the bathroom may have you chasing the *helados* (ice-cream) cart.

MISSION DOLORES
CHURCH

Map p328 (Misión San Francisco de Asís; ☎415-621-8203; www.missiondolores.org; 3321 16th St; adult/child $5/3; ⊗9am-4pm Nov-Apr, to 4:30pm May-Oct; ☐22, 33, Ⓑ16th St Mission, ⓂJ) The city's oldest building and its namesake, whitewashed adobe Misión San Francisco de Asís was founded in 1776 and rebuilt in 1782 with conscripted Ohlone and Miwok labor – note the ceiling patterned after native baskets. Recent restorations revealed a hidden mural behind the altar painted by Ohlone artisans: a sacred heart, pierced by a sword and dripping with blood.

The building's nickname, Mission Dolores (Mission of the Sorrows), was taken from a nearby lake but it turned out to be tragically apt. With harsh living conditions and little resistance to introduced diseases, some 5000 Ohlone and Miwok died in mission measles epidemics in 1814 and 1826. In the cemetery beside the adobe mission, a replica Ohlone hut commemorates their mass burial in the graveyard, among early Mexican and European settlers.

Surrounding the Ohlone memorial, you'll notice graves dating from the Gold Rush. Alongside mission founders are buried Don Luis Antonio Arguello, the first governor of Alta California under Mexican rule, and Don Francisco de Haro, the first mayor of San Francisco. Hitchcock fans looking for the grave of Carlotta Valdes will be disappointed: the tomb was only a prop for the film *Vertigo*.

Today the modest adobe mission is overshadowed by the adjoining ornate Churrigueresque basilica, built in 1913 after an 1876 brick Gothic cathedral collapsed in the 1906 earthquake. The front doors are usually only open during services, so you'll need to pass through the original adobe mission structure and cross a courtyard to enter a side door.

Your eyes may take a moment to adjust once you're inside, because most of the light is filtered through the basilica's splendid stained-glass windows. The choir windows show St Francis beaming beatifically against an orange background, and lower windows along the nave feature the 21 California missions from Santa Cruz to San Diego and mission builders Father Junípero Serra and Father Francisco Palou. True to Mission Dolores' name, seven panels depict the Seven Sorrows of Mary: one above the main door and three on each of the side balconies.

CREATIVITY EXPLORED   ART GALLERY
Map p328 (☎415-863-2108; www.creativity explored.org; 3245 16th St; donations welcome; ☺10am-3pm Mon-Fri, to 7pm Thu, noon-5pm Sat-Sun; ; 14, 22, 33, 49, B16th St Mission, MJ) Brave new worlds are captured in inspired artworks destined for museum retrospectives, major collections from New York to New Zealand and even Marc Jacobs handbags – all by the local developmentally disabled artists who create at this nonprofit center. Intriguing themes

range from superheroes to architecture and openings are joyous celebrations with the artists, their families and rock-star fan base.

CLARION ALLEY   MURALS
Map p328 (btwn 17th & 18th Sts, off Valencia St; 14, 22, 33, B16th St Mission, MJ) FREE Trial by fire is nothing compared to Clarion Alley's street-art test: unless a piece is truly inspired, it's going to get peed on or painted over. Very few pieces survive for years, such as Megan Wilson's daisy-covered *Capitalism Is Over (If You Want It)* or Jet Martinez' view of Clarion Alley inside a man standing in a psychedelic forest.

Even art-prankster Banksy respected the rules of this road: instead of infringing on local turf curated by Balmy Alley's collective of street artists, Banksy's stencil of a Native American holding a No Trespassing sign went up in Sycamore St, the next alley over. Incontinent art critics seem to have taken over the east end of Balmy Alley – pee-eew! – so topical murals usually go up on the west end.

GALERÍA DE LA RAZA   ART GALLERY
Map p328 (☎415-826-8009; www.galeriadela raza.org; 2857 24th St; ☺noon-6pm Tue-Sat; ; 10, 14, 33, 48, 49, B24th St Mission) Art never forgets its roots at this nonprofit that has showcased Latino art since 1970. Recent standouts include Victor De La Rosa's digital textiles woven of Mission stories, group shows exploring SF's Latin gay culture, and urban Native American graffiti-folklore painting. Outside is the Digital Mural Project, a billboard featuring slogans like '*Venceremos*/We shall overcome' instead of the usual cigarette advertisements.

WOMEN'S BUILDING   NOTABLE BUILDING, MURALS
Map p328 (☎415-431-1180; www.womensbuild ing.org; 3543 18th St; ; M18th St, B16th St Mission) The nation's first female-owned-and-operated community center has been quietly doing good work with 170 women's organizations since 1979, but the 1994 addition of the *Maestrapeace* mural showed this building for the landmark that it truly is. An all-star team of *muralistas* covered the building with images of women trailblazers, including activist Rigoberta Menchú, poet Audre Lorde and former US Surgeon General Dr Joycelyn Elders.

SOUTHERN EXPOSURE ART GALLERY

Map p328 (415-863-2141; www.soex.org; 3030 20th St; donations welcome; noon-6pm Thu-Sat; 12, 22, 27, 33, 16th St Mission) Art really ties the room together at nonprofit arts center Southern Exposure, where works are carefully crafted not just with paint and canvas but a sense of community. Recent projects include Sandra Ono's coral reef installation made of plastic sandwich bags and Mat Dryhurst's musical performance with percussion on vintage calculating machines.

Don't miss SoEx's annual Monster Drawing Rally, where major Bay Area artists draw live and the audience snaps up works for $60 while the ink's still wet.

ELEANOR HARWOOD GALLERY ART GALLERY

Map p328 (415-867-7770; www.eleanorhar wood.com; 1295 Alabama St; 11am-6pm Wed-Sat; 10, 27, 33, 48, 24th St Mission) **FREE** On a sleepy Mission street, this eye-opening gallery showcases Bay Area talents, including Francesca Pastine, who creates haunting drawings by blacking out news-paper columns like a censor, leaving only margins. Breakout gallery stars include US Venice Biennale artist Emily Prince, whose daily drawings form poignant catalogs: all the hats in her house, say, or all the US soldiers killed in Iraq.

GUERRERO GALLERY ART GALLERY

Map p328 (415-400-5168; www.guerrero gallery.com; 2700 19th St; 11am-7pm Tue-Sat, noon-5pm Sun; 22, 27, 33, 16th St Mission) **FREE** Social critiques can come across heavy-handed in words, but the artists featured at Guerrero Gallery have a way of slyly slipping them into captivating art. Witness Erin M Riley's tapestries inspired by blurry party-girl Polaroids, Hilary Pecis' collage of famous guys named John and Andrew Schoultz's gold-leafed American flag that's rough around the edges.

RATIO 3 ART GALLERY

Map p328 (415-821-3371; www.ratio3.org; 2831A Mission St; 10am-5pm Tue-Sat; 12, 14, 48, 49, 16th St Mission) Art-fair buzz begins at this trippy stark-black gallery that

---

WORTH A DETOUR

POTRERO GULCH

San Francisco's Design District has found its edge with the arrival of avant-garde galleries, showing art that easily upstages beige sofas. Between SoMa and Potrero Hill is a gulch dotted with warehouse showrooms overlooked not long ago, unless you were in the business of selecting window treatments. But ever since **California College of the Arts** (1-800-447-1278; www.cca.edu; 1111 8th St at 16th St; 11am-7pm Tue & Thu, to 6pm Wed, Fri & Sat; 10, 19, 22, 33) **FREE** creatively repurposed the neighborhood's old bus depot for its campus, Potrero Gulch has become downright eye-catching. Stop inside CCA to discover fresh provocations in the Wattis Gallery, which recently featured Lebanese painter-poet Etel Adnan, and in PLAySPACE, the student-curated gallery.

Head under the highway overpass to discover **SOMArts** (Map p324; 415-863-1414; www.somarts.org; 934 Brannan St; gallery noon-7pm Tue-Fri, to 5pm Sat), a nonprofit community hub for creative thinking that hosts shows featuring edible murals, cave paintings of internet memes, and live-action Samoan tattooing performances. Just down the street, San Francisco Center for the Book (p172) features shows of hand-made pop-up books and matchbook-sized 'zines.

The magnetic creative pull of Potrero Gulch is irresistible now that two of San Francisco's leading galleries have moved to the neighborhood. **Catharine Clark Gallery** (Map p328; 415-399-1439; www.cclarkgallery.com; 248 Utah St; 11am-6pm Tue-Sat; 9, 10, 19, 22, 27, 33) **FREE** instigates art revolutions with Al Farrow's stunning miniature religious monuments meticulously crafted from used ammunition, while **Hosfelt Gallery** (Map p328; 415-495-5454; 260 Utah St; 10am-6pm Tue-Sat; 9, 10, 22, 27, 33) mesmerizes visitors with works like Rina Banerjee's massive pink plastic Taj Mahal made from recycled tourist souvenirs. Friendly art debates start over drinks and parking-lot BBQ served by Top Chef contestants at **Thee Parkside** (Map p330; www.theeparkside.com; 1600 17th St; 2pm-2am; 10, 19, 22) – but once bluegrass or punk bands play, artistic differences are settled and dancing begins.

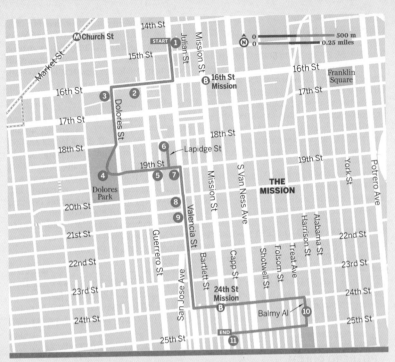

Neighborhood Walk
The Mission's Most Colorful Characters

START FOUR BARREL
END MISSION PIE
LENGTH 2.7 MILES; THREE HOURS

Begin by fueling up with house roast in the parklet at ❶ **Four Barrel** (p162) and buzz right past boutiques to ❷ **Creativity Explored** (p152), where the window showcases works by developmentally disabled artists. Ahead is the city's first building: adobe ❸ **Mission Dolores** (p151), built by some 5000 native Ohlone and Miwok. You can glimpse the Miwok memorial hut through the mission fence on Chola Lane.

To see how San Francisco has evolved, climb to the upper southwest corner of ❹ **Dolores Park** (p151) for panoramic views. Walking down 19th St, you'll pass Daniel Doherty's Impressionist-inspired 2009 mural ❺ **Dejeuner Dolores**, showing Dolores Park's regular cast of characters including frolicking pugs, handlebar-mustachoied men in matching Speedos and families in their Sunday best. Swing left on

Lapidge to spot Georgia O'Keefe and goddesses galore in ❻ **Women's Building** (p152) murals.

Back on Valencia, you'll spot the Chris Ware mural and storefront art installation of ❼ **826 Valencia** (p151), where you can duck inside for pirate supplies. Down the street, pause to pay respects to bygone celebrities at ❽ **Dog-Eared Books** (p171) – the front window features hand-drawn obituary cartoons of luminaries from Liz Taylor to Susan Sontag. Along the block is the mossy storefront of ❾ **Viracocha** (p166), where cats snuggle up to vintage typewriters.

Turn down 24th St and then swing down ❿ **Balmy Alley** (p151), where you may recognize assassinated activist Archbishop Romero and Surrealist painter Frida Kahlo among the colorful characters illuminating garage doors in this mural-covered backstreet. After this slice of Mission life, join locals for a slice of strawberry-rhubarb pie at ⓫ **Mission Pie** (p159).

regularly delivers on its promise to 'bring vastness to mind.' While some gallery artists are recognizable from frequent *Artforum* and Miami Basel appearances, gallerist Chris Perez also showcases artworks that remain inexplicably unknown – including Mitzi Pederson's shattered, glittered concrete or meticulous paintings by pioneering SF street artist Margaret Kilgallen.

ROOT DIVISION
ART GALLERY

Map p328 (☑415-863-7668; www.rootdivision.org; 3175 17th St; donations welcome; ☺2-6pm Wed-Sat; ☐14, 22, 33, 49, ☒16th St Mission) **FREE** Everyone's a winner at this arts nonprofit, which hosts curated shows on such themes as wordplay and strange bedfellows. Root Division keeps the inspiration coming, offering artists subsidized studio space in exchange for providing low-cost community art classes from painting to electronics. Don't miss interactive events like December's Misfit Toy Workshop, where artists create factory-second toys like Santa's rebel elves.

MUSEUM OF CRAFT & DESIGN
MUSEUM

Map p330 (☑415-773-0303; www.sfmcd.org; 2569 3rd St; adult/child $8/5; ☺11am-6pm Tue-Sat, noon-5pm Sun; ☐22, 48, ☒T) Pistol-packing tricycles, woven metal jellyfish, Gothic cardboard picture frames: dazzling, experimental designs not meant for mass production reignite wonder at the Museum of Craft & Design. Check the online schedule for hands-on workshops for kids and Etsy Meet & Make nights, where accomplished artisans lead hands-on projects related to museum shows, from wire crochet jewelry to art made with living moss.

☒ EATING

★ LA TAQUERIA
MEXICAN $

Map p328 (☑415-285-7117; 2889 Mission St; burritos $6-8; ☺11am-9pm Mon-Sat, to 8pm Sun; ☑; ☐12, 14, 48, 49, ☒24th St Mission) The definitive burrito at La Taqueria has no debatable saffron rice, spinach tortilla or mango salsa – just perfectly grilled meats, slow-cooked beans and classic tomatillo or mesquite salsa wrapped in a flour tortilla. If you skip the beans, you'll pay extra, because they pack in more meat – but spicy pickles and *crema* (Mexican sour cream) bring complete burrito bliss.

★ CRAFTSMAN & WOLVES
BAKERY, CALIFORNIAN $

Map p328 (☑415-913-7713; http://craftsman-wolves.com; 746 Valencia Street; pastries $3-7; ☺7am-9pm Mon-Thu, to 10pm Fri, 8am-10pm Sat, 8am-9pm Sun; ☐14, 22, 33, 49, ☒16th St Mission, ☒J) Exquisite checkered black sesame/white coffee cube cakes are ideal for celebrating SF half-birthdays, foggy days and imaginary holidays. Conventional breakfasts can't compare to the Rebel Within: savoury sausage-spiked asiago cheese muffin with a silken soft-boiled egg baked inside. Blue Bottle espresso calls for sandwich cookies – cocoa shortbread with peanut-butter ganache – and matcha coconut traveler's cake for the road.

UDUPI PALACE
INDIAN $

Map p328 (☑415-970-8000; www.udupipalaceca.com; 1007 Valencia St; mains $8-10; ☺11am-10pm Mon-Thu, to 10:30pm Fri-Sun; ☐14, 33, 49, ☒24th St Mission) Tandoori in the Tenderloin is for novices – SF foodies swoon over the bright, clean flavors of South Indian *dosa* (light, crispy lentil-flour pancake) dipped in mildly spicy vegetable *sambar* (soup) and coconut chutney. Don't miss the *medhu vada* (savory lentil donuts with *sambar* and chutney) or *bagala bhath* (yogurt rice with cucumber and nutty toasted mustard seeds).

MISSION CHEESE
CHEESE $

Map p328 (☑415-553-8667; missioncheese.net; 736 Valencia St; ☺11am-9pm Tue-Thu, to 10pm Fri-Sat; ☐14, 22, 33, 49, ☒J, ☒16th St Mission) Smile and say wine at this cheese bar, serving up sublime pairings with expert advice and zero pretension. The all-domestic cheese menu ranges from triple-creamy to extra-stinky, raw cow's milk to sheep's milk, and California wines reign supreme. When in dairy doubt, try 'mongers choice' surprise-cheese platters with pickles, nuts and dried fruit. Order at the bar; note early closing.

PANCHO VILLA
MEXICAN $

Map p328 (☑415-864-8840; www.sfpanchovilla.com; 3071 16th St; burritos $7-8.50; ☺10am-midnight; ☐14, 22, 33, 49, ☒16th St Mission) The hero of the downtrodden and burrito-deprived, Pancho Villa supplies tinfoil-wrapped meals the girth of your forearm and lets you add ammunition at the fresh, heaping salsa bar. The line moves fast going in, and as you leave, the door is held

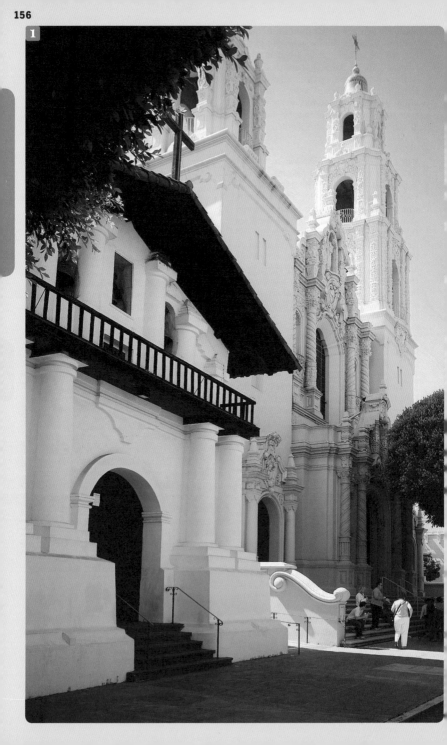

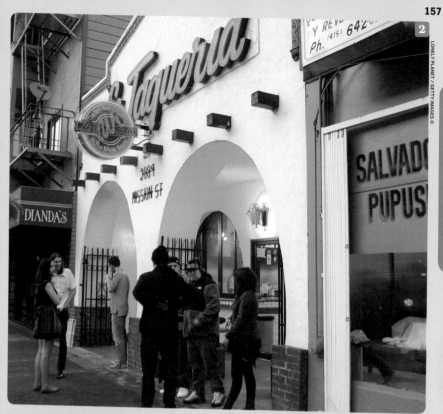

LONELY PLANET / GETTY IMAGES ©

JUDY BELLAH / GETTY IMAGES ©

1. Mission Dolores (p151)
This complex – after which the neighborhood is named – includes the Misión San Francisco de Asís (the city's oldest building) and a grand 1913 basilica.

2. La Taqueria (p155)
Head here for some of the best burritos and tacos in town; choice ingredients such as spicy pickles and *crema* (Mexican sour cream) have made this a local institution.

3. Carnaval San Francisco (p21)
The Mission bursts with color on the last weekend of May, as crowds fill the streets for this vibrant celebration of Latin American and Caribbean music and culture.

SF À LA MODE: BEST LOCAL ICE CREAM

Humphry Slocombe (Map p328; ☎415-550-6971; www.humphryslocombe.com; 2790 Harrison St; ice cream $2.75-5; ⊙noon-9pm Mon-Thu, to 10pm Fri-Sun; 🖐; 🚍12, 14, 49, ⓑ24th St Mission) ✒ Indie-rock organic ice cream may permanently spoil you for Top 40 flavors. Once Thai Curry Peanut Butter and Magnolia Brewery Stout have rocked your taste buds, cookie dough seems so obvious, and ordinary sundaes can't compare to Secret Breakfast (bourbon and corn flakes) and Vietnamese Coffee drizzled with hot fudge and olive oil.

Bi-Rite Creamery (Map p328; ☎415-626-5600; www.biritecreamery.com; 3692 18th St; ice cream $3-7; ⊙11am-10pm Sun-Thu, to 11pm Fri & Sat; 🖐; 🚍33, ⓑ16th St Mission, ⓂJ) ✒ Velvet ropes at clubs seem pretentious in laid-back San Francisco, but at organic Bi-Rite Creamery they make perfect sense: once temperatures pass 70 degrees, the line wraps around the corner for organic salted caramel ice cream with housemade hot fudge, or Sonoma honey-lavender ice cream packed into organic waffle cones. For a quicker fix, get balsamic strawberry soft-serve at the window (1pm-9pm).

Mitchell's Ice Cream (Map p328; ☎415-648-2300; www.mitchellsicecream.com; 688 San Jose Ave; ice cream $3-6; ⊙11am-11pm; 🚍14, 49, ⓑ24th St Mission, ⓂJ) An otherwise mellow Mission block is thronged with grinning grown-ups and kids doing happy dances as they make their Mitchell's selections: classic Kahlua mocha cream or exotic tropical macapuno (young coconut)? The avocado and ube (purple yam) are acquired tastes but they've been local favorites for generations – Mitchells has kept San Francisco coming back for seconds since 1953.

Mr & Mrs Miscellaneous (Map p330; ☎415-970-0750; 699 22nd St; ice cream $3.50-9; ⊙11:30am-6pm Wed-Sat, to 5pm Sun; Ⓜ22nd St) Black and Tan beer, toasted-sesame halva, cinnamon-y horchata and browned butter are among the many savory, Miscellaneous flavors that make this ice creamery worth the trek to Dogpatch.

open for you and your newly acquired Pancho's paunch. Stick around for serenades by roving mariachis.

RADISH
CALIFORNIAN CREOLE $

Map p328 (☎415-834-5441; www.radishsf.com; 3465 19th St; mains $8-16; ⊙5-10pm Mon-Tue, 10am-10pm Wed-Thu, 10am-11pm Fri-Sat, 9am-9pm Sun; 🚍14, 22, 33, ⓑ16th St Mission) ✒ Hedonists and food revolutionaries converge at Radish, where decadent Southern-inspired food is made with lavish helpings of organic Californian produce and sustainable meats. Mission barflies recover with eggs and house-cured bacon in homemade biscuits and bottomless mimosas, while N'Orleans transplants get catfish po'boy sandwiches piled with tangy slaw, and vegetarians revel in roasted beets with candied pecans and sheep's feta.

OLD JERUSALEM
MIDDLE EASTERN $

Map p328 (☎415-642-5958; http://oldjsf.com; 2976 Mission St; mains $7-11; ⊙11am-10pm Sun-Thu, to 11pm Fri & Sat; 🕗; 🚍12, 14, 48, 49, ⓑ24th St Mission) Foodies scouring the Mission for the ultimate taco shouldn't overlook this outpost of Middle Eastern authenticity, complete with Dome of the Rock poster and pristine hummus that doesn't overdo the tahini. Get the classic falafel, *shwarma* (marinated, roasted lamb) or *shish taouk* (marinated grilled chicken) with all the fixings: hummus, onion, eggplant, potato and tangy purple sumac, with optional hot-pepper paste.

WISE SONS JEWISH DELICATESSEN
DELI, CALIFORNIAN $

Map p328 (☎415-787-3354; www.wisesonsdeli.com; 3150 24th St; sandwiches $10-12.50; ⊙8am-3pm Wed-Fri, from 9am Sat-Sun; 🚍12, 14, 48, 49, ⓑ24th St Mission) ✒ A Wild West East Coast deli, where the bialy comes with house-smoked wild Pacific salmon and artisan Sierra Nevada cream cheese. You're in SF, already, so get the vegetarian Reuben on rye with smoked trumpet mushrooms instead of pastrami. If the schlep to 24th St is too much, find Wise Sons at the Jewish Contemporary Museum (p86) and Ferry Building market (p79).

MISSION PIE AMERICAN, BAKERY **$**

Map p328 (☑415-282-1500; www.missionpie.
com; 2901 Mission St; pie $3-5; ⊙7am-10pm
Mon-Fri, from 8am Sat, from 9am Sun; 🛜🅿🚼;
🚇12, 14, 48, 49, 🅱24th St Mission) 🍴 Like
mom used to make, only better: hot-from-
the-oven pies at this certified-green bakery
range from savory organic chicken pot pies
($7) to all-American heirloom apple ($5 per
slice with free organic whipped cream).
The sunny Victorian storefront doubles
as a neighborhood hangout with board
games, blocks for kiddies and a library of
conscientious cookbooks to inspire your
own food revolution.

TARTINE BAKERY **$**

Map p328 (☑415-487-2600; www.tartinebakery.
com; 600 Guerrero St; pastries $3-6, sandwiches
$10-13; ⊙8am-7pm Mon, 7:30-7pm Tue & Wed,
7:30-8pm Thu & Fri, 9am-8pm Sat & Sun; 🅿;
Ⓜ18th St, 🅱16th St Mission) Riches beyond
your wildest dreams: butter-golden *pain
au chocolat*, cappuccino with ferns drawn
in dense foam and *croque monsieurs* turbo-
loaded with ham, two kinds of cheese and
béchamel. Don't be dismayed by the inevitable line out the door – it moves fast – but
be aware that lolling in Dolores Park is the
only possible post-Tartine activity.

★ICHI SUSHI SUSHI **$$**

(Map p328; ☑415-525-4750; www.ichisushi.
com; 3369 Mission St; sushi $4-8; ⊙5:30-10pm
Mon-Thu, to 11pm Fri-Sat; 🚇14, 49, 🅱24th St
Mission, Ⓜ J) Alluring on the plate and posi-
tively obscene on the tongue, Ichi Sushi is
a sharp cut above other fish joints. Chef
Tim Archuleta slices silky, sustainably
sourced fish with a jeweler's precision,
balances it atop well-packed rice, and tops
it with tiny but powerfully tangy dabs of
gelled yuzu and microscopically cut spring
onion and chili daikon that make soy
sauce unthinkable.

★NAMU GAJI KOREAN, CALIFORNIAN **$$**

Map p328 (☑431-6268; www.namusf.com; 499
Dolores St; small plates $8-22; ⊙11:30am-10pm
Tue-Thu & Sun, to 11pm Sat & Sun; 🚇22, 33, Ⓜ J,
🅱16th St Mission) 🍴 SF's unfair culinary advantages – organic local ingredients, Silicon Valley inventiveness and Pacific Rim
roots – are showcased in Namu's Korean-
inspired soul food. Menu standouts include
ultra-savory shiitake mushroom dumplings, meltingly tender marinated beef
tongue, and Namu's version of *bibimbap*:

Marin Sun Farms grass-fed steak, organic
vegetables, spicy gojuchang and Sonoma
farm egg atop rice, served sizzling in a
stone pot.

The extensive drink menu runs from
specialty *sochu* (grain liquor) to Natural
Process Alliance's organic Napa sauvignon
blanc wine, dispensed from a reused metal
canteen.

PIZZERIA DELFINA PIZZERIA **$$**

Map p328 (☑415-437-6800; www.delfinasf.com;
3611 18th St; pizzas $11-17; ⊙11:30am-10pm
Tue-Thu, to 11pm Fri, noon-11pm Sat & Sun, 5:30-
10pm Mon; 🅿) One bite explains why SF is
so obsessed with pizza lately: Delfina's thin
crust supports the weight of fennel sausage
and fresh mozzarella without drooping
or cracking, while white pizzas let chefs
freestyle with Cali-foodie ingredients like
maitake mushrooms, broccoli rabe and
artisan cheese. No reservations; sign up
on the chalkboard and wait with wine at
Delfina bar next door.

LOCANDA ITALIAN **$$**

Map p328 (☑415-863-6800; www.locandasf.
com; 557 Valencia St; share plates $10-24;
⊙5:30pm-10pm Mon-Wed, to 11pm Thu-Sat,
5-10pm Sun; 🚇14, 22, 33, 49, 🅱16th St Mission)
Friends, Romans, San Franciscans – join
the crowd for pizza bianca with figs and
prosciutto, scrumptious tripe melting
into rich tomato-mint sauce, Roman fried

TOP 5 MISSION TACOS

La Palma Mexicatessen (p161)
Carnitas (braised pork shoulder) with
pickled red onion on tortillas made
fresh in-house with organic masa.

Pancho Villa (p155) Pollo verde
(green-chili-stewed chicken) with
escabeche (spicy pickled) carrots and
crema (Mexican sour cream).

Namu Gaji (p159) Korean steak
tacos, with grass-fed beef and spicy
sauce rolled into a seaweed wrapper.

Tacolicious (p160) Seasonal vegetarian taco with roasted butternut
squash, poblano peppers and *pepitas*
(spiced pumpkin seeds).

La Taqueria (p155) *Lengua* (marinated beef tongue) with onions, cilantro
and pickled jalapeno.

artichokes and tender fried sweetbreads. Pasta dishes are less adventurous than small plates invented with market-fresh organic ingredients, like the poached farm egg with squash blossoms and shavings of *bottarga (*cured fish roe).

MAVERICK   CALIFORNIAN $$
Map p328 (☏415-863-3061; www.sfmaverick. com; 3316 17th St; share plates $12-25; ⊙5:30-10pm Mon-Thu, to 11pm Fri & Sat, 5:30-9pm Sun, brunch 10:30am-2:30pm Sat & Sun; ☐14, 22, 33, 49, Ⓑ16th St Mission) 🍷 Cowboys start California dreaming at this tiny Mission bistro, where pasture-raised meats are spruced up with sensational California-grown sides – think Southern fried chicken with pan-seared broccoli rabe and whiskey gravy, or sweetbreads with pickled cherries and edible nasturtium flowers. Go Mondays or Wednesdays for two-person fried chicken buckets with braised greens, house-pickled beans and fluffy biscuits for $25.

TACOLICIOUS   CAL-MEX $$
Map p328 (☏415-626-1344; 741 Valencia St; ⊙11:30am-midnight; 🍷; ☐14, 22, 33, 49, Ⓑ16th St Mission, ⓂJ) Never mind the name: once you get a mouthful of *carnitas* (braised-pork) tacos and passionfruit-habanero margaritas, you're in no position to argue authenticity or grammar, or say anything besides *uno mas, por favor* (another, please). Choose four tacos for $14, including seasonal vegetarian options. No reservations, but while you wait you can work through the 100-tequila menu at the bar.

MISSION CHINESE   CAL-CHINESE $$
Map p328 (Lung Shan; ☏415-863-2800; www.missionchinesefood.com; 2234 Mission St; dishes $9-16; ⊙11:30am-10:30pm Mon-Tue, Thu-Sun; ☐14, 33, 49, Ⓑ16th St Mission) Extreme gourmets and Chinese takeout fans converge on Danny Bowien's cult-food dive. Tiki pork belly with pickled pineapple and spicy lamb-face noodles are big enough for two – though not for the salt-shy – and satisfy your conscience: 75¢ from each main is donated to San Francisco Food Bank. Wine corkage is $10; cash only, parties of eight or less.

MR POLLO   CAL-ECUADORIAN $$
Map p328 (☏415-374-5546; 2823 Mission St; 4-dish tasting menu $20; ⊙6-10pm; ☐12, 14, 48, 49, Ⓑ24th St Mission) Mission-Mex devotees are in for a culinary awakening at this South American supper club showcasing

organic Californian ingredients. Prepare for a parade of salt-pork *arepas* (corn-cakes), empanadas (stuffed pastries), seasonal mains like crispy salmon belly with ginger and housemade lychee ice cream. This bolt-hole hidden among Mission St dollar stores seats about 15, so come early and expect a 20-minute wait.

EL TECHO DI LOLINDA   LATIN AMERICAN $$
Map p328 (Lolinda Rooftop; ☏415-550-6970; http://lolindasf.com; 2518 Mission St; small plates $8-17; ⊙5:30-11pm Sun-Thu, to midnight Fri-Sat; ☐14, 33, 49, Ⓑ24th St Mission) Come here for Latin street food six floors above Mission St, with views over cinema marquees, palm trees and low-riders all the way to downtown. Sunny days call for *ono ceviche*, a Royal Bermuda Yacht Club (white rum, lime, curacao and Velvet Falernum) and sunblock; foggy days require chicken empanadas, the Lone Palm (spiced rum with grapefruit, honey and bitters) and a windbreaker.

★COMMONWEALTH   CALIFORNIAN $$$
Map p328 (☏415-355-1500; www.commonwealthsf.com; 2224 Mission St; small plates $11-16; ⊙5:30-10pm Sun-Thu, to 11pm Fri & Sat; 🍷; ☐14, 22, 33, 49, Ⓑ16th St Mission) California's most imaginative farm-to-table dining isn't in some quaint barn, but the converted cinderblock Mission dive where chef Jason Fox serves sensational salads of green strawberries and black radishes with fennel pollen, and poached oysters atop foraged succulents and rhubarb ice that looks like a tide-pool and tastes like a dream. Savor the $75 prix fixe, knowing $10 is donated to charity.

RANGE   CALIFORNIAN $$$
Map p328 (☏415-282-8283; www.rangesf.com; 842 Valencia St; mains $20-28; ⊙6-10:30pm Mon-Thu, from 5:30-Sun; 🍷; ☐14, 33, 49, Ⓑ16th St Mission, ⓂJ) Inspired American dining is alive and well within Range. Local king salmon practically sings on the plate with pickled chili, olives and basil, and pasta with fava beans, goat's milk feta and pistachio pistou is a cure for common mac 'n' cheese. Desserts are made in-house. Although the beer fridge is a repurposed medical cabinet, Range won't cost you an arm or leg.

FOREIGN CINEMA   CALIFORNIAN $$$
Map p328 (☏415-648-7600; www.foreign cinema.com; 2534 Mission St; ⊙6-10pm Mon-Thu, 5:30-11pm Fri & Sat, 5:30-10pm Sun, brunch 11am-

GOURMET SUPPLIES

Bi-Rite (Map p328; ☎415-241-9760; www.biritemarket.com; 3639 18th St; sandwiches $7-10; ☺9am-9pm; ♿; ➡14, 22, 33, 49, Ⓑ16th St Mission) 🌿 Nemesis of grocery budgets and ally of gourmands whose cooking repertoire is limited to reheating, Bi-Rite is a San Francisco foodie's version of breakfast at Tiffany's. Local artisan chocolates, sustainable cured meats and organic fruit are displayed like jewels, and the selection of Californian wines and cheeses is downright dazzling. Get deli sandwiches to go to Dolores Park.

Rainbow Grocery (Map p328; ☎415-863-0620; www.rainbowgrocery.org; 1745 Folsom St; ☺9am-9pm; ♿; ➡9, 12, 33, 47) 🌿 The legendary cooperative attracts masses to buy eco/organic/fair-trade products in bulk, sample the bounty of local cheeses and flirt in the artisan chocolate aisle. To answer your questions about where to find what in the Byzantine bulk section, ask a fellow shopper – staff can be elusive. Small though well-priced wine and craft beer selections; no meat products.

La Palma Mexicatessen (Map p328; ☎415-647-1500; 2884 24th St; ☺8am-6pm Mon-Sat, to 5pm Sun; ➡14, 48, Ⓑ24th St Mission) Follow the hand-slapping sound of organic tortilla-making in progress to La Palma and hit the take-out counter for handmade tamales, *pupusas* (tortilla-pockets) filled with potato and *chicharones* (pork crackling), *carnitas* (slow-roasted pulled pork) by the pound, *cotija* (Oaxacan cheese) and La Palma's own tangy tomatillo sauce. Now all you need is a small army to finish off that meal you've assembled...

3pm Sat & Sun; ➡12, 14, 33, 48, 49, Ⓑ24th St Mission) Reliably tasty dishes like spiced apricot quail and grilled ancho-chili pork chops with roast fig are the main attractions, but Luis Buñuel and François Truffaut provide an entertaining backdrop with movies screened in the courtyard, with subtitles you can follow when the conversation lags. For the red-carpet treatment, there's valet parking ($12) and a well-stocked oyster bar.

🍷 DRINKING & NIGHTLIFE

★ELIXIR
BAR

Map p328 (☎415-522-1633; www.elixirsf.com; 3200 16th St; ☺3pm-2am Mon-Fri, noon-2am Sat & Sun; Ⓑ16th St Mission) 🌿 Do the planet a favor and have another drink at SF's first certified-green bar in an actual 1858 Wild West saloon serving knockout cocktails made with farm-fresh mixers and small-batch, organic, even biodynamic spirits. Consult the bartender for sneak-up-on-you seasonal cocktails – dastardly tasty organic basil Negronis and cucumber-infused vodka Collins will get you air-guitar-rocking to the killer jukebox.

Drink-for-a-cause Wednesdays encourage imbibing, with proceeds from 9pm until close supporting local charities.

ZEITGEIST
BAR

Map p328 (☎415-255-7505; www.zeitgeistsf.com; 199 Valencia St; ☺9am-2am; ➡22, 49, Ⓑ16th St Mission) You've got two seconds flat to order from tough-gal barkeeps used to putting macho bikers in their place – but with 40 beers on draft, beer lovers are spoiled for choice. Regulars head straight to the bar's huge graveled beer garden to sit at long picnic tables and smoke out. Bring cash for the bar and late-night food vendors.

TRICK DOG
BAR

Map p328 (☎415-471-2999; www.trickdogbar.com; 3010 20th St; ☺3pm-2am; ➡12, 14, 49) Drink in style with designer cocktails meticulously calibrated to match a Pantone color palette. Choose your drink by paint swatch color: Razzle Dazzle Red gets you local Hangar One vodka with house cordials, strawberries and lime, while Gypsy Tan means Rittenhouse rye with Fernet, lemon-ginger and nutmeg. Arrive early for bar stools or hit the mood-lit loft for high-concept bar bites.

RITUAL COFFEE ROASTERS
CAFE

Map p328 (☎415-641-1011; www.ritualroasters.com; 1026 Valencia St; ☺6am-10pm Mon-Fri, 7am-10pm Sat, 7am-9pm Sun; ☎; ➡14, 49, Ⓑ24th St Mission) Cults wish they inspired the same devotion as Ritual, where regulars solemnly queue for house-roasted cappuccino with ferns drawn in foam and specialty drip coffees with some genuinely bizarre flavor profiles – descriptions comparing roasts to grapefruit peel or hazelnut aren't exaggerating. Electrical outlets are limited to encourage conversation, so you can eavesdrop on dates, art debates and political protest plans.

20 SPOT
WINE BAR

Map p328 (📞415-624-3140; www.20spot.com; 3565 20th St; ⏰5pm-1am Thu-Sat, to midnight Sun, Mon & Wed; 🚇14, 22, 33, Ⓑ16th St Mission) Pull up an Eames rocker and find your California mellow at this midcentury wine lounge. After decades as Force of Habit punk record shop – note the vintage sign – this corner joint has earned the right to unwind with a glass of Baker Lane Sonoma Pinot Noir and not get any guff. Caution: deviled duck eggs could become a habit.

ROCK BAR
BAR

(Map p328; 📞415-550-6664; http://rockbarsf. com; 80 29th St; ⏰4pm-2am Mon-Sat, from 10am Sun; 🚇14, 24, 49, Ⓜ J) Eureka: inside these rock-veneer walls, you're golden with original concoctions made of craft spirits and priced to move ($7 to $10). Happy hours from 4pm to 7:30pm feature house-specialty cocktails like the Dirty Metaphoric, with Tito's vodka, olive juice and muddled Fresno chili. Order fried chicken across the street at Front Porch and they'll deliver it to your stool. Cash only.

MONK'S KETTLE
PUB

Map p328 (📞415-865-9523; www.monkskettle. com; 3141 16th St; ⏰noon-2am; 🚇22, 33, 49, Ⓑ16th St Mission) Unlike trendy gastropubs, Monk's Kettle realizes you're here for the beer – and delivers, with 25 cult brews ranging in hue from Japanese Hitachino white ale to Sonoma's Death & Taxes black lager. Regulars waiting an hour for seats are probably here for 100+ Belgian-style saison ales, accompanied by food with enough mustard and salt to perk thirst for more beer.

LEXINGTON CLUB
LESBIAN BAR

Map p328 (📞415-863-2052; www.lexington club.com; 3464 19th St; ⏰3pm-2am; 🚇14, 33, 49, Ⓑ16th St Mission) SF's all-grrrrl bar can be cliquish at first so be strategic: compliment someone on her skirt (she made it

herself) or tattoo (she designed it herself) and casually mention you're undefeated at pinball, pool or thumb-wrestling. When she wins (because she's no stranger to the Lex), pout just a little and maybe she'll buy you a $4 beer.

HOMESTEAD
BAR

Map p328 (📞415-282-4663; www.homesteadsf. com; 2301 Folsom St; ⏰2pm-2am; 🚇12, 14, 22, 33, 49, Ⓑ16th St Mission) Your friendly Victorian corner dive c 1893, complete with carved-wood bar, pressed-tin ceiling, salty roast peanuts in the shell and salty Mission characters. On any given night, SF's creative contingent pack the place to celebrate art openings, dance shows and fashion launches with cheap draft beer – and when Iggy Pop or David Bowie hits the jukebox, stand back.

FOUR BARREL COFFEE
CAFE

Map p328 (📞415-252-0800; www.fourbarrel coffee.com; 375 Valencia St; ⏰7am-8pm; 🈴; 🚇14, 22, 🚲16th St Mission) Surprise: the hippest cafe in town is also the friendliest. Taxidermied boars glower atop industrial roastery walls, but the baristas are upbeat, and having no outlets or wi-fi keeps the scene sociable. Drip roasts are complex and powerful; the fruity espresso is an acquired taste. Caffeinating crowds mingle in a sunny parklet with bike parking and patio seating.

Opt for the Slow Pour at the front bar and your barista will explain growing, roasting and cupping methods in charmingly geeky detail.

FIZZARY
SODA FOUNTAIN

Map p328 (📞877-368-4608; www.fizzary. com; 2949 Mission St; ⏰11:45am-7pm Tue-Sun; 🚇12, 14, 27, 49, Ⓑ24th St Mission) Nostalgia-inducing soda pop is the drug of choice at this modern 'apothecary,' from alarmingly red strawberry Ski soda to Capone's Black Cherry soda. Classic flavors like grape and cream soda glow enticingly in backlit prayer niches, but adventurous drinkers glug Always Avery's Zombie Brain-Juice, Mr Q's fizzy cucumber concoction and house-made Taylor's Tonics Espresso Cola – all $2 each, or four for $6.

If your soda of choice isn't in the fridge, pop your pop in the immersion chiller for five minutes while you shop for salt-water taffy. One piece is free with soda purchase; get the chili mango.

TRUCK
GAY BAR

Map p328 (📞415-252-0306; www.trucksf.com; 1900 Folsom St; ⏰4pm-2am Mon-Fri, from 2pm Sat-Sun; 🚌12, 22, 33, Ⓑ16th St Mission) Local artists, out-of-face drag queens, off-duty DJs and underground scenesters mingle at Truck over pinball, stiff drinks and pop-up patio suppers. The scene is gay neighborhood bar most nights but drag happens at Cocktailgate Sundays, and Fridays get shirtless by 6pm. Dirty boys: get the password for Tuesday's speakeasy for $1 shots all night.

ST VINCENT TAVERN
WINE BAR

Map p328 (📞415-285-1200; www.stvincentsf. com; 1270 Valencia St; ⏰5:30-10pm Mon-Thu, to 11pm Fri, noon-3pm & 5:30-11pm Sat; 🚌12, 14, 48, 49, Ⓑ24th St Mission) Dive into the deep end of the list of 100 bottles under $100 compiled by sommelier/owner David Lynch - if you're not drinking ambitiously, he'll serve you half a bottle of Cep Russian River Pinot Noir Rosé (bet you'll drink the other half). Food isn't an afterthought: bone marrow with smoked Calabrian chili is meant for obscure, earthy Croatian red wines.

Saturday afternoons the cellar is open for tastings and pairings, usually 5–6 tastes for $20–25.

LATIN AMERICAN CLUB
BAR

Map p328 (📞415-647-2732; 3286 22nd St; ⏰6pm-2am Mon-Fri, from 3pm Sat-Sun; 🚌12, 14, 49, ⒷMission St) Margaritas go the distance here - just don't stand up too fast. Ninja *piñatas* and *papel picado* (cut-paper banners) add a festive atmosphere, and rosy lighting and generous pours enable shameless flirting outside your age range.

DOC'S CLOCK
BAR

Map p328 (www.docsclock.com; 2575 Mission St; ⏰5pm-2am Mon-Thu, 4pm-2am Fri & Sat, 8pm-midnight Sun; 🅟; 🚌12, 14, 49, Ⓑ24th St Mission) 🌿 Follow the siren call of the dazzling neon sign into this mellow, green-certified dive for your choice of 14 local craft brews, free shuffleboard, Pac-Man, tricky pinball and easy conversation. Happy hours run 9pm to 2am daily and all day Sundays; first Saturday of each month is 4pm to 8pm Doggie Happy Hour, with proceeds to support city dog rescues.

BORDERLANDS
CAFE

Map p328 (📞415-970-6998; www.borderlands -cafe.com; 870 Valencia St; ⏰8am-8pm; 🚌14, 33, 49, Ⓑ16th St Mission) A delicious outlier in high-tech SF, Borderlands has unplugged its wi-fi and credit-card machines and provided lo-fi reading material: racks of magazines and paperback mysteries available for thumbing or the 1950s purchase price of 50¢. West Coast coffeehouse culture is staging a comeback here, complete with hairless cats, creaky wood floors, top-notch hot chocolate and sociable sofas for offline conversation.

BERETTA
BAR

Map p328 (📞415-695-1199; www.berettasf.com; 1199 Valencia St; ⏰5:30pm-1am Mon-Fri, from 11am Sat & Sun; Ⓑ24th St Mission) After shopping locally and seasonally on Valencia St, nothing hits the spot like Beretta's cocktails, made with fresh everything. Order your Death Proof special (chartreuse, gin, lime and craft root beer) before or after peak dinner hours, when the small storefront restaurant-and-bar gets packed and deafeningly loud. You might be inclined to come back for cocktail classes.

⭐ ENTERTAINMENT

⭐ROXIE CINEMA
CINEMA

Map p328 (📞415-863-1087; www.roxie.com; 3117 16th St; regular/matinee $10/7; 🚌14, 22, 33, 49, Ⓑ16th St Mission) A little neighborhood nonprofit cinema with major international clout for distributing indie films and showing controversial films and documentaries banned elsewhere. Tickets to film festival premieres, rare revivals and raucous annual Oscars telecasts sell out fast - but if the main show is packed, check out documentaries in teensy next-door Little Roxy instead. No ads, plus personal introductions to every film.

⭐OBERLIN DANCE COLLECTIVE
DANCE

Map p328 (ODC; 📞box office 415-863-9834, classes 415-863-6606; www.odctheater.org; 3153 17th St; drop-in class $14, shows $25-50; ⏰shows vary; 🚌12, 14, 22, 33, 49, Ⓑ16th St Mission) For nearly 40 years, ODC has been redefining dance with risky, raw performances and the sheer joy of movement. ODC's season runs September–December, but its stage presents year-round shows featuring local and international artists. ODC Dance Commons is a hub and hangout for the dance community offering 200 classes a week, from flamenco to vogue; all ages and levels welcome.

1. 22nd St Parklet

One of San Francisco's growing number of curbside parklets, this piece of reclaimed real estate is a great vantage point from which to take in the passing Mission scene.

2. Anchor Brewing Company (p171)

Take a tour of Potrero Hill's 1937 landmark building and see not only the workings of the brewery but sample the delicious end-product.

3. Dolores Park (p151)

This gathering point in the Mission neighborhood plays host to protests, taco picnics, sports, movies, mime peformances and everything in between.

WORTH A DETOUR

DOGPATCH CREATIVE CORRIDOR

Techies have staked out turf atop Potrero Hil, but upstart creatives have the run of waterfront warehouses downhill around 22nd and 3rd St. After the shipping business moved to Oakland in the 1950s, this neighborhood was left in dry-dock for decades – even waterfront dive bars like Tom's Dry Dock closed (though the sign remains). But sprawling brick shipping warehouses proved ideal for San Francisco Art Institute's MFA graduate student studios, and now that **Muni's T line** has made the area accessible from downtown, the Museum of Craft & Design (p155) moved in down the block. Around the corner, **Triple Aught Design** (Map p330; ☎415-318-8252; www.tripleaughtdesign.com; 660 22nd St; ⏰11am-6pm Tue-Sun; 🚌22, 48, Ⓜ T) produces thoughtfully designed, multi-functional menswear worthy of James Bond, with sleek Stealth Hoodies and trousers with reinforced knees perfect for parties or parkour.

This industrial waterfront may not look much like Napa Valley, but urban wineries and wine bars have sprouted up here like dandelions in the sidewalk. **Sutton Cellars** (Map p330; ☎707-874-9466; www.suttoncellars.com; 601 22nd St; ⏰call for tastings; Ⓜ T) offers $5 tastings that range from cult Rose of Carignane to botanical vermouth that's too tasty to mix into martinis. Across the street, wine bar **Yield** (Map p330; ☎415-401-8984; www.yieldsf.com; 2490 3rd St; ⏰4.30pm-midnight Tue-Sat; 🚌22) specializes in organic wine pairings with seasonal small plates. For no-fuss brews and burgers on a sunny dock, head down to the **Ramp** (Map p330; ☎415-621-2378; www.theramprestaurant.com; 855 Terry Francois St; ⏰11am-9pm Mon-Fri, from 9:30am Sat-Sun; 🚌22, 48, Ⓜ T).

Dogpatch's dock-workers' neighborhood has some of San Francisco's oldest Victorians and brick buildings, miraculously standing their ground through quakes and development schemes. One prime example is the 1859 **Yellow Building**, whose latest incarnation includes a sister branch for Hayes Valley's MAC (p198) clothing store and **Dig** (Map p330; ☎415-648-6133; http://digwinesf.com; 1005 Minnesota St; ⏰noon-7pm Tue-Sat; 🚌22, 48, Ⓜ T), a well-curated collection of wines from small producers in Italy, France and Austria.

Artisan food industries are bringing new flavour to the waterfront. Mr & Mrs Miscellaneous (p158) factory-outlet ice cream parlour does a brisk business in bourbon caramel ice cream, while Recchiuti Chocolate concocts experimental candy and chocolate tasting menus at the Dogpatch **Chocolate Lab** (Map p330; ☎415-489-2881; http://chocolatelabsf.com; 801 22nd St; desserts under $10, mains $10-20; ⏰11am-10pm Tue-Thu, to 11pm Fri-Sat, to 5pm Sun; 🚌22, 48, Ⓜ T) before launching them at the Ferry Building (p110). **Kitchenette** (Map p330; www.kitchenettesf.com; 958 Illinois St; sandwiches $5-10; ⏰11:30am-1:30pm Mon-Fri; 🚌22, 48, Ⓜ T) supplies downtown offices with memorable organic sandwiches, but at its dockside Dogpatch kitchen, the obvious lunch choice is the Dogpatch Millionaire: an Indian fried chicken sandwich drizzled with garam masala honey and loaded with spicy slaw.

★ **THE CHAPEL**   LIVE MUSIC

Map p328 (☎415-551-5157; www.thechapelsf.com; 777 Valencia St; tickets $15-22; 🚌14, 33, Ⓜ J, Ⓑ16th St Mission) Musical prayers are answered in a 1914 California Craftsman landmark with heavenly acoustics. The 40ft roof is regularly raised by shows like Preservation Hall Jazz Band jamming with Nick Lowe, Polyphonic Spree's full-choir ruckus and Radiohead's *OK Computer* lipsynched by an all-star drag revue. Many shows are all-ages, except when comedians like W Kamau Bell test edgy material.

VIRACOCHA   LIVE MUSIC, SPOKEN WORD

Map p328 (☎415-374-7048; www.viracochasf.com; 998 Valencia St; ⏰noon-6pm Wed-Fri, to 7pm Sat & Sun; Ⓑ18th St, Ⓑ24th St Mission) Shotgun-shack Western home decor boutique by day, by night Viracocha hosts oddball songwriters, shy poets and occasional foraged-food events in its downstairs gallery and back-room vintage library (see website). Bang away on the badly tuned piano if you like – it's that kind of place – but try not to dribble foraged-mushroom pastries onto 1920s typewriters or driftwood sculpture.

EL RIO — NIGHTCLUB

Map p328 (☏415-282-3325; www.elriosf.com; 3158 Mission St; admission $3-8; ☺1pm-2am; ☻; 🚌12, 14, 27, 49, Ⓑ24th St Mission) The DJ mix at El Rio takes its cue from the patrons: eclectic, fearless, funky and sexy, no matter your orientation. Come for shuffleboard and free oysters on the half shell on Fridays at 5:30pm, and powerful margaritas will soon get you bopping to disco-post-punk mash-ups and flirting shamelessly in the back garden. Cash only.

MARSH — THEATER, COMEDY

Map p328 (☏415-826-5750; www.themarsh. org; 1062 Valencia St; tickets $15-35; Ⓑ24th St Mission) Choose your seat wisely: you may spend the evening on the edge of it. With one-acts and monologues that involve the audience in the creative process, this is San Francisco experimental theater at its most exciting. Sliding-scale pricing structure allows everyone to participate and a few reserved seats are sometimes available ($50 per ticket).

Performances range from the unbelievable life story of Ram Dass, Harvard psychologist turned '60s celebrity psychedelic guru, to HBO comedian Marga Gomez' riffs on SF public nudity and her experience as a lesbian cruise entertainer.

BRAVA THEATER — THEATER

Map p328 (☏415-641-7657; www.brava.org; 2781 24th St; prices vary; 👪; 🚌9, 27, 33, 48) Brava's been producing women-run theater for more than 20 years, hosting acts from comedian Sandra Bernhardt to V-day monologist Eve Ensler, and it's the nation's only company with a commitment to producing original works by lesbians and women of color. Brava honors the Mission's Mexican heritage with folkloric music and dance celebrations, plus hand-painted show posters modeled after Mexican cinema billboards.

ELBO ROOM — LIVE MUSIC

Map p328 (☏415-552-7788; www.elbo.com; 647 Valencia St; admission $6-25; ☺5pm-2am; 🚌14, 22, 33, Ⓑ16th St Mission) Funny name, because there isn't much to speak of upstairs in this vintage 1935 honky-tonk with crowd-favorite shows of dancehall dub DJs, live sweater funk, offbeat indie bands and Bombshell Betty Burlesque. Come any night for $2 pints from 5pm to 9pm at the chilled downstairs bar (admission free).

AMNESIA — LIVE MUSIC

Map p328 (☏415-970-0012; www.amnesiathe bar.com; 853 Valencia St; admission free-$10; ☺5:30pm-2am; 🚌14, 33, 49, Ⓑ16th St Mission) A closet-sized Boho dive with outsized swagger, serving cold Belgian beer and red-hot jazz to ragtag hipsters. Just to keep the crowds guessing, musical acts range from Monday bluegrass jams to gypsy punk, plus Wednesday accordion jazz, random readings and cinema shorts; check the website or just go with the flow.

REVOLUTION CAFE — LIVE PERFORMANCE

Map p328 (☏415-642-0474; www.facebook.com/ RevCafe; 3248 22nd St; suggested donation $5-20; ☺9am-midnight Sun-Thu, to 2am Fri-Sat; ☻; 🚌14, 49, Ⓑ24th St Mission) Musicians, you're among friends here: classically trained musicians jam here daily. Hot days call for iced coffee and live gypsy jazz, and even Mondays are redeemed with Belgian brews and rollicking chamber music with in-house Classical Revolution. Arrive by 7pm to snag a table, or hang on the sidewalk with free wi-fi.

DOUBLE DUTCH — DJ BAR

Map p328 (☏415-373-1042; www.thedouble dutch.com; 3192 16th St; free-$5; ☺7pm-2am Tue-Thu & Sun, from 5pm Fri-Sat; 🚌14, 22, 33, 49, Ⓑ16th St Mission) Bust a move – you gotta give up a little Harlem shake for Double Dutch DJs spinning old-school rap and R&B on vinyl. The boom-box wall, b-boying videos and '80s Air Jordans dangling from the ceiling set the scene, so go ahead and funk up the dance floor. Weeknights you'll have plenty of room; weekends pack. Hey laaaaadieeees: free entry.

LITTLE BAOBAB — LIVE MUSIC

Map p328 (☏415-643-3558; www.bissapbaobab. com; 3388 19th St; free-$5; ☺7pm-2am Thu-Sat; Ⓜ18th St) A Senegalese restaurant early in the evening, Baobab brings on the DJ or live act around 10pm – and before you can say 'tamarind margarita,' tables are getting shoved out of the way to make more room on the dance floor. Midweek Cuban mambo, Thursday reggae and Friday and Saturday Paris-Dakar Afrobeat get the Mission in a universal groove.

SUB-MISSION — LIVE MUSIC

Map p328 (☏415-255-7227; www.sf-submission. com; 2183 Mission St; shows $5-13; ☺6-11pm Mon-Thu, 6pm-1am Fri-Sat, 8-11pm Sun; 🚌14, 22,

33, B24th St Mission) Punk comes roaring out from the underground at SUB-Mission, with local punk bands inflaming weeknights and weekend-visitor bands from LA to Argentina leaving anyone within earshot with a nasty itch for more. Everything you'd expect from an underground Mission punk club is here: anarchic sets, unlockable bathrooms, surly bartenders and cheap, tasty tacos to warm hardcore hearts.

CAFE COCOMO   LATIN MUSIC
Map p330 (☑415-410-4012; www.cafecocomo. com; 650 Indiana St; admission $10-15; ☺7pm-midnight Mon, 6pm-midnight Thu, 6pm-2am Sat; ☐10, 22, MT) *Muy caliente* (very hot) Cocomo is one of the top Latin clubs nationwide, with big-name bands and a kicking dance floor Friday and Saturday nights. Dance lessons get the party started with tango Mondays, salsa Tuesdays and *bachata* Wednesdays. Dancers mingle on the cool mezzanine and romantic garden patio. Dress suave to pass the doormen, who aren't impressed by baseball caps.

MIGHTY   CLUB
Map p328 (☑415-762-0151; www.mighty119.com; 119 Utah St; admission $10-20; ☺10pm-4am Thu-Sat; M16th St) A Potrero warehouse packs a Mighty wallop with a booming sound system, underground dance music, graffiti-inspired art and cool local crowd who don't fuss about dress codes. Weekend DJs veer towards electronic, dance-house and hip-

> **WORTH A DETOUR**
> ### BOTTOM OF THE HILL
> Quite literally at the bottom of Potrero Hill, **Bottom of the Hill** (Map p330; ☑415-621-4455; www.bottomof thehill.com; 1233 17th St; admission $5-12; ☺shows 9/10pm Tue-Sat; ☐10, 19, 22) is definitely out of the way but always top of the list for seeing fun local bands, from notable alt-rockers like Deerhoof to newcomers worth checking out for their names alone (Truckstop Honeymoon, Strawberry Smog, You Are Plural). The smokers' patio is ruled by a cat that enjoys music more than people – totally punk rock. Anchor Steam on tap but it's a cash-only bar; check the website for lineups.

hop; on other nights, events vary wildly from geek-out SF Next Tech meet-ups to indie designer showcases (check website).

MAKE-OUT ROOM   LIVE MUSIC
Map p328 (☑415-647-2888; www.makeoutroom. com; 3225 22nd St; cover free-$10; ☺6pm-2am; ☐12, 14, 49, B24th St Mission) Velvet curtains and round booths invite you to settle in for the evening's entertainment, which ranges from punk-rock fiddle to '80s one-hit-wonder DJ mash-ups and painfully funny readings at Writers with Drinks. Booze is a bargain, especially during 6pm-to-9pm weeknight happy hours – but the bar is cash-only.

MISSION
BOWLING CLUB   BOWLING
Map p328 (☑415-863-2695; http://missionbowl ingclub.com; 3176 17th St; ☺3-11pm Mon-Wed, to midnight Thu-Sat, 11am-11pm Sat-Sun; ☐12, 22, 33, 49, B16th St Mission) Don't mock until you try bowling Mission-style: six lanes in a mood-lit warehouse, where the bar pours a mean tangerine sour with egg-white foam and the 3pm-to-6pm happy-hour menu is local and seasonal. Soul & Bowl Mondays get your week started right; book lanes in advance online (yes, really). Under-21s allowed only on weekends before 7pm.

VERDI CLUB   NIGHTCLUB
Map p328 (☑415-861-9199; www.verdiclub. net; 2424 Mariposa St; ☐22, 27, 33) Throwing swanky soirees since 1916, the Verdi Club hosts the Porchlight storytelling series, punk homecoming dances and regular Tuesday swing-dancing lessons. Thursday-night tango at the Verdi features live *bandoneón* (free-reed, accordion-like instrument) players and sharply dressed dancers circling the floor. Check website for events and bring cash for the bar.

RITE SPOT CAFE   LIVE MUSIC
Map p328 (☑415-552-6066; www.ritespot-cafe.net; 2099 Folsom St; free, musician tips appreciated; ☺4pm-2am; ☐12, 22, 33, B16th St Mission) The vintage dive-bar neon in the middle of warehouse nowhere-land is pointing you in the Rite direction for offbeat performances banged out on a tinkling house piano nightly. Check the online calender for enchantingly kooky acts like Uni and Her Ukelele or Reuben Rye playing post-punk piano, or just follow a hunch and discover the next Tom Waits.

ROCCAPULCO SUPPER CLUB
SALSA CLUB

Map p328 (📞415-648-6611; www.roccapulco. com; 3140 Mission St; admission $10-20; ⏰8pm-2am; 🚌12, 14, 27, 49, 🅱24th St Mission) Get your salsa, rumba and *bachata* (Dominican dance) on at this high-ceilinged, stadium-sized Latin venue that books sensational international touring acts. Most nights it's a straight bar, ripe with cologne and hormones; women and gay newcomers to the scene may feel more comfortable in a group. Supper is not actually served, just hot beats. Dress like you mean it.

🛍 SHOPPING

For prime boutique shopping, hit 16th St between Valencia and Dolores Sts, Valencia from 15th to 24th St, and 24th St West of Bryant St. Dogpatch has design boutiques around 22nd and Third Sts and Potrero Gulch has upstart galleries wedged between design showrooms.

★GRAVEL & GOLD
HOUSEWARES, GIFTS

Map p328 (📞415-552-0112; www.gravelandgold. com; 3266 21st St; ⏰noon-7pm Mon-Sat, to 5pm Sun; 🅼24th St Mission, 🅱24th St Mission) Get back to the land and in touch with your roots, without ever leaving sight of a Mission sidewalk. Gravel & Gold celebrates California's hippie homesteader movement with a line of trippy totes, smock-dresses and throw pillows alongside vintage artifacts like silkscreened '60s Osborne/Woods ecology posters, rare books on '70s beach-shack architecture and hand-thrown hippie stoneware mugs.

★NEEDLES & PENS
GIFTS, BOOKS

Map p328 (📞415-255-1534; www.needles-pens. com; 3253 16th St; ⏰noon-7pm; 🚌14, 22, 33, 49, 🅱16th St Mission) Do it yourself or DIY trying: this scrappy zine/how-to/art gallery delivers the inspiration to create your own artworks on paper, magazines, rehabbed T-shirts or album covers. Nab Brendan Monroe's *Islands* comic illustrating traffic islands and man as an island, Tahiti Pehrson's three-dimensional, hand-cut paper mandalas, plus alphabet buttons to pin your own credo onto a handmade messenger bag.

★BETABRAND
CLOTHING

Map p328 (📞800-694-9491; www.betabrand. com; 780 Valencia St; ⏰11am-6pm Mon-Thu, to 7pm Fri-Sat, noon-6pm Sun; 🚌14, 22, 33, 49, 🅱16th St Mission) Crowdsource your fashion choices at Betabrand, where experimental designs are put to an online vote and winners are produced in limited editions. Recent approved designs include lunch-meat-patterned socks, reversible smoking jackets, disco-ball windbreakers and bike-to-work pants with reflective-strip cuffs. Some styles are clunkers – including 'sweans,' sweatpant jeans – but at these prices you can afford to take fashion risks.

NOOWORKS
CLOTHING

Map p328 (📞415-829-7623; www.nooworks.com; 395 Valencia St; ⏰11am-7pm Tue-Sat, to 5pm Sun & Mon; 🚌14, 22, 33, 49, 🅱16th St Mission) Artist-designed graphic prints give Noow-orks a streetwise edge over other Mission designers. Nooworks' Muscle Beach maxidresses show an SF sense of humor, with a psychedelic print of rainbows and flexing bodybuilders that look like California ex-governor Arnold Schwarzenegger. Surreal men's tees featuring cat-headed professors and Victorian-print unisex satchels are good to go to any Mission gallery opening.

AQUARIUS RECORDS
MUSIC STORE

Map p328 (📞415-647-2272; www.aquariusrecords. org; 1055 Valencia St; ⏰11am-8pm Sun-Wed, to 9pm Thu-Fri, 10am-10pm Sat; 🚌14, 48, 49, 🅱16th St Mission) When pop seems played out, this is the dawning of the age of Aquarius Records, featuring Armenian blues, Oakland warehouse-party bands and rare Japanese releases. Recent staff favorites include *Sounds of North American Frogs*, groovy '60s Brazilian tropicália from Os Mutantes, Mauritanian Muslim funk band compilations and SF's own Prizehog, enthusiastically described as 'dirgey doom pop slowcore!'

COMMUNITY THRIFT
CLOTHING, VINTAGE

Map p328 (📞415-861-4910; www.community thriftsf.org; 623 Valencia St; ⏰10am-6:30pm; 🚌14, 22, 33, 49, 🅱16th St Mission) 🦮 When local collectors and retailers have too much of a good thing, they donate it to Community Thrift, where proceeds go to community organizations – all the more reason to gloat over your $5 totem-pole teacup, $20 vintage '70s suede jacket and $35 art deco cigar humidor. Donate your castoffs (until 5pm daily) and show some love to the Community.

DEMA
CLOTHING, ACCESSORIES

Map p328 (📱415-206-050; www.godemago.com; 1038 Valencia St; ⏰11am-7pm Mon-Fri, noon-7pm Sat, noon-6pm Sun; 🚌12, 14, 48, 49, 🚇24th St Mission) BART from Downtown lunches to Mission restaurants in vintage-inspired chic by San Francisco's own Dema Grim. House specialties are flattering bias-cut dresses and floaty silk blouses in original prints, with buttons that look like gumdrops. At this indie designer, you get what you pay for here in squealed compliments – but check bins and sales racks for 60% off scores.

ACCIDENT & ARTIFACT
GIFTS, ACCESSORIES

Map p328 (📱415-437-9700; www.accidentandartifact.com; 381 Valencia St; ⏰noon-7pm Wed-Sun; 🚌14, 22, 🚇16th St Mission) A highly curious curiosity shop, even by Mission standards. Decorative dried fungi and redwood burls make regular appearances on the scavenged wood displays alongside vintage Okinawan indigo textiles, industrial molds and artfully redrawn topographical maps. Better curation than most galleries and priced accordingly.

GOOD VIBRATIONS
ADULT TOYS

Map p328 (📱415-522-5460; www.goodvibes.com; 603 Valencia St; ⏰10am-9pm Sun-Thu, to 11pm Fri & Sat; 🚌14, 22, 33, 49, 🚇16th St Mission) 'Wait, I'm supposed to put that where?' The understanding salespeople in this worker-owned cooperative are used to giving rather explicit instructions so don't hesitate to ask. Margaret Cho is on the board here, so you know they're not shy. Check out the display of antique vibrators, including one that looks like a floor-waxer – thank goodness for modern technology.

MISSION SKATEBOARDS
CLOTHING, ACCESSORIES

Map p328 (📱415-647-7888; www.missionsk8boards.com; 3045 24th St; ⏰11am-7pm; 🚌12, 14, 48, 49, 🚇24th St Mission) Street cred comes easy with locally designed Mission decks, custom tees to kick-flip over and cult skate shoes at this shop owned by SF street-skate legend Scot Thompson. This shop is handy to Potrero del Sol/La Raza Skatepark (p172), and for newbies too cool for kneepads, SF General. Check the website for events, including street races and documentary premieres.

SCRAP (SCROUNGERS' CENTER FOR RE-USABLE ART PARTS)
ACCESSORIES

(📱415-647-1746; www.scrap-sf.org; 801 Toland St; ⏰9am-5pm Mon-Sat; 🚼; 🚌9, 15, 23, 24, 44) 🍃 Renew, recycle and rediscover your creativity with postindustrial arts and crafts materials from SCRAP. Take a workshop at SCRAP for inspiration and make your own recycled glass mosaic, bracelet made from Lego blocks or recycled shag rug. DIY classes are held most Saturdays (see website for listings); the entrance to SCRAP is at the confluence of Hwy 101 and Hwy 280.

AGGREGATE SUPPLY
CLOTHING, GIFTS

Map p328 (📱415-643-4847; www.AggregateSupplySF.com; 806 Valencia St; ⏰11am-7pm; 🚌14, 33, 49, 🚇16th St Mission) In this storefront showcase, a think tank of three SF designers caters to SF obsessions: streetwise graphics, fog-chill prevention and organic everything. Designer Turk + Taylor contributes pop-art California T-shirts and African-print windbreakers, Acacia home decor offers Western striped wool beach blankets and Heliotrope makes fragrance-free skincare from organic ingredients for dewy skin on sunny days.

ADOBE BOOKS & BACKROOM GALLERY
BOOKSTORE, ART

Map p328 (📱415-864-3936; www.adobebookshop.com; 3130 24th St; ⏰noon-8pm Mon-Fri, from 11am Sat-Sun; 🚌14, 🚇24th St Mission) Come here for every book you never knew you needed used and cheap, plus zine launch parties, poetry readings and art openings. Navigate the obstacle course of sofas, cats, art books and German philosophy to see Backroom Gallery shows – artists who debuted here have gone on to success at international art fairs and Whitney Biennials.

VOYAGER
CLOTHING, ACCESSORIES

Map p328 (📱415-779-2712; www.thevoyagershop.com; 365 Valencia St; ⏰11am-7pm; 🚌14, 22, 33, 49, 🚇16th St Mission) Post-apocalyptic art-school surf-shack is the general vibe inside this curated storefront. The communal lovechild of the Haight's Revolver and Mollusk surf shop plus sundry Mission bookstores and galleries, items for sale range from '70s-stye rough leather belts and cultish Dutch Scotch and Soda denim to surfwear and art books in the geodesic submarine gallery.

PAXTON GATE
GIFTS

Map p328 (📱415-824-1872; www.paxton-gate.com; 824 Valencia St; ⏰11am-7pm; Ⓜ Valencia

WORTH A DETOUR

BERNAL HEIGHTS

For a quick getaway from Mission's urban grit, veer off Mission St south of 30th St onto colorful **Cortland Ave**, lined with quirky Victorian storefront boutiques and laid-back local hangouts. Weekends start just over the hill at **Alemany Market** (www. facebook.com/pages/Alemany-Flea-Market/238369190114; 100 Alemany Blvd (off Hwy 101); ☺flea market 6am-3pm Sunday, farmers market dawn-dusk Saturdays), where California's first farmers market has been held on Saturdays since 1943 – it's also the site of Sunday morning flea markets that unearth hidden treasures from Victorian attics. Urban hikers summit Bernal Heights and go flying down the **double hillside slides** at Esmeralda and Winfield Sts – adults and kids alike – to get good and hungry for brunches at **Liberty Cafe** (Map p328; ☏415-695-1223; www.thelibertycafe.com; 410 Cortland Ave; ☺lunch Tue-Fri, dinner Tue-Sun, brunch Sat & Sun, 5:30-9:30pm Thu-Sat wine bar; 🚌24) or savory potato dumplings at **Anda Piroshki** (☏415-821-9905; www.anda-piroshki.com; 331 Cortland Ave; ☺10am-5pm Wed-Mon). Legend has it that Janis Joplin once got lucky on the pool table at landmark lesbian bar **Wild Side West** (Map p328; ☏415-647-3099; 424 Cortland Ave; ☺2pm-2am Mon-Sat, to midnight Sun; Ⓜ Mission St) but sunny days are ultra-mellow in the blooming back garden.

St, Ⓑ16th St Mission) Salvador Dalí probably would've shopped here for all his taxidermy and gardening needs. With puppets made with animal skulls, terrariums sprouting from lab specimen jars and teddy bear heads mounted like hunting trophies, this place is beyond surreal. The new kids' shop down the street (766 Valencia St) maximizes playtime with volcano-making kits, sea-monster mobiles and solar-powered dollhouses.

BLACK & BLUE TATTOO
BODY ART

Map p328 (☏415-626-0770; www.blackandblue tattoo.com; 381 Guerrero St; ☺noon-7pm; 🚌14, 22, 33, 49, Ⓑ16th St Mission) This women-owned tattoo parlor gets it in ink with designs ranging from octopus-tentacle armbands to shoulder-to-shoulder spans of the Golden Gate Bridge. Check out artists' work at the shop or online, then book a consultation. Once you've talked over the design, you can book your tattoo – you'll need to show up sober, well-fed and clear-headed for your transformation.

DOG-EARED BOOKS
BOOKS

Map p328 (☏415-282-1901; www.dogearedbooks. com; 900 Valencia St; ☺10am-10pm Mon-Sat, to 9pm Sun; 🚼; 🚌14, 22, 26, 33, 49, Ⓑ24th St Mission) Novels, remainders and graphic novels pack the shelves, but intriguing new stuff gets its due in esoteric sections (especially Pirate Literature) and trusty staff picks (including the latest Miranda July project and adult fiction by Daniel Handler, aka Lemony Snicket).

Don't miss hand-drawn obituaries to celebrities like Susan Sontag, James Brown and Edward Said displayed in the front window.

🏃 SPORTS & ACTIVITIES

Excellent hands-on cooking classes are available at 18 Reasons and La Cocina (p28) – spots fill up quickly so book early.

⭐ANCHOR BREWING COMPANY
BREWERY TOUR

Map p330 (☏tour bookings 415-863-8350 ext 0; www.anchorbrewing.com; 1705 Mariposa St; 🚌10, 19, 22) FREE Beer-lovers, here's your best-ever excuse for day-drinking: Anchor Brewing Company offers free weekday public tours with free beer. The 45-minute tour covers Anchor's 1937 Potrero Hill landmark building and shiny-copper equipment, followed by a 45-minute beer-tasting course with six half-pints of different Anchor brews. Make reservations by phone at *least* a month in advance (three in summer).

MISSION CULTURAL CENTER FOR LATINO ARTS
ARTS CLASSES

Map p328 (☏415-643-5001; www.mission culturalcenter.org; 2868 Mission St; ☺5-10pm Mon, 10am-10pm Tue-Fri, 10am-5:30pm Sat; 🚼; 🚌14, 49, Ⓑ24th St Mission) Join a class in tango, take up the congas, get crafty with your kids or create a protest poster at the

SAN FRANCISCO 49ERS

The 49ers were the National Football League dream team from 1981–94, claiming five Superbowl championships. But lately fans have put up with a decade-long dry spell and fumbled 2012 Superbowl bid – not to mention the fog at bayfront Monster/Candlestick Park. After decades shivering through games, the 49ers have a new home in 2014: Santa Clara's brand-new Levi's Stadium. To reach the stadium, take CalTrain one hour south to Santa Clara station, then catch the game-day shuttle.

Some fans grumble that the team should be renamed, since Santa Clara is 38 miles from downtown San Francisco – but other fans are too excited about hosting Superbowl 50 in 2016 to quibble. Since the new stadium is in Silicon Valley, it's tricked out with technology, from the power-generating solar roof to wi-fi-only tickets and concessions. Maybe there's hope yet: in a superstitious effort to align the team with San Francisco Giants' bearded winning streak, the team's bread-loving mining mascot Sourdough Sam now sports a beard.

printmaking studio at this happening Latino cultural center. Teachers are friendly and participants range from *niños* (kids) to *abuelos* (grandparents). Check the online calendar for upcoming gallery openings; don't miss **Día de los Muertos** altar displays in November.

POTRERO DEL SOL/LA RAZA
SKATEPARK
SKATING

Map p328 (25th & Utah Sts; ☺8am-9pm; ☒9, 10, 27, 33, 48, Ⓑ24th St Mission) Grab air with newbies and pros blasting ollies off SF's best concrete bowls. Downsides: the bathroom is sketchy and graffiti on the concrete can make for a slippery ride. Wait for a clean area of the bowl to bust big moves and leave room for little skaters. For gear, hit up nearby Mission Skateboards (p170).

SAN FRANCISCO CENTER
FOR THE BOOK
ART CLASSES

Map p330 (☏415-565-0545; www.sfcb.org; 300 De Haro St; admission free; classes vary; ☺10am-5pm Mon-Fri, noon-4pm Sat; Ⓜ16th St) **FREE** Beautiful books are handmade daily at San Francisco's community press. Beyond traditional binding workshops, this nonprofit offers hands-on classes that teach you to make books that fit into matchboxes, pop

up into cityscapes and unfold into prison guard towers. SFCB also hosts September's **Roadworks Street Fair**, where artists use a three-ton construction steamroller to make prints on the street.

DANCE MISSION
DANCE CLASSES

Map p328 (☏415-826-4441; www.dancemission.com; 3316 24th St; ⓗ; ☒12, 14, 48, 49, Ⓑ24th St Mission) Step out and find your niche at this nonprofit Mission dance hub, featuring contact improv, dance jams and classes in styles from Afro-Haitian to Bollywood. Check the website for dance showcases in the 140-seat theater, plus events and guest-artist workshops ranging from beginner taiko drumming to dancing in stilts.

YOGA TREE
YOGA

Map p328 (☏415-647-9707; www.yogatreesf.com; 1234 Valencia St; class $18, three-class introductory pass $20; ☺10am-10pm; ☒12, 14, 48, Ⓑ24th St Mission) Relax and breathe easier in this clean, warm, colorful studio with personable instructors and drop-in classes, primarily in mellow Hatha yoga. Check the website for additional classes at Yoga Tree studios in the Castro, Hayes Valley, Haight and another Mission location on Shotwell, where weekday 6:30pm classes are donation-based.

The Castro & Noe Valley

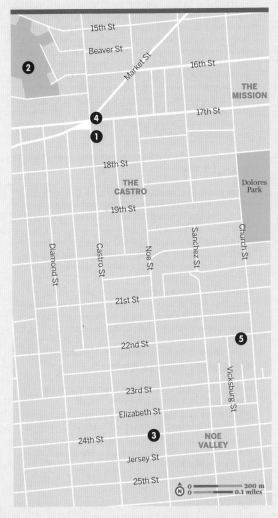

Neighborhood Top Five

1 Catching a classic film at the **Castro Theatre** (p181) and hearing the Mighty Wurlitzer's pipes roar before showtime.

2 Climbing **Corona Heights** (p175) at sunset and watching Market St light up below.

3 Dodging baby strollers on **24th St** as you window-shop indie stores (p182).

4 Watching for kooky naked dudes at **Jane Warner Plaza** (p175).

5 Not going over the handlebars while biking down SF's steepest street, **22nd St** (p175).

For more detail of this area, see Map p336 and p337 ➡

Lonely Planet's Top Tip

Historic streetcars run like toy trains along the waterfront and up Market St, from Fisherman's Wharf to the Castro, via Downtown. Trouble is, trains sometimes get stuck in traffic and you can wait forever. Check arrival times at www.next muni.com, which uses GPS tracking; use the 'live map' to determine trains' exact locations. If the F-Market is far away or running slow, take underground-metro K, L or M trains, which move (much) faster beneath Market St – same ticket, same price.

Best Places to Eat

→ Frances (p177)
→ Starbelly (p176)
→ Anchor Oyster Bar (p176)
→ Chow (p176)
→ Dinosaurs (p177)

For reviews, see p176

Best Places to Drink

→ Cafe Flore (p177)
→ Blackbird (p177)
→ 440 Castro (p177)
→ Moby Dick (p180)
→ Twin Peaks Tavern (p180)

For reviews, see p177 →

Best Places to Shop

→ Sui Generis (p181)
→ Unionmade (p181)
→ Ambiance (p182)
→ Omnivore (p182)
→ Cliff's Variety (p181)

For reviews, see p181 →

Explore the Castro & Noe Valley

The Castro's main crossroads is at the intersection of Market, 17th and Castro Sts. Noe Valley extends along 24th St, a scant mile down Castro, over the (gigantic) 21st St hill. You can explore both neighborhoods in a few hours.

Mornings are quiet. The Castro is busiest afternoons and evenings, especially weekends, when crowds come to people-watch, shop and drink; at night expect to see 20-somethings stumbling down Castro. Noe Valley is best midday and in the afternoon – there's not much open after 7pm, just some bars and restaurants.

If the 21st St Hill atop Castro St proves too daunting, bus 24-Divasadero connects the two neighborhoods but it's notorious for gaps in service: expect to wait or check www.nextmuni.com for real-time arrivals. In Noe Valley, shops on 24th St extend between Diamond and Sanchez Sts; and on Church St, the restaurants and shops continue until the last stop on the J-Church line, around 29th St. Castro-area shops line Market St, between Church and Castro Sts, and Castro St, from Market to 19th Sts, with a few scattered along 18th St. Both neighborhoods are surrounded by residential streets, good for strolling, with many pretty Victorians.

Local Life

→**Hangouts** The Wednesday afternoon Castro Farmers Market (March through November) provides the best glimpse of locals, especially from sidewalk tables at Cafe Flore (p177).

→**Drinking** The Castro is packed with bars, but most don't get going till evening. For listings, pick up a copy of *BarTab* magazine – supplement to the local, gay *Bay Area Reporter* newspaper.

→**What (not) to wear** You may be tempted to flaunt your gym-toned physique in the sexy Castro, but once afternoon fog blows, carry a jacket or shiver – locals spot tourists by their shorts and tank tops.

Getting There & Away

→**Metro** K, L and M trains run beneath Market St to Castro Station. J trains serve Noe Valley.

→**Streetcar** Vintage streetcars operate on the F-Market line, from Fisherman's Wharf to Castro St.

→**Bus** The 24 and 33 lines operate to the Castro but may have long waits between buses. The 24 and 48 lines serve Noe Valley.

◉ SIGHTS

CASTRO THEATRE   THEATER

Map p336 (📞415-621-6120; www.thecastro
theatre.com; 429 Castro St; ⊘Tue-Sun; ⓜCastro)
The city's grandest movie palace opened in
1922. The Spanish-Moorish exterior yields
to mishmash styles inside, from Italianate
to oriental. Ask nicely and staff may let you
peak. For the best photos of the blue-and-
pink lights, shoot the downhill side from
across the street.

GLBT HISTORY MUSEUM   MUSEUM

Map p336 (📞415-777-5455; www.glbthistory.
org/museum; 4127 18th St; admission $5;
⊘11am-7pm Mon-Sat, noon-5pm Sun; ⓜCastro)
America's first gay-history museum cobbles
ephemera from the community – Harvey
Milk's campaign literature, matchbooks
from long-gone bathhouses, the dress Laura Linney wore as Mary Anne Singleton in
the TV adaptation of *Tales of the City* – together with harder-hitting installations,
such as audiovisual interviews with Gore
Vidal and pages of the 1950s penal code
banning homosexuality.

Though fascinating to see pieces of the
gay collective past, the curatorial vision
sometimes feels timid. But it's well worth
a look and you can pick up great gay-SF
souvenir T-shirts, including one of Milk,
emblazoned with his famous inspirational
quotation, 'You gotta give 'em hope.' Indeed.

HARVEY MILK &
JANE WARNER PLAZAS   SQUARE

(Market & Castro Sts; ⓜCastro) A huge rainbow
flag flaps above Castro and Market Sts, officially **Harvey Milk Plaza** (Map p336; 📶24, 33,
F, Castro St). Look closer and spot a plaque
honoring the man whose legacy is gay civic
pride and political clout. Across Castro, by
the F-train terminus, at **Jane Warner Plaza**
(Map p336), ragtag oddballs and kids too
young for the bars congregate at public tables and chairs.

For more on Milk, head down the Muni-
metro stairs to see text and images of his
life. Jane Warner was a much-loved lesbian
police officer. Compared with loud-mouth
Harvey, Jane was modest – which makes
it doubly ironic that in 2012 her namesake
plaza attracted international attention for
public nudity. Several flagrant exhibition-
ists lollygagged here dawn till dusk, casually splaying their legs at oncoming traffic.
Their passive-aggressive behavior incited

such outcry that public nudity in SF was
eventually dubbed illegal – but not a sex
crime, just an infraction. Now it's legal to
strip only at a handful of public events, like
Folsom Street Fair. You can still sometimes
spot the 'naked guys' at the plaza, only now
they wear socks on their penises, posing for
pictures with tourists by F-Market trains.

CORONA HEIGHTS PARK   PARK

Map p336 (btwn 16th St & Roosevelt Way; 📶37,
ⓜCastro) Scramble up the rocky 520ft Corona Heights summit (aka Museum Hill
or Red Rocks) for jaw-dropping, eastward
180-degree views. Come evening, the city
unfurls below in a carpet of light. Take tiny
Beaver St uphill to the steps through the
bushes, then cut right of the tennis courts,
up the trail. For an easier hike, enter via the
Roosevelt Way side.

RANDALL
JUNIOR MUSEUM   CHILDREN'S MUSEUM

Map p336 (📞415-554-9600; www.randallmuse-
um.org; 199 Museum Way; ⊘10am-5pm Tue-Sat;
♿; 📶24, 37, ⓜCastro) **FREE** Kids go cuckoo
for live-animal exhibits of urban wildlife –
racoons, owls, more racoons – at this oh-
so-cute nature museum near the summit
of Corona Heights Park. Saturday is the
best day to visit, when incredible **Golden
Gate Model Railroad Club** (www.ggmrc.
org; ⊘10am-4pm Sat) **FREE** opens its doors.
Check the website for wonder-inspiring
hands-on workshops.

NOBBY CLARKE MANSION HISTORICAL BUILDING

Map p336 (250 Douglass St, at Caselli Ave; ⓜCas-
tro) Built 1892 by an attorney who wanted
sunnier weather than fashionable Nob Hill
afforded, this gorgeous Queen Anne mansion went uninhabited after its construction: Snob Hill socialites dubbed the house
'Nobby Clarke's Folly' and his wife refused
to move in. It served briefly as a hospital;
now it's apartments.

22ND ST HILL   STREET

Map p337 (22nd St, btwn Church & Vicksburg Sts;
ⓜJ) The prize for the steepest is shared between two SF streets: Filbert St (between
Hyde and Leavenworth) and here. Both
have 31.5% grades (17-degree slope), but
there's barely any traffic on 22nd. Nothing
quite beats the thrill of cycling down 22nd,
grabbing two fistfuls of brakes, trying not
to go over the bars – not for the faint of
heart.

✖ EATING

Most Castro restaurants lie on Market St, from Church to Castro Sts, and around the intersection of Castro and 18th Sts; eat to-go food at tables in the curbside parklet (Map p336; 544 Castro St). In Noe Valley, find quick lunch spots along 24th St, between Church and Diamond Sts.

CHILE PIES   NEW MEXICAN $

Map p336 (http://greenchilekitchen.com; 314 Church St; dishes $5-9; ◷noon-10pm; ⓜChurch) ✎ This tiny bakery and quick-lunch counter spins all-American classic pies with a Southwestern zip: drawing inspiration from New Mexico, Chile Pies integrates not-hot green chillies into sweet and savory pastries, made with organic ingredients and flaky all-butter crusts. Standouts include sweet green chili-apple pie and savory chicken pot pies with green-chili stew.

JUMPIN' JAVA   CAFE

Map p336 (☑415-431-5282; 139 Noe St; ◷7am-8pm; 🛜; 🚌37, ⓜF, N) Alterna-dorks hunch over MacBooks at Castro's quietest cafe, nicknamed 'Laptop Library.' Nobody talks. Bring a computer or be bored. Fun fact: this chapter was penned here.

STARBELLY   CALIFORNIAN, PIZZA $$

Map p336 (☑415-252-7500; www.starbellysf. com; 3583 16th St; dishes $6-19; ◷11:30am-11pm, till midnight Fri & Sat; ⓜCastro) ✎ The seasonal small plates at always-busy Starbelly include standout *salumi,* market-fresh salads, scrumptious pâté, roasted mussels with housemade sausage and thin-crusted pizzas. The barnlike rooms get loud; sit on the heated patio for quieter conversation. If you can't score a table, consider its neighboring burger joint, **Super Duper Burger** (Map p336; www.superdupersf.com; 2304 Market St; ◷11am-11pm; ⓜCastro) ✎ for all-natural burgers and milkshakes.

ANCHOR OYSTER BAR   SEAFOOD $$

Map p336 (www.anchoroysterbar.com; 579 Castro St; mains $15-25; ◷11:30am-10pm Mon-Sat, 4-9:30pm Sun; ⓜCastro) Since its founding in 1977, Anchor's formula has been simple: seafood classics, like local oysters, crab cakes, Boston clam chowder and copious salads. The nautical-themed room seats just 24 at shiny stainless-steel tables; you can't make reservations, but for faster serv-

ice you can sit at the marble-top bar. Or you can wait outside with vino on the bench until you're called.

L'ARDOISE   FRENCH $$

Map p336 (☑415-437-2600; www.ardoisesf.com; 151 Noe St; mains $17-29; ◷5:30-10pm Tue-Sat; ⓜF, K, L, M, N) For date night with an all-local crowd, this storefront neighborhood charmer on a leafy side street is perfectly placed for some strolling hand-in-hand after dining on classic French-bistro fare, including perfect *steak-frites.* Dim lighting adds sex appeal but the room gets noisy – especially weekends – when the cheek-by-jowl tables fill. Make reservations.

CHOW   AMERICAN $$

Map p328 (☑415-552-2469; www.chowfoodbar. com; 215 Church St; mains $9-14; ◷11am-11pm; ✎; ⓜChurch) Chow's diverse menu appeals to all tastes, with everything from pizza to pork chops and Thai-style noodles to spaghetti and meatballs. The wood-floored room is big, loud and always busy. Avoid tables alongside the bar (you'll get jostled); request a table on the back patio for quiet(er) conversations. Call ahead for the 'no-wait' list.

LA MÉDITERRANÉE   MIDDLE EASTERN $$

Map p336 (☑415-431-7210; www.lamediterra nee.net; 288 Noe St; mains $12-15; ◷11am-10pm Sun-Thu, to 11pm Fri & Sat; ✎ 👪; ⓜCastro) Zesty, lemon-laced Lebanese fare at friendly prices makes La Méd the Castro's neighborhood meet-up spot. Chicken kebabs on rice pilaf are pleasingly plump; the *kibbe* harmoniously blends pine nuts, ground lamb and cracked wheat, and the smoky eggplant in the baba ghanoush was roasted for hours and isn't the least bit bitter about it. There's a branch in **Pacific Heights** (Map p331; www. cafelamed.com; 2210 Fillmore St; mains $11-14; ◷11am-10pm).

CHILANGO   MEXICAN $$

Map p328 (☑415-552-5700; www.chilangorestau rantsf.com; 235 Church St; dishes $8-12; ◷11am-10pm; ⓜChurch) ✎ Upgrade from taqueria to sit-down restaurant at this casual Mexican spot that uses all-organic ingredients in its Mexico City–derived cooking. Meals are served at tile-top tables embedded with Frida Kahlo images. Everything is made to order, including guacamole and tortillas. Favorite dishes: filet-mignon tacos, duck *flautas* (deep-fried flour tortilla with filling) and succulent *carnitas* (roast pork).

CHEAP EATS: THE CASTRO & NOE VALLEY

Dinosaurs (Map p336; http://dinosaursrestaurant.com; 2275 Market St, lower level; sandwiches $5; ⊙10am-10pm; MCastro) Stellar Vietnamese sandwiches on crusty French bread – our fave for quick eats.

Burgermeister (Map p336; www.burgermeistersf.com; 138 Church St; burgers $8-12; ⊙11am-11pm; ♿; MChurch) All-natural burgers and fries.

Taqueria Zapata (Map p336; 4150 18th St; dishes $5-9; ⊙11am-10pm; ♿; MCastro) Castro's best burritos.

Mollie Stone's Market (Map p336; www.molliestones.com; 4201 18th St; ⊙7am-11pm; MCastro) High-end grocery with prepared foods.

Noe Valley Bakery (Map p337; www.noevalleybakery.com; 4073 24th St; dishes $4-8; ⊙7am-7pm Mon-Fri, to 6pm Sat & Sun; ♿; ◻24, 48) Sandwiches on house-baked bread, croissants and éclairs.

Barney's Burgers (Map p337; www.barneyshamburgers.com; 4138 24th St; burgers $8-12; ⊙11am-10pm; ⏞♿; ◻24, 48) All-natural burgers and big salads.

TATAKI
SUSHI $$
(Map p337; ☎415-282-1889; www.tatakisushibar.com; 1740 Church St; dishes $12-20; ⊙5-9:30pm; MJ) ⏞ Sister to the groundbreaking Pacific Heights sushi bar (p177), this second branch of Tataki has the same high standards for sustainably sourced fish, smartly paired with unusual ingredients. And it's right on the J-Church streetcar line.

LOVEJOY'S TEA ROOM
BAKERY $$
Map p337 (☎415-648-5895; www.lovejoystearoom.com; 1351 Church St; tea $10-15; ⊙11am-5pm Wed-Sun; MJ) All the chintz you'd expect from an English tearoom but with a San Francisco crowd: curators talk video-installation art over Lapsang souchong, scones and clotted cream, while dual dads take their daughters and dolls out for 'wee tea' of tiny sandwiches, petits fours and hot chocolate. Make reservations.

★FRANCES
CALIFORNIAN $$$
Map p336 (☎415-621-3870; www.frances-sf.com; 3870 17th St; mains $27-28; ⊙5-10.30pm Tue-Sun; MCastro) Chef/owner Melissa Perello earned a Michelin star for fine dining, then ditched downtown to start this market-inspired neighborhood bistro. Daily menus showcase bright, seasonal flavors and luxurious textures: cloudlike sheep's-milk ricotta gnocchi with crunchy breadcrumbs and broccolini, grilled calamari with preserved Meyer lemon, and artisan wine served by the ounce, directly from Wine Country.

🍷 DRINKING & NIGHTLIFE

Castro bars open earlier than in other neighborhoods; on weekends most open at noon.

★CAFE FLORE
CAFE
Map p336 (☎415-621-8579; www.cafeflore.com; 2298 Market St; ⊙7am-midnight Sun-Thu, to 2am Fri & Sat; 🛜; MCastro) You haven't done the Castro till you've lollygagged on the sun-drenched patio at the Flore – everyone winds up here sooner or later. Weekdays present the best chance to meet neighborhood regulars, who colonize the tables outside. Weekends get packed. Great happy-hour drink specials, like two-for-one margaritas. The food's good, too. Wi-fi weekdays only; no electrical outlets.

BLACKBIRD
GAY BAR
Map p336 (☎415-503-0630; www.blackbirdbar.com; 2124 Market St; ⊙3pm-2am; MChurch) Castro's first-choice lounge-bar draws an unpretentious mix of guys in tight T-shirts and their gal-pals for seasonally changing cocktails made with bitters and tinctures, good wine and craft beer by the glass, billiards and – everyone's favorite bar amenity – the photo booth. Ideal spot to begin a Castro pub crawl but it's crowded on weekends.

440 CASTRO
GAY BAR
Map p336 (☎415-621-8732; www.the440.com; 440 Castro St; ⊙noon-2am; MCastro) The most happening bar on the street, 440 draws bearded, gym-fit 30- and 40-something

BARRY WINIKER / GETTY IMAGES ©

LATITUDESTOCK (BILL BACHMANN / GETTY IMAGES ©

1. F-Market Streetcar (p174)
Travel to the Castro in retro style on the F streetcar that runs down Market St from Fisherman's Wharf.

2. Castro Theatre (p175)
The city's grandest movie palace continues to draw crowds to its often-raucous screenings.

3. Castro Street Scene
Rainbow pride flags and buskers pepper the Castro and Market streetscapes.

4. 24th St Shopping (p182)
A parklet provides respite from heavy-duty shopping amongst Noe Valley's boutiques.

RACHAEL NUSBAUM / GETTY IMAGES ©

FELLINI'S "AMARCORD"

dudes – especially for Thursday's 'CDXL', when go-go boys twirl – and an odd mix of Peter Pans for Monday's underwear night.

MOBY DICK
GAY BAR

Map p336 (415-861-1199; www.mobydicksf. com; 4049 18th St; noon-2am; Castro) The name overpromises, but not regarding the giant fish tank behind the bar, which provides a focal point for shy boys who would otherwise look at their shoes. Weekdays it's a mellow spot for pool, pinball and meeting neighborhood 20-to-40-somethings.

TWIN PEAKS TAVERN
GAY BAR

Map p336 (415-864-9470; www.twinpeakstav ern.com; 401 Castro St; noon-2am Mon-Fri, from 8am Sat & Sun; Castro) Don't call it the glass coffin. Show some respect: Twin Peaks was the world's first gay bar with windows open to the street. The jovial crowd skews (way) over 40, but they're not chicken hawks (or they wouldn't hang here) and they love it when happy kids show up to join the party.

Ideal for a tête-à-tête after a film at the Castro, or for cards, Yahtzee or backgammon (BYO).

MIX
GAY BAR

Map p336 (415-431-8616; www.sfmixbar.com; 4086 18th St; 7am-2am Mon-Fri, from 6am Sat & Sun; Castro) The last Castro bar to open at 6am, Mix is a must on a pub crawl. We like the low-ceilinged pool and bar area but prefer the open-roofed smokers patio. Expect gal-next-door lesbians, 20-something gay boys, trannie pals and the odd stumbling drag queen. Great drink specials keep everyone wasted. On Mondays there's free pool.

HITOPS
SPORTS BAR

Map p336 (hitopssf.com; 2247 Market St; 4pm-12am Mon-Wed, 4pm-2am Thu-Fri, 11am-2am Sat, noon-2am Sun; Castro) If you thought homosexuality and team sports were incompatible, you haven't spent Sunday at Castro's fist gay sports bar, doing shots with softball leaguers, scarfing down fries and screaming at giant-screen TVs. Hard not to love its collegial pub vibe, full-length shuffleboard table, fat comfy bar stools and cutie-pie barkeeps – but damn, it's loud.

LOOKOUT
GAY BAR

Map p336 (415-431-0306; www.lookoutsf. com; 3600 16th St; 3:30pm-2am Mon-Fri, from 12:30pm Sat & Sun; Castro) A favorite for its street-view balcony, Lookout packs in gym-fit 30-somethings. Monday's karaoke provides fun on Castro's quietest night; DJs spin other evenings. Hot rugby players come by on Sunday afternoons for Jock. No cat-calling from the balcony, please!

SAMOVAR TEA LOUNGE
CAFE

Map p336 (415-626-4700; www.samovartea. com; 498 Sanchez St; 8am-10pm; ; Castro) Zen-chic Samovar's sunny Castro location specializes in organic, fair-trade teas and provides a fresh alternative to the bars. Sandwiches and cheese plates, paired with tea, provide reason to linger.

EDGE
GAY BAR

Map p336 (qbarsf.com/edge; 4149 18th St; noon-2am; Castro) When you're feeling kinda ratty and you're looking for a daddy, it's the Edge. And who says drag queens and leather men can't be friends?

BADLANDS
GAY BAR

Map p336 (415-626-9320; www.badlands-sf. com; 4121 18th St; Castro) The Castro's long-standing dance bar gets packed with gay college boys, their screaming straight girlfriends and chicken hawks. If you're over 30, you'll feel old. Expect lines on weekends.

THE CAFE
GAY NIGHTCLUB

Map p336 (www.cafesf.com; 2369 Market St; 5pm-2am Mon-Fri, from 3pm Sat & Sun; Castro) The Cafe draws a just-over-21 crowd – especially Fridays for Boy Bar – to its upstairs dance floor with kick-ass sound and high-tech lighting. Parties range from Latino to lesbian; check the calendar. If you're not dancing, cruise the open-air smokers lounge or shoot pool beneath trippy lights that make it hard to aim after your second cocktail.

QBAR
GAY BAR

Map p336 (415-864-2877; www.qbarsf.com; 456 Castro St; 4pm-2am Mon-Fri, from 2pm Sat & Sun; Castro) Barely 20-somethings pack shoulder-to-shoulder to shout over ear-splitting pop and dance on the tiny floor. Smokers fill the patio. Occasional go-go boys add spice but lately QBar's been going straight – except at Wednesday's staple, Booty Call.

TOAD HALL
GAY BAR

Map p336 (415-621-2811; www.toadhallbar. com; 4146 18th St; 3pm-2am; Castro) Posses of pals get their drink on fast with Toad Hall's specials. Dig the smokers patio and little dance floor. The name derives from Castro's original gay bar, forgotten until the film *Milk,* but this bears no resemblance.

MIDNIGHT SUN   GAY BAR

Map p336 (☎415-861-4186; www.midnightsunsf. com; 4067 18th St; ⊙2pm-2am; Ⓜ Castro) A favorite of khaki-clad suburbanites who aren't entirely comfortable gay-socializing without something to divert attention, Midnight Sun is a video bar. The *Dynasty* era marked its heyday, but crowds still come for *American Idol* and it remains a reliable place to... well, watch TV. Best time: early evening.

☆ ENTERTAINMENT

★ CASTRO THEATRE   CINEMA

Map p336 (☎415-621-6120; www.thecastrothea tre.com; 429 Castro St; adult/child $11/8.50; ⊙Tue-Sun; Ⓜ Castro) The Mighty Wurlitzer organ rises from the orchestra pit before evening performances and the audience cheers for classics from the Great American Songbook, ending with (sing along, now): 'San Francisco open your Golden Gate/You let no stranger wait outside your door...' If there's a cult classic on the bill, say, *Whatever Happened to Baby Jane?,* expect participation. Otherwise, crowd are well-behaved and rapt.

CAFE DU NORD/SWEDISH
AMERICAN HALL   LIVE MUSIC

Map p336 (☎415-861-5016; www.cafedunord.com; 2170 Market St; cover varies; Ⓜ Church) Rockers, chanteuses, comedians, raconteurs and burlesque acts perform nightly at this former basement speakeasy with bar and showroom, and the joint still looks like it did in the '30s. The hall upstairs, with balcony seating and Scandinavian woodwork, hosts miscellaneous events. Check online calendar.

🛍 SHOPPING

🛍 The Castro

SUI GENERIS   CLOTHING, ACCESSORIES

Map p336 (www.suigenerisconsignment.com; men's shop 2231 Market St, women's shop 2265 Market St; Ⓜ Castro) Emerge with confidence from his-and-her designer-consignment boutiques certain nobody but you will be

working your new look. The well-curated collection of contemporary and vintage clothing skews dressy – best for those with fat wallets who fit runway-model sizes.

CLIFF'S VARIETY   HOUSEWARES

Map p336 (www.cliffsvariety.com; 479 Castro St; ⊙8:30am-8pm Mon-Fri, 9:30am-6pm Sat, 11am-6pm Sun; Ⓜ Castro) None of the hardware maestros at Cliff's will raise an eyebrow if you express a dire need for a jar of rubber nuns, silver body paint and a case of cocktail toothpicks, though they might angle for an invitation. The window displays at Cliff's, a community institution since 1936, are a local landmark.

UNIONMADE   CLOTHING, SHOES

Map p336 (www.unionmadegoods.com; 493 Sanchez St; Ⓜ Castro) Upgrade your casual-Friday look with Unionmade's mix of classic quality labels – American-heritage brands like Pendleton and Levi's Vintage, plus European staples like Il Bisonte leather goods.

ALFIO   MEN'S CLOTHING

Map p336 (www.alfioboutique.com; 526 Castro St, 2nd fl; ⊙11am-8pm Mon-Sat, to 7pm Sun; Ⓜ Castro) The line between Euro and gay blurs at this swank upstairs boutique, specializing in clothing by lesser-known Italian designers, imported directly from Milan. Stellar shopping for those particular about cut and fit but expect to spend. Great for denim.

BOOKS INC   BOOKSTORE

Map p336 (www.booksinc.net; 2275 Market St; ⊙10am-10pm; Ⓜ Castro) The Castro's indie bookstore carries new-release hardcovers, good fiction, extensive magazines and travel books. Check bulletin boards for readings and literary events.

DE LA SOLE   SHOES

Map p336 (www.delasole.com; 549 Castro St; Ⓜ Castro) SF gets its kicks at De La Sole, from mod Duckie Brown-Florsheim wingtips to radiator-vented sandals by Montreal brand Industry. Says the sales rep to a customer squeezing into a 60%-off Palladium boot: 'Don't worry, it won't always be so tight.' Chimes in a fellow customer, without missing a beat: 'That's what they all say.'

HUMAN RIGHTS CAMPAIGN
ACTION CENTER & STORE   GIFTS, CLOTHING

Map p336 (shop.hrc.org; 575 Castro St; ⊙10am-8pm Mon-Sat, to 7pm Sun; Ⓜ Castro) Make more than a fashion statement in signature HRC tees designed by Marc Jacobs, Kenneth Cole and other fashion-forward thinkers, with proceeds supporting LGBT civil-rights initiatives. Hopeful romantics shop for sterling-silver soul-mate rings, while activists scan the bulletin board and petitions.

If this storefront seems familiar, you're right: this was once Harvey Milk's camera shop and one of the locations used in the Academy Award–winning *Milk*.

KENNETH WINGARD HOUSEWARES

Map p336 (www.kennethwingard.com; 2319 Market St; ⊙11am-7pm; MCastro) Upgrade from ho-hum IKEA to mod housewares that are positively scrumptious: glossy tangerine vases, vintage tiki-fabric cushions and mood-setting, ecofriendly, cork-shaded lamps, all priced for mass consumption.

WORN OUT WEST ACCESSORIES

Map p336 (www.wornoutwest.com; 582 Castro St; ⊙noon-7pm Sun-Fri, from 11am Sat; MCastro) Find leathers, original-cut Levi's 501s, cockrings and tanks at this old-school-Castro used-clothing store and dress like a slutty local. Good fetish wear at great prices. Not much for gals, alas.

🏠 Noe Valley

AMBIANCE CLOTHING, ACCESSORIES

Map p337 (www.ambiancesf.com; 3985 & 3989 24th St; ⊙11am-7pm; 🚌24, 48, MJ) Expect to find some super-cute outfit requiring you hit the town. Dresses are particularly good, emphasizing girly-girl casual. For bargains, start next door at the shoe-and-sale store. Shop sister locations at 1458 Haight St for teen-appropriate prom dresses and 1858 Union St in the Marina for cocktail attire.

RABAT CLOTHING, SHOES

Map p337 (📞415-282-7861; www.rabatsshoes.com; 4001 24th St; ⊙10:30am-7pm Mon-Sat, 11am-6pm Sun; 🚌24, 48, MJ) With frenetic collections of high-end and local designers – some of whom work in-store – Rabat offers style without sacrificing function, with trim Nanette Lapore jackets and Michael Stars tees. The owner hits Europe's shows to personally select the bounce-in-your-step men's shoes and snazzy-but-flat women's shoes and boots – be prepared to spend for such stylish imports.

OMNIVORE BOOKSTORE

Map p337 (www.omnivorebooks.com; 3885a Cesar Chavez St; ⊙11am-6pm Mon-Sat, noon-5pm Sun; MJ) Salivate over signed cookbooks by chef-legend Alice Waters, A16's 'James Beard Rising Star Chef' Nate Appelbaum and signed copies of *The Omnivore's Dilemma* by Michael Pollan. Check the calendar for standing-room-only in-store events with star chefs. Don't miss the collection of vintage cookbooks and rarities, such as a Civil War–era recipe book, written longhand.

ISSO CLOTHING, ACCESSORIES

Map p337 (www.issosf.com; 3789 24th St; ⊙11am-7pm Mon-Sat, noon-6pm Sun; 🚌48, MJ) 'Made, found or designed in the Bay Area' is the motto of this purveyor of women's apparel that also designs its own line – expect updated classics with little zings, such as angle-pocket pencil skirts made of vintage fabric. Local designers round out the collection.

GLOBAL EXCHANGE FAIR TRADE CRAFT CENTER GIFTS, HOUSEWARES

Map p337 (www.globalexchangestore.org; 4018 24th St; ⊙11am-7pm Tue-Fri, 10am-7pm Sat, 11am-6pm Sun-Mon; 🚌24, 48, MJ) 🌿 Consumerism with heart. Inventories constantly change but typically include baskets, ceramics, fairtrade chocolates, exceptional jewelry and sweatshop-free clothing, with proceeds going right back to the community cooperatives that made them, via nonprofit Global Exchange.

The Haight, NoPa & Hayes Valley

Neighborhood Top Five

1 Bringing the Summer of Love back to **Haight St** (p185): wear flowers, draw up a manifesto, sing freestyle folk songs on the corner of Haight and Ashbury Sts, or follow in the footsteps of psychedelic-rock giants.

2 Toasting jazz giants between sets at **SFJazz** (p194) in front of Sandow Birk's tiled music history mural.

3 Glimpsing San Francisco's towering achievements atop **Alamo Square** (p186), from Victorian mansions that housed hippie communes to City Hall's risen-from-the-ashes rotunda.

4 Grazing your way around **Patricia's Green** (p192) in Hayes Valley.

5 Picking up a new skill at the **Makeshift Society** (p199), from graffiti calligraphy to concocting cocktail bitters.

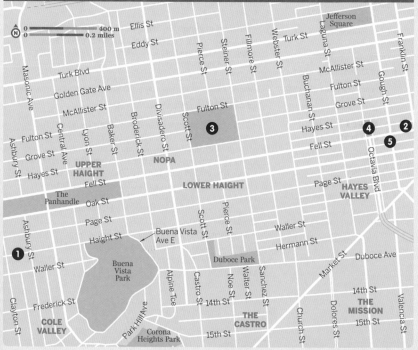

For more detail of this area, see Map p338 and p340 ➡

Lonely Planet's Top Tip

Ever since the '60s, America's youth have headed to the Haight as a place to fit in, no questions asked. But in 2010 San Francisco passed the controversial Sit/Lie Ordinance, making 7am-to-11pm sidewalk loitering punishable by $50 to $100 fines. Critics note the law has been primarily enforced in the Haight, ticketing homeless teens – but with 1300 shelter beds to accommodate 6500 to 13,000 homeless citywide, many youth have no place else to go. Spare change is a short-term fix; consider donations to youth-service nonprofits instead.

✕ Best Places to Eat

➡ Rich Table (p189)
➡ Jardinière (p189)
➡ Rosamunde Sausage Grill (p186)
➡ Bar Crudo (p188)
➡ Zuni Cafe (p189)

For reviews, see p186 ➡

☐ Best Places to Drink

➡ Smuggler's Cove (p193)
➡ Toronado (p189)
➡ Alembic (p192)
➡ Two Sisters Bar & Books (p193)
➡ Hôtel Biron (p193)

For reviews, see p189 ➡

Explore Hayes Valley, NoPa & the Haight

Stroll Hayes Valley's trendy restaurants and glam boutiques, then discover its down-to-earth side on Patricia's Green. Fog permitting, pick up picnic fixings in NoPa (North of Panhandle) for lunch atop Alamo Square Park. Otherwise, hop the bus straight to the Upper Haight for a walking tour through hippie history. After admiring the Victorians ringing Alamo Square, amble down to NoPa for shopping and dining. Browse your way down Haight St for Rosamunde sausages and Toronado beer, until you're ready to brave karaoke at the Mint, show tunes at Martuni's or even the Scorpion Bowl at Smuggler's Cove.

Local Life

➡ **Cheap eats and fancy drinks** Go high/low with Rosamunde sausages (p186) and Toronado Belgian ales (p189), oyster po' boy sliders and rare bourbon at Alembic (p192), Nojo chicken yakatori skewers (p189) and agricole rum drinks at Smuggler's Cove (p193).

➡ **Hangouts** Aspiring flower children and original-issue hippies gather at Coffee to the People (p188), skaters hit Haight St's downhill slide to Lower Haight bars and grab bites in NoPa before shows at the Independent (p194).

➡ **Musical stylings** Go acoustic on the corner of Haight and Ashbury Sts, belt it out at the Mint (p194), sing along at Martuni's (p193) or rock out at free concerts at Amoeba Music (p194).

Getting There & Away

➡ **Bus** Market St buses 6 and 71 run up Haight St to Golden Gate Park. The 22 links Lower Haight to the Mission and Japantown/Marina. Number 24 runs along Divisadero, connecting NoPa and the Haight to the Castro and Pacific Heights. Bus 43 connects Upper Haight with the Marina, and 33 runs through Upper Haight between the Richmond and the Mission. Buses 21 and 5 connect Hayes Valley with Downtown and Golden Gate Park.

➡ **Streetcar** The N line offers a shortcut from Downtown and Lower Haight to Upper Haight.

➡ **BART** Civic Center BART is four blocks east of Hayes Valley.

WENDY CONNETT / GETTY IMAGES ©

TOP SIGHT
HAIGHT ST

Was it the fall of 1966 or the winter of '67? As the Haight saying goes, if you can remember the Summer of Love, man, you probably weren't there. The fog was laced with Nag Champa incense and burning draft cards, entire days were spent contemplating DayGlo Grateful Dead posters, and the corner of Haight and Ashbury Sts became the turning point of a generation.

Unlikely Landmarks

Flashbacks are a given in the Haight, which still has its swinging '60s tendencies. Only a very mysterious, very local illness could explain the number of neighborhood medical marijuana clubs, and tie-dyes and ideals have never entirely gone out of fashion here – hence the highly prized vintage psychedelic rock tees on the wall at Wasteland and Bound Together Anarchist Book Collective. Some '60s memories are better left behind: habits were kicked in the neighborhood's many rehabs and many an intimate itch has been mercifully treated gratis at the Haight Ashbury Free Clinic. To relive the highlights of the era, a short **walking tour** (p187) passes the former flophouses of the Haight's most famous and infamous residents.

Lower & Upper Haight

Since the '60s, Haight St has divided into two major splinter factions, delineated by a **Divisadero St** strip of indie boutiques, trendy bars and restaurants. The **Upper Haight** specializes in potent coffee, radical literature and retail therapy for rebels, while the **Lower Haight** has better bars, more economic and ethnic diversity, and a pot-club mellow occasionally disrupted by gang activity northeast of Fillmore and Haight Sts.

DON'T MISS...

➡ Haight Flashback walking tour
➡ Mysterious 4:20 clock at Haight & Ashbury Sts
➡ *Anarchists of the Americas* mural at Bound Together Anarchist Book Collective
➡ Lower Haight bars

PRACTICALITIES

➡ Map p338
➡ Haight St btwn Fillmore & Stanyan Sts
➡ Ⓜ Haight St

⊙ SIGHTS

HAIGHT ST STREET
See p185.

ALAMO SQUARE PARK PARK
Map p338 (Hayes & Scott Sts; ☀; ☐5, 21, 22, 24)
FREE The pastel Painted Ladies of famed
Postcard Row on Alamo Square's east side
pale in comparison with the colorful characters along the north side of the park. Here
you'll spot true Barbary Coast baroque,
with facades bedecked with fish-scale shin-
gles and gingerbread trim dripping from
peaked roofs.

On the park's northwest corner, the
olive-green, gilded Stick Italianate Victorian capped by an ornamental watchtower
was built by candy mogul William West-
erfield in 1889 and survived subsequent
tenancies by Russian bootleggers, Fillmore
jazz musicians and hippie communes.
Filmed rituals held in the tower by Church
of Satan founder Anton LaVey apparently
involved hundreds of candles and coaxing a
grumpy lion up four flights of stairs.

BUENA VISTA PARK PARK
Map p338 (http://sfrecpark.org; Haight St, btwn
Central Ave & Baker St; ⊙sunrise-sunset; ☐6, 37,
43, 71) True to its name, this park founded
in 1867 offers splendid vistas over the city to
Golden Gate Bridge as a reward for hiking
up the steep hill ringed by stately century-
old California oaks. Take Buena Vista Ave
West downhill to spot Victorian mansions
that survived the 1906 earthquake and fire.
After-hours boozing or cruising is risky,
given petty criminal activity.

GRATEFUL DEAD HOUSE NOTABLE BUILDING
Map p338 (710 Ashbury St; ☐6, 33, 37, 43, 71)
Like surviving members of the Grateful
Dead, this purple Victorian sports a touch
of gray – but during the Summer of Love,
this was where Jerry Garcia and bandmates
blew minds, amps and brain cells. After
their 1967 drug bust, the Dead held an infamous press conference here, claiming if
everyone who smoked marijuana were arrested, San Francisco would be empty.

**HUNTER S THOMPSON
CRASH PAD** NOTABLE BUILDING
(318 Parnassus Ave; Ⓜ︎N) On the unremarka-
ble bay-windowed facade, you might notice
patched bullet holes – mementos of Hunter
S Thompson's 1960s tenancy, when parties
degenerated into Hell's Angels orgies and
shoot-outs. Thompson narrowly survived
to write *Hell's Angels: The Strange and Terrible Saga of the Outlaw Motorcycle Gang*,
founding Gonzo journalism with this motto: 'When the going gets weird, the weird
turn pro.'

✗ EATING

✗ The Haight

★**ROSAMUNDE SAUSAGE GRILL** SAUSAGES $
Map p338 (☎415-437-6851; http://rosamunde-
sausagegrill.com; 545 Haight St; sausages $4-6;
⊙11:30am-10pm; ☐6, 22, 71, Ⓜ︎N) Impress a
dinner date on the cheap: load up classic
Brats or duck-fig links with complimentary roasted peppers, grilled onions, whole-
grain mustard and mango chutney, and
enjoy with your choice of 100 beers at Toronado next door. But to impress a local lunch
date, call ahead or line up by 11:30 Tuesdays
for massive $6 burgers with grilled onions.

ESCAPE FROM NEW YORK PIZZA PIZZA $
Map p338 (☎415-668-5577; www.escapefrom-
newyorkpizza.com; 1737 Haight St; slices $3-5;
⊙11am-midnight Sun-Thu, to 2am Fri & Sat; ☐6,
22, 33, 43, 71) The Haight's obligatory mid-
bender stop for a hot slice. Pesto with roasted garlic and potato will send you blissfully
off to carbo-loaded sleep, but the sundried
tomato with goat cheese, artichoke hearts
and spinach will recharge you to go another
round. Art donated by fans includes signed
rocker head-shots (hello, Elvis Costello and
Metallica) and cartoons by *The Simpsons'*
Matt Groening.

SUNRISE DELI MIDDLE EASTERN $
Map p338 (☎415-355-1555; www.sunrisedeli.net;
1671 Haight St; Sandwiches $7-9; ⊙11am-8pm; ✈;
☐6, 33, 37, 43, 71, Ⓜ︎N) Vegetarians swear by
Sunrise for its crispy falafel sandwich – best
supersized with eggplant and/or avocado –
but even meat-eaters will be won over by
smoky *baba ghanoush* (eggplant dip) and
hearty *mujeddrah* (lentil-rice with crispy
onions). Enjoy yours in the sunny storefront
or order to go for Golden Gate Park picnics.
For broader deli selections, visit the **Sunset
location** (Map p342; ☎415-664-8210; 2115 Irving St; dishes $4-7; ⊙9am-9pm Mon-Sat, 10am-
8pm Sun; ✈; Ⓜ︎Judah St).

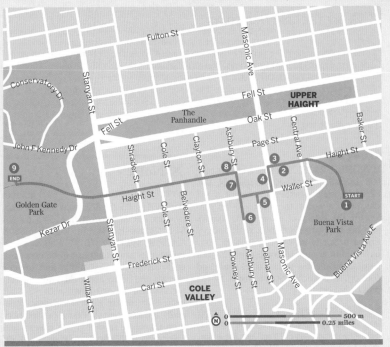

Neighborhood Walk
Haight Flashback

START BUENA VISTA PARK
END GOLDEN GATE PARK
LENGTH 1.3 MILES; ONE HOUR

Start your trip back in time in ① **Buena Vista Park** (p186), with panoramic city views that moved surviving San Franciscans to tears after the fire of 1906.

Heading west up Haight St, you may recognize Emma Goldman and Sacco and Vanzetti in the *Anarchists of the Americas* mural at ② **Bound Together Anarchist Book Collective** (p195) – if you don't, staff can provide you with some biographical comics by way of introduction. Continuing west, you can't miss ③ **Magnolia Brewpub** (p188), the corner microbrewery and organic eatery named after a Grateful Dead song.

It's believed the Symbionese Liberation Army once used ④ **1235 Masonic Ave** as a safehouse to hold Patty Hearst, the kidnapped heiress turned revolutionary bank robber.

Turning right off Masonic Ave onto Waller St, you'll notice a narrow lane leading uphill. In 1978 ⑤ **32 Delmar St** was the site of Sid Vicious' overdose that finally broke up the Sex Pistols.

Pay your respects to the former flophouse of Jerry Garcia, Bob Weir and Pigpen, at the ⑥ **Grateful Dead House** (p186) at 710 Ashbury St, site of an infamous drug bust in 1967. Down the block, ⑦ **635 Ashbury St** is one of many known San Francisco addresses for Janis Joplin, who had a pretty hard time hanging onto leases in the 1960s – but, as she sang, 'Freedom's just another word for nothin' left to lose.'

At the corner of Haight and Ashbury, you'll notice that the ⑧ **clock** overhead always reads 4:20, better known in 'Hashbury' as International Bong Hit Time. Follow the beat of your own drummer to the drum circle at ⑨ **Hippie Hill in Golden Gate Park**, where free spirits have gathered since the '60s to tune in, turn on and attempt to hit a workable groove.

❶ OFF THE GRID THURSDAYS

Peace and love come easy in the Haight, but dinnertime can suddenly divide friends into warring factions – one party insists on Chinese, while a splinter group demands dessert. From 5 to 9pm Thursdays, there's a diplomatic dinner solution at the corner of Stanyan and Waller: Off the Grid. A dozen food trucks pull into the empty lot across from McDonald's – and for little more than a McMeal, you can go gourmet with pork-belly buns from Chairman (p28), empanadas from El Sur (p28) and mini-carrot-cakes from Kara's Cupcakes. Instead of debating dinner, you can have your cake and dance to live music too.

AXUM CAFE
ETHIOPIAN $

Map p338 (☑415-252-7912; www.axumcafe.com; 698 Haight St; mains $8-15; ⊙5-10pm; ☑; ☐6, 22, 24, 71, Ⓜ️N) Whether you've got a hot date with a vegan, the hunger of an athlete or the salary of an activist, Axum's vegetarian platter for two with spongy *injera* bread is handy. Dig in with your bare hands, try not to hog lip-tingling red lentils and mellow yellow chickpeas, and cool off with Anchor Steam brews by the pint or pitcher.

COFFEE TO THE PEOPLE
CAFE

Map p338 (☑415-626-2435; 1206 Masonic Ave; ⊙6am-8pm Mon-Fri, from 7am Sat & Sun; 📶☑📶; ☐6, 33, 37, 43, 71) 🖋 The people united will never be decaffeinated at this radical coffee house – though dairy-free hemp milk and vegan cookies are optional. Grab seats at bumper-sticker-covered tables, admire hippie macramé on the walls and browse consciousness-raising books. But beware the quadruple-shot Freak Out, which has enough fair-trade espresso to reinvigorate the Sandinista movement. Five percent of purchases supports community organizations.

MAGNOLIA
BREWPUB
CALIFORNIAN, AMERICAN $$

Map p338 (☑415-864-7468; www.magnoliapub. com; 1398 Haight St; mains $11-20; ⊙11am-midnight Mon-Thu, to 1am Fri, 10am-1am Sat, 10am-midnight Sun; ☐6, 33, 43, 71) 🖋 Organic pub grub and homebrew samplers keep conversation flowing at communal tables, while grass-fed Prather Ranch burgers satisfy stoner appetites in booths – it's like the Summer of Love all over again, only with better food. Magnolia microbrews its own for morning-after brunches of quinoa hash with brewer's yeast plus Stout of Circumstance strong enough to revive the Grateful Dead.

🍴 NoPa

LITTLE CHIHUAHUA
MEXICAN $

Map p338 (☑415-255-8225; www.thelittlechihuahua.com; 292 Divisadero St; tacos $4-5, burritos $8-11; ⊙11am-11pm Mon-Fri, 10am-11pm Sat & Sun; ☑📶; ☐6, 21, 24, 71) 🖋 Who says sustainable, organic food has to be expensive or French? Grass-fed meats and organic veggies and beans are packed into organic tortillas, all washed down with $3 draft beer. Burritos are a two-meal deal, especially the decadent Al Pastor (grilled pork with pineapple salsa and jack cheese) and savory-sweet Black Bean Plantain. Kids' menu available.

BAR CRUDO
SEAFOOD $$

Map p338 (☑415-409-0679; www.barcrudo.com; 655 Divisadero St; small plates $10-14; ⊙5-10pm Tue-Thu & Sun, to 11pm Fri-Sat; ☐5, 6, 21, 24, 71) An international idea that's pure California: choice seafood served raw Italian-style, with pan-Asian condiments and East–West beers. Start with Japanese Hitachino white ale with velvety avocado-*uni* (sea urchin) toast and graduate to potent Belgian Tripel ales with crudo platters featuring wasabi-spiked Arctic char. Don't miss happy hour (5pm to 6:30pm), when specials include $1 oysters, $5 chowder and $5 wine.

RAGAZZA
PIZZA $$

Map p338 (☑415-255-1133; www.ragazzasf.com; 311 Divisadero St; pizza $13-18; ⊙5-10pm Mon-Thu, to 10:30 Fri & Sat; 📶; ☐6, 21, 24, 71) 'Girl' is what the name means, as in, 'Oooh, *girl*, did you try the potato-leek pizza?!' Artisan salumi is the star of many Ragazza pies, from the Amatriciana with pecorino, bacon and egg to the pork belly with Calabrian chili and beet greens – best with carafes of Sardinian reds or weighty white Roero. Arrive early to nab garden patio tables.

✕ Hayes Valley

CHANTAL GUILLON MACARONS   DESSERT **$**
Map p340 (☏415-864-2400; www.chantalguillon. com; 437 Hayes St; macarons $1.80; ⏰11am-7pm Tue-Sat, noon-6pm Sun & Mon; ☖5, 21, 47, 49) Sorry, Oreo. The competition for the ultimate sandwich cookie is down to two of Chantal Guillon's French macarons: Sicilian pistachio and passion fruit. Declare a winner from sunny sidewalk seats, or go for a second championship round: caramel *fleur-de-sel* (sea salt) and jasmine green tea.

★RICH TABLE   CALIFORNIAN **$$**
Map p340 (☏415-355-9085; http://richtablesf. com; 199 Gough St; meals $30-40; ⏰5:30-10pm Sun-Thu, to 10:30pm Fri-Sat; ☖5, 6, 21, 47, 49, 71, Ⓜ Van Ness) 🍴 Licking plates is the obvious move after finishing chilled apricot soup with pancetta or rabbit cannelloni with nasturtium cream. Here, married co-chefs and owners Sarah and Evan Rich invent playful, exquisite Californian food like the Dirty Hippie: a crock of silky goat-buttermilk panna cotta topped with nutty sunflower seeds and hemp – a dish as offbeat and entrancing as the drum circle at Hippie Hill.

Check the website for food events and bargain $35 prix fixe menus. Book two to four weeks ahead (call the restaurant directly) or arrive before 5:30 to bide your time at the barn-wood bar and hope for an opening before the California wine on tap runs dry.

NOJO   JAPANESE **$$**
Map p340 (☏415-896-4587; www.nojosf.com; 231 Franklin St; small plates $4-15; ⏰11:30am-2pm & 5:30-10pm Wed-Fri, 5:30-9:30pm Mon, 11am-2:30pm & 5-9:30pm Sun, 5:30-10:30pm Sat; ☖5, 6, 21, 47, 49, 71, Ⓜ Van Ness) 🍴 Everything you could possibly want skewered and roasted at happy hour, except maybe your boss. Tasting-portion-size Japanese *izakaya* (bar snacks) specialties include grilled chicken *yakitori* (skewers), miso-glazed trout and beef tongue slathered in savory-sweet *tare* sauce. Local, organic produce brightens every dish. Trust staff on wine, beer and sake pairings, but don't miss Buddha's Hand cocktails at Sunday brunch.

CHEZ MAMAN WEST   FRENCH **$$**
Map p340 (☏415-355-9067; www.chezmamansf. com; 401 Gough St; meals $15-30; ⏰11:30am-11pm Mon-Fri, from 10:30am Sat & Sun; ☖5, 21, 47,

49, Ⓜ Van Ness) Quit pretending you're considering the sensible Niçoise salad and go for the restorative brunch everyone needs mid-shopping-spree: buckwheat crepes plumped with decadent fillings like prosciutto with bechamel or chicken with creamy mustard sauce. Bubbly by the glass and cinnamon-laced berry *pain perdu* for dessert will leave you ready to take sales racks by storm.

★JARDINIÈRE   CALIFORNIAN **$$$**
Map p340 (☏415-861-5555; www.jardiniere.com; 300 Grove St; mains $19-37; ⏰5-10:30pm Tue-Sat, to 10pm Sun & Mon; ☖5, 21, 47, 49, Ⓜ Van Ness) 🍴 Iron Chef, Top Chef Master and James Beard Award winner Traci Des Jardins champions sustainable, salacious California cuisine. She has a way with California's organic vegetables, free-range meats and sustainably caught seafood that's probably illegal in other states, lavishing housemade tagliatelle with bone marrow and topping velvety scallops with satiny sea urchin. On Monday, $49 scores three decadent courses with wine pairings.

ZUNI CAFE   CALIFORNIAN, AMERICAN **$$$**
Map p340 (☏415-552-2522; www.zunicafe.com; 1658 Market St; mains $14-29; ⏰11:30am-11pm Tue-Thu, to midnight Fri & Sat, 11am-11pm Sun; ☖6, 71, 47, 49, Ⓜ Van Ness) Gimmickry is for amateurs – Zuni has been turning basic menu items into gourmet staples since 1979. Reservations and fat wallets are handy, but the see-and-be-seen seating is a kick and the food is beyond reproach: Caesar salad with house-cured anchovies, brick-oven-roasted free-range chicken with horseradish mashed potatoes, and mesquite-grilled organic-beef burgers on focaccia (shoestring fries $6 extra, and recommended).

🍷 DRINKING & NIGHTLIFE

🍸 The Haight

★TORONADO   PUB
Map p338 (☏415-863-2276; www.toronado. com; 547 Haight St; ⏰11:30am-2am; ☖6, 22, 71, Ⓜ N) Glory hallelujah, beer lovers: your prayers have been answered. Be humbled before the chalkboard altar that lists

Victorians

DANIEL OSTERKAMP / GETTY IMAGES ©

The city's signature architectural style was labeled 'Victorian,' but demure Queen Victoria would surely blush to see the eccentric architecture perpetrated in her name in San Francisco. Few of the older buildings you'll see in SF were actually built during Victoria's 1837–1901 reign, including steeply gabled Gothic Revivals. The rest are cheerfully inauthentic San Franciscan takes on a vaguely Anglo-Continental style, with rococo flourishes that made mansions and bordellos look alike.

Local 'Painted Ladies' have candy-color palettes, gingerbread woodworking bedecking peaked roofs, and gilded stucco garlands swagging huge, look-at-me bay windows. The 1906 quake and fire destroyed many of the city's 19th-century treasures and much of its kitschy excess. Of the 19th-century Painted Ladies that have stood the test of trends and tremors, many belong to other architectural categories:

1. Alamo Square (p186), Haight **2.** Grateful Dead House (p186), Haight **3.** Haas-Lilienthal House (p138), Pacific Heights

Stick (1880s)

In the Lower Haight, Mission and Pacific Heights, you'll notice squared-off Victorians built to fit into narrow lots side-by-side, typically with flat fronts and long, narrow windows.

Queen Anne (1880s–1910)

Architects pulled out all the stops on Queen Anne mansions, adding balconies, turrets, chimneys, bay windows and gables. Alamo Square (p186) has several exuberant examples with fish-scale shingle decoration, rounded corner towers and decorative bands to lift the eye skyward.

Edwardian (1901–1914)

Most of the 'Victorians' you'll see in San Francisco are actually from the postfire Edwardian era – art nouveau, Asian-inspired, and Arts and Crafts details are the giveaways. You'll spot original Edwardian stained-glass windows and false gables in the inner Richmond, Haight and Castro neighborhoods.

LOCAL KNOWLEDGE

SHIPPING-CONTAINER GOURMET SCENE

After the 1989 earthquake damaged freeway ramps around Fell and Octavia Streets, urban blight struck the neighborhood – until San Franciscan voters nixed the overpass and reinvented Octavia Boulevard as a walkable, palm-tree-lined community hub. The social center is **Patricia's Green** (Map p340; http://sfrecpark.org), with a playground, handy picnic tables and rotating sculpture displays inspired by Burning Man. But the main gourmet action is east of the green in two formerly vacant lots, where food trucks park and shipping containers now house three key gourmet attractions.

Smitten Ice Cream (Map p340; www.smittenicecream.com; 432 Octavia St; ⊗noon-10pm daily; ₪5, 7, 21) Ice cream is made to order with liquid nitrogen and seasonal ingredients, yielding extra-creamy but subtle flavors such as olive oil-lavender and spearmint-chip.

Ritual Coffee Roasters (Map p340; www.ritualroasters.com; 434 Octavia St; ⊗7am-7pm daily; ₪5, 7, 21) The outpost of the Mission roastery offers creamy espresso and powerful pour-overs to rival Blue Bottle around the corner.

Biergarten (Map p340; http://biergartensf.com; 424 Octavia St; ⊗3-9pm Wed-Sat, 1-7pm Sun; ₪5, 7, 21) The faintest ray of sunshine brings lines down the block for beer and bratwurst at Biergarten – wear sunblock, order two rounds and get the pickled deviled eggs and pretzels to share with newfound friends at communal picnic tables.

50-plus beers on tap and hundreds more bottled, including spectacular seasonal microbrews. Bring cash and order sausages from Rosamunde next door to accompany ale made by Trappist monks. It may get too loud to hear your date talk, but you'll hear the angels sing.

ALEMBIC
BAR

Map p338 (☑415-666-0822; www.alembicbar. com; 1725 Haight St; ⊗noon-2am; ₪6, 33, 37, 43, 71, Ⓜ︎N) The tin ceilings are hammered and floors well-stomped, but drinks expertly crafted from 250 specialty spirits are not made for pounding – hence the 'No Red Bull/ No Jägermeister' sign and duck-heart bar snacks. Toast the Haight with a Lava Lamp (rosé bubbly with walnut bitters) or be rendered speechless by Charlie Chaplin, a sloe gin, lime and apricot liqueur concoction.

AUB ZAM ZAM
BAR

Map p338 (☑415-861-2545; 1633 Haight St; ⊗3pm-2am; ₪6, 22, 33, 43, 71, Ⓜ︎N) Arabesque arches, an *Arabian Nights*–style mural, 1930s jazz on the jukebox and top-shelf cocktails at low-shelf prices keep restless romantics happy for the night at this Haight St mainstay. Legendary founder Bruno used to throw you out for ordering a vodka martini, but he was a softie in the end, bequeathing his beloved bar to regulars who had become friends. Cash only.

NOC NOC
BAR

Map p338 (☑415-861-5811; www.nocnocs.com; 557 Haight St; ⊗5pm-2am Mon-Thu, from 3:30pm Fri, from 3pm Sat & Sun; ₪6, 22, 24, 71, Ⓜ︎N) Who's there? Nearsighted graffiti artists, anarchist hackers, electronica DJs practicing for Burning Man and other characters straight out of an R Crumb comic, that's who. Happy hour from 5pm to 7pm daily brings $3 local drafts, but those soju cocktails will knock-knock you off your steampunk scavenged-metal stool.

UVA ENOTECA
WINE BAR

Map p338 (☑415-829-2024; www.uvaenoteca. com; 568 Haight St; ⊗5-10pm Mon, to 11pm Tue-Fri, 11:30am-11:30pm Sat, 3:30-10pm Sun; ₪6, 22, 24, 71, Ⓜ︎N) Boys with shags and girls with bangs discover the joys of Bardolino and Barbera by the tasting glass. A staff of tattooed Lower Haight hotties pair drinks with inventive local veggie plates and cheese and charcuterie boards. Daily happy hours (5pm to 6:30pm) bring $5 house wine and a bargain bar menu.

🍷 NoPa

MADRONE ART BAR
BAR

Map p338 (☑415-241-0202; www.madroneartbar. com; 500 Divisadero St; cover free-$5; ⊗5pm-2am Tue-Sat, 6pm-2am Sun & Mon; ₪5, 6, 21, 24, 71)

Expect the unexpected at this Victorian bar with the bomb-shaped disco ball, rotating art installations and Motown nights featuring the Ike Turner drink special: Hennessy served with a slap. But nothing beats jaw-dropping Purple Thriller mash-ups at the monthly Prince vs Michael Jackson party, when the tiny place packs. Cash only; acts range from punk-bluegrass to rock-piano.

VINYL COFFEE & WINE BAR   CAFE, WINE BAR

Map p338 (☑415-621-4132; www.vinylsf.com; 359 Divisadero St; ⏲7am-11pm Mon-Thu, 8am-midnight Fri & Sat, 8am-9pm Sun; 🚌6, 21, 24, 71) Like a superhero in disguise, Vinyl by day is a slightly nerdy cafe serving Blue Bottle roasts to start-up founders – but once the lights are dimmed and happy hour kicks in with $6 wine (5:30pm to 7pm), this place gets action-packed. Check events listings for Brainstorm Trivia nights and Pizza Hacker pop-ups for margherita pizza baked in a modified Weber grill.

CANDYBAR   BAR

Map p338 (☑415-673-7078; www.candybarsf.com; 1335 Fulton St; ⏲6-10pm Tue-Thu & Sun, to midnight Fri & Sat; 🚌5, 21, 24) Other bars mock froufrou drinks and inexpert dart players, but here you can shamelessly order a Strawberry Kiss (bubbly with frozen strawberries and ginger ale) and cheat at board games around candlelit tables. Yes, you can turn Candyland into a drinking game – loser buys the next round of Drunken S'mores with rum, chocolate sauce and toasted marshmallows.

🍷 Hayes Valley

★SMUGGLER'S COVE   BAR

(Map p340; ☑415-869-1900; www.smugglerscovesf.com; 650 Gough St; ⏲5pm-1:15am; 🚌5, 21, 49, Ⓜ Van Ness) Yo-ho-ho and a bottle of rum... or maybe a Dead Reckoning with Angostura bitters, Nicaraguan rum, tawny port and vanilla liqueur, unless someone will share the flaming Scorpion Bowl? Pirates are bedeviled by choice at this Barbary Coast shipwreck tiki bar, hidden behind a tinted-glass door. With 400 rums and 70 cocktails gleaned from rum-running around the world, you won't be dry-docked long.

BLUE BOTTLE COFFEE COMPANY   CAFE

Map p340 (☑415-252-7535; www.bluebottlecoffee.net; 315 Linden St; ⏲7am-6pm Mon-Fri, 8am-6pm Sat & Sun; 🚌5, 21, 47, 49, Ⓜ Van Ness) 🍃 Don't mock SF's coffee geekery until you've tried the elixir emerging from this back-alley garage-door kiosk. The Bay Area's Blue Bottle built its reputation with micro-roasted fair-trade organic coffee – especially mood-altering bittersweet mochas and cappuccinos with foam so stiff, the frothy ferns barely budge when stirred. Expect a wait and seats outside on creatively repurposed traffic curbs.

Stop by the Ferry Building kiosk for a quick Blue Bottle fix or the downtown 66 Mint St coffee lab to witness coffee coursing through the mad-scientist glass tubing of Blue Bottle's $20,000 coffee siphon.

HÔTEL BIRON   WINE BAR

Map p340 (☑415-703-0403; www.hotelbiron.com; 45 Rose St; ⏲5pm-2am; 🚌6, 71, 21, 47, 49, Ⓜ Van Ness) Duck into the alley to find this walk-in wine closet, with standout Californian, Provençal and Tuscan vintages and a cork-studded ceiling. The vibe is French underground, with exposed-brick walls, surreally romantic art, a leather couch and just a few tables for two. Barkeeps let you keep tasting until you find what you like; pair with decadent cheese and salumi platters.

MARTUNI'S   GAY

Map p340 (☑415-241-0205; http://martunis.ypguides.net; 4 Valencia St; ⏲2pm-2am; 🚌6, 71, Ⓜ Van Ness) Slip behind the velvet curtains to see who's tickling the ivories at the city's last piano bar, where gay and straight, salt-and-pepper regulars seem to have committed the Great American Songbook to memory. You'll be singing too, after a couple of top-notch watermelon, lemon-drop or Godiva chocolate martinis under $10.

TWO SISTERS BAR & BOOKS   BAR

Map p340 (☑415-863-3655; 579 Hayes St; ⏲4-11pm Tue-Thu, to midnight Fri, 11am-midnight Sat, noon-10pm Sun; 🚌5, 21) Witty banter is helped along by wine and conversation-starting books in this cozy Victorian nook. Trade *Twilight* for *Fahrenheit 451* – there's a take-one, leave-one honor system – and order the truffled deviled eggs or a weeknight special (4pm to 6pm), including $5 cheese plates and cocktails.

⭐ ENTERTAINMENT

★ SFJAZZ CENTER   JAZZ

Map p340 (☎866-920-5299; www.sfjazz.org; 201 Franklin St; ☺showtimes vary; 🚌5, 7, 21, Ⓜ Van Ness) Jazz greats coast-to-coast and from Argentina to Yemen are showcased at America's newest, largest jazz center. The SF Jazz Festival takes place here in July, but year-round the calendar features legends such as McCoy Tyner, Regina Carter, Béla Fleck and Tony Bennett (who left his heart here, after all). Upper-tier cheap seats are more like stools, but offer clear stage views.

The LEED-certified glass-and-concrete auditorium offers clear views to the street, with an artist-in-residence program encouraging collaborations like pianist Jason Moran's performance with skateboarders improvising balletic moves on indoor ramps. At intermission, don't miss craft cocktails on the balcony, or the Sandow Birk tile murals capturing the history of jazz on the East Coast, in the Midwest, and in California. Check the website for family matinees and master classes on subjects ranging from congas to dance-percussion.

THE INDEPENDENT   LIVE MUSIC

Map p338 (☎415-771-1421; www.theindependent-sf.com; 628 Divisadero St; tickets $12-45; ☺box office 11am-6pm Mon-Fri, to 9:30pm show nights; 🚌5, 6, 21, 71) Shows earn street creds at the intimate Independent, featuring indie dreamers (Magnetic Fields, Rogue Wave), rock legends (Courtney Love, Marky Ramone), alterna-pop (Imagine Dragons, Vampire Weekend), comedians (Dave Chapelle, Comedians of Comedy) and such wacky events as the US Air Guitar Championships. Ventilation is poor, but drinks are cheap – and movie nights offer free shows with a two-drink minimum.

BOOKSMITH   BOOK READINGS

Map p338 (☎415-863-8688; www.booksmith.com; 1644 Haight St; ☺10am-10pm Mon-Sat, to 8pm Sun; 🛗; Ⓜ Haight St) SF is one of America's top three book markets, and authors who swing through town on tours make Booksmith's Author Series a literary destination. Recent readings include Neil Gaiman, Khaled Hosseini, Pulitzer Prize–winning Adam Johnson, *Cooked* author Michael Pollan and comics-journalist Wendy McNaughton. Check the online calendar for book swaps and open-bar Literary Clown Foolery nights.

CLUB DELUXE   JAZZ

Map p338 (☎415-552-6949; 1511 Haight St; ☺4pm-2am Mon-Fri, 2pm-2am Sat & Sun; 🚌6, 33, 37, 43, 71) Blame it on the bossa nova or the punch bowls of Deluxe Spa Collins (gin, cucumber, ginger, lemon and soda). Cover is either free or $5 for swinging jazz bands, comedy acts and monthly appearances by Little Minsky's Burlesque Show. Expect mood lighting, cats who wear hats well and dolls who can swill highballs without losing their matte red lipstick.

SF LESBIAN GAY BISEXUAL
TRANSGENDER COMMUNITY CENTER   GAY

Map p340 (☎415-865-5555; www.sfcenter.org; 1800 Market St; ☺noon-10pm Mon-Fri, 10am-9pm Sat; Ⓜ Market St) The glass-walled teal Victorian is a gorgeous place to see and be seen, but because of poor endowment, too-high rental rates and weak programming, it hasn't panned out as a GLBT community hangout. Still, it's worth a look to see if something's on during Pride month (June).

🛍 SHOPPING

🏠 The Haight

AMOEBA MUSIC   MUSIC

Map p338 (☎415-831-1200; www.amoeba.com; 1855 Haight St; ☺11am-8pm; Ⓜ Haight St) Enticements are hardly necessary to lure the masses to the West Coast's most eclectic collection of new and used music and video,

---

WORTH A DETOUR

KARAOKE AT THE MINT

Die-hard singers pore over giant books of 30,000 tunes in every genre at mixed straight-gay karaoke bar the **Mint** (Map p340; ☎415-626-4726; www.themint.net; 1942 Market St; ☺3pm-2am Mon-Fri, 2pm-2am Sat & Sun; Ⓜ Market St), where big voices rattle pennies in the basement of the US mint just uphill. Coinage won't get you far here, though: standard karaoke-jockey tip is $1 a song. Billy Idol is fair game for a goof, but only serious belters take on Barbra. Two-song maximum and two-drink minimum help keep American Idolatry from getting too serious.

but Amoeba offers listening stations, a free music zine with uncannily accurate reviews, a free concert series that recently starred X (John Doe/Exene Cervenka), Lana Del Rey and the Dandy Warhols, plus a foundation that's saved 1000-plus acres of rainforest.

BOUND TOGETHER
ANARCHIST BOOK COLLECTIVE   BOOKSTORE
Map p338 (☎415-431-8355; http://bound-togetherbooks.wordpress.com; 1369 Haight St; ⏰11:30am-7:30pm; ◻6, 33, 37, 43, 71) Since 1976 this volunteer-run, nonprofit anarchist bookstore has kept free thinkers supplied with organic farming manuals, prison literature and radical comics, while coordinating the Anarchist Book Fair and restoring its 'Anarchists of the Americas' storefront mural – which makes us tools of the state look like slackers. Hours are impressively regular, but call ahead to be sure.

GOORIN BROTHERS HATS   ACCESSORIES
Map p338 (☎415-436-9450; www.goorin.com; 1446 Haight St; ⏰11am-8pm; ◻6, 33, 37, 43, 71) Peacock feathers, high crowns and local-artist-designed embellishments make it easy for SF hipsters to withstand the fog while standing out in a crowd. Straw fedoras with striped tie-silk bands bring the shade in style, as do flat-brim selvedge-denim baseball caps with embroidery designed by San Francisco tattoo artist Yutaro Sakai.

TANTRUM   GIFTS
(Map p338; ☎415-504-6980; www.shoptantrum.com; 858 Cole St; ⏰11am-7pm; 👶; ◻6, 33, 37, 43, 71, Ⓜ N) All the cool stuff you wish you'd had as a kid is here: tiddlywinks in a wooden mushroom, cuddly blue elephants and mix-and-match brass charms to string into a mysterious hammer and bunny necklace. Midcentury modern circus is the design aesthetic in new and vintage items, including mod candy-striped hula-hoops and vintage pinafores worthy of Alice in Wonderland.

LOVED TO DEATH   GIFTS, TAXIDERMY
Map p338 (☎415-551-1036; www.lovedtodeath.net; 1681 Haight St; ⏰11:30am-7pm Mon-Thu, to 8pm Fri & Sat, noon-7pm Sun; ◻6, 33, 37, 43, 71, Ⓜ N) Deer stare unblinking from the walls alongside a rusty saw and devotional ex-voto miniatures: the signs are ominous – and for sale. Head upstairs for Goth gifts, including Victorian hair lockets and port-able last rites kits handy for exorcisms. Not for the faint of heart, or vegans – though as store proprietors note, no animal was killed specifically for these taxidermy designs.

WASTELAND   CLOTHING, ACCESSORIES
Map p338 (☎415-863-3150; www.wastelandclothing.com; 1660 Haight St; ⏰11am-8pm Mon-Sat, noon-7pm Sun; ◻6, 33, 37, 43, 71, Ⓜ N) ✈ The catwalk of thrift, this vintage superstore adds instant style with barely worn Marc Jacobs smock-frocks, '70s Missoni sweaters and a steady supply of go-go boots. Hip occasionally verges on hideous with sequined sweaters and '80s power suits, but at reasonable (if not bargain) prices anyone can afford fashion risks. If you've got excess baggage, they buy clothes noon to 6pm daily.

PIEDMONT BOUTIQUE   CLOTHING, ACCESSORIES
Map p338 (☎415-864-8075; www.piedmontsf.com; 1452 Haight St; ⏰11am-7pm; ◻6, 33, 37, 43, 71) 'No food, no cell phones, no playing in the boas,' says the sign at the door, but inside, that last rule is gleefully ignored by cross-dressers, cabaret singers, strippers and people who take Halloween dead seriously. All the getups are custom-designed in-house and built to last – so, like certain escorts, they're not as cheap as they look.

XAPNO   GIFTS, ACCESSORIES
Map p338 (☎415-863-8199; www.xapno.com; 678 Haight St; ⏰11am-7pm Tue-Thu & Sun, 10am-9pm Fri & Sat; ◻6, 33, 37, 43, 71, Ⓜ N) Antique typewriter ribbon tins, sea-breezy soaps for scrubbing sailors, succulents dripping from blown-glass bottles: such unusual gifts lead grateful recipients to believe you've spent weeks and small fortunes in San Francisco curiosity shops. But Xapno regularly stocks rare finds at reasonable prices and will wrap them for you, too. Hours are erratic.

SFO SNOWBOARDING & FTC SKATEBOARDING   OUTDOOR GEAR
Map p338 (☎415-626-1141; www.sfosnow.com; 1630-32 Haight St; ⏰11am-7pm; ◻6, 33, 37, 43, 71, Ⓜ N) Big air and big style are the tip at this local snowboard and skateboard outfitter. Show some local flair as you grab air on a Western Edition deck with drawings of ramshackle Victorian houses, or hit the slopes with Tahoe-tested gear (mostly for dudes, some unisex). Ask staff about upcoming SF street games, pro expos and Tahoe snow conditions.

THE HAIGHT, NOPA & HAYES VALLEY SHOPPING

1. Haight & Ashbury Sts
This intersection – and the famous legs extending from Piedmont Boutique – mark the heart of Flower Power–era SF.

2. Flight 001 (p198)
Visit this NoPa store and stock up on airplane accessories before your next zero-legroom flight.

3. The Independent (p194)
Indie bands, rock legends and comedians alike take the stage at this Lower Haight venue.

4. Toronado (p189)
Beer is the word here, with 50-plus brews available on tap and many more awaiting you in bottled form.

URBAN MERCANTILE   HOUSEWARES, GIFTS
(Map p338; ☑415-643-6372; http://urbanmer-cantile.com; 85 Carl St; ☺11am-6pm Tue-Sat, noon-5pm Sun; ☒6, 33, 37, 43, 71, Ⓜ N) A design sourcebook come to life, this little storefront could be the beginning of your next big home-decor overhaul. It starts with nubby linen napkins or a hand-thrown celadon cup and progresses rapidly to ultra-plush bath towels and graphite porcelain dinnerware. For gifts, there's a vast selection of letterpress cards and tiny, delicate modern jewelry.

UPPER PLAYGROUND   CLOTHING, ACCESSORIES
Map p338 (☑415-861-1960; www.upperplayground. com; 220 Fillmore St; ☺noon-7pm; ☒6, 22, 71, Ⓜ N) Blend into the SF scenery with locally designed 'Left Coast' hoodies, bragadocious 'SanFranf*ckingciso' tees, and collegiate pennants for city neighborhoods (the Tenderloin totally needs a cheering section). Men's gear dominates, but there are women's tees, kids' tees in the back room and slick graffiti art in the Fifty24SF Gallery next door.

BRAINDROPS BODY ART   BODY ART
Map p338 (☑415-621-4162; www.braindrops.net; 1324 Haight St; ☺noon-7pm Sun-Thu, to 8pm Fri & Sat; ☒6, 33, 37, 43, 71) New Yorkers and Berliners fly in for original custom designs by top tattoo artists here – bring design ideas to your consultant or trust them to make suggestions. Piercings are done gently without a gun, with body jewelry ranging from subtle nose studs to mondo jade ear spools.

REVOLVER   CLOTHING, ACCESSORIES
Map p338 (☑415-583-3363; www.revolversf.com; 136 Fillmore St; ☺noon-8pm; ☒6, 22, 71, Ⓜ N) Entering this boutique is like wandering into the bedroom of some Western novelist-stoner, with pieces in soft natural fabrics strewn across wooden crates. Preps meet hipsters halfway with moccasins, slim-fit Scotch & Soda green chinos, Farm Tactics' California-made cotton baseball shirts and walnut-rimmed wayfarer sunglasses. Women's wear is relaxed sailing attire: tank sundresses, linen shorts, nautical jackets.

🏠 NoPa

RARE DEVICE   GIFTS
Map p338 (☑415-863-3969; www.raredevice. net; 600 Divisadero St; ☺noon-8pm Mon-Fri, 11am-7pm Sat, 11am-6pm Sun; ☒5, 6, 21, 24, 71) Sly SF wit is the rare device that makes this well-curated selection of gifts for all ages so irresistible. Blue-and-white china gets updated with modern urban scenes, stackable wooden alligators are an improvement on ordinary toy blocks, and Little Otsu's Alpine Songs planner puts the joy back into busy schedules.

🏠 Hayes Valley

★RELIQUARY   CLOTHING, ACCESSORIES
Map p340 (☑415-431-4000; www.reliquarysf. com; 537 Octavia Blvd; ☺11am-7pm Mon-Sat, noon-6pm Sun; ☒5, 21, 47, 49) Enter the well-traveled walk-in closet of Leah Bershad, a former designer for the Gap whose folksy jet-set aesthetic is SF's antidote to khaki-and-fleece global domination. Hand-crafted vintage – embroidered peasant blouses, Santa Fe woolen blankets, silver jewelry banged together by Humboldt hippies – shares the spotlight with cult American designs like Raleigh denim, Majestic tissue-tees and Claire Vivier envelope clutches.

FLIGHT 001   ACCESSORIES
Map p340 (☑415-487-1001; www.flight001.com; 525 Hayes St; ☺11am-7pm Mon-Sat, to 6pm Sun; ☒5, 21, 47, 49) Enjoying a flight in the zero-legroom era becomes possible with help from Flight 001. Clever carry-ons built to fit international size regulations come with just the right number of pockets for collapsible water bottles, caution-orange adapters you won't leave behind and the first-class Jet Comfort Kit with earplugs, sleep mask, booties, neck rest, candy and cards.

NANCY BOY   BEAUTY PRODUCTS
Map p340 (☑415-552-3636; www.nancyboy.com; 347 Hayes St; ☺11am-7pm Mon-Fri, to 6pm Sat & Sun; ☒5, 21, 47, 49) All you closet pomaders and after-sun balmers: wear those products with pride, without feeling like the dupe of some cosmetics conglomerate. Clever Nancy Boy knows you'd rather pay for the product than for advertising campaigns featuring the starlet du jour, and delivers locally made products with plant oils that are tested on boyfriends, never animals.

MAC   CLOTHING, ACCESSORIES
Map p340 (☑415-863-3011; www.modern-appealingclothing.com; 387 Grove St; ☺11am-7pm Mon-Sat, noon-6pm Sun; ☒5, 21, 47, 49) 'Modern Appealing Clothing' is what it promises and what it delivers for men and women,

with streamlined chic from Maison Martin Margiela, sculptural dresses from Comme des Garçons and splashy limited-edition tees by developmentally disabled artists at Oakland's Creative Growth. Staff are on your side, rooting for you to score something from the 40%-to-75%-off sales rack.

Check out the second location showcasing California designers in Dogpatch (p166).

GIMME SHOES   SHOES
Map p340 (415-864-0691; www.gimmeshoes.com; 416 & 381 Hayes St; 11am-7pm Mon-Sat, noon-6pm Sun; Hayes St) Don't let SF hills become your arch-rivals: head to Gimme Shoes and kick up those high-end heels. Bide your time, and Dries van Noten silver slingbacks and Ellen Verbeek birch-wood wedges at the spotlit 381 Hayes showcase might hit 40%-to-60%-off racks across the street at 416 Hayes. Men have their pick of tawny Paul Smith oxfords or polka-dotted Marc Jacobs brogues.

GREEN ARCADE   BOOKSTORE
Map p340 (415-431-6800; www.thegreenarcade.com; 1680 Market St; noon-8pm Mon-Sat, to 7pm Sun; 6, 47, 49, 71, Van Ness) From mushroom foraging to worm composting to running for office on an environmental platform, this bookstore emphasizes helpful how-to books over eco-apocalypse treatises, so you'll leave with a rosier outlook on making the world a greener place.

ISOTOPE   COMICS
Map p340 (415-621-6543; www.isotopecomics.com; 326 Fell St; 11am-7pm Tue-Fri, to 6pm Sat & Sun; 5, 21, 47, 49) The toilet seats signed by famous cartoonists over the front counter show just how seriously Isotope takes comics. Newbies tentatively flip through Daniel Clowes and Chris Ware in the graphic-novel section, while fanboys eye new titles from Berkeley's Adrian Tomine and SF's Last Gasp Publishing and head upstairs to lounge with local cartoonists – some of whom teach at Isotope's Comics University.

FATTED CALF   FOOD & DRINK
Map p340 (414-400-5614; www.fattedcalf.com; 320 Fell St; 10am-8pm; 5, 21, 47, 49, Van Ness) Hostess gifts that win you return invitations to SF dinner parties come from Fatted Calf. This Bay Area salumi maker's showcase is also a one-stop shop for Californian artisan foods, with out-

standing selections of local goat cheeses, heirloom beans, chutney and specialty meats, from sausage to duck fat.

GANGS OF SAN FRANCISCO   CLOTHING
Map p340 (www.gangsofsanfrancisco.com; 66 Gough St; noon-6pm Sat & Sun; 21, 47, 49, Van Ness) Brazil-born SF silk-screener Laureano Faedi has unearthed insignia for every thuggish clique to claim an SF street corner, from the San Francisco Vigilance Committee – known for conducting kangaroo trials and swift hangings during SF's Gold Rush era – to the Richmond Beer Town Brawlers, who malingered near Golden Gate Park, c 1875–96.

SPORTS & ACTIVITIES

MAKESHIFT SOCIETY   WORKSHOPS
Map p340 (415-625-3220; http://makeshiftsociety.com; 235 Gough St; workshops $25-75; 9am-6pm Mon-Fri, plus after-hours workshops) Learn something new at this creative clubhouse for adults, where free brown-bag sessions spark ideas over lunch, and evening workshops range from classical calligraphy to iPhonography (the art of using your phone for creative purposes). Stick around to pick up essential SF skills for building terrariums, concocting cocktail bitters and plein-air paintings of the Golden Gate Bridge.

WORKSHOP   WORKSHOPS
Map p338 (415-874-9186; www.workshopsf.org; 1798 McAllister St; workshops $35-98; class times vary; 5, 21, 43) Silicon Valley tech titans go low-tech in their downtime at Workshop, with hands-on courses in the not-quite-lost arts of letterpress printing, mozzarella-stretching, metalsmithing, tea-blending and hand-sewing. Instructors are patient and enthusiastic, and most classes cost under $50 – the party nail art class costs less than a salon mani/pedi, and the kimchi cocktail course less than a round at the bar.

AVENUE CYCLERY   CYCLING
Map p338 (415-387-3155; www.avenuecyclery.com; 756 Stanyan St; bikes per hr/day $8/30; 10am-6pm; 5, 6, 33, 71, N) In one of the more bicycle-friendly parts of the city, Avenue Cyclery has an extensive selection of bicycles for rent (price includes helmet) and for sale.

Golden Gate Park & the Avenues

THE RICHMOND | THE SUNSET

Neighborhood Top Five

1 Doing what comes naturally in **Golden Gate Park** (p202): skipping, lolling or lindy-hopping through America's most outlandish stretch of urban wilderness, and racing the buffalo towards the Pacific Ocean.

2 Following Andy Goldsworthy's sidewalk fault lines to groundbreaking art inside the **MH de Young Museum** (p203).

3 Enjoying sunsets on the wildflower-topped roof and wild nights at **California Academy of Sciences** (p203).

4 Numbing toes in the Pacific and expanding horizons to Asia at **Ocean Beach** (p206).

5 Catching end-of-the-world views and glimpses of Sutro Sam the river otter at **Sutro Baths** (p205).

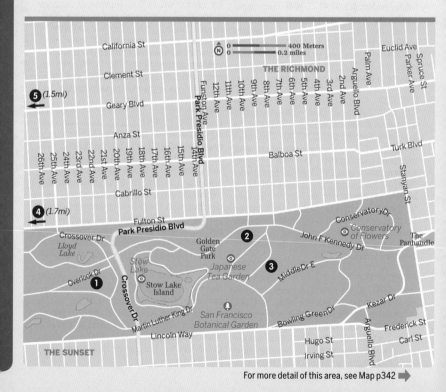

For more detail of this area, see Map p342 ➡

Explore Golden Gate Park & the Avenues

Civilization is overrated, with its traffic jams and office blocks – but once you reach the Conservatory of Flowers (p204) in Golden Gate Park, that's all behind you. Hang out with blue butterflies in the rainforest dome at the California Academy of Sciences (p203), or globe-trot from Egyptian goddesses to James Turrell light installations in the worldly arts exhibits of the MH de Young Museum (p203). Enjoy a moment of Zen and green tea in the Japanese Tea Garden (p204), then summit Strawberry Hill for views past Stow Lake (p204) to the Pacific as red-tailed hawks swoop past.

Wander to San Francisco Botanical Garden (p204) for respite in the redwood grove before hopping the N streetcar all the way to Ocean Beach (p206). Stroll the 4-mile stretch of sand to the Richmond for dinner at Aziza (p210) and tequila school at Tommy's Mexican Restaurant (p211), or stay put in the Sunset for surf-shopping at Mollusk (p213) and dinner at Outerlands (p211). With food and fog like this, you must be in heaven.

Local Life

→**Foggy days** Stay warm with Trouble Coffee (p212), hoodies from Mollusk (p213), matinees at Balboa Theatre (p213), and rainforest strolls inside the California Academy of Sciences (p203) and Conservatory of Flowers (p204).

→**Goose bumps, guaranteed** Get delicious chills with bare feet on Ocean Beach (p206), eerily lifelike ceremonial masks at MH de Young Museum (p203), cliff's-edge views along the Coastal Trail (p205) and ice-cream cocktails at Trad'r Sam (p212).

→**Outposts of cool** Outlandishness is a way of life at Park Life (p213) art openings, Hollow (p212) art-installation coffee breaks and musical interludes in the garden at General Store (p213).

Getting There & Away

→**Bus** Numbers 1, 31 and 38 run from Downtown through the Richmond, while 71 and 6 head from Downtown to the Sunset. Buses 5 and 21 skirt the north edge of Golden Gate Park, while north–south buses 28, 29 and 44 cut across the park. Number 2 covers Clement St, 33 connects to the Haight and Castro, and 18 spans the Great Highway.

→**Streetcar** The N line runs from Downtown through the Sunset to Ocean Beach.

Lonely Planet's Top Tip

Hear that echo across Golden Gate Park? It's probably a concert and very likely a free one. Opera divas, indie acts, bluegrass greats and hip-hop heavies take turns rocking SF gratis, from the wintry days of June through golden October afternoons. Most concerts are held in Sharon Meadow or Polo Fields on weekends; for upcoming events, consult the park calendar at www. golden-gate-park.com.

✕ Best Places to Eat

→ Aziza (p210)

→ Outerlands (p211)

→ Kabuto (p207)

→ Spruce (p210)

→ Thanh Long (p211)

For reviews, see p207 →

◻ Best Places to Drink

→ Tommy's Mexican Restaurant (p211)

→ Beach Chalet (p212)

→ Trouble Coffee (p212)

→ Hollow (p212)

→ Plough & Stars (p213)

For reviews, see p211 →

⊙ Best Urban Wildlife Sightings

→ Bison in Golden Gate Park (p202)

→ Bank swallows at Fort Funston (p206)

→ Penguins at California Academy of Sciences (p203)

For reviews, see p205 →

GOLDEN GATE PARK & THE AVENUES

SABRINA DALBESIO / GETTY IMAGES ©

TOP SIGHT
GOLDEN GATE PARK

When San Franciscans refer to 'the park,' there's only one that gets the definite article: Golden Gate Park. Everything San Franciscans hold dear is here: free spirits, free music, redwoods, Frisbee, protests, fine art, bonsai and buffalo.

The scenery turns surreal at California Academy of Sciences (p203), Renzo Piano's LEED–certified home for 38,000 weird and wonderful animals under a 'living roof' of California wildflowers. Across the Music Concourse, you can see from Oceania to California via ancient Egypt inside Herzog & de Meuron's sleek MH de Young Museum (p203), clad with copper that's oxidizing green to blend into the park.

This scenery seems far-fetched now, but former mayor Frank McCoppin's park project seemed impossible in 1866. Even Frederick Law Olmsted, architect of New York's Central Park, was daunted by the prospect of transforming 1017 acres of dunes into park. San Francisco's green scheme fell to young, tenacious civil engineer William Hammond Hall, who insisted that instead of casinos, resorts, race tracks and an igloo village, primary park features should include botanical gardens, the Japanese Tea Garden (p204) and boating on scenic Stow Lake (p204).

The east end of the park covers San Francisco history from the 1860s to the present day. In the northeast corner, the Conservatory of Flowers Victorian greenhouse (p204) flanks the **Dahlia Garden** (Map p342). West of **Hippie Hill** drum circles on **Sharon Meadow** are the quietly quaint Lawn Bowling Club (p214) and contemplative valley of the **AIDS Memorial Grove**. On the park's southeast corner is the city's biggest **children's playground**, complete with vintage carousel.

DON'T MISS...

➡ MH de Young Museum
➡ California Academy of Sciences
➡ San Francisco Botanical Garden
➡ Japanese Tea Garden
➡ Conservatory of Flowers

PRACTICALITIES

➡ Map p342
➡ http://sfrecpark.org
➡ 🚻🎫
➡ 🚌5, 18, 21, 28, 29, 33, 44, 71, Ⓜ N

Near 9th Avenue are unexpected finds: **Druid altars** behind the **baseball diamond**, ruins of a Spanish monastery at the SF Botanical Garden (p204) and the **Shakespeare Garden** collection of 150 plants mentioned in Shakespeare's writings. Sundays when JFK Drive closes to traffic around 9th Ave, there's roller disco and lindy-hopping (p214) in the park.

West around Martin Luther King Jr Dr are the polo fields where the 1967 Human Be-In took place and free concerts are still held during **Hardly Strictly Bluegrass**. At the park's wild western edge, quixotic bison stampede in their paddock toward windmills and Ocean Beach (p206) sunsets.

MH de Young Museum

The oxidized copper building keeps a low profile, but there's no denying the park's star attraction: the **MH de Young Museum** (Map p342; ☑415-750-3600; www.famsf.org/deyoung; 50 Hagiwara Tea Garden Dr; adult/child $10/6, discount with Muni ticket $2, 1st Tue of month free; ☺9:30am-5:15pm Tue-Sun, to 8:45pm Fri mid-Jan–Nov; ☐5, 44, 71, Ⓜ N). The cross-cultural collection featuring African masks and Meso-American sculpture alongside California crafts and painting has been broadening artistic horizons for a century – its acclaimed building by Swiss architects Herzog & de Meuron is equally daring.

The 144ft twisting sci-fi medieval armored **tower** is one architectural feature that seems incongruous with the park setting, but access to the tower viewing room is free and the elevator by Ruth Asawa's mesmerizing filigreed pods is worth the wait.

Upstairs, don't miss 19th-century **Oceanic collection** ceremonial oars and stunning Afghani rugs from the 11,000-plus **textile collection. Blockbuster basement shows** range from Bulgari jewels to Vermeer paintings, but even more riveting are **main floor installations**.

Access to the **garden cafe** is free and offers views of the **Osher Sculpture Garden**.

California Academy of Sciences

Leave it to San Francisco to dedicate a glorious monument entirely to freaks of nature: the **California Academy of Sciences** (Map p342; ☑415-379-8000; www.calacademy.org; 55 Music Concourse Dr; adult/child $34.95/24.95, discount with Muni ticket $3; ☺9:30am-5pm Mon-Sat, 11am-5pm Sun; ♿; ☐5, 6, 31, 33, 44, 71, Ⓜ N) ✎. Its tradition of weird science dates from 1853, with thousands of live animals and 46 scientists now under a 2.5-acre wildflower-covered roof. Butterflies alight on visitors to the glass **Rainforest Dome**, a rare white alligator stalks a mezzanine swamp and penguins paddle the tank in the **African Hall**.

WILD NIGHTS AT THE ACADEMY

....

The penguins nod off to sleep, but night owls roam after-hours events at the California Academy of Sciences. At the over-21 **NightLife**, rainforest-themed cocktails are served and strange mating rituals observed among shy internet daters (ID required; $12 entry; events 6pm to 10pm Thursdays). Kids may not technically sleep during Academy Sleepovers, but they might kick off promising careers as research scientists (ages 5 and up; $99 per person; events 6pm-8am). Book ahead online.

....

Though a local newspaper once cautioned that Golden Gate Park's scenic benches led to 'excess hugging,' San Franciscans have flocked to the park since its inception. On a single sunny day in 1886, almost a fifth of the city's entire population made the trip to the park – canoodling shamelessly, no doubt.

In the basement aquarium, kids duck inside a glass bubble to enter an **Eel Forest**, find Nemos in the tropical-fish tanks and befriend starfish in the aquatic **petting zoo**.

Glimpse into infinity in **Morrison Planetarium** and ride the elevator to the blooming **Living Roof** for park panoramas.

San Francisco Botanical Garden

Sniff your way around the world inside the 55-acre **San Francisco Botanical Garden** (Strybing Arboretum; Map p342; ⬚415-661-1316; www.strybing.org; 1199 9th Ave; adult/child $7/5; free 2nd Tue of month; ☺9am-6pm Apr-Oct, to 5pm Nov-Mar; bookstore 10am-4pm; 🚻; 🚌6, 43, 44, 71, Ⓜ︎N) ♿, from South African savannah grasses to Japanese magnolias. Don't miss the California native-plant meadow, redwood grove and Ancient Planet Garden. **Free tours** take place daily; for details, stop by the bookstore inside the entrance. Last entrance is one hour before closing.

Japanese Tea Garden

Since 1894 this 5-acre **garden** (Map p342; ⬚tea ceremony reservations 415-752-1171; www.japaneseteagardensf.com; 75 Hagiwara Tea Garden Dr; adult/child $7/5, Mon, Wed & Fri before 10am free; ☺9am-6pm Mar-Oct, to 4:45pm Nov-Feb; 🚌5, 44, 71, Ⓜ︎N) has blushed with cherry blossoms in spring, turned flaming red with maple leaves in fall and lost all track of time in the meditative **Zen Garden**. The 100-year-old bonsai grove was cultivated by the Hagiwara family, who returned from WWII Japanese American internment camps to discover their prized miniature evergreens had been sold – and spent decades recovering these trees.

Free tours cover the garden's history Mondays and Saturdays at 9:30am; tea ceremonies are held Wednesdays and Fridays in spring at 10:30am, 11:15am and noon ($25; booking required).

Conservatory of Flowers

Flower power is alive and well at San Francisco's **Conservatory of Flowers** (Map p342; ⬚info line 415-831-2090; www.conservatoryofflowers.org; 100 John F Kennedy Dr; adult/child $7/5; ☺10am-4:30pm Tue-Sun). Inside this recently restored 1878 Victorian greenhouse, orchids command center stage like opera divas, lilies float contemplatively in ponds and carnivorous plants give off odors that smell exactly like insect belches.

Stow Lake

A park within the park, **Stow Lake** (Map p342; www.sfrecpark.org; ☺sunrise-sunset; Ⓜ︎9th Ave) offers steep hikes up a picturesque island called **Strawberry Hill**. Pedal boats, rowboats and electric boats are available in good weather at the 1946 **boathouse** (Map p342; www.stowlakeboathouse.com; 50 Stow Lake Dr; boats per hr $14-29; ☺10am-6pm Mon-Fri, from 9am Sat & Sun; 🚌5, 29, 44, 71).

HUNGRY?

For sit-down meals, Academy Café (p203), Golden Gate Golf Clubhouse (p215) and Beach Chalet (p212) are the most reliable, reasonable options inside the park. Inexpensive, tasty alternatives near the park include Underdog (p211), Nan King Road Bistro (p211), Masala Dosa (p210), San Tung (p211) and Nopalito (p211). Otherwise, look for hot-dog carts along JFK Drive and street-food trucks on the Music Concourse (between MH de Young Museum and California Academy of Sciences).

⊙ SIGHTS

⊙ The Richmond

GOLDEN GATE PARK   PARK
See p202.

SUTRO BATHS   PARK
Map p342 (www.nps.gov/goga/historyculture/ sutro-baths.htm; Point Lobos Ave; ⊙sunrise-sunset; visitor center hours 9am-5pm; **P**; 🚍5, 31, 38) ✔ **FREE** Hard to imagine from these ruins, but Victorian dandies and working stiffs once converged here for bracing baths and workouts in itchy wool rental swimsuits. Millionaire Adolph Sutro built hot and cold indoor pools to accommodate 10,000 unwashed masses in 1896, but the masses apparently preferred dirt and the baths closed in 1952. There's just one part-time resident: river otter **Sutro Sam**.

Above the baths are the new **Land's End Lookout** visitor center and cafe plus the **Sutro Heights Park** public gardens, built in 1885 and restored with native plants. The path down to the baths is steep, but worth it at low tide to discover a hidden gem: a **sea-cave tunnel** that leads to end-of-the-world views of Marin Headlands. If the baths look familiar, you must be a film buff: these splendid ruins made a fitting backdrop for 1971's May–December comedy classic *Harold & Maude*.

LEGION OF HONOR   MUSEUM
Map p342 (📞415-750-3600; http://legionofhonor.famsf.org; 100 34th Ave; adult/child $10/6, discount with Muni ticket $2, 1st Tue of month free; ⊙9:30am-5:15pm Tue-Sun; 🚻; 🚍1, 18, 38) A museum as eccentric and illuminating as San Francisco itself, the Legion showcases a wildly eclectic collection ranging from Monet water lilies to John Cage soundscapes, ancient Iraqi ivories to R Crumb comics. Upstairs are blockbuster shows of Surrealists and Impressionists, but don't miss exhibits from the Legion's Achenbach Foundation for Graphic Arts, which range from Rembrandt to Ed Ruscha.

A marble-clad replica of Paris' Légion d'Honneur, the Legion is a monumental tribute to Californians killed in France in WWI. It was built by Alma de Bretteville Spreckels, a larger-than-life sculptor's model who donated her fortune to gift this museum to San Francisco. The centerpiece of 'Big Alma's' legacy is Rodin's *The Kiss* – but at 4pm on weekends, pipe organ recitals steal the show in the Rodin gallery.

COASTAL TRAIL   TRAIL
Map p342 (www.californiacoastaltrail.info; Fort Funston to Lincoln Park; ⊙sunrise-sunset; 🚍1, 18, 38) Hit your stride on the 9-mile stretch of Coastal Trail starting at Fort Funston, crossing 4 miles of sandy Ocean Beach, wrapping around the Presidio and ending at the Golden Gate Bridge. Casual strollers can pick up the trail near Sutro Baths, head around Land's End for end-of-the-world views, then duck into the Legion of Honor at Lincoln Park.

LINCOLN PARK   PARK
Map p342 (Clement St; ⊙sunrise-sunset; 🚍1, 18, 38) John McLaren took time off his 56-year job as Golden Gate Park's superintendent to establish lovely Lincoln Park. The 45-minute hike around Land's End follows a partially paved coastline trail with staircases, Golden Gate views and low-tide sightings of coastal shipwrecks; pick up the trailhead north of the Legion of Honor. Book ahead for scenic Lincoln Park Golf (p215).

FRANKENART MART   GALLERY
Map p342 (📞415-221-2394; www.frankenartmart. com; 515 Balboa St; ⊙4-9pm Thu-Fri, 1-8pm Sat, 1-6pm Sun; 🚍5, 31, 33, 44) Itchy palms frustrated by hands-off museums find sweet hands-on relief at this participatory art gallery. Create artwork on show themes such as Dream Job, Infiltration and Space Station, swap artwork with others and contribute haiku for Poetry in a Can. Saturday afternoon Playshop art workshops are free with purchase of a 'billustration' (sliding-scale art priced at a $25 to $75 utility-bill cost).

Kids are welcome with adult companions to supervise, though not all art may be suitable for all ages. Occasionally open Tuesday evenings; see online calendar for free-hot-dog Sundays and other special events.

COLUMBARIUM   NOTABLE BUILDING
Map p342 (📞415-771-0717; www.neptune-society .com; 1 Loraine Ct; ⊙8:30am-5pm Mon-Fri, 10am-3pm Sat & Sun; 🚍5, 31, 33, 38) **FREE** San Francisco's Victorian Columbarium is lined with art nouveau stained-glass windows under its sheltering dome, illuminating more than 8000 niches honoring dearly

GOLDEN GATE PARK & THE AVENUES SIGHTS

departed relations, dogs and rabbits. The ancient Roman tradition of memorial buildings for cremated remains was revived in San Francisco in 1898, when burial grounds were crowding San Francisco's 7-by-7-mile peninsula.

The Columbarium was largely abandoned from 1934 until its 1979 restoration by the Neptune Society, a cremation advocacy group. Many visitors today come to admire the Victorian neoclassical architecture and pay respects to the niche of pioneering gay city supervisor Harvey Milk, who was killed by a political opponent.

◉ The Sunset

OCEAN BEACH   BEACH
Map p342 (☑415-561-4323; www.parksconservancy.org; Great Highway; ☺sunrise-sunset; ☐5, 18, 31, Ⓜ N) Golden Gate Park ends at this blustery beach, too chilly for bikini-clad clambakes but ideal for hardcore surfers braving riptides (casual swimmers beware). Bonfires are permitted in artist-designed fire pits only; no alcohol allowed. On Ocean Beach's south end, beachcombers spot sand dollars and 19th-century shipwrecks. Stick to paths in fragile dunes, where skittish snowy plover shorebirds shelter in winter.

FORT FUNSTON   PARK
(Map p342; ☑415-561-4323; www.parksconservancy.org; Skyline Blvd; Ⓟ🐕🚻; ⓜJudah St) 🐾 Grassy dunes up to 200ft high at Fort Funston give an idea what the Sunset looked like until the 20th century. A defunct military installation, Fort Funston still has 146-ton WWII guns aimed seaward and abandoned Nike missile silos near the parking lot. Nuclear missiles were never launched from Fort Funston, but flocks of hang gliders launch and land here.

Butterflies and shorebirds have the run of Fort Funston, which is now part of the Golden Gate National Recreation Area. Loop trails and hang-glider launches are wheelchair- and stroller-accessible, and dogs are allowed off-leash in many areas. The National Park Service is gradually replacing invasive ice plants with native vegetation, and volunteers are welcome to join the effort at the Fort Funston Native Plant Nursery (see website for details). If you're driving, bicycling or walking here, follow the Great Hwy south and turn right on Skyline Blvd; park entrance is past Lake Merced, on the right-hand side.

SAN FRANCISCO ZOO   ZOO
(Map p342; ☑415-753-7080; www.sfzoo.org; 1 Zoo Rd; adult/child ages 4-14 $15/9; ☺10am-5pm (including holidays); 🚻; ☐18, 23, Ⓜ L) Even those who object to zoos in theory have been known to break down and take the kids here – after being begged for, oh, the thousandth time – only to discover that there are actually some well-kept habitats. Of note are the Savannah, featuring giraffes, zebras and ostrich, and the Lemur Forest, hosting cuddly Madagascan primates in a woodland setting.

This is quite an improvement over a few years ago, when the elephant herd began dying of pneumonia and had to be relocated from the foggy Sunset to a more suitable climate. The zoo's biggest attractions are the Great Ape Forest, the barnyard-style petting zoo and the gorgeous Dentzel carousel ($2 per ride). The Big Cat exhibit is now upgraded, after a 2007 tiger attack killed one person and injured two others. New interactive storybook features are activated with a Zoo Key ($3) and jeep strollers and wheelchairs are available for rent ($11 and $10, respectively).

THE FOG BELT
Not sure what to wear to a day in Golden Gate Park or dinner in the Avenues? Join the club. Downtown may be sunny and hot, while the Avenues are blanketed in coastal fog that lowers temperatures by as much as 20°F (10°C).

The fog bank usually begins around the Haight, so the area to the west is known as the fog belt. For a more exact assessment of the fog situation, view satellite imagery on the National Oceanic and Atmospheric Administration (NOAA) website (www.wrh.noaa.gov/mtr). When the fog wears out its welcome, take a bus to the Castro or the Mission on the sunnier side of town – and when the fog reaches the Mission, hop BART to sunny Berkeley across the bay (p217).

EATING

✕ The Richmond

SPICES
SICHUAN **$**

Map p342 (☎415-752-8884; www.spicesrestaurantonline.com; 294 8th Ave; mains $7-13; ⊙11am-10:30pm; ☒1, 2, 38, 44) The menu reads like an oddly dubbed Hong Kong action flick, with dishes labeled 'fire-burst!!' and 'stinky!', but zesty chili-oil-pickled Napa cabbage, silky mapo tofu and brain-curdling spicy chicken are definitely worthy of exclamation. When you head toward the kitchen for the bathroom, the chili aroma will make your eyes well up...or maybe that's just gratitude. Cash only.

PRETTY PLEASE BAKESHOP
BAKERY **$**

Map p342 (☎415-347-3733; www.prettypleasesf.com; 291 3rd Ave; baked goods $1.50-5; ⊙11am-7pm Tue-Fri, to 6pm Sat, to 5pm Sun; ✖; ☒1, 2, 33, 38, 44) Since you asked nicely, pastry chef Alison Okabayashi will hand over your choice of all-American treats: mini-cheesecakes, red velvet cupcakes and salted caramel brownies. Best of all are her upscale, preservative-free versions of Hostess (RIP) cakes: Ding Dongs are buttercream-filled chocolate cakes dipped in Guitard ganache, and Twinks are cream-filled sponge cakes in seasonal pumpkin or classic vanilla.

GENKI
DESSERT, GROCERIES **$**

Map p342 (☎415-379-6414; www.genkicrepes.com; 330 Clement St; crepes $5-6; ⊙2-10:30pm Mon, 10:30am-10:30pm Tue-Thu & Sun, 10:30am-11:30pm Fri & Sat; ✖; ☒1, 2, 33, 38) Life is always sweet at Genki, with aisles of packaged Japanese gummy candies nonsensically boasting flavors 'shining in the cheeks of a snow-country child,' a dozen variations on tapioca bubble tea, and French crepes by way of Tokyo with green-tea ice cream and Nutella. Stock up in the beauty supply and Pocky aisle to satisfy sudden hair-dye or snack whims.

WING LEE
DIM SUM **$**

Map p342 (☎415-668-9481; 503 Clement St; dim sum $1.60-3.50; ⊙10am-5pm; ☒1, 2, 38, 44) To feed two famished surfers for $10, just Wing Lee it. Line up with small bills and walk away loaded with shrimp-and-leek dumplings, BBQ pork buns (baked or steamed), chicken *shu mai* (open-topped

dumplings), potstickers and crispy sesame balls with chewy red bean centers. Fluorescent-lit lunch tables aren't made for dates, but these dumplings won't last long anyway.

KABUTO
SUSHI **$$**

Map p342 (☎415-752-5652; www.kabutosushi.com; 5121 Geary Blvd; sushi $6-10; ⊙11:30am-2:30pm & 5:30-10:30pm Tue-Sat, 5:30-9:30pm Sun; ☒1, 2, 28, 31, 38) Even Tokyo traditionalists and seafood agnostics squeal over innovative sushi served in this converted hot-dog drive-in. Sushi chefs top nori-wrapped rice with wahoo, grapefruit and basil cream, *hamachi* (yellowtail) with pear and wasabi mustard, and – eureka! – the '49er oyster with sea urchin, caviar, a quail's egg and gold leaf, chased with sake. Reserve ahead; maximum party of four.

TON KIANG RESTAURANT
DIM SUM **$$**

Map p342 (☎415-387-8273; www.tonkiang.net; 5821 Geary Blvd; dim sum $3-7; ⊙10am-9pm Mon-Thu, to 9:30pm Fri, 9:30am-9:30pm Sat, 9am-9pm Sun; ✖; ☒1, 29, 31, 38) This dim sum champion runs laps around the competition, laden with fragrant, steaming bamboo baskets. Choose on aroma, or order *gao choy gat* (shrimp and chive dumplings), *dao miu gao* (pea tendril and shrimp dumplings) and *jin doy* (sesame balls). A tally is kept at your table, so you could quit around the $20 mark – but wait, here's another round...

BURMA SUPERSTAR
BURMESE **$$**

Map p342 (☎415-387-2147; www.burmasuperstar.com; 309 Clement St; mains $9-22; ⊙11:30am-3:30pm & 5-10pm Mon-Thu & Sun, to 10:30pm Fri & Sat; ☒1, 2, 33, 38, 44) Yes, there's a wait, but do you see anyone walking away? Blame it on fragrant catfish curries and traditional Burmese green-tea salads tarted up with lime and dried shrimp. Reservations aren't accepted – ask the host to call you at the cafe across the street so you can enjoy a glass of wine while you wait, or head to small-plates sister restaurant **B Star Bar** (Map p342; 127 Clement St).

HALU
JAPANESE **$$**

Map p342 (☎415-221-9165; 312 8th Ave; yakitori $2.50-4, ramen $10-12; ⊙5-10pm Tue-Sat; ☒1, 2, 38, 44) Between Beatles memorabilia plastering the walls and fragrant *yakitori* (skewers) drifting past, dinner at this snug five-table joint feels like stowing away on a Japanese Yellow Submarine. Ramen

GOLDEN GATE PARK & THE AVENUES EATING

ROBERTO SONCIN GEROMETTA / GETTY IMAGES ©

1. California Academy of Sciences (p203)

Meet some butterflies (but don't touch them) under the glass of the Rainforest Dome at this zoologist's delight nestled in Golden Gate Park.

2. Ocean Beach (p206)

Golden Gate Park ends at this blustery beach, perfect for beachcombers and hardcore surfers.

3. Beach Chalet (p212)

Take in a Pacific sunset and some live music over a house microbrew at this bar overlooking Ocean Beach.

4. MH de Young Museum (p203)

This oxidised copper building, designed by Herzog & de Meuron, houses rich cross-cultural collections of art and objects, making it Golden Gate Park's star attraction.

ROBERTO SONCIN GEROMETTA / GETTY IMAGES ©

LOCAL KNOWLEDGE

SEA FORAGING WITH KIRK LOMBARD

If restaurant menus aren't adventurous enough for you, try something off the menu and on the beaches. Sealife expert Kirk Lombard was nominated for a 2013 James Beard Award for introducing urbanites to the bounty of San Francisco Bay on his Sea Foraging Adventures (p294).

While working for US Fish & Game, Lombard noticed that many anglers were ignoring meals in San Francisco's midst: bullwhip kelp perfect for pickling on Ocean Beach, smelt netted on Baker Beach ideal for panko-crusting and pan-frying, and barbecue-ready monkeyface prickleback eels sniggled right under the Golden Gate Bridge.

'People can't believe we have so much edible food in the Bay,' he says. 'They know big, deep-water ocean fish are endangered, but don't realize it can be healthier and more sustainable to eat lower down the food chain.'

Lombard is a transplant from New York, where his grandfather took him fishing on the Hudson River. 'Back when I was a kid, the Hudson was so polluted, it caught fire a couple times – now that's a clear sign you don't want to eat the fish,' he jokes. 'Foraging around the Bay makes people more aware of what a healthy, diverse aquaculture looks and tastes like, and it's the best motivation I can think of to keep it that way.'

is respectably toothsome, but the house specialties are skewered and barbecued. Get anything wrapped in bacon – scallops, quail eggs, *mochi* (rice-cake) – and if you're up for offal, have a heart.

CASSAVA
BAKERY, CALIFORNIAN $$

Map p342 (☑415-640-8990; www.cassavasf.com; 3519 Balboa St; brunch $10-15; ◎7am-2:45pm Mon & Wed-Fri, 8am-2:45pm Sat & Sun; ☐5, 18, 31, 38) Early risers and park joggers are rewarded with SF-roasted Ritual coffee and Cassava's housemade, multilingual breakfasts – the correct description in any language for poached-egg panini, Japanese-curry puff pastries or truffle-chorizo hash is 'mmmm.' Grab panini before a Balboa Theatre matinee or reserve online for pop-up dinners ($50 to $60). Communal tables are packed indoors – make room for new friends.

★AZIZA
MOROCCAN, CALIFORNIAN $$$

Map p342 (☑415-752-2222; www.aziza-sf.com; 5800 Geary Blvd; mains $16-29; ◎5:30-10:30pm Wed-Mon; ☐1, 29, 31, 38) Chef Mourad Lahlou's inspiration is Moroccan and his ingredients organic Californian, but the flavors are out of this world: Sonoma duck confit melts into caramelized onion inside flaky pastry *basteeya*, while saffron infuses slow-cooked local lamb atop barley. Chef Mourad trounced *Iron Chef* competitors with Moroccan–California crossroads cuisine, and pastry chef Melissa Chou's apricot bavarian is a goodnight kiss.

SPRUCE
CALIFORNIAN $$$

(Map p342; ☑415-931-5100; www.sprucesf.com; 3640 Sacramento St; mains $14-39; ◎11:30am-2:30pm & 5-10pm Mon-Fri, 5-11pm Sat, 5-10pm Sun; ☐1, 2, 33, 43) ✎ VIP all the way, with Baccarat crystal chandeliers, tawny leather chairs and 1000 wines. Ladies who lunch dispense with polite conversation, tearing into grass-fed burgers on house-baked English muffins loaded with pickled onions, zucchini grown on the restaurant's own organic farm and an optional fried egg. Want fries with that? Oh yes, you do: Spruce's are cooked in duck fat.

✖ The Sunset

MASALA DOSA
INDIAN $

Map p342 (☑415-566-6976; www.masaladosasf.com; 1375 9th Ave; dishes $6-14; ◎11:30am-11pm Wed-Mon, 11am-4pm Tue; ☑ ♿; ☐6, 33, 43, 44, 71, MN) Warm up on the south side of the park with South Indian fare in a mood-lit storefront bistro. The house specialty is paper dosa, a massive crispy lentil-flour pancake served with *sambar* (spicy soup) and chutney – but onion and pea *uthappam* is heartier and equally gluten-free. Standout mains include chicken Madras rich with coconut milk and fragrant wild salmon masala.

YUM YUM FISH
JAPANESE, SUSHI $

Map p342 (☑415-566-6433; www.yumyumfish-sushi.com; 2181 Irving St; sushi $1-8; ◎10:30am-7:30pm; ☐28, 71, MN) Be the envy of seagulls with Ocean Beach picnics from Yum Yum. A fish market with just three tables, Yum Yum makes sushi to order with generous slabs of fresh fish at bargain prices. Instead of gimmicky *maki*, Yum Yum creates California rolls with actual California crab. Fish is labeled so you can check sustainability ratings with Seafood Watch.

NAN KING ROAD BISTRO   CHINESE $
Map p342 (☑415-753-2900; http://nankingroad-bistro.net; 1360 9th Ave; mains $7-12; ☺11:30am-10pm Mon-Fri, from noon Sat & Sun; ☑ ⓐ; ☐6, 43, 44, 71, Ⓜ N) Shake off the chill on foggy days with Nan King Road's spicy Mongolian beef and definitive kung pao chicken lunch special ($7), with the right ratio of chili to roast peanuts. Chinese opera characters stare you down from massive paintings to ensure you finish your vegetables – and with caramelized eggplant and smoky dry-braised string beans, that's not hard.

UNDERDOG   HOT DOGS $
Map p342 (☑415-665-8881; www.underdog-organic.com; 1634 Irving St; hot dogs $4-5; ☺11am-9pm; ☑ ⓐ; ☐28, 29, 71, Ⓜ N) ⬤ For cheap, organic meals on the run in a bun, Underdog is the surprise winner. Roasted garlic and Italian pork sausages are USDA-certified organic, and smoky veggie chipotle hot dogs could make dedicated carnivores into fans of fake meat. Beef on wheat is a winner, but vegan versions and gluten-free buns are also available – and even the condiments are organic.

SAN TUNG   DIM SUM $
Map p342 (☑415-242-0828; www.santung-restaurant.com; 1031 Irving St; mains $8-13; ☺11am-9:30pm Thu-Tue; ⓐ; ☐6, 43, 44, 71, Ⓜ N) Arrive at 5:30pm on a Sunday and already the place is packed – it's that crowded for a reason. Actually four reasons: first is the dry braised chicken wings (tender, moist morsels that defy the very name), followed by housemade dumplings and noodles. But the kicker is the bill: a three-course meal for two for $20.

★OUTERLANDS   CALIFORNIAN $$
Map p342 (☑415-661-6140; www.outerlandssf.com; 4001 Judah St; sandwiches & small plates $8-9, mains $12-27; ☺11am-3pm & 6-10pm Tue-Fri, 10am-3pm & 5:30-10pm Sat & Sun; ⓐ; ☐18, Ⓜ N) ⬤ When windy Ocean Beach leaves you feeling shipwrecked, drift into this beach-shack bistro for organic, seed-

to-table California comfort food. Brunch demands Dutch pancakes in iron skillets with housemade ricotta, lunch brings $12 grilled artisan cheese combos with farm-inspired soup, and slow-cooked lamb shoulder slouches on flatbread at dinner. Reserve ahead, arrive early and sip wine outside until seats open up indoors. Angle for a spot where you can watch chef Brett Cooper and part of his team cooking

THANH LONG   VIETNAMESE $$
Map p342 (☑415-665-1146; www.anfamily.com; 4101 Judah St; mains $10-18; ☺5-9:30pm Tue-Thu & Sun, to 10pm Fri & Sat; ⓐ; ☐18, Ⓜ N) Since 1971, San Franciscans have lingered in the outer Sunset after sunset for two reasons, both at Thanh Long: roast pepper crab and garlic noodles. One crab serves two (market price runs $34 to $40) with noodles ($9), but shaking beef and mussels make a proper feast. The wine list offers good-value local pairings, especially Navarro's dry Gewürztraminer.

NOPALITO   MEXICAN $$
Map p342 (☑415-233-9966; www.nopalitosf.com; 1224 9th Ave; ☺11:30am-10pm Mon-Sat, from 10:30am Sun; ⓐ; ☐6, 43, 44, 71, Ⓜ N) ⬤ Head south of Golden Gate Park's border for upscale, sustainably sourced Cal-Mex, including tasty *tortas* (sandwiches on round Mexican flatbread), tender *carnitas* (slow-braised pork) tacos and cinnamon-laced Mexican hot chocolate. Reservations aren't accepted, but on sunny weekends when every Park dawdler craves margaritas and tangy fish ceviche, call one to two hours ahead to join the wait list.

🍷 DRINKING & 🍸 NIGHTLIFE

TOMMY'S MEXICAN RESTAURANT   BAR
Map p342 (☑415-387-4747; www.tommysmexican.com; 5929 Geary Blvd; ☺noon-11pm Wed-Mon; ☐1, 29, 31, 38) Welcome to SF's temple of tequila served since 1965. Tommy's serves enchiladas as a cover for day-drinking until 7pm, when margarita pitchers with blanco, reposado or añejo tequila rule. Cuervo Gold is displayed 'for educational purposes only' – it doesn't meet Tommy's strict criteria of unadulterated 100% agave, aged in small barrels. Luckily for connoisseurs, 211 tasty tequilas do.

HOLLOW

Between simple explanations and Golden Gate Park, there's **Hollow** (Map p342; ☑415-242-4119; www.hollowsf.com; 1435 Irving St; ⊗8am-5pm Mon-Fri, 9am-5pm Sat & Sun; ☐28, 29, Ⓜ N): an enigma wrapped in a mystery inside an espresso bar. House coffee is made with SF's cultish Ritual roasts and the secret ingredient in the cupcakes is Guinness – but that doesn't begin to explain those shelves. Magnifying glasses, beard balms and robot tea-strainers are inexplicably for sale here in galvanized tin pails, obsessive-compulsively organized into a kind of shelf haiku. There are only a couple of marble tables indoors but there's a sociable curb outside, plus more arty shopping in the next-door annex.

BEACH CHALET
BREWERY, BAR
Map p342 (☑415-386-8439; www.beachchalet.com; 1000 Great Hwy; ⊗9am-11pm Mon-Thu, 9am-midnight Fri, 8am-midnight Sat, 8am-11pm Sun; ⊕; ☐5, 18, 31) Microbrews with views: watch Pacific sunsets through pint glasses of the Beach Chalet's house beer, with live music on Tuesdays and Fridays. Downstairs, 1930s Works Project Administration (WPA) frescoes highlight San Francisco history and the development of Golden Gate Park. The backyard Park Chalet hosts raucous 'Recovery Brunch Buffets' with bottomless champagne on Sundays ($27.50), plus Wednesday-to-Friday happy hours (3-6pm).

TROUBLE COFFEE
CAFE
Map p342 (www.troublecoffee.com; 4033 Judah St; ⊗7am-7pm Mon-Fri, 8am-8pm Sat, 8am-5pm Sun; ☐18, Ⓜ Judah St) 🍴 Coconuts are unlikely near blustery Ocean Beach, but here comes Trouble with the 'Build Your Own Damn House' $8 breakfast special: coffee, thick-cut cinnamon-laced toast and an entire young coconut. On rare sunny mornings, join surfer regulars on the driftwood bench out front – otherwise, house-roasted 'The Hammer' organic espresso breaks through morning fog at the reclaimed wood counter.

TRAD'R SAM
TIKI BAR
Map p342 (☑415-221-0773; 6150 Geary Blvd; ⊗11am-2am; ☐1, 29, 31, 38) Island getaways in rattan booths at this vintage tiki lounge will cure that Ocean Beach chill. You won't find beer on tap, but you may discover an ice-cream island in your minty Grasshopper cocktail. Classic-kitsch lovers order the Hurricane, which comes with two straws to share for a reason: drink it by yourself and it'll blow you away.

540 CLUB
BAR
Map p342 (☑415-752-7276; www.540-club.com; 540 Clement St; ⊗11am-2am; 🎤; ☐1, 2, 38, 44) Party like a mortgage broker post-bailout in this converted bank. Look for the neon pink elephant over the archway, and enter the former savings and loan office for weekday happy hours (4pm to 7pm), Saturday soul and Catholic School Karaoke (see website calendar). Loosen up for darts or pool with a dozen brews on tap, including Guinness, Stella Artois and Hoegaarden. Free wi-fi.

VELO ROUGE CAFÉ
CAFE
Map p342 (☑415-752-7799; 798 Arguello Blvd; ⊗6:30am-5pm Mon & Tue, 6:30am-10pm Wed-Fri, 8am-10pm Sat, 8am-5pm Sun; ☐5, 21, 31, 33, 38) Bike one block from Golden Gate Park and you've earned a Blue Bottle coffee break or a frosty mug of Chimay beer surrounded by charming pre-doping-scandal Tour de France memorabilia. Grilled panini and mega-salads get you geared up to take on the Golden Gate Bridge – return at around 6pm for live music and $4 wine at happy hour.

BITTER END
PUB
Map p342 (☑415-221-9538; 441 Clement St; ⊗4pm-2am Mon-Fri, 11am-2am Sat & Sun; ☐1, 2, 38, 44) Don't be bitter if tricky Tuesday-night trivia games don't end with decisive wins – near-victories are fine excuses for another beer or pear cider at this local haunt with well-worn wood floors, Irish bartenders and passable pub grub. Sore losers can challenge trivia champs to a friendly grudge match at the pool tables and dart board on the balcony.

SOCIAL
BREWERY
Map p342 (☑415-681-0330; www.socialkitchenandbrewery.com; 1326 9th Ave; ⊗4pm-midnight Mon-Thu, to 2am Fri, 11:30am-2am Sat, 10:30am-midnight Sun; ☐6, 43, 44, 71, Ⓜ N) In every Social situation, there are a couple of troublemakers – specifically the bitter but golden Rapscallion and the dangerously seductive

Belgian Beach House Blonde. This snazzy, skylit modern building looks like an architect's office but tastes like a neighborhood brewpub, and just happens to serve addictive sweet potato tempur and lime-laced Brussels-sprout chips – but hey, hogging the bowl is anti-Social.

⭐ ENTERTAINMENT

BALBOA THEATRE
CINEMA

Map p342 (☑415-221-8184; www.balboamovies. com; 3630 Balboa St; adult/child & matinee $10/7.50; ☺showtimes vary; 🚼; 🚌5, 18, 31, 38) First stop, Cannes; next stop, Balboa and 37th, where Russian documentaries split the bill with first-run movies, family-friendly classic matinees and raucous screening events. Filmmakers vie for marquee spots at this 1926 neighborhood movie palace run by the non-profit San Francisco Neighborhood Theater Foundation, which keeps tickets affordable and programming exciting.

Summertime brings something for everyone at the Balboa: superhero flicks, the SF Indie Documentary Festival, Saturday morning kids' matinees with free popcorn and dance performances screened in their entirety.

PLOUGH & STARS
LIVE MUSIC, PUB

Map p342 (☑415-751-1122; www.theploughand-stars.com; 116 Clement St; ☺3pm-2am Mon-Thu, 2pm-2am Fri-Sun, showtime 9pm; 🚌1, 2, 33, 38, 44) Bands who sell out shows from Ireland to Appalachia and headline San Francisco's Hardly Strictly Bluegrass festival jam here on weeknights, taking breaks to clink pint glasses of Guinness at long union-hall tables. Mondays compensate for no live music with an all-day happy hour, plus free pool and blarney from regulars; expect modest cover charges ($6–12) for weekend shows.

NECK OF THE WOODS
CLUB, DANCING

Map p342 (☑415-387-6343; http://neckofthe woodssf.com; 406 Clement St; ☺6pm-2am; 🚌1, 2, 33, 38, 44) A vast new two-story venue with all the right moves, from Salsa Mondays ($20 per class) to weekend indie rock and alterna-pop acts pounding the upstairs stage. Downstairs is a sleek-yet-cozy lounge with happy hour $3 well drinks and beer, and wholly unpredictable open mic nights.

🛍 SHOPPING

⭐ PARK LIFE
ART, GIFTS

Map p342 (☑415-386-7275; www.parklifestore. com; 220 Clement St; ☺noon-8pm Mon-Thu, 11am-9pm Fri-Sat, 11am-7pm Sun; 🚌1, 2, 33, 38, 44) The Swiss Army knife of hip SF stores: design store, indie publisher and art gallery, all in one. Park Life is exceptionally gifted with presents too good to wait for birthdays, including Golden State pendants, Sutro Sam otter tees, Park Life's catalog of utopian visions by Shaun O'Dell and Ian Johnson's portrait of John Coltrane radiating prismatic thought waves.

⭐ MOLLUSK
SURFBOARDS, CLOTHING

Map p342 (☑415-564-6300; www.mollusksurf-shop.com; 4500 Irving St; ☺10am-6:30pm Mon-Sat, to 6pm Sun; Ⓜ Judah St) The geodesic-dome tugboat marks the spot where ocean meets art in this surf gallery. Legendary shapers (surfboard makers) create limited-edition boards for Mollusk, and signature big wave T-shirts and hoodies win nods of recognition on Ocean Beach. Kooks (newbies) get vicarious big-wave thrills from coffee-table books on California surf culture, Thomas Campbell ocean collages and other works by SF surfer-artists.

GREEN APPLE BOOKS
BOOKSTORE

Map p342 (☑415-387-2272; www.greenapple-books.com; 506 Clement St; ☺10am-10:30pm Sun-Thu, to 11:30pm Fri & Sat; 🚌1, 2, 33, 38, 44) Blissed-out booklovers emerge blinking at sunset after days browsing three floors of new releases, used titles and staff picks more reliable than *New York Times* reviews. To find out what's on SF's mind lately, check the local interest section and stick around for author events. Don't miss remainders piled near the entry, or the fiction/music annex two doors down.

GENERAL STORE
GIFTS, ACCESSORIES

Map p342 (☑415-682-0600; http://shop-generalstore.com; 4035 Judah St; ☺11am-7pm Mon-Fri, 10am-7pm Sat & Sun; 🚌18, Ⓜ N) Anyone born in the wrong place or time to be a Nor-Cal hippie architect can still look the part, thanks to a) beards and b) General Store. Pine-lined walls showcase handcrafted indigo scarves, slingshots, wicker bangles, organic hair powder and SF topographical maps. On weekends, smokers flirt on driftwood sidewalk benches and folkies strum in the backyard garden.

GOLDEN GATE PARK & THE AVENUES SHOPPING

FOGGY NOTION
GIFTS, ACCESSORIES

Map p342 (415-683-5654; www.foggy-notion. com; 275 6th St; noon-7pm Wed-Sun; 1, 2, 38, 49) Local makers conspire to produce SF's most original, hyper-local souvenir selection: California-shaped chalkboards, Pacific driftwood candle-holders, tea towels silkscreened with SF's Sutro Tower and honey from Golden Gate Park hives. Dashingly handsome recycled leather bags are made by store owner Alissa Anderson, who has a Mason jar obsession – look for them repurposed as soap dispensers, pepper grinders and sippy cups.

SEEDSTORE
CLOTHING

Map p342 (415-386-1600; www.seedstoresf. com; 212 Clement St; 11am-7pm Mon-Thu, to 8pm Fri & Sat, to 6pm Sun; 1, 2, 33, 3, 44) Raid the closet of a Western movie star and you'd fit right in at Seedstore. The old-timey shingle hung over the door is misleading: no gardening supplies are sold here, but you will find Pendelton suspender trousers, wood-heeled clogs, Navajo-pattern cardigans and filmy Free People peasant blouses.

URBAN BAZAAR
GIFTS

Map p342 (415-664-4422; http://urban-bazaarsf.com; 1371 9th Ave; noon-7pm Mon, Tue-Sat 11am-7pm, 11am-5:30pm Sun; 6, 43, 44, 71, N) Show some SF love with gifts for adults and kids made by local artisans and fair-trade collectives, including Ocean Beach–scented soap, Victorian Painted Lady stamp sets and guitar picks made from recycled SF street signs. Check the website for workshops with SF artisans, and hang out with the neighborhood over free fair-trade coffee in the garden on Sundays.

SPORTS & ACTIVITIES

GOLDEN GATE PARK BIKE & SKATE
BICYCLING

Map p342 (415-668-1117; www.goldengateparkbikeandskate.com; 3038 Fulton St; skates per hr $5-6, per day $20-24, bikes per hr $3-5, per day $15-25, tandem bikes per hr/day $15/75, discs $6/25; 10am-6pm; 5, 31, 44) Besides bikes and skates (both quad-wheeled and inline), this little rental shop just outside the park rents disc putters and drivers for the nearby free Frisbee golf course. Call ahead to confirm it's open if the weather looks iffy.

GOLDEN GATE JOAD
ARCHERY

Map p342 (www.goldengatejoad.com; Golden Gate Park Archery Range, Fulton St & 47th Ave; 2-hour lesson including archery gear rental $20; classes Saturday mornings; 5, 18, 31) Blockbuster movies like *The Avengers*, *The Hunger Games* and *Brave* have revived San Francisco's Victorian-era archery craze, and you can take aim Saturday mornings in Golden Gate Park with nonprofit Junior Olympic Archery Division (JOAD) club. Patient, certified coaches offer traditional bow archery classes for adults and kids ages eight and up (with guardian consent). Book online well in advance; beginner classes fill quickly.

LINDY IN THE PARK
DANCE

Map p342 (www.lindyinthepark.com; John F Kennedy Dr, btwn 8th & 10th Ave; 11am-2pm Sun; MFulton St) FREE Sundays swing at the free lindy-hopping dance party in Golden Gate Park, on a sidewalk near the MH de Young Museum (weather permitting). All are welcome; dancers range from first-timers to semiprofessionals, hipsters to grandparents. Free half-hour lessons begin at noon, but you can always just watch or wing it.

LAWN BOWLING CLUB
BOWLING

Map p342 (415-487-8787; www.golden-gatepark.com; Bowling Green Dr, Golden Gate Park; 5, 21, 33, 71, N) Pins seem ungainly and bowling shirts unthinkable once you've joined sweater-clad enthusiasts on America's first public bowling green. Free lessons are available from volunteers at noon on Wednesdays. Flat-soled shoes are mandatory, but otherwise bowlers dress for comfort and the weather – though all-white clothing has been customary at club social events since 1901.

SAN FRAN CYCLO
BICYCLING

Map p342 (415-831-8031; http://sanfrancyclo.com; 746 Arguello Blvd; rental bicycle per hr $8-12, kid's bicycle per day $20, helmet per day $10; 11am-7pm Mon-Fri, 10am-6pm Sat, 10am-5pm Sun; 5, 31, 33, 38) Glide around Golden Gate Park and zip across the Bridge on sleek new bikes, including hybrid options and electric bikes. Storefront for pickup/drop-off is just north of Golden Gate Park near the Velo Rouge Café (p212), a handy pit-stop and SF cycling-scene hub.

SAN FRANCISCO'S TOP 3 URBAN GOLF COURSES

Golden Gate Municipal Golf Course (Map p342; 415-751-8987; www.golden-gateparkgolfcourse.com; 47th Ave & Fulton St, Golden Gate Park; adult/child Mon-Thu $15/5, Fri-Sun $19/7; 6am-8pm; 5, 18, 31) This challenging nine-hole, par-27 course is built on sand dunes, with 100yd drop-offs and 180yd elevated greens. No reservations are taken, but it's busiest before 9am weekdays and after school. On weekend afternoons, bide your time waiting with excellent clubhouse wood-fired BBQ sandwiches (their sauce secret: Anchor Steam beer). Equipment rentals and practice range available; kids welcome.

Lincoln Park Golf Course (Map p342; 415-221-9911, reservations 415-750-4653; http://sfrecpark.org/parks-open-spaces/golf-courses; 34th Ave & Clement St, Lincoln Park; Mon-Thu $38, Fri-Sun $42, cart $26; sunrise-sunset; 1, 18, 38) For game-sabotaging views, this hilly, 18-hole course wraps around Land's End and the Legion of Honor to face Golden Gate Bridge. It has the most iconic SF vistas, so watch out for daydreaming hikers and brides posing for wedding pictures – fore!

Harding Park Municipal Golf Course (Map p342; 415-664-4690; www.tpc.com/tpc-harding-park; 99 Harding Rd, at Skyline Blvd; 9-hole course Mon-Thu $27, Fri-Sun $32, 18-hole course Mon-Thu $155, Fri-Sun $175; sunrise-sunset; 18, 29) Tournaments play San Francisco's lush 18-hole landscape partially shaded by cypress trees beside Lake Merced, while walk-ins are welcome at the adjoining Jack Flemming nine-hole course. Cart is included with 18-hole Harding Park greens fees or costs $9.50 on the Flemming course. Call to reserve tee times at Harding; a booking fee of $10 per person applies.

SAN FRANCISCO CROQUET CLUB CROQUET
(Map p342; 415-928-5525; www.croquetworld.com/sfcc.html; 19th Ave & Wawona St, Stern Grove; 17, 23, 28, K, L, M) FREE Croquet is not just for mad queens and chi-chi garden parties anymore at this nonprofit club. Members are hardcore about wickets and all-white attire, but nonmembers can join free sessions the first three Saturdays each month or plan group parties ($15/person, $150 minimum); kids are welcome. Drinking, picnicking and genteel heckling ('Tsk-tsk, wristy swing!') are permitted on sideline benches.

SAN FRANCISCO
MODEL YACHT CLUB BOATING
Map p342 (415-386-1037; www.sfmyc.org; Spreckels Lake, Golden Gate Park; sunrise-sunset; 5, 18, 31) America's Cup is bigger, but miniature remote-controlled regattas on Spreckels Lake are more exciting. Kids go wild for scale-model yachts built and operated by local collectors on this oversized fountain around 1pm to 4pm. Spreckels Lake is a refuge for wayward and abandoned turtles, which sunbathe on the shore. When members are around, check out vintage boats in the clubhouse.

SAN FRANCISCO
DISC GOLF SPORTS
Map p342 (www.sfdiscgolf.org; Marx Meadow Dr, at Fulton St btwn 25th & 30th Ave; sunrise-sunset; 5, 28, 29, 31, 38) FREE Wander the tranquil fairy-tale woods of outer Golden Gate Park and you'll find fierce Frisbee golf games in progress at a permanent 18-hole disc-golf course. Rent tournament discs at Golden Gate Park Bike & Skate to mingle with disc-tossing singles on Sundays (8:30am to 10am; $5) or join Tuesday twilight doubles tournaments (from $5:30pm; $5) – winners take home cash.

FLYCASTING CLUB FISHING
Map p342 (www.ggacc.org; John F Kennedy Dr, McLaren Anglers' Lodge & Casting Pools, Golden Gate Park; sunrise-sunset; 2, 29, N) Across from the buffalo paddock in Golden Gate Park are casting pools with targets open to the general public. Fly casters practice here in their waders, gracefully setting a fly from a thin line that looks about a mile long. Check the website for upcoming free casting lessons and casting tournaments.

GOLDEN GATE PARK & THE AVENUES SPORTS & ACTIVITIES

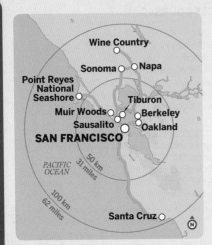

Day Trips from San Francisco

Berkeley p217
Home to a world-famous university, socially progressive activists, a 'Gourmet Ghetto' and summer weather up to 20°F warmer than in SF.

Muir Woods & Muir Beach p220
Some of the world's tallest trees reach skyward in primordial forests near breezy Pacific shores, just across the Golden Gate Bridge.

Sausalito & Tiburon p221
Picturesque bayside towns, perfect for strolling and shopping, are a ferry ride away in Marin County. Linger for sunset drinks by the water.

Napa Valley p225
Fancy-pants Napa vineyards first put the US on the world's viticulture map. Cycle among rolling hillsides, tipple top-tier wines and nab seats at star chefs' tables.

Sonoma Valley p233
With its 19th-century California mission town, farm-to-table kitchens and pastoral wineries that welcome picnicking, Sonoma retains its folksy ways.

Berkeley

Explore

You can't legally walk around nude anymore, but 'Berserkeley' remains the Bay Area's radical hub, crawling with university students, skateboarders and aging hippies. Not much has changed since the 1960s heyday – except the bumper stickers, 'No Blood for Oil' replacing 'Make Love Not War.'

The main destinations of day-trippers are downtown Berkeley and the University of California (UC) campus. Just north of campus on Shattuck Ave lies North Berkeley's 'Gourmet Ghetto.' Berkeley is also home to a large South Asian community, as evidenced by the abundance of sari and spice shops along University Ave. The hills above Berkeley are crisscrossed with hiking trails through Tilden Regional Park, which has bird's-eye views over the Bay Area.

The Best...

➡ **Sight** University of California, Berkeley (p217)

➡ **Place to Eat** Chez Panisse (p219)

➡ **Place to Drink** Caffe Strada (p219)

Top Tip

If you're coming to explore the UC campus and downtown Berkeley during the day, avoid driving or taking BART trains during weekday rush hours.

Getting There & Away

➡ **Car** Bay Bridge to I-80 east; exit University Ave.

➡ **Train** Downtown Berkeley's **BART** (☑511, 510-465-2278; www.bart.gov) station is most convenient ($3.70, 25 minutes).

➡ **Bus AC Transit** (☑511; www.actransit.org) runs frequent buses from San Francisco's Transbay Temporary Terminal (Howard, Main & Beale Sts) to Berkeley ($4.10, 45 minutes), with connecting buses available.

Need to Know

➡ **Area Code** 510

➡ **Location** 11 miles northeast of San Francisco.

➡ **Tourist office** (☑800-847-4823, 510-549-7040; www.visitberkeley.com; 2030 Addison St; ⊙9am-5pm Mon-Fri)

◉ SIGHTS

UNIVERSITY OF CALIFORNIA, BERKELEY
UNIVERSITY

(www.berkeley.edu) The campus of UC Berkeley – aka 'Cal' – is California's oldest, founded in 1866. From Telegraph Ave, enter via **Sproul Plaza**, ground zero for people-watching, soapbox oration and pseudo-tribal drumming. The adjacent **Visitor Services Center** (☑510-642-5215; http://visitors.berkeley.edu; 101 Sproul Hall; ⊙tours usually 10am Mon-Sat & 1pm Sun) offers free guided campus tours (reservations required). Alternatively, enter campus off Center St, a short walk east of the Downtown Berkeley BART station.

The **Campanile** (Sather Tower; adult/child $2/1; ⊙10am-3:45pm Mon-Fri, to 4:45pm Sat, 10am-1:30pm & 3-4:45pm Sun; ⊞) was modeled on St Mark's Basilica in Venice. The 307ft spire has knockout views and some of the carillon's 61 bells are as big as a Volkswagen. Recitals take place daily at 7:50am, noon and 6pm, with a longer piece on Sundays at 2pm.

At the **UC Berkeley Art Museum** (☑510-642-0808; www.bampfa.berkeley.edu; 2626 Bancroft Way; adult/child $10/7; ⊙11am-5pm Wed-Sun), 11 galleries showcase works from Ancient Chinese to cutting-edge contemporary. Scheduled to move to a new Oxford St location in 2014, the complex also houses the avant-garde Pacific Film Archive (p219).

Reopening in 2014, the **Phoebe Hearst Museum of Anthropology** (☑510-643-7648; http://hearstmuseum.berkeley.edu; Kroeber Hall) showcases the diversity of indigenous human cultures, with artifacts from ancient Peru, Egypt and Africa. A large collection also highlights Native Californians.

Uphill east of the main campus, the **UC Botanical Garden at Berkeley** (☑510-643-2755; http://botanicalgarden.berkeley.edu; 200 Centennial Dr; adult/child $10/2; ⊙9am-5pm, closed 1st Tue each month) protects more than 13,000 species of plants, making it one of the USA's most varied flora collections.

TELEGRAPH AVE
STREET

Running south of campus, Telegraph Ave is the heart of Berkeley's student village, a constant flow of shoppers, buskers and street vendors. Expect an odd mix of greying hippies, hipsters and ponytailed panhandlers. It's not for everyone – some find it trashy and obnoxious – but if you're on the hunt for books, vinyl records or bumper stickers, this is the place.

East Bay

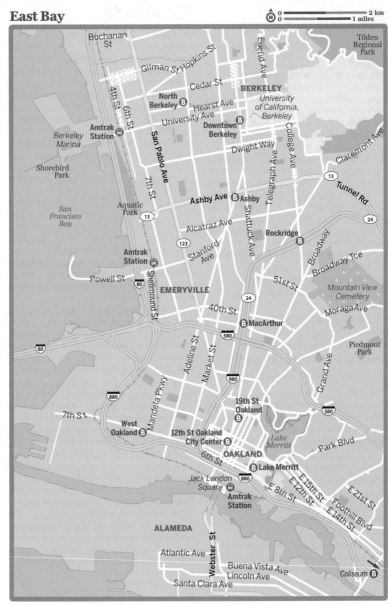

TILDEN REGIONAL PARK   PARK

(www.ebparks.org/parks/tilden) Escape to Berkeley's hills and revel in nearly 40 miles of hiking and biking trails, a botanical garden, seasonal swimming at Lake Anza and plenty of kids' stuff, including a merry-go-round and mini steam train. AC Transit bus 67 runs to and around the park on weekends and holidays from the Downtown Berkeley BART station, but only stops at the entrance (and doesn't go inside the park) on weekdays ($2.10, 20 minutes).

EATING

CHEESE BOARD PIZZA PIZZERIA $

(http://cheeseboardcollective.coop; 1512 Shattuck Ave; slice/half-pizza $2.50/10; ⊙11:30am-3pm & 4:30pm-8pm Tue-Sat; 🅿️🚇) A Gourmet Ghetto mainstay, this worker-owned collective crafts only one wildly creative flavor of crispy, veggie pizza each day. Live music often jams at night. The next-door bakery vends artisanal cheeses and oven-fresh bread.

VIK'S CHAAT CORNER INDIAN $

(www.vikschaatcorner.com; 2390 4th St; meals under $9; ⊙11am-6pm Mon-Thu, to 8pm Fri-Sun) At the back of a South Asian grocery store, this airy cafeteria serves freshly made, order-at-the-counter authentic Indian street food – no tikka masala here. Daily curry specials are plated with all the trimmings.

JUICE BAR COLLECTIVE HEALTH FOOD $

(www.thejuicebar.org; 2114 Vine St; dishes $4-8; ⊙10am-4:30pm Mon-Sat) Tiny North Berkeley storefront makes tasty polenta–black bean casserole, veggie quiche, tofu banh mi sandwiches, organic salads, from-scratch soups and orchard-fresh fruit smoothies.

CREAM DESSERTS $

(www.creamnation.com; 2399 Telegraph Ave; items $2-4; ⊙noon-midnight Mon-Wed, to 2am Thu-Fri, 11am-2am Sat, 11am-11pm Sun) Near campus, concoct your own wacky mix-and-match ice-cream sandwiches – salted caramel with snickerdoodle cookies, anyone? Cash only.

LA NOTE FRENCH $$

(☎510-843-1535; www.lanoterestaurant.com; 2377 Shattuck Ave; mains $9-20; ⊙8am-2:30pm Mon-Fri, 8am-3pm Sat & Sun, 6-10pm Thu-Sat) A sociable spot to fuel up downtown before exploring, La Note serves a classic French cafe menu of omelettes, Niçoise salads, baguette sandwiches and hearty bowls of ratatouille.

⭐CHEZ PANISSE CALIFORNIAN $$$

(☎cafe 510-548-5049, restaurant 510-548-5525; 1517 Shattuck Ave; cafe dinner mains $18-28, restaurant prix-fixe dinner $65-100; ⊙cafe 11:30am-2:45pm & 5-10:30pm Mon-Thu, to 3pm & to 11:30pm Fri & Sat; restaurant seatings 6-6:30pm & 8:30-9:15pm Mon-Sat) 🥐 The temple of Alice Waters – doyenne of California cuisine – remains at the pinnacle of Bay Area dining. Reserve one month ahead for legendary dinners in the cozy Craftsman-style dining room, where no substitutions are allowed

on the daily-changing restaurant menu. If you'd prefer to order à la carte, book the less expensive but equally lovely upstairs cafe.

GATHER CALIFORNIAN $$$

(☎510-809-0400; www.gatherrestaurant.com; 2200 Oxford St; mains lunch $11-18, dinner $16-28; ⊙11:30am-2pm Mon-Fri, from 10am Sat & Sun, also 5-10pm daily; 🅿️) 🥐 When vegan foodies and passionate farm-to-table types dine out together, they often end up downtown at Gather, where a salvaged-wood interior is punctuated by an open kitchen. Swoon over seasonal Californian dishes created from locally sourced ingredients and sustainably raised meats.

🍷 DRINKING & NIGHTLIFE

CAFFE STRADA CAFE

(2300 College Ave; ⊙6am-midnight; 📶) Caffeine-wired students mob the outdoor patio to study, ardently philosophize and flirt.

JUPITER BAR

(2181 Shattuck Ave; ⊙11:30am-1am Mon-Thu, to 1:30am Fri, noon-1:30am Sat, noon-midnight Sun) For a sociable introduction to NorCal's craft beer scene, head to this brewpub's back patio. Live music or a DJ most nights.

⭐ ENTERTAINMENT

PACIFIC FILM ARCHIVE CINEMA

(PFA; ☎510-642-5249; www.bampfa.berkeley.edu; 2575 Bancroft Way; adult/child $9.50/6.50) Renowned movie theater explores the art of film-making, including rare, new and historic prints from around the globe. It's moving to Oxford St in 2014.

FREIGHT & SALVAGE COFFEEHOUSE LIVE MUSIC

(☎510-644-2020; http://thefreight.org; 2020 Addison St; tickets $5-30) This all-ages, alcohol-free coffeehouse dating from the radical '60s hosts traditional folk and world music – fiddle, guitar, strings and soul.

BERKELEY REPERTORY THEATRE THEATER

(☎510-647-2949; www.berkeleyrep.org; 2025 Addison St; tickets $35-100) Some San Franciscans cross the bay just to see Berkeley Rep's bold versions of classical and contemporary plays.

(☎510-642-9988; www.calperfs.berkeley.edu; Zellerbach Hall; tickets from $18) UC's premier stage showcases top-flight dance troupes and musical ensembles from the US and abroad.

Muir Woods & Muir Beach

Explore

Coastal redwoods are the tallest living things on earth and exist only on the West Coast, extending north from California's Big Sur into southern Oregon. Only 4% of original redwood forest remains, but to-day you can amble around a glorious old-growth stand just 10 miles from the Golden Gate Bridge. You could spend as little as an hour in Muir Woods, following crowds along the main paths, but for perspective on the ancient forest, hike the park's longer trails, which lift you above the big trees onto rugged ridgelines where ocean panoramas unfurl. Afterward, continue to the coast and along Hwy 1 to pebbly Muir Beach – but you'd do well to bring a sweater, not a bikini: chances are it'll be chilly.

The Best...

⇒ **Sight** Cathedral Grove (p221)
⇒ **Trail** Dipsea Trail (p221)
⇒ **Place to Eat & Drink** Pelican Inn (p221)

Top Tip

To beat the crowds, come early in the day, late afternoon or midweek; otherwise the parking lots fill up. During summer, ride the shuttle bus to Muir Woods.

EAST BAY BY BART

To escape San Francisco's famous fog, especially in summer, chase some California sunshine over in the East Bay by hopping a BART train to:

⇒ **Downtown Berkeley Station** It's close to UC Berkeley, Shattuck Ave's restaurants and bars, and Telegraph Ave's funky shops and street vendors.

⇒ **Rockridge Station** Straddling the Berkeley/Oakland border, College Ave is a pretty street for strolling, with a bevy of eateries and locally owned shops.

⇒ **19th St Oakland Station** Walk six blocks east to Lake Merritt, then follow the lakeside recreational path south to the seafood bar and grill at **Lake Chalet** (☎510-208-5253; www.thelakechalet.com; 1520 Lakeside Dr; mains $11-29; ⊙11am-10pm Mon-Thu, to 11pm Fri, 10am-11pm Sat, 10am-10pm Sun) for happy-hour oysters and beer, or book ahead for a **gondola cruise** (☎510-663-6603; http://gondolaservizio.com; 1520 Lakeside Dr; 30min cruise from $40).

⇒ **Lake Merritt Station** Continue south to the **Oakland Museum of California** (OMCA; ☎888-625-6873, 510-318-8400; www.museumca.org; 1000 Oak St; adult/child 9-17yr $12/6; ⊙11am-5pm Wed-Sun, to 9pm Fri; ♿). Or head north along the lakeshore to the botanical gardens, **boating center** (☎510-238-2196; www2.oaklandnet.com; 568 Bellevue Ave; boat rentals per hr $10-24; ⊙open daily Mar-Oct, Sat & Sun only Nov-Feb), whimsical 1950s **Children's Fairyland** (☎510-452-2259; www.fairyland.org; 699 Bellevue Ave; admission $8; ⊙10am-4pm Mon-Fri, to 5pm Sat & Sun Jun-Aug, off-season hr vary; ♿) and pint-sized **nature center** (☎510-238-3739; www2.oaklandnet.com; 600 Bellevue Ave; ⊙9am-3pm Tue-Sat; ♿) FREE.

⇒ **12th St Oakland City Center Station** Wander south into the Old Oakland Historic District, with happening cafes and restaurants around the intersection of Washington & 9th Sts. Keep going down Broadway to waterfront Jack London Square, where the writer's Klondike Gold Rush-era log cabin stands next to the saloon **Heinhold's First & Last Chance** (http://heinolds.com; 48 Webster St).

⇒ **Coliseum Station** Check out big-name musical acts and touring shows or Golden State Warriors basketball at Oracle Arena, or watch Oakland A's baseball or Oakland Raiders football at O.co Coliseum.

Getting There & Away

➡**Car** Take Hwy 101 north across the Golden Gate Bridge, exiting at Hwy 1. Continue north along Hwy 1/Shoreline Hwy to Panoramic Hwy (a right-hand fork). Follow Panoramic Hwy almost a mile, then turn left onto Muir Woods Rd.

➡**Ferry & Bus** On weekends and holidays from May through October, **Marin Transit** (☑415-455-2000, 511; www.marintransit.org) bus 66F ('Muir Woods Shuttle') operates from Sausalito's ferry terminal (round-trip adult/child $5/free, 50 minutes), connecting every hour or so with Golden Gate Ferry (p60) service from San Francisco (one-way adult/child $9.75/4.75, 30 minutes).

Need to Know

➡**Area code** 415

➡**Location** 12 miles northwest of San Francisco

SIGHTS

MUIR WOODS
NATIONAL MONUMENT FOREST
Map p222 (☑415-388-2595; www.nps.gov/muwo; Muir Woods Rd, Mill Valley; adult/child $7/free; ⊙8am-7:30pm, closes earlier mid-Sep–mid-Mar) The closest stand of coastal redwoods to San Francisco, this old-growth forest dates back to time immemorial. Even at peak times, when the park is jam-packed with local families and tourists, a short hike will get you out of the densest crowds and onto trails with unforgettable vistas.

These trees were initially eyed by loggers, and Redwood Creek, as the area was known, seemed ideal for a dam. Those plans were halted when congressman and naturalist William Kent bought a section of Redwood Creek in 1905 and later donated 295 acres to the federal government. President Theodore Roosevelt declared the site a national monument in 1908, its name honoring John Muir, naturalist and founder of the Sierra Club environmental group.

The 1-mile **Main Loop Trail** is easy, leading alongside Redwood Creek to 1000-year-old trees at Cathedral Grove. The **Dipsea Trail** is a strenuous 2-mile hike to the top of aptly named Cardiac Hill, but it's beautiful for views – a half-mile steep grade through fern-fringed forest leads from the canyon to

an exposed ridge, from which you can see Mt Tamalpais, the Pacific and San Francisco. For a longer stint, keep trekking down to the tiny coastal town of **Stinson Beach**.

You can also walk down into Muir Woods via trails from the Panoramic Hwy (such as the Bootjack Trail from Bootjack picnic area) or nearby Mt Tamalpais State Park's Pantoll Station (via the Stapleveldt and Ben Johnson Trails).

MUIR BEACH BEACH
Map p222 (www.nps.gov/goga; off Pacific Way) **FREE** The turnoff to Muir Beach from Hwy 1 is marked by the coast's longest row of mailboxes near mile marker 5.7, just before the Pelican Inn. Immediately north on Hwy 1 there are stunning coastal views from **Muir Beach Overlook**. During WWII, watch for invading Japanese ships was kept from the surrounding concrete lookouts.

EATING & DRINKING

MUIR WOODS TRADING COMPANY CAFE $
Map p222 (☑415-388-7059; www.muirwoodstradingcompany.com; Muir Woods Rd, Mill Valley; dishes $3-10; ⊙from 9am daily, closing varies 5:30pm to 7pm; 🖐) ✔ It's pricey, but this little cafe near the park entrance serves melty-good grilled cheese sandwiches, savory soups and hot drinks that hit the spot on foggy days.

PELICAN INN PUB $$$
Map p222 (☑415-383-6000; www.pelicaninn.com; 10 Pacific Way; mains lunch $11-23, dinner $16-34; 🖐) Hikers, cyclists and families come for pub lunches at the Tudor-style timbered restaurant and cozy bar, perfect for a pint, a game of darts and warming-up fireside. The British fare is respectable enough, but it's the setting that's magical.

Sausalito & Tiburon

Explore

Perched above Richardson Bay, Sausalito is cosseted with art galleries, houseboats and picture-postcard bay vistas. It's often sunnier than San Francisco. The town becomes

Marin County

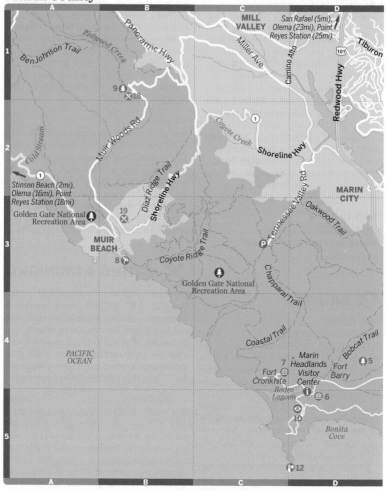

a victim of its charm on summer weekends, when day-trippers jam the sidewalks, shops and restaurants. For the locals' scene, wander one block inland to Caledonia St.

On a small peninsula jutting out into the bay, Tiburon (Spanish for 'shark') isn't at the forefront of most tourists' minds, although it's a popular jumping-off point for trips to Angel Island (p228). Browse boutique shops inside historic clapboard buildings on Main St, grab a bite to eat by the docks and you've done Tiburon. During summer, Tiburon throws its Main St block party, kicking off at 6pm on Friday nights.

The Best...

➡ **Sight** Bay Model Visitor Center (p224)
➡ **Place to Eat** Fish (p225)
➡ **Place to Drink** Wellingtons Wine Bar (p225)

Top Tip

Rent a bicycle in San Francisco, cycle over the Golden Gate Bridge, then take the ferry back from Sausalito. If you drive, expect weekend traffic jams in town.

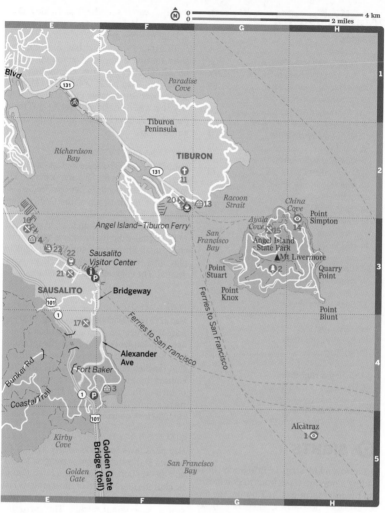

Getting There & Away

➡ **Ferry** Golden Gate Ferry (p60) sails from San Francisco's Ferry Bldg to Sausalito ($9.75, 30 minutes). Blue & Gold Fleet (p75) sails to Sausalito from Fisherman's Wharf ($11, 30 minutes), and to Tiburon from both Fisherman's Wharf and the Ferry Bldg ($11, 30 minutes).

➡ **Car** To Sausalito: take Hwy 101 north across the Golden Gate Bridge, then the immediate Alexander Ave or main Sausalito exit; for Tiburon, continue to the Tiburon Blvd/E Blithedale Ave exit.

➡ **Bus Golden Gate Transit** (☏ 415-455-2000, 511; http://goldengatetransit.org) bus 10 runs hourly to Sausalito from downtown San Francisco ($4.50, one hour).

Need to Know

➡ **Area code** 415

➡ **Location** Sausalito is 5 miles north of San Francisco; Tiburon is 12 miles north-northeast.

➡ **Tourist office** (Map p222; ☏ 415-332-0505; www.sausalito.org; 780 Bridgeway Blvd, Sausalito; ⊙ 11:30am-4pm Tue-Sun)

Marin County

◉ SIGHTS

Sausalito's main strip is Bridgeway Blvd, leading along the waterfront to downtown and the ferry terminal. In Tiburon, the ferry also lands downtown, where old houseboats have metamorphosed into shops on Main St's Ark Row.

BAY MODEL VISITOR CENTER   MUSEUM
Map p222 (☑415-332-3871; www.spn.usace. army.mil; 2100 Bridgeway Blvd, Sausalito; admission by donation; ☺9am-4pm Tue-Fri, 10am-5pm Sat & Sun late May-early Sep, 9am-4pm Tue-Sat early Sep-late May; ⊕) Until computers rendered it obsolete, this enormous 1.5-acre hydraulic scale model of the entire San Francisco Bay and delta helped scientists understand the effects of tides and currents on the land. A 24-hour period is represented in only 15 minutes. Look in the

deepest water – under the Golden Gate Bridge – to understand the incredible force of tidal movements.

To explore the actual bay yourself, consider renting a kayak or stand-up paddle boarding (SUP) set from nearby **Sea Trek Kayaking** (Map p222; ☑415-332-8494; www. seatrek.com; Schoonmaker Point Marina, 85 Liberty Ship Way, Sausalito; SUP set & kayak rental per hr $20-35, tours $45-110), which also offers guided trips.

BAY AREA DISCOVERY MUSEUM   MUSEUM
Map p222 (☑415-339-3900; www.baykidsmuseum. org; 557 McReynolds Rd, Sausalito; admission $11, free 1st Wed each month; ☺9am-5pm Tue-Sun; ⊕) Under the north tower of the Golden Gate Bridge at Fort Baker, this hands-on activity museum is fun for kids up to eight years old. Multilingual exhibits include a wave workshop, small underwater tunnel and outdoor play area with a faux-shipwreck to romp around. The cafe sells healthful nibbles.

RAILROAD &
FERRY DEPOT MUSEUM   MUSEUM
Map p222 (www.landmarks-society.org; 1920 Paradise Drive, Tiburon; suggested donation $5; ☺1-4pm Wed-Sun Apr-Oct) Formerly the terminus of a ferry to San Francisco and a railroad that reached north to Ukiah, this late 19th-century building showcases a scale model of turn-of-the-20th-century Tiburon's commercial hub. Take a look at the restored stationmaster's quarters upstairs.

OLD ST HILARY'S   CHURCH
Map p222 (www.landmarks-society.org; 201 Esperanza St, Tiburon; suggested donation $5; ☺1-4pm Sun Apr-Oct) This deconsecrated Catholic church (1888) is one of the country's last examples of Carpenter Gothic architecture still in its original setting. The surrounding hillsides of **Old St Hilary's Open Space Preserve** nurture a trove of rare wildflowers, best in spring.

✗ EATING & DRINKING

GOLDEN GATE MARKET   MARKET, DELI $
Map p222 (☑415-332-3040; 221 2nd St, Sausalito; sandwiches from $6; ☺8am-9pm Mon-Sat, 9am-7pm Sun) Grab deli sandwiches and salads, local cheeses, wine and beer for waterfront picnics at this tiny grocery store on the south side of Sausalito, convenient for cyclists.

FISH
SEAFOOD $$

Map p222 (☑415-331-3474; www.fish311. com; 350 Harbor Dr, Sausalito; mains $12-25; ☺11:30am-8:30pm; 🚼) 🍴 This dockside joint hooks locals with sustainable, line-caught fish and bayside seating at picnic tables. Sustainability and organics have their price, but it's worth it – especially come salmon season. Devour oak-grilled fish fillets, BBQ oysters and Dungeness crab rolls. Cash only.

SUSHI RAN
JAPANESE $$$

Map p222 (☑415-332-3620; http://sushiran.com; 107 Caledonia St, Sausalito; shared plates $3-33; ☺11:45am-2:30pm Mon-Fri, 5pm-10pm Sun-Thu, to 11pm Fri & Sat) One of the Bay Area's top sushi spots melds East-West tastes of land and sea, from grilled octopus dolloped with popcorn puree to sliced hand rolls of spicy crab, grilled eel and fresh avocado. A wine and sake bar eases the pain of long waits – better yet, reserve ahead.

SAM'S ANCHOR CAFE
SEAFOOD $$$

Map p222 (☑415-435-4527; www.samscafe.com; 27 Main St, Tiburon; mains $12-30; ☺11am-10pm Mon-Fri, from 9:30am Sat & Sun; 🚼) Everyone wants to eat outdoors, but you can't reserve waterfront patio tables at this seafood and burger shack, Tiburon's oldest restaurant (look for the trapdoor used to spirit booze straight from ship to saloon). The food's so-so. Watch for seagulls swooping in to steal your fries.

WELLINGTONS WINE BAR
BAR

Map p222 (☑415-339-8836; www.wellingtons winebar.com; 300 Turney St, Sausalito; ☺4pm-9pm Mon, to 10pm Tue-Thu, 3pm-11pm Fri & Sat; 🎣) Before catching the ferry home, cozy up with a glass of wine at this wine bar and pub with drop-dead bay vistas. You'd not be the first to miss your boat for all the fun you're having here.

Napa Valley

Explore

California's most glamorous farmland, the 30-mile-long Napa Valley is famous for Cabernet Sauvignon and Chardonnay,

DAY TRIPS FROM SAN FRANCISCO NAPA VALLEY

MARIN HEADLANDS

Jaggedly rising on the north side of the Golden Gate Bridge, the rugged beauty of these windswept headlands is all the more striking given that they're only a few miles from San Francisco's crowded streets. A few forts and bunkers are left over from more than a century of use by the US military.

Today this development-free open space is protected by **Golden Gate National Recreation Area** (Map p222; www.nps.gov/goga). Rugged hiking and cycling trails wind through the headlands, affording panoramic cliff-edge views of the sea, the bridge and the city. Some trails lead to isolated natural beaches, picnic spots and campgrounds.

Near the **Marin Headlands Visitor Center** (Map p222; ☑415-331-1540; www.nps.gov/goga/marin-headlands.htm; Fort Barry, Bldg 948; ☺9:30am-4:30pm Sat-Mon Apr-Sep), you can peek into the open studios of the **Headlands Center for the Arts** (Map p222; ☑415-331-2787; www.headlands.org; 944 Simmonds Rd; ☺noon-5pm Sun-Thu) FREE. Then visit the wildlife hospital at the eco-conscious, educational **Marine Mammal Center** (Map p222; ☑415-289-7325; www.tmmc.org; 2000 Bunker Rd; admission by donation; ☺10am-5pm; 🚼) 🍴.

It's a steep half-mile hike from the end of Conzelman Rd to 1877 **Point Bonita Lighthouse** (Map p222; www.nps.gov/goga/pobo.htm; off Field Rd; ☺12:30-3:30pm Sat-Mon) FREE, reached via a suspension bridge and tunnel. History hounds will want to join a guided walk around **Nike Missile Site SF-88** (Map p222; ☑415-331-1453; www.nps.gov/goga/nike-missile-site.htm; off Field Rd; ☺12:30pm-3:30pm Thu-Sat) FREE, a genuine Cold War–era relic.

If you're driving, take the Alexander Ave exit off Hwy 101 northbound immediately after crossing the Golden Gate Bridge, then turn left under the freeway onto Bunker Rd and follow the signs to the visitor center. On Saturdays, Sundays and holidays, Muni (p287) bus 76 runs hourly from downtown San Francisco to the visitor center ($2, 45 minutes), usually between 9:30am and 5:30pm.

1. Houseboats at Sausalito (p221)
Enjoy the quirky charm of this city across the Golden
Gate Bridge.

2. Napa Valley Vineyards (p225)
This 30-mile-long valley is the most-visited part of
California's Wine Country region.

**3. Muir Woods National Monument
(p221)**
Hike in this forest amongst 1000-year-old redwoods.

**4. University of California, Berkeley
(p217)**
Sproul Plaza is at the heart of the UC Berkeley campus.

ANGEL ISLAND

Rising from the middle of San Francisco Bay, Angel Island has served as a military base, immigration station, WWII Japanese internment camp and Nike missile site. Today the island is a **state park** (Map p222; ☑415-435-5390; www.parks.ca.gov) FREE with interesting and thought-provoking forts, interpretive exhibits and bunkers to explore.

Families spread out picnics in protected coves overlooking the close but immeasurably distant urban grid. Escape the crowds and get back to nature on 13 miles of hiking trails – including up Mt Livermore (788ft) for panoramic views when it's not foggy – or on the mostly paved 6-mile perimeter cycling loop.

Nicknamed the 'Ellis Island of the West,' Angel Island's early 20th-century **US Immigration Station** (USIS; Map p222; ☑415-435-5537; www.aiisf.org; adult/child 6-17yr $5/3, incl tour $7/5; ⊙museum 11am-3pm Mon-Fri, to 4pm Sat & Sun, daily tour schedules vary) is a 1.5-mile walk or bike ride from the ferry dock. Reserve guided tours in advance or try your luck buying tickets upon arrival (bring cash).

The best times to visit the island are summer weekends, when more historic buildings are open, or during spring wildflower season. Take the **Angel Island–Tiburon Ferry** (Map p222; ☑415-435-2131; www.angelislandferry.com; 21 Main St, Tiburon; round-trip adult/child/bike $13.50/11.50/1) from Tiburon (round-trip adult/child $13.50/11.50) or **Blue & Gold Fleet** ferries (p75) from San Francisco (round-trip adult/child $17/9.50). Rental bicycles (per hour/day $12.50/40) are available near the island's ferry dock and **cafe** (Map p222; ☑415-435-3392; www.angelisland.com; items $3-14; ⊙10am-3pm, weather permitting; ☎🖶).

winery art collections, top-drawer chefs, volcanic-mud baths and architect-designed monuments to ego. It's the most-visited part of Wine Country – Hwy 29 slows to a standstill on summer weekends, so come midweek if possible. Napa can be done as a day trip, but you'd be smart to stay at least one night – not only for convenience, but also romance.

The riverside city of Napa, farthest south, surprisingly lacks much charm. Calistoga, in the north, is the least-gentrified town, freckled with historic hot-springs resorts. Posh mid-valley destinations include the small towns of St Helena, where traffic snarls, and Yountville, a 19th-century stagecoach stop that has more Michelin-starred eateries per capita than anywhere else in the nation.

The Best...

➡ **Sight** di Rosa Art + Nature Preserve (p229)

➡ **Place to Eat** French Laundry (p232)

➡ **Place to Drink** Hess Collection (p229)

Top Tip

Legally many Napa Valley wineries cannot receive drop-in visitors (or allow picnicking). Book well ahead for tastings at famous-name winemakers. Carry your cellphone for making last-minute reservations.

Getting There & Away

➡ **Car** To Napa, take Hwy 101 to Hwy 37 east. At the Hwy 121/37 split, take Hwy 121 north, which veers east toward Napa; at Hwy 29, turn north. From downtown San Francisco, the Bay Bridge is quicker (about an hour) but a little less scenic: take I-80E to Hwy 37 west, then go north on Hwy 29.

➡ **Ferry & Bus** Possible, but slow: from San Francisco's Ferry Bldg, take **Vallejo Baylink Ferry** (☑877-643-3779; www.baylinkferry.com) ($13, one hour), then **Vine Transit** (☑707-251-2800; www.ridethevine.com) buses to Napa ($1.50 to 3.25, 30 to 55 minutes), with onward buses to other valley towns.

Need to Know

➡ **Area Code** 707

➡ **Location** 50 miles northeast of San Francisco

➡ **Tourist office** (☑855-333-6272, 707-251-5895; www.visitnapavalley.com; 600 Main St; ⊙9am-5pm Sep-Apr, 9am-5pm Mon-Thu, to 6pm Fri-Sun May-Oct)

⊙ SIGHTS

Many wineries require advance reservations, so make one or two appointments and plan your day around them. Don't try to visit more than a few wineries in one day. If you're driving, take faster Hwy 29 north from Napa or follow the scenic Silverado Trail, which runs parallel up the valley.

★ DI ROSA ART + NATURE
PRESERVE   GALLERY, GARDEN

(☑707-226-5991; www.dirosaart.org; 5200 Hwy 121, Napa; admission $5, tours $12-15; ☺10am-4pm Wed-Sun, to 6pm Wed-Sun Apr-Oct) When you notice scrap-metal sheep grazing in Carneros vineyards, you've spotted one of the best-anywhere collections of modern and contemporary Northern California art. Reservations are recommended for tours covering everything from Tony Oursler's grimacing video projections in the wine cellar to million-dollar Robert Bechtle abstracts hanging from the ceiling.

★ HESS COLLECTION   WINERY, GALLERY

(☑707-255-8584; www.hesscollection.com; 4411 Redwood Rd, Napa; tasting $10; ☺10am-5pm) ∅ Blue-chip art and big reds are the pride of Hess Collection, a winery and art gallery northwest of downtown Napa. Monster Cabernet Sauvignon and oaky Chardonnay are paired with large canvas and mixed-media art by mega-modernists such as Robert Motherwell. Ready yourself for a winding mountain road. Reservations suggested.

FROG'S LEAP   WINERY

(☑707-963-4704; www.frogsleap.com; 8815 Conn Creek Rd, Rutherford; tasting $15, incl tour $20; ☺10am-4pm; 🚻🐾) ∅ Meandering paths wind through fruit-bearing orchards and gardens surrounding an 1884 barn with cats and chickens roaming the farmstead. Here the family-friendly, down-to-earth vibe exemplifies old Napa. The LEED-certified, solar-powered winery makes excellent Sauvignon Blanc and Cabernet Sauvignon. Tour reservations required.

ROBERT SINSKEY   WINERY

(☑707-944-9090; www.robertsinskey.com; 6320 Silverado Trail, Napa; tasting $25, incl tour $50-75; ☺10am-4:30pm) ∅ For hilltop views and food-friendly wines, visit this chef-owned winery, whose tasting room resembles a miniature cathedral. Small seasonal bites accompany tasting pours of organic-certified wines, with especially noteworthy Pinot Noir from Carneros vineyards. Reserve ahead for farm-to-table and wine cave tours.

PRIDE MOUNTAIN   WINERY

(☑707-963-4949; www.pridewines.com; 3000 Summit Trail, St Helena; tasting $10, incl tour $15-75; ☺by appointment) High atop Spring Mountain, cult-favorite Pride straddles the Sonoma–Napa county border and makes stellar Cabernet Sauvignon and Merlot, and elegant Chardonnay and Viognier. Picnicking at the unfussy hilltop estate is spectacular, but you must first have a tasting appointment.

MUMM NAPA   WINERY, GALLERY

(☑800-686-6272; www.mummnapa.com; 8445 Silverado Trail, Rutherford; tastings $8-40, tour $25; ☺10am-4:45pm) The valley views are as spectacular as the fine-art photography exhibits at Mumm. Appointments are only necessary if you want to sample sparkling wines while seated on a terrace overlooking the vineyards – ideal for impressing your date. Tip: the 10am winery tour is complimentary (tasting surcharge applies).

REGUSCI   WINERY

(☑707-254-0403; www.regusciwinery.com; 5584 Silverado Trail, Napa; tastings $25-30, incl tour $30-60; ☺10am-5pm) One of Napa's oldest wineries dates from the late 1800s. Vineyards wrap around a stone building on the valley's quieter eastern side in the premier Stag's Leap District. Enjoy Bordeaux-style blends and a lovely oak-shaded picnic area. Tour reservations required.

CASA NUESTRA   WINERY

(☑866-844-9463; www.casanuestra.com; 3451 Silverado Trail, St Helena; tasting $10; ☺by appointment) ∅ A peace flag and portrait of Elvis greet you in the tasting barn at this old-school, '70s-vintage, mom-and-pop winery with playful goats beside a little picnic area. Diverse varietals bottled here include Chenin Blanc grapes from 50-year-old organic vines. Call ahead.

CASTELLO DI AMOROSA   WINERY, CASTLE

(☑707-967-6272; www.castellodiamorosa.com; 4045 Hwy 29, Calistoga; admission & tasting $18-28, incl guided tour $33-69; ☺9:30am-6pm, to 5pm Nov-Feb) It's a near-perfect recreation of a 13th-century Tuscan castle, complete with moat, frescoes hand-painted by Italian artisans and a torture chamber filled with

DAY TRIPS FROM SAN FRANCISCO NAPA VALLEY

Wine Country

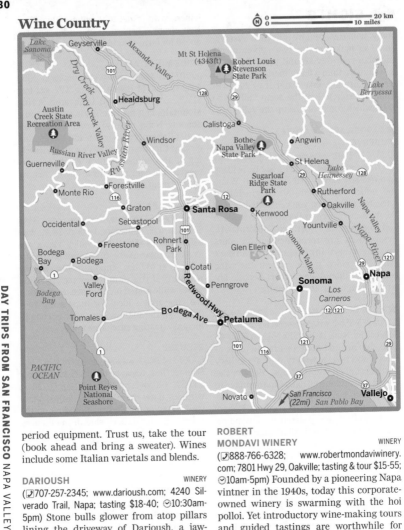

period equipment. Trust us, take the tour (book ahead and bring a sweater). Wines include some Italian varietals and blends.

DARIOUSH   WINERY
(☎707-257-2345; www.darioush.com; 4240 Silverado Trail, Napa; tasting $18-40; ☺10:30am-5pm) Stone bulls glower from atop pillars lining the driveway of Darioush, a jaw-dropping, over-the-top winery styled after the ancient Persian temples of Persepolis. It's known for monumental Shiraz, Cabernet Sauvignon, Merlot and Malbec.

CADE   WINERY
(☎707-965-2746; www.cadewinery.com; 360 Howell Mountain Rd S, Angwin; tastings $35-60; ☺by appointment) 🍃 Ascend Mt Veeder for drop-dead vistas and hawks riding thermals at Napa's oh-so-swank, first-ever all organically farmed, LEED gold-certified winery, partly owned by ex-SF mayor Gavin Newsom. Reservations required.

ROBERT MONDAVI WINERY   WINERY
(☎888-766-6328; www.robertmondaviwinery.com; 7801 Hwy 29, Oakville; tasting & tour $15-55; ☺10am-5pm) Founded by a pioneering Napa vintner in the 1940s, today this corporate-owned winery is swarming with the hoi polloi. Yet introductory wine-making tours and guided tastings are worthwhile for novices – make reservations.

ROBERT LOUIS STEVENSON STATE PARK   PARK
(☎707-942-4575; www.parks.ca.gov; Hwy 29; ☺sunrise-sunset) FREE The long-extinct volcanic cone of Mt St Helena marks Napa Valley's northern end at this undeveloped state park near Calistoga. It's a strenuous 5-mile climb to the summit (4343ft), but what a view – 200 miles all the way to Mt Shasta on a clear day. The much easier Table Rock Trail ends at drop-dead valley views; it's a 4-mile round-trip.

Check weather conditions before setting out. Temperatures are best from February through May, during wildflower season. Autumn is also pretty, when the vineyards change colors.

EATING

Napa Valley is an outpost of San Francisco's food scene – plan to have a lingering lunch or dinner mid-valley. Make reservations whenever possible; even on weekdays during winter, many restaurants sell out quickly. Most restaurants don't serve late – average Napa visitors get too drunk during the daytime to stay up for a 9pm table.

St Helena also has a haute **farmers market** (www.sthelenafarmersmkt.org; Crane Park, off Grayson Ave; ⊙7:30am-noon Fri May-Oct; ⊞).

OXBOW PUBLIC MARKET MARKET $
(☑707-226-6529; www.oxbowpublicmarket.com; 644 1st St, Napa; dishes from $3; ⊙9am-7pm Mon-Sat, 10am-5pm Sun) ⏀ Oxbow's gourmet marketplace showcases local, sustainably produced artisanal food, such as Hog Island oysters, rotisserie chicken and chicory Caesar salads from Kitchen Door, Model Bakery's baked goods and Three Twins certified-organic ice cream. Come hungry and plan to graze. Tuesday is locals night, with many discounts. Tuesday and Saturday mornings, there's a farmers market.

GOTT'S ROADSIDE AMERICAN $$
(☑707-963-3486; http://gotts.com; 933 Main St, St Helena; dishes $3-14; ⊙7am-9pm, to 10pm May-Sep; ⊞) Wiggle your toes in the grass at this 1950s drive-in diner with modern 21st-century sensibilities: burgers are all-natural beef, organic chicken or sushi-grade tuna, with chili-dusted sweet-potato fries and thick handmade milkshakes on the side. To avoid hunger-inducing waits, avoid peak meal times or call ahead for takeout and beat the line. There's another branch at downtown Napa's Oxbow Public Market.

BOUNTY HUNTER WINE BAR & SMOKIN' BBQ BARBECUE $$
(☑707-226-3976; www.bountyhunterwinebar.com; 975 1st St, Napa; dishes $4-24; ⊙11am-10pm Sun-Thu, to midnight Fri & Sat; ⊞) With pressed-tin ceilings and trophy heads on the walls, Bounty Hunter evinces an Old

---

CALISTOGA'S MUD-BATH SPAS

Celebrated 19th-century author Robert Louis Stevenson said of Calistoga, 'the whole neighborhood of Mt St Helena is full of sulfur and boiling springs... Calistoga itself seems to repose on a mere film above a boiling, subterranean lake.'

Indeed, it does. Calistoga is synonymous with the mineral water bearing its name, bottled here since 1924. Its springs and geysers have earned it the nickname the 'hot springs of the West.'

The town itself is famous for its old-time spas and mud-bath emporiums, where you're buried like a tree root in hot mud, made with volcanic ash from nearby Mt St Helena. Afterward you'll soak in a tub filled with clear, hot mineral water, then step into a steam room and later take a catnap while wrapped in blankets.

The first-choice classic is serene **Indian Springs Spa** (☑707-942-4913; www.indianspringscalistoga.com; 1712 Lincoln Ave, Calistoga; ⊙by appointment 9am-8pm), which mines its own volcanic ash. Mud baths ($85) include access to a giant spring-fed swimming pool (pack a swimsuit).

Vintage 1950s **Dr Wilkinson's Hot Springs Resort** (☑707-942-4102; www.drwilkinson.com; 1507 Lincoln Ave, Calistoga; ⊙by appointment 8:30am-3:45pm) uses more peat moss for lighter mud baths ($89). Tiny, garden-filled **Lavender Hill Spa** (☑800-528-4772, 707-942-4495; http://lavenderhillspa.com; 1015 Foothill Blvd, Calistoga; ⊙by appointment 9am-9pm Thu-Mon, to 7pm Tue & Wed) offers even lighter lavender-infused mud baths ($89).

Ultra-contemporary **Spa Solage** (☑707-226-0825; www.solagecalistoga.com/spa; 755 Silverado Trail, Calistoga; ⊙by appointment 8am-8pm) is the chic choice for DIY paint-on mud treatments ($98), including an optional soak before or afterward in a co-ed mineral-springs pool (swimwear required). Ask about private experiences for couples.

ℹ️ ALTERNATIVES TO DRIVING IN NAPA VALLEY

Calistoga Bike Shop (📞707-942-9687; www.calistogabikeshop.com; 1318 Lincoln Ave, Calistoga) Extensive selection of rental bikes (from $35 a day) at the valley's quiet northern end. Also organizes self-guided tours ($89) that include free tastings and wine pickup. Reservations advised.

Getaway Adventures (📞800-499-2453, 707-568-3040; http://getawayadventures.com; tours $149) Offers 'Sip-n-Cycle' tours around Calistoga and Carneros, including a picnic lunch at a winery. Reservations required.

Napa Valley Adventure Tours (📞707-259-1833, 707-224-9080; www.napavalley adventuretours.com; 1147 1st St, Napa) Wine-tasting bicycle trips ($95 to $170) with lunch starting from Napa, Carneros and St Helena. Also rents bikes (from $35 a day). Reservations essential.

Napa River Velo (📞707-258-8729; www.naparivervelo.com; 680 Main St, Napa) Pro bike shop in downtown Napa rents hybrid, road, mountain and tandem bicycles ($40 to $85 per day).

Napa Valley Wine Train (📞800-427-4124, 707-253-2111; www.winetrain.com; 1275 McKinstry St, Napa; tours $99-205) Cushy, touristy three-hour train trips on a historic rail line through the valley, with an optional stop at a winery.

West vibe, a fitting backdrop for superb 'cue, made with house-smoked meats and whole chickens roasted over cans of beer. It's great for a no-fuss meal in downtown Napa, with dozens of wines, whiskeys and tequila by the glass.

⭐ FRENCH LAUNDRY   CALIFORNIAN $$$
(📞707-944-2380; www.frenchlaundry.com; 6640 Washington St, Yountville; prix-fixe dinner $270; ⏱seatings 11am-1pm Fri-Sun, 5:30pm-9:15pm daily) A high-wattage culinary experience on par with the world's best, Thomas Keller's French Laundry is ideal for marking lifetime achievements – a 40th birthday, say, or a Nobel Prize. Book exactly two months (to the day) ahead: call at 10am sharp, or log onto www.opentable.com at precisely midnight. If you can't score a reservation, console yourself at Keller's nearby note-perfect French bistro, **Bouchon** (📞707-944-8037; www.bouchonbistro.com; 6354 Washington St, Yountville; mains $18-45; ⏱11am-midnight Mon-Fri, from 10am Sat & Sun), which is (much) easier to book, or with phenomenal pastries at next-door **Bouchon Bakery** (📞707-944-2253; http://bouchonbakery.com; 6528 Washington St, Yountville; items from $3; ⏱7am-7pm).

AD HOC   CALIFORNIAN $$$
(📞707-944-2487; www.adhocrestaurant.com; 6476 Washington St, Yountville; prix-fixe dinner from $52; ⏱5-10pm Wed-Sun, also 10am-1pm Sun) Don't bother asking for a menu at Thomas Keller's innovative comfort-food restaurant,

where chefs concoct a daily four-course, market-driven menu. No substitutions (unless you mention dietary restrictions), but none are needed – every dish is garden-fresh and spot-on. Monday's fried-chicken night has a religious following; book ahead. Pick up gourmet seasonal lunches to go at next-door **Addendum** (www.adhocrestaurant.com/addendum; box lunch $16.50; ⏱11am-2pm Thu-Sat Mar-Oct; 🚲).

WINE SPECTATOR
GREYSTONE RESTAURANT   CALIFORNIAN $$$
(📞707-967-1010; www.ciarestaurants.com; 2555 Main St, St Helena; dinner mains $22-34; ⏱11:30am-2:30pm & 5-9pm Mon-Fri, 11:30am-9pm Sat, noon-7:15pm Sun; 🐟) An imposing 1889 stone chateau houses the Culinary Institute of America's fine-dining restaurant, casual bakery-cafe and a gadget-filled cooking shop. Book ahead for dinner in the restaurant, where a seasonally changing New American menu might dish lamb carpaccio, brown-butter ricotta ravioli and blood-orange sorbet. Popular weekend cooking demos and wine-tasting classes.

BISTRO DON GIOVANNI   ITALIAN $$$
(📞707-224-3300; www.bistrodongiovanni.com; 4110 Howard Ln, Napa; mains $14-39; ⏱11:30am-10pm Sun-Thu, to 11pm Fri & Sat) Often winning locals' vote for their favorite Hwy 29 roadhouse, this Italian ristorante dishes modern pastas, wood-roasted fish and meats, and crispy pizzas topped with heirloom

tomatoes and imported cheeses. Reservations are essential, especially on weekends, which get pretty packed and loud. Good luck getting a patio table!

 **SLEEPING**

If you can't swing the rates in Napa, consider suburban Vallejo, 15 miles south of downtown Napa, where less expensive motels and chain hotels line the I-80 Fwy.

CHABLIS INN   MOTEL $$

(☑707-257-1944; www.chablisinn.com; 3360 Solano Ave, Napa; r $105-179; ❋@🛜🏊) A multistory motel on Napa's suburban strip off Hwy 29, here the crisp, modern and reasonably spacious rooms don't cut any corners – some even have jetted tubs for couples.

EUROSPA & INN   MOTEL $$

(☑707-942-6829; www.eurospa.com; 1202 Pine St, Calistoga; r incl breakfast $145-195; ❋🛜🏊) Immaculate single-story motel on a quiet side street in Calistoga has just 13 rooms, some with gas-burning fireplaces and two-person whirlpool tubs. Skip the on-site spa.

CALISTOGA INN   INN $$

(☑707-942-4101; www.calistogainn.com; 1250 Lincoln Ave, Calistoga; r with shared bath incl breakfast $119-149; 🛜) Downtown Calistoga's newly renovated turn-of-the-20th-century inn is upstairs from a lively brewery-restaurant (bring earplugs). Most rooms have one queen bed. No TVs.

★INDIAN SPRINGS RESORT   RESORT $$$

(☑707-942-4913; www.indianspringscalistoga. com; 1712 Lincoln Ave, Calistoga; r/cottage from $199/229; ❋@🛜🏊) At Calistoga's finest mineral-springs resort, historic bungalows face a central lawn with palm trees, shuffleboard, bocce, hammocks and BBQ grills. Two dozen rooms inhabit the restored 1930s Spanish-style lodge, a short walk from the soothing spa and two naturally heated swimming pools.

ANDAZ NAPA   HOTEL $$$

(☑707-687-1234; http://andaznapa.com; 1450 1st St, Napa; r from $269; ❋@🛜) Downtown Napa's newest lodgings feel like a big-city hotel, where business-class rooms are styled with chocolate-leather headboards, walk-in waterfall showers and plush rugs. Mingle at complimentary evening wine tastings.

Sonoma Valley

Explore

There are three Sonomas: the town, valley and county. Think of them as Russian dolls.

Anchoring the bucolic 17-mile-long Sonoma Valley, the town of Sonoma makes a great jumping-off point for exploring Wine Country. Its 19th-century buildings surround Sonoma Plaza, California's largest town square. Halfway up the valley, tiny Glen Ellen is like a Norman Rockwell painting come to life – in stark contrast to the suburban sprawl of Santa Rosa.

The Sonoma Hwy (Hwy 12) runs all the way through Sonoma Valley, passing wineries especially revered for Zinfandel and Syrah, before turning west at Santa Rosa toward Sebastopol, south of the Russian River. Running parallel up Sonoma Valley's west side to Glen Ellen, Arnold Dr has less traffic than Hwy 12, but fewer wineries.

The Best...

➡ **Sight** Sonoma Plaza (p234)
➡ **Place to Eat** Cafe La Haye (p237)
➡ **Place to Drink** Bartholomew Park Winery (p235)

Top Tip

If you're not up for driving, hit downtown Sonoma and the tasting rooms around tree-shaded Sonoma Plaza, where it's legal to drink wine on the grass after 11am.

Getting There & Away

➡ **Car** From San Francisco to downtown Sonoma (about one hour), take Hwy 101 north to Hwy 37 east. At the Hwy 37/121 split, take Hwy 121 north, then Hwy 12 north.

DAY TRIPS FROM SAN FRANCISCO SONOMA VALLEY

TRAFFIC ALERT

Hwys 121 and 37 pass by Sonoma Raceway, which on major auto-racing event days causes huge traffic backups lasting for miles. Check the calendar at www.racesonoma.com. If there's a race, take Hwy 101 north to Santa Rosa instead, then drop back down Hwy 12 south into Sonoma Valley.

WORTH A DETOUR

POINT REYES NATIONAL SEASHORE

On an entirely different tectonic plate from California's mainland, the windswept peninsula of Point Reyes juts 10 miles out to sea and lures marine mammals, migratory birds and whale-watching tourists. It enfolds 110 sq miles of pristine ocean beaches, sand dunes, lagoons and wind-tousled ridges. Bring warm clothing, as even the sunniest days can quickly turn cold and foggy.

Though it may seem counter-intuitive, winter is the best season to visit for wildlife-spotting – whales breaching offshore, elephant seals giving birth and birds alighting everywhere. Miles of hiking trails crisscross the peninsula, some leading to hidden beaches. The beaches on the peninsula's western side get hammered by powerful surf and aren't safe for swimming – never turn your back on the ocean.

A mile west of Olema, orient yourself at **Bear Valley Visitor Center** (☑415-464-5100; www.nps.gov/pore; ⊙10am-5pm Mon-Fri, from 9am Sat & Sun), then traipse the short Earthquake Trail outside. Another easy walk leads to a reproduction Miwok village. Off Limantour Rd, you can trek atop ocean bluffs past grazing herds of tule elk for nearly 5 miles each way to Tomales Point, separating Tomales Bay from the Pacific. To paddle a kayak out into the bay, make reservations with **Blue Waters Kayaking** (☑415-669-2600; www.bwkayak.com; rentals/tours from $50/70; ▣).

Crowning the peninsula's westernmost tip, **Point Reyes Lighthouse** (end of Sir Francis Drake Blvd; ⊙2:30pm-4pm Thu-Mon, weather permitting) **FREE** is buffeted by ferocious winds. It sits 600ft below the headlands, down 308 steps, so that its light can shine below the fog that usually blankets the point. On weekends and holidays between late December and mid-April, all visitors must ride the shuttle bus from Drakes Beach to reach the lighthouse and **Chimney Rock**, where you can spy on a braying elephant-seal colony and migratory gray whales. Buy seasonal shuttle tickets (adult/child $5/free) at oceanview **Kenneth C Patrick Visitor Center** (☑415-669-1250; www.nps.gov/pore; Drakes Beach Rd; ⊙usually 10am-5pm Sat, Sun & hol).

Two miles north of Olema, the tiny town of **Point Reyes Station** has cozy bakeries and cafes, a roadside diner and upscale restaurants. Gather a picnic lunch at **Tomales Bay Foods & Cowgirl Creamery** (www.cowgirlcreamery.com; 80 4th St; sandwiches $6-12; ⊙10am-6pm Wed-Sun; ▣) ⬤ or warm yourself with handmade, seasonal Cal-Italian cuisine at **Osteria Stellina** (☑415-663-9988; http://osteriastellina.com; 11285 Hwy 1; mains $14-24; ⊙11:30am-2:30pm & 5-9pm; ▣) ⬤.

The entrance to Point Reyes National Seashore is just over 30 miles northwest of San Francisco, at least an hour's drive without traffic.

➤**Bus** Service is infrequent and slow; call for trip-planning assistance. From San Francisco, take **Golden Gate Transit** (☑415-455-2000, 511; http://goldengate.org) buses to Santa Rosa ($10.75, two to three hours), then catch **Sonoma County Transit** (☑800-345-7433, 707-576-7433; www.sctransit.com) buses to downtown Sonoma ($3.50, 70 minutes) via Sonoma Valley towns.

Need to Know
➤**Area Code** 707
➤**Location** 45 miles north–northeast of San Francisco
➤**Tourist office** (☑866-996-1090, 707-996-1090; www.sonomavalley.com; 453 1st St E; ⊙9am-5pm Mon-Sat, from 10am Sun)

◉ SIGHTS

More laid-back and less commercial than Napa, Sonoma Valley shelters over 70 wineries alongside Hwy 12 – and unlike Napa, most welcome picnicking. You don't usually need appointments to taste, but call ahead for tours. For vineyard picnics, bring your own food and buy a bottle of your host's wine – it's only polite.

SONOMA PLAZA   SQUARE
(btwn Napa, Spain & 1st Sts, Sonoma) Century-old trees cast sun-dappled shade on the plaza, a great spot for a picnic with a bottle of Sonoma Valley wine. Historic buildings line the plaza's north side. Smack in the center, the Mission Revival-style **City Hall** (1908) has identical facades

on four sides, reportedly because plaza business owners all demanded it face their direction.

SONOMA STATE
HISTORIC PARK   HISTORIC SITE
(☑707-938-9560; www.parks.ca.gov; adult/child $3/2; ☺10am-5pm) Glimpse early California history at **Mission Solano San Francisco** (114 E Spain St, Sonoma; ☺tours 11am-2pm Fri-Sun). Founded in 1823, it once covered 10,000 acres, farmed by nearly 1000 conscripted Native Californian workers. The E Spain St wing remains largely intact, with a reconstructed chapel. Nearby at the **Adobe Barracks** (20 E Spain St, Sonoma), Sonoma settlers surprised Mexican soldiers in 1850 by declaring the independent Bear Flag Republic.

Also part of the park, the **Toscano Hotel** (20 E Spain St, Sonoma; ☺tours 1pm-4pm Sat-Mon) opened as a store and library in 1851, later becoming travelers' lodgings. Peek into the lobby – except for the traffic outside, you'd swear you've stepped back in time.

GUNDLACH-BUNDSCHU WINERY   WINERY
(☑707-939-3015; www.gunbun.com; 2000 Denmark St, Sonoma; tasting $10, incl tour $20-50; ☺11am-4:30pm, to 5:30pm Jun-mid-Oct) ✐ Down a winding country road that beckons to cyclists, 'Gun-Bun' is one of Sonoma's oldest and prettiest wineries. Founded in 1858 by Bavarian immigrant Jacob Gundlach, it looks just like a storybook castle. Perched above tidy rows of grapevines and a reclaimed-water lake, the solar-powered winery produces legendary Tempranillo and signature Gewürztraminer. Make reservations for farm and vineyard tours.

★BARTHOLOMEW PARK WINERY   WINERY
(☑707-939-3024; www.bartpark.com; 1000 Vineyard Lane, Sonoma; tasting $10, incl tour $20; ☺11am-4:30pm) ✐ Inside a 400-acre nature preserve perfect for picnicking, these family-owned vineyards were first cultivated in 1857. Now organic-certified, they yield citrusy Sauvignon Blanc and smoky-midnight Merlot. After tasting, peruse the tiny historical museum or go for a walk among wildflower fields on three miles of hiking trails. Weekend tours require reservations. 'Bart Park' is a great bike-to destination.

KUNDE   WINERY
(☑707-833-5501; www.kunde.com; 9825 Hwy 12, Kenwood; tasting & tour $10-40; ☺10:30am-

5pm) ✐ Let your spirit be uplifted at this hillside estate winery, where 20 varietals of sustainably grown grapes are harvested in small batches, then transformed into premium wines aged in volcanic lava-rock caves. Lemon-zest Sauvignon Blanc, berry Zinfandel and chocolate-noted Cabernet Sauvignon are award winners. Book ahead for mountaintop tastings, vineyard tours and guided hikes.

JACK LONDON
STATE HISTORIC PARK   PARK
(☑707-938-5216;   www.jacklondonpark.com; 2400 London Ranch Rd, Glen Ellen; per car $8, tour adult/child $4/2; ☺9:30am-5pm Thu-Mon) Off Hwy 12, obey the call of the wild where adventure-novelist Jack London built his dream house – it burned down on the eve of completion in 1913. Tour the original writer's cottage or browse memorabilia inside the small **museum** standing in a redwood grove. Twenty miles of hiking and mountain-biking trails weave through the park's 1400 rural hilltop acres.

CORNERSTONE SONOMA   GARDEN
(☑707-933-3010; www.cornerstonegardens.com; 23570 Arnold Dr, Hwy 121, Sonoma; ☺10am-4pm; 🐾) **FREE** There's nothing traditional about this tapestry of gardens, which showcase the work of 25 avant-garde landscape designers. Kids can run around while you explore garden shops, sip wine at tasting rooms, play bocce by the market cafe or gather winery maps at the satellite **Sonoma Valley Visitors Center** (☑866-996-1090, 707-996-1090; www.sonomavalley.com; ☺10am-4pm). To get here, turn at the giant oversized blue chair.

KAZ WINERY   WINERY
(☑707-833-2536; www.kazwinery.com; 233 Adobe Canyon Rd, Kenwood; tasting $5; ☺11am-5pm Fri-Mon, by appointment Tue-Thu; 🐾🍷) ✐ Veer off Hwy 12 to Sonoma's in-the-know local fave. Always crazy-fun, Kaz pours organically grown wines and ports at a wooden barrel-top tasting bar inside a barn. Discover lesser-known varietals like Alicante Bouschet and Lenoir. Kids get Play-Doh, grape juice and a playground, while adults sift through vinyl LPs and pop them on the turntable.

CLINE CELLARS   WINERY
(☑800-546-2070,   707-940-4030;   www.cline cellars.com; 24737 Arnold Dr, Sonoma; tasting

free, tours $20-40; ⊘tasting room 10am-6pm, museum 10am-4pm, tours 11am, 1pm & 3pm) 🅿 Balmy days are made for pond-side picnics, and rainy ones for fireside tastings of value-priced, old-vine Zinfandel and Mourvedre inside an 1850s farmhouse with rooftop solar panels. Stroll out back to the **museum**, housing 1930s miniature-scale replicas of California's original 21 Spanish colonial missions.

BR COHN
WINERY

(☑800-330-4064, 707-938-4064; www.brcohn. com; 15000 Sonoma Hwy, Glen Ellen; tasting $10; ⊘10am-5pm) Picnic like a rock star at BR Cohn. Its founder Bruce Cohn managed '70s superband the Doobie Brothers before moving on to make organic olive oils and crowd-pleasing, if high-priced, wines – including gold-medal Chardonnay and Cabernet Sauvignon.

BENZIGER
WINERY

(☑707-935-4527, 888-490-2739; www.benziger. com; 1883 London Ranch Rd, Glen Ellen; tasting $10-20, tram tour adult/child $20/5; ⊘10am-5pm, tram tours 11:30am-3:30pm weather permitting; ♿) 🅿 Pastoral, biodynamic Benziger gives newbies an excellent crash course in winemaking with its open-air tram tour (reservations recommended) of biodynamic vineyards, the crush pad and barrel caves, with mass-market wine tasting afterward.

WELLINGTON
WINERY

(☑800-816-9463; www.wellingtonvineyards. com; 11600 Dunbar Rd, Glen Ellen; tastings $5; ⊘10:30am-4:30pm) 🅿 West of Hwy 12, some of Sonoma Valley's best buys await at low-key Wellington, where the under-$30 wines include unusual white port and peppery Zinfandels produced by century-old vines that miraculously survived Prohibition.

BEYOND SONOMA VALLEY

Even more stand-out wineries await in other corners of Sonoma County. West of Hwy 101 and Santa Rosa, the woodsy Russian River Valley is home to prized Pinot Noir grapes. Further north on Hwy 101, well-heeled Healdsburg is the gateway to down-to-earth Dry Creek and Alexander Valley vineyards, which craft earthy Zinfandel and Cabernet Sauvignon, respectively.

RAVENSWOOD WINERY
WINERY

(☑707-933-2332; www.ravenswoodwinery.com; 18701 Gehricke Rd, Sonoma; tasting $10, incl tour $15; ⊘10am-4:30pm) With the slogan 'no wimpy wines,' this buzzing hilltop tasting room that's always hectic pours a full slate of estate-grown, single-vineyard and vintner's blend Zinfandels. Wine newbies welcome. Tour reservations requested.

🍴 EATING

SONOMA MARKET
DELI, MARKET $

(☑707-996-3411; www.sonoma-glenellenmkt. com; 500 W Napa St, Sonoma; sandwiches from $6; ⊘6am-10pm) Superior grocery store, bakery and deli makes hot-pressed panini and picnic fixings like Sonoma cheeses, California olives, alongside a hot-and-cold salad bar. Also in **Glen Ellen** (13751 Arnold Dr, Glen Ellen; ⊘6am-8pm).

FREMONT DINER
AMERICAN $$

(☑707-938-7370; http://thefremontdiner.com; 2698 Fremont Dr, Sonoma; breakfast & lunch mains $6-14; ⊘8am-3pm Mon-Wed, to 9pm Thu-Sun; ♿) 🅿 Lines snake out the door on weekends at this farm-to-table roadside diner with Southern flavor. When the sun shines, nab an outdoor picnic table and wolf down ricotta pancakes, fried chicken and waffles, oyster po' boys and savory BBQ pulled-pork sandwiches. Arrive early to avoid waiting.

FIG CAFE & WINEBAR
FRENCH $$

(☑707-938-2130; www.thefigcafe.com; 13690 Arnold Dr, Glen Ellen; mains $10-20; ⊘10am-3pm Sat & Sun, 5:30pm-9pm daily) For Californian twists on country French comfort food – imagine organic salads, steamed mussels, butcher's steak and duck cassoulet – visit this convivial brasserie in Glen Ellen village. No reservations or corkage fee on BYOB wine. Book ahead for its more famous sister bistro, **The Girl & the Fig** (☑707-938-3634; www.thegirlandthefig.com; 11 W Spain St, Sonoma; mains $15-25; ⊘11:30am-10pm Mon-Thu, to 11pm Fri, 11am-11pm Sat, 10am-10pm Sun), in downtown Sonoma.

RED GRAPE
ITALIAN $$

(☑707-996-4103; http://theredgrape.com; 529 1st St W, Sonoma; mains $10-20; ⊘11:30am-10pm; ♿) Step inside a sunlight-filled pizzeria for

WORTH A DETOUR

HWY 1 SOUTH TO SANTA CRUZ

The 70 miles of coastal Hwy 1 unspooling south of San Francisco are bordered by craggy beaches, sea-salted lighthouses, organic farm stands and tiny towns. Make time for beckoning vista points to spot migratory whales breaching offshore in winter or kitesurfers skimming waves like giant mosquitoes. Half Moon Bay is an easy day trip from the city, but the money shots lie further south toward Santa Cruz.

The beauty prize-winning beaches begin less than 10 miles south of San Francisco in **Pacifica**, past the gargantuan Devil's Slide Tunnels. About 5 miles south of town, **Montara State Beach** (www.parks.ca.gov; ⏲8am-sunset) FREE is a local favorite for its pristine sand. Further south along Hwy 1 at Moss Beach, **Fitzgerald Marine Reserve** (www.fitzgeraldreserve.org; end of California Ave; ⏲8am-sunset; 👪) FREE protects tide pools teeming with sea life, best viewed at low tide.

Next up is 4-mile-long, crescent-shaped **Half Moon Bay State Beach** (www.parks.ca.gov; per car $10; 👪). Turn off at **Pillar Point Harbor** and climb the sand dunes above **Mavericks** surf break, where in winter death-defying surfers ride 40ft-plus swells past rocky cliffs. When the bay is calm, get out on the water with **Half Moon Bay Kayak Co** (☎650-773-6101; www.hmbkayak.com; Pillar Point Harbor; kayak rentals/tours from $25/75). Half Moon Bay's tastiest seafood shack is **Flying Fish Grill** (☎650-712-1125; www.flyingfishgrill.net; 211 San Mateo Rd; dishes $5-17; ⏲11am-8:30pm Wed-Mon; 👪), off Hwy 92, not far from downtown's quaint Main St.

Fifteen miles further south, **Pescadero State Beach** (www.parks.ca.gov; per car $8; ⏲8am-sunset) attracts beachcombers and birders to its marshy nature preserve. Detour a few miles inland to Pescadero village for bakery-deli **Arcangeli Grocery Co** (www.normsmarket.com; 287 Stage Rd; ⏲10am-6pm) and family-owned **Harley Farms Cheese Shop** (☎650-879-0480; www.harleyfarms.com; 250 North St; ⏲10am-5pm Thu-Sun; 👪) 🍃, which offers goat-dairy farm tours by reservation.

Five miles south of the Pescadero turn-off, **Pigeon Point Lighthouse** stands on a windswept coastal perch off Hwy 1. Another 5 miles south, **Año Nuevo State Park** (☎tour reservations 800-444-4445; www.parks.ca.gov; entry per car $10, tour per person $7; ⏲8:30am-5pm, last entry 3:30pm Apr-Aug, to 4pm, last entry 3pm Sep-Nov, tours only mid-Dec–Mar) is home to the world's largest colony of northern elephant seals. Call ahead to reserve space on a 2½-hour, 3-mile guided walking tour during the cacophonous winter birthing and mating season.

It's 20 more miles south to countercultural **Santa Cruz**, famous for its beaches, surf scene, university and radical activists. Head directly to the **Santa Cruz Beach Boardwalk** (☎831-423-5590; www.beachboardwalk.com; 400 Beach St; rides $3-6, all-day pass $32; ⏲daily late May-early Sep, off-season hr vary; 👪), the West Coast's oldest beachfront amusement park. The neighboring **municipal wharf** is stuffed with take-out seafood counters, or grab a bite at the **Picnic Basket** (http://thepicnicbasketsc.com; 125 Beach St; items $3-8; ⏲7am-9pm, shorter off-season hr; 👪) across the street.

Head west along West Cliff Dr to **Lighthouse Point**, which overlooks **Steamers Lane** surf break, and the lighthouse's tiny **surfing museum** (www.santacruzsurfingmuseum.org; 701 W Cliff Dr; admission by donation; ⏲10am-5pm Wed-Mon Jul 4-early Sep, noon-4pm Thu-Mon early Sep-Jul 3). Best for sunsets, tide pools and roosting monarch butterflies in winter, **Natural Bridges State Beach** (www.parks.ca.gov; 2531 W Cliff Dr; per car $10; ⏲8am-sunset) awaits at the end of West Cliff Dr, 3 miles from the wharf.

Downtown Santa Cruz buzzes along **Pacific Ave**, where eclectic cafes and unique boutiques draw a wacky mix of characters.

thin-crust pies topped with local cheeses and cured meats, lunchtime panini sandwiches, or fresh, handmade pastas for dinner, plus small-production Sonoma wines by the glass or bottle.

★**CAFE LA HAYE** CALIFORNIAN $$$
(☎707-935-5994; www.cafelahaye.com; 140 E Napa St, Sonoma; mains $20-30; ⏲5:30pm-9pm Tue-Sat) 🍃 It's still downtown Sonoma's top pick for earthy New American cooking,

made with produce sourced from within 60 miles. The charmingly tiny dining room is cheek-by-jowl and service borders on perfunctory, but the clean simplicity and flavor-packed cooking make it many foodies' first choice. Reserve far ahead.

ZAZU RESTAURANT & FARM   CALIFORNIAN **$$$**
(☏707-523-4814; www.zazurestaurant.com; 3535 Guerneville Rd, Santa Rosa; dinner mains $20-30; ☺5:30pm-8:30pm Wed-Sun, also 9am-2pm Sun) ✐ West of Hwy 101, this farm-to-table roadhouse that raises its own chickens serves organic veggies from the back garden, house-made black pig salumi and warm, honey-drizzled Sonoma County cheeses. From late May through October, ask about discounted prix-fixe dinners on Monday nights. Make reservations.

EL DORADO KITCHEN   CALIFORNIAN **$$$**
(☏707-996-3030; www.eldoradosonoma.com; 405 1st St W, Sonoma; mains lunch $12-18, dinner $19-31; ☺8am-11am daily, 11:30am-9:30pm Sun-Thu, to 10pm Fri & Sat) ✐ Biodynamic salads, braised pork-belly sandwiches with smoked tomato aioli, housemade lemon-ricotta ravioli and roasted Petaluma chicken are among the ravishing dishes coming from this ultra-modern exhibition kitchen. In summer, dine under the stars in the courtyard. Reservations recommended.

🏃 SPORTS & ACTIVITIES

WINE COUNTRY CYCLERY   BICYCLING
(☏707-966-6800; www.winecountrycyclery.com; 262 W Napa St, Sonoma) The town of Sonoma is ideal for biking – not too hilly – and multiple wineries are within easy reach of downtown. Book ahead for bicycle rentals (from $30 a day), especially on weekends and holidays.

🛌 SLEEPING

At the valley's northern end, Santa Rosa has more affordable motels near Hwy 101. So does Petaluma, off Hwy 101 west of Sonoma town.

SONOMA HOTEL   HISTORIC HOTEL **$$**
(☏800-468-6016, 707-996-2996; www.sonomahotel.com; 110 W Spain St, Sonoma; r incl breakfast $115-240) Old-fashioned rooms squeeze together inside this 19th-century landmark on bustling Sonoma Plaza. There's a two-night minimum stay on most weekends. No elevator or parking lot.

BEST WESTERN SONOMA VALLEY INN   MOTEL **$$**
(☏800-334-5784, 707-938-9200; www.sonomavalleyinn.com; 550 2nd St W, Sonoma; r from $150; ✳@🛜🐕🐾) ✐ Don't let the chain-gang name fool you: this deluxe motel just two blocks from Sonoma Plaza has a saltwater swimming pool, hot tub and sauna. Big rooms come with eco-friendly bath goodies and most have gas-burning fireplaces.

GAIGE HOUSE INN   B&B **$$$**
(☏800-935-0237, 707-935-0237; www.gaige.com; 13540 Arnold Dr, Glen Ellen; d incl breakfast from $275; 🛜🐕🐾) Nearby vineyards, Asian-chic rooms and fireplace suites adorn the historic main house, with pebbled meditation courtyards waiting outside by the pool. Socialize over the breakfast buffet and at evening wine-and-cheese receptions.

BELTANE RANCH   B&B **$$$**
(☏707-996-6501; www.beltaneranch.com; 11775 Hwy 12, Glen Ellen; d incl breakfast $150-265; 🛜) Surrounded by horse pastures, this cheerful, lemon-yellow 1890 ranch house has wide porches dotted with swings and wicker chairs. The five peaceful B&B rooms and private garden cottage are phone- and TV-free.

Sleeping

San Francisco is the birthplace of the boutique hotel. You'll find standard-issue chains with basic comforts, four-stars with upmarket amenities and five-stars with top-flight luxuries, but it's the little places that stand out – elegant Victorians on neighborhood side streets, artsy downtowners with intimate bars and cozy inns that smell of freshly baked cookies.

When to Book

Travelers often only consider the cost of an airline ticket when deciding when to travel, but we highly recommend you first confirm the availability of good hotel rates before booking flights. 'City-wide sellouts' happen several times a year when there's a big convention or event in town. To help choose dates, check the **SF Convention & Visitors Bureau** (www.sanfrancisco.travel/meeting-planners) convention calendar, which shows the expected bed count each convention requires. The city has 33,600 total rooms; if the calendar says a convention (such as Oracle) will require over 10,000 beds, choose other dates or expect to pay a premium – sometimes double or even triple the normal rates.

Room Rates & Fees

San Francisco is in a boom cycle – this is the epicenter of tech and the whole world wants to be here. There simply aren't enough beds. Since this book's last edition, prices at many downtown hotels have jumped 20% to 30%. Day-to-day rates fluctuate wildly. Prices in this chapter reflect the average cost of a basic double room, April to October, excluding city-wide sellout periods when hotels charge 'compression rates' – a handy term when negotiating with hotels.

To get the best prices at chains, rates at which fluctuate daily, call the hotel during business hours and speak with in-house reservations, rather than toll-free central reservations, for up-to-date information about inventories and specials. Some hotels have internet-only deals, but when booking online, know that 'best rate' does not necessarily mean lowest-available rate. When in doubt, call the hotel directly. Online booking engines (eg Priceline) offer lower rates but have many restrictions and may be non-refundable.

Although hostels and budget hotels are cheapest, rooms are never truly cheap in SF: expect $80 for a private hostel room, $120 for a budget motel and $150+ for midrange hotels. Note the hefty 16% room tax on top of quoted rates. Most hotels offer free wi-fi (only luxury hotels charge, claiming it's for secured lines). Prices run higher June to August and plummet from November to April. Ask about weekly rates. On weekends and holidays, rates for business and luxury hotels decrease but increase for tourist hotels; weekdays the opposite is true.

Hotels vs Boutique Hotels

When we say 'boutique hotel,' we're referring to mid- and upmarket hotels with fewer than 100 rooms, unique decor and/or service and amenities distinguishing them from cookie-cutter chains or simpler small hotels. Luxury hotels are their own class, too big to be boutique. Some stylish hotels fall between chain and boutique; we label them 'design hotels.' Charming small hotels that serve breakfast are B&Bs; otherwise we just call them 'small hotels' if they lack the high style of a real boutique.

NEED TO KNOW

Prices
Rates quoted here are for double rooms, with bath, in high season (summer); you can sometimes do better, except when there's a convention.

$ under $100
$$ $100–200
$$$ more than $200

Parking
Hotel parking costs $35 to $50 per night extra. When there's a *free* self-service lot, we've included the parking symbol. Hotels without parking often have valet parking or an agreement with a nearby garage; call ahead.

Reconfirming
If you're arriving after 4pm, guarantee with a credit card or your reservation may be cancelled.

Tipping
Tipping housekeepers in US hotels is standard practice; leave a couple of dollars on your pillow each morning and be guaranteed excellent housekeeping.

Breakfast
Breakfast is not included in rates unless specified.

What's a Double?
In the US, a double room means accommodations for two people in one bed. If you want two beds in one room, specify this.

SLEEPING

Lonely Planet's Top Choices

Argonaut Hotel (p243) Nautical-themed hotel at Fisherman's Wharf.

Hotel Drisco (p250) Stately boutique hotel in civilized Pacific Heights.

Hotel Vitale (p247) Contemporary downtowner with knockout waterfront vistas.

Orchard Garden Hotel (p248) San Francisco's first all-green-practices hotel.

Hotel Bohème (p248) Artsy boutique charmer in the heart of North Beach.

Best by Budget

$
San Remo Hotel (p248) Spartan furnishings, shared baths, great rates.

Pacific Tradewinds Hostel (p248) Downtown hostel with snappy design.

Coventry Motor Inn (p242) Value-priced motel with big rooms.

HI San Francisco Fisherman's Wharf (p242) Waterfront hostel with amazing views.

Marina Inn (p242) Simple small hotel.

$$
Hotel Monaco (p243) Snazzy design, useful amenities, central location.

Hotel Carlton (p245) Freshly redesigned with good-value rooms.

Golden Gate Hotel (p250) Old-fashioned small hotel with resident cat.

Hotel Zetta (p244) Tech-centric downtowner full of art.

Steinhart Hotel & Apartments (p249) Good-value apartment hotel.

$$$
Mandarin Oriental (p246) Great service; knockout views.

W Hotel (p248) Party central for clubbing conventioneers.

Palace Hotel (p246) Stately hotel at century-old landmark.

Inn at the Presidio (p243) Small luxury inn surrounded by national-park land.

Argonaut Hotel (p243) Nautically themed hotel at Fisherman's Wharf.

Hotel Drisco (p250) Luxury hotel atop Pacific Heights.

Best for Kids

Hotel del Sol (p242) Colorful theme rooms, plus a heated outdoor pool.

Hotel Tomo (p249) Japantown hotel styled in splashy colors of Japanimé.

Seal Rock Inn (p252) Oceanfront family motel, far from the city center.

Argonaut Hotel (p243) The Wharf's best hotel, with a giant lobby to explore.

Americania Hotel (p247) Above-average motel with pool.

Best for Views

Mandarin Oriental (p246) Bridge-to-bridge views from a five-star skyscraper.

Sir Francis Drake (p247) Playful 1920s tower hotel above Union Square.

Mark Hopkins Intercontinental (p250) Nob Hill address for stately charm.

Fairmont San Francisco (p250) Hilltop vistas plus SF's grandest lobby.

Hotel Vitale (p247) Shagadelic with a Bay Bridge view.

Argonaut Hotel (p243) The Wharf's best, with fab bayfront vistas.

Where to Stay

Neighborhood	For	Against
The Marina, Fisherman's Wharf & the Piers	Near the northern waterfront; good for kids; lots of restaurants and nightlife at the Marina; many motels on Lombard St – with parking.	Fisherman's Wharf is all tourists; parking at the Marina and Wharf is a nightmare.
Downtown, Civic Center & SoMa	Biggest selection of hotels; near all public transportation, including cable cars; walkable to many sights, shopping and theaters. Parts of SoMa are close to major downtown sights; great nightlife and restaurants.	Downtown quiet at night; Civic Center feels rough – the worst area extends three blocks in all directions from Eddy and Jones Sts; parking is expensive.
North Beach & Chinatown	Culturally colorful; great strolling; lots of cafes and restaurants; terrific sense of place.	Street noise; limited choices and transport; next-to-impossible parking.
The Hills & Japantown	Stately, classic hotels atop Nob Hill; good nightlife and shopping in Japantown and Pacific Heights.	The Hills are steep, hard on the out-of-shape; parking difficult; slightly removed from major sights.
The Mission & Potrero Hill	Mission's flat terrain makes walking easier; good for biking; easy access to BART.	Limited choice; distance from sights; gritty street scene on main thoroughfares.
The Castro & Noe Valley	Great nightlife, especially for GLBT travelers; provides a good taste of local life; easy access to Market St transit.	Distance from major tourist sights; few choices; limited parking.
The Haight & Hayes Valley	Lots of bars and restaurants; Hayes Valley near cultural sights; the Haight near Golden Gate Park.	Limited public transportation in the Haight; gritty street scene at night on major thoroughfares; parking difficult.
Golden Gate Park & the Avenues	Quiet nights; good for outdoor recreation; easier parking.	Very far from major sights; foggy and cold in summer; limited transportation.

SLEEPING

🛏 The Marina, Fisherman's Wharf & the Piers

★ HI SAN FRANCISCO
FISHERMAN'S WHARF   HOSTEL $

Map p316 (☑415-771-7277; www.sfhostels.com; Bldg 240, Fort Mason; dm $30-40 incl breakfast, r $65-100; P @ 🛜; 🚌28, 30, 47, 49) Trading downtown convenience for a glorious park-like setting with million-dollar waterfront views, this hostel occupies a former army hospital building, with bargain-priced private rooms and dorms (some co-ed) with four to 22 beds (avoid bunk numbers 1 & 2 – they're by doorways). Huge kitchen. No curfew, but no heat during daytime: bring warm clothes. Limited free parking.

COVENTRY MOTOR INN   MOTEL $

Map p316 (☑415-567-1200; www.coventry motorinn.com; 1901 Lombard St; r $95-165; P ✳🛜; 🚌22, 28, 30, 43) Of the many motels lining Lombard St (Hwy 101), the generic Coventry has the highest quality-to-value ratio with spacious, well-maintained (if plain) rooms and extras like air-con (good for quiet sleeps) and covered parking. Parents: there's plenty of floor space to unpack kids' toys, but no pool.

MARINA INN   HOTEL $

Map p316 (☑800-274-1420, 415-928-1000; www. marinainn.com; 3110 Octavia St; r $89-119; 🛜; 🚌28, 30, 47, 49) An excellent value in the Marina, this vintage 1920s hotel has small, clean rooms with cabbage-rose decor, offering a cozier alternative to a motel. Single-pane glass means street noise; bring earplugs. Close to Union St shopping and bars.

TUSCAN INN   DESIGN HOTEL $$

Map p314 (☑800-648-4626, 415-561-1100; www. tuscaninn.com; 425 North Point St; r $169-299; ✳@🛜✖; 🚌47, 🚋Powell-Mason, Ⓜ F) 🖉 Staying at touristy Fisherman's Wharf doesn't mean you have to settle for plain-jane chains like Hilton. The Tuscan Inn – managed by fashion-forward Kimpton – is as comfortable but has way more character, with spacious rooms styled in jewel-tone colors and bold patterns. Kids love the in-room Nintendo; parents love the afternoon wine hour.

HOTEL DEL SOL   THEME MOTEL $$

Map p316 (☑877-433-5765, 415-921-5520; www. thehoteldelsol.com; 3100 Webster St; d $189-269; P ✳@🛜✖; 🚌22, 28, 30, 43) 🖉 The spiffy, kid-friendly Marina District del Sol is a riot of color, with tropical-themed decor. A quiet, revamped 1950s motor lodge with palm-lined central courtyard, it's one of the few San Francisco hotels with a heated outdoor pool. Family suites have trundle beds and board games. Free parking.

WHARF INN   MOTEL $$

Map p314 (☑800-548-9918, 415-673-7411; www. wharfinn.com; 2601 Mason St; r $179-259; P 🛜✖; 🚌47, 🚋Powell-Mason, ⓂF) This standard-issue, two-story motor lodge at the Wharf has clean, nothing-special rooms, ideal for kids who make messes. Some rooms are loud; bring earplugs. Rates fluctuate wildly with the tourist tide.

MARINA MOTEL   MOTEL $$

Map p316 (☑800-346-6118, 415-921-9406; www. marinamotel.com; 2576 Lombard St; r $139-199; P 🛜✖; 🚌28, 30, 41, 43, 45) Established in 1939 to accommodate visitors arriving via the new Golden Gate Bridge, the Marina has an inviting Spanish-Mediterranean look,

---

WEBSITES

Lonelyplanet.com (www.lonelyplanet.com/usa/san-francisco/hotels) For more accommodation reviews by Lonely Planet authors; you can also book online here.

Deal Angel (www.dealangel.com) Booking engine that compares lowest-rate deals.

Guest Mob (www.guestmob.com) Searches mid- to high-end hotels; eliminates opaque bookings; allows refunds.

HotelTonight (www.hoteltonight.com) Smartphone app for discount same-day bookings.

Kayak (www.kayak.com) Compares multiple booking sites.

with a quiet bougainvillea-lined courtyard. Rooms are homey, simple and well maintained (never mind occasional scuffs); some have full kitchens (extra $10–20). Rooms on Lombard St are loud; request one in back.

★ARGONAUT HOTEL   DESIGN HOTEL $$$
Map p314 (☎866-415-0704, 415-563-0800; www.argonauthotel.com; 495 Jefferson St; r $205-325, with view $305-550; ❋❂☎; ☐19, 47, 49, ☐Powell-Hyde) ☞ Fisherman's Wharf's top hotel was built as a cannery in 1908 and has century-old wooden beams and exposed brick walls. Rooms sport an over-the-top nautical theme, with porthole-shaped mirrors and plush, deep-blue carpets. Though all have the amenities of an upper-end hotel – ultra-comfy beds, iPod docks – some rooms are tiny with limited sunlight.

Pay extra for a mesmerizing bay view. Kids meet other kids in the big lobby.

INN AT THE PRESIDIO   HOTEL $$$
Map p318 (☎415-800-7356; www.innatthepresidio.com; 42 Moraga Ave; r incl breakfast $195-300, ste $300-350; ℗❂☎; ☐43; PresidiGo Shuttle) ☞ Built in 1903 as bachelor quarters for army officers, this three-story red-brick building in the Presidio was transformed in 2012 into a spiffy national-park lodge, styled with leather, linen and wood. Oversized rooms are plush, including feather beds with Egyptian-cotton sheets. Suites have fireplaces. Nature surrounds you, with hiking trailheads out back, but taxis downtown cost $25.

🛏 Downtown & Civic Center

HI SAN FRANCISCO DOWNTOWN   HOSTEL $
Map p320 (☎415-788-5604; www.sfhostels.com; 312 Mason St; dorm $39-45, r incl breakfast $89-135; @☎; Ⓜ Powell, Ⓑ Powell) Location, location – a block from Union Square, this well-managed hostel got a total makeover in 2009 and looks fresh, clean and colorful. Dorms have four beds; private rooms sport low-slung platform beds (beware sharp corners) and some even have down pillows (by request). Extras include free breakfast, quiet area, social lounge, clean kitchen and full activities calendar.

FITZGERALD HOTEL   HOTEL $
Map p322 (☎800-334-6835, 415-775-8100; www.fitzgeraldhotel.com; 620 Post St; s $89-119, d $99-139; ☎; ☐2, 3, 27, 38) Upgrade from hostel to hotel at this good-value hotel decorated with mismatched furniture liquidated from fancier hotels. The old-fashioned building (built in 1910) needs upgrades (note the temperamental elevator), rooms are tiny and have occasional scuff marks and torn curtains, but baths are clean, rooms have fridges and microwaves, and there's a cute wine bar downstairs.

ADELAIDE HOSTEL   HOSTEL $
Map p322 (☎877-359-1915, 415-359-1915; www.adelaidehostel.com; 5 Isadora Duncan Lane; dm $28-35, r $75-120, incl breakfast; @☎; ☐38) Down a hidden alley, the 22-room Adelaide has up-to-date furnishings and marble-tiled baths – also the occasional rust stain and dust bunny. Extras include $5 dinners, group activities and two common areas (one quiet). Good service; friendly crowd. Note: your private room may wind up being in the nearby Dakota or Fitzgerald Hotels; of the two, the Fitzgerald is the better.

HI SAN FRANCISCO CITY CENTER   HOSTEL $
Map p322 (☎415-474-5721; www.sfhostels.org; 685 Ellis St; dm incl breakfast $25-40, r $85-110; @☎; ☐19, 38, 47, 49) A converted seven-story, 1920s apartment building, this better-than-average hostel has private baths in all rooms, including dorms. All-you-can-eat pancakes or eggs cost $1. The neighborhood, on the edge of the gritty Tenderloin, is sketchy but nearby are good bars and cheap eats.

USA HOSTELS   HOSTEL $
Map p322 (☎877-483-2950, 415-440-5600; www.usahostels.com; 711 Post St; dm $30-42, r $93-119 incl breakfast; ☎; ☐2, 3, 27, 38) Built in 1909, this former hotel is now a spiffy hostel resembling a college dormitory, bustling with international students. Private rooms sleep three or four and have a fridge, microwave and TV. Dorms have built-in privacy screens with a reading light and electrical outlet, and lockers contain outlets to charge electronics. Common areas include a big kitchen, laundry and games space.

★HOTEL MONACO   DESIGN HOTEL $$
Map p322 (☎866-622-5284, 415-292-0100; www.monaco-sf.com; 501 Geary St; r $179-269; ❋@☎; ☐38, ☐Powell-Hyde, Powell-Mason) ☞ Snazzy Monaco gets details right, with guestrooms a riot of color – lipstick-red lacquer, navy-blue velvet and shiny-purple silk – plus substantive amenities like high-thread-count sheets, ergonomic workspaces,

multiple electrical outlets, and ample drawer, closet and bathroom-vanity space. Extras include in-room goldfish, spa with Jacuzzi, gym, evening wine, bicycles and bragging rights to a stylin' address.

HOTEL ZETTA   HOTEL $$

Map p320 (☑855-212-4187, 415-543-8555; www.hotelzetta.com; 55 5th St; r $189-249; ❈@🛜🐾; ⒷPowell St, ⓂPowell St) 🐾 Opened 2013, this snappy eco-conscious downtowner by the Viceroy group plays to techies who work too much, with a mezzanine-level 'play room' with billiards, shuffleboard and two-story-high Plinko wall rising above the art-filled lobby. Upstairs, bigger-than-average rooms look sharp with padded black-leather headboards and low-slung platform beds; web-enabled flat-screen TVs link to your devices.

HOTEL TRITON   DESIGN HOTEL $$

Map p320 (☑800-800-1299, 415-394-0500; www.hoteltriton.com; 342 Grant Ave; r $175-275, ste $350; ❈@🛜🐾; ⓂMontgomery, ⒷMontgomery) 🐾 The Triton's lobby thumps with high-energy music and pops with color like the pages of a comic book. Self-consciously hip rooms sport SF-centric details, like wallpaper repeating two random columns of Kerouac's *On the Road*, redeemed by snappy colors, ecofriendly amenities and shag-worthy beds. Baths have limited space but there's unlimited Häagen-Dazs ice cream on request.

Don't miss tarot-card readings and chair massages during nightly wine hour. Kids get special amenities.

HOTEL DIVA   BOUTIQUE HOTEL $$

Map p322 (☑800-553-1900, 415-885-0200; www.hoteldiva.com; 440 Geary St; r $169-289; ❈@🛜🐾; 🚃38, 🚃Powell-Hyde, Powell-Mason) Favored by midbudget fashionistas and traveling club kids, industrial-chic Diva's stainless-steel and black-granite aesthetic conveys a sexy urban look. Beds are comfy, with good sheets, feather pillows and down comforters adding much-needed softness to the hard-edged design. Best for a party but if you're here on business, escape your room to work in one of the artist-designed lounges.

GALLERIA PARK   BOUTIQUE HOTEL $$

Map p320 (☑800-738-7477, 415-781-3060; www.jdvhotels.com; 191 Sutter St; r $189-229; ❈@🛜🐾; ⓂMontgomery, ⒷMontgomery) 🐾 Exuberant staff greet your arrival at this downtown boutique charmer, a 1911 hotel styled with con-temporary art and handsome furnishings in soothing jewel tones. Some rooms (and beds) run small but include Frette linens, down pillows, high-end bath amenities, free evening wine and – most importantly – good service. Rooms on Sutter St are noisier but get more light; interior rooms are quietest.

SERRANO HOTEL   DESIGN HOTEL $$

Map p322 (☑415-885-2500, 866-289-6561; www.serranohotel.com; 405 Taylor St; $149-229; ❈@🛜🐾; 🚃38) The grand Spanish-Revival lobby of the 17-story Serrano was completely restored to 1928 specifications, with eye-popping jewel tones and Moroccan patterns – colors and fabrics that repeat upstairs in small, well-priced rooms that would cost more in a better neighborhood (thank goodness for double-pane windows). Evening wine hour and onsite gastropub add value.

If relevant, request a room with strong wi-fi reception.

MYSTIC HOTEL   HOTEL $$

Map p320 (☑415-400-0500; www.mystichotel.com; 417 Stockton St; r $179-259; @🛜🐾; 🚃30, 45, ⒷMontgomery) Built in 1904 and redone in 2010, the Mystic's austere design plays to hip cats, with simple small rooms enhanced by smoked mirrors and fresh-looking white-on-white design elements. Baths run small – so does the elevator – but new owner Charlie Palmer is determined to make the old building swank. No air-con means open windows above loud streets (bring earplugs).

Confirm that you're getting a recently renovated room. Don't miss the downstairs Burritt Room (p99) bar.

HOTEL ABRI   HOTEL $$

Map p320 (☑415-392-8800, 888-229-0677; www.hotelabrisf.com; 127 Ellis St; r $169-249; ❈@🛜🐾; ⓂPowell, ⒷPowell) Inside a remodeled early-20th-century building, the Abri has a contemporary sensibility, with bold black-and-tan motifs, pillow-top beds with feather pillows, iPod docks, flat-screen TVs and big workstations. Few baths have tubs but rainfall showerheads compensate. The hotel's popularity has meant wear-and-tear on the once-fresh furnishings, but rooms remain comfy, the staff friendly and accommodating.

Request a quiet room, *not* above the Subway sandwich shop to avoid the pervasive smell of baking bread.

HOTEL CARLTON
DESIGN HOTEL **$$**

Map p322 (☑415-673-0242; www.jdvhotels.com; 1075 Sutter St; $139-199; @🛜❄; 🚍2, 3, 19, 38, 47, 49) ✍ Renovated in 2013, this fresh-looking hotel trades convenience for value – it's a ten-minute walk to Union Square – but feels inviting for its playful design that nods to North Africa and its spotlessly clean rooms with colorful bedspreads that get laundered after each guest (a rarity among hotels). Downstairs there's a terrific Middle Eastern restaurant.

Rooftop solar panels provide power and the hotel claims carbon-neutral status. Ninth-floor rooms have blackout window shades; quietest are those with suffix -08 to -19.

WARWICK SAN FRANCISCO HOTEL HOTEL **$$**

Map p322 (☑800-203-3232, 415-928-7900; www.warwicksf.com; 490 Geary St; r $129-269; @🛜; 🚍38) If you prefer high heels to hiking boots but can't afford the Ritz, the Warwick presents a way-less-expensive alternative. Though rooms are small-ish, they convey discreet tastefulness with European antiques and Chinese porcelain – beds even have triple-sheeting, but you'll have to request feather pillows. The hotel was slated for renovations in 2014; request a remodeled room.

CHANCELLOR HOTEL
HOTEL **$$**

Map p320 (☑415-362-2004; www.chancellorhotel.com; 433 Powell St; r $145-250; @🛜; 🚍2, 3, 38, 🚋Powell-Mason, Powell-Hyde) Built in 1914, the family-owned Chancellor has simple, if small, rooms with double-pane glass that blocks the noise of passing cable cars. Best are the bathroom's deep tubs, relics from before water conservation. Expect good value – and distance from the grit a few blocks downhill. For quiet, book rear-facing rooms.

HOTEL UNION SQUARE
HOTEL **$$**

Map p320 (☑800-553-1900, 415-397-3000; www.hotelunionsquare.com; 114 Powell St; r $151-239; ✻@🛜❄; Ⓜ️Powell, Ⓑ️Powell) Hotel Union Square looks sharp, with smart design touches complementing the original brick walls. The main drawbacks are lack of sunlight and very small rooms, but designers compensated with cleverly concealed lighting, mirrored walls and plush fabrics. Convenient location near major transport – never mind the panhandlers outside. Not all rooms have air-con.

PHOENIX HOTEL
MOTEL **$$**

Map p322 (☑800-248-9466, 415-776-1380; www.thephoenixhotel.com; 601 Eddy St; r incl breakfast $119-229; 🅿️🛜❄; 🚍19, 31, 47, 49) The city's rocker crash pad draws minor celebs and Dionysian revelers to a 1950s motor lodge with basic rooms dolled up with tropical decor. The former coffee shop is now the happening, sexy gastro-lounge Chambers. Check out the cool shrine to actor-director Vincent Gallo opposite room 43. One complaint: noise – bring earplugs. Parking is free, as is admission to Kabuki Springs & Spa (p148).

BERESFORD ARMS HOTEL
HOTEL **$$**

Map p322 (☑800-533-5633, 415-673-2600; www.beresford.com; 701 Post St; r $149-179, w/ kitchen $179-209; @🛜; 🚍2, 3, 27, 38) Because its 1912 building originally housed apartments, the Beresford has bigger-than-average rooms, some with kitchens. We appreciate the fancy-looking lobby, large well-kept (if conservatively decorated) rooms, reasonable minibar prices and respectable location just beyond the riffraff of the Tenderloin, but service is decidedly perfunctory. Request a recently remodeled room – if you can charm front-desk staff into cooperating.

HOTEL CALIFORNIA
HOTEL **$$**

Map p322 (☑800-227-4223, 415-441-2700; www.hotelca.com/sanfrancisco; 580 Geary St; r $149-179; @🛜❄; 🚍27, 38) Alas, no pink champagne on ice, but it does provide frosted tequila shots upon check-in and wine and cheese nightly. This bay-windowed, vintage-1920s hotel has small rooms with laminate floors and sometimes-thin walls but also cheery yellow paint jobs, fluffy beds and double-pane windows that (generally) block street noise (request a quiet room).

ANDREWS HOTEL
HOTEL **$$**

Map p322 (☑800-926-3739, 415-563-6877; www.andrewshotel.com; 624 Post St; r incl breakfast $109-199; 🛜; 🚍2, 3, 27, 38, 🚋Powell-Mason, Powell-Hyde) Just two blocks west of Union Square, this 1905 hotel has friendly, personable staff, small but comfortable rooms (the quietest are in back) and a good Italian restaurant downstairs. Though it's nothing fancy, we love the homey feel – it's like staying at your aunt's house, without having to pet the cat.

STRATFORD HOTEL
HOTEL **$$**

Map p320 (☏415-397-7080, 888-504-6835; www.
hotelstratford.com; 242 Powell St; r incl breakfast
$109-189; @🛜; MPowell, BPowell) A good-
value hotel at Union Square, the eight-story
Stratford has simple white-walled rooms
with plain furnishing and occasional scuff
marks – but they're clean, as are the baths
which have rainfall showerheads but no
tubs. Rooms on Powell St are loud. The el-
evator is s-l-o-w.

HOTEL BERESFORD
HOTEL **$$**

Map p322 (☏415-673-9900; www.beresford.com;
635 Sutter St; r $139-159; @🛜; 🚌2, 3, 27, 🚋Pow-
ell-Hyde, Powell-Mason) Built in 1910, this old-
fashioned tourist hotel has creaky floors
but provides good-value accommodations
and adjoins an English-style pub. Guest
rooms are clean and simple, with conservative Colonial-style furnishings and double-
pane glass that blocks noise from weekend
revelers. Avoid -03 rooms; they're adjacent
to the (loud) elevator, but compensate with
jetted bathtubs. Good location, just off Union Square.

HOTEL DES ARTS
ART HOTEL **$$**

Map p320 (☏800-956-4322, 415-956-3232;
www.sfhoteldesarts.com; 447 Bush St; r $119-159,
without bath $79-99; 🛜; MMontgomery, BMont-
gomery) Finally a midbudget hotel for art
freaks. All rooms have been painted with
jaw-dropping murals by underground art-
ists. Service is weak, linens thin and some
bathrooms have separate hot and cold taps,
but the art provides the feeling of sleeping
inside a painting. Rooms with private bath
require a seven-night stay. Bring earplugs.

MANDARIN ORIENTAL
LUXURY HOTEL **$$$**

Map p319 (☏800-622-0404, 415-276-9888;
www.mandarinoriental.com/sanfrancisco; 222
Sansome St; r from $495; ❄@🛜❄; 🚋Califor-
nia, MMontgomery, BMontgomery) On the top
11 floors of SF's third-tallest building, the
Mandarin offers sweeping, unobstructed
views from every room. There's nothing
risky about the classical decor but details
are perfect, beds sumptuous and oh, those
vistas... For a splurge, book a 'Golden Gate
Mandarin' room (from $895) with bathtub
surrounded by floor-to-ceiling windows
and bird's-eye views of *both* the Golden
Gate and Bay Bridges.

Alas, no pool – hence the four-star des-
ignation – but there's a spa and service
equals, or even bests, the city's five-stars.

TAJ CAMPTON PLACE
LUXURY HOTEL **$$$**

Map p320 (☏866-969-1825, 415-781-5555; www.
tajhotels.com; 340 Stockton St; r from $289;
❄@🛜; 🚌30, 45, MMontgomery) Impeccable
service sets Campton Place apart – this is
where to put your fur-clad rich aunt when
she wants discretion above all. Details are
lavish, if beige. Cheapest rooms are tiny;
pay to upgrade or be imprisoned in a jewel-
ry box. Excellent on-site formal restaurant.

PALACE HOTEL
HOTEL **$$$**

Map p320 (☏800-325-3535, 415-512-1111; www.
sfpalace.com; 2 New Montgomery St; r from $229;
❄@🛜❄❄; MMontgomery, BMontgomery)
The 1906 landmark Palace stands as a monument to turn-of-the-century grandeur, aglow
with 100-year-old Austrian crystal chandeliers. Cushy (if staid) accommodations cater
to expense-account travelers but prices drop
on weekends. Even if you're not staying here,
see the opulent **Garden Court**, one of Northern California's most beautiful rooms, and
sip tea beneath a translucent glass ceiling.

There's also a spa; kids love the big pool.

HOTEL PALOMAR
DESIGN HOTEL **$$$**

Map p320 (☏866-373-4941, 415-348-1111; www.
hotelpalomar-sf.com; 12 4th St; r $229-325;
❄@🛜❄; MPowell, BPowell) 🐾 The sexy
Palomar is decked out with crocodile-print
carpets, stripy persimmon-red chairs,
chocolate-brown wood and cheetah-print
bathrobes. Hugh Hefner would definitely
approve. Beds are dressed with feather-
light down comforters and Frette linens,
and there's plenty of floor space for in-room
yoga (request supplies at check-in). Our only
complaint: sometimes-spotty service.

Don't miss drinks at the swank **Fifth
Floor** restaurant.

INN AT UNION SQUARE
BOUTIQUE HOTEL **$$$**

Map p320 (☏800-288-4346, 415-397-3510; www.
unionsquare.com; 440 Post St; r $229-299, ste
$309-359; ❄@🛜; 🚋Powell-Hyde, Powell-Mason,
MPowell, BPowell) 🐾 Traditionalists love the
conservative chintz decor and personalized
service of this understated boutique charmer, best for older travelers who want both
quiet and central location. Extras include
twice-daily maid service and a fireside
breakfast. Great for shopping and theaters.

WESTIN ST FRANCIS HOTEL
HOTEL **$$$**

Map p320 (☏800-228-3000, 415-397-7000; www.
westin.com; 335 Powell St; r $229-449; ❄@🛜❄;
🚋Powell-Mason, Powell-Hyde, MPowell, BPowell)

This is one of SF's most storied hotels – Gerald Ford was shot right outside. Tower rooms have stellar views but feel architecturally generic. We prefer the original building's old-fashioned charm, with its high ceilings and crown moldings. Westin beds set the industry standard for comfort but service is decidedly business-class, not first.

KENSINGTON PARK HOTEL
BOUTIQUE HOTEL **$$$**

Map p320 (☎415-788-6400; www.kensington-parkhotel.com; 450 Post St; r $189-289; ✳ @ 🛜 🐾; 🚋Powell-Hyde, Powell-Mason, MPowell, BPowell) The dramatic 1925 Spanish-Moorish lobby plays a broody counterpoint to the guestrooms' sophisticated mash-up of Queen Anne and contemporary furnishings. Some rooms are small but have extras like down pillows. Downstairs is the top-flight seafood restaurant **Farallon**. Central location, just off Union Square, apart from the sketchy Tenderloin.

SIR FRANCIS DRAKE HOTEL
HOTEL **$$$**

Map p320 (☎800-795-7129, 415-392-7755; www.sirfrancisdrake.com; 450 Powell St; r $189-320; ✳ @ 🛜; 🚋Powell-Mason, Powell-Hyde, MPowell, BPowell) 🐾 The city's most famous doormen, clad like cartoon Beefeaters, stand sentinel at this 1920s tower with a magnificent Spanish-Moorish lobby that gets defaced with tacky posters when a convention's in town. Rooms are styled in bold prints on neutral greige and have requisite business-class amenities and proper beds. Book 16th-to-20th-floor rooms for expansive views. Alas, service is lackluster.

If you can get someone's attention, ask about the secret room between elevator platforms, where during Prohibition the hotel operated a speakeasy.

🛏 SoMa

BEST WESTERN CARRIAGE INN
DESIGN MOTEL **$$**

Map p324 (☎800-780-7234, 415-552-8600; www.carriageinnsf.com; 140 7th St; r $129-189; ✳ @ 🛜 🐾; MCivic Center, BCivic Center) An upmarket motor lodge with bigger-than-average rooms, styled with colorful textiles, the Carriage Inn gives good bang for your buck, but it's on a sometimes-sketchy street. Alas, unlike many other motels, self-parking costs $25. The pool is across the street at the Americania.

AMERICANIA HOTEL
DESIGN MOTEL **$$**

Map p324 (☎415-626-0200; www.americaniahotel.com; 121 7th St; r $129-189; @ 🛜 🐾; MCivic Center, BCivic Center) Rooms at this restyled motor lodge face a central courtyard and look sharp, with a retro-'70s aesthetic incorporating black-and-teal-checked carpeting, white-vinyl headboards, pop art and playful extras. Kids love the small outdoor heated pool. Parents love the microbrews at the excellent downstairs burger joint – but may dislike the sometimes-gritty neighborhood and $25 charge for self-parking.

GOOD HOTEL
DESIGN HOTEL **$$**

Map p324 (☎800-444-5819, 415-621-7001; www.thegoodhotel.com; 112 7th St; r $109-169; @ 🛜 🐾; MCivic Center, BCivic Center) 🐾 A revamped motel attached to a restyled apartment hotel, Good Hotel places a premium on green with reclaimed-wood headboards, light fixtures of repurposed bottles, and fleece bedspreads made from recycled soda bottles and cast-off fabrics. It's like a smartly decorated college dorm – youthful and fun. Drawbacks are a sometimes-sketchy neighborhood and street noise; book in back.

The front desk rents bikes. For air-con – or if you have lots of luggage to unload – book the motel side. Self-parking costs $25. The pool is across the street at the Americania.

MOSSER HOTEL
HOTEL **$$**

Map p324 (☎800-227-3804, 415-986-4400; www.themosser.com; 54 4th St; r $119-189, w/ shared bath $109-129; @ 🛜; MPowell, BPowell) A tourist-class hotel with semi-stylish details, the Mosser has tiny rooms and tinier baths but rates are (usually) a bargain. Service can be lackluster and the building is old, but it's centrally located and rooms are half the price of the neighboring Marriott, a boon for conventioneers on a budget.

HOTEL VITALE
DESIGN HOTEL **$$$**

Map p324 (☎888-890-8688, 415-278-3700; www.hotelvitale.com; 8 Mission St; r from $255; ✳ @ 🛜 🐾; MEmbarcadero, BEmbarcadero) The ugly exterior disguises a fashion-forward shagadelic hotel, with echoes of midcentury-modern design, enhanced by up-to-the-minute luxuries. Beds are dressed with silky-soft, 450-thread-count sheets. There is an excellent on-site spa with two rooftop hot tubs. Best rooms face the bay and have spectacular bridge views.

SLEEPING SOMA

W HOTEL
HOTEL **$$$**

Map p324 (☎877-946-8357, 415-777-5300; www.whotel.com; 181 3rd St; r from $249; ✳@☎☎; MMontgomery, BMontgomery) Sexy door-men stand sentinel like bouncers at a disco and club-kids-turned-conventioneers crowd the lobby, blaring with thump-thump music. Though forced in its cool, the look is hot – wear something tight, blend right in. High-floor rooms in the 31-story tower have spectacular views; all have upholstered window seats, stereos with chill music and sumptuous beds.

Though its concept is definitely corporate, W does a stellar job capitalizing on sex and rock and roll – the drugs are up to you.

HARBOR COURT HOTEL
BOUTIQUE HOTEL **$$$**

Map p324 (☎866-792-6283, 415-882-1300; www.harborcourthotel.com; 165 Steuart St; r from $269; ✳@☎☎; MEmbarcadero, BEmbarcadero) Rooms are tiny at this repurposed, vintage-1928 YMCA hotel, but designers compensated with pull-out drawers under platform beds and attractive textures and colors. Book a bay-view room (trust us). Downstairs, guests gather fireside in the handsome bayside common area. Lively bars and restaurants line the street outside. The adjoining Y (extra charge) has an excellent gym and pool.

🛏 North Beach & Chinatown

SAN REMO HOTEL
SMALL HOTEL **$**

Map p334 (☎800-352-7366, 415-776-8688; www.sanremohotel.com; 2237 Mason St; d $79-129; @☎☎; ☐30, 47, ☐Powell-Mason) One of the city's best-value stays, the San Remo dates to 1906 and is long on old-fashioned charm. Rooms are simply done with mismatched turn-of-the-20th-century furnishings and all rooms share baths. Think reputable, vintage boarding house. Note: least-expensive rooms have windows onto the corridor, not the outdoors. Family suites accommodate up to five. No elevator.

PACIFIC TRADEWINDS HOSTEL
HOSTEL **$**

Map p334 (☎888-734-6783, 415-433-7970; www.sanfranciscohostel.org; 680 Sacramento St; dm $30; @☎; ☐1, ☐California, BMontgomery) San Francisco's smartest-looking all-dorm hostel has a blue-and-white nautical theme, fully equipped kitchen, spotless glass-brick showers and no lockout time. Bunks are bolted to the wall so there's no bed-shaking when your bunkmate shifts. Alas, no elevator means hauling bags up three flights but it's worth it. Great service, fun staff.

GRANT PLAZA
HOTEL **$**

Map p334 (☎800-472-6899, 415-434-3883; www.grantplaza.com; 465 Grant Ave; r $95-140; ☎; ☐1, ☐California St) Many rooms overlook the blinking neon and exotic streetscape of Grant Ave (expect noise); they're quite clean (never mind the excessive air-freshener) but blandly decorated with generic furniture. Bathrooms have soap, not shampoo. Still, it's great value. And to be in the heart of Chinatown, this is the place.

⭐ORCHARD GARDEN HOTEL
ECO HOTEL **$$**

Map p334 (☎888-717-2881, 415-399-9807; www.theorchardgardenhotel.com; 466 Bush St; r $189-259; ✳@☎; ☐2, 3, 30, 45, BMontgomery) 🍃 San Francisco's first all-green-practices hotel uses sustainably grown wood, chemical-free cleaning products and recycled fabrics in its soothingly quiet rooms. Don't think you'll be trading comfort for conscience: rooms have unexpectedly luxe touches like high-end down pillows and Egyptian-cotton sheets. Don't miss the sunny rooftop terrace – a lovely spot at day's end.

⭐HOTEL BOHÈME
BOUTIQUE HOTEL **$$**

Map p334 (☎415-433-9111; www.hotelboheme.com; 444 Columbus Ave; r $174-224; @☎; ☐10, 12, 30, 41, 45) Our favorite boutique hotel is a love letter to the Beat era, with moody orange, black and sage-green color schemes nodding to the 1950s, inverted Chinese umbrellas hanging from the ceiling and photos from the Beat years on the walls. Rooms are smallish, some front on noisy Columbus Ave (quieter rooms are in back) and baths are teensy, but it's smack in the middle of North Beach's vibrant street scene. No elevator.

SW HOTEL
HOTEL **$$**

Map p334 (☎888-595-9188, 415-362-2999; www.swhotel.com; 615 Broadway; r $149-219; ✳☎; ☐10, 12, 30, 45) The notorious Sam Wong has been totally overhauled, and now it's a respectable, good-value hotel, heavy on the pastels and air-freshener. Its number-one selling point is location – on the Broadway axis dividing North Beach and Chinatown – but some rooms are incredibly loud: bring earplugs or use air-con (not available in cheaper rooms). Parking not always available.

WASHINGTON SQUARE INN
B&B $$$

Map p334 (☑800-388-0220, 415-981-4220; www.wsisf.com; 1660 Stockton St; r incl breakfast $199-349; @🛜; 🚌30, 41, 45, 🚋Powell-Mason) On leafy, sun-dappled Washington Square, this inn looks decidedly European and caters to the over-40 set, with tasteful rooms styled with a few choice antiques, including carved, wooden armoires. Least-expensive rooms are tiny, but what a stellar address. Wine and cheese each evening and breakfast in bed are lovely extras. No elevator.

🛏 Nob Hill, Russian Hill & Fillmore

HOTEL KABUKI
THEME HOTEL $$

Map p331 (☑800-533-4567, 415-922-3200; www.hotelkabuki.com; 1625 Post St; r $169-269; @🛜💪; 🚌2, 3, 38) The Kabuki nods to Japan, with *shoji* (rice-paper screens) on the windows and orange-silk dust ruffles beneath platform beds. The boxy 1960s architecture is plain, but rooms are spacious (if in need of some upgrading). Best details: deep Japanese soaking tubs with adjoining showers and free passes to Kabuki Springs & Spa (but only when you book directly through JDV hotels).

HOTEL TOMO
THEME HOTEL $$

Map p331 (☑888-822-8666, 415-921-4000; www.hoteltomo.com; 1800 Sutter St; r $175-275; 🅿✳@🛜; 🚌2, 3, 22, 38) Japanese pop culture informs the Tomo's aesthetic, with big-eyed anime characters blinking on the lobby's TV screens. The blond minimalist room furniture and fat-boy beanbags make it feel a bit like a college dorm, but it's great fun for families and anime nuts, if not for high-heeled sophisticates. Rates vary wildly, depending on occupancy.

HOTEL REX
BOUTIQUE HOTEL $$

Map p332 (☑800-433-4434, 415-433-4434; www.jdvhotels.com; 562 Sutter St; r $159-229; ✳@🛜💪; 🚋Powell-Hyde, Powell-Mason, Ⓜ Powell, ⒷPowell) 🐾 French gramophone music fills the intimate lobby and lounge, conjuring New York's Algonquin in the 1920s. Rooms likewise feel inviting (despite compact size) with their traditional masculine aesthetic, hand-painted lampshades and local art. Beds are particularly great, with crisp linens and down pillows. Caveats: rear-facing rooms lack sunlight but are quiet; street-facing rooms are bright, but noisy. Request air-con.

WHITE SWAN INN
BOUTIQUE HOTEL $$

Map p332 (☑800-999-9570, 415-775-1755; www.whiteswaninnsf.com; 845 Bush St; r incl breakfast $179-259; 🅿@🛜; 🚌2, 3, 27) Like an English country inn, the romantic White Swan is styled with cabbage-rose wallpaper, red-plaid flannel bedspreads and polished Colonial-style furniture. Each oversized room has a gas fireplace – cozy on a foggy night – and there's wine and cheese in the library. Hipsters may find it stifling but if you love Tudor style, you'll feel right at home.

QUEEN ANNE HOTEL
B&B $$

Map p331 (☑800-227-3970, 415-441-2828; www.queenanne.com; 1590 Sutter St; r incl breakfast $129-189, ste $223-279; @🛜; 🚌2, 3) The Queen Anne occupies a lovely 1890 Victorian mansion, formerly a girls' boarding school. Though the chintz decor borders on frilly, it matches the stately house. Rooms are comfy (some are tiny) and have a mishmash of antiques; some have romantic wood-burning fireplaces.

PETITE AUBERGE
BOUTIQUE HOTEL $$

Map p332 (☑800-365-3004, 415-928-6000; www.petiteaubergesf.com; 863 Bush St; r incl breakfast $189-269; 🛜; 🚌2, 3, 27) Petite Auberge feels like a French country inn, with floral-print fabrics, sunny-yellow colors and in-room gas fireplaces – one of downtown's most charming mid-priced stays. Alas, several rooms are dark (especially tiny number 22) and face an alley where rubbish collectors rattle cans early (request a quiet room). Breakfast and afternoon wine are served fireside in the cozy salon.

STEINHART HOTEL & APARTMENTS
APARTMENT HOTEL $$

Map p332 (☑800-533-1900, 415-928-3855; www.steinharthotel.com; 952 Sutter St; studio per week $1150, 1br apt per week from $1400; 🛜💪; 🚌2, 3, 27, 38) If you're staying for a week or longer, the Steinhart is a great address, an early-20th-century building with high ceilings and swank art-deco furnishings. Small studios have galley-style kitchenettes; larger studios and one-bedroom apartments have full kitchens. Rates include weekly housekeeping, free wi-fi and local calls, and use of the backyard patio and grill.

CARTWRIGHT HOTEL
HOTEL $$

Map p332 (☑415-421-2865; www.cartwrightunionsquare.com; 524 Sutter St; r $129-159; @🛜💪; 🚋Powell, Ⓜ Powell) Built 1915 and overhauled

2008, the fresh-faced Cartwright has a monochromatic, earth-tone color scheme and clean lines. Bathrooms are tiny but have good rainfall showerheads. There's nothing risky to the Spartan aesthetic but it's smartly done and presents a reasonable alternative to Union Square's splashier boutiques.

GOLDEN GATE HOTEL   HOTEL $$

Map p332 (☑800-835-1118, 415-392-3702; www.goldengatehotel.com; 775 Bush St; r $115, w/ bath $175; @ 🖥; 🚇2, 3, 🚋Powell-Hyde, Powell-Mason) Like an old-fashioned *pensione*, the Golden Gate has kindly owners and simple rooms with mismatched furniture, inside a 1913 Edwardian hotel safely up the hill from the Tenderloin. Rooms are small, clean and comfortable and most have private baths (some with antique claw-foot tubs). Enormous croissants, homemade cookies and a resident cat provide TLC after long days of sightseeing.

HOTEL VERTIGO   HOTEL $$

Map p332 (☑888-444-4605, 415-885-6800; www.hotelvertigosf.com; 940 Sutter St; r $129-189; @ 🖥; 🚇2, 3, 27) Alfred Hitchcock shot scenes from *Vertigo* here and a recent refurbishment nods to the master with Spirograph-like artwork reminiscent of the opening sequence. The snappy aesthetic blends cool colors and low-slung wingchairs beside platform beds dressed with down duvets. It's a 10-minute walk to reach anywhere noteworthy, but this translates to lower-than-average rates – plus bragging rights to movie history.

NOB HILL HOTEL   HOTEL $$

Map p332 (☑415-885-2987; www.nobhillhotel.com; 835 Hyde St; r $120-200; @ 🖥🖥; 🚇2, 3, 27) Rooms in this 1906 hotel have been dressed up in heavy Victoriana, with brass beds, fringed lampshades and floral-print carpet. The twee look borders on grandma-lives-here, but it's definitely not cookie-cutter and service is personable. Rooms on Hyde St are loud; book in back. Expect ten-minute walks to get anywhere.

★HOTEL DRISCO   BOUTIQUE HOTEL $$$

Map p316 (☑800-634-7277, 415-346-2880; www.hoteldrisco.com; 2901 Pacific Ave; r $245-425; @ 🖥; 🚇3, 24) The only hotel in Pacific Heights, a stately 1903 apartment-hotel tucked between mansions, stands high on the ridgeline. We love the architecture, attentive service and chic rooms, with their elegantly austere decor, but the high-on-a-hill location is convenient only to the Marina; anywhere else requires bus or taxi. Still, for a real boutique hotel, it's tops.

HUNTINGTON HOTEL   LUXURY HOTEL $$$

Map p332 (☑800-227-4683, 415-474-5400; www.huntingtonhotel.com; 1075 California St; r from $239; ❄ @ 🖥🖥; 🚋California St) Other nearby hotels are showier but the Huntington is Nob Hill's discrete grande dame, the go-to address of society ladies who prefer the comfort of tradition over the garishness of style. Request a high-floor park-view room ('PVR') and don't even think of wearing workout clothes in the white-glove lobby. The chic on-site **Nob Hill Spa** is among the city's best.

FAIRMONT SAN FRANCISCO   LUXURY HOTEL $$$

Map p332 (☑800-441-1414, 415-772-5000; www.fairmont.com; 950 Mason St; r from $299; ❄ @ 🖥🖥; 🚋California St) Presidents and heads of state choose the Fairmont, the magnificent lobby of which is decked out with crystal chandeliers, marble floors and towering yellow-marble columns. Notwithstanding the opulent Presidential suite, rooms have traditional business-class furnishings and lack the finer details of top-end luxury hotels. Still, few addresses can compare. For old-fashioned character, reserve the original 1906 building; for jaw-dropping views, the tower.

MARK HOPKINS INTERCONTINENTAL   HOTEL $$$

Map p332 (☑800-327-0200, 415-392-3434; www.markhopkins.net; 999 California St; r $179-339; ❄ @ 🖥; 🚋California St) Glistening marble floors reflect glowing crystal chandeliers in the lobby of the 1926 Mark Hopkins, a San Francisco landmark. Detractors call it staid but its timelessness is precisely why others (including Michelle Obama) love it. Rooms are done in business-classy style, with Frette linens, and most have knockout hilltop views, but some details miss: anticipate four-, not five-star service.

🛏 The Mission

INN SAN FRANCISCO   B&B $$

Map p328 (☑415-641-0188, 800-359-0913; www.innsf.com; 943 S Van Ness Ave; r $185-295, with shared bath $135-185, cottage $325-385, all incl breakfast; 🅿 @ 🖥; 🚇14, 49) 🌿 The stately

Inn San Francisco occupies an elegant 1872 Italianate-Victorian mansion, impeccably maintained and packed with period antiques. All rooms have fresh-cut flowers and sumptuous beds with fluffy featherbeds; some have Jacuzzi tubs. There's also a freestanding garden cottage that sleeps up to six. Outside there's an English garden and redwood hot tub open 24 hours (a rarity). Limited parking: reserve ahead. No elevator.

The Castro & Noe Valley

PARKER GUEST HOUSE GLBT, B&B $$
Map p336 (☑888-520-7275, 415-621-3222; www. parkerguesthouse.com; 520 Church St; r incl breakfast $159-269; @☎; ☒33, ⓜJ) The Castro's stateliest gay digs occupy two side-by-side Edwardian mansions. Details are elegant and formal, never froufrou. Rooms feel more like a swanky hotel than a B&B, with super-comfortable beds and down duvets. Bath fixtures gleam. The garden is ideal for a lovers' tryst – as is the steam room. No elevator.

INN ON CASTRO GLBT, B&B $$
Map p336 (☑415-861-0321; www.innoncastro. com; 321 Castro St; r $155-185, without bath $115-145, incl breakfast, self-catering apt $175-210; ☎; ⓜCastro) A portal to the Castro's disco heyday, this Edwardian townhouse is decked out with top-end '70s-mod furnishings. Rooms are retro-cool and spotlessly kept. Exceptional breakfasts – the owner is a chef. Several nearby, great-value apartments are also available for rental. No elevator.

WILLOWS INN GLBT, B&B $$
Map p336 (☑415-431-4770; www.willowssf. com; 710 14th St; r with shared bath $110-150; ☎; ⓜChurch) Willows has the homey comforts of a B&B, without any fuss. None of the 12 rooms has private bath but all have sinks. Shared kitchenette. Rooms on 14th St are sunnier and have good street views, but they're noisier; ask when you book. No elevator.

BECK'S MOTOR LODGE GLBT, MOTEL $$
Map p336 (☑800-227-4360, 415-621-8212; www. becksmotorlodge.com; 2222 Market St; r $130-165; Ⓟ❉☎; ⓜCastro St) Though technically not gay, its placement at the center of the Castro makes it the de facto gay favorite. We don't recommend bringing kids, espe-

cially during big gay events, when rooms are reserved months ahead. Book a rear-facing unit for quiet, a room in front to cruise with your blinds open.

24 HENRY GLBT, B&B $$
Map p336 (☑800-900-5686, 415-864-5686; www.24henry.com; 24 Henry St; r $149, without bath $105-125; @☎; ⓜChurch) A converted Victorian on a beautiful, quiet side street, 24 Henry's rooms are simply decorated with cast-off ersatz antiques and utilitarian furniture. Best for no-fuss gay travelers. No elevator.

The Haight, NoPa & Hayes Valley

HAYES VALLEY INN SMALL HOTEL $
Map p340 (☑800-930-7999, 415-431-9131; www. hayesvalleyinn.com; 417 Gough St; s $80-92, d $84-120, queen $125-145 incl breakfast; @☎❉; ☒21, ⓜVan Ness) Like a European *pension*, this amazingly reasonable find has simple, small rooms with shared baths, a border collie panting in the parlor and staff who want to mother you. Two rooms have bunks, two others have single beds – ideal for families or friends. Our only complaints are street noise and too-few baths. Good shopping nearby. No elevator.

METRO HOTEL SMALL HOTEL $
Map p338 (☑415-861-5364; www.metrohotelsf. com; 319 Divisadero St; r $88-138; @☎; ☒6, 24, 71) On a thoroughfare bisecting the Upper and Lower Haight districts, this straightforward, no-frills hotel provides cheap, clean rooms with private bath, an outdoor garden patio and 24-hour reception. Some rooms have two double beds; one room sleeps six ($150). The location is largely residential but you can walk to the Haight's bars and restaurants. No elevator.

RED VICTORIAN
BED, BREAKFAST & ART B&B $
Map p338 (☑415-864-1978; www.redvic.net; 1665 Haight St; r $159-189, without bath $99-139, incl breakfast; ☎; ☒33, 43, 71) ✔ The year 1967 lives on at the tripped-out Red Vic. Each room in the 1904 landmark building pays tribute to peace, ecology and global friendship, with themes like Sunshine, Flower Children and, of course, the Summer of Love. Only four of 18 rooms have baths; all include breakfast in the organic **Peace Café**. Reduced rates for longer stays. No elevator.

CHATEAU TIVOLI   B&B $$

(Map p338; ☑800-228-1647, 415-776-5462; www.chateautivoli.com; 1057 Steiner St; r incl breakfast $170-215, without bath $115-135, ste $275-300; ☎; ☐5, 22) This imposing, glorious chateau on a secondary thoroughfare near Alamo Square once hosted Isadora Duncan and Mark Twain, and though its two-toned gabled roofs have faded, its grand domed turrets, cornices and gorgeous carved woodwork retain their luster. Guestrooms are full of soul, character and, rumor has it, the ghost of a Victorian opera diva. No elevator, no TVs.

SLEEP OVER SAUCE   B&B $$

Map p340 (☑415-252-1423; www.sleepsf.com; 135 Gough St; r $129-189; @☎; Ⓜ Van Ness) We like the homey vibe of this eight-room inn, set above a pretty good dinner house and bar. Rooms are simple, with dark-wood furniture and nothing froufrou; guests share a big common area with fireplace. Baths are sparkling clean but some are across the hall. No elevator, no front desk – check in at the restaurant downstairs.

PARSONAGE   B&B $$$

Map p340 (☑888-763-7722, 415-863-3699; www.theparsonage.com; 198 Haight St; r $220-270; @☎; ☐6, 71, Ⓜ F) A 23-room Italianate-Victorian convenient to Market St transit, the Parsonage retains gorgeous original details, including rose-brass chandeliers and Carrera-marble fireplaces. The spacious, airy rooms are lovely with oriental rugs, period antiques and, in some cases, wood-burning fireplaces. Take breakfast in the formal dining room, from 8am to 10am, then brandy and chocolates before bed. Charming owners. No elevator.

🛏 Golden Gate Park & the Avenues

SEAL ROCK INN   MOTEL $$

Map p342 (☑888-732-5762, 415-752-8000; www.sealrockinn.com; 545 Point Lobos Ave; s $125-157, d $135-167; Ⓟ☎⛱; ☐38) Far from downtown, this vintage-1950s ocean-side motel has big rooms (many sleep four); all have refrigerators, some have microwaves. It's best for families wanting to linger near the beach or hike the coast. Ping-pong keeps kids from getting antsy; ask if the pool has re-opened. Reserve way ahead for upgraded 3rd-floor fireplace rooms.

Plan ahead for meal times: the on-site restaurant keeps erratic hours and there's little else nearby.

Understand
San Francisco

San Francisco Today

Small as it is, this 7-by-7-mile peninsula looms large in the imagination – and on smart-phones, thanks to locally invented social media and mobile apps. Saloons, urban farms and pot clubs are sprouting across SF's 43 hills, and now same-sex couples can declare love and propose marriage from these very hilltops. SF has its ups and downs, but as anyone who's clung onto the side of a cable car will tell you, this town gives one hell of a ride.

Best on Film

Milk (2008) Sean Penn won an Oscar for his portrayal of America's first openly gay elected official.

Tales of the City (1993) Laura Linney unravels a mystery in SF's swinging '70s disco scene.

Harold & Maude (1971) Conservatory of Flowers and Sutro Baths make metaphorically apt backdrops for May-to-December romance.

Chan Is Missing (1982) When Chan disappears, two cabbies realize they don't know Chan, Chinatown or themselves.

Best in Print

Howl and Other Poems (Allen Ginsberg; 1956) Mind-altering, law-changing words defined a generation of 'angel-headed hipsters.'

Time and Materials (Robert Hass; 2007) Every Pulitzer Prize–winning syllable is as essential as a rivet in the Golden Gate Bridge.

On the Road (Jack Kerouac; 1957) Banged out in a San Francisco attic, Kerouac's travelogue set post-war America free.

Slouching Towards Bethlehem (Joan Didion; 1968) Scorching truth burns through San Francisco fog during the Summer of Love.

Green City, USA

According to the North American Green Cities Index, San Francisco is the greenest of them all. Anything you might want to do here, you can do with a clean, green conscience. You can eat, drink, shop, sleep and even cavort sustainably – just look for the sustainable icon (🌱) in this guide.

San Francisco is on track to become a zero-waste city by 2020 and to that end mandates citywide composting and bans plastic bags. Practices that are standard-setting elsewhere are mainstream here, including electric buses, LEED-certified attractions and restaurants featuring California-grown produce and foraged ingredients. San Francisco raises the bar with more than 230 city-certified green businesses, 1400 electric-hybrid taxis, 40 certified local farmers markets, 30 community urban farms, even organic cocktail bars.

Social-Mediated SF

If you're not on Twitter, Facebook, Instagram, Pinterest, YouTube, Yelp, Google+ or LinkedIn, are you sure you still have a pulse? San Francisco will try to convince you to use one of these Bay Area–based social media platforms to validate your existence. After all, a lot of local jobs depend on it.

But there is a backlash in this technology hub. In a city where telecommuters have turned public spaces into satellite offices, cafes are removing electrical outlets and stores are posting signs saying 'No phone calls. No excuses.' That's right: even Apple and Google products don't get a pass for being local. SF's early adopters are now returning social media to its initial use: to touch base and plan to meet in person.

Extravagant Indulgence

Blame SF for any number of temptations: chocolate bars, designer jeans, martinis, TV broadcasts, online shopping and LSD. Lately, San Francisco's saloon revival has been putting spitoons and absinthe fountains back into active service – and only a very local ailment could explain why one of every six San Franciscans has a prescription to the city's 41 pot clubs.

Yet despite their many indulgences and slacker reputations, San Franciscans hold more patents per capita than any other US city, read more books and rack up more degrees than other Americans. As a tech hub, the Bay Area currently leads the nation in job creation. But the city has also earned a reputation for compassion, building family homeless shelters, pioneering hospice care and funding more nonprofits than any other US city.

Homelessness in SF

San Francisco has been a refuge for anyone who doesn't fit in elsewhere since the Gold Rush, but the city's resources are currently strained. With only 1300 shelter beds citywide, many homeless San Franciscans are left on the streets – including vulnerable youth and families. The closure of veterans' facilities, public mental health clinics and rehabs across California have also left patients with few options for care and shelter outside the Bay Area. Nonprofits providing essential services are concentrated in the Tenderloin and SoMa, so homelessness is most evident in these areas.

Solutions aren't simple, since low-income housing is increasingly scarce in the Bay Area. The technology boom has raised the average house price to $1 million and driven rents upward to rival New York. To see positive developments at work – including new family shelters under construction – visit or volunteer at Glide Memorial (p88).

Always a Bridesmaid

San Francisco was the first city to authorize same-sex marriages back in 2004 – but some 4036 honeymoons were abruptly ended when their marriages were legally invalidated by the state. Court battles ensued and California voters narrowly passed 2008's California Proposition 8 measure to legally define marriage as between a man and a woman. Countersuits were initiated, arguing that limiting marriage rights runs contrary to civil rights protections in California's constitution.

But for star-crossed San Francisco couples, there is a happy ending. In 2013, the US Supreme Court upheld California courts' ruling that state civil rights protections invalidate Prop 8, setting a nationwide precedent. The day of the decision, many longtime partners got hitched at City Hall – some for the second or third time, to the same person.

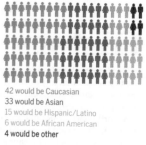

if San Francisco were 100 people

42 would be Caucasian
33 would be Asian
15 would be Hispanic/Latino
6 would be African American
4 would be other

politics
(% of population)

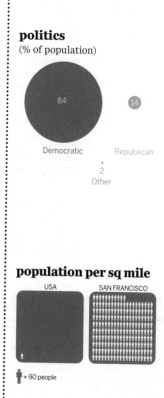

84 Democratic

14 Republican

2 Other

population per sq mile

USA   SAN FRANCISCO

🯅 ≈ 90 people

History

Native Californians had found gold in California long before 1849 but it hardly seemed worth mentioning, as long as there were oysters for lunch and venison for dinner. But once word circulated, San Francisco was transformed almost overnight from bucolic trading backwater to Gold Rush metropolis. One hundred and sixty-odd (make that very odd) years of booms, busts, history-making hijinks and lowdown dirty dealings later, San Francisco remains the wildest city in the west – and still dreams of oysters for lunch and venison for dinner.

Top 5 Sites for Native History

Mission Dolores (the Mission)

Alcatraz

The Presidio

Rincon Center Murals (Financial District)

San Francisco Historical Society (Downtown)

Cowboys on a Mission

When Spanish cowboys brought 340 horses, 302 head of cattle and 160 mules to settle Misión San Francisco de Asís (Mission San Francisco) in 1776, there was a slight hitch: the area had already been settled by Native Americans for over 14,300 years. Since there were enough shellfish and wild foodstuffs to go around, the arrival of Captain Juan Bautista de Anza, Father Francisco Palou and their livestock was initially met with no apparent resistance – until the Spaniards began to demand more than dinner.

The new arrivals expected the local Ohlone to build them a mission and to take over its management within 10 years. In exchange, the Ohlone were allowed one meager meal a day, if any, and a place in God's kingdom – which came much sooner than expected for many. Smallpox and other introduced diseases decimated the Ohlone population by almost three-quarters during the 50 years of Spanish rule in California. While some Ohlone managed to escape the short life of obligatory construction work and prayer, others were caught, returned to the adobe barracks and punished.

As the name suggests, Mission Dolores ('mission of the sorrows') settlement never really prospered. The sandy, scrubby fields were difficult to farm, fleas were a constant irritation and the 20 soldiers who manned the local Presidio army encampment were allotted one scanty shipment of provisions per year. Spain wasn't especially sorry to hand over the troublesome settlement to the newly independent nation of

TIMELINE	June 1776	1835	1846
	Captain Juan Bautista de Anza and Father Francisco Palou arrive in SF with cattle and settlers. With Ohlone conscripts, they build the Misión San Francisco de Asís (now Mission Dolores).	President Andrew Jackson's emissary makes an offer of $500,000 to buy Northern California. Mexico testily refuses and tries to sell California to England.	The Mexican–American War breaks out and drags on for two years, with much posturing but little actual bloodshed in California.

Mexico, but Mexico soon made this colony a profitable venture with a bustling hide and tallow trade at Yerba Buena Cove, where the Financial District now stands.

Meanwhile, US–Mexico relations steadily deteriorated, made worse by rumors that Mexico was entertaining a British buy-out offer for California. The Mexican–American War broke out in 1846 and dragged on for two years before ending with the Treaty of Guadalupe Hidalgo. This treaty formally ceded California and the present-day southwestern states to the USA – a loss that was initially reckoned by missionizing Church fathers in souls but within months could be counted in ingots.

'Gold! Gold! Gold!'

Say what you will about Sam Brannan, but the man knew how to sell a story. In 1848, the San Francisco real-estate speculator and tabloid founder published sensational news of a find 120 miles away near Sutter's Mill, where sawmill employees had found gold flakes in the water. Hoping to scoop other newspapers and maybe sell swampland to rubes back East, Brannan published rumors of the find as solid fact. When San Franciscans proved skeptical, Brannan traveled to Sutter's Fort and convinced fellow Mormons to entrust him with a vial of gold for the church, swearing to keep their secret. Brannan kept his word for about a day. Upon his arrival, he ran through Portsmouth Square, brandishing the vial and shouting, 'Gold! Gold! Gold on the American River!'

But Brannan's plan backfired. Within weeks San Francisco's population shrank to 200, as every able-bodied individual headed to the hills to pan for gold. Brannan's newspaper folded; there was no one around to read, write or print it. Good thing Brannan had a backup plan: he'd bought every available shovel, pick and pan and opened a general store near Sutter's Fort. Within its first 70 days, Brannan & Co sold $36,000 in equipment – almost a million bucks in today's terms.

Luckily for Brannan's profit margins, other newspapers around the world weren't that scrupulous about getting their facts straight either, hastily publishing stories of 'gold mountains' near San Francisco. Boatloads of prospectors arrived from Australia, China, South America and Europe while another 40,000 prospectors trudged overland, eager to scoop up their fortunes on the hillsides. Prices for mining supplies shot up tenfold and Brannan was raking in $150,000 a month, almost $4 million in today's terms. Food wasn't cheap, either: a dozen eggs could cost as much as $10 in San Francisco in 1849, the equivalent of $272 today.

1848

Gold is discovered near present-day Placerville. San Francisco's newspaper publisher Sam Brannan lets word out and the Gold Rush is on.

Town center, Placerville

1849–51

San Francisco's waterfront 'Sydney-Town' area becomes a target of resentment and attacks; Australian boarding houses are torched repeatedly by arsonists.

Lawless, Loose & Lowdown

By 1850, the year California was fast-tracked for admission as the 31st state in the Union, San Francisco's population had skyrocketed from 800 a year earlier to an estimated 25,000. But for all the new money in town, it wasn't exactly easy living. The fleas were still a problem and the rats were getting worse – but at least there were plenty of distractions.

Most of the early prospectors (called '49ers, after their arrival date) were men under the age of 40, and to keep them entertained – and fleece the gullible – some 500 saloons, 20 theaters and numerous venues of ill repute opened within five years. A buck might procure whiskey, opium or one of the women frolicking on swings along San Francisco's 'Barbary Coast.' At gaming tables, luck literally was a lady: women card dealers dealt winning hands to those who engaged their back-room services. In 1851, visiting French journalist (and noted brothel expert) Albert Bernard de Russailh reported, 'There are also some honest women in San Francisco, but not very many.'

Wise prospectors arrived early and got out quick – but there weren't very many of those, either. As gold became harder to find, backstabbing became more common, sometimes literally. Successful Peruvians and Chileans were harassed and denied renewals to their mining claims, and most left California by 1855. Native Californian laborers who had helped the '49ers strike it rich were also denied the right to hold claims. Despite San Francisco's well-earned notoriety for freewheeling lawlessness, crime was swiftly and conveniently blamed on Australian newcomers. From 1851 to 1856, San Francisco's self-appointed Vigilance Committee tried, convicted and hung suspect 'Sydney Ducks' in hour-long proceedings that came to be known as 'kangaroo trials.' Along with Australians, Chinese – the most populous group in California by 1860 – were at the receiving end of misplaced resentment.

After bawdy Jenny Lind Theater became SF's first city hall in 1852, competitor Bella Union ran this advertising campaign: 'As sweet and charming creatures as ever escaped a female seminary. Lovely tresses! Lovely lips! Buxom forms! at the BELLA UNION. And such fun! If you don't want to risk both optics, SHUT ONE EYE.'

Chinatown's Gold Mountain

Within a year of the 1849 Gold Rush, Chinatown was already established in San Francisco – better known in Cantonese as 'Gold Mountain.' At first Chinatown wasn't exclusively Chinese at all, but a bachelor community of Mexican, American, European, African American and Chinese miners who bunked, prospected and caroused side by side. But when gold prices came crashing down with the discovery of gold in Australia, miners turned irrational resentments on resident Australians and Chinese. Australian lodging houses were burned to the ground, anti-Chinese riots broke out and Chinese land claims were rendered null and void. In 1870, San Francisco officially restricted housing and employment for anyone born in China.

1850	1851	1861–65	May 1869
With hopes of solid-gold tax revenues, the US hastily dubs California the 31st state.	Gold discovery in Australia leads to cheering in the streets of Melbourne and panic in the streets of San Francisco as the price for California gold plummets.	While US Civil War divides North from South back East, SF perversely profits in the West as industry diverted from factories burdened by the war effort heads to San Francisco.	The Golden Spike completes the first transcontinental railroad. The news travels via San Franciscan David Brooks' invention, the telegraph.

The 1882 US Chinese Exclusion Act prevented new immigration from China, barred Chinese from citizenship until 1943 and spurred the passage of 100 parallel ordinances limiting rights for Japanese San Franciscans. Not coincidentally, anti-Chinese laws served the needs of local magnates looking for cheap labor to build the first cross-country railroad. With little other choice of legitimate employment, an estimated 12,000 Chinese laborers did the dangerous work of dynamiting rail tunnels through the Sierra Nevada.

After the 1906 fire, city officials planned to oust Chinese residents altogether and develop the prime property of Chinatown, but the Chinese consulate and rifle-toting Chinatown merchants persuaded the city otherwise. Today Chinatown is a major economic boon to the city as one of its top tourist attractions, yet many residents scrape by on less than $10,000 a year – not exactly a Gold Mountain. Better-off residents tend to leave Chinatown, new arrivals move in and the cycle begins anew.

Keeping the West Wild

As gold, silver and railroad money flowed into San Francisco, the city grew. It didn't exactly blossom at first, though – public works were completely neglected and heavily populated sections of the city were mired in muck. Eventually the debris-choked waterfront filled in and streets were graded and paved. As soon as Andrew Hallidie made the formidable crag accessible by cable car in 1873, Nob Hill sprouted mansions for millionaires, including the 'Big Four' railroad barons: Leland Stanford, Collis P Huntington, Mark Hopkins and Charles Crocker. Wherever there was green in the city, real-estate speculators saw greenbacks, cleverly repackaging even the flea-plagued cattle pastures of the Mission District and Cow Hollow as desirable residential districts. The Gold Rush was officially over; the land rush was on.

Naturalist John Muir came through San Francisco in 1868 but quickly left with a shudder for Yosemite. However, the early environmentalist organization he founded, the Sierra Club, would eventually find its major backers in San Francisco. The unspoiled wilderness that Muir and his organization successfully lobbied to protect includes one of San Francisco's most popular escapes: Muir Woods.

San Franciscans, determined to preserve the city's natural splendors, pushed to establish the city's first park in 1867, when squatters were paid to vacate the area now known as Buena Vista Park. With a mandate from San Francisco voters to transform sand dunes into a vast city park, tenacious engineer William Hammond Hall saw the development of Golden Gate Park through to completion from 1870 to 1887 – despite

GOLDEN GATE PARK

William Hammond Hall briefly quit his job building Golden Gate Park in 1886 over proposals to convert the park into a racetrack lined with tract homes. When a casino and carnival were established for the 1893 Midwinter's Fair, Hammond Hall fought to get the park returned to its intended purpose.

1873	1882	April 18, 1906
When a skittish driver declines to test the brakes of Andrew Hallidie's 'wire rope railway,' aka cable car, Hallidie jumps in and steers the car downhill as crowds cheer.	The US Chinese Exclusion Act suspends new immigration from China and these racially targeted laws remain until 1943.	A massive earthquake levels entire blocks of SF in 47 seconds flat, setting off fires that rage for three days. Survivors start rebuilding while the town is still smoldering.

ANGUS OBORN / GETTY IMAGES ©

Cable car on California St

developers' best attempts to scuttle park plans in favor of casinos, amusement parks, resorts, racetracks and an igloo village. Populist millionaire Adolph Sutro decided that every working stiff should be able to escape Downtown tenements for the sand dunes and sunsets of Ocean Beach, accessible for a nickel on his public railway. Sutro's idea proved wildly popular, and by way of thanks, he was elected mayor in 1894.

Double Disaster

Built in 1907, soon after the earthquake, the Great American Music Hall still shows the determined flamboyance of post-earthquake San Francisco, with carved gilt decor recalling the city's Gold Rush heyday and scantily clad frescoed figures hinting at other possible backstage entertainments.

By the 20th century, San Francisco had earned a reputation for scandal, corruption, earthquakes and other calamities – none of it good for business. To redirect attention from its notorious waterfront fleshpots to its comparatively underexposed urban assets, the city commissioned Chicago architect Daniel Burnham to give San Francisco a beaux arts Civic Center to rival Baron Haussmann's Paris. This elaborate plan had just been finalized when disaster struck – twice.

On April 18, 1906, a quake estimated at a terrifying 7.8 to 8.3 on today's Richter scale struck the city. In 47 seconds, San Franciscans discovered just how many corners had been cut on government contracts. Unreinforced buildings collapsed, including City Hall. The sole functioning water source was a fountain donated to the city by opera prodigy Lotta Crabtree. Assembly lines were formed to haul buckets of water from Lotta's Fountain, but the water couldn't reach the crest of steep hills fast enough. Nob Hill mansions with priceless Old Master and Impressionist art collections were reduced to ashes; inhabitants were lucky to escape with their lives. Survivors fled to Potrero Hill and Buena Vista Park, and for three days watched their city and its dreams of grandeur go up in smoke.

The Show Must Go On

Yet San Francisco had learned one thing through 50 years of booms and busts: how to stage a comeback. All but one of the city's 20 historic theaters had been completely destroyed by the earthquake and fire, but theater tents were soon set up amid the rubble. The smoke wafting across makeshift stages wasn't a special effect when surviving entertainers began marathon performances to keep the city's spirits up. Opera divas sang their hearts out to San Francisco gratis – though the world's most famous tenor, Enrico Caruso, vowed never to return to the city after the quake jolted him out of bed at the Palace Hotel. Soprano Luisa Tetrazzini ditched New York's Metropolitan Opera to return to San Francisco and sang on Market St to an audience of 250,000 – virtually every surviving San Franciscan.

1910	1913	1914	1915
Angel Island opens as the West Coast immigration station. Over 30 years, 175,000 arrivals from Asia are subjected to months or years of interrogation and prison-like conditions.	California's Alien Land Law prohibits property ownership by Asians, including Japanese, Koreans and Indians. Lawyer Juichi Soyeda immediately files suit; he wins in 1952, 23 years after his death.	The Red Light Abatement Act prohibits dancing in the city's 2800 bars; police arrest female barkeeps, burlesque dancers and prostitutes.	Postquake San Francisco hosts the Panama–Pacific International Exposition. The city cements its reputation as a showplace for new technology, outlandish ideas and the arts.

San Franciscans rose to the occasion and rebuilt their city at an astounding rate of 15 buildings a day. In a show of popular priorities, San Francisco's theaters were rebuilt long before City Hall's grandiose Civic Center was completed. Most of the Barbary Coast had gone down in flames, so the theater scene and most red-light entertainments decamped to the Tenderloin, where they remain.

But San Francisco's greatest comeback performance was the 1915 Panama–Pacific International Exposition, held in celebration of the completion of the Panama Canal. Earthquake rubble was used to fill 635 marshy acres of the Marina, where famous architects built elaborate pavilions showcasing San Francisco's Pacific Rim connections, exotic foods and forward thinking. Crowds gasped at displays of the latest, greatest inventions, including the world's first steam locomotive, a color printing press and early typewriter (at 14 tons, not exactly a laptop). When the party ended, Bernard Maybeck's Palace of Fine Arts plaster folly was the one temporary exhibit San Franciscans couldn't bear to see torn down, so the structure was recast in concrete.

The Left Coast

San Francisco's port thrived in 1934, but local longshoremen pulling long hours unloading heavy cargo for scant pay didn't see the upside of the shipping boom. When they protested dangerous working conditions, shipping tycoons sought dockworkers elsewhere – only to discover San Francisco's longshoremen had coordinated their strike with 35,000 workers along the West Coast. After 83 days, police and the National Guard broke the strike, killing 34 strikers and wounding 40 sympathizers. Public sympathy forced concessions from shipping magnates and local Diego Rivera murals and Coit Tower Works Project Administration (WPA) frescoes reflect the pro-worker sentiment that swept the city – known henceforth as America's 'Left Coast.'

When WWII brought a shipbuilding boom to town, women and 40,000 African American arrivals claimed key roles in San Francisco's workforce. But with misplaced anxiety about possible attacks from the Pacific, Japanese San Franciscans and Japantown became convenient targets for public animosity. Two months after the attack on Pearl Harbor, President Franklin Delano Roosevelt signed Executive Order 9066 ordering the relocation of 120,000 Japanese Americans to internment camps. The San Francisco–based Japanese American Citizens League (JACL) immediately challenged the grounds for internment and lobbied tirelessly for more than 40 years to overturn the executive order, gain symbolic reparations for internees and restore the community's

1927	1934	1937	February 1942
After a year of tinkering, 21-year-old Philo Farnsworth transmits the first successful TV broadcast of…a straight line.	A West Coast longshoremen's strike ends with 34 strikers and sympathizers shot by police. A mass funeral and citywide strike follow; longshoremen win historic concessions.	After four years of dangerous labor in treacherous Pacific tides, the Golden Gate Bridge is complete.	Executive Order 9066 mandates internment of 120,000 Japanese Americans. The Japanese American Citizens League files civil rights claims.

standing with a formal letter of apology signed by President George HW Bush in 1988. By setting key legal precedents from the 1940s onward, JACL paved the way for the 1964 Civil Rights Act.

Beats: Free Speech, Free Spirits

Members of the armed services dismissed from service for homosexuality and other 'subversive' behavior during WWII were discharged onto the streets of San Francisco, as if that would teach them a lesson. Instead, the new arrivals found themselves at home in the low-rent, laissez-faire neighborhoods of North Beach and the Haight. So when the rest of the country took a sharp right turn with McCarthyism in the 1950s, rebels and romantics headed for San Francisco – including one Jack Kerouac. By the time *On the Road* was published in 1957 chronicling his westward journey, the motley crowd of writers, artists, dreamers and unclassifiable characters Kerouac called 'the mad ones' had found their way to like-minded San Francisco.

San Francisco didn't always take kindly to the nonconformists derisively referred to in the press as 'beatniks,' and police and poets were increasingly at odds on the streets of North Beach. Officers tried to fine 'beatnik chicks' for wearing sandals, only to be mercilessly taunted in verse by self-described African American Jewish voodoo anarchist and street-corner Beat poet Bob Kaufman. Poet Lawrence Ferlinghetti and bookstore manager Shigeyoshi Murao of City Lights were arrested for 'willfully and lewdly' printing Allen Ginsberg's magnificent, incendiary epic poem *Howl*. But artistic freedom prevailed in 1957, when City Lights won its landmark ruling against book banning.

The kindred Beat spirits Ginsberg described in *Howl* as 'angel-headed hipsters burning for the ancient heavenly connection' experimented with art, radical politics, marijuana and one another, defying 1950s social-climbing conventions and Senator Joe McCarthy's alarmist call to weed out 'communists in our midst.' When McCarthy's House Un-American Activities Committee (HUAC) convened in San Francisco in 1960 to expose alleged communists, UC Berkeley students organized a disruptive, sing-along sit-in at City Hall. After police turned fire hoses on the protesters, thousands of San Franciscans rallied and HUAC split town, never to return. It was official: the '60s had begun.

> **Top 5 for Beats**
>
> City Lights (North Beach)
>
> Beat Museum (North Beach)
>
> Vesuvio (North Beach)
>
> Li Po (Chinatown)
>
> Bob Kaufman Alley (North Beach)

Flower Power

San Francisco was a testing ground for freedom of expression in the 1960s, as comedian Lenny Bruce uttered the F-word on stage and burlesque dancer Carol Doda bared it all for titillated audiences in North

1957
City Lights wins a landmark ruling against book banning over the publication of Allen Ginsberg's *Howl*, and free speech and free spirits enjoy a reprieve from McCarthyism.

January 1966
The Trips Festival is organized by techno-futurist Stewart Brand and features author Ken Kesey, the Grateful Dead, Janis Joplin, Native American activists and Hells Angels.

City Lights bookstore (p131), North Beach

Beach clubs. But neither jokes nor striptease would pop the last button of conventional morality in San Francisco – no, that was a job for the CIA. In a pronounced lapse in screening judgment, the CIA hired local writer Ken Kesey to test psychoactive drugs intended to create the ultimate soldier. Instead, they unwittingly inspired Kesey to write the novel *One Flew Over the Cuckoo's Nest,* drive psychedelic busloads of Merry Pranksters across country, and introduce San Francisco to LSD and the Grateful Dead at the legendary Acid Tests.

After the Civil Rights movement anything seemed possible, and for a while it seemed that the freaky force of free thinking would stop the unpopular Vietnam War. At the January 14, 1967 Human Be-In in Golden Gate Park, trip-master Timothy Leary urged a crowd of 20,000 to dream a new American dream and 'turn on, tune in, drop out.' Free music rang out in the streets, free food was provided by the Diggers, free LSD was circulated by Owsley Stanley, free crash pads were all over the Haight and free love transpired on some very dubious free mattresses. For the duration of the Summer of Love – weeks, months, even a year, depending who you talk to and how stoned they were at the time – it seemed possible to make love, not war.

But a chill soon settled over San Francisco and for once it wasn't the afternoon fog. Civil rights hero Martin Luther King Jr was assassinated on April 8, 1968, followed by the fatal shooting of Robert Kennedy on June 5, right after he'd won California's presidential primary. Radicals worldwide called for revolution and separatist groups like Oakland's Black Panther Party for Self-Defense took up arms. Meanwhile, recreational drug-taking was turning into a thankless career for many, a distinct itch in the nether regions was making the rounds and still more busloads of teenage runaways were arriving in the ill-equipped, wigged-out Haight. Haight Ashbury Free Clinic helped with the rehabbing and the itching, but disillusionment seemed incurable when Hell's Angels beat protestors in Berkeley and turned on the crowd at a free Rolling Stones concert at Altamont.

Many idealists headed 'back to the land' in the bucolic North Bay, jumpstarting California's organic farm movement. A dark streak emerged among those who remained, including young Charles Manson, the Symbionese Liberation Army (better known post-1974 as Patty Hearst's kidnappers) and an evangelical egomaniac named Jim Jones, who would oblige 900 followers to commit mass suicide in 1978. By the time Be-In LSD supplier Stanley was released from a three-year jail term in 1970, the party seemed to be over. But in the Castro, it was just getting started.

HISTORY FLOWER POWER

Best Ways to Revive the Summer of Love

Give a free concert on Haight St or give freely to any local nonprofit

Commune with nature in Golden Gate Park

Walk on the wild side of hippie history on the Haight Flashback walking tour

Read '60s manifestos at Bound Together Anarchist Book Collective

Write your own manifesto, fueled by hemp-milk lattes at Coffee to the People

October 1966	January 1967	1969	November 20, 1969
In Oakland, Huey Newton and Bobby Seale found the Black Panther Party for Self-Defense, demanding 'Land, Bread, Housing, Education, Clothing, Justice and Peace.'	The Summer of Love kicks off with the Human Be-In, with draft cards used as rolling papers, free Grateful Dead gigs and Allen Ginsberg naked as usual.	The first computer link is established between Stanford Research Institute and UCLA via ARPANET and an unsolicited group message is sent across the network: spam is born.	Native American activists reclaim the abandoned island of Alcatraz as reparation for broken treaties. The occupation lasts 19 months until FBI agents forcibly oust the activists.

PROTEST

Pride

By the 1970s, San Francisco's gay community was fed up with police raids, done with hetero Haight squats and ready for music with an actual beat. In 1959, after an opponent accused then-mayor George Christopher of allowing San Francisco to become 'the national headquarters of the organized homosexuals,' Christopher authorized crackdowns on gay bars and started a blacklist of gay citizens.

Never one to be harassed or upstaged, WWII veteran and drag star José Sarria became the first openly gay man to run for public office in 1962, on a mayoral platform to end police harassment of gay San Franciscans. He won 5600 votes. Undaunted, he declared himself Absolute Empress of San Francisco, the widow and true heir of Emperor Norton. When local media echoed the Empress' criticism of the continuing raids, the crackdown stopped – a feat not achieved for years elsewhere, until New York's 1969 Stonewall protests.

By the mid-1970s, the rainbow flag was flying high over gay businesses and homes in the out-and-proud Castro and the sexual revolution was in full swing at gay clubs and bathhouses on Polk St and in SoMa. The Castro was triumphant when Castro camera-store owner Harvey Milk was elected city Supervisor, becoming the nation's first openly gay elected official – but as Milk himself predicted, his time in office would be cut short by an act of extremist violence. Dan White, a washed-up politician hyped on Hostess Twinkies, fatally shot Milk and then-mayor George Moscone at City Hall in 1978. The charge was reduced to manslaughter due to the infamous 'Twinkie Defense' faulting the ultrasweet junk food, sparking an outpouring of public outrage dubbed the 'White Riot.' But White was deeply disturbed and committed suicide a year after his 1984 release.

By then San Francisco had other matters weighing heavily on its mind. A strange illness began to appear at local hospitals and it seemed to be hitting the gay community especially hard. The first cases of AIDS reported in 1981 were initially referred to as GRID (Gay-Related Immune Deficiency) and a social stigma became attached to the virus. But San Francisco health providers and gay activists rallied to establish global standards for care and prevention, with vital early HIV/AIDS health initiatives funded not through federal agencies but with tireless local fundraising efforts. Yet unmarried same-sex partners had no legal standing to make lifesaving medical decisions.

Civil rights organizations, religious institutions and GLBT organizations increasingly popped the question: why couldn't same-sex couples get married too? Early backing came from the Japanese American Citizens League, which publicly endorsed marriage for same-sex couples as

On November 20, 1969, 79 Native American activists and their families defied Coast Guard blockades to symbolically reclaim Alcatraz as native land. Hundreds of supporters joined the protest, until ousted by FBI raids on June 11, 1971. Public support for protesters strengthened self-rule for Native territories, signed into law by Richard Nixon.

April 16, 1977	1977	November 18, 1978	1981
The Apple II is introduced in SF at the first West Coast Computer Faire and stuns the crowd with its computing speed (1MHz).	Harvey Milk becomes the first openly gay man elected to US public office. Milk sponsors a gay-rights bill and trend-setting 'pooper-scooper' ordinance before his murder by Dan White.	After moving his People's Temple from SF to Guyana, Jim Jones orders the murders of a congressman and four journalists and mass suicide of 900 followers.	The first cases of AIDS are identified. The disease has since taken 30 million lives, but early intervention in SF instituted key prevention measures and established global treatment standards.

a civil right in 1994. Just 45 days after taking office in 2004, San Francisco mayor Gavin Newsom authorized same-sex weddings in San Francisco. The first couple to be married were Phyllis Lyon and Del Martin, a San Francisco couple who had spent 52 years together. California courts ultimately voided their and 4036 other San Francisco same-sex marriage contracts but Lyon and Martin weren't dissuaded: they married again on June 18, 2008, with Mayor Newsom personally officiating. Martin passed away two months later at age 83, her wife by her side.

California courts struck down the 2008 law as unconstitutional in 2010, and upon appeal, the US Supreme Court upheld the state ruling in July 2013. In San Francisco, same-sex couples are once again getting hitched at City Hall – some of them for the second or third time to the same person, without ever getting divorced.

San Francisco 3.0

Industry dwindled steadily in San Francisco after WWII, as Oakland's port accommodated container ships and the Presidio's military presence tapered off. But onetime military tech contractors found work in a stretch of scrappy firms south of San Francisco, an area known today as Silicon Valley. When a company based in a South Bay garage called Hewlett-Packard introduced the 9100A 'computing genie' in 1968, a generation of unconventional thinkers and tinkerers took note.

Ads breathlessly gushed that Hewlett-Packard's 'light' (40lb) machine could 'take on roots of a fifth-degree polynomial, Bessel functions, elliptic integrals and regression analysis' – all for the low, low price of $4,900 (about $29,000 today). Consumers didn't know what to do with such a computer, until its potential was explained in simple terms by Stewart Brand, an LSD tester for the CIA with Ken Kesey and organizer of the first Trips Festival in 1966. In his 1969 *Whole Earth Catalog*, Brand reasoned that the technology governments used to run countries could empower ordinary people. That same year, University of California, Los Angeles, professor Len Kleinrock sent the first rudimentary email from his computer to another at Stanford. The message he typed was 'L,' then 'O,' then 'G' – at which point the computer crashed.

The next wave of California techies was determined to create a personal computer that could compute and communicate without crashing. When 21-year-old Steve Jobs and Steve Wozniak introduced the Apple II at San Francisco's West Coast Computer Faire in 1977, techies were abuzz about the memory (4KB of RAM!) and the microprocessor speed (1MHz!). The Mac II originally retailed for the equivalent today of $4300 (or for 48KB of RAM, more than twice that amount) – a staggering investment

Best Ways to Show Gay Pride

Join the Pride Parade

Get introduced to fabulous, fearless pioneers at GLBT Historical Society

Peruse petitions at Human Rights Campaign

Shop until there's a cure at AIDS fundraising boutique Under One Roof

Come out and play in the Mission, Castro and SoMa

HISTORY SAN FRANCISCO 3.0

October 17, 1989

The Loma Prieta earthquake hits 6.9 on the Richter scale; a freeway in SF and a Bay Bridge section collapse in 15 seconds, killing 41 people.

March 2000

After the NASDAQ index having peaked at double its value, the dot-com bubble pops and share prices plummet. Businesses across SF close within a month.

DAVID L. RYAN / GETTY IMAGES ©

Building damaged by the Loma Prieta earthquake

for what seemed like a glorified calculator/typewriter. Even if machines could talk to one another, pundits reasoned, what would they talk about?

A trillion web pages and a couple of million mobile apps later, it turns out machines have plenty to communicate. By the mid-1990s the dot-com industry boomed in SoMa warehouses, as start-up ventures rushed to put news, politics, fashion and, yes, sex online. But when venture capital funding dried up, multimillion-dollar sites shriveled into online oblivion. The paper fortunes of the dot-com boom disappeared on one nasty NASDAQ-plummeting day, March 10, 2000, leaving San Francisco service-sector employees and 26-year-old vice-presidents alike without any immediate job prospects. City dot-com revenues vanished; a 1999 FBI probe revealed that a windfall ended up in the pockets of real-estate developers. Today San Francisco is again sprouting startups that aim for the success of locally founded ventures like San Francisco–based Twitter, Pinterest, Yelp and Instagram – and just south of the city, Facebook, LinkedIn, YouTube, Apple, Google, Yahoo! and more.

Meanwhile, inside shiny new glass towers at SoMa's Mission Bay, biotech start-ups are putting down roots and yielding research. Biotech is nothing new here: since Genentech was founded over beer at a San Francisco bar in 1976, the company has cloned human insulin and introduced the hepatitis B vaccine. California voters approved a $3 billion bond measure in 2004 for stem cell research and by 2008 California had become the biggest funder of stem cell research. With so many global health crises demanding researchers' attention and funding, many cures still seem a distant, if not impossible dream – but if history is any indication, the impossible is almost certain to happen in San Francisco.

Top 5 for Weird Technology

Exploratorium
(Fisherman's Wharf)

Musée Mécanique
(Fisherman's Wharf)

Audium
(Japantown)

Wave Organ
(Marina)

Children's Creativity Museum (SoMa)

2004	February 2004	2010	2013
Google's IPO raises a historic $1.67 billion at $85 per share. By 2013, shares were worth more than ten times that amount and the company's worth had reached $114 billion.	Defying a Californian ban, SF mayor Gavin Newsom licenses 4037 same-sex marriages. Courts declare the marriages void but the civil rights challenge stands.	After SF couples file suit, California courts declare Proposition 8 prohibiting same-sex marriage unconstitutional due to equal rights protections.	Retrofit of the Bay Bridge is completed. Within weeks, 32 bolts are busted. Estimated cost to fix: $10 million; estimated completion: early 2014.

Local Cuisine & Drinks

Two secret ingredients have transformed this small city into a global culinary capital: dirt and competition. Almost anything grows in the fertile farmland around San Francisco and rocky hillsides yield fine wines in nearby Sonoma and Napa. Add Pacific seafood and coastal pasture-raised meats, and it seems like a no-fail recipe for a feast. But chefs need to work even harder to stand out in San Francisco, where everyone has access to top-notch ingredients and there's about one restaurant for every 227 people – more than anywhere else in the USA and twice as many as in New York. San Franciscans even grow their own food in 35 official community gardens, with 30 more proposed this year. Mock if you must but people have been known to move to SF for the food (ahem).

History

Before San Francisco became part of the US it belonged to Mexico, which established NorCal ranching and farming traditions. Early arrivals to California's Gold Rush came from around the Pacific Rim, and since most were men not accustomed to cooking for themselves, they relied on makeshift restaurants. SF's cross-cultural cravings began with '49er favorites: Chinese chow mein, local oysters and French wines. Between hot meals, miners survived on chocolate bars, invented in San Francisco by Domingo Ghirardelli.

Fishing and farming brought fresh ingredients and new dishes to San Francisco. Before the first Italian restaurant in the USA opened in 1886 at North Beach, Italian fishermen cooked up vats of *cioppino* (seafood stew) dockside. The 1942–64 US Bracero Program importing Mexican agricultural labor brought local variations on Mexican staples, including megameals wrapped in flour tortillas known as burritos.

After the 1960s, many disillusioned idealists concluded that the revolution was not about to be delivered on a platter – but chef Alice Waters thought otherwise. In 1971 she opened Chez Panisse (p219) in a converted house in Berkeley, with the then-radical notion of highlighting the ultrafresh flavors of the Bay Area's seasonal, sustainably produced bounty – and diners tasted the difference for themselves. Today, Waters' call for good, clean, fair food has become a worldwide Slow Food manifesto and a rallying call for Bay Area chefs like Evan and Sarah Rich.

Food Specialties

California Cuisine

What other cities might call fusion fare or California cuisine, San Francisco just calls dinner. There's nothing fussy or forced about mixing cuisines here – after 150 years, it's become a reflex. Dishes are prepared with a light touch, highlighting ingredients grown locally with San Francisco's worldly, adventurous eaters in mind: Cantonese choy sum, Treviso radicchio, Blenheim apricots. But don't be fooled into thinking it's easy. A single dish may use knife skills learned from Asian neighbors and cooking techniques borrowed from the Mediterranean, where the climate and soil are similar to the Bay Area's.

Ethnic Comfort Food

Since one out of three San Franciscans is born overseas, SF's go-to comfort foods aren't just burgers and pizza – though you'll find plenty of those – but *pho* (Vietnamese noodles), tandoori chicken, *kimchi* (Korean fermented vegetables) and, above all, dim sum and burritos. Anyone attempting to leave San Francisco without trying these last two favorites should be turned back at the airport for their own good – though once you try them, you might not want to leave.

Dim sum is Cantonese for what's known in Mandarin as *xiao che* (small eats); some also call it *yum cha* (drink tea). Waitstaff roll carts past your table with steaming baskets of dumplings, platters of garlicky sautéed greens and, finally, plates of sweet crispy sesame balls and creamy egg custard.

The most hotly debated local dish is the SF burrito, which is nothing like imposters you'll find elsewhere. San Franciscans have religious convictions about correct fillings: beans (pinto, black or, heaven help you, refried), meats (grilled, stewed or, blessed be, fried pork carnitas) and salsas (tomato-onion *pico de gallo,* tangy green tomatillo or smoky mesquite). This is all loaded onto a flour tortilla and rolled into a foodstuff the approximate length and girth of a forearm. No one finishes, but leftovers rival cold pizza as SF's guilty-pleasure breakfast.

Seafood

The Pacific offers a haul of seafood to San Francisco diners but there's trouble in those waters: some species have been overfished and their extinction could throw the local aquaculture off balance. Monterey Bay Aquarium has been monitoring local fish stock for decades and its Seafood Watch program helps diners identify best options, good choices

---

Top 5 Dim Sum

Chairman food truck (Off the Grid; Marina)

Ton Kiang Restaurant (the Richmond)

City View (Chinatown)

Great Eastern Restaurant (Chinatown)

San Tung (the Sunset)

EVAN RICH: CHEF & RESTAURATEUR

East Coast v West Coast

I was born and raised in Queens and I thought the New York restaurant scene had it all. San Francisco proved me wrong...but I had to eat at Chez Panisse twice to really understand Californian cuisine. The first time I thought, right, it's basically a classic rustic French approach to food. Then after being here a year, I went back to Chez Panisse and I recognized all the subtleties I'd missed, the way each preparation highlighted the varietal characteristics of a particular ingredient. That takes finesse.

Getting Fresh in SF

Working with Daniel [Patterson, at Coi] I learned there's a life force, an energy to produce when it's freshly picked, so you have to think fast to maximize that flavor. Ideally I'd like to serve a dish made with ingredients harvested within a couple hours – we're working on planting a kitchen garden down the block.

Innovation Served Nightly

We're around the corner from SFJazz Center, so yeah, the pressure is on to improvise with the best. Our neighborhood regulars are from Apple and Google, technology leaders who trust us to innovate but also execute at a certain level. We can't afford to have an off-night here or we'll hear about it from our customers all over Twitter and Yelp – because they invented that stuff.

Evan Rich is co-chef/owner with spouse and fellow chef Sarah Rich of Rich Table (p189), 2013 James Beard nominee for Best New Restaurant in America.

Taco, chips and salsa at Mijita (p94) in the Ferry Building

and items to avoid on local seafood menus – find out which of your seafood favorites are on the best list at www.montereybayaquarium.org/cr/seafoodwatch.aspx. Delicious, sustainable, local seafood choices found almost year-round include wild Dungeness crab, locally farmed oysters and locally farmed caviar.

Sourdough Bread

San Francisco is famous for its sourdough bread, although the pucker-inducing aftertaste can be an acquired taste. The most famous 'mother dough' in town dates back to 1849, when baker Isidore Boudin hit on a combination of wild yeast and bacteria that's been kept alive ever since. You'll see people eating sourdough bowls filled with clam chowder down at Fisherman's Wharf, but be warned: the combination of starchy, salty glop with the very occasional clam has yet to be proven digestible.

Vegetarian & Vegan Food

To all you beleaguered vegetarians, accustomed to eating out at places where the only non-animal dish is some unspeakable vegetarian lasagna: you're in San Francisco now. While fine dining chefs elsewhere stake their reputations on French truffle-strewn steaks, California-grown fruits and vegetables are not side dishes to Bay Area chefs, but tasting-menu highlights. On the cheaper side, vegetarian options abound at taquerias, pizzerias, noodle joints, Middle Eastern delis, food trucks and groceries. With the most farmers markets of any metropolitan area in the US (30 and counting), you're not about to run out of veggie options anytime soon. There are plenty of great choices for vegans on local menus, including fine-dining prix fixes at Coi (p125) and all-vegan Millennium (p96).

Top 5 for Local & Sustainable Seafood

Tataki (Pacific Heights)

Benu (SoMa)

Jardinière (Hayes Valley)

Hog Island Oyster Company (Ferry Building)

La Mar Cebicheria (Embarcadero)

Drink Specialties

Wine

Wine bars are the newest, oldest trend on the SF drinking scene. Wine has been the local drink ever since Mission Solano was established in Sonoma with acres of vineyards, more than strictly necessary for communion wine. While Gold Rush miners who struck it rich splashed out for imported champagne at SF bars, others found solace in beverages from Napa and Sonoma. Some local vines survived federal scrutiny during Prohibition, on the grounds that the grapes were needed for sacramental wines back east – a bootlegging bonanza that kept SF speakeasies well supplied.

Drinking snobbery is reversed in SF: wine drinkers don't mind something local and on tap, while beer drinkers fuss over their monk-brewed triple Belgians and debate relative hoppiness levels. It's not that SF wine drinkers are always so easy to please – the local selection's just that good. Many of the USA's best wines are produced nearby, including excellent cabernet, zinfandel, syrah, pinot noir (and rosé of pinot noir), viognier, chardonnay, sauvignon blanc and sparkling wines.

VIP bottle service and Kristal are so LA: there's no reason to get fancy just to get a decent glass of wine in SF, where bars like Barrique just roll out the barrels from local wineries and pour the good stuff straight from the tap. But at restaurants, many wine lists outsize the food menu and feature cult wines that aren't distributed outside California. Consult your sommelier to help you find daring parings by the glass or bottle, or take tips from Benu's acclaimed sommelier Yoon Ha (p102).

Top 5 Wine Bars

RN74 (SoMa)

Terroir Natural Wine Merchant (SoMa)

Barrique (Financial District)

Hôtel Biron (Hayes Valley)

20 Spot (the Mission)

Beer

Blowing off steam took on new meaning during the Gold Rush, when entrepreneurs trying to keep up with the demand for drink started brewing beer at higher temperatures. The result was a full, rich flavor and such powerful effervescence that when a keg was tapped, a mist would rise like steam. The much-beloved Anchor Brewing Company has made its signature Anchor Steam amber ale this way with copper distilling equipment since 1896. Other favorite local brews include Trumer Pils, Sierra Nevada Pale Ale, Speakeasy Big Daddy IPA and Boont Amber Ale, plus local seasonal microbrews. Head to the City Beer Store & Tasting Room for a drinkable education and leave a tipsy connoisseur.

Historic Cocktails

The highest honorific for a bartender in San Francisco isn't mixologist (too technical) or artisan (too medieval), but drink historian. Cocktails have appeared on San Francisco happy-hour menus since its Barbary Coast days, when they were used to sedate sailors and shanghai them onto outbound ships. Now bartenders are researching old recipes and reviving SF traditions: ladling rum punch from crystal bowls, topping Pisco sours with traditional foamy egg whites as though no one had ever heard of veganism or salmonella, and apparently still trying to knock sailors cold with Old Fashioneds made with bourbon, bitters, zest and vengeance.

Every self-respecting SF bartender holds strong opinions on the martini, first mentioned in an 1887 bartending guide by Professor Jerry Thomas. Legend has it that the martini was invented when a boozehound walked into an SF bar and demanded something to tide him over until he reached Martinez across the bay. The original was made with vermouth, gin, bitters, lemon, maraschino cherry and ice, though by the 1950s the recipe was reduced to gin with vermouth vapors and an olive or a twist. Today Comstock Saloon (p127) offers a version of the original Martinez, and Aub Zam Zam (p192) a Sinatra Rat Pack version.

Top 5 for Researched Cocktails

Bar Agricole (SoMa)

Smuggler's Cove (Hayes Valley)

Bourbon & Branch (the Tenderloin)

Rickhouse (Union Square)

Comstock Saloon (North Beach)

Literary
San Francisco

San Francisco has more writers than any other US city and hoards three times as many library books as the national average. The truth of San Francisco is stranger than its fiction: where else could poetry fight the law and win? Yet that's exactly what happened in the 1957 landmark anti-censorship ruling People v Ferlinghetti. Though it may seem anachronistic here in the capital of new technology, San Franciscans continue to buy more books per capita than other US cities.

Required Reading

Any self-respecting SF bookshelf hosts plenty of poetry (Beat authors obligatory), a graphic novel, nonfiction essays about the San Francisco scene and at least one novel by a Bay Area author.

Poetry

San Francisco's Kenneth Rexroth popularized haiku here back in the 1950s and residents still enjoy nothing more than a few well-chosen words. When SF has you waxing poetic, hit an open mic in the Mission.
   Key titles:

➡ *Howl and Other Poems* (Allen Ginsberg) Each line of Ginsberg's epic title poem is an ecstatic improvised mantra, chronicling the waking dreams of the Beat generation that rejected postwar conformity.

➡ *Time and Materials* (Robert Hass) Each word in these Pulitzer Prize–winning poems by the Berkeley-based US poet laureate is as essential and grounding as a rivet in the Golden Gate Bridge.

➡ *A Coney Island of the Mind* (Lawrence Ferlinghetti) This slim 1958 collection by San Francisco's poet laureate is an indispensable doorstop for the imagination, letting fresh air and ideas circulate.

Fiction

Many San Franciscans seem like characters in a novel and after a few days here, you'll swear you've seen Armistead Maupin's corn-fed Castro newbies, Dashiell Hammett's dangerous redheads and Amy Tan's American-born daughters explaining slang to Chinese-speaking moms.
   Key titles:

➡ *Tales of the City* (Armistead Maupin) The 1976 *San Francisco Chronicle* serial follows true San Francisco characters: pot-growing landladies of mystery, ever-hopeful Castro club-goers and wide-eyed Midwestern arrivals.

➡ *The Joy Luck Club* (Amy Tan) The stories of four Chinese-born women and their American-born daughters are woven into a textured history of immigration and aspiration in San Francisco's Chinatown.

➡ *The Maltese Falcon* (Dashiell Hammett) In this classic noir novel, private eye Sam Spade risks his reputation on a case involving an elusive redhead, a gold statuette, the Holy Roman Empire and an unholy cast of thugs.

**Best for
Spoken
Word**

*Yerba Buena
Center for the
Arts (SoMa)*

*Edinburgh Castle
(the Tenderloin)*

*Make-Out Room
(the Mission)*

*Amnesia (the
Mission)*

*Marsh (the
Mission)*

272

LITERARY SAN FRANCISCO

Nonfiction & Memoir

People-watching rivals reading as a preferred San Francisco pastime and close observation of antics that would seem bizarre elsewhere pays off in stranger-than-fiction nonfiction – hence Hunter S Thompson's gonzo journalism and Joan Didion's core-shaking truth-telling.

Key titles:

➡ *Slouching Towards Bethlehem* (Joan Didion) Like hot sun through San Francisco fog, Didion's 1968 essays burn through the hippie haze to reveal glassy-eyed teenagers adrift in the Summer of Love.

➡ *On the Road* (Jack Kerouac) The book Kerouac banged out on one long scroll of paper in a San Francisco attic over a couple of sleepless months of 1951 shook America awake.

➡ *Hell's Angels: A Strange and Terrible Saga* (Hunter S Thompson) This spare-no-details account of the outlaw Bay Area motorcycle club invented gonzo journalism and scandalized the nation.

➡ *The Electric Kool-Aid Acid Test* (Tom Wolfe) His florid style seems dated, but Wolfe had extraordinary presence of mind to capture the '60s with Ken Kesey, the Merry Pranksters, the Grateful Dead and Hell's Angels.

Graphic Novels

Ambrose Bierce and Mark Twain set the San Francisco standard for sardonic wit, but recently Bay Area graphic novelists like R Crumb and Daniel Clowes have added a twist to this tradition with finely drawn, deadpan behavioral studies. For more, don't miss the Cartoon Art Museum (p85).

Key titles:

➡ *Ghost World* (Daniel Clowes) The Oakland-based graphic novelist's sleeper hit follows recent high-school grads Enid and Rebecca as they make plans, make do, grow up and grow apart.

➡ *All Over Coffee* (Paul Madonna) The San Francisco-based artist combines watercolor landscapes of the city with stories that may have taken place there, if anywhere.

Zines

The local 'zine scene has been the underground mother lode of riveting reading since the '70s brought punk, a DIY ethic and V Vale's groundbreaking *RE/Search* to San Francisco. The most successful local zine of all, McSweeney's, is the initiative of Dave Eggers, who achieved first-person fame with *A Heartbreaking Work of Staggering Genius* and generously sunk the proceeds into 826 Valencia, a nonprofit writing program for teens. McSweeney's also publishes an excellent map of literary San Francisco so you can walk the talk.

Spoken Word

San Francisco's literary tradition doesn't just hang out on bookshelves. Allen Ginsberg's ecstatic readings of *Howl* continue to inspire slam poets at Litquake (p23) and Beat authors like Kerouac freed up generations of open-mic monologuists from the tyranny of tales with morals and punctuation.

Best for Comics & Graphic Novels

Cartoon Art Museum gift shop (SoMa)

Isotope (Hayes Valley)

Kinokuniya Books & Stationery (Japantown)

Alternative Press Expo (Month by Month)

Best for Zines

San Francisco Main Library Zine Reading Area (Civic Center)

Needles & Pens (the Mission)

826 Valencia (the Mission)

Adobe Books (the Mission)

Bound Together Anarchist Book Collective (the Haight)

Visual Arts

Art explodes from frames and jumps off the pedestal in San Francisco, where murals, street performances and impromptu sidewalk altars flow from alleyways right into galleries. Velvet ropes would only get in the way of SF's enveloping installations and interactive new-media art – often provocative and occasionally off-putting, but never standoffish.

Media & Methods

San Francisco has some unfair artistic advantages: it's a photogenic city with a colorful past, with 150-year-old photography and painting traditions to prove it. Homegrown traditions of '50s Beat collage, '60s psychedelia, '70s punk, '80s graffiti, '90s skater-graphics and 2000s new-media art keep San Francisco's art scene vibrant.

Best for Photography

MH de Young Museum (Golden Gate Park)

Fraenkel Gallery at 49 Geary (Union Square)

Yerba Buena Center for the Arts (SoMa)

Chinese Historical Society of America (Chinatown)

Photography

Pioneering 19th-century photographer Pirkle Jones saw expressive potential in California landscape photography, but it was SF native Ansel Adams' photos of Northern California's sublime wilds and his accounts of photography in Yosemite in the 1940s that would draw legions of camera-clutching visitors to San Francisco. Adams founded Group f/64 with Edward Weston, who kept a studio in SF and made frequent visits from his permanent base in nearby Carmel.

Dorothea Lange spent many years based in San Francisco, photographing Californians grappling with the hardship of the Great Depression and Japanese Americans forced to leave their San Francisco homes for WWII internment camps. This legacy of cultural critique continues with the colorful Californian suburban dystopias of Larry Sultan and Todd Hido.

Social Commentary

The 1930s social realist movement brought Mexican muralist Diego Rivera to San Francisco – and with him came bold new approaches to public art. The Depression-era Work Projects Administration (WPA) sponsored several SF muralists, and from the 1970s their larger-than-life figures and leftist leanings have been reprised in works by Mission *muralistas*, such as the Women's Building.

Offsetting high-minded revolutionary art is gutsy, irreverent SF satire. Tony Labatt's 1970s video of disco balls dangling from his nether regions sums up SF's disco-era narcissism, while Lynn Hershman Leeson's performances as alter-ego Roberta Breitmore chronicled 1970s encounters with feminism, self-help and diet fads. San Francisco provocateur Enrique Chagoya serves comic relief for banking-crisis hunger pangs with his Warhol-esque 'Mergers, Acquisitions and Lentils' soupcans at Electric Works.

RICK GERHARTER / GETTY IMAGES ©

Diego Rivera's mural *The Making of a Fresco* in the Diego Rivera Gallery (p136)

Abstract Thinking

Local art schools attracted major abstract expressionist talents during SF's vibrant postwar period, when Clyfford Still, David Park and Elmer Bischoff taught at the San Francisco Art Institute. Still and Park founded the misleadingly named Bay Area Figurative Art movement, an elemental style often associated with San Francisco painter Richard Diebenkorn's fractured, color-blocked landscapes. Diebenkorn influenced San Francisco Pop artist Wayne Thiebaud, who tilted Sunset street grids into giddy Bay Area abstract cityscapes.

Best for Inspired Abstract Art

....

Haines Gallery at 49 Geary (Union Square)

....

Eli Ridgway (SoMa)

....

Gregory Lind Gallery at 49 Geary (Union Square)

....

Eleanor Harwood Gallery (the Mission)

High Concept, High Craft

San Francisco's peculiar dedication to craft and personal vision can get obsessive. Consider *The Rose,* the legendary painting Beat artist Jay DeFeo began in the 1950s and worked on for eight years, layering it with 2000lb of paint until a hole had to be cut in the wall of her apartment to forklift it out. Ruth Asawa started weaving not with wool but metal in the 1950s, creating intricate MH de Young Museum sculptures that look like jellyfish within onion domes within mushrooms. SF's most famous obsessive is Matthew Barney, raised in San Francisco, who made his definitive debut at SFMOMA with *Cremaster Cycle* videos involving vats of Vaseline.

Street Smarts

With Balmy Alley murals as inspiration, SF skateboard decks and Clarion Alley garage doors were transformed in the 1990s with boldly outlined, oddly poignant graphics, dubbed 'Mission School' for their storytelling *muralista* sensibilities and graffiti-tag urgency. The Mission School's professor emeritus was the late Margaret Kilgallen, whose closely observed character studies blended hand-painted street signage, comic-book pathos and a miniaturist's attention to detail.

Clare Rojas expanded on these principles with urban folk-art wall paintings, featuring looming, clueless California grizzly bears and tiny, fierce girls in hoodies. Barry McGee's assemblages include piles of found bottles painted with freckled, feckless characters and jumpy animations shown on beat-up TVs. Some Mission School art is fairly derided as the faux-naive work of stoned MFAs – but when its earnestness works, it hits you where it counts.

New Media

The technological expertise of the Bay Area is hard to match and it's no surprise that local artists are putting it to creative use in new media artwork. Since the '80s, Silicon Valley artist Jim Campbell has been building motherboards to misbehave – in one case, a running figure freezes as soon as it senses viewers approaching and, like a frightened doe, will resume activity only if you stay stock-still. Rebecca Bollinger's grouped sketches are inspired by images found through a web keyword search, while Kota Ezawa created special cartoon-image software to turn the OJ Simpson trial into the multichannel cartoon animation it actually was.

San Francisco's interactive artists invite you to burp the art and change its DNA. John Slepian programmed a hairy rubber nub swaddled in blankets to sob disconsolately, until you pick it up and pat its posterior. New media artist Scott Snibbe created an app that allows users to not only remix but alter the musical DNA of Bjork's *Biophilia* compositions by attacking songs with visual viruses and splicing new cells into the melodies.

Public Sculpture

San Franciscans have had strong feelings about public sculpture since at least 1894, when vigilante art critics pulled down a statue of dentist Henry D Cogswell over a Washington Square Park drinking fountain he'd donated.

The WPA commissioned all-stars to adorn the Aquatic Park Bathhouse with art, including a totemic seal by Beniamino Bufano and a green-slate nautical frieze by pioneering African American artist Sargent Johnson. Bufano also sculpted Chinese revolutionary Sun Yat-sen's statue in Chinatown and San Francisco City College's 1968 *St Francis of the Guns,* made of 1,968 guns collected in a San Francisco gun-buyback scheme. St Francis' mosaic robe features four assassinated leaders: Abraham Lincoln, Dr Martin Luther King, Jr, and John Fitzgerald and Robert Kennedy.

The sculptor who made the biggest impact on the San Francisco landscape in sheer scale is Richard Serra, from the rooftop sculpture garden at SFMOMA to University of California San Francisco's Mission Bay campus. Serra's massive rusted-metal minimalist shapes have been favorably compared to ship's prows – and less generously, Soviet factory seconds.

Some San Francisco public sculptures are not above cheap puns – or hot debate. A gift to the city from SF-based founders of the Gap, Claes Oldenburg & Coosje van Bruggen's 2002 *Cupid's Span* represents the city's reputation for romance with a giant bow and arrow sunk into the Embarcadero. But the city wasn't smitten: a recent poll ranks it among SF's most despised public artworks. Tony Bennett's musical anthem 'I Left My Heart in San Francisco' inspired SF General's Hearts in San Francisco fundraising project, but the cartoon hearts have been regularly graffitied, denounced as eyesores by public park advocates and marked by territorial canine critics.

VISUAL ARTS MEDIA & METHODS

Best for Murals

San Francisco Art Institute's Diego Rivera Gallery (Russian Hill)

Coit Tower (North Beach)

WPA Murals at Rincon Annex (SoMa)

Balmy Alley (the Mission)

Best for New Media

di Rosa Art + Nature Preserve (Napa Valley)

Catharine Clark Gallery (SoMa)

Southern Exposure (the Mission)

MH de Young Museum (Golden Gate Park)

San Francisco Music

Only an extremely eclectic DJ can cover SF's varied musical tastes. Classical, blue-grass, Latin music and Chinese and Italian opera have survived fire and earthquakes in San Francisco. Music trends that started around the Bay never really went away: '50s free-form jazz and folk; '60s psychedelic rock; '70s disco bathhouse anthems; and '90s west-coast rap and Berkeley's punk revival. Today, DJ mash-ups put SF's entire back catalog to work.

Classical Music & Opera

Since conductor Michael Tilson Thomas was wooed away from London Symphony Orchestra to take the baton here in 1995, San Francisco Symphony has raked in international accolades. The Symphony has won more Grammys than Lady Gaga and you can see why: Thomas conducts on the tips of his toes, enthralling audiences with full-throttle Mahler and Beethoven and some genuinely odd experimental music.

San Francisco Opera is the USA's second-largest opera company after New York's Metropolitan Opera, but it's second to none with risk-taking. You'd never guess San Francisco's opera roots go back to the 19th century from avant-garde productions like *Dangerous Liaisons, Harvey Milk, Dead Man Walking* and the definitive revival of Puccini's California Gold Rush opera *The Girl of the Golden West* featuring Pavarotti successor Salvatore Licitra.

Rock

San Francisco's rock of choice lately is preceded by the prefix alt- or in-die- at music extravaganzas like Outside Lands, Noise Pop and the free Mission Creek Oakland Festival. SF acts like Rogue Wave, Peggy Honeywell and Joanna Newsom add acoustic roots stylings even when they're not playing the FolkYeah! and Hardly Strictly Bluegrass festivals, while Black Rebel Motorcycle Club and Deerhoof throw Mission grit into their seismic walls of sound. Metalheads need no introduction to the mighty Metallica, the triumphant survivors of a genre nearly smothered in the '80s by its own hair.

Before you arrived, you may have had the impression San Francisco's rock scene had ODed long ago. Fair enough. San Francisco has the ignominious distinction of being a world capital of rocker drug overdoses. In the Haight, you can pass places Janis nearly met her maker; 32 Delmar St, where Sid Vicious went on the heroin bender that finally broke up the Sex Pistols; and the Grateful Dead flophouse, where the band was drug-raided. Grateful Dead guitarist Jerry Garcia eluded the bust and survived for decades, until his death in rehab in 1995. Jerry's former band mates still periodically tour under the name Furthur.

Baby boomers keep the sound of San Francisco in the '60s alive and much of it stands the tests of time and sobriety. After Joan Baez and Bob Dylan had their Northern California fling, folk turned into folk rock and Jimi Hendrix turned the American anthem into a tune suitable for an acid trip. When Janis Joplin and Big Brother & the Holding Company applied their rough musical stylings to 'Me and Bobby McGee,' it was like applying that last necessary pass of sandpaper to the sometimes clunky, wooden verses of traditional folk. Jefferson Airplane held court at the Fillmore, turning Lewis Caroll's opium-inspired children's classic into the psychedelic anthem 'White Rabbit' with singer Grace Slick's piercing wail.

The '60s were quite a trip but the '70s rocked on. Crosby, Stills, Nash & Young splintered, but Neil Young keeps 'rockin' in the free world' from his ranch south of San Francisco with his earnest, bluesy whine. Since the 1970s, California-born, longtime Marin resident Tom Waits has been singing in a gruff, after-hours, Western honky-tonk voice with a permanent catch in the throat. SF's own Steve Miller Band turned out stoner hits like 'The Joker,' and Mission-born, lifelong San Franciscan Carlos Santana combined a guitar moan and Latin backbeat in 'Black Magic Woman,' 'Evil Ways' and 'Oye Como Va' – and made a crossover comeback with 1999's Grammy-winning *Supernatural* and 2005 *All That I Am,* featuring fellow San Franciscan Kirk Hammett of Metallica.

Funk & Hip-Hop

The '60s were perhaps best summed up by freaky-funky, racially integrated San Francisco supergroup Sly and the Family Stone in their creatively spelled 1969 number-one hit: 'Thank You (Falettinme Be Mice Elf Agin).' San Francisco's '70s funk was mostly reverb from across the bay in Oakland, where Tower of Power worked a groove with taut horn arrangements.

All this trippy funk worked its way into the DNA of the Bay Area hip-hop scene, spawning the jazz-inflected, free-form Charlie Hunter Trio and the infectious wokka-wokka baseline of rapper Lyrics Born. Oakland's MC Hammer was an '80s crossover hip-hop hitmaker best known for inflicting harem pants on the world, though his influence is heard in E-40's bouncing hyphy sound. Political commentary and pop hooks became East Bay hip-hop signatures with Michael Franti and Spearhead, Blackalicious and the Coup. But the Bay Area is still best known as the home of the world's most talented and notorious rapper: Tupac Shakur, killed in 1996 by an assailant out to settle an East Coast/West Coast gangsta rap rivalry.

Best for Rock & Punk

Fillmore Auditorium (Japantown)

Warfield (Union Square)

Bottom of the Hill (Potrero Hill)

Great American Music Hall (the Tenderloin)

Slim's (SoMa)

SAN FRANCISCO MUSIC FUNK & HIP-HOP

SF ECLECTIC HITS PLAYLIST

Take Five by Dave Brubeck Quartet (1959)

Make You Feel That Way by Blackalicious (2002)

Everyday People by Sly and the Family Stone (1968)

Evil Ways by Santana (1969)

Come Out and Play (Keep 'Em Separated) by The Offspring (1994)

Lights by Journey (1978)

Uncle John's Band by The Grateful Dead (1970)

Stay Human (All the Freaky People) by Michael Franti & Spearhead (2007)

San Francisco Anthem by San Quinn (2008)

Welcome to Paradise by Green Day (1992)

The American in Me by The Avengers (1979)

Come Back from San Francisco by Magnetic Fields (1999)

California by Rogue Wave (2005)

Me and Bobby McGee by Janis Joplin (1971)

Punk

London may have been more political and Los Angeles more hardcore, but San Francisco's take on punk was weirder. Dead Kennedys frontman Jello Biafra ran for mayor in 1979 with a platform written on the back of a bar napkin: ban cars, set official rates for bribery and force businessmen to dress as clowns. He received 6000 votes and his political endorsement is still highly prized. But for oddity even Jello can't top The Residents, whose identities remain unknown after 60 records and three decades of performances wearing giant eyeballs over their heads.

Today, punk's not dead in the Bay Area – in fact, it's getting mainstream radio play. Ska-inflected Rancid and pop-punk Green Day brought punk staggering out of Berkeley's 924 Gilman into the mass-media spotlight. Hardcore punks sneered at Green Day's chart-topping hits, but the group earned street cred (and Grammys) in 2004 with the dark social critique of *American Idiot* – at least until that album became a Broadway musical. Following the early success of *Punk in Drublic,* San Francisco–based NOFX recorded an impressively degenerate show at Slim's called *I Hear They've Gotten Worse Live!* Punk continues to evolve in San Francisco, with queercore Pansy Division, the brass-ballsiness of Latin ska-punk La Plebe, and all-girl, all-badass rockers the Donnas.

Jazz

Best for Jazz

....

SFJazz (Hayes Valley)

....

Yoshi's (Japantown)

....

Intersection for the Arts (the Mission)

....

Yerba Buena Center for the Arts (SoMa)

....

The Chapel (Mission)

Ever since house bands pounded out ragtime hits to distract Barbary Coast audiences from bar-room brawls, San Francisco has echoed with jazz. The new SFJAZZ Center is the nation's second jazz center and a magnet for global talents as artists-in-residence.

SF swung in the 1950s with West Coast jazz innovated by the legendary Dave Brubeck Quartet, whose *Time Out* is among the best-selling jazz albums of all time. Bebop had disciples among the Beats and the SF scene is memorably chronicled in Kerouac's *On the Road.* Billie Holiday and Miles Davis recorded here and John Coltrane is revered as a saint at the African Orthodox Church of St John Coltrane.

During the '60s, the SF jazz scene exploded into a kaleidoscope of styles. Trumpeter Don Cherry blew minds with Ornette Coleman's avant-garde ensemble, while Dixieland band Turk Murphy kept roots jazz relevant. At legendary Yoshi's and Preservation Hall West's The Chapel, tempos shift from Latin jazz to klezmer, acid jazz to swing, and jazz traditionalists regularly play Hardly Strictly Bluegrass Festival. Even jazz newbies recognize native San Franciscan Vince Guaraldi's score for *A Charlie Brown Christmas*, a beloved antidote to standard Christmas carols.

San Francisco Architecture

Superman wouldn't be so impressive in San Francisco, where most buildings are low enough for even a middling superhero to leap in a single bound. The Transamerica Pyramid and Ferry Building clock tower are helpful pointers to orient newcomers and Coit Tower adds emphatic punctuation to the city skyline – but San Francisco's low-profile buildings are its highlights, from Mission adobe and gabled Victorians to forward-thinking grass-covered roofs. Keeping a low profile in the midst of it all are Western storefronts, their jagged rooflines as lopsided and charming as a cowboy's smirk.

The Mission & Early SF

Not much is left of San Francisco's original Ohlone-style architecture, beyond the grass memorial hut you'll see in the graveyard of Spanish Mission Dolores and the wall of the original Presidio (military post), both built in adobe with conscripted Ohlone labor. When the Gold Rush began, buildings were slapped together from ready-made sawn timber components, sometimes shipped from the East Coast or Australia – a sign of postwar prefab ahead.

In SF's Barbary Coast days, City Hall wasn't much to look at, at least from outside: it was housed in the burlesque Jenny Lind Theater at Portsmouth Square. Most waterfront buildings from SF's hot-headed Wild West days were lost to arson, including San Francisco's long-lost neighborhoods of Sydneytown and Chiletown, named for early Gold Rush arrivals. Eventually, builders of Jackson Square got wise and switched to brick.

But masonry was no match for the 1906 earthquake and fire, which left the waterfront almost completely leveled – with the mysterious, highly explosive exception of the Italianate 1866 AP Hotaling's Warehouse, which at the time housed SF's largest whiskey stash. The snappiest comeback in SF history is now commemorated in a bronze plaque on the building: 'If, as they say, God spanked the town/For being over-frisky/Why did He burn His churches down/And spare Hotaling's whiskey?'

Uphill toward North Beach, you'll spot a few other original 1860s–80s Italianate brick storefronts wisely built on bedrock: elevated false facades are capped with jutting cornices, a straight roofline and graceful arches over tall windows.

Victoriana

To make room for new arrivals with the gold, railroad and shipping booms, San Francisco had to expand – and fast. Wooden Victorian row houses cropped up almost overnight with a similar underlying floor plan, but with eye-catching embellishments so inhabitants stumbling home after Barbary Coast nights could recognize their homes. Some of these 'Painted Ladies' proved surprisingly sturdy: several upstanding Victorian row-houses remain in Pacific Heights, the Haight and the Mission.

Best for Early Architecture

Mission Dolores
(Mission)

Presidio (Marina & Presidio)

Cottage Row
(Fillmore)

Jackson Square
(Downtown)

Old St Mary's Cathedral & Square
(Chinatown)

Octagon House
(Cow Hollow)

The Victorian era was a time of colonial conquest and the culmination of the European Age of Discovery, and Victorians liked to imagine themselves as the true successors of great early civilizations. San Franciscans incorporated designs from ancient Rome, Egypt and the Italian Renaissance into grand mansions around Alamo Square, giving fresh-out-of-the-box San Francisco a hodge-podge instant culture.

Pacific Polyglot Architecture

A trip across town or even down the block will bring you face to facade with San Francisco's Spanish and Mexican heritage, Asian ancestry and California Arts and Crafts roots. San Francisco's cinemas and theaters dispense with geographical logic in favor of pure fantasy, from the scalloped Moorish arches of the 1913 Exotic Revivalist Alcazar Theater at 650 Geary St to the Italianate bordello baroque of the 1907 Great American Music Hall.

Best for Victorian Architecture

....

Alamo Square (the Haight)

....

Haight Flashback walking tour (the Haight)

....

Haas-Lilienthal House (Pacific Heights)

....

Conservatory of Flowers (Golden Gate Park & Avenues)

....

Columbarium (Golden Gate Park & Avenues)

....

Chateau Tivoli (the Haight)

Mission & Meso-American Influences

Never mind that Mexico and Spain actually fought over California, and missionaries and Aztecs had fundamental religious and cultural differences: San Francisco's flights of architectural fancy paved over historical differences with cement, tile and stucco. Meso-American influences are obvious in the stone-carved Aztec motifs on Sansome St banks and 1929 Mayan-Deco gilt reliefs that add jaw-dropping grandeur to the lobby of architect Timothy Pfleuger's 450 Sutter St dental office building.

San Francisco's 1915–35 mission revival paid tribute to California's Hispanic heritage, influenced by the 1915 Panama–Pacific International Exposition held in San Francisco. Spanish baroque fads flourished with the 1918 construction of a new *churrigueresque* (Spanish baroque) Mission Dolores basilica, replacing the earlier brick Gothic cathedral damaged in the 1906 earthquake. The look proved popular for secular buildings, such as the Spanish baroque Castro Theatre marquee.

Chinatown Deco

Distinctive Chinatown Deco became a cornerstone of Chinatown's redevelopment initiative after the 1906 quake. A forward-thinking group of Chinatown merchants led by Look Tin Eli consulted with a cross-section of architects and rudimentary focus groups to reinvent brothel-lined Dupont St as tourist-friendly, pagoda-topped Grant St, with dragon lanterns and crowd-pleasing modern chinoiserie buildings.

The first licensed female architect in California and the chief architect of over-the-top Spanish-Gothic-Greek folly Hearst Castle, Julia Morgan showed tasteful restraint and finesse combining cultural traditions in her designs for the pagoda-topped brick Chinatown YWCA (now the Chinese Historical Society of America) and graceful Italianate Emanu-el Sisterhood Residence (now home to the San Francisco Zen Center).

California Arts & Crafts

California Arts and Crafts style combines Mission influences with English Arts and Crafts architecture, as seen in Bay Area Craftsman cottages and earthy ecclesiastical structures like San Francisco's Swedenborgian Church.

Berkeley-based architect Bernard Maybeck reinvented England's Arts and Crafts movement with the down-to-earth California bungalow, a small, simple single-story design derived from summer homes

The Contemporary Jewish Museum (p86), designed by Daniel Libeskind

favored by British officers serving in India. Though Maybeck's Greco-Roman 1915 Palace of Fine Arts was intended as a temporary structure, the beloved almost-ruined fake ruin was recast in concrete in the 1960s and it continues to serve as San Franciscans' favorite wedding-photo backdrop.

Modern Skyline

Once steel-frame buildings stood the test of the 1906 earthquake, San Francisco began to think big with its buildings. The city aspired to rival the capitols of Europe and commissioned architect Daniel Burnham to build a grand City Hall in the neoclassical Parisian beaux arts or 'city beautiful' style. But City Hall was reduced to a mere shell by the 1906 earthquake and it wasn't until 1924 that architect Timothy Pfleuger built San Francisco's first real skyscraper: the Gothic Deco, 26-storey 1924 Pacific Telephone Building on 140 New Montgomery St. Recently restored, the telecom megalith is now the headquarters of Yelp and other tech companies.

Flatirons

Chicago and New York were already raising skylines to new heights and San Francisco borrowed their flatiron style to maximize prime real estate along Market St. The street cuts a diagonal across San Francisco's tidy east-west grid, leaving both flanks of four attractive, triangular flatiron buildings exposed to view.

Among the XXX cinemas surrounding 1020 Market St at Taylor, you'll find the lacy, white flatiron featured as broody Brad Pitt's apartment in the film *Interview with a Vampire*. On a more respectable block above the Powell St cable car turnaround is the stone-cold silver

Top 5 Low-Profile SF Landmarks

California Academy of Sciences (Golden Gate Park)

MH de Young Museum (Golden Gate Park)

Swedenborgian Church (the Presidio)

Chinese Historical Society of America (Chinatown)

Xanadu Gallery (Union Square)

fox known as the James Flood Building, a flinty character that has seen it all: fire, earthquakes and the Gap's attempts to revive bell-bottoms at its ground-floor flagship store. Flood's opulent cousin is the 1908 Phelan Building at 760 Market St, while that adorable little slip of a building on the block at 540 Market St is the 1913 Flatiron Building.

Debates are rising over SoMa's new high-rise **Mission Bay** development. Proponents describe it as a forward-thinking green scheme. Critics argue that such costly real estate attracts only chain stores and high-priced retailers, excluding affordable mom-and-pop businesses and cultural institutions.

SAN FRANCISCO ARCHITECTURE MODERN SKYLINE

Streamlined SF

San Francisco became a forward-thinking port city in the 1930s, with 1939 Streamline Moderne Aquatic Park Bathhouse that looks like an ocean liner and SF's sleek signature art-deco Golden Gate Bridge. But except for the exclamation point of Coit Tower, most new SF buildings kept a low, sleek profile. Until the '60s, San Francisco was called 'the white city' because of its unbroken swaths of white stucco.

Skyscrapers

SF's skyline scarcely changed until the early 1960s, when seismic retrofitting and innovations made upward mobility possible in this shaky city. The 1959 Crown Zellerbach Building at 1 Bush St became a prototype for downtown buildings: a minimalist, tinted-glass rectangle with open-plan offices. The Financial District morphed into a Manhattanized forest of glass boxes, with one pointed exception: the Transamerica Pyramid. High-rises are now springing up in SoMa's southern Mission Bay district, with slots for 'urban village' shops, condos, restaurants and cafes. This latest attempt at instant culture is consistent with the city's original Victorian vision – only bigger and blander.

Prefab Chic

Amid Victorian-prefab row houses in San Francisco neighborhoods, you might also spot some newcomers that seem to have popped right out of the box. Around Patricia's Green in Hayes Valley, shipping containers have been repurposed into stores, a cafe, ice-cream parlor and a beer garden. San Francisco's *Dwell* magazine championed architect-designed, eco-prefab homes innovated in the Bay Area and you can spot some of the results in Diamond Heights and Bernal Heights. The exteriors can seem starkly minimal but interior spaces make the most of air and light.

Some Victorian mansions are now B&Bs, so you too can live large in swanky San Francisco digs of yore: see Sleeping options in the Haight, Pacific Heights, Mission and Castro.

Adaptive Reuse

Instead of starting from scratch, avant-garde architects are repurposing San Francisco's eclectic architecture to meet the needs of a modern city. Architect Daniel Libeskind's design for the 2008 Contemporary Jewish Museum turned a historic power station into the Hebrew letter for life, with a blue-steel pavilion as an emphatic accent. San Francisco's neglected, partially rotten Piers 15 and 17 sheds were retrofitted and connected with Fujiko Nakaya's Fog Bridge to form a stunning, solar-powered new home for the Exploratorium.

But raising the roof on standards for adaptive reuse is the 2008 LEED–certified green building for the California Academy of Sciences. Pritzker Prize–winning architect Renzo Piano incorporated the previous building's neoclassical colonnaded facade, gutted the interior to make way for a basement aquarium and four-story rainforest, and capped it with a domed 'living roof' of California wildflowers perforated with skylights to let air circulate.

Earthquakes

No region is completely free of earthquakes and thousands of minor tremors happen around the world daily. Given San Francisco's history, earthquakes are a sensitive subject for many around here. But for others, it's a calculated risk to live in a city that is – geologically as well as culturally – resilient and outlandish.

The Science of Quakes

San Francisco is rough around the edges, geologically speaking. Jagged coastal ranges and the still-rising Sierra Nevada to the east reveal rough edges of continental and ocean tectonic plates slowly crushed together as the North American continent drifted westward over hundreds of millions of years.

About 30 million years ago, the ocean plates stopped colliding and instead started sliding against each other, creating points of friction that became a mighty rift: California's 810-mile San Andreas Fault. This is the fault that runs through San Francisco; the epicenters for San Francisco's major 1906 and 1989 earthquakes were located along this fault.

East of San Francisco, there's another seismic hotspot between the Pacific and North American tectonic plates: the 74-mile-long Hayward Fault. Risk assessors estimate that the next earthquake in the Bay Area is likely to happen along the Hayward Fault and that an earthquake at a magnitude of 6.9 on the Richter scale could cause significant damage in San Francisco. That said, San Francisco survived four earthquakes of 6.8 or higher from 1836 to 1911, when few buildings were seismically reinforced. Odds are that you won't experience a quake on your visit to San Francisco.

The Big Ones

California has the toughest seismic building standards and most earthquake drills worldwide – but the state learned standard-setting the hard way, through two epic San Francisco quakes. To experience the big ones for yourself, check out the California Academy of Science Shake House (p203), where the '06 and '86 earthquakes are safely simulated inside a San Francisco Victorian.

1906 Great Quake & Fire

For 47 horrifying seconds on April 18, 1906, streets buckled, windows popped and brick buildings imploded across San Francisco. The quake was a teeth-rattling 7.8 to 8.3 on today's Richter scale. Unreinforced structures – including City Hall – collapsed in ruins. Wooden structures were set ablaze by toppled chimneys and ruptured gas mains spread the fire.

But this was an unnatural disaster. City maintenance funds had been pocketed by unscrupulous officials, so fire hydrants and water mains didn't work. Firebreaks were created by dynamiting troughs

EARTHQUAKE PREPAREDNESS

Beyond San Francisco, many countries and cities are seismically active – from Tokyo to London, New Zealand to Turkey. Learn the drill to keep your family and community safe at www.shakeout.org and download guides at www.fema.gov/earthquake/earthquake-safety-home. Some basics:

➡ When you feel a tremor, drop, cover and hold on. Unsecured objects and unreinforced masonry may fall and there could be aftershocks.

➡ Keep ID, emergency contact numbers and three days' worth of essential medication on you.

➡ Earthquakes can disrupt utilities, so you might keep bottled water and cash handy in case faucets and ATMs don't work.

along Van Ness Ave – but instead of containing the conflagration, the explosions set off new fires. Firefighters couldn't haul equipment and water through rubble-choked streets, and in a city surrounded by water on three sides, fires raged.

After three days and two nights, the death toll topped 3000 and 100,000-plus city residents were left homeless. But the city rallied: while SF entertainers gave marathon free performances, San Francisco rebuilt 15 buildings a day.

1989 Loma Prieta Quake

At 5:04pm on October 17, 1989, a quake along the San Andreas Fault hit 6.9 on the Richter scale near Loma Prieta in the Santa Cruz Mountains. Lasting 10 to 15 seconds, the quake was short and severe: 57 deaths were caused by the earthquake and 3000 people rendered homeless. Santa Cruz was hit hard and 74 homes in San Francisco's land-filled Marina district became uninhabitable.

During the quake, a 50-foot section of the eastern span of the Bay Bridge collapsed. Voters approved bond measures to fund a retrofit completed in 2013, heralded with a 25,000 LED-light installation. But within weeks, faulty bolts were identified in the repaired span. A plan was proposed to fix the bolts – for another $10 million. So while visitors marvel at the twinkling lights, San Franciscans maintain a love/hate relationship with the Bay Bridge.

The '89 quake happened during a World Series grudge match between Bay Area baseball rivals: the Giants and Oakland Athletics. Fans nationwide watched in horror as the live broadcast captured the quake, dubbed 'The World Series Quake.'

Giants fans claim the '89 quake cursed the team, who lost to Oakland. But with lucky beards and thongs, the Giants managed to shake the quake, winning World Series in 2010 and 2012.

Survival Guide

Transportation

ARRIVING IN SAN FRANCISCO

Service from three Bay Area airports makes getting to San Francisco quick and convenient. Direct flights to SF from LA take about 90 minutes; from Chicago about 4 hours; from Atlanta 5 hours; and from New York 5½ to 6 hours. Bargain fares can be found online year-round, but don't forget to factor in additional transit time and costs to get to SF if you're flying into San Jose or Oakland instead of San Francisco.

Consider getting here by train instead of car or plane to enjoy spectacular scenery en route, without unnecessary traffic hassles and excess carbon emissions.

Air

San Francisco International Airport

One of the busiest airports in the country, **San Francisco International Airport** (SFO; www.flysfo.com) is 14 miles south of downtown off Hwy 101 and accessible by BART.

GETTING TO/FROM SAN FRANCISCO INTERNATIONAL AIRPORT

BART (Bay Area Rapid Transit; www.bart.gov; one way $8.25) Offers a fast, direct 30-minute ride to/from downtown San Francisco. The SFO BART station is connected to the International Terminal; tickets can be purchased from machines inside the station entrance.

SamTrans (www.samtrans.com; one way $5) Express bus KX takes about 30 minutes to reach Temporary Transbay Terminal in the South of Market (SoMa) area.

Airport Shuttles (one way $15-17) Depart from baggage-claim areas, taking 45 minutes to most SF locations. For service to the airport, call to reserve a pickup from any San Francisco location at least 4 hours in advance of departure time. Companies include **SuperShuttle** (800-258-3826; www.supershuttle.com), **Quake City** (415-255-4899; www.quakecityshuttle.com), **Lorrie's** (415-334-9000; www.gos-fovan.com) and **American Airporter Shuttle**. (415-202-0733; www.americanairporter.com)

Taxi Taxis to downtown San Francisco cost $35 to $50, departing from the yellow zone on the lower level of SFO.

Car The drive between the airport and the city can take as little as 20 minutes, but allow an hour during morning and evening rush hours. If you're headed to the airport via Hwy 101, take the San Francisco International Airport exit. Don't be misled by the Airport Rd exit, which leads to parking lots and warehouses.

Oakland International Airport

Travelers arriving at **Oakland International Airport** (OAK; 510-563-3300; www.oaklandairport.com), 15 miles east of Downtown, will have a little further to go to reach San Francisco.

GETTING TO/FROM OAKLAND INTERNATIONAL AIRPORT

BART The cheapest way to get to San Francisco from the Oakland Airport. AirBART shuttles ($3) run every 10 to 20 minutes to the Coliseum station, where you can catch BART to downtown SF ($3.85, 25 minutes).

Taxi Leave curbside from Oakland airport and average $22 to $35 to Oakland and $50 to $70 to SF.

SuperShuttle (800-258-3826; www.supershuttle.com) Offers shared van rides to downtown SF for $27 to $35.

Airport Express (800-327-2024; www.airportexpressinc.com; 5:15am-9:15pm) Runs a scheduled shuttle every two hours (from 6am to midnight) between Oakland Airport and Sonoma ($34) and Marin ($26) counties.

Norman y Mineta San Jose International Airport

Fifty miles south of downtown San Francisco, **Norman y**

CLIMATE CHANGE & TRAVEL

Every form of transport that relies on carbon-based fuel generates CO_2, the main cause of human-induced climate change. Modern travel is dependent on airplanes, which might use less fuel per kilometer per person than most cars but travel much greater distances. The altitude at which aircraft emit gases (including CO_2) and particles also contributes to their climate change impact. Many websites offer 'carbon calculators' that allow people to estimate the carbon emissions generated by their journey and, for those who wish to do so, to offset the impact of the greenhouse gases emitted with contributions to portfolios of climate-friendly initiatives throughout the world. Lonely Planet offsets the carbon footprint of all staff and author travel.

Mineta San Jose International Airport (SJC; 408-501-0979; www.sjc.org) is a straight shot into the city by car via Hwy 101. The VTA Airport Flyer (bus 10; tickets $2; from 5am to midnight) makes a continuous run between the Santa Clara Caltrain station (Railroad Ave and Franklin St) and the airport terminals, departing every 15 to 30 minutes. From Santa Clara station, Caltrain (one way $9; 90 minutes) runs several trains every day to the terminal at 4th and King Sts in SF.

Bus

Until the new terminal is complete in 2017, SF's inter-city hub remains the **Temporary Transbay Terminal** (Howard & Main Sts). From here you can catch the following buses:

AC Transit (www.actransit. org) Buses to the East Bay.

Golden Gate Transit (Map p324; www.goldengatetransit. org) North-bound buses to Marin and Sonoma counties.

Greyhound (800-231-2222; www.greyhound.com) Buses leave daily for Los Angeles ($59, 8 to 12 hours), Truckee near Lake Tahoe ($31, 5½ hours) and other destinations.

SamTrans (www.samtrans. com) South-bound buses to Palo Alto and the Pacific coast.

Train

Easy on the eyes and carbon emissions too, train travel is a good way to visit the Bay Area and beyond.

Caltrain (www.caltrain.com; cnr 4th & King Sts) Caltrain connects San Francisco with Silicon Valley hubs and San Jose.

Amtrak (800-872-7245; www.amtrakcalifornia.com) Amtrak serves San Francisco via its stations in Oakland and Emeryville (near Oakland). Amtrak offers rail passes good for seven days of travel in California within a 21-day period (from $159). It also runs free shuttle buses from its stations in Emeryville and Oakland's Jack London Sq to San Francisco's Ferry Building and Caltrain station.

Amtrak is good for longer-distance travel as well. The Coast Starlight (LA to Emeryville from $59, Oakland to Portland from $105, Seattle from $128, LA to Seattle from $114) offers a spectacular 35-hour run from Los Angeles to Seattle via Emeryville/Oakland, with meals served on china in the Dining Car, local wines and artisan cheeses served in the Pacific Parlor Car and an Arcade Room in which to play video games. The California Zephyr (Chicago to Oakland from $313) takes its time (51 hours), traveling from Chicago through the Rockies and snow-capped Sierra Nevada en route to Oakland.

GETTING AROUND SAN FRANCISCO

When San Franciscans don't have somewhere else to be right quick – and even when they do – most people walk, bike or take Muni instead of a car or cab. Those slackers are smart: this is the best way to take in San Francisco and helps preserve the city's natural charm by curbing carbon emissions and other pollutants.

Bus, Streetcar & Cable Car

Muni (Municipal Transit Agency; 511; www.sfmta.com) Muni operates bus, streetcar and cable car lines. Buses and streetcars are referred to interchangeably as Muni and are denoted in this guide by the Ⓜ icon. Some areas are better connected than others, but Muni spares you the costly hassle of driving and parking in San Francisco and it's often faster than driving during rush hour.

Schedules

For fastest routes and the most exact departure times, consult http://transit.511. org. Arrival times can also be viewed on digital displays or guesstimated by consulting schedules posted inside bus shelters. Nighttime and weekend service is less

BUSES AROUND THE BAY

Three public bus systems connect San Francisco to the rest of the Bay Area. Most buses leave from clearly marked bus stops; for transit maps and schedules, see the bus system websites.

AC Transit (www.actransit.org) Offers East Bay bus services from the Temporary Transbay Terminal. For public transport connections from BART in the East Bay, get an AC Transit transfer ticket before leaving the BART station and then pay an additional 75¢ to $1.

Golden Gate Transit (Map p324; www.goldengatetransit.org) Connects San Francisco to Marin (tickets $4.40 to $5.50) and Sonoma counties (tickets $10.25 to $12.60), but be advised that service can be slow and erratic.

SamTrans (☑800-660-4287; www.samtrans.com) [FREE] Runs buses between San Francisco and the South Bay, including bus services to/from SFO. Buses pick up/drop off from the Temporary Transbay Terminal and other marked bus stops within the city.

frequent. Owl service (from 1am to 5am) is offered on a limited number of lines, with departures about every half-hour.

System Maps

A detailed Muni Street & Transit Map is available free online (www.sfmuni.com).

Tickets

Standard fare for buses or streetcars is $2; tickets can be bought onboard buses and streetcars (exact change required) and at underground Muni stations. Cable car tickets cost $6 per ride, and can be bought at cable car turnaround kiosks or onboard from the conductor. Hang onto your ticket even if you're not planning to use it again: if you're caught without one by the transit police, you're subject to a $100 fine (repeat offenders may be fined up to $500).

Transfers

At the start of your Muni journey, free transfer tickets are available for additional Muni trips within 90 minutes (not including cable cars or BART). After 8:30pm, buses issue a Late Night Transfer good for travel until 5:30am the following morning.

Discounts & Passes

MUNI PASSPORTS

A **Muni Passport** (1/3/7 days $14/22/28) allows unlimited travel on all Muni transport, including cable cars. It's sold at the Muni kiosk at the Powell St cable car turnaround on Market St, SF's Visitor Information Center, the TIX Bay Area kiosk at Union Square and from a number of hotels. One-day passports can be purchased from cable car conductors.

CLIPPER CARDS

Downtown Muni/BART stations issue the **Clipper Card**, a reloadable transit card with a $3 minimum that can be used on Muni, BART, AC Transit, Caltrain, SamTrans, and Golden Gate Transit and Ferry (not cable cars). Clipper Cards automatically deduct fares and apply transfers – only one Muni fare is deducted in a 90-minute period.

FAST PASS

Monthly Muni Fast Pass (adult/child $64/22) offers unlimited Muni travel for the calendar month, including cable cars. Fast Passes are available at the Muni kiosk at the Powell St cable car turnaround and from businesses that display the Muni Pass sign in their window.

Bus

Muni buses display their route number and final destination on the front and side. If the number is followed by the letter A, B, X or L, then it's a limited-stop or express service.

KEY ROUTES

22 Fillmore From Dogpatch (Potrero Hill), through the Mission on 16th St, along Fillmore St past Japantown to Pacific Heights and the Marina.

33 Stanyan From San Francisco General Hospital, through the Mission, Castro and Haight, past Golden Gate Park to Clement St.

38 Geary From the Temporary Transbay Terminal, along Market to Geary Blvd, north of Golden Gate Park through the Richmond district to Ocean Beach.

71 Noriega From the Temporary Transbay Terminal, along Market and Haight Sts, along the southeast side of Golden Gate Park through the Sunset and to the Great Hwy at the beach.

Streetcar

Muni Metro streetcars run from 5am to midnight on weekdays, with limited schedules on weekends. The L and N lines operate 24 hours, but above ground Owl buses replace streetcars between 12:30am and 5:30am. The F-Market line runs vintage streetcars above ground along Market St to the Embarcadero, where they turn north to Fisherman's Wharf. The T line heads south along the Embarcadero through SoMa and Mission Bay, then down 3rd St. Other streetcars run underground below Market St Downtown.

KEY ROUTES

F Fisherman's Wharf and Embarcadero to the Castro.

J Downtown to the Mission, the Castro and Noe Valley.

K, L, M Downtown to the Castro.

N Caltrain and SBC Ballpark to the Haight, Golden Gate Park and Ocean Beach.

T The Embarcadero to Caltrain and Bayview.

Cable Car

In this age of seat belts and air bags, a rickety cable-car ride is an anachronistic thrill. There are seats for about 30 passengers, who are often outnumbered by passengers clinging to creaking leather straps. For more on cable car maps, service and history, see p43.

KEY ROUTES

California St Runs east to west along California St, from the Downtown terminus at Market and Davis Sts through Chinatown and Nob Hill to Van Ness Ave.

Powell-Mason Runs from the Powell St cable car turnaround past Union Square, turns west along Jackson St, and then descends north down Mason St, Columbus Ave and Taylor St towards Fisherman's Wharf. On the return trip it takes Washington St instead of Jackson St.

Powell-Hyde Follows the same route as the Powell-Mason line until Jackson St, where it turns down Hyde St to terminate at Aquatic Park; coming back it takes Washington St.

BART

Venues readily accessible by **BART** (Bay Area Rapid Transit; www.bart.gov) are denoted by the B icon in this guide. The fastest link between Downtown and the Mission District also offers transit to SF airport, Oakland ($3.20) and Berkeley ($3.80). Four of the system's five lines pass through SF before terminating at Daly City or SFO. Within SF, one-way fares start at $1.75.

Tickets

BART tickets are sold at BART stations and you'll need a ticket to enter and exit. If your ticket still has value after you exit the station, it is returned to you with the remaining balance. If your ticket's value is less than needed to exit, use an Addfare machine to pay the appropriate amount. The Clipper Card can be used for BART travel.

Transfers

At San Francisco BART stations, a 25¢ discount is available for Muni buses and streetcars; look for transfer machines before you pass through the turnstiles.

Taxi

Fares start at $3.50 at the flag drop and run about $2.75 per mile. Add at least 10% to the taxi fare as a tip ($1 minimum).

The following taxi companies have 24-hour dispatches:

DeSoto Cab (☑415-970-1300)

Green Cab (☑415-626-4733; www.626green.com) Fuel-efficient hybrids; worker-owned collective.

Luxor (☑415-282-4141)

Yellow Cab (☑415-333-3333)

Car & Motorcycle

If you can, avoid driving in San Francisco: traffic is a given, street parking is harder to find than true love and meter readers are ruthless.

Traffic

San Francisco streets mostly follow a grid bisected by Market St, with signs pointing toward tourist zones such as North Beach, Fisherman's Wharf and Chinatown. Try to avoid driving during rush hours: 7:30am to 9:30am and 4:30pm to 6:30pm, Monday to Friday. Before heading to any bridge, airport or other traffic chokepoint, call 511 for a traffic update.

Parking

Parking is tricky and often costly, especially Downtown – ask your hotel about parking, and inquire about validation at restaurants and entertainment venues.

GARAGES

Downtown parking garages charge from $2 to $8 per hour and $25 to $50 per day, depending on how long you park and whether you require in-and-out privileges. The most convenient Downtown parking lots are at the Embarcadero Center, at 5th and Mission Sts, under Union Square and at Sutter and Stockton Sts. For more public parking garages, see www.sfmta.com; for a map of garages and rates, see http://sfpark.org.

PARKING RESTRICTIONS

Parking restrictions are indicated by the following color-coded sidewalk curbs:

Blue Disabled parking only; identification required.

Green Ten-minute parking zone from 9am to 6pm.

Red No parking or stopping.

White For picking up or dropping off passengers only.

Yellow Loading zone from 7am to 6pm.

TOWING VIOLATIONS

Desperate motorists often resort to double-parking or parking in red zones or on sidewalks, but parking authorities are quick to tow cars. If this should happen to you, you'll have to retrieve your car at **Autoreturn** (☎415-865-8200; www.autoreturn.com; 450 7th St, SoMa; ⏲24hr; Ⓜ27, 42). Besides at least $73 in fines for parking violations, you'll also have to fork out a towing and storage fee ($453.75 for the first four hours, $63.50 for the rest of the first day, $63.50 for every additional day, plus a $26 transfer fee if your car is moved to a long-term lot). Cars are usually stored at 415 7th St, corner of Harrison St.

Rental

Typically a small rental car might cost $55 to $70 a day or $175 to $300 a week, plus 9.5% sales tax. Unless your credit card covers car-rental insurance, you'll need to add $10 to $20 per day for a loss/damage waiver. Most rates include unlimited mileage; with cheap rates, there's often a per-mile charge above a certain mileage.

Booking ahead usually ensures the best rates and airport rates are generally better than those in the city. As part of SF's citywide green initiative, rentals of hybrid cars and low-emissions vehicles from rental agencies at SFO are available at a discount.

To rent a motorcycle, contact **Dubbelju** (☎415-495-2774; www.dubbelju.com; 689a Bryant St); rates start at $99 per day. **Go Car** (http://www.gocartours.com/) rents mini-cars with audio GPS instructions to major attractions in multiple languages; rates start at $55/hour.

To get around town techie-style, you can rent a Segway from **Segway SF Bay** (http://www.segwaysfbay.com) for use on bike lanes and trails (they're banned on sidewalks). Rates start at $45 per 90 minutes, including free lessons and map. Guided Segway tours (from $60 per 2 hours) are available from **City Segway Tours** (http://citysegwaytours.com).

Major car-rental agencies include the following:

Alamo Rent-a-Car (☎800-327-9633, 415-693-0191; www.alamo.com; 750 Bush St, Downtown; ⏲7am-7pm; 🚋Powell-Mason, Powell-Hyde, Ⓜ2, 3, 4, 76)

Avis (☎800-831-2847, 415-929-2555; www.avis.com; 675 Post St, Downtown; ⏲6am-6pm; Ⓜ2, 3, 4, 76)

Budget (☎800-527-0700, 415-292-8981; www.budget.com; 321 Mason St, Downtown; ⏲6am-6pm; Ⓜ2, 3, 4, 38)

Dollar (☎800-800-5252; www.dollarcar.com; 364 O'Farrell St, Downtown; ⏲7am-7pm; Ⓜ2, 3, 4, 38)

Hertz (☎800-654-3131, 415-771-2200; www.hertz.com; 325 Mason St, Downtown; ⏲6am-6pm Mon-Thu, to 8pm Fri & Sat; Ⓜ2, 3, 4, 38)

Thrifty (☎800-367-2277, 415-788-6906; www.thrifty.com; 350 O'Farrell St, Downtown; ⏲7am-7pm; Ⓜ2, 3, 4, 38)

Car Share

Car sharing is a convenient alternative to rentals that spares you pick-up/drop-off and parking hassles: reserve a car online for an hour or two or all day and you can usually pick up/drop off your car within blocks of where you're staying. It also does the environment a favor: fewer cars on the road means less congestion and pollution, especially with fuel-efficient and hybrid share-cars.

Zipcar (☎866-494-7227; www.zipcar.com) rents Prius Hybrids and Minis by the hour for flat rates starting at $8.25 per hour, including gas and insurance, or by day for $89; a $25 application fee and $50 prepaid usage are required in advance. Drivers without a US driver's license should follow instructions on the website. Once approved, cars can be reserved online or by phone. Check the website for pick-up/drop-off locations.

Roadside Assistance

Members of **American Automobile Association** (AAA; ☎800-222-4357, 415-773-1900; www.aaa.com; 160 Sutter St; ⏲8:30am-5:30pm Mon-Fri) can call the 800 number any time for emergency road service and towing. AAA also provides travel insurance and free road maps of the region.

FURTHER AFIELD: LOS ANGELES & LAS VEGAS

For muscle beaches, celebrity sightings and camera-ready wackiness, head south on coastal Hwy 1 to Los Angeles. It'll take 12 hours depending on traffic and how often you stop. A quicker jaunt is less-scenic Hwy 101 (nine hours); the fastest route is boring inland I-5, which takes about six hours.

Las Vegas, Nevada, is a nine-hour non-stop drive from San Francisco. Cross the Bay Bridge to 580 east, to I-5 south, veering off towards 99 south (at exit 278), to 58 east, then I-15 the last 160 miles. A slower, gloriously scenic option is to go east through Yosemite National Park on Hwy 120 (summer only; verify by calling 800-GAS-ROAD) and south on Hwy 395, east on Hwy 190 through Death Valley National Park then south on Hwy 95 straight into Sin City.

BIKING AROUND THE BAY AREA

➡ **Within SF** Muni has racks that can accommodate two bikes on some of its commuter routes, including 17, 35, 36, 37, 39, 53, 56, 66, 76, 91 and 108.

➡ **Marin County** Bikes are allowed on the Golden Gate Bridge, so getting north to Marin County is no problem. You can transport bicycles on Golden Gate Transit buses, which usually have free racks available (first-come, first-served). Ferries also allow bikes aboard when space allows.

➡ **Wine Country** To transport your bike to Wine Country, take Golden Gate Transit or the Vallejo Ferry. Within Sonoma Valley, take Arnold Dr instead of busy Hwy 12; through Napa Valley, take the Silverado Trail instead of Hwy 29 to avoid drivers U-turning for wineries. The most spectacular ride in Wine Country is sun-dappled, tree-lined West Dry Creek Rd in Sonoma's Dry Creek Valley.

➡ **East Bay** Cyclists can't use the Bay Bridge until the planned bike paths are complete, so you'll need to take your bike on BART. Bikes are allowed on uncrowded BART trains, but during rush hours special limits apply. Between 6:30am and 9am and from 4pm to 6:30pm, people with bikes can't travel on the first three cars. During commute hours, you can also travel with your bike across the bay via the **Caltrans Bay Bridge Bicycle Commuter Shuttle** (☎510-286-0876; http://www.dot.ca.gov/dist4/shuttle.htm; tickets $1; ⊙6:20-8:30am & 3:50-6:15pm Mon-Fri) which operates from the corner of Folsom and Main Sts in San Francisco and MacArthur BART station in Oakland.

Boat

With the revival of the Embarcadero and reinvention of the Ferry Building as a gourmet dining destination, commuters and tourists alike are taking the scenic ferry across the bay.

Alcatraz

Alcatraz Cruises (Map p315; ☎415-981-7625; www.alcatrazcruises.com; adult/child day $26/16, night $33/19.50) has ferries departing from Pier 33 for Alcatraz every half-hour from 9am to 3:55pm and at 6:10pm and 6:45pm for night tours.

East Bay

Blue & Gold Fleet Ferries (Map p319; www.blueandgoldfleet.com) operates ferries from the Ferry Building, Pier 39 and Pier 41 at Fisherman's Wharf to Jack London Square in Oakland (one way $6.25). During baseball season, a Giants ferry service runs directly from the landing at AT&T Park's Seals Plaza entrance to Oakland and Alameda.

Ticket booths are located at the Ferry Building and Piers 39 and 41.

Marin County

Golden Gate Transit Ferries (Map p319; ☎415-455-2000; www.goldengateferry.org; ⊙6am-9:30pm Mon-Fri, 10am-6pm Sat & Sun) runs regular ferry services from the Ferry Building to Larkspur and Sausalito (one way adult/child $9.75/4.75). Transfers are available to Muni bus services and bicycles are permitted. Blue & Gold Fleet Ferries also provides service to Tiburon or Sausalito (one way $11).

Napa Valley

Get to Napa car-free via **Vallejo Ferry** (Map p319; ☎877-643-3779; www.baylinkferry.com; adult/child $13/6.50) with departures from Ferry Building docks about every hour from 6:30am to 7pm weekdays and every two hours from 11am to 7:30pm on weekends; bikes are permitted. From the Vallejo Ferry Terminal, take Napa Valley Vine bus 10 to downtown Napa, Yountville, St Helena or Calistoga.

Caltrain

From the depot at 4th and King Sts in San Francisco, **Caltrain** (www.caltrain.com; cnr 4th & King Sts) heads south to Millbrae (connecting to BART and SFO, 30 minutes), Palo Alto (one hour) and San Jose (1½ hours). This is primarily a commuter line, with frequent departures during weekday rush hours and less often between non-rush hours and on weekends.

Bicycle

Bike sharing is new to SF in 2013 (check out http://bayareabikeshare.com), but there are still not enough bike lanes for safe biking east of Van Ness Avenue. Bicycles can be carried on BART, but not on crowded trains or the first three trains during weekday rush hours. On Amtrak, bikes can be checked as baggage for $5.

Directory A–Z

Business Hours

Standard business hours are as follows. Nonstandard hours are listed in specific reviews.

Banks 9am to 4:30pm or 5pm Monday to Friday (occasionally 9am to noon Saturday).

Offices 8:30am to 5:30pm Monday to Friday.

Restaurants Breakfast 8am to noon, lunch noon to 3pm, dinner 5:30pm to 10pm; Saturday and Sunday brunch 10am to 2pm.

Shops 10am to 6pm or 7pm Monday to Saturday and noon to 6pm Sunday.

Customs Regulations

Each person over the age of 21 is allowed to bring 1L of liquor and 200 cigarettes duty-free into the USA. Non-US citizens are allowed to bring in $100 worth of duty-free gifts. Should you be carrying more than $10,000 in US and foreign cash, traveler's checks or money orders, you need to declare the exact amount – undeclared sums in excess of $10,000 may be subject to confiscation.

Discount Cards

Some green-minded venues, such as the MH de Young Museum, the California Academy of Sciences and the Legion of Honor, also offer discounts to ticket-bearing Muni riders.

City Pass (www.citypass. com; adult/child $84/59) This pass covers cable cars, Muni and entry to four attractions, including California Academy of Sciences, Blue & Gold Fleet Bay Cruise, Aquarium of the Bay and either the Exploratorium or the MH de Young Museum.

PRACTICALITIES

Newspapers & Magazines

San Francisco Bay Guardian (www.sfbg.com) SF's free, alternative weekly covers politics, theater, music, art and movie listings.

San Francisco Chronicle (www.sfgate.com) Main daily newspaper with news, entertainment and event listings online.

SF Weekly (www.sfweekly.com) Free weekly with local gossip and entertainment.

Radio

For local listening in SF and online via podcasts/streaming audio, check out these stations:

KQED 88.5 FM (www.kqed.org) National Public Radio (NPR) and Public Broadcasting (PBS) affiliate offering podcasts and streaming video.

KALW 91.7 FM (www.kalw.org) Local NPR affiliate: news, talk, music, original programming.

Volunteering

VolunteerMatch (www.volunteermatch.org) Matches your interests, talents and availability with a local nonprofit where you could donate your time, if only for a few hours.

Craigslist (http://sfbay.craigslist.org/vol) Lists opportunities to support the Bay Area community, from nonprofit fashion-show fundraisers to teaching English to new arrivals.

Go Card ([📞]800-887-9103; www.gosanfranciscocard.com; adult/child 1-day $55/45, 2-day $80/65, 3-day $110/80) Offers access to the city's major attractions, plus discounts on packaged tours and waterfront restaurants and cafes.

Electricity

120v/60hz

120v/60hz

Electric current in the USA is 110 to 115 volts, 60Hz AC. Outlets may be suited for flat two-prong or three-prong plugs. If your appliance is made for another electrical system, pick up a transformer or adapter at Walgreens.

Emergencies

Police, Fire & Ambulance ([📞]emergency 911, nonemergency 311)

San Francisco General Hospital ([📞]emergency room 415-206-8111, main hospital 415-206-8000; www.sfdph.org; 1001 Potrero Ave; [Ⓜ]Potrero Ave)

Drug & Alcohol Emergency Info Line ([📞]415-362-3400)

Trauma Recovery & Rape Treatment Center ([📞]415-437-3000; www.traumarecoverycenter.org) A 24-hour hotline.

Internet Access

SF has free wi-fi hot spots citywide – locate one nearby with www.openwifispots.com. Places listed in this guide that offer wi-fi are denoted by the [📶] icon. You can connect for free at most cafes and hotel lobbies, as well as at the following locations:

Apple Store (www.apple.com/retail/sanfrancisco; 1 Stockton St; ⊗9am-9pm Mon-Sat, 10am-8pm Sun; [📶]; [Ⓜ]Powell St) Free wi-fi and internet terminal usage.

San Francisco Main Library (Map p322; www.sfpl.org; 100 Larkin St; ⊗10am-6pm Mon & Sat, 9am-8pm Tue-Thu, noon-5pm Fri & Sun; [📶]; [Ⓜ]Civic Center) Free 15-minute internet terminal usage; spotty wi-fi access.

Legal Matters

San Francisco police usually have more urgent business than fining you for picking a protected orange California poppy on public land (up to $500), littering ($250 and up), loitering on sidewalks against the Sit/Lie law ($100-to-$500 ticket), jaywalking (ie crossing streets outside a pedestrian crosswalk, which can run from $75 to $125) or failing to clean up after your puppy ($50 in some places, plus shaming glares from fellow dog-owners).

Drinking alcoholic beverages outdoors is not officially allowed, though beer and wine is often permissible at street fairs and other outdoor events. You may be let off with a warning for being caught taking a puff on a joint, but don't count on it – possessing marijuana for personal use is still a misdemeanor in this lenient city, though legal with a prescription inside a medicinal marijuana club. In recent years the police have cracked down on park squatters, so maybe you should change your plans if you were hoping to relive the Summer of Love at Golden Gate Park.

If you are arrested for any reason, it's your right to remain silent, but never walk away from an officer until given permission or you could be charged with resisting arrest. Anyone arrested gets the right to make one phone call. If you want to call your consulate, the police will give you the number on request.

Medical Services

Before traveling, contact your health-insurance provider to find out what types of medical care they will cover outside your hometown (or home country). Overseas visitors should acquire travel insurance that covers medical situations in the US, where nonemergency care for uninsured patients can be very expensive.

For nonemergency appointments at hospitals, you'll need proof of insurance or cash. Even with insurance, you'll most likely have to pay up front for nonemergency care, and then wrangle with your insurance company afterwards in order to get your money reimbursed. That said, San Francisco has reputable medical facilities as well as alternative medical practices and herbal apothecaries.

Clinics

American College of Traditional Chinese Medicine (☑415-282-9603; www.actcm.edu; 450 Connecticut St; ☺8:30am-9pm Mon-Thu, 9am-5:30pm Fri & Sat; ☐10, 19, 22) Acupuncture, herbal remedies and other traditional Chinese medical treatments provided at low cost.

Haight Ashbury Free Clinic (☑415-762-3700; www.healthright360.org; 558 Clayton St; ☺by appointment; ☐6, 33, 37, 43, 71, Ⓜ N) Services are offered by appointment only; provides substance abuse and mental health services.

Lyon-Martin Women's Health Services (☑415-565-7667; www.lyon-martin.org; ste 201, 1748 Market St; ☺11am-7pm Mon & Wed, 9am-5pm Tue & Fri, noon-5pm Thu; ☐6, 71, Ⓜ F) Women's clinic with affordable gynecological, recovery, HIV and mental health services, by appointment only; lesbian- and transgender-friendly.

Emergency Rooms

Davies Medical Center (☑415-600-6000; www.cpmc.org; 45 Castro building, cnr Noe St & Duboce Ave; ☺24hr; ☐6, 22, 24, 71, Ⓜ J, N) Offers 24-hour emergency services.

San Francisco General Hospital (☑emergency 415-206-8111, main hospital 415-206-8000; www.sfdph.org; 1001 Potrero Ave; ☺24hr; ☐9, 10, 33, 48) Provides care to uninsured patients, including psychiatric care; no documentation required beyond ID.

University of California San Francisco Medical Center (☑415-476-1000; www.ucsfhealth.org; 505 Parnassus Ave; ☺24hr; ☐6, 43, 71, Ⓜ N) Leading medical advances nationwide.

Pharmacies

Pharmaca (☑415-661-1216; www.pharmaca.com; 925 Cole St; ☺8am-8pm Mon-Fri, 9am-8pm Sat & Sun; ☐6, 37, 43, Ⓜ N) Pharmacy plus naturopathic and alternative remedies; weekend chair massage available.

Walgreens (☑415-861-3136; www.walgreens.com; 498 Castro St, cnr 18th St; ☺24hr; ☐24, 33, 35, Ⓜ F, K, L, M) Pharmacy and over-the-counter meds; dozens of locations citywide (see website).

Money

US dollars are the only accepted currency in San Francisco, though barter is sometimes possible on **Craigslist** (http://sfbay.craigslist.org). Debit/credit cards are accepted widely but bringing a combination of cash, cards and traveler's checks is wise.

ATMs

Most banks have ATMs, which are open 24 hours a day, except in areas where street crime is a problem (such as near the BART stop at 16th and Mission Sts). For a small service charge, you can withdraw cash from an ATM using a credit card; check with your provider about applicable fees.

Changing Money

Though there are exchange bureaus located at airports, the best rates are generally at banks in the city. For the latest exchange rates, visit currency converter website www.xe.com.

American Express (Amex; ☑415-536-2600; www.americanexpress.com/travel; 455 Market St; ☺8:30am-5:30pm Mon-Fri, 9:30am-3:30pm Sat; Ⓜ Embarcadero, Ⓑ Embarcadero) Exchanges money and also sells traveler's checks.

Bank of America (☑415-837-1394; www.bankamerica.com; 1 Powell St, downstairs; ☺9am-6pm Mon-Fri, to 2pm Sat; Ⓜ Powell St, Ⓑ Powell St) Though most banks do exchange currency, this branch of the Bank of America is the most centrally located and convenient.

Traveler's Checks

In the US, traveler's checks in US dollars are virtually as good as cash; you don't necessarily have to go to a bank to cash them, as some establishments will accept them just like cash. The major advantage of traveler's checks in US dollars over cash is that they can be replaced if lost or stolen.

Organized Tours

Precita Eyes Mission Mural Tours (Map p328; ☑415-285-2287; www.precitaeyes.org; adult $15-20 child $5; ☺see website calendar for tour dates; ♿) Muralists lead two-hour tours on foot or bike covering 60 to 70 murals in a six- to 10-block radius of mural-bedecked Balmy Alley; proceeds fund mural upkeep at this community arts nonprofit.

Sea Foraging Adventures (www.seaforager.com; from $45 per person; ☺calendar and reservations online)

California sealife expert Kirk Lombard leads guided adventures to secret foraging spots around San Francisco's waterfront, finding urban edibles ranging from bullwhip seaweed to eels under the Golden Gate Bridge.

Chinatown Alleyway Tours (📞415-984-1478; www. chinatownalleywaytours.org; adult/student $18/12; ⊙11am Sat & Sun; 👪) Neighborhood teens lead two-hour community nonprofit tours for up-close-and-personal peeks into Chinatown's past (weather permitting). Book five days ahead or pay double for Saturday walk-ins; cash only.

Green Tortoise (📞415-956-7500, 800-867-8647; www.greentortoise.com) Quasi-organized, easygoing, bargain travel on customized, biodiesel-fueled buses with built-in berths that run from San Francisco to points across California and beyond, including Bay Area day tours to Russian River and Santa Cruz (from $40); three-day round trips to Mendocino, Yosemite or Death Valley (from $249); and three- to seven-day coastal trips south to Monterey, Big Sur and LA (from $249).

Public Library City Guides (www.sfcityguides. org; tours free; donations/tips welcome) Volunteer local historians lead nonprofit tours organized by neighborhood and theme: Art Deco Marina, Gold Rush Downtown, Secrets of Fisherman's Wharf, Telegraph Hill Stairway Hike and more. See website for upcoming tours.

Tree Frog Treks (play night $35, day camp $100; 👪) Meet red-footed tortoises and blue-tongued skinks at scientific play dates on Saturday nights and occasional nature discovery day-camps (for kids age 5

and up) in Golden Gate Park, the Presidio and Fort Funston.

Fire Engine Tours (Map p314;📞415-333-7077; www. fireenginetours.com; departs Beach St, at the Cannery; adult/child $50/30; ⊙tours depart 9am, 11am, 1pm, 3pm) Hot stuff: a 75-minute ride in an open-air vintage fire engine over Golden Gate Bridge. Dress warmly in case of fog.

Pets

San Franciscans have more pets than kids, so this town is definitely pet-friendly – although dogs still have to stay on a leash in many parts of town, and you're required by law to clean up your dog's little gifts to nature (fines run up to $50). San Francisco's pioneering 'poop scoop' ordinance was America's first, championed by Supervisor Harvey Milk.

Leash Laws

To check out the best locations for Rover to roam free, see San Francisco Dog Parks (http://www.sfdogparks. com) and bone up on local leash laws at **SF Dog** (www. sfdog.org).

Pet Housing

To find SF hotels that allow dogs, check out www.dog-friendly.com.

Wag Hotel (📞415-876-0700; www.waghotels.com; 14th St; 🐾) If you need to go away for a few days, you might check your pet into the swanky Wag Hotel. Rates begin at $30 for a 'kitty condo', $48 for a doggie room and $80 to $150 for a posh canine suite; luxury extras available.

Community

There are opportunities galore for pet lovers to connect in SF, including two SF-based websites: www.catster.com and www.dogster.com.

Post

Check www.usps.com for post office locations throughout San Francisco. Following are the most conveniently located post offices for visitors:

Civic Center Post Office (Map p322;📞800-275-8777; 101 Hyde St; ⊙9am-5pm Mon-Fri, 10am-2pm Sat; Ⓜ Civic Center, Ⓑ Civic Center)

Rincon Center Post Office (Map p319;📞800-275-8777; www.usps.gov; 180 Steuart St; ⊙8am-6pm Mon-Fri, 9am-2pm Sat; Ⓜ Embarcadero, Ⓑ Embarcadero) Postal services plus historic murals in historic wing.

US Post Office (Map p320; 📞415-397-3333; 170 O'Farrell St; ⊙10am-5:30pm Mon-Sat, 11am-5pm Sun; 🚋 Powell-Mason & Powell-Hyde, Ⓜ Powell St, Ⓑ Powell St) Located at Macy's department store.

Public Holidays

Most shops remain open on public holidays (with the exception of Independence Day, Thanksgiving, Christmas and New Year's Day), while banks, schools and offices are usually closed. Holidays that may affect travelers include the following:

New Year's Day January 1

Martin Luther King Jr Day Third Monday in January

Presidents' Day Third Monday in February

Easter Sunday (and Good Friday and Easter Monday) in March or April

Memorial Day Last Monday in May

Independence Day July 4

Labor Day First Monday in September

Columbus Day Second Monday in October

Veterans Day November 11

Thanksgiving Fourth Thursday in November

Christmas Day December 25

Safe Travel

Keep your city smarts and wits about you, especially at night in the Tenderloin, South of Market (SoMa) and the Mission. The Bayview-Hunters Point neighborhood south of Potrero Hill along the water is plagued by a high crime rate and violence and isn't particularly suitable for wandering tourists. After dark, Dolores Park, Buena Vista Park and the entry to Golden Gate Park at Haight and Stanyan Sts are used for drug deals and casual sex hookups.

Taxes

SF's 9.5% sales tax is added to virtually everything, including meals, accommodations and car rentals. Groceries are about the only items not taxed, and unlike European Value Added Tax, sales tax is not refundable. There's also a 15.5% hotel room tax to take into consideration when booking hotel accommodations.

In response to city laws mandating healthcare benefits for restaurant workers, some restaurants are passing along those costs to diners by tacking an additional 3% to 4% 'Healthy SF' charge onto the bill – a slippery business practice mentioned in the fine print that may eventually be eliminated, given City Hall audits and widespread diner protest on restaurant review websites.

Telephone

The US country code is ☏1 and San Francisco's city code is ☏415. To make an international call from the Bay Area, call ☏011 + country code + area code + number. When calling Canada, there's no need to dial the international access code ☏011. When dialing another area code, the code must be preceded by ☏1. For example, to dial an Oakland number from San Francisco, start with ☏1-510.

Area Codes in the Bay Area

East Bay ☏510

Marin County ☏415

Peninsula ☏650

San Francisco ☏415

San Jose ☏408

Santa Cruz ☏831

Wine Country ☏707

Local calls from a public pay phone usually start at 50¢. Hotel telephones will often add heavy surcharges. Toll-free numbers start with 800 or 888, while phone numbers beginning with 900 usually incur high fees.

Cell Phones

Most US cell phones besides the iPhone operate on CDMA, not the European standard GSM – make sure you check compatibility with your phone service provider. North American travelers can use their cell phones in San Francisco and the Bay Area, but should check with their carrier about roaming charges.

Operator Services

International operator ☏00

Local directory ☏411

Long-distance directory information ☏1 + area code + 555-1212

Operator ☏0

Toll-free number information ☏800-555-1212

Phonecards

For international calls from a public pay phone, it's a good idea to use a phone card, available at most corner markets and drug stores. Otherwise, when you dial ☏0, you're at the mercy of the international carrier who covers that pay phone.

Time

San Francisco is on Pacific Standard Time (PST), three hours behind the East Coast's Eastern Standard Time (EST) and eight hours behind Greenwich Mean Time (GMT/UTC). Summer is Daylight Saving Time in the US.

Toilets

Citywide Self-cleaning, coin-operated outdoor kiosk commodes cost 25¢; there are 25 citywide, mostly located at North Beach, Fisherman's Wharf, the Financial District and the Tenderloin. Toilet paper isn't always available and there's a 20-minute time limit. Public library branches and parks throughout the city also have restrooms.

Downtown Clean toilets and baby-changing tables can be found at Westfield San Francisco Centre and Macy's.

Civic Center San Francisco Main Library has restrooms.

Haight-Ashbury & Mission District Woefully lacking in public toilets; you may have to buy coffee, beer or food to gain access to locked customer-only bathrooms.

Tourist Information

San Francisco Visitor Information Center (Map p320; ☏415-391-2000, events 415-391-2001; www.onlyinsanfrancisco.com; Market & Powell Sts, lower level, Hallidie Plaza; ⊙9am-5pm Mon-Fri, to 3pm

Sat & Sun; ⓖPowell-Mason, Powell-Hyde, ⓜPowell St, ⒷPowell St) Provides practical information for tourists, publishes glossy tourist-oriented booklets and runs a 24-hour events hotline.

Golden Gate National Recreation Area Headquarters (Map p314;☑415-561-4700; www.nps.gov/goga; 495 Jefferson St; ☺8:30am-4:30pm Mon-Fri; ☐19, 30, 47, ⓖPowell-Hyde, ⓜF) Find out everything hikers need to know about accessing the Golden Gate National Recreation Area. On offer is a wealth of maps and information about camping, hiking and other programs for these and other national parks in the Pacific West region (including Yosemite).

For further tourist information, check out the following websites:

Lonely Planet (www.lonelyplanet.com)

SFGate.com (www.sfgate.com)

SFist (www.sfist.com)

Travelers with Disabilities

All Bay Area transit companies offer wheelchair-accessible service and travel discounts for travelers with disabilities. Major car-rental companies can usually supply hand-controlled vehicles with one or two days' notice. For people with visual impairment, major intersections emit a chirping signal to indicate when it is safe to cross the street. Check the following resources:

San Francisco Bay Area Regional Transit Guide (www.transit.511.org/disabled/index.aspx) Covers accessibility for people with disabilities.

Muni's Street & Transit (www.sfmta.com) Details which bus routes and streetcar stops are wheelchair-friendly.

Independent Living Resource Center of San Francisco (☑415-543-6222; www.ilrcsf.org; ☺9am-4:30pm Mon-Thu, to 4pm Fri) Provides further information about wheelchair accessibility on Bay Area public transit and in hotels and other local facilities.

Visas
Canadians

Canadian citizens currently only need proof of identity and citizenship to enter the US – but check the US Department of State for updates, as requirements may change.

Visa Waiver Program

USA Visa Waiver Program (VWP) allows nationals from 37 countries to enter the US without a visa, provided they are carrying a machine-readable passport. For the updated list of countries included in the program and current requirements, see the **US Department of State** (http://travel.state.gov/visa) website.

Citizens of VWP countries need to register with the US Department of Homeland Security (https://esta.cbp.dhs.gov/esta/) three days before their visit. There is a $14 fee for registration application; when approved, the registration is valid for two years.

Visas Required

You must obtain a visa from a US embassy or consulate in your home country if you:

➡ Do not currently hold a passport from a VWP country.

➡ Are from a VWP country, but don't have a machine-readable passport.

➡ Are from a VWP country, but currently hold a passport issued between October 26, 2005, and October 25, 2006, that does not have a digital photo on the

information page or an integrated chip from the data page. (After October 25, 2006, the integrated chip is required on all machine-readable passports.)

➡ Are planning to stay longer than 90 days.

➡ Are planning to work or study in the US.

Work Visas

Foreign visitors are not legally allowed to work in the USA without the appropriate working visa. The most common, the H visa, can be difficult to obtain. It usually requires a sponsoring organization, such as the company you will be working for in the US. The company will need to demonstrate why you, rather than a US citizen, are most qualified for the job.

The type of work visa you need depends on your work:

H visa For temporary workers.

L visa For employees in intra-company transfers.

O visa For workers with extraordinary abilities.

P visa For athletes and entertainers.

Q visa For international cultural-exchange visitors.

Women Travelers

Women should apply their street smarts in San Francisco as in any other US city, just to be on the safe side. SF is an excellent destination for solo women travelers: you can eat, stay, dine and go out alone without anyone making presumptions about your availability, interests or sexual orientation.

The **Women's Building** (Map p328; ☑415-431-1180; www.womensbuilding.org; 3543 18th St; ♿; ⓜ18th St, Ⓑ16th St Mission) has a Community Resource Room offering information on healthcare, domestic violence, childcare, harassment, legal issues, employment and housing.

Behind the Scenes

SEND US YOUR FEEDBACK

We love to hear from travelers – your comments keep us on our toes and help make our books better. Our well-traveled team reads every word on what you loved or loathed about this book. Although we cannot reply individually to postal submissions, we always guarantee that your feedback goes straight to the appropriate authors, in time for the next edition. Each person who sends us information is thanked in the next edition – the most useful submissions are rewarded with a selection of digital PDF chapters.

Visit **lonelyplanet.com/contact** to submit your updates and suggestions or to ask for help. Our award-winning website also features inspirational travel stories, news and discussions.

Note: We may edit, reproduce and incorporate your comments in Lonely Planet products such as guidebooks, websites and digital products, so let us know if you don't want your comments reproduced or your name acknowledged. For a copy of our privacy policy visit lonelyplanet.com/privacy.

OUR READERS

Many thanks to the travelers who used the last edition and wrote to us with helpful hints, useful advice and interesting anecdotes: Anna Flore, Gary Hays & Daniel Pförtsch

AUTHOR THANKS

Alison Bing

Heartfelt thanks to Lonely Planet guidebook mastermind Suki Gear, managing editor Sasha Baskett and adventurer extraordinaire John Vlahides; to intrepid research companions Sahai Burrowes, Haemin Cho, Lisa Park, Yosh Han, Rebecca Bing, Tony Cockrell and Akua Parker; but above all to Marco Flavio Marinucci, who made a Muni bus ride into the trip of a lifetime. Alison dedicates this book to Bluford Moor, writer and rescuer of lost toys on Tenderloin sidewalks. He loved San Francisco, and in its infinite wisdom, the city loved him right back.

Sara Benson

Thanks to Suki Gear, Sasha Baskett, Alison Lyall and everyone else at LP for making this book happen. I'm grateful to the many Bay Area residents who generously shared their local expertise. Big thanks to friends and family too, especially the Picketts, Alex Leviton, Beth Kohn and Evan Baxter.

John A Vlahides

I owe great thanks to my commissioning editor Suki Gear and co-author Alison Bing, who encouraged me to accept this assignment. I'm so happy they did. In San Francisco, I'm grateful to Karl Soehnlein, Kevin Clarke, Christine Murray and Gabriel Lasa for help researching; Adam Young for distracting me; and barista Salvador Flores for the many cups of coffee. Most importantly I'm grateful to you, dear reader, for helping me see San Francisco through your eyes. Thanks for letting me be your guide.

ACKNOWLEDGMENTS

Climate map data adapted from Peel MC, Finlayson BL & McMahon TA (2007) 'Updated World Map of the Köppen-Geiger Climate Classification', Hydrology and Earth System Sciences, 11, 1633-44.

Illustration pp54-5 by Michael Weldon.

Cover photograph: Powell-Hyde cable car with Alcatraz in the distance, San Francisco, CA, Ron Niebrugge/Alamy.

THIS BOOK

This 9th edition of Lonely Planet's *San Francisco* guidebook was researched and written by Alison Bing and John A Vlahides. Sara Benson wrote the Day Trips from San Francisco chapter. The previous two editions were written by Alison and John. This guidebook was commissioned in Lonely Planet's Oakland office and produced by the following:

Commissioning Editor
Suki Gear

Coordinating Editor
Elizabeth Jones

Senior Cartographer
Alison Lyall

Coordinating Layout Designer Frank Deim

Managing Editors
Sasha Baskett, Brigitte Ellemor

Managing Layout Designer
Chris Girdler

Assisting Editors
Judith Bamber,
Christopher Pitts

Cover Research
Naomi Parker

Internal Image Research
Kylie McLaughlin

Thanks to Nicholas Colicchia, Ryan Evans, Larissa Frost, Genesys India, Jouve India, Wayne Murphy, Trent Paton, Martine Power, Kerrianne Southway, Lyahna Spencer, Gerard Walker

BEHIND THE SCENES

Index

See also separate subindexes for:

🍴 **EATING P304**

🍷 **DRINKING & NIGHTLIFE P306**

☆ **ENTERTAINMENT P307**

🛍 **SHOPPING P307**

🏃 **SPORTS & ACTIVITIES P308**

🛏 **SLEEPING P309**

San Francisco Maps

Sights

- Beach
- Bird Sanctuary
- Buddhist
- Castle/Palace
- Christian
- Confucian
- Hindu
- Islamic
- Jain
- Jewish
- Monument
- Museum/Gallery/Historic Building
- Ruin
- Sento Hot Baths/Onsen
- Shinto
- Sikh
- Taoist
- Winery/Vineyard
- Zoo/Wildlife Sanctuary
- Other Sight

Activities, Courses & Tours

- Bodysurfing
- Diving
- Canoeing/Kayaking
- Course/Tour
- Skiing
- Snorkeling
- Surfing
- Swimming/Pool
- Walking
- Windsurfing
- Other Activity

Sleeping

- Sleeping
- Camping

Eating

- Eating

Drinking & Nightlife

- Drinking & Nightlife
- Cafe

Entertainment

- Entertainment

Shopping

- Shopping

Information

- Bank
- Embassy/Consulate
- Hospital/Medical
- Internet
- Police
- Post Office
- Telephone
- Toilet
- Tourist Information
- Other Information

Geographic

- Beach
- Hut/Shelter
- Lighthouse
- Lookout
- Mountain/Volcano
- Oasis
- Park
- Pass
- Picnic Area
- Waterfall

Population

- Capital (National)
- Capital (State/Province)
- City/Large Town
- Town/Village

Transport

- Airport
- BART station
- Border crossing
- Boston T station
- Bus
- Cable car/Funicular
- Cycling
- Ferry
- Metro/Muni station
- Monorail
- Parking
- Petrol station
- Subway/SkyTrain station
- Taxi
- Train station/Railway
- Tram
- Underground station
- Other Transport

Note: Not all symbols displayed above appear on the maps in this book

Routes

- Tollway
- Freeway
- Primary
- Secondary
- Tertiary
- Lane
- Unsealed road
- Road under construction
- Plaza/Mall
- Steps
- Tunnel
- Pedestrian overpass
- Walking Tour
- Walking Tour detour
- Path/Walking Trail

Boundaries

- International
- State/Province
- Disputed
- Regional/Suburb
- Marine Park
- Cliff
- Wall

Hydrography

- River, Creek
- Intermittent River
- Canal
- Water
- Dry/Salt/Intermittent Lake
- Reef

Areas

- Airport/Runway
- Beach/Desert
- Cemetery (Christian)
- Cemetery (Other)
- Glacier
- Mudflat
- Park/Forest
- Sight (Building)
- Sportsground
- Swamp/Mangrove

MAP INDEX

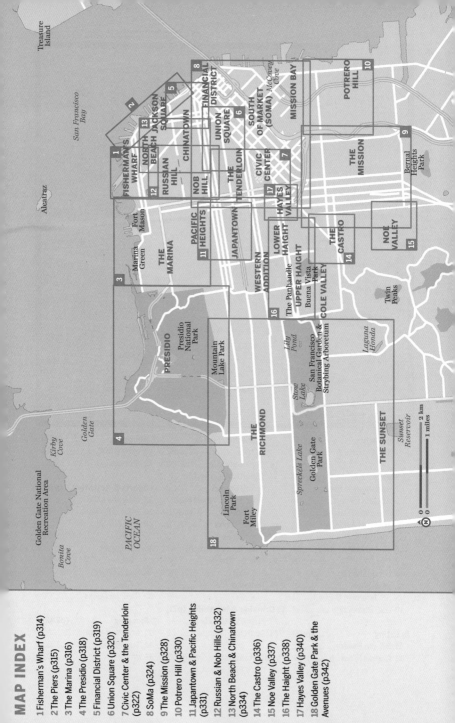

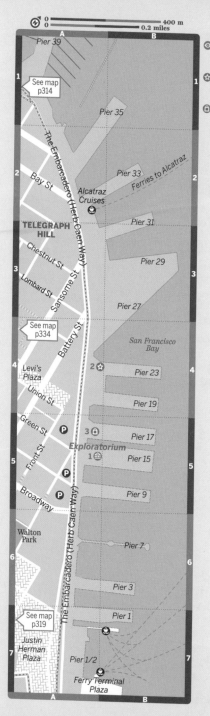

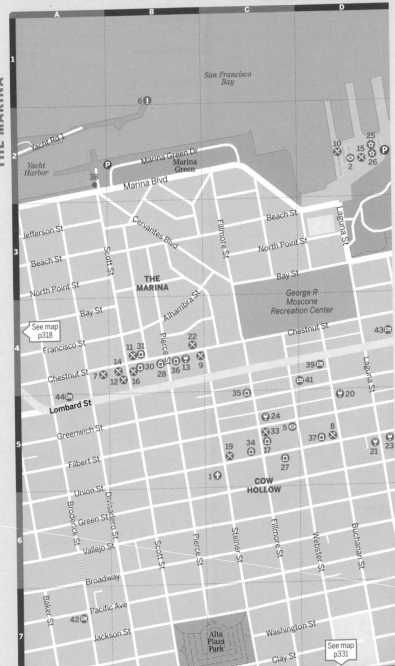

San Francisco Bay

Yacht Rd 1

Yacht Harbor

Marina Green Dr

Marina Green

Marina Blvd

Jefferson St

Beach St

Cervantes Blvd

Fillmore St

Beach St

North Point St

North Point St

Scott St

Bay St

THE MARINA

Alhambra St

Bay St

George R Moscone Recreation Center

Chestnut St

Laguna St

See map p318

Francisco St

Pierce St

Chestnut St

Lombard St

Laguna St

Greenwich St

Filbert St

Union St

Divisadero St

Green St

Broderick St

Vallejo St

Broadway

COW HOLLOW

Steiner St

Pierce St

Scott St

Fillmore St

Webster St

Buchanan St

Baker St

Pacific Ave

Jackson St

Alta Plaza Park

Washington St

Clay St

See map p331

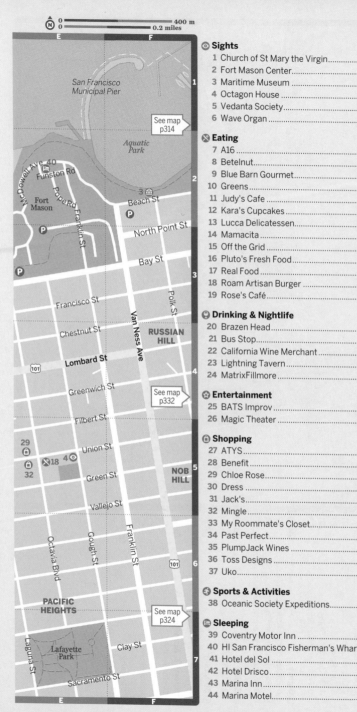

◎ **Sights** (p63)
1 Church of St Mary the Virgin.............C5
2 Fort Mason Center................................D2
3 Maritime Museum F2
4 Octagon House E5
5 Vedanta Society...................................C5
6 Wave Organ...B1

✪ **Eating** (p67)
7 A16 ....A4
8 Betelnut..D5
9 Blue Barn Gourmet............................B4
10 Greens..D2
11 Judy's Cafe B4
12 Kara's Cupcakes B4
13 Lucca Delicatessen.............................B4
14 Mamacita..B4
15 Off the Grid D2
16 Pluto's Fresh Food.............................B4
17 Real Food...C5
18 Roam Artisan Burger E5
19 Rose's Café C5

◉ **Drinking & Nightlife** (p71)
20 Brazen Head...D5
21 Bus Stop...D5
22 California Wine Merchant..................B4
23 Lightning Tavern.................................D5
24 MatrixFillmore.....................................C5

✪ **Entertainment** (p72)
25 BATS Improv...D2
26 Magic Theater D2

🛍 **Shopping** (p73)
27 ATYS..C5
28 Benefit..B4
29 Chloe Rose...E5
30 Dress B4
31 Jack's..B4
32 Mingle...E5
33 My Roommate's Closet.....................C5
34 Past Perfect...C5
35 PlumpJack Wines C5
36 Toss Designs..B4
37 Uko..D5

🎯 **Sports & Activities** (p74)
38 Oceanic Society Expeditions.............A2

🛏 **Sleeping** (p242)
39 Coventry Motor Inn D4
40 HI San Francisco Fisherman's Wharf........E2
41 Hotel del Sol D4
42 Hotel Drisco A7
43 Marina Inn..D4
44 Marina Motel.......................................A5

THE PRESIDIO

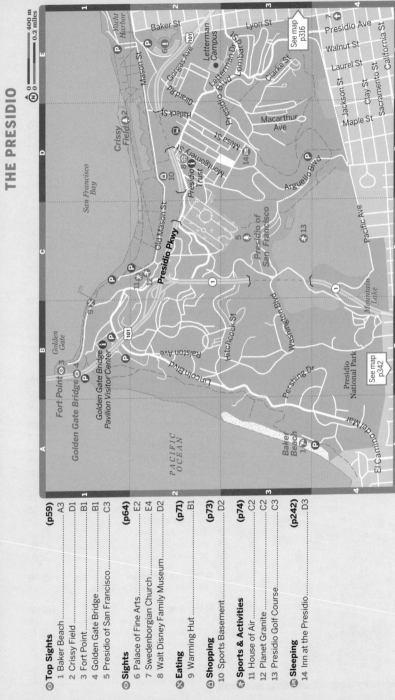

FINANCIAL DISTRICT

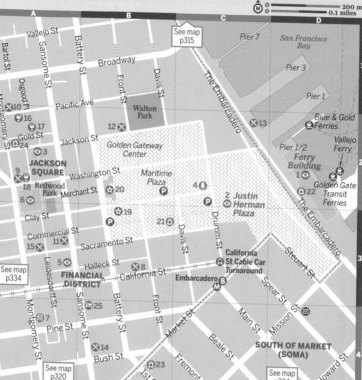

See map p315

See map p334

See map p320

See map p324

UNION SQUARE

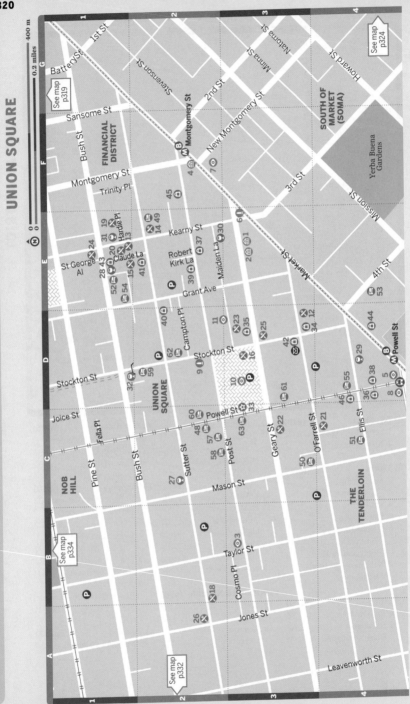

See map p319

See map p324

See map p334

See map p332

Battery St

1st St

Sansome St

Stevenson St

Montgomery St

2nd St

Minna St

Natoma St

Howard St

New Montgomery St

SOUTH OF MARKET (SOMA)

Yerba Buena Gardens

3rd St

Mission St

4th St

Bush St

FINANCIAL DISTRICT

Montgomery St

Trinity Pl

Kearny St

Market St

Robert Kirk La

Maiden La

Grant Ave

Campton Pl

Stockton St

UNION SQUARE

Powell St

Geary St

O'Farrell St

Ellis St

Post St

Sutter St

Bush St

Pine St

Fella Pl

Joice St

Stockton St

NOB HILL

Mason St

Taylor St

Cosmo Pl

Jones St

THE TENDERLOIN

Leavenworth St

St George Al

Hardie Pl

Claude La

Powell St

Powell St

Sights (p83)
1 49 Geary.....................................E3
2 77 Geary.....................................E3
3 Bohemian Club.....................B3
4 Crocker Bank Building........F2
5 James Flood Building...........D4
6 Lotta's Fountain.....................E3
One Montgomery Terrace......(see 4)
7 Palace Hotel............................F2
8 Powell St Cable Car
   Turnaround...........................D4
Rena Bransten Gallery...........(see 2)
9 Ruth Asawa Fountain...........D2
10 Union Square..........................D3
Westin St Francis Hotel
   Glass Elevators...................(see 63)
11 Xanadu Gallery: Folk Art
   International.........................D2

Eating (p92)
12 Bio...D3
13 Boxed Foods.............................E1

14 Bread & Cocoa.......................E2
15 Cafe Claude.............................E1
16 Emporio Rulli.........................D3
17 Farmerbrown..........................C5
18 Fleur de Lys............................B2
19 Galette 88................................E1
20 Gitane......................................E1
21 Johnny Foley's........................C4
22 Lefty O'Douls.........................C3
23 Mocca on Maiden Lane.........D3
24 Muracci's Curry......................E1
25 Rotunda...................................D3
26 Sweet Woodruff.....................A2

Drinking & Nightlife (p98)
Burritt Room..............................(see 59)
27 Cantina....................................C2
Clock Bar.....................................(see 63)
28 Irish Bank................................E1
29 John's Grill...............................D4
30 Otis Lounge.............................E2
31 Rickhouse.................................E1

32 Tunnel Top...............................D1

Entertainment (p105)
Starlight Room...........................(see 60)
33 TIX Bay Area...........................C3

Shopping (p109)
34 Barneys....................................D3
35 Britex Fabrics..........................D3
36 DSW..D4
37 Gump's.....................................E2
38 H&M..D4
39 Icebreaker...............................E2
40 Le Sanctuaire.........................D2
41 Loehmann's.............................E2
42 Macy's......................................D3
43 Margaret O'Leary...................E1
44 Original Levi's Store...............D4
45 Under One Roof.......................F2
46 Uniqlo......................................D4
47 Westfield San Francisco
   Centre....................................D5

Sleeping (p243)
48 Chancellor Hotel....................C2
49 Galleria Park............................E2
50 HI San Francisco
   Downtown.............................C3
51 Hotel Abri................................C4
52 Hotel des Arts.........................E1
53 Hotel Palomar.........................E4
54 Hotel Triton.............................E1
55 Hotel Union Square...............D4
56 Hotel Zetta..............................D5
57 Inn at Union Square..............C2
58 Kensington Park
   Hotel......................................C2
59 Mystic Hotel...........................D2
Palace Hotel...............................(see 7)
60 Sir Francis Drake
   Hotel......................................C2
61 Stratford Hotel.......................D3
62 Taj Campton Place.................D2
63 Westin St Francis
   Hotel......................................C3

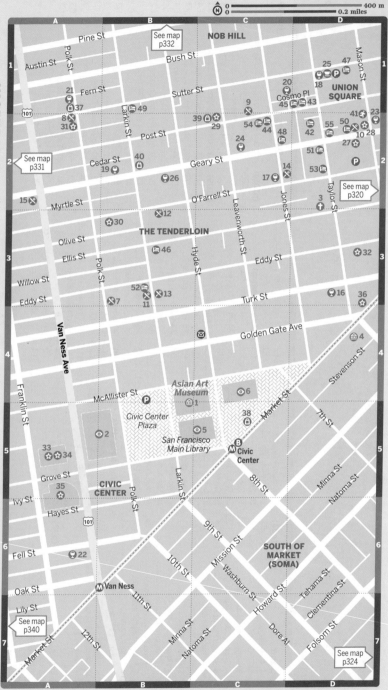

400 m
0.2 miles

NOB HILL

UNION SQUARE

Cosmo Pl

THE TENDERLOIN

See map p332

See map p331

See map p320

See map p324

See map p340

Asian Art Museum

Civic Center Plaza

San Francisco Main Library

Civic Center

CIVIC CENTER

SOUTH OF MARKET (SOMA)

Van Ness

Pine St
Austin St
Polk St
Bush St
Fern St
Sutter St
Larkin St
Post St
Cedar St
Geary St
Myrtle St
O'Farrell St
Olive St
Ellis St
Eddy St
Turk St
Polk St
Eddy St
Golden Gate Ave
Van Ness Ave
McAllister St
Grove St
Ivy St
Hayes St
Fell St
Oak St
Lily St
Market St
Franklin St
Hyde St
Leavenworth St
Jones St
Taylor St
Mason St
Larkin St
7th St
8th St
9th St
10th St
11th St
12th St
Minna St
Natoma St
Mission St
Washburn St
Howard St
Dore Al
Stevenson St
Tehama St
Clementina St
Folsom St
Willow St

CIVIC CENTER & THE TENDERLOIN

Key on p326

SOMA

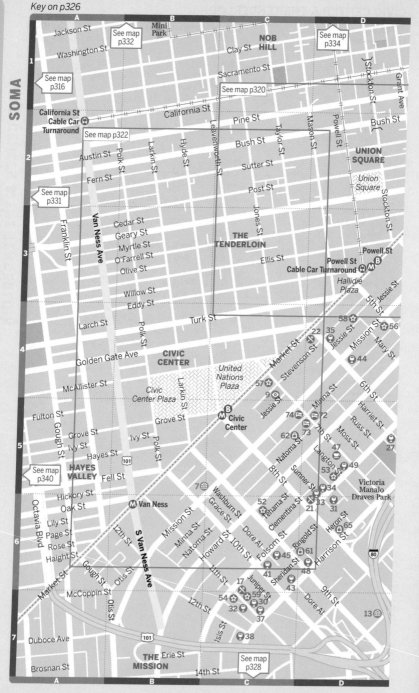

See map
p332

See map
p334

See map
p316

See map
p320

See map
p322

See map
p331

See map
p340

See map
p328

NOB
HILL

Jackson St

Washington St

Clay St

Sacramento St

California St
Cable Car
Turnaround

California St

Pine St

Bush St

Austin St

Fern St

Polk St

Larkin St

Hyde St

Leavenworth St

Bush St

Sutter St

Taylor St

Mason St

Powell St

Stockton St

Grant Ave

Bush St

UNION
SQUARE

Union
Square

Stockton St

Franklin St

Van Ness Ave

Cedar St

Geary St

Myrtle St

O'Farrell St

Olive St

Willow St

Eddy St

Post St

Jones St

THE
TENDERLOIN

Ellis St

Powell St
Cable Car Turnaround

Powell St

Hallidie
Plaza

5th St

Jessie St

Larch St

Golden Gate Ave

Turk St

58

22

35

Jessie St

Mission St

56

44

Mary St

CIVIC
CENTER

McAllister St

Larkin St

United
Nations
Plaza

Civic
Center Plaza

Market St

Stevenson St

6th St

Harriet St

Russ St

Moss St

27

Fulton St

Grove St

Ivy St

Gough St

Grove St

Ivy St

Hayes St

Polk St

57

9

Jessie St

Civic
Center

74

72

62

73

Minna St

7th St

Natoma St

Langton St

47

53

49

HAYES
VALLEY

Fell St

Hickory St

Oak St

Octavia Blvd

Lily St

Page St

Rose St

Haight St

12th St

S Van Ness Ave

Van Ness

7

Washburn St

Mission St

Grace St

Minna St

Natoma St

Howard St

10th St

Dore Al

52

Tehama St

Clementina St

34

21

33

31

Ringold St

Heron St

65

Harrison St

80

McCoppin St

Gough St

Otis St

11th St

Folsom St

45

61

48

41

Sheridan St

43

Dore Al

9th St

13

Sumner St

8th St

Victoria
Manalo
Draves Park

12th St

Duboce Ave

Brosnan St

THE
MISSION

Erie St

14th St

Mini
Park

Mission St

Natoma St

17

Juniper St

54

59

32

30

37

38

13th St

11th St

SOMA

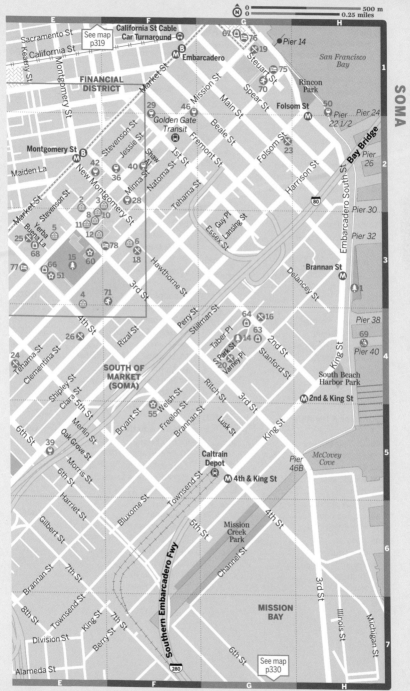

0 — 500 m
0 — 0.25 miles

Sacramento St

California St Cable
Car Turnaround

See map
p319

California St

Keary St

Montgomery St

Montgomery St

**FINANCIAL
DISTRICT**

Market St

**California St Cable
Car Turnaround**

67 76

19 Pier 14

Embarcadero

Steuart St

Spear St

75

70

Rincon
Park

Folsom St

San Francisco
Bay

29

46

Mission St

Main St

50
Pier
22 1/2

Pier 24

Bay Bridge

**Golden Gate
Transit**

Montgomery St

42

New Montgomery St

Stevenson St

Jessie St

Shaw

Beale St

Fremont St

1st St

Minna St

Folsom St

23

Pier
26

Maiden La

Market St

Stevenson St

36

40

28

Natoma St

Tehama St

Harrison St

Pier 30

80

Pier 32

2

3

8

10

Yerba
Buena La

5

11

12

25

68

15

60

78

6

18

Essex St

Guy Pl

Lansing St

Brannan St

Delancey St

1

Pier 38

77

66

51

4

71

3rd St

Hawthorne St

Perry St

Stillman St

64

16

King St

69

Pier 40

26

4th St

Rizal St

Taber Pl

63

14

Park St

220

Varney Pl

2nd St

Stanford St

South Beach
Harbor Park

24

Tehama St

Clementina St

Shipley St

Clara St

5th St

Bryant St

55

Welsh St

Freelon St

Brannan St

Ritch St

Lusk St

3rd St

King St

2nd & King St

McCovey
Cove

6th St

Merlin St

Oak Grove St

39

6th St

Morris St

Harriet St

Bluxome St

Townsend St

**Caltrain
Depot**

4th & King St

Pier
46B

4th St

Gilbert St

Brannan St

7th St

8th St

Townsend St

King St

7th St

Berry St

Southern Embarcadero Fwy

5th St

**Mission
Creek
Park**

Channel St

4th St

**MISSION
BAY**

3rd St

Illinois St

Michigan St

Division St

280

6th St

See map
p330

Alameda St

**SOUTH OF
MARKET
(SOMA)**

SOMA *Map on p324*

◉ Sights (p85)
1 Brannan Street Wharf.................................H3
2 California Historical Society
　　Museum...E2
3 Cartoon Art Museum.................................F2
4 Children's Creativity Museum..................E3
5 Contemporary Jewish Museum...............E3
6 Crown Point Press.....................................F3
7 Electric Works..B5
8 Eli Ridgway...E3
9 Federal Building..C4
10 GLBT Historical Society............................E3
11 Museum of the African Diaspora.............E3
12 San Francisco Museum of
　　Modern Art..E3
13 SOMArts..D7
14 South Park...G4
15 Yerba Buena Gardens...............................E3

◉ Eating (p96)
16 21st Amendment Brewery.......................G4
17 Basil Thai Canteen....................................C6
18 Benu..F3
19 Boulevard...G1
20 Butler & the Chef......................................G4
21 Citizen's Band..D6
22 Dottie's True Blue Café............................D4
23 Prospect..G2
24 Tin Vietnamese...E4
25 Tropisueño..E3
26 Zero Zero...E4

◉ Drinking & Nightlife (p101)
27 1015 Folsom..D5
28 111 Minna..F2
29 83 Proof...F2
30 Bar Agricole..C7
31 Bloodhound...D6
32 Butter...C7
33 Cat Club..D5
34 City Beer Store & Tasting Room.............D5
35 Club OMG..D4
36 Dada..F2
37 DNA Lounge..C7
38 Eagle Tavern...C7
39 EndUp..E5
40 Harlot..F2
41 Hole in the Wall...C6

42 House of Shields...E2
43 Lone Star Saloon.......................................C6
44 Monarch..D4
45 Powerhouse..C6
46 RN74...F1
47 Sightglass Coffee......................................D5
48 Stud...D6
49 Terroir Natural Wine Merchant...............D5
50 Waterbar..H1

◉ Entertainment (p107)
51 AMC Loews Metreon 16.............................E3
52 AsiaSF...C6
53 Brainwash...D5
54 Honey Soundsystem..................................C7
55 Hotel Utah Saloon......................................F5
56 Intersection for the Arts...........................D4
57 Kunst Stoff..C4
58 Mezzanine...D4
59 Slim's...C7
60 Yerba Buena Center for the Arts.............E3

◉ Shopping (p112)
61 Branch...D6
62 General Bead..C5
63 Isda & Co Outlet..G4
64 Jeremy's..G4
65 Madame S & Mr S Leather........................D6
66 Metreon..E3
67 San Francisco Railway Museum Gift
　　Shop..G1
68 SFMOMA Museum Store...........................E3

◉ Sports & Activities (p113)
69 City Kayak...H4
70 Embarcadero YMCA...................................G1
　　Spinnaker Sailing............................(see 69)
71 Yerba Buena Center Ice Skating &
　　Bowling...F3

◉ Sleeping (p247)
72 Americania Hotel.......................................D5
73 Best Western Carriage Inn.......................D5
74 Good Hotel..C5
75 Harbor Court Hotel....................................G1
76 Hotel Vitale...G1
77 Mosser Hotel...E3
78 W Hotel..F3

THE MISSION *Map on p328*

THE MISSION

See map p330

See map p324

See map p338

See map p336

Key on p327

400 m
0.2 miles

Vermont St
McKinley Square
San Bruno Ave
James Lick Fwy
San Bruno Ave
Utah St
Potrero Ave
Division St
Alameda St
15th St
16th St
Franklin Square
17th St
Mariposa St
18th St
19th St
20th St
Treat Ave
Erie St
Shotwell St
14th St
15th Ave
S Van Ness Ave
Capp St
Mission St
Julian St
15th St
Guerrero St
Brosnan St
Clinton Park
Duboce Ave
Dolores St
THE CASTRO
Chula La
Landers St
Church St
Sharon St
Dearborn St
Dorland St
Linda St
San Carlos St
Valencia St
16th St Mission
Dolores Park
Dolores St
Hancock St
18th St
19th St
Cumberland St

THE MISSION

San Bruno Ave
Utah St
San Francisco General Hospital
22nd St
25th St
Potrero del Sol Park
★ 99
Potrero Ave
Hampshire St
York St
★ 61
Bryant St
25 ✕
8 ⊞
Florida St
Bryant St
21st St
23rd St
Florida St
York St
24th St
Alabama St
⊞ 7
Alabama St
Harrison St
24 ✕
100 ✦
⊙ 2
Garfield Square
Harrison St
Precita Park
Treat Ave
90 ⓘ
Treat Ave
Lucky St
Folsom St
Folsom St
★ 97
Precita Ave
Shotwell St
80 42
✕
ⓘ
Shotwell St
THE MISSION
22nd St
Shotwell St
S Van Ness Ave
Precita Ave
ⓘ 102
Capp St
⊞ 12
32 ✕
26 ✕
31 ✕ 56
Cesar Chavez St
ⓘ 47
24th St Mission
98
✦
34 ✕
Mission St
96
ⓑ
★ 73
Mission St
22 ✕
23 ✕
Bartlett St
66
63 ✦
✕ 41
ⓘ 82
51 71
✕ 45
Valencia St
89
ⓘ
78
86 ⓘ
67 ★
54 ⓘ
101 ✦
55 ⓘ
ⓘ 87
Liberty St
21st St
Hill St
23rd St
San Jose Ave
Guerrero St
Ames St
Fair Oaks St
Fair Oaks St
Quane St
Dolores St
Jersey St
Clipper St
26th St
NOE VALLEY
Chattanooga St
Church St
Cesar Chavez St
Vicksburg St
27th St
Sanchez St
See map p337

ichi Sushi (0.3mi);
Liberty Café (0.7mi);
Wild Side West (0.7mi)

Mitchell's Ice Cream (0.2mi);
Rock Bar (0.2mi)

POTRERO HILL

0 400 m
0 0.2 miles

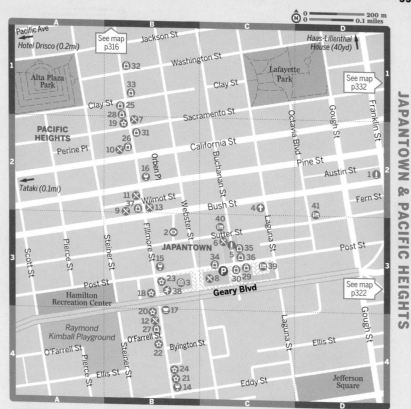

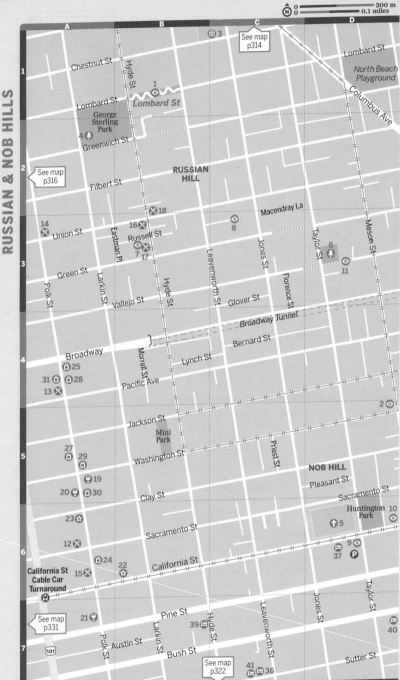

200 m
0.1 miles

See map
p314

Chestnut St

Lombard St

North Beach
Playground

Columbus Ave

Lombard St

1

Lombard St

George
Sterling
Park

4

Greenwich St

See map
p316

Filbert St

**RUSSIAN
HILL**

Macondray La

18

14

Union St

16

8

Russell St

7 **17**

6

11

Green St

Eastman Pl

Larkin St

Polk St

Hyde St

Leavenworth St

Jones St

Taylor St

Mason St

Vallejo St

Glover St

Florence St

Broadway Tunnel

Broadway

Bernard St

Lynch St

25

31 **28**

Morrell St

Pacific Ave

13

2

Jackson St

Mini
Park

27 **29**

Washington St

Priest St

NOB HILL

Pleasant St

19

Sacramento St

20 **30**

Clay St

23

Huntington
Park

10

5

12

Sacramento St

9

24

22

California St

37

15

**California St
Cable Car
Turnaround**

Jones St

Taylor St

See map
p331

21

Pine St

39

40

Polk St

Larkin St

Hyde St

Leavenworth St

Austin St

Bush St

Sutter St

See map
p322

41 **36**

RUSSIAN & NOB HILLS

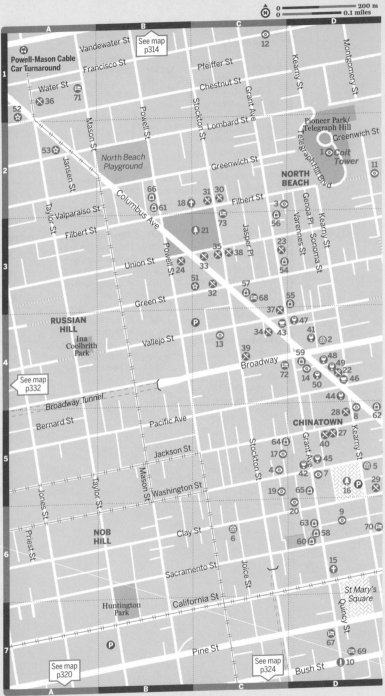

200 m
0.1 miles

Powell-Mason Cable Car Turnaround

Vandewater St

See map p314

Pfeiffer St

Francisco St

Chestnut St

Kearny St

Montgomery St

Water St

36   71

52

Powell St

Stockton St

Lombard St

Grant Ave

Pioneer Park/
Telegraph Hill

Greenwich St

53

Mason St

Jansen St

North Beach
Playground

Telegraph Hill Blvd

Coit
Tower

1

11

Greenwich St

NORTH
BEACH

Valparaiso St

Columbus Ave

66

61   18   31 30

Filbert St

3

56

Genoa Pl

Kearny St

Varennes St

Sonoma St

Taylor St

Filbert St

Powell St

21

73

Jasper Pl

23

54

Union St

35

33   38

24

RUSSIAN
HILL

51   32

Green St

57

68

55

37

47

34   43

41

2

See map
p332

Ina
Coolbrith
Park

Vallejo St

13

39

Broadway

59

48
49
22
46

72   14

50

44

Broadway Tunnel

Bernard St

Pacific Ave

28   8   62

CHINATOWN

27

40

Jackson St

64

17

4

45

42   7

Stockton St

Grant Ave

Kearny St

5

29

16

Washington St

19   65

20

9

70

63

58

NOB
HILL

Clay St

6

60

Jones St

Taylor St

Mason St

Joice St

15

Priest St

Sacramento St

St Mary's
Square

Huntington
Park

California St

Quincy St

See map
p320

Pine St

See map
p324

67

69

Bush St

10

◎ **Top Sights** (p117)
1 Coit Tower D2

◎ **Sights** (p118)
2 Beat Museum D4
3 Bob Kaufman Alley C2
4 Chinatown Alleyways C5
5 Chinese Culture Center D5
6 Chinese Historical Society
   of America C6
7 Chinese Telephone
   Exchange D5
8 Columbus Tower.................D5
9 Commercial Street.............. D6
10 Dragon's Gate....................D7
11 Filbert Street Steps D2
12 Francisco St Steps C1
13 Good Luck Parking Garage. C4
14 Jack Kerouac Alley D4
15 Old St Mary's Cathedral &
   Square D6
16 Portsmouth Square.............D5
17 Ross Alley...........................C5
18 Saints Peter & Paul
   Church................................B2
19 Spofford Alley.....................C5
20 Tien Hau Temple.................. D6
21 Washington Square C3

◎ **Eating** (p124)
22 Brioche Bakery..................... D4
23 Cafe Jacqueline...................C3
24 Cinecittà..............................B3
25 City View E6
26 Coi.....................................E4
27 Great Eastern Restaurant....D5
28 House of Nanking D5
29 Jai Yun...............................D5
30 Liguria Bakery C2
31 Mama's...............................C2
32 Mara's Italian Pastry........... C3
33 Mario's Bohemian Cigar
   Store Cafe C3
34 Molinari C4
35 Park Tavern C3
36 Pat's Cafe...........................A1
37 Ristorante Ideale.................C4
38 Tony's Coal-Fired Pizza &
   Slice House....................... C3

39 Yuet Lee...............................C4
40 Z & Y D5

◎ **Drinking & Nightlife** (p127)
41 15 Romolo............................D4
42 Buddha Lounge....................D5
43 Caffe Trieste.......................C4
44 Comstock Saloon D4
45 Li Po....................................D5
46 Réveille................................D4
47 Saloon D4
48 Specs Museum Cafe D4
49 Tosca Cafe...........................D4
50 Vesuvio D4

◎ **Entertainment** (p130)
51 Beach Blanket Babylon........C3
52 Bimbo's 365 Club A1
53 Cobb's Comedy Club A2

◎ **Shopping** (p131)
54 101 Music C3
55 Al's Attire D3
56 Aria C3
57 Buyer's Best Friend
   Mercato...............................C3
58 Chinatown Kite Shop D6
59 City Lights............................D4
60 Clarion Music Center D6
61 Double Punch.......................B2
62 Eden & Eden D5
63 Far East Flea Market............D6
64 Golden Gate Fortune
   Cookie Company C5
65 Red Blossom Tea
   Company D5
66 Rock Posters &
   Collectibles........................B2

◎ **Sleeping** (p248)
67 Grant Plaza..........................D7
68 Hotel Bohème C3
69 Orchard Garden Hotel D7
70 Pacific Tradewinds
   Hostel.................................D6
71 San Remo Hotel...................A1
72 SW Hotel..............................C4
73 Washington Square
   Inn.......................................C3

THE CASTRO

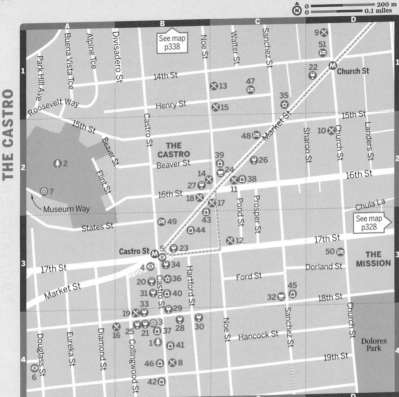

0 ____ 200 m
0 ____ 0.1 miles

NOE VALLEY

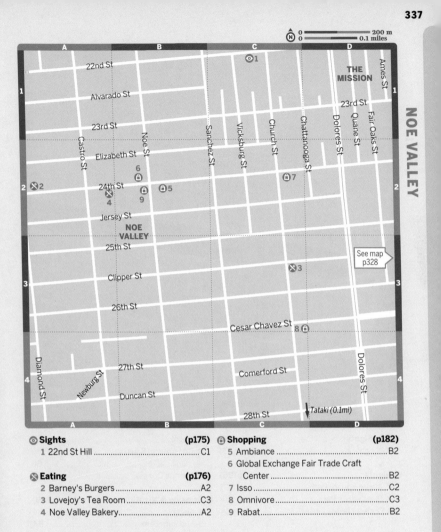

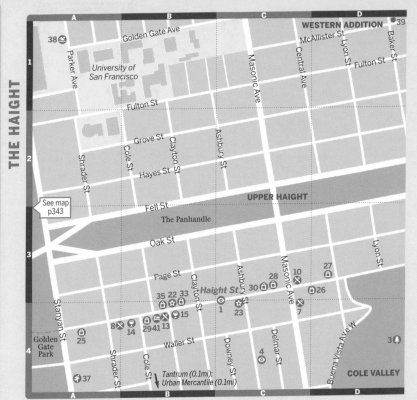

◎ **Top Sights** **(p185)**
1 Haight St C4

◎ **Sights** **(p186)**
2 Alamo Square Park.......................F1
3 Buena Vista Park D4
4 Grateful Dead House...................C4

✖ **Eating** **(p186)**
5 Axum Cafe G3
6 Bar Crudo....................................E1
7 Coffee to the People...................C4
8 Escape from New York Pizza A4
9 Little Chihuahua.........................F3
10 Magnolia Brewpub......................C3

11 Ragazza F3
12 Rosamunde Sausage
   Grill G3
13 Sunrise Deli B4

◙ **Drinking & Nightlife** **(p189)**
14 Alembic......................................B4
15 Aub Zam Zam B4
16 Candybar.....................................E1
17 Madrone Art Bar..........................F2
18 Noc Noc......................................G3
19 Toronado....................................G3
20 Uva Enoteca................................G3
21 Vinyl Coffee & Wine
   Bar...F2

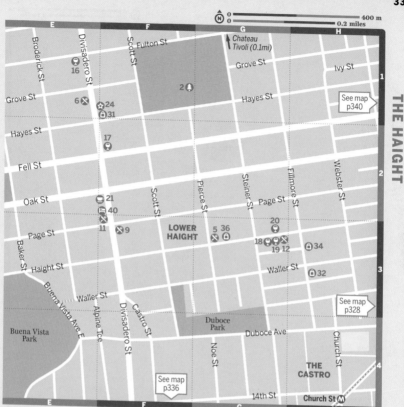

THE HAIGHT

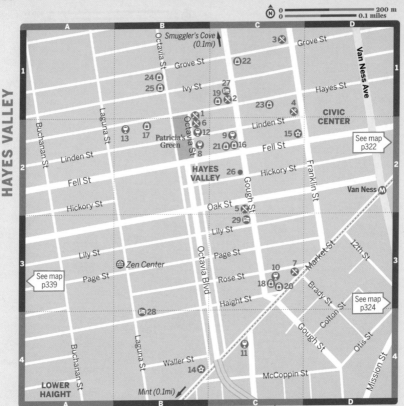

N
0 ————————— 200 m
0 ————————— 0.1 miles

HAYES VALLEY

GOLDEN GATE PARK & THE AVENUES *Map on p342*

GOLDEN GATE PARK & THE AVENUES

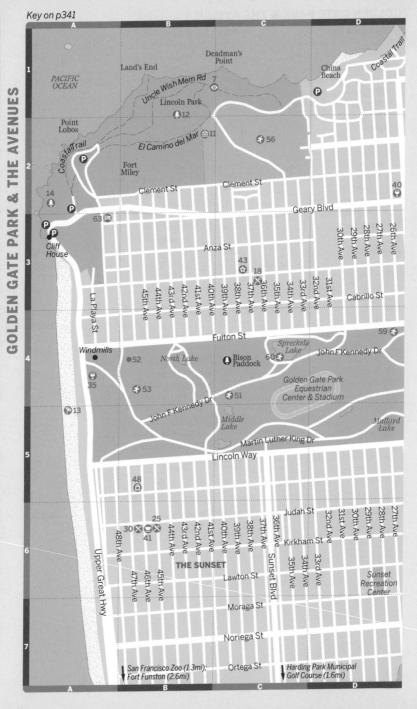

PACIFIC OCEAN

Deadman's Point

Land's End

China Beach

Coastal Trail

Uncle Wish Mem Rd
7

Lincoln Park
12

Point Lobos

Coastal Trail

El Camino del Mar 11

56

Fort Miley

Clement St

Clement St

14

Geary Blvd

40

63

Cliff House

Anza St

43
18

45th Ave
44th Ave
43rd Ave
42nd Ave
41st Ave
40th Ave
39th Ave
38th Ave
37th Ave
36th Ave
35th Ave
34th Ave
33rd Ave
32nd Ave
31st Ave

30th Ave
29th Ave
28th Ave
27th Ave
26th Ave

Cabrillo St

La Playa St

Fulton St

Spreckels Lake

59

Windmills
52

North Lake

Bison Paddock
60

John F Kennedy Dr

35

53

Golden Gate Park Equestrian Center & Stadium

51

13

John F Kennedy Dr

Middle Lake

Mallard Lake

Martin Luther King Dr

Lincoln Way

48

Judah St

31st Ave
30th Ave
29th Ave
28th Ave
27th Ave

25
30

41

48th Ave
47th Ave
46th Ave
45th Ave
44th Ave
43rd Ave
42nd Ave
41st Ave
40th Ave
39th Ave
38th Ave
37th Ave
36th Ave

Kirkham St

32nd Ave

35th Ave
34th Ave
33rd Ave

THE SUNSET

Lawton St

Sunset Blvd

Sunset Recreation Center

Upper Great Hwy

Moraga St

Noriega St

San Francisco Zoo (1.3mi);
Fort Funston (2.6mi)

Ortega St

Harding Park Municipal Golf Course (1.6mi)

0 1 km
0 0.5 miles

Presidio
National Park

See map
p318

Mountain
Lake Park

Mountain
Lake

Lake St

Sacramento St

California St

California St

Spruce (0.1mi)

California St

Clement St

28 47 46 44 19 26
                   45

THE
RICHMOND

Geary Blvd

39 15

20 33 36 17
           16

31

21

7th Ave
6th Ave
5th Ave
4th Ave

8

Rossi
Playground

Anza St

58

Balboa St

25th Ave
24th Ave
23rd Ave
22nd Ave
21st Ave
20th Ave
19th Ave
18th Ave
17th Ave
16th Ave
15th Ave
14th Ave
Funston Ave
12th Ave
11th Ave
10th Ave
9th Ave
8th Ave

10

3rd Ave
2nd Ave
Arguello Blvd

42

54

Fulton St

See map
p338

MH de Young
Museum 5

57

Conservatory
of Flowers

2

9

John F Kennedy Dr

Lloyd
Lake

California
Academy of
Sciences

Golden
Gate Park 3

62

4

1

55

61

Japanese
Tea Garden

AIDS
Memorial
Grove

Children's
Playground

Stow
Lake

Strawberry
Hill Island

Shakespeare
Garden

Kezar Dr

Elk Glen
Lake

6

San Francisco
Botanical Garden

Martin Luther King Dr

Lincoln Way

24

5th Ave
4th Ave
2nd Ave

50

Carl St

32

Irving St

34

22 38

27

37

49 23

29

26th Ave
25th Ave
24th Ave
23rd Ave
21st Ave
20th Ave
19th Ave
18th Ave
17th Ave
16th Ave
15th Ave
14th Ave
Funston Ave
12th Ave
11th Ave
10th Ave
9th Ave
8th Ave

7th Ave

Kirkham St

Interior
Park Belt

Grand
View
Park

Mt Sutro
(918m)

Laguna
Honda

Sunset
Reservoir

San Francisco
Croquet Club (0.9mi)

Midtown Terrace
Recreation Center

Our Story

A beat-up old car, a few dollars in the pocket and a sense of adventure. In 1972 that's all Tony and Maureen Wheeler needed for the trip of a lifetime – across Europe and Asia overland to Australia. It took several months, and at the end – broke but inspired – they sat at their kitchen table writing and stapling together their first travel guide, *Across Asia on the Cheap*. Within a week they'd sold 1500 copies. Lonely Planet was born.

Today, Lonely Planet has offices in Melbourne, London and Oakland, with more than 600 staff and writers. We share Tony's belief that 'a great guidebook should do three things: inform, educate and amuse'.

Our Writers

Alison Bing

Coordinating Author; North Beach & Chinatown; The Mission & Potrero Hill; The Haight, NoPa & Hayes Valley; Golden Gate Park & the Avenues
Over 15 years in San Francisco, Alison has done everything you're supposed to do in the city and many things you're not, including falling in love on the Haight St bus and quitting a Silicon Valley day job to write about travel. Alison holds degrees in art history and international diplomacy – respectable credentials she regularly undermines with opinionated culture commentary for mobile guides, magazines, radio and books, including Lonely Planet's *California*, *USA*, *Coastal California*, *California Trips*, *San Francisco* and *Pocket San Francisco*. Join further adventures as they unfold on Twitter @AlisonBing.

Sara Benson

Day Trips from San Francisco After graduating from college in Chicago, Sara jumped on a plane to San Francisco with just one suitcase and $100 in her pocket. She has bounced around California ever since, including stints working as a national park ranger in the Sierra Nevada. The author of 55 travel and nonfiction books, Sara hiked across Point Reyes, cycled around Angel Island and tippled Napa and Sonoma wines while researching this guide. Follow her latest adventures online at www.indietraveler.blogspot.com and @indie_traveler on Twitter.

Read more about Sara at:
lonelyplanet.com/members/sara_benson

John A Vlahides

The Marina, Fisherman's Wharf & the Piers; Downtown, Civic Center & SoMa; Nob Hill, Russian Hill & Fillmore; The Castro & Noe Valley; Sleeping
John A Vlahides co-hosts the TV series *Lonely Planet: Roads Less Travelled*, screening internationally on National Geographic Channels and in the US on Travel Channel. John studied cooking in Paris, and he's a former luxury-hotel concierge and member of Les Clefs d'Or, the international union of the world's elite concierges. John lives in San Francisco, where he sings tenor with the Grammy-winning San Francisco Symphony and spends free time on the beach beneath the Golden Gate Bridge. For more, see JohnVlahides.com and Twitter.com/JohnVlahides.

Read more about John at:
lonelyplanet.com/members/johnvlahides

Published by Lonely Planet Publications Pty Ltd
ABN 36 005 607 983
9th edition – Feb 2014
ISBN 978 1 74220 734 6
© Lonely Planet 2014   Photographs © as indicated 2014
10 9 8 7 6 5 4 3 2 1
Printed in China